WORD MEANING AND MONTAGUE GRAMMAR

Studies in Linguistics and Philosophy

Volume 7

The titles published in this series are listed at the end of this volume.

DAVID R. DOWTY

WORD MEANING AND MONTAGUE GRAMMAR

The Semantics of Verbs and Times in Generative Semantics and in Montague's PTQ

Kluwer Academic Publishers

Dordrecht / Boston / London

Library of Congress Cataloging in Publication Data

CIP

Dowty, David R
Word meaning and Montague grammar.

(Synthese language library; v. 7)
Bibliography: p.
Includes index.
1. Semantics. 2. Montague grammar. 3. Generative grammar. 4. English language–Grammar, Generative. I. Title. II. Series.
P325.5.G45D6 415 79-19332
ISBN 90-277-1008-2
ISBN 90-277-1009-0 pbk.

Published by Kluwer Academic Publishers,
P.O. Box 17, 3300 AA Dordrecht, The Netherlands.

Kluwer Academic Publishers incorporates
the publishing programmes of
D. Reidel, Martinus Nijhoff, Dr W. Junk and MTP Press.

Sold and distributed in the U.S.A. and Canada
by Kluwer Academic Publishers,
101 Philip Drive, Norwell, MA 02061, U.S.A.

In all other countries, sold and distributed
by Kluwer Academic Publishers Group,
P.O. Box 322, 3300 AH Dordrecht, The Netherlands.

First published 1979
Reprinted with new preface 1991

Printed on acid-free paper

Printed in the Netherlands

FOREWORD

The most general goal of this book is to propose and illustrate a program of research in word semantics that combines some of the methodology and results in linguistic semantics, primarily that of the generative semantics school, with the rigorously formalized syntactic and semantic framework for the analysis of natural languages developed by Richard Montague and his associates, a framework in which truth and denotation with respect to a model are taken as the fundamental semantic notions. I hope to show, both from the linguist's and the philosopher's point of view, not only why this synthesis can be undertaken but also why it will be useful to pursue it. On the one hand, the linguists' decompositions of word meanings into more primitive parts are by themselves inherently incomplete, in that they deal only in distinctions in meaning without providing an account of what meanings really are. Not only can these analyses be made complete by a model-theoretic semantics, but also such an account of these analyses renders them more exact and more readily testable than they could ever be otherwise. On the other hand, I have tried to dispel the misconception widely held by philosophers that all the interesting and important problems of natural language semantics have to do with so-called logical words and with compositional semantics rather than with word-semantics, as well as with the more basic misconception that it is possible even to separate these two kinds of problems. Cases are explored where the compositional semantics of tenses and time adverbials is so completely intertwined with the semantics of verbs as to preclude an analysis of the former without treating the latter as well.

The best way in which to advocate a program of research is to provide a concrete illustration of how it can be carried out. Thus a more specific but equally important goal of this book is to present analyses, carried out within this framework, of a set of interrelated problems centering around the semantics of the so-called "Aristotelian" verb classification (in Zeno Vendler's terminology, the distinctions among *states, activities, accomplishments* and *achievements*) and the grammatical constructions which provide the diagnostic tests that have been used to delimit these classes in English.

A third goal of this book is to shed further light on the traditional controversy in transformational grammar over the question of how the semantic interpretation of a sentence is best correlated with its syntactic structure, in particular, the way the analysis of word meaning relates to this problem. Here I think a number of issues that remained cloudy in the inconclusive debate on this topic in the late 1960's and early 1970's can be brought clearly into focus by the very powerful yet explicit framework presented in Montague's 'Universal Grammar' (Montague, 1970b), of which the PTQ grammar (i.e., 'The Proper Treatment of Quantification in Ordinary English', Montague, 1973) is the best known example.

Chapter 1 introduces the "Universal Grammar" theory and shows how several linguistic theories which differ from one another in the "division of labor" between syntax and semantics can all be seen as special instances of that theoretical framework. This allows the issues connected with the three goals mentioned above to be stated more clearly and concretely, and it prepares the way for their investigation in what follows.

In Chapter 2 the "Aristotelian" verb classification (which I will refer to as an *aspectual classification* of verbs) is approached from two standpoints simultaneously: first, from the linguist's methodology of seeking out minimal semantic distinctions which manifest themselves repeatedly, if in subtle ways, in the syntactic and lexical patterns of the language itself, and second, from the logician's methodology of constructing for a formalized language definitions of truth and entailment with respect to a model that match our intuitions about the corresponding English sentences. Because generative semantics offers the most highly structured version of decomposition analysis, I adopt it here, but it will become apparent that the results of this chapter are equally compatible with other ways of relating word meaning to surface structure besides the generative semantics theory.

My concern with this verb classification problem over the years has convinced me that no account of these distinctions in verbs can ever be deemed satisfactory unless it also leads to an explanation of just why the syntactic and semantic diagnostic tests which isolate these classes behave as they do. I believe that all previous treatments of this problem (including my own) are fatally defective in this way. The remaining chapters, therefore, examine the syntax and semantics of English constructions in which the consequences of distinctions in verb class can be observed, providing at the same time an illustration of how research in word semantics and syntax must interact extensively in a compositonal theory such as Montague's.

Chapter 3 concerns the progressive tense, which is crucially involved in distinguishing among several types of verbs. The English progressive, like the similar phenomenon of imperfective aspect in other languages, provides the greatest challenge to Anthony Kenny's thesis (which I adopt) that accomplishments are partly defined by the changes of state with which they terminate. Moreover, the analysis of the progressive leads to the major innovation of taking truth relative to an interval of time (rather than a moment of time) as the basic semantic definition, and this in turn leads to a new view of the verb classification.

Chapter 4 shows how the semantic analyses of Chapters two and three can be correlated explicitly in the PTQ theory with the variety of surface syntactic patterns of English that manifest each verb class, e.g. single verbs, verbs whose obligatory complements are prepositional phrases, adjectives or nouns, and the important problem of how an optional modifier of a verb can convert a verb phrase from one aspectual class to another.

Chapter 5 is concerned with linguistic evidence pertaining to the generative semantics claim that decomposed lexical structures are best regarded as underlying syntactic structures of English (rather than simply as aspects of semantic interpretation). Interactions of word meaning with the scope of adverbials and quantifiers (which, incidentally, provide a strong *semantic* motivation for decomposition) are used to argue that the method of relating syntax to meaning offered by PTQ is superior to both generative semantics and Katz' interpretive semantics in certain ways.

As one of the prime manifestations of distinctions in aspectual class in English is in processes of word formation (e.g. the intransitive achievement *awaken* is lexically derived from the stative adjective *awake*, and the transitive accomplishment verb *awaken* is further derived from intransitive *awaken*), I have included as Chapter 6 a theory of *lexical rules* for Montague Grammar. As the proper relationship between lexical and syntactic rules has been a difficult and controversial problem in linguistic theory, I believe this chapter is essential if important data such as the relation between *awake*, transitive *awaken* and intransitive *awaken* is to be seen in proper perspective.

Chapter 7 introduces syntactic and semantic rules for English tenses, auxiliary verbs (modals, perfective *have* and progressive *be*), time adverbials (*yesterday, since Thursday*, etc.) and "aspectual adverbials" such as *for an hour* and *in an hour*. As no fully formalized treatment of many of these problems has appeared, this chapter may be of interest quite independently of the matter of lexical semantics. These analyses are presented in an English fragment that includes lexical rules and a lexicon (words treated in this book and their translations) as well as the usual syntactic and semantic rules. As each rule and lexical item of the fragment is accompanied by page references to discussions earlier in the text, the fragment also serves as a summary of and index to the analyses of the book.

From the linguist's point of view, no discussion of semantics would be complete these days without mention of the question of the "psychological reality" of semantic analyses. My view on this issue is outlined briefly in Chapter 8. I have placed this chapter at the end of the book because I think the relevance of my treatments of word meaning to the psychology of language understanding are best comprehended after one sees just what the analyses consist of. However, this chapter could instead be read before the other chapters, if desired.

The approach to linguistic research taken in this book can be contrasted with the more usual strategy by saying that my work is "vertical" rather than "horizontal". While the usual tack is to focus on a single "level of linguistic structure" (semantics, pragmatics, syntax, morphology, lexicon, etc.) and explore as wide a range of data at that level as possible, I have here focused on a small set of semantic problems but explored their repercussions at many levels of the grammar–model-theoretic semantics, componential semantics, the syntax of verb phrases, the syntax of tenses and adverbials, and lexical rules. I hope the novel perspective gained by this approach will be enlightening enough to suggest its application elsewhere. This strategy is closely linked with my belief in the importance of placing any treatment of a semantic problem in natural language within a completely formalized fragment. The goal of giving completely formalized if limited grammars, which once characterized transformational research but has come to be ignored in recent years, is now fortunately taken seriously again in Montague Grammar. It should go without saying that my inclusion of a fragment does not imply that I consider myself to have given a definitive treatment of my subject. On the contrary, the goal of formalization in linguistic research is to enable subsequent researchers to see the defects of an analysis as clearly as its merits; only then can further progress be made efficiently.

As a large part of the audience for which this book is ultimately intended does not yet have the facility with Montague Grammar needed to follow all the analyses in this book with ease (and is hindered from acquiring such facility by the impenetrability of Montague's own writings and the lack of an adequate textbook), I had originally intended to include here an extensive introduction to Montague's PTQ. Though existing introductions by Barbara Partee (Partee, 1974) and by Richmond Thomason (Montague, 1974) are indeed admirable in what they accomplish in a limited space, I do not believe they are sufficiently detailed to bring the reader whose background is linguistic semantics to a clear and coherent picture of this complicated system as a whole (at least, not without a further sizeable investment of time and energy). This introductory section was in fact written, but it turned out to be too long to be included in this book. Since then, Stanley Peters and Robert E. Wall have invited me to join them as collaborator on their planned textbook on Montague Grammar, in which my introductory material is now included. As the textbook was intended to appear at the same time as or before this book, I felt it was no longer necessary to include an introduction here. Since the publication of the textbook has however been slightly delayed, I am pleased that the Indiana University Linguistics Club (310 Lindley Hall, Bloomington, IN 47401) has decided to distribute on a temporary basis my original introduction for this book, under the title *A Guide to Montague's PTQ*.

If the textbook just mentioned, my *Guide*, or another equally detailed introduction is available to the reader with no prior knowledge of Montague Grammar, these will provide far quicker access to Montague Grammar than a reading of Montague's work in the original. PTQ might be likened to an abridged version of Chomsky's *Aspects of the Theory of Syntax* in which all formal definitions and rules have been retained but all intervening prose has been deleted. Though deceptively short, PTQ (not to mention "Universal Grammar") certainly does equal if not exceed the *Aspects* theory in scope and complexity. Since readers' approaches to my book will vary, I will briefly sketch the kind of knowledge of Montague Grammar which is desirable for reading it.

As PTQ is the version of Montague Grammar best known to linguists and is, in my opinion, the version most suited to linguistic analysis, I have employed the PTQ version throughout. How PTQ fits into the general theory of "Universal Grammar" is explained in Chapter 1, and no prior acquaintance with "Universal Grammar" is assumed. To ease the reader's notational burden, I have followed the notational conventions of PTQ exactly. But following Bennett (1974), I have simplified this system slightly in dispensing with Montague's awkward and not completely successful use of individual concepts as members of the extensions of nouns and intransitive verbs; cf. Wall, Peters and Dowty (to appear), which likewise employs this simplification and explains why it is desirable. Instead, nouns and intransitive verbs will denote sets of individuals directly. Thus the distinction between $\mathbf{walk}'(x)$ and $\mathbf{walk}'_*(u)$ vanishes: $\mathbf{walk}'$ denotes a set of individuals, the variables x, y and z denote individuals, and the notation $\mathbf{walk}'_*$ and the variables u and v are unnecessary. Otherwise, translations appear exactly like their counterparts in PTQ.

The most important knowledge of Montague Grammar which the reader can bring to this book is the ability to think of meanings in terms of abstract set-theoretic "semantical objects" such as basic entities, properties of entities (functions from indices to sets of entities), propositions (sets of indices), properties of properties of entities, etc. These "semantical objects" are not linguistic entities in any sense but are the non-linguistic objects (if abstract ones) that are denoted by expressions of languages or serve as the intensions of expressions. By contrast, the formulas of intensional logic that are exhibited as translations of sentences are not the end-points of semantic description (as are the "logical forms" or "semantic representations" of many linguistic theories) but are significant only insofar as they represent the semantical objects (propositions, etc.) which are the "real" meanings in this theory. It is important to keep in mind that *entailment, logical equivalence, logical truth*, etc. are ultimately defined entirely in terms of the relation of sentences to these semantical objects, not just in terms of formulas of intensional logic.

The second most useful ability is some skill in computing and in simplifying the translations of English sentences. The simplification of translations is technically a non-essential step, but in practice, skill in performing such simplifications is extremely useful, for it enables one to view a novel translational rule such as those given in this book and perceive immediately what its "real" semantic effect will be. The reader who is not adept at simplifying translations is advised to try out a sample derivation and simplification of its translation for each new rule, in order to be sure of the rule's import.

Though I have had to presuppose this basic knowledge of Montague Grammar, I have definitely not written this book with only the specialist in Montague grammar in mind but have tried to take the novice into consideration at all times. Thus I have explained formal definitions in prose whenever I feel they might be confusing to some readers, have occasionally given step-by-step translations, and have elaborated on points of potential misunderstanding. While this approach has made this book longer than it might have been, I believe this strategy will actually reduce rather than increase the time it takes to absorb its contents. It should also be pointed out that the semantical Chapters 2 and 3 (as well as Chapters 1 and 8) can be read without any explicit knowledge of Montague Grammar at all, assuming one is familiar with the rudiments of the formal interpretation of tense and modal logic. Though even the remaining chapters can be read if one is willing to take my word for it that rules will do exactly what I claim they will, I must hasten to add that I think one of the reasons linguistic semantics finds itself in a dire state today is *because* readers have been too willing to assume that "somehow or other" a derivation will work itself out in the right way.

Many of the ideas in this book have appeared in print in one form or another over the years, though often in quite a different form from what they take here. The decomposition analyses of Chapter 2 stem from my Ph.D. dissertation (Dowty, 1972). The treatment of the progressive in Chapter 3 is largely that of Dowty (1977) and the ideas for incorporating decomposition analyses into PTQ appeared in rudimentary form in Dowty (1976). The theory of lexical rules from Chapter 6 first appeared in Dowty (1975).

The earlier stages of my work on this project were supported by grants from the American Council of Learned Societies and from the Institute for Advanced Study. The final preparation of the manuscript was assisted by a grant from the College of Humanities of The Ohio State University. I have benefitted from the advice and comments of a number of people, most especially Stanley Peters, Barbara Partee, Richmond Thomason, M. J. Cresswell, David Lewis, Gregory Carlson, Arnold Zwicky and Marion Johnson. For reading the entire manuscript and providing comments, special thanks are due to James McCawley, Per-Kristian Halvorsen and most of all to Susan Schmerling, for her very thorough critique. But obviously none of these people is responsible for (and in some cases will be quite surprised to see) what I have made of their suggestions. For a heroic task of typing, much thanks goes to Marlene Deetz Payha, who has become so proficient at Montague's notation that she is able to type out well-formed expressions of intensional logic flawlessly from the most illegibly scribbled manuscript. I am grateful to Doug Fuller and Greg Stump for help with editing. Finally, thanks also to friends Dory Levy and David Snyder for their own important contributions to the completion of this work.

Ohio State University, October 1978 D. R. DOWTY

TABLE OF CONTENTS

PREFACE TO THE SECOND PRINTING

On the occasion of the reprinting this book some dozen years after its initial appearance, it seems appropriate to add this preface for two reasons. Due to the regrettable absence of a summarizing chapter in the original to explain the relationship among the various results of the book clearly (an omission that was as much a consequence of the author's inability to grasp these fully himself at that point as to the pressure of time), its overall conclusions have proved all too easy to misinterpret for readers who could not study the whole book in detail. I will try to clarify here the most problematic point, the relationship between the two different aspectual theories in the book. Secondly, because of the great amount of research in aspect and aktionsart that has been done since the book appeared, it may be useful to try to say in which ways the results of the book have been superseded by subsequent research and in which ways (in my view at least) they have not.

It is important to realize that not one but two theories of aspect are the subject of this book, the *decompositional theory* of chapter two (in which Vendler's four verb types are analyzed in terms of characteristic types of formulas that include the operators DO, CAUSE and BECOME), and the theory introduced in chapter three and subsequent chapters based on *interval semantics*, a theory which the first theory is, to an extent, rejected in favor of. One indication that this fact has been misunderstood by some recent writers is that references can be found to "the theory of aspect of Dowty (1979)" whose authors actually turn out to refer to the decompositional theory only, i.e. the "rejected" one. Such an author has missed the main point of the book.

The two theories are not however incompatible. Indeed, it is a major concern of the book to show not only how the two can be combined (i.e. by interpreting the CAUSE and BECOME operators in terms of an interval-based temporal possible worlds semantics, leading to a two-step analysis in which English verbs are first translated into formulas with these operators, then the formulas are interpreted in an interval-based temporal model theory) but also that there are virtues to doing so: the combination explains things that neither individual theory can by itself. For example, the combined theory, but not an interval semantics analysis alone, can account for the generalization (due, in effect, to Kenny and Vendler) that the telic predicates, which are the "non-subinterval predicates" of Bennett-Partee and Taylor (the originators of the interval semantics theory), are apparently just those predicates that entail the bringing about of a change of state.

But it is the second theory, the interval semantics account of aspect (first introduced for verbs themselves – i.e. what we today term their *aktionsart* – on pp. 163–186), in which the most important work of the book is done. It this theory that:

(i) gives a semantics for durative adverbials like *for an hour* vs. non-durative *in an hour* that is not only intuitively right but explains just why it is that these should be diagnostics for atelic (stative and activity) vs. telic (accomplishment and achievement) aktionsarten. (This analysis is "buried" on pp. 332–339 with little surrounding discussion, which is quite unfortunate because it should actually have been made a key feature of the interval semantics account of aspect.)

(ii) is the necessary basis for the analysis of the progressive tense in chapter three (on this analysis cf. below).

(iii) as is made more fully clear in important recent work, primarily by Manfred Krifka (see below), will eventually explain how the contrast between *drink a glass of beer* and *drink beer* is the source of a contrast in the aspect of a sentence, just as the contrast in lexical choice of verb of presence of a "Goal" prepositional phrase (e.g. *to the bank*) is.

(iv) more generally, leads to a fully *compositional* theory of aspect, in which the role of each of the contributors to the aspect of a sentence (verb, prepositional phrase, tense, adverbs) is formalized.

Though the combined theory gives a nice account of the great majority of sentences, there is a residue of cases for which the decompositional theory fails (because here the Kenny-Vendler generalizations fall short): (a) not all activity predicates can reasonably be analyzed as having DO in their translations (cf. pp. 163–166), and (b) not all telic (accomplishment) predicates can be analyzed as having BECOME in their translations (pp. 186,187). These can be described, up to a point anyway, in interval semantics, but this failure of complete correspondence implies that the combined theory is not quite the fully general account of aspect that the book had aspired to. (At least, it cannot be achieved with this particular decompositional system: the possibility exists that a different decompositional analysis might succeed, but I personally do not hold out much hope for that.)

Thus the book leaves the two theories in a somewhat uneasy alliance. Because of the intuitive naturalness and broad applicability of the decompositional analysis across the lexicon, the tantalizing hope remains that it, like similar ones advocated (*sine* formal interpretation) by Ray Jackendoff and others, may have true cognitive significance, even for cognition outside of language processing. I myself regard the question of such significance as still an open one, a problem for future cognitive science to resolve with at least partially extra-linguistic methods. But the book does not appeal to this motivation in the end but simply offers the use of Montogovian translations employing the formally-interpreted CAUSE and BECOME operators as a practically useful means for describing some of the entailments of a very wide variety of English constructions economically and perspicuously yet precisely, a use amply demonstrated in the last four chapters. That these operators persist to the final pages of the book should not, I emphasize again, mislead the casual reader into thinking that lexical decomposition is "the theory of aspect" of this book. Since decompositional analyses of lexical meaning have become popular again in recent years in some offshoots of Government Binding theory (and elsewhere), I hope their proponents will eventually take account the difficulties and limitations of purely decompositional theories of aspect that this book presents – after chapter two.

With respect to subsequent research on aspect, the most important issue is the relationship of the "interval semantics" model of temporal semantics of this book (and other research of that period, especially by Max Cresswell) to more modern research which takes *event* as a primitive and does not directly appeal to "truth of a predicate with respect to an interval of time", a change of viewpoint suggested early by Emmon Bach's 1986 "The Algebra of Events" (*Linguistics and Philosophy* 4:159–219) and developed notably in Erhard Hinrichs' 1985 Ohio State University dissertation *A Compositional Semantics for Aktionsarten and NP reference in English* (to be published in revised form in Kluwer's SLAP series), by Goedehard Link in 1987 in "Algebraic Semantics of Event Structures" (*Proceedings of the Sixth Amsterdam Colloquium*, ed. J. Groenendijk et al, Foris), by Manfred Krifka in "Nominal Reference and Temporal Constitution: Towards a Semantics of Quantity" (prepublication in 1987 and publication to appear in *Semantics and Contextual Expressions*, ed. R. Bartsch et al, Foris) and in his book *Nominalreferenz und Zeitkonstitution* (Fink, 1989), Peter Lasersohn's Ohio State University dissertation *A Semantics for Groups and Events* (also to appear in revised form), and in papers by others. (These are representative of what may be called *algebraic* event-based semantics; a less algebraically-oriented but philosophically broader study of aspect and events is Terence Parsons' forthcoming *Events in the Semantics of English*, MIT Press.)

The point to which I would draw attention is that the key relationship, in algebraic event-based semantics, of one event (denoted by a sentence) being a subpart of second event (denoted by the same or a different sentence) corresponds to the relationship, in the interval-semantics analysis of aspect, between the case of a sentence being true of one interval and the case of the same sentence – or a different one – being true of a superinterval of the first interval. In terms of these corresponding important relationships in each theory, for example, the difference between a telic and an atelic sentence is defined in parallel ways, and the relationships between the two kinds of aspectual adverbials are given parallel explanations. In other words, the two kinds of theories are isomorphic in their accounts of the fundamentals of aspect – up to a point at least. This is not to deny that are significant details for which the two are not isomorphic (see Krifka's 1989 book for some comparisons), much less obscure the now well-recognized fact that the event-based paradigm is conceptually simpler, easier to formalize, and has substantive advantages, e.g. in issues of the intensionality of events and the analysis of collective and other complex events. But my point is that the modern algebraic event-based account of aspect should naturally be seen not as an outright abandonment of the interval-based theory of aspect (as is sometimes suggested) but as the result of a rather monotonic line of development that began with Bennett-Partee's and Barry Taylor's seminal papers and continued with the present book and its interval-semantics contemporaries.

One not so minor improvement of the new paradigm lies in the way it has afforded of describing the "change of state" entailments of telics (e.g. *painting the house red* entails the house coming to be red). The BECOME operator which plays such a central role in this book is an attempt to carry over the intuition of von Wright's Logic of Change from an instant-based to an interval-based system. The details of the BECOME semantics given here were criticized, appropriately, but a more important defect is its intuitive implication that when an event of change takes place over an interval of time, the change in some sense does not "take effect" until the end of the interval. The analysis of telicity by Krifka (cf. above) and others in terms of an object-to-event homomorphism in event-based semantics allows us to say more intuitively that the change involved in painting a house red can consist of many temporally included subevents, each of which is the painting red of some part of the house: the change of state is permitted to be temporally distributed into many successive and small constituent changes of state. This is clearly on the right track, but what remains to be done is to apply this technique to all the other ways of expressing a change of state in language for which BECOME is invoked in this book: change of state verbs derived by a productive lexical process from adjectives (*flatten, harden, widen, blacken*, etc.), Source and Goal prepositional phrases (*to the bank, from the bank*) and the telicity introduced by them, and how the semantics of the progressive tense interacts with telicity (see below). This book may remain useful as a guide to these. A feature of the book to which there has been much reaction is its analysis of the English progressive and its "imperfectivity" properties. (It should not be overlooked that my 1977 article on the progressive in *Linguistics and Philosophy* 1:45–78 contains some further applications of this analysis not included in this book itself.) Some undesirable consequences of the analysis were quickly pointed out, and this led Frank Vlach, Emmon Bach, Terence Parsons, Robin Cooper, Erhard Hinrichs and a number of others to devise new analyses of the problem I called the "imperfective paradox" (a bad choice of terminology, some have complained) in one way or another (see Hinrichs', Krifka's and Parsons' books cited above for references). That there is as yet however no single widely-accepted solution to this puzzle means that the book may remain a useful statement of the problem. Many analyses (e.g. Parsons') attempt to avoid a modal semantics for the progressive entirely, but I still believe that is a mistake. Analyses that arise naturally out of the object-to-event homomorphism idea, for example, account for "partitive" uses of the progressive but not for the "intensional" ones. Consider for example the case where I have just begun the process of writing a book: here one could imagine it might truly be said that I am writing a book, even though there may exist as yet no actual part of the book such that I have written that part: it is such cases as this for which partitive analyses seem to be inadequate as they stand, though at least the homomorphism analysis is probably an important step forward.

Also in need of a comment is the compositional semantic interaction of tenses with time adverbials in the large fragment in chapter seven. The syntax for such interactions is unfortunately handled in this fragment by syncategorematic rules which add a verb tense and an adverbial to a phrase in a single operation, leading to a syntax that, from the vantage point of 1991, looks clumsy and inelegant. A better method is to treat a quasi-Reichenbachian "reference time" as an independent temporal parameter (of the recursive semantic definitions) from the usual "speech time" parameter, which allows tenses and adverbs to be syntactically independent. My 1982 paper "Tenses, Time Adverbials, and Compositional Semantic Theory" (*Linguistics and Philosophy* 5:28–58) compares the two methods, and John Nerbonne's 1982 Ohio State University dissertation *German Temporal Semantics: Three-Dimensional Tense Logic and a GPSG Fragment* has the most thorough development I know of of this "neo-Reichenbachian" technique. (As suggested by Hans Kamp, Barbara Partee, Hinrichs and myself, compositional tense semantics within a sentence should perhaps be part of the more general matter of temporal discourse reference across sentence boundaries, which in turn implies that the best way to deal with natural language tenses will ultimately be resolved partly by the currently active debate on the proper way of handling pronominal reference across sentences.) But to return to the present book, I would like to emphasize that the unattractive *syntactic* approach should not be allowed to obscure the worthwhile points of the *compositional semantic* interactions of tenses and adverbs in these analyses, for these compositional semantic interactions can after all be reconstructed in most any one of several current syntactic frameworks. For those with the patience to dig through these syntactic rules, I believe these analyses raise some semantic questions that are still unsolved and worthy of attention, e.g. how and why do the scopes of *in-* and *for-* adverbials with respect to present perfect and progressive tenses seem to depend on their position in the sentence (cf. pp. 342–348; 368–371) and how are semantically "word-internal" readings of durative adverbials to be analyzed (250–285; 368,9)?

In addition to the compositional tense analysis, there are two other parts of the book which I would today write quite differently (and investigate more thoroughly had I the time), but with which I still have sympathy in the existing form. One is the proposal in chapter six that the distinction between lexically-derived and syntactically-derived constructions cross-cuts the distinction between "words" versus "phrases", a suggestion that has occasionally been embraced in subsequent literature but is still insufficiently developed in light of current morphological research. The second is my attempt in chapter eight to reconstruct, in my own way, Hilary Putnam's thesis that a semantic theory of truth and reference is in one sense a totally different enterprise from an (abstractly) psychological, mental theory of the human language-using capacity ("linguistic competence"), though is also an enterprise from which this second enterprise can immediately profit and in any event will ultimately depend for complete adequacy. Though the later chapter is out of place in that its concerns are in no way specific to aktionsart and aspect, the subject of the chapter is increasingly relevant in a day when cognitive science recognizes that one of its goals is to explain why linguistic ability, like other cognitive abilities, is a valuable adaptation of the human species. I only hope that today's readers will find their interest piqued by these short chapters so as to investigate these topics further on their own.

CHAPTER 1

MONTAGUE'S GENERAL THEORY OF LANGUAGES AND LINGUISTIC THEORIES OF SYNTAX AND SEMANTICS

1.1. THE MEANING OF "UNIVERSAL" IN "UNIVERSAL GRAMMAR"

Montague's 'Universal Grammar' (Montague, 1970b, henceforth UG) provides the general theory of languages of which the grammar in 'The Proper Treatment of Quantification in Ordinary English' (Montague, 1973, henceforth PTQ) and the grammar in 'English as a Formal Language' (Montague, 1970a) are but particular instances. It is important to realize that Montague did not have the linguist's usual understanding of the phrase *universal grammar* in mind here, according to which it would refer to the problem of characterizing just the class of possible human languages. Instead, he deliberately aimed to create a much more powerful and general theory capable of comprehending the syntax and semantics of all the known artificial languages of logicians as well as that of natural languages and, no doubt, of countless varied, as yet unimagined, "unnatural" languages.

It is sometimes suggested that this feature of Montague's program renders it totally irrelevant to the linguist's concerns, since it makes no "empirical claims" about the class of possible human languages. While I would agree that the goal of Linguistics is to characterize this narrower class of the possible human languages, I maintain that Montague's UG will in fact be quite useful to linguists in pursuing this goal. But its purpose will be to serve not as a linguistic theory *per se* but as a reference framework within which to formalize, study, and compare various theories of possible human language. Because of its combination of extreme generality and absolutely explicit formalization, it should give us a better perspective not just on what is being included by a particular theory of natural language, but what is being excluded as well.

In the remainder of this chapter I will illustrate this suggestion, and at the same time set the stage for the remaining chapters of this book, by discussing several versions of transformational grammar (henceforth TG) and generative semantics (henceforth GS) from the point of view of the universal grammar theory (UG). While I will presuppose familiarity with the PTQ theory here and especially an understanding of intensional semantics, I will not presuppose that the reader has any acquaintance with UG, and I will explain notions from the latter theory as the need for them arises. (Ladusaw and Halvorsen (1977) is to be recommended as an introduction to UG for the linguist).

To be sure, not every conceivable theory of language is encompassed by the UG theory. General though it is, it embodies some very specific claims about the fundamental nature of meaning and about the way in which syntax and meaning are systematically correlated. Stated in the simplest way possible, this systematic condition embodies the familiar Fregean view that the meaning of every expression of the language is a function of the meanings of its immediate constituents and of the syntactic rule used to form it, and, significantly, nothing but the meanings of these constituents and the rule used.

From the principle of compositionality, it follows directly that any complex expression having more than one meaning must be producible in more than one way from the syntactic rules. (To say that the meaning of an expression is a *function* of the meaning of its constituents and the rule forming it is of course to say that for any combination of expressions and rules combining them, there is a *unique* meaning that will be assigned to the resulting expression.) But for technical reasons to be discussed later, the UG theory requires that the same syntactic expression may *not* be produced in more than one way, by using different rules or different component expressions.

Since natural languages obviously have syntactically ambiguous expressions of various sorts, this requirement cannot literally be satisfied. To resolve the conflict, the universal grammar theory distinguishes between the expressions of a *language* proper, and corresponding expressions of a *disambiguated language* which lies at the heart of every language; only expressions of the disambiguated language must meet this strict no-ambiguity condition. Expressions of the language proper may correspond to more than one expression of the disambiguated language, and since it is expressions of the disambiguated language that are interpreted semantically, an expression of the language proper may be assigned more than one interpretation, according to the various corresponding disambiguated expressions it is associated with.

Already from this brief exposition, the phrases *underlying structure* and *surface structure* will spring to the reader's mind as equivalents for the phrases *expression of the disambiguated language* and *expression of the language proper* respectively. One must beware, however, of making this association too facilely. To understand to what extent this analogy between transformational grammar and Montague's theory can and should be applied, it is necessary to examine the definitions of *language, disambiguated language,* and *interpretation for a language* more carefully.

1.2. SYNTAX IN THE UG THEORY AND IN LINGUISTIC THEORIES

1.2.1. Language *and* Disambiguated Language *in Universal Grammar*

A *disambiguated language* is defined as a sequence $\langle A, F_\gamma, X_\delta, S, \delta_0\rangle_{\gamma \in \Gamma, \delta \in \Delta}$. Here,

1. Δ is the set of *syntactic categories* of the language (or more precisely, the set of *names* of categories, since categories themselves are defined as sets of expressions).
2. X_δ (for each δ in the set Δ) is the sequence of sets of *basic expressions* (i.e. "lexical items") for each category δ in Δ. As the reader will recall from PTQ, there is no distinction between "lexical" and "non-lexical" categories, and some categories (e.g., sentences) may be devoid of basic expressions.
3. F_γ (for each γ in Γ) are the *structural operations* of the language, indexed by the set Γ. For example, in PTQ the set of structural operations is the set $\{F_0, F_1, F_2, F_{3,0}, F_{3,1}, \ldots F_{3,n}, F_4, \ldots, F_9, F_{10,0}, F_{10,1}, \ldots, F_{10,n}, F_{11}, \ldots F_{15}\}$, the operations which concatenate expressions, perform case agreement, insert tenses and negation, etc., and in the case of the operation schemas $F_{3,n}$ and $F_{10,n}$, replace pronouns having a specified subscript.
4. S is the set of *syntactic rules*, each of them in the form of a sequence consisting of a structural operation, followed by the syntactic category or categories that are input(s) to the rule, followed by the category which is the output of the rule. For example, the PTQ rule S5 for combining a transitive verb with its object to form an IV-phrase would be identified in this format with the sequence $\langle F_5, \langle TV, T\rangle, IV\rangle$, where F_5 is the operation concatenating the two inputs and changing the second to its objective case form if it is a pronoun.
5. The last item in the definition of *disambiguated language*, δ_0, is the category of *declarative sentences*.
6. I have deferred until last the discussion of the set A, which is called the set of *proper expressions*. This set contains all the basic expressions and all expressions that can be formed from them by application or repeated application of the structural operations.

This set A is not the same as the set of all expressions which are well-formed according to the syntactic rules, since A contains all these and others besides. The reason for this is that A contains expressions that can be formed by applying operations to any inputs without regard to syntactic category, e.g. the result of applying to a sentence and an IV-phrase an operation intended (according to S) to apply only to a TV and T phrase. The set A would thus not seem to be of much linguistic interest, but it is convenient for Montague to include it because he takes advantage of the fact that $\langle A, F_\gamma\rangle_{\gamma \in \Gamma}$ defines an *algebra* (with $\bigcup_{\delta \in \Delta} X_\delta$ as its *generator set*, F_γ, $\gamma \in \Gamma$ as its *operations*, and A as its *field*) in defining *interpretation* and *translation* later on. It is not necessary to concern ourselves with the details of these algebraic definitions here. (It is actually the whole set A which is required to be "disambiguated" in the strong sense alluded to earlier – that is, the result of applying an operation F_γ to any sequence of inputs (whether or not the inputs and outputs are "well-formed" according to S, i.e. are of the appropriate category for F_γ) must be distinct from any other basic or non-basic expression in A.)

A *language* is then defined as consisting of a disambiguated language plus an "ambiguating relation." Montague thus represents a language formally as $\langle\langle A, F_\gamma, X_\delta, S, \delta_0\rangle_{\gamma \in \Gamma, \delta \in \Delta}, R\rangle$, where the first part is the disambiguated language as before and R is the "ambiguating relation."

What did Montague intend the ambiguating relation R to be? Formally, no conditions whatsoever are placed on R by the UG theory, except for the (obvious) requirement that the domain of R be included in A. The domain of R thus might be A itself or, say, just the well-formed expressions of the disambiguated language, or some proper subset of these. R might be a one-to-many relation, a many-to-one relation, a many-to-many relation or a one-to-one relation (in which case the language is *syntactically unambiguous*). The elements in the range of R could bear great similarity to their disambiguated counterparts, or no similarity whatsoever.

1.2.2. *Montague's Use of the Ambiguation Relation R*

In the English fragment in UG, the ambiguating relation R happens to be defined as a function applying to A such that for all expressions ζ, $R(\zeta)$ is the result of deleting all parentheses and "variables" from ζ. For example, a sentence of the disambiguated English fragment of UG is (1):

(1) **{Jones (seeks a {horse such v_5 that {it v_5 speaks}})}**

and the corresponding expression of the language proper is thus (2):

(2) **Jones seeks a horse such that it speaks**

(The use of distinctive kinds of parenthesization, as illustrated in (1), is introduced into the grammar of the disambiguated language in UG to help insure that the strong distinctiveness requirement on A mentioned above is satisfied.)

In PTQ a slightly different tack is taken. Though the PTQ grammar is not literally constructed within the UG format, it is by design compatible with it, and from comments in PTQ (p. 255, Thomason edition) it is clear that the ***analysis trees*** themselves are to be taken as expressions of the "underlying" (Montague's word) disambiguated language, the ambiguating relation thus being that function which erases all but the top node of an analysis tree and erases even the structural operation index attached to that node. For example, (3) would be a disambiguated expression in PTQ, and its corresponding expression of the language proper would be (4):

(3)

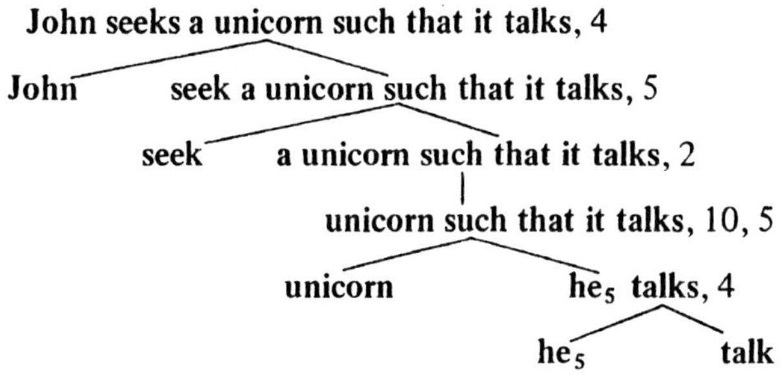

(4) **John seeks a unicorn such that it talks**

(In PTQ, the structural operation indices in the analysis tree take over the role played by the distinctive parentheses in UG; that is, they insure that the strong disambiguation requirement is met. For example, the result of applying $F_{10,3}$ to a sentence might sometimes be the same sentence as the result of applying $F_{10,5}$ to that same input – specifically, when there are no occurrences of either **he**$_3$(**him**$_3$) or **he**$_5$(**him**$_5$) in the input sentence – but by virtue of these indices the analysis trees are nevertheless distinct.)

The strategy Montague was employing in both these fragments thus seems clear: he constructed the disambiguated language underlying the English fragment as close as possible to (surface) English as the strong no-ambiguity conditions on the algebra $\langle A, F_\gamma \rangle_{\gamma \in \Gamma}$ would allow, adding disambiguation devices such as fancy parentheses, subscripted variables and operation indices to insure that these requirements are met. Then R simply erases these extraneous devices. (It will be recalled that Montague distrusted TG as he knew it, hence "surface English" *was* English in his view.)

1.2.3. *Other Ways of Construing the Ambiguating Relation R: Cresswell's System*

M. J. Cresswell, whose analyses of natural language were profoundly influenced by Montague, seems to have adopted in his book *Logics and Languages* (Cresswell, 1973) the same strategy as Montague with respect to this ambiguity problem. Borrowing terms from TG, Cresswell calls the sentences of his underlying disambiguated language λ-*deep structures*, and the more English-like, sometimes ambiguous sentences which are correlated with these in his theory as *surface structures*. As Cresswell points out, however, the connection between the two kinds of expressions is quite different than in standard transformational theory. An example of a deep structure in Cresswell's theory is (5), and the corresponding surface structure is (6).

(5) $\langle$**Arabella**, $\langle\lambda, x_1, \langle\langle\lambda, x_{\langle 0,0\rangle}, \langle\langle\lambda, y_1, \langle\langle$**loves**$, x_1, y_1\rangle, x_{\langle 0,0\rangle}\rangle\rangle$, **no one**$\rangle\rangle$, **tenderly**$\rangle\rangle\rangle$

(6) **Arabella loves no one tenderly**

Here, as with all deep and surface structures in Cresswell's theory, the surface structure is produced from the deep structure simply by erasing all brackets, all λ-operators, and all variables. Thus Cresswell's "ambiguating relation" is in effect the same as Montague's in UG and PTQ. (Actually, this is an over-simplification of Cresswell's system. What is derived from the deep structure by the erasing operation is called a *shallow structure*. The *surface structure* in the proper sense is derived from the shallow structure by another operation that roughly corresponds to the linguist's "morphological spelling out rules;" (cf. Cresswell, 1973; pp. 127, 128, 209 ff.). Though the ambiguating relation itself performs the same erasure operation in Cresswell's theory and in UG, Cresswell's overall syntactic system is quite different from UG. Cresswell does not give his syntactic operations the power to concatenate expressions in different specified orders, substitute, or permute parts of expressions in specified ways as Montague's operations do. Instead, the operations are restricted to simple concatenation, though a functor expression (corresponding to an A/B category in PTQ) and its argument category (a B category) are always allowed to concatenate in either order. This flexibility is needed to produce all the necessary word orders of English sentences. The result is that if a given English shallow structure is well-formed, then any permutation of the words of that shallow structure whatsoever also counts as well-formed and can be given the same interpretation as the first.[1] To filter out undesirable word orders, Cresswell appeals to a set of *acceptability principles* but makes no attempt to describe any of these principles.[2] While this result may seem unsatisfactory for a linguistic theory – pending further elucidation of the acceptability principles – the simple system which results suits Cresswell's purposes well.

1.2.4. *The Relation R as Transformational Component*

Nothing in the general theory of UG requires that the ambiguating relation R be restricted to a bracket-erasing operation, of course. An alternative view of the R relation which immediately suggests itself to the linguist (and which is suggested by Cresswell's terms) is that the disambiguated language be construed as the "language" of deep structures in a classical TG (such as the *Aspects* theory, Chomsky, 1965), and that the expressions correlated with deep structures by R be the surface structures which are derived from deep structures by some transformational component. That is, suppose that the deep structures of some transformational theory T (or structures which closely resemble them) can be successfully enumerated by a grammar which meets the requirements of a *disambiguated language* according to UG. (The fact that languages generated by an "outside-in" context-free phrase structure grammar can be generated equally well by an "inside-out" recursive definition like Montague uses is intuitively obvious; cf. Wall, 1972, Ch. 8.) Supposing further that the transformational component of T can be rigorously formalized. Then the ambiguating relation R is explicitly defined as follows: $\zeta R \zeta'$ wherever ζ is a sentence of the disambiguated language (and thus a Deep Structure in T), ζ' is a surface structure according to T, and there exists a transformational derivation according to T in which ζ is the first and ζ' the last member of the derivation. (One immediate difference between this and the earlier construal of R is that R is now a many-to-many relation, since the presence of optional transformations allows one deep structure to be associated with several surface structures. In the "erasure" version of R, R is a many-to-one relation.)

From a certain point of view it would be more appropriate to treat R as the transformational and phonological components together, so that $\zeta R \zeta'$ is the case whenever ζ' is the surface phonetic representation derived from a surface structure which is in turn derived from the deep structure ζ by the transformational component. This would be desirable because surface structures are actually treated as bracketed expressions themselves, hence even two distinct surface structures can sometimes correspond to the same phonetic string, e.g. in the case of the sentence *Old men and women were present.*

For all we know, Montague may have foreseen this transformational specification of *R* for future UG-type fragments of English having a richer English syntax than the limited fragments he himself constructed in UG and PTQ, assuming the transformations could be specified in a way that met his standards of rigor. In fact, David Lewis, one of Montague's colleagues who was more favorably disposed towards transformational grammar than Montague himself, proposed in his "General Semantics" (Lewis, 1970) a theory very much in the spirit and form of UG in which a transformational component is to be explicitly included to relate the unambiguous underlying structures to their surface counterparts. As Lewis points out, his proposals are compatible with several versions of transformational theory, including those that contain global rules (and even those that contain surface-structure interpretation rules, if we are willing to follow Lakoff's suggestion (Lakoff, 1970, §3) to regard these as "notational variants" of (one kind of) global constraint so that meaning is still determined by the deepest underlying structure alone. Cf. Lewis, 1970, pp. 186-191 for further discussion.) GS is not excluded from Lewis' theory because nothing requires the basic expressions (i.e. English words) at surface structure to be the same basic expressions as those in the underlying disambiguated sentences. Nor does the UG theory exclude this, since the objects in the range of *R* could be objects of a quite different sort from those in the domain.

1.2.5. *R and the Potential Vacuity of the Compositionality Thesis*

What then, if anything, *cannot* count as an ambiguating relation for a grammar? Though UG itself puts no restrictions at all on *R*, any remotely reasonable account of a language (natural or artificial) must surely do so. Since for any interesting language (and all natural languages) the domain of *R* is infinite, a minimum requirement is that the value of *R* be effectively computable for each argument. For any grammar of a natural language to be of serious interest, the underlying unambiguous sentence (or sentences) corresponding to any surface structure must also be computable from the surface structure by some effective algorithm (even if it is the procedure of computing a (finite) number of deep-to-surface derivations to see which ones turn out to produce the initially given surface structure).

But perhaps we should require even more of *R* for any linguistic theory. If we accept my suggestion to regard Montague's version of the Fregean compositionality of languages as an interesting and significant claim about natural languages, then this claim has intuitive content and practical testability only to the extent that the connection between the disambiguated level (at which compositionality is strictly observed) and the "surface" level is straightforward and direct.

Unfortunately, ideas of what constitutes a "straightforward and direct" relationship of this sort will vary greatly from investigator to investigator. A few cases are uncontroversial. For example, it can hardly be doubted that an ambiguous example like (7) (though it is in fact often not ambiguous in spoken language, cf. Lehiste, 1973) is best related to unambiguous structures having as minimum additions the bracketing in (8) or (9):

(7) Steve or Sam and Bob will come

(8) [Steve or [Sam and Bob]] will come

(9) [[Steve or Sam] and Bob] will come

But such simple cases are in the minority. For a transformational grammarian, a long and complex derivation from a fairly abstract underlying structure may seem quite "straightforward and direct" if the transformations involved are well-motivated from his point of view on independent grounds. A Generative Semanticist may feel the same way about an even longer, globally constrained derivation from a still more abstract underlying structure. It is almost certain that Montague would have regarded both these kinds of derivations with great suspicion, regarding them quite possibly as a denial of his view that meaning in natural languages is compositional.

At present, then, there can be no explicit criteria for a "straightforward and direct" connection between underlying and surface levels that will be acceptable to all. But I will continue to assume that adherence to this notion, in some unspecified form, is a desired goal of an acceptable theory of natural language grammars.

1.2.6. *Trade-Offs between R and the Syntactic Operations*

A further complicating factor is that because the UG theory places no constraints (beyond the strong no-ambiguity conditions) on the structural operations $F_\gamma, \gamma \in \Gamma$, considerable "trade-off" is allowed between the contribution made by these operations to the final surface form, vis-à-vis the contribution made by R. We could, of course, decide to restrict one of these "components" with the aim of keeping the other one simple. Montague, in UG and PTQ, seems to have tried to let the structural operations do as much of the work as possible (while adhering to the no-ambiguity conditions), whereas if we took classical TG as a model (regarding the structural operations of the syntactic rules as the base component, and R as the transformational component), we would restrict the operations $F_\gamma, \gamma \in \Gamma$, to those that could be performed by a context-free phrase structure grammar (or whatever type of phrase-structure grammar we desire for our base component), allowing R to perform all the more complex (transformational) manipulations needed to produce a surface structure.

A convenient way to observe just what such trade-offs can involve is to compare the original PTQ grammar with the transformational "metamorphosis" of it presented in Cooper and Parsons (1976) and Cooper (1975). To take just one rule as an example, consider the PTQ rule S14, which quantifies into sentences with term phrases:

S14. If $\alpha \in P_T$ and $\phi \in P_t$, then $F_{10,n}(\alpha, \phi) \in P_t$, where either (i) α does not have the form **he**$_k$, and $F_{10,n}(\alpha, \phi)$ comes from ϕ by replacing the first occurrence of **he**$_n$ or **him**$_n$ by α and all other occurrences of **he**$_n$ or **him**$_n$ by **he/she/it** or **him/her/it** respectively, according as the gender of the first B_{CN} or B_T in α is masc./fem./neuter, or (ii) $\alpha =$ **he**$_k$, and $F_{10,n}(\alpha, \phi)$ comes from ϕ by replacing all occurrences of **he**$_n$ or **him**$_n$ by **he**$_k$, or **him**$_k$, respectively.

Now a transformational grammar does not allow a phrase-structure rule to perform operations such as replacing parts of a tree by new sub trees, so this rule must be split between the phrase-structure component and the transformational component. What is essential for unambiguous semantic interpretation of this rule – and thus must be present in deep structure – is that there be two constituents consisting of a sentence and a term phrase to act as quantifier, plus an indication of which variables in the sentence are to be interpreted as bound by the term phrase (i.e. the variables with the subscript n in Montague's rule). Also, the latter transformation must be able to tell which variables in the embedded sentence should be replaced or turned into pronouns. Thus Cooper and Parsons propose in their transformational grammar the following phrase-structure rule:

(10) S → NP Vbl S

which generates the quantifying term phrase (NP) and an instance of the quantified variable outside the sentence in which it will ultimately appear. This rule's transformational counterpart is the following:

(11) $NP[x_i]_{Vbl}[X[he_i]_{NP}(Y\ he_i)^*Z]_S$

SD: 1 2 3 4 5 6 7

SC: ϕ ϕ 3 1 5 **he/she/it/he$_j$** 7

(Conditions on pronoun choice are omitted here; cf. Cooper and Parsons (1976), p. 318. The notation $(\alpha)^*$ stands for any number of consecutive occurrences of α, including zero occurrences – a "non-Boolean" condition.) This rule is quite similar in effect to the Quantifier Lowering transformation of GS. It is clear that the combined effect of these two rules is exactly that of S14 in PTQ.[3]

The theories adopted by Cresswell (1973) and Lewis (1970) in effect follow the option of keeping the structural operations simple and relegating all other manipulations to (their equivalent of) the R-relation; both their grammars, unlike PTQ, use *pure* categorial grammars to define the syntax of the disambiguated language – that is, simple concatenation is the only structural operation, and the syntactic rules themselves (determining what can be concatenated with what) are determined entirely by the way the categories are named.

Is there any way of deciding which of these two ways of dividing the labor between the structural operations and R is to be preferred, or whether a mixture of "work" by the two components is desirable? At the level of generality of the present discussion, it seems to me that we have no reason whatsoever for a preference. More specific considerations must be brought in to decide this issue in a rational way, if it is to be decided. (Of course, individuals will have decided intuitive preferences, such as the preference of transformational linguists for the second of the two options.) For example, Partee's 'Montague Grammar and the Well-Formedness Constraint' (Partee, to appear), suggests that by restricting R to erasure of disambiguation devices and variable subscripts as in PTQ or UG (or even making it the identity relation) and by limiting the structural operations to recursively-definable combinations of a few basic "sub-operations", the existing semantic constraint of compositionality and the requirements of the disambiguated language may together go a long way toward characterizing possible natural languages syntactically. (See below for more of Partee's views). Other approaches than this are no doubt possible.

1.2.7. *Transformations as Independent Syntactic Rules*

There is yet another way of reconstructing a kind of transformational grammar within the UG theory that complicates this picture even more, this procedure stemming from Partee (1975). This is to add meaning-preserving transformations not via the ambiguating relation R, but to add them as syntactic rules along with the other, "formative" syntactic rules. This is legitimate in Montague's program as long as the meaning of the sentence resulting from such a syntactic rule can be correctly defined as some function of the meaning of the original sentence. If the transformation is "meaning-preserving," then this semantic function is quite simply the identity mapping. What cannot be added to the syntactic rules in this way (at least, so long as we adhere to the fundamental form of Montague's theory) is an obligatory transformation. The syntactic rules are together understood as a simultaneous recursive definition of the sets of well-formed expressions in each syntactic category, and it is essential to this end that, for example, any expression defined as belonging to the category t (sentences) by successive application of syntactic rules be regarded as well-formed, no matter how many rules have been used. Instead, the effect of obligatory transformations is most naturally captured through the relation R or by incorporating the effect of such transformations into certain crucial "formative" syntactic rules as Montague did. As an example of the latter method, note that Montague incorporates the effect of the obligatory transformation of Subject-Verb agreement into the structural operation of the subject-predicate rule (S4). Though the subject-predicate rule itself is technically "optional," it happens that the only way of getting sentences (phrases of category t) in the PTQ grammar is by the use of this rule. (Actually, the sentence adverb (S9), sentence conjunction (S11) and sentence quantification rules (S14) form sentences as well, but since these require sentences as input, one application of the subject-predicate rule is inevitable in each finite clause.) Other familiar obligatory transformations can be treated similarly; PTQ incorporates case marking in the verb-object rule (S5), and Thomason (1976, pp. 87, 88) incorporates reflexivization in the subject-predicate rule. All the operations associated with relative clauses could be incorporated into one relative clause formation rule, though Rodman (1976) does not choose to do this in his treatment of relative clauses.

Transformations that "change meaning" also cannot be incorporated among the syntactic rules if the way in which they change meaning is not describable by a general rule entirely in terms of the meaning of the input sentence. To take a familiar example from the literature, suppose it were the case that, as Lakoff and Chomsky once claimed, an unconstrained Passive transformation would change meaning by restricting the possible understanding of scope relationships between subject and object quantifiers. (This claim may well be false, but it will serve as a useful example.) Since the meaning of a sentence is, in the PTQ theory, a proposition (a set of possible worlds), no function taking the meanings of sentences as arguments could ever determine from a proposition itself what quantifier scopes if any might have been represented in the sentence that originally determined that proposition.

It could be objected that Partee's method of incorporating transformations into the syntactic rules violates the spirit of a Fregean semantics for natural language. In Montague's version of the Fregean approach, each syntactic rule has a specific and crucial contribution to make to the meaning of the whole expression. Transformations are a kind of rule that makes no such semantic contribution, but rather they supply additional, sometimes optional syntactic "frills" not directly related to meaning. For this reason it might seem more appropriate to consider them part of *R*. Whether or not this objection is cogent and significant, there is nothing in the UG theory that literally rules Partee's proposal out. Moreover, there could be good reasons for adding transformations in this way. "Transformations" can sometimes be formulated in a somewhat novel manner in MG in such a way that they do make non-vacuous (and well-defined) contributions to meaning. For example, Partee (1975) formulates Passive Agent deletion so that it deletes a free variable, but the semantic interpretation of this operation is to bind this variable with an existential quantifier. This accounts for the meaning properly. If it could be shown that certain reformulations of this sort were preferable to their original transformational formulations, and that certain other "semantically vacuous" transformations had to apply *before* these "semantic" transformations in certain derivations, then this would be an excellent reason for formulating the semantically vacuous transformations as real syntactic rules as well. (Some novel formulations of traditional transformations as rules that necessarily contribute to meaning are discussed in Dowty (1978a)).

1.3. SEMANTICS IN UG

1.3.1. *The Compositionality of Meanings*

Montague's theory of semantics in UG is provided in two forms, *Semantics: Theory of Meaning* and *Semantics: Theory of Reference* (pp. 227-231). These two sections do not as might appear from the titles present theories of two complementary aspects of semantics (on a par with, say, Grice's (1973) *asserted* versus *implicated* meaning, or Jackendoff's (1972) four parts of meaning), but rather give first a very general and then a more specific treatment of the same subject. The *Theory of Meaning* gives general structural properties that meanings are required to have and specifies how meanings are to be correlated compositionally with expressions of the language in a systematic way, but it does not say what *meanings* really are. The *Theory of Reference* fills in content for the preceding section, defining in almost exactly the same way as in the model-theoretic interpretation of the intensional logic in PTQ, *sense* (*intension* in PTQ), *denotation* (*extension* in PTQ) categorized according to the same *types* as in PTQ, *truth* relative to a model, and *entailment*. (Unfortunately, the term *meaning* is given a specific technical definition in this second section, in addition to its general definition in the first section. I will use it only in its earlier, more general definition.)

An *interpretation* for a disambiguated language (as defined in the general theory of meaning) is a system $\langle B, G_\gamma, f\rangle_{\gamma \in \Gamma}$. Here,

1. B is the set of meanings; it includes both the meanings assigned to basic expressions and the meanings assigned to complex expressions, and possibly even other meanings which are not assigned to any expression of the language.

2. G_γ, for $\gamma \in \Gamma$, is a sequence of operations on meanings. Since the result of performing any of these operations on meanings in B is also required to be in B (i.e. the set B is *closed* under the operations $G_\gamma, \gamma \in \Gamma$), the sequence $\langle B, G_\gamma\rangle_{\gamma \in \Gamma}$ defines an *algebra* of meanings, just as $\langle A, F_\gamma\rangle_{\gamma \in \Gamma}$ defined a syntactic algebra. Moreover, $\langle A, F_\gamma\rangle_{\gamma \in \Gamma}$ and $\langle B, G_\gamma\rangle_{\gamma \in \Gamma}$ are required to be *similar*, which is to say that to each operation F_γ there corresponds exactly one operation G_γ, and this corresponding operation is of the same number of places (i.e., both are one-place operations (functions), or two-place operations, or three-place operations, etc.).

3. f is a function assigning some meaning in B to each basic expression of the disambiguated language.

By formulating both the syntax of the language and the overall structure of the meanings (whatever they are) as similar algebras, Montague is able to specify the compositional relationship of meaning to syntax using the convenient notion of a *homomorphism* between two algebras. This notion is intuitively characterized by Halvorsen and Ladusaw (1977) as "a structure-preserving transformation of one algebra into another." They continue, "the idea of one algebra being homomorphic to another is that the structure of the second is reflected in that of the first in the sense that the structure of the first is a refinement of (or is identical to) the structure of the second." (p. 60). The most familiar example is probably the following (cited also by Halvorsen and Ladusaw): We take an algebra to be defined over the base-ten numerals $\{0, 1, 2, \ldots\}$, together with some operations closed in this set – let us take base-ten addition and base-ten multiplication as our operations – and then we consider a second algebra defined over the set of binary numerals $\{0, 1, 10, 11, 100, 101, \ldots\}$ with the two corresponding operations of binary addition and binary multiplication. It turns out that the function which converts a base-ten numeral to its binary counterpart is a homomorphism from the first algebra to the second. A computer can take advantage of this fact and perform addition or multiplication on base-ten numbers by first converting them to their binary counterparts, then performing the corresponding binary operation on these counterparts, and finally converting the result back to base-ten notation. This works in part because the result of first performing any base-ten operation on two base-ten numerals and then converting the result to a base-two numeral is equal to the result of first converting the original base-ten numerals to binary numerals and then performing the corresponding binary operations on those binary numerals. This is just what the definition of a homomorphism says, in more general terms: If h is the converting function from algebra $\langle A, F_\gamma \rangle_{\gamma \in \Gamma}$ to $\langle B, G_\gamma \rangle_{\gamma \in \Gamma}$, then it is a *homomorphism* from the first to the second just in case for all corresponding operations F_γ and G_γ, and for all sequences $\langle x_0, x_1, x_2, \ldots x_n \rangle$ of appropriate length n of objects in A,

$$h(F_\gamma(\langle x_0, x_1, x_2, \ldots x_n \rangle)) = G_\gamma(\langle h(x_0), h(x_1), h(x_2), \ldots h(x_n) \rangle).$$

(In the example of the numeral systems, the converting function is a one-to-one correspondence and thus also determines a homomorphism from the second algebra back to the first – this accounts for the computer's last step – but this situation does not obtain with all homomorphisms.)

Montague's general theory of meaning insures that the function f giving a meaning to each basic expression will determine a unique homomorphism from the syntactic algebra $\langle A, F_\gamma \rangle_{\gamma \in \Gamma}$ to the semantic algebra $\langle B, G_\gamma \rangle_{\gamma \in \Gamma}$. That is, there is a unique semantic operation corresponding to each syntactic operation in the language, and the meaning assigned to any expression is a function of the meaning of its parts and the syntactic rule used to form it – namely, this meaning is the result of applying to the meanings of the parts the semantic operation G_γ that corresponds to the syntactic operation F_γ that formed the expression. This is a formal statement of Frege's principle of compositionality which is precise yet surprisingly general, since it makes no assumptions about what meanings are.

1.3.2. *Katz' Early Theory as an Instance of the General Theory of Meanings*

It is interesting to note that even Katz' early theory of semantics (Fodor and Katz, 1963; Katz, 1966) can be accommodated to a great degree within this very general theory of meaning. Katz' *dictionary* corresponds to the function f that assigns a meaning (which Katz calls a *lexical reading*) to each basic expression of the language. The *projection rules* in Katz' theory can be regarded as the semantic operations G_γ, for $\gamma \in \Gamma$, since there is a projection rule corresponding to each phrase structure rule. (Katz says there is a projection rule corresponding to each "grammatical relation", which seems to amount to the same thing; cf. Katz, 1966, p. 165. This feature of Katz' theory has since been modified in Katz, 1973.) These projection rules are described as combining recursively the readings of expressions lower in the Deep Structure tree to produce readings for each node immediately dominating lower nodes. The set of all readings for all expressions can then be seen as the set B in Montague's definitions. Since in the versions of transformational grammar accepted in the middle 1960's (cf. Katz and Postal, 1964) semantic interpretation was supposed to be determined on the basis of Deep Structure alone, the entire transformational theory of syntax and semantics fits fairly neatly into the UG format: the phrase-structure rules are the syntactic rules in UG; the transformation component defines the ambiguating relation R; the dictionary gives the assignment f of meanings to basic expressions, and the projection rules are the semantic operations G_γ, for γ in Γ. (There are, to be sure, aspects of Katz' theory which do not fit so clearly this format. For example, Katz' dictionary actually assigns *sets* of readings to words, and the projection rules can likewise give sets of readings. Semantically ambiguous words are assigned a set with more than one reading in it. Though meanings could indeed be sets in the UG theory, this treatment of lexical ambiguity would not fit well with the theory of reference. Rather, semantically ambiguous words should be treated as formally distinct basic expressions in the disambiguated language, though they can be identical expressions in the language proper.)

It is also perhaps worthy of note that Montague defines *synonymy* in this general theory – it is given as simply identity of meanings, and as long as meanings are well-defined, this notion makes sense no matter what sorts of things meanings are. The more vital notions of *entailment* (and the family of notions definable in terms of it – *logical equivalence, tautology,* and *contradiction* –) can only be defined later in terms of the full theory of reference, where *truth relative to a model* is defined. Katz also defines synonymy as a matter of identity between readings produced by the projection rules. (Like Montague, Katz defines synonymy for all categories of expressions, not just sentences.) Katz' theory is of course distinctive in its attempt to define entailment not in terms of classes of models (as in the model-theoretic method) nor in terms of inferences in some formal deductive system, but rather in terms of *containment* of (parts of) one reading in another, and it is this feature of his program that critics have found most inadequate.

Of course it has frequently been pointed out that Katz' theory, Jackendoff's theory (Jackendoff, 1972), some versions of Generative Semantics and in fact all linguists' *structural* theories of semantics (in the sense of Lyons, 1968) are deficient in an essential way, in that they lack a theory of reference altogether. This point now is too familiar to need repetition here (cf. Vermazen, 1967; Lewis, 1970; Partee, 1975; Cresswell, 1978a; for example). I am, as before, assuming here that the reader understands the essentials of how *intension, truth, reference* and *entailment* are characterized in "possible worlds" semantics as in PTQ, Lewis (1970) or Cresswell (1973) and thus will understand the full force of this criticism without further elaboration.

1.3.3. *The Theory of Reference in UG*

I will not discuss the UG theory of reference in detail, since I am assuming the reader is already acquainted with one very rich instance of this theory – the interpretation of the intensional logic of PTQ. (Note that we are not yet talking about interpreting English by means of translation, so the intensional logic is the *only* disambiguated language whose interpretation is under discussion at this point.) A *Fregean interpretation*, which is the central notion of the theory of reference, must be based on some assignment of the categories of the disambiguated language into logical *types*, a requirement being that sentences get the type t. Sets of possible senses and possible denotations are prescribed for each type in the same way as in PTQ with respect to a set of individuals, a set of worlds, and a set of times. (Actually, I overlook a few differences between PTQ and UG here which are of no consequence to our discussion.) A function f (signified by F in PTQ) assigns intensions to the basic expressions (i.e., to the *constants* of intensional logic in PTQ).

What is interesting to note is how the Fregean interpretation (of, say, the intensional logic) satisfies the general definition of meaning given earlier. In the algebra of meanings $\langle B, G_\gamma, f\rangle_{\gamma \in \Gamma}$ defined by this interpretation, the set B will now consist of the two truth values, the individuals named by the names of the language, the properties of and the relations-in-intension among individuals etc. denoted by constants and all the other propositions, properties, and such "semantical objects" of various types that can be denoted by complex as well as basic expressions. The set G_γ for $\gamma \in \Gamma$ is the set of semantic operations corresponding to the formation rules of the intensional logic. For example, binary operations on truth values will correspond to the syntactic operations forming $[\phi \wedge \psi]$, $[\phi \vee \psi]$, $[\phi \rightarrow \psi]$ and $[\phi \leftrightarrow \psi]$, the operation of applying a function to its argument will correspond to the syntactic operation forming $\delta(\alpha)$, and so on. Finally, *f* is the function assigning intensions to basic expressions, and it uniquely determines a homomorphism from the syntactic algebra of the intensional logic into this algebra of meanings. Here, the compositional correspondence between language and the things called "meanings" has the same general form as in the Katz theory as reconstructed above, but whereas the things correlated with language were other symbolic objects called "readings" in Katz' theory, here they are the non-linguistic objects referred to by expressions – objects named, truth-values denoted, propositions (sets of possible worlds) expressed, and so on.

1.3.4. *Generative Semantics as an Instance of UG*

Some versions of GS do explicitly or implicitly propose that a theory of reference (model theory) be added to interpret the logical structures of the theory – cf. Keenan (1972), Dowty (1972), and Lakoff (1972), though Lakoff here (and in later writings) seems somewhat equivocal on the relevance of model-theoretic interpretation. With the addition of model theory, it seems to me that GS is formalizable in the UG theory without undue distortion, and that when so formalized, it would embody enough of the important aspects of Montague's semantic and syntactic treatments of English to be of serious relevance to contemporary Montague Grammarians. (In fact, the formalization of GS in intensional logic has been suggested by Heidrich (1975).) Several specific points will require comments, however. A difficulty in discussing these points about GS is that there is not and never has been a "standardized" version of GS, but rather there are at least as many versions as researchers who have written under this rubric. In what follows, I attempt to base my assumptions about GS loosely on Lakoff (1968; 1972), McCawley (1973), Keenan (1972), and Dowty (1972).

In outline, GS can be seen as an instance of the UG theory in the following way. The disambiguated language is here represented by the "language" of *logical structures* (also known as *semantic representations*), and these are defined by the syntactic rules of the disambiguated language. (In GS these may be viewed as either phrase structure rules or recursive definitions, and, I believe, what McCawley calls "well-formedness conditions on semantic representations.") The basic expressions of this disambiguated language do not look like words or morphemes of English, but rather resemble the variables, individual constants, predicates and logical symbols of first-order logic and modal logic, with some new logical symbols added. The ambiguating relation is defined thus: $\zeta R \zeta'$ if and only if ζ is a well-formed logical structure and there exists a sequence of phrase markers (a derivation) such that ζ is the initial phrase marker (sentences of the disambiguated language can easily be regarded as phrase markers), ζ' is the final phrase marker, and this sequence satisfies all of the given list of *derivational constraints*. These constraints include both local derivational constraints (conditions on adjacent pairs of phrase-markers in the sequence, also known as *transformations*), and *global derivational constraints* (conditions on non-adjacent pairs of phrase markers, or on entire derivations). When $\zeta R \zeta'$, ζ' will bear little resemblance to ζ, since the basic expressions in ζ will have been replaced in large chunks by English words in ζ', and multiply-embedded sentences will typically be condensed to single clauses. The expressions of the disambiguated language will be given a *Fregean interpretation* as described above.

Specific comment is required, first of all, on the logical structures. Most GS literature is oblivious to logical types, and so logical structures will have to be "cleaned up" to observe type-theoretic well-formedness. It has been seen as one of the virtues of GS that it requires only a very few categories in logical structure, probably only the three categories *noun phrase, verb* and *sentence* (also called *argument, predicate* and *sentence*). This view derives from the assumption that there are few "kinds" of semantic entities. When we begin to take model theory for logical structures seriously, this becomes a problem rather than a virtue. Quantifiers, for example, are claimed to belong to the same category as predicates in logical structure. But quantifiers cannot be interpreted model-theoretically in the same way as predicates (of individuals) are interpreted, so the two classes may be distinguished for semantic purposes. Since the surface syntax of English quantifiers is likewise totally different from that of "predicates" of the class Noun, Verb and Adjective (the sole exception being archaic sentences like *The men who left were many*, though most English quantifiers don't in fact occur in this construction at all), I fail to see how the literal treatment of quantifiers as "higher predicates" has much to recommend it. The claim that quantifiers come from higher predicates is to be clearly distinguished here from the claim that quantifiers originate in *higher sentences*, since this latter claim is perfectly consistent with type theory and the usual treatment of quantifiers in logical languages. Thus I propose to assume that the undifferentiated class of "atomic predicates" in GS is categorized into their most obviously appropriate types, following the pattern of type assignment in PTQ and UG. For example, a reference to the "two-place predicate BELIEVE" that occurs in formulas BELIEVE (α, ϕ) (where α is an individual term and ϕ is a formula) is to be understood as reference to a constant BELIEVE of type $\langle\langle s, t\rangle, \langle e, t\rangle\rangle$, hence the formula is understood as BELIEVE $(\alpha, {}^\wedge\phi)$. This example brings up the point that the intensional types of Montague's intensional logic (types $\langle s, a\rangle$, for all types a) have no precedent in GS. But here again I think that to adopt them, along with the operators "$^\vee$" and "$^\wedge$" is not to do great violence to GS. Since GS explicitly postulates modal operators and operators representing propositional attitude verbs that create opaque contexts, an intensional semantic treatment is required for these. In any case, a system of intensional semantic interpretation can be developed quite similar to Montague's in UG and PTQ which avoids the distinction between intensional and extensional types altogether (and thus avoids the operators "$^\wedge$" and "$^\vee$" in the object language). This approach makes the definition of *intension* the primary recursive semantic definition. Extensions can still be defined in terms of intensions in the metalanguage, though no object-language expressions directly denote extensions. Cresswell (1973), Lewis (1970) and Montague (1970a) all adopt versions of this simpler procedure.

It has been suggested by generative semanticists (cf. Lakoff, 1972, pp. 569-587) that presuppositions of sentences be represented somehow or other in the Logical Structure. Recently, Karttunen and Peters (1975) have developed a means for generating the presuppositions of complex expressions (or rather, the *conventional implicature* of complex expressions, a term of Grice's they adopt to avoid confusion over various understandings of *presupposition*) in terms of the meanings and implicatures of the component expressions with appropriate "filtering", these implicatures being derived ultimately from implicatures and denotations assigned to the basic expressions in a complex expression. This system generates implicatures compositionally in tandem with denotations, and is based on the PTQ-grammar. (See also Gazdar (1977), which also involves the UG framework.) Also, it is sometimes suggested (Lakoff, 1971) that the presuppositions must be taken into account in determining grammatical well-formedness of sentences, but I believe this is a misapprehension that is adequately corrected by Karttunen (1974, p. 192).

Another proposal actually associated with GS is the higher performative analysis (cf. Sadock, 1974; Ross, 1970; Lakoff, 1972). However, I believe that David Lewis' proposal for the "underlying structure" of non-declaratives (which relies, in turn, on his theory of language use in Lewis (1969)) is preferable to the usual GS versions of "higher performatives."

Thus I conclude that the essential features of the GS theory (or to be more accurate, what to *me* have always seemed the most important features) can all be accommodated as a special instance of the UG theory. It is true that an enormous amount of work would be needed to produce a small, explicit fragment of English in this framework, a fragment explicit in all details and comparable with the English fragment in PTQ, but this is because many aspects of GS have never been made precise in any form, not because of any theoretical or notational incompatibility. In fact, I believe GS would have a great deal to gain from being viewed in this way, because Montague's semantic apparatus (i.e., the intensional model-theory) is both extremely well developed already and eminently suitable to serving as the model-theoretic interpretation for the logical structures of GS. (In the next chapter, I will try to show just how useful model-theory is in sharpening and testing the lexical decomposition analyses of GS.) The UG theory will unfortunately not really help in formalizing the derivational constraints of GS, and I can offer little help in this formidable task.

1.4. INTERPRETATION BY MEANS OF TRANSLATION

1.4.1. *Translations and Semantic Representation*

I have deliberately avoided up to this time discussing the two-stage translation process of PTQ and the general definitions for translations in UG. As the reader will be aware from his knowledge of PTQ, English sentences are not interpreted directly but are translated, constituent by constituent, by means of a set of translation rules into expressions of Montague's intensional logic. It is worthwhile to note that the translation procedure is purely compositional and thus can be viewed as assigning *meanings* to all English expressions (though it only indirectly assigns senses and denotations to them, by way of the Fregean interpretation of the intensional logic). Thus the translation procedure constitutes an interpretation $\langle B, G_\gamma, f\rangle_{\gamma \in \Gamma}$ because (1) there is an assignment function f of meanings (in this case translations) to basic expressions of English, (2) there are operations corresponding to each syntactic rule (actually to each syntactic function) that operate on translations and give new translations – these are specified in the translation rules, the most common operation being to take the two translations α' and β' and form them into $\alpha'(\hat{}\beta')$, and (3) there will be a set B consisting of all the translations of basic expressions and translations that can be produced from them by applications of the operations given in the translation rules.

A homomorphism is determined from the syntactic algebra to this "translation algebra"[4] by f, since in PTQ the translation of a syntactically derived expression is equal to the result of performing the operation in the appropriate translation rule on the translations of the constituent expressions used to form that derived expression.

It is naturally tempting to linguists to think of the translation of an expression into intensional logic in PTQ as a "semantic representation", since these translations look like the formal objects that are called semantic representations or semantic structures in various linguistic theories. In fact, "semantic representation" is not a wholly inappropriate term since this translation in a sense "represents" the semantical object which is to be the extension (and also indirectly the one which is the intension) of the English expression.

1.4.2. *Classical GS and Upside-Down GS*

Given these similarities between the translations into intensional logic and linguists' semantic representations, a quite different way of seeing GS as an instance of the UG theory suggests itself, this way first noticed by Stanley Peters, I believe. This is to view the logical structures of GS as corresponding in UG to the *translations* of English sentences into intensional logic, rather than to expressions of the primary disambiguated language. The English surface structures in the GS theory would then correspond to the expressions of the primary disambiguated language of UG, i.e. to expressions produced by the "syntax of English" in the PTQ theory. The Derivational Constraints in GS would on this view appear in the UG theory as the translation rules. This reconstruction of GS embodies at least the fundamental idea that GS is essentially a system for pairing English surface structures with sentences of a highly "abstract" formal language that represent the meaning of the surface structures in a direct way, and that there is no significant level of "Deep Structure" between the two. (This is not to deny, however, that this second "reconstruction" of GS overlooks a number of differences. For example, this second reconstruction involves an independent syntactic characterization of surface structures by a set of rules, while GS holds that surface structures can only be appropriately characterized derivatively from logical structures by means of derivations. My expository purpose in considering this second reconstruction will become apparent later on.)

To facilitate understanding and comparison of these two ways of viewing GS, I have included a chart (Figure 1) showing side-by-side "component

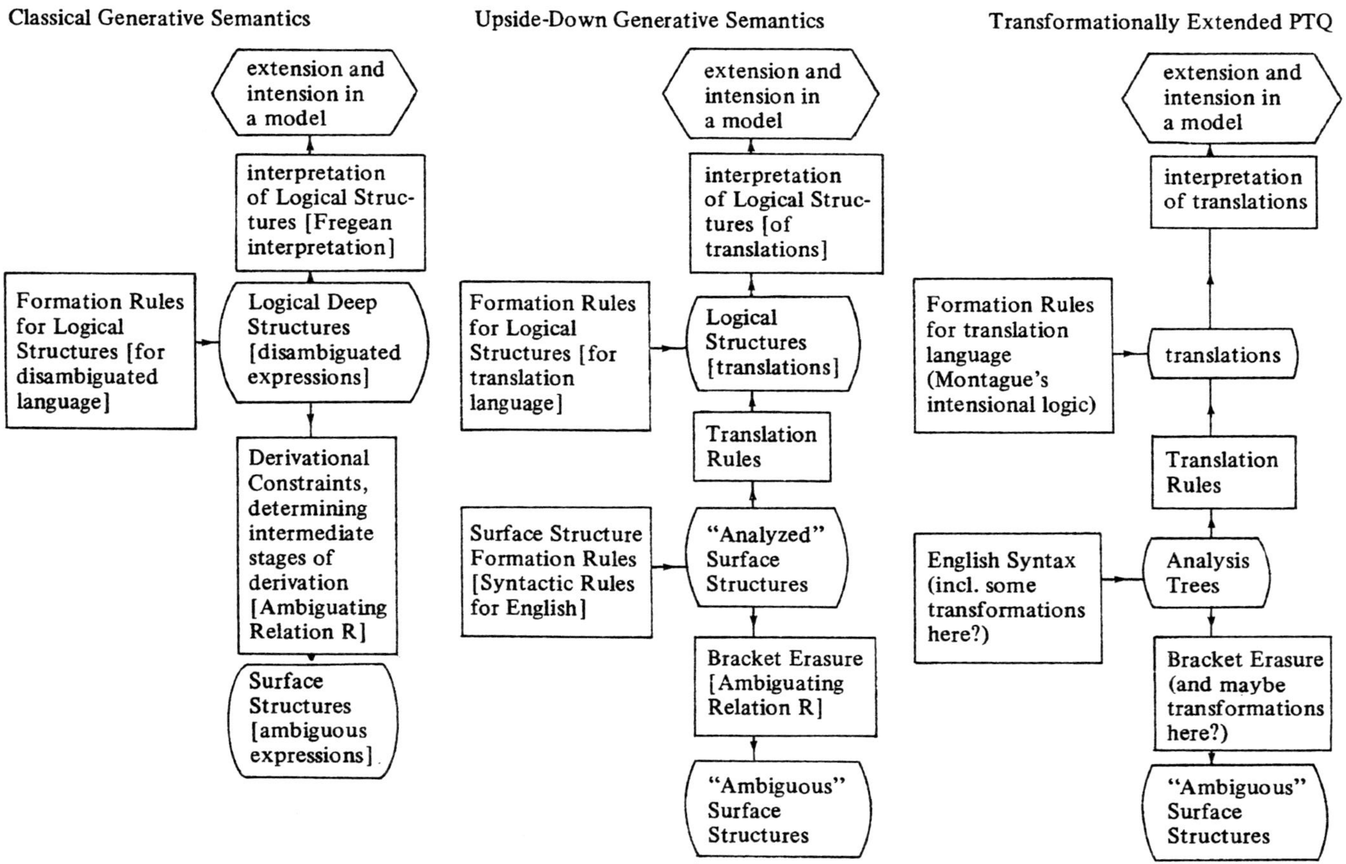
Classical Generative Semantics
extension and intension in a model
interpretation of Logical Structures [Fregean interpretation]
Formation Rules for Logical Structures [for disambiguated language]
Logical Deep Structures [disambiguated expressions]
Derivational Constraints, determining intermediate stages of derivation [Ambiguating Relation R]
Surface Structures [ambiguous expressions]
Upside-Down Generative Semantics
extension and intension in a model
interpretation of Logical Structures [of translations]
Formation Rules for Logical Structures [for translation language]
Logical Structures [translations]
Translation Rules
Surface Structure Formation Rules [Syntactic Rules for English]
"Analyzed" Surface Structures
Bracket Erasure [Ambiguating Relation R]
"Ambiguous" Surface Structures
Transformationally Extended PTQ
extension and intension in a model
interpretation of translations
Formation Rules for translation language (Montague's intensional logic)
translations
Translation Rules
English Syntax (incl. some transformations here?)
Analysis Trees
Bracket Erasure (and maybe transformations here?)
"Ambiguous" Surface Structures

Fig. 1.

diagrams" of these two different formalizations of GS. I refer to the first one I presented as *Classical GS* and the second one just now mentioned as *Upside-Down GS*. For further comparison, I have also included a third diagram, purporting to represent the kind of transformationally extended PTQ advocated by Partee.

How different is this Upside-Down GS from Classical GS? From a comment once made by Jerry Morgan (1970, p. 49) about the Generativist/Interpretivist controversy, one might wonder whether there would be any important difference at all:

> It seems to me that McCawley is correct in claiming, with Lakoff, Ross, and others that there is no autonomous level of deep structure intervening between semantic representation and surface structure. However, it seems likely that for those who reject this view and accept the position outlined by Chomsky in recent papers, many rules long considered to be syntactic transformations will come to have the status of "semantic interpretation rules", and deep structure will turn out to be considerably less deep that has been supposed in much of the literature. If so, then the two opposing theories may eventually evolve into notational variants of each other.

Would the Upside-Down GS theory as I have characterized it constitute the "notational variant" of Classical GS that Morgan here envisages? On the contrary, there would be a number of differences between the two, and we will want to look at these one by one.

1.4.3. *Directionality*

Perhaps the most obvious difference in the two GS theories is in the *directionality* of the mapping between logical structures and surface structures. The derivations of Classical GS are often conceived of as mapping logical structures into surface structures, while the inverted theory maps (near-) surface structures into logical translations.

However, the relevance of the notion of "directionality" in a derivation has frequently been called into question on both sides of the debate between proponents of GS and proponents of interpretative semantics, as is perhaps reflected in the Morgan quote above. Chomsky (1970) points out that if a grammar is conceived of as some device for enumerating pairs (S, s), where S is a semantic representation and s is a surface structure, then it makes no sense at a general level of discussion to ask whether the device should map S onto s, or rather map s onto S. Lakoff (1971) follows this claim with the (slightly stronger) one that "the notion of the directionality in a derivation is meaningless" and Katz (1971) argues roughly that there is no real issue in choosing between generative semantics and interpretive semantics, because transformations and interpretive semantic rules are merely inverses of each other.

In an important article, Zwicky (1972) disputes the view that any discussion of directionality of a derivation is pointless, and since his reasons will become extremely relevant to our discussion of lexical decomposition later on, we will examine them here. Zwicky agrees with Chomsky that if we only evaluate devices for generating pairs by looking at the set of pairs produced, then "at a general level of discussion" there is no basis for choosing one device over another if they both enumerate the same sets. But if we also take into account the structure of different devices that specify the same set of pairs, we may find a real sense in which one of the devices takes one of the members of the pair as "basic" and derives the other member of the pair from it, hence possesses a distinct "directionality". Zwicky illustrates this point by considering various devices for enumerating the set SQ of all pairs (A, B) where A is a positive whole number in decimal notation and B is its square, also in decimal notation. One way of enumerating the members of SQ is by the following recursive definition:

1. $(1, 1) \in \text{SQ}$
2. If $(x, y) \in \text{SQ}$, then $(x + 1, y + 2x + 1) \in \text{SQ}$

For example, the fact that $(4, 16) \in \text{SQ}$ can be demonstrated by a sequence of steps showing that $(1, 1), (2, 4), (3, 9)$, and then finally $(4, 16)$ are all members of SQ. For this device there seems to be no sense in which one of the members of the pair is taken as "more basic" than the other.

As Zwicky observes, this device is "not the one that leaps first to mind". Rather, one is likely to think instead of a device which takes the first member of any pair (A, B) as basic and derives the second member B from it by multiplying A by itself by means of the standard multiplication algorithm. A third device would take the second member B as basic, then by means of some square root algorithm, determine whether there exists a whole member A such that $(A, B) \in \text{SQ}$, and if so, what that (unique) A is.

Zwicky suggests there may be good reasons for the intuition that the second device is somehow a better or simpler way of enumerating SQ than the first or the third – "that within some definitional framework, the set of squares can be defined on the basis of the set of whole numbers and certain fundamental operations, but not vice versa, or that given certain computational devices, the standard algorithm involves the fewest steps or the least amount of 'scratch space'," adding that some limits on "definitional frameworks" may have to be assumed to make this statement actually true.

Zwicky goes on to propose that within sufficiently narrow assumptions about the nature of a linguistic theory, rules that serve to pair two stages x and y of a derivation may be meaningfully said to be "directional" in a sense similar to the directionality of the "better" device for enumerating the set SQ – that is, it may be that the appropriate set of pairs (x, y) can be simply and easily described by some algorithm which gives for any first member x an appropriate y, but that the inverse algorithm giving the first member x for any y is either impossible to define or else can be defined only in a very awkard or complex way. As an example of this situation he suggests the unbounded movement transformations of Ross (1967) may be definable in only one direction in the *Aspects* model. On the other hand, Dative Movement (Green, 1974) could be cited as an example of a transformation that possess no such directionality, since it can be formulated with equal ease in either "direction". Since a whole derivation is a linearly ordered set of expressions, if various rules that each relate adjacent stages in a derivation have this directional property, (hopefully, all these will have the *same* inherent direction), then the derivation as a whole can meaningfully be said to be directional.

Of course, to say that the "simpler" formulation of a rule is always preferred to an "awkward" or "complex" version is but a crude way of characterizing the criteria by which linguists evaluate different analyses, and different theories. Rather, the real goal is the admittedly somewhat vague and subjective one of finding the analysis and ultimately the theory that best and most simply reflects the over-all regularities and patterns evidenced in the language itself. A more complex treatment of one specific phenomenon may turn out to be more preferable from the larger perspective because it better fits general patterns set by other rules. This is a criterion of "simplicity and elegance" again, now viewed from a larger perspective. Though linguists would go farther than this (as Zwicky does) and say that "psychological reality" is also ultimately a criterion, I think that we can avoid this controversial point temporarily, because in practice the criterion of "best reflecting the over-all patterns and regularities evidenced in the language itself" is the guiding one for linguists in syntactic analysis, and I believe this is a criterion to which philosophers working in MG as well as linguists can readily subscribe.

As Zwicky points out, a further problem with the traditional debate on directionality among the generative semanticists and interpretive semanticists was that people saw it as a single question that would be answered one way or the other for a number of different aspects of the grammar, whereas it really should have been treated as a number of independent issues. That is, the question whether quantification should be treated by rules mapping "surface" determiners and pronouns into predicate-logic-like representations of quantification or vice versa is really independent of the question whether monomorphemic causatives (like *kill*) should be mapped into "decomposed" paraphrases or vice versa, and this in turn is independent of other questions about the transformational versus lexical generation of derived nominals, multiple versus uniform lexical insertion, the use of derivational constraints versus surface structure interpretation rules, etc. Though these issues are to *some* extent interrelated, I do not believe they are nearly so interrelated as many have assumed.

Besides mere directionality, another difference between the classical GS theory and the inverted GS theory as I have formulated them here is that the notion of a *derivation* having multiple stages is essential in the former in a way that it is not in the latter. If we compare a transformational derivation and Montague's procedure for translation of a complex expression, we find that though it is true that both involve a series of *steps*, these are not at all parallel. In a transformational derivation a whole clause is operated on again and again by successive transformations, whereas in a translation each constituent of a clause is operated on by a separate translation rule, but only one translation rule applies to each constituent. A completed translation will exactly reflect the constituent structure of the expression which it translated (though the corresponding parts will often have additional internal structure as well), but the last stage of a completed transformational derivation need not reflect at all the structure of the first stage.

1.5. PRELIMINARIES TO THE ANALYSIS OF WORD MEANING

1.5.1. *The Direction of Decomposition*

The preceding discussion of the inverted GS theory and its relationship to the classical generative semantics theory is preliminary to making the following observations about the analysis of word meaning:

In the chapters that follow, particularly in Chapter 5, one of the most important questions we will be concerned with is whether the "lexical decomposition" of certain kinds of words (both monomorphemic words and complex words derived by word formation) should be described by sequences of syntactic operations that have the effect of mapping complexes of expressions of an abstract, "logical" language into words of English, in the way that classical GS has suggested, or whether instead the same pairing of words with such complex expressions is best accomplished by a translation function of the PTQ variety, that prescribes "in one step" a mapping from words of English into complex expressions.

In accord with Zwicky's suggestion, I do not regard this question of directionality as a meaningless one to ask within some well-defined framework, and the two forms of the UG theory described above will serve as such a framework. In spite of their protests about the meaninglessness of directionality, the generative semanticists have presented what I think should be taken as arguments that the theory mapping complex expressions by stages into English words captures more linguistic generalizations than one with an inverse mapping, not because these GS mappings are literally simpler in isolation but simpler in terms of systematic patterns found in the language as a whole. We will want to examine these carefully. Whether or not the semantic interpretation rules in Katz' theory are really just inverses of the GS "pre-lexical transformations" as he claims, I think it will be clear that the translation function in PTQ is *not* equivalent to pre-lexical transformations "played backwards". Some important consequences will emerge from these differences.

Also in accord with Zwicky's suggestion, I will assume, initially at least, that this particular question of directionality is independent of other points of controversy that existed between the generative semanticists and interpretive semanticists, such as the treatment of quantification, performatives, derived nominals, etc.

Thus I will not really be discussing evidence for and against the two versions of GS I outlined as formalizations of the whole GS theory *per se*, but only evidence for the treatment of certain lexical decomposition analyses in the two ways represented by these two theories. The treatment of word meaning in what I called the inverted GS theory is really to be regarded here as compatible with the possible inclusion of some transformation-like rules in the "surface" syntax of English, and the treatment of quantifiers and bound pronouns found in PTQ. In other words, the question of choosing between the inverted GS theory and the third theory I have included in Fig. 1, the transformationally-extended PTQ theory, will not really be at issue here. (Those interested in comparing an explicit formalization of a "deep-to-surface" treatment of quantifiers and bound pronouns with an explicitly formalized "surface-to-semantics" treatment of the same phenomena are invited to compare the two transformational reformulations of the PTQ theory found in Cooper and Parsons (1976). In that work the authors are not concerned with showing why one or the other of these formulations is preferable on any particular grounds, but only with the more basic task of showing in a rigorous way that exactly the *same* pairings of English sentences with semantic interpretations can be achieved by either of these two methods for a restricted fragment of English, namely the PTQ fragment. The reader may, of course, draw his own conclusions as to which might be preferable for whatever reasons. I believe I am correct in assuming that Cooper and Parsons, like most current investigators in Montague Grammar, including myself, feel that we do not yet have significant reason for preferring one of these formulations or the original PTQ formulation over another. I think this contrasts with the lexical decomposition analyses discussed in this book, where some reasons for preferring one version stand out clearly. See also Cooper (1975) for yet another interesting reformulation of the same matters. This, however, goes outside the scope of the UG theories entirely in altering the notion of *disambiguated language*.)

1.5.2. *Is a Level of "Semantic Representation" Necessary?*

There are, however, much more fundamental questions to concern ourselves with about lexical decomposition analyses than just this directionality issue. Linguists have almost invariably assumed that a semantic representation of some sort – whether it resemble those suggested by the generative semanticists, Katz, Jackendoff, or others – is an essential part of any adequate theory of meaning and furthermore that in this semantic representation the meanings of words are not indicated by single units but by complexes of "semantic primes" of some kind of other. But these assumptions are called into question by the UG theory and will have to be explicitly examined.

From inspection of the PTQ grammar, it may well seem that the step of translating English into intensional logic is necessary to what Montague wishes to accomplish, and that this translation of an English sentence corresponds fairly closely to the notion of a semantic representation in linguistic theories of meaning. This is not quite so, for reasons that become somewhat clearer when we turn to UG where the definition of *interpretation induced by translation* is given. Recall that the syntax of a disambiguated language embodies an algebra $\langle A, F_\gamma \rangle_{\gamma \in \Gamma}$, and that the translation function is defined so as to be a homomorphism from the syntactic algebra of the first language (English) into the syntactic algebra of the second (intensional logic). (Actually, this is an oversimplification; since Montague wants to let certain syntactic operations of English translate by means of complex expressions of intensional logic – as where the result of forming **every** α in English translates into $\lambda P \Lambda x[\alpha'(x) \rightarrow P\{x\}]$ – this homomorphism is not really into the syntactic algebra of intensional logic but rather into an expanded version of that algebra containing *derived syntactic operations*, such as one that produces the entire expression above from α'.) Likewise, we noted that the Fregean interpretation of intensional logic (its model-theoretic interpretation) has the form of a homomorphism from the syntactic algebra of intensional logic into the algebra of meanings (here denotations) of the model-theory. Now comes the pay-off of these algebraic formulations. Montague can now use the mathematical device of letting these two homomorphisms induce a third one, a homomorphism directly from English into model-theoretic denotations. That is, if k is the translation function (homomorphism from English to logic) and h is the meaning assignment for the intensional logic (homomorphism from the logical algebra to the algebra of denotations), the *composition* of the two functions h and k (or their *relative product*) is a meaning assignment giving a direct model-theoretic interpretation for English. I refer the reader to UG (pp. 231-233) and Halvorsen and Ladusaw (1977) for the exact definitions, since it is not important to fully understand these here, but merely to see that it is this direct model-theoretic interpretation for English which results from this process which is ultimately of interest, not the two-stage translation/interpretation process itself. All the important semantic notions for English expressions – truth and denotation, entailment and logical equivalence – are adequately defined in terms of this direct model-theoretic interpretation without reference to the mediating translation into intensional logic.

Thus it would be possible to define an equivalent model-theoretic interpretation for English in other ways besides via the translation procedure. To take one rule for a concrete example, note the translation of **every** α in PTQ:

> **every** α translates into $\lambda P \Lambda x[\alpha'(x) \rightarrow P\{x\}]$, where α' is the translation of α.

If we had the model theory of PTQ but not the intensional logic, then we might write the semantic rule for this English expression something like the following:

> **every** α denotes, with respect to $\mathfrak{A}$, i, j, and g, that function h with domain $D_{\langle s,\langle e, t\rangle\rangle}$ and range $\{0, 1\}$ such that for all $k \in D_{\langle s,\langle e, t\rangle\rangle}$, $h(k) = 1$ if and only if for all $a \in D_e$, if the extension of α with respect to $\mathfrak{A}, i, j$ and g yields 1 when applied to a, then $k(\langle i, j\rangle)(a) = 1$; and $h(k) = 0$ otherwise.

Despite the differences in appearance, this rule gives exactly the same model-theoretic interpretation to all phrases **every** α as does the PTQ translation into intensional logic (assuming we have equivalent interpretations for all CN-phrases α here).

The translation procedure apparently served Montague as an expository device and as a matter of convenience. To me at least it does seem that the interpretations of English sentences in PTQ are more readily understood via their (simplified) translations than if these must be understood entirely by means of direct definitions like that above, and that these translations are more workable for demonstrating entailments. However, this may be a matter of opinion. In his seminar at Princeton in the fall of 1974, David Lewis formulated the PTQ theory in terms of direct definitions like this one and without the translation procedure because he considered the direct definitions more natural.

Given this subservient role that the translations themselves play in the UG theory, and the feasibility of constructing a model-theoretic semantics in the UG theory which contains no "level of structure" that seems to correspond to linguists' semantic representation at all, we are bound to ask just what role, if any, the lexical decomposition analyses of the kind found in GS or other linguistic theories should play in a model-theoretic semantics for English of the UG sort. This, in fact, is the most fundamental question to be answered in this study.

1.5.3. *Lexical Decompositions and the Description of Entailments*

First of all, I will try to show that the kind of decomposition analysis produced in GS can form a useful basis for expanding the class of entailments among English sentences that are formally provable in the theory, entailments which are of a good deal of interest in their own right and are not presently treated in PTQ fragments. Though some philosophers – perhaps including even Montague – have maintained a distinction between "logical words" and "non-logical words" and have believed that there is no interest in theoretical semantics in entailments dependent on properties of the latter class, I will try to show that this is a short-sighted position. Though there are to be sure semantic relationships between individual words which are of no great semantic interest – say, for example, the words *horse* and *cow* – there are nevertheless interesting semantic relationships among certain classes of non-logical words – such as the aspectual classes of verbs in the present study – which are illuminated by model-theoretic analysis. Moreover, the proper analysis of some traditional "logical words" in natural languages such as tenses, modals and some aspects of natural language quantification will interact with non-logical words and will depend more and more on a clear understanding of these kinds of non-logical words as the analyses of logical words become more detailed. From this point of view, decomposition analyses will at the very least serve the same purpose that the decomposition of **every** and other words served for Montague in PTQ – that of a convenient and perspicuous way of formalizing these entailments. This in itself is a more than adequate motivation for some decomposition analysis.

1.5.4. *Decomposition and Structuralism*

For the linguist, decomposition analyses have traditionally had quite a different significance. When pursued in a careful way, this kind of analysis is thought to reveal important "units of meaning" that form part of the structural organization of meanings in the language as a whole, units that are hoped to have some psychological significance. I hope to demonstrate that some inherent limitations of this purely structural approach to semantics can be overcome only if these structurally-motivated "units of meaning" are attached to a theory of reference such as that provided by Montague. Only then can we begin to ask in any rigorous way how adequate these decompositional analyses are and whether they really have the cross-vocabulary generality that is ascribed to them. The question whether we can really expect the best-motivated structural analyses to correspond to some kind of psychological reality, as linguists since Chomsky have claimed, is a difficult one that I will deliberately defer to Chapter 8.

One particular way in which the "basic structural units" of word meanings are thought to be revealed in natural languages is in the prefixes, suffixes and other methods of deriving words from other words that appear in natural languages, affixes which reappear from one language to the next with enough semantic similarity to make them candidates for universal units of natural language meaning. Thus it is important to have an explicit theory of word derivation for MG, and such a theory is developed in Chapter 6.

1.5.5. *Possible Word Meanings in Natural Language*

Since a professed goal of modern linguists is to characterize the class of possible human languages in as narrow a way as possible, a necessary part of this goal is to try to characterize the class of possible word meanings of natural languages in as narrow a way as possible. Decomposition analyses have traditionally been viewed in linguistics as a step towards this goal. That is, as decompositional analysis is supposed to reveal a universal set of fundamental "units of meaning", a constructional view of word meanings leads to the viewpoint that a possible word meaning (and a possible sentence meaning as well?) is anything that can be constructed out of these fundamental units by some specified method of putting them together (cf. Lyons, 1968, pp. 470-481). Naive and ephemeral though this goal may sound to some today when stated in this form, I think that it is fair to say that, because of our structuralist heritage, we linguists have not given up this goal and cannot be expected to abandon it unless and until it has been explored in much greater depth and found either successful or ultimately unworkable.

For this reason it will be valuable for linguists to approach this question from the referential notion of possible word meaning that the UG semantic theory provides. Here as before, the UG theory cannot be taken as a theory of natural language word meaning as it stands, but rather its usefulness is as a framework in which to construct and test such theories. From the point of view of reference, the notion of possible word meaning in UG is as broad as one could possibly imagine, and thus provides us with a "null hypothesis" as to the limits on how words may refer. Since the class of possible intensions of words will differ from logical type to logical type, let us take just one type to use as an illustration: the type $\langle s, \langle e, t\rangle\rangle$ (properties of individuals) which serves as the intensions of intransitive verbs, common nouns, and probably some adjectives. What the UG/PTQ theory allows is that an intension of this type may pick out absolutely any set of objects (individuals) whatsoever in a situation, and this extension may vary in any way whatsoever from one possible world to the next, one time to the next, and according to whatever additional parameters we include in the *n*-tuple called an index, such as place, speaker, hearer, etc. This is exactly what is meant by saying that the set of possible denotations of type $\langle s, \langle e, t\rangle\rangle$ is the set of *all* functions from indices to sets of individuals, i.e. the set $(\{0, 1\}^{D_e})^{I \times J}$. Thus according to the UG theory (or in fact any standard "possible worlds" referential theory) a noun or intransitive verb might very well denote with respect to some time, some world, and some suitably comprehensive model the set containing Richard

Nixon's left ear, the Eiffel Tower and Lake Michigan, while on alternate Thursdays it denoted not this set but instead the set of all albino wombats, and if used in Chicago would denote certain unicorns plus all currently existing cheese soufflés. One's intuitions of course rebel at the thought of such a "word" in any natural language, and it is a sobering thought to the linguist who would adopt a referential semantic theory to realize that this sort of thing is what the unadorned basic theory allows. Of course, the denotations of natural language nouns, verbs and adjectives do vary across possible worlds (cf. *actual* and *imaginary*), time (cf. *extinct, temporary, anticipated*), place (*nearby, distant*), speaker and hearer (cf. *yours, mine*) and many other contextual parameters, and they may be small sets or large (cf. *pope* and *electron*). But intuitively, even these words with varying denotations nevertheless denote things that have "something in common from a human viewpoint", they share some property in the ordinary language sense of *property*, rather than this quite general set-theoretic definition of *property* used in PTQ. (It is important, by the way, not to forget that the property variables P, Q, P', etc. in PTQ range over properties in this large, general set-theoretic sense and not the intuitively natural sense.) The question is, is there any principled way to single out the kinds of properties that may serve as intensions of natural language nouns, verbs and adjectives from the other "non-natural" properties in $(\{0, 1\}^{D_e})^{I \times J}$ and to do the same for word meanings of other logical types?

One possible answer to this question – and for all we know today, the appropriate answer – is that there is no principled way at all to segregate natural language intensions from this larger set. It may be that man with his varied interests, perceptual capacities and his current and yet-to-be-invented technological tools is potentially capable of finding any previously "unrelated" collection of things or events varying across worlds, times, places, etc. to be of interest, and that man's languages will always be ready to respond with a word for denoting such a collection. Since for all I know there may be cognitive limits of sorts on this potentiality, perhaps a better way of phrasing this response is to say that there is no interest to the theory of *semantics* in trying to determine limits of possible word meanings.

Though such pessimism is perhaps not unjustified, I think one can at least reasonably entertain the hope that there be principled ways of *excluding* certain subsets of the possible denotations in UG from being candidates for intensions of words, even though the precise limits of possible word meanings remain otherwise unresolved. The most promising area for such investigation I know of may be the ways in which verb denotations may vary with times;

this topic will be taken up in Chapter 2, Section 2.4. It may turn out that decomposition analyses of verbs – either via a translation procedure or by an abstract underlying disambiguated language – may provide a way of stating these limits that would not be possible otherwise, and this possibility is one of the motivations for pursuing the lexical decomposition analyses of linguists within model-theoretic semantics.

To summarize this section briefly, there are two fundamental questions to be asked concerning lexical decomposition analyses:

I. Is lexical decomposition as found in GS and in other linguistic theories desirable, given Montague's semantic program for natural languages?

II. If the answer to (I) is yes, then is a grammar best formulated as mapping 'decomposed' structures into single natural language words (as in classical GS), or as mapping 'whole words' into decomposed translations?

There may be as many as three distinct reasons for advancing certain decomposition analyses in Montague's program, and these reasons should be distinguished carefully:

1. To facilitate the perspicuous statement of important entailment relations among words and sentences of English (or other languages). This is presumably Montague's motivation for decomposing *be, necessarily,* names and determiners in PTQ. From this point of view, decomposition is a convenient but theoretically non-essential device. (It may turn out, however, that some decompositions can be shown to be *necessary* to capture certain kinds of entailments; this possibility is discussed in section 5.8.2.)

2. To capture what linguists feel to be significant paradigmatic and syntagmatic relationships among classes of word meanings in a (all) natural language(s), i.e. relationships which they hope may have psychological significance, and to come closer to capturing the notion of "possible word meaning in a natural language", perhaps only by excluding certain classes of possible intensions of the UG theory from being candidates for word meanings in some language.

3. To satisfy the "independent syntactic arguments" presented in GS that such decomposed structures must be part of the *syntactic* structures underlying surface sentences of English.

Because of the way certain combinations of positions on these questions and reasons have been associated with various schools of linguistics, it is important to point out that they have a degree of independence which may not always have been recognized. If decomposition is desirable because of reasons (1) and/or (2), question (II) is not thereby answered automatically; we must still look at reason (3) and other considerations to decide it. But conversely, if reason (3) is rejected, some "semantic" decomposition analyses may still be useful because of (1) or (2).

NOTES

[1] This is easy to demonstrate, once one observes that because of the lambda-operators, there is for any λ-deep structure an equivalent λ-deep structure with any word transposed to the beginning or end (and therefore, another equivalent λ-deep structure with another word transposed, etc.); cf. Ruttenberg (1976) for discussion.

[2] See Goodman (1976) for a formulation of these principles as a transformational syntax for deriving surface structures from λ-deep structures.

[3] Actually, Cooper and Parsons use this same transformation to effect "quantifier lowering" for quantifications over CN and IV phrases, as well as over sentences. Thus the label "S" in the structural description should really be replaced by the disjunctive label "S or CN or VP". The phrase structure rules that initially produce these other input quantifier structures are thus different from (10) though similar to it.

[4] As mentioned later in the text, this "translation algebra" is not really the same thing as the syntactic algebra of the intensional logic itself, but rather consists of the later algebra "expanded" to include derived syntactical rules formed by combining two or more operations. For example, the translation rule that gives $\alpha'(\hat{}\beta')$ is really the composition of the operation producing $\delta(\gamma)$ from δ and γ with the operation producing $\hat{}\zeta$ from ζ.

CHAPTER 2

THE SEMANTICS OF ASPECTUAL CLASSES OF VERBS IN ENGLISH

In this chapter I will present a set of lexical decomposition analyses of classes of verbs in English. Their place in the present work is to provide a "case study" from a natural language with which to illustrate the theoretical issues presented at the end of the last chapter. These analyses are based in part on my own previous work in this area (Dowty, 1972), but aside from my own familiarity with this area, there are good reasons for choosing this topic here. The problems connected with these verb classes touch on the best-known kinds of analyses of word meaning in generative semantics (with the possible exception of those in Postal's 'Remind' (Postal, 1970)) and the strongest independent syntactic arguments for this kind of analysis. Whether or not the problems that arise here are really typical of those that would arise with many other kinds of word meanings, they are in any case central as far as existing research goes. Also, this case study provides a good example of how the analysis of "logical words" (here tenses and time adverbials) can depend on the semantic analysis of "non-logical" words. Finally, these classes of verbs have a tradition of study in philosophy that goes back to Aristotle.

The plan of the chapter is to begin with a brief introduction to the generative semantics theory of lexical decomposition, then to present the analyses from the implicit point of view of the "classical GS" theory along with an explanation of the "structural motivation" that linguists might recognize as supporting such analyses – that is, citation of syntactic, morphological and semantic patterns and regularities that these analyses can be said to explain in some sense. At the same time, these decomposition analyses are treated as forming a fragment of a "Natural Logic" for which explicit model-theoretic interpretation is given. In later chapters we will modify these analyses, examine the independent syntactic motivation for treating them as underlying syntactic structures of English, and consider the alternative of capturing the same semantic effect of these decomposition analyses by using the translation function and other constraints on model-theoretic interpretation, rather than by appealing to abstract deep structures.

2.1. THE DEVELOPMENT OF DECOMPOSITION ANALYSIS IN GS

2.1.1. *Pre-GS decomposition analyses*

As mentioned in the introduction, decomposition analysis of word meaning in modern linguistics originates with the early structuralist writings of Hjelmslev (1953) and Jakobson (1936), if not earlier. The standard Hjelmslev example, the data for which is repeated below, is motivated by purely *paradigmatic* considerations at the semantic level.

(1)			
	woman	man	child
	cow	bull	calf
	mare	stallion	foal
	hen	rooster	chick

That is, when attention is paid to the way members of the same paradigm (the same distributional class, which is in this case common nouns) contrast with each other semantically, certain contrasts appear repeatedly. In this set of words, all the words in the first column contrast with the third in the same way, and all the words in a row contrast with corresponding words in some other row in the same way. This systematic relationship is described by assigning the semantic component (or *semantic feature* or *semantic marker*) *female* to all the words in the first column, the component *male* to those words in the second column, the component *adult* to the words in both the first two columns, the component *non-adult* to the third column, and components such as *human, bovine, equine*, etc. to various rows. When one has gone through the entire vocabulary of the language postulating and assigning semantic markers in this way, one should in theory be able to distinguish the meaning of any word from that of any other by inspecting the semantic markers assigned to each of them, in exactly the same way as one distinguishes in phonological theory any phoneme of the language from any other by inspecting the phonological features assigned to them. If this feature system is adequate to represent all the semantic *contrasts* evidenced in the language and is the "optimal" feature system for doing so, then according to structuralist semantic theories, the task of semantics is done. We need not inquire further what sort of entities these features *adult, female, human*, etc. are, but may safely take them as primitives of the semantic theory. Though more recent versions of structural theories such as Katz' have been enlarged and modified in various ways, this basic view of the componential analysis of word meaning seems to have survived intact. If one looks at Katz' recent analysis of the meaning of *chair*, exactly the same motivation seems to be present (Katz, 1972, p. 40):

(2) (Object) (Physical) (Non-living) (Artifact) (Furniture) (Portable) (Something with legs) (something with a back) (something with a seat) (seat for one)

Here, (Object) distinguishes the meaning of *chair* from that of abstract words like *number*, (Physical) distinguishes it from *deity*, (Non-living) from *tree*, (Artifact) from *mountain*, (Furniture) from *house*, (Portable) from *bed*, (Something with legs) from *wastebasket*, (Something with a back) from *stool*, (Something with a seat) from *table*, (Seat for one) from *bench*. Katz is of course not the only modern proponent of this approach. A recent textbook in "linguistic semantics" (Dillon, 1977) is concerned largely with analysis into primitive components of just this sort.

My point here is not to argue the usefulness of this sort of decomposition, (though I am inclined to doubt that it has great value). Rather, I want to point out that if we ask what consequences such analysis will have in a theory of reference, there seems to be only one possible answer: what is going on here is simply that the denotations of extensional predicates are being defined in terms of the intersections of the denotations of other, supposedly more basic extensional predicates. As Cresswell points out (Cresswell, 1975, p. 14), Katz' analysis of *chair* is, from a referential point of view, tantamount to saying that *x is a chair* is analyzed as a conjunction (3),

(3) $object'(x) \ \& \ physical'(x) \ \& \ \ldots \ \& \ seat\text{-}for\text{-}one'(x)$

where *object'*, *physical'*, . . . *seat-for-one'* are all extensional first-order predicates of an artificial language of linguistic theory, since clearly chairs are just those things which are objects, physical, . . . and seats for one. If we add binary semantic features to our repertory (i.e., a feature of the form $-\alpha$ for each feature α, such as $-$*human*, as well as $+$*human*), then we have in effect added negation as well as conjunction to our "markerese" language.[1] We must regard these predicates as essentially *non-logical constants*, in the sense that nothing whatsoever is said in Katz' theory that would determine *which* individuals are to be in the extension of each of these predicates.

One thing that this "conjunctive" decomposition of course buys us is the ability to reduce certain entailments in natural language among apparently "non-logical" words to logical entailments that are definable in terms of the sentential operators &, $\vee$, $\neg$, and $\rightarrow$. Thus for example, if we do not decompose *bachelor* and *unmarried man*, example (4) will at best have the logical form (5), and this formula will not (in the absence of meaning postulates or other restrictions on possible interpretations) count as a valid (or analytic) formula.

(4) Every bachelor is an unmarried man.

(5) $\bigwedge x[bachelor(x) \rightarrow [\neg married(x) \,\&\, man(x)]]$

If however we decompose *bachelor* into the markers (*− married*), (*adult*), and (*male*) and decompose *man* as (*adult*) and (*male*), then the resulting logical form of (4) will be a valid formula of standard first-order logic:

(6) $\bigwedge x[[\neg married(x) \,\&\, adult(x) \,\&\, male(x)] \rightarrow [\neg married(x) \,\&\, adult(x) \,\&\, male(x)]]$

(If "$\neg$*married*" were represented as a single marker (*unmarried*), or if it were further decomposed into a conjunction of predicates, then the formula would be valid just the same.) Given this apparent equivalence between semantic markers of this sort and conjunctions of predicates, it is hard to see how Katz' definition of *entailment* in terms of containment of one reading (group of markers) in another is anything but a degenerate or equivalent version of entailment as defined in first-order logic. Whether *all* entailments in natural language among extensional predicates can be captured economically by this method remains an open question, since no thorough treatment of this sort of a large segment of the vocabuluary of any language exists.

I will have nothing more to say about such conjunctive, purely extensional decompositions. The decomposition analyses to be considered below are supported linguistically by quite a different sort of evidence than the purely paradigmatic considerations illustrated above, and as they involve modal and tense operators and connectives rather than extensional predicates, the semantic problems in constructing a referential basis for them are much more complex.

2.1.2. *Causatives and Inchoatives in Lakoff's Dissertation*

The development of the verb analysis we will be concerned with begins in part with Lakoff (1965).[2] One set of sentence forms that Lakoff was concerned with were triads like (7a-c) and (8a-c).

(7) a. The soup was cool
b. The soup cooled
c. John cooled the soup

(8) a. The metal was hard
b. The metal hardened
c. John hardened the metal

As similar triads can be found with quite a large number of verbs in English, a systematic syntactic relationship is clearly involved from the point of view of the transformational grammarian of 1965. That is, the same "deep grammatical relation" is intuitively evident (or seemed evident then) between subject and predicate in the (a) and (b) sentences of the sets, and a similar relation holds between verb and object in (c). Parallel selectional restrictions also hold for the three kinds of sentence – that is, if we pick an inappropriate subject for the (a) example (**The prime number is cool*), then we can correctly predict that the (b) example (**The prime number cooled*) and the (c) example (**John cooled the prime number*) will be equally inappropriate. As these three sentences could not be derived from the same deep structure under the then universally accepted hypothesis that transformations preserve meaning, Lakoff had to seek distinct though related deep structure sources for the (b) and (c) examples. He noted the following types of sentences:

(9) a. The soup cooled.
b. The soup became cool.
c. The soup came to be cool.
d. It came about that the soup was cool.
e. That the soup was cool came about.

As examples of the form of (9a) and (9b) are virtually synonymous and differ very little in syntactic form, Lakoff noted that it would be plausible that they were derived from the same or almost the same deep structure. Assuming that this was in fact the case, Lakoff made a similar observation about (9b) and (9c). But (9c) can be seen as a transformed version of (9d), the transformation in this case being the well-motivated Raising-to-Subject transformation (at that time known as *It*-replacement). And (9d) is the extraposed form of (9e). (Some treatments of Raising would derive (9c) directly from (9e), without extraposition.) If all the sentences (9a)-(9e) come from the same or nearly the same deep structure source, then this source or sources most closely resemble (9e), where there is a sentential subject *The soup is cool* and an intransitive verb *come about*. As abstract deep structure elements with semantic significance were coming into vogue at that time (cf. Katz and Postal's (1964) *Neg* and *Q*), (9a) was considered by Lakoff to differ from the others in having an abstract verb with the feature +INCHOATIVE where the others had real verbs *become* or *come about* with about the same meaning. As the deep structure of (7a) is contained within that of (7b) under this analysis, the coincidence of grammatical relations and selectional restrictions is thereby predicted.

The situation with (7c) is quite parallel. One can find paraphrases of (7c) which are plausibly transformational variants of it but have one more clause than (7b), just as (7b) has one more clause than (7a):

(10) a. John cooled the soup.
b. John caused the soup to cool.
c. John made the soup cool.
d. John caused the soup to become cool.
e. John brought it about that the soup was cool.
f. John caused it to come about that the soup was cool.

If all of (10a)-(10f) come from the same or at least structurally identical deep structures, then those structures will contain the deep structure of (7b) embedded in a higher sentence which has the main verb *cause, make*, or the semantically similar abstract verb with the feature +CAUSATIVE. Here again, the parallel grammatical relations, selectional restrictions and meaning between (7b) and (7c) are accounted for. Lakoff's deep structures for (7b) and (7c) are (7b′) and (7c′) respectively. The feature +PRO indicates that the verbs are abstract.

(7b′)

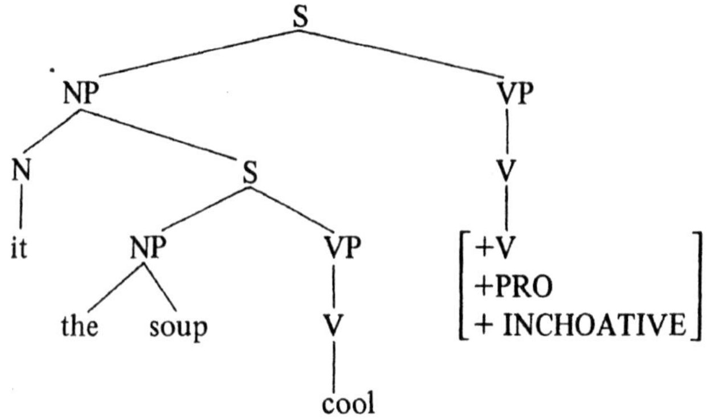

(7c′)

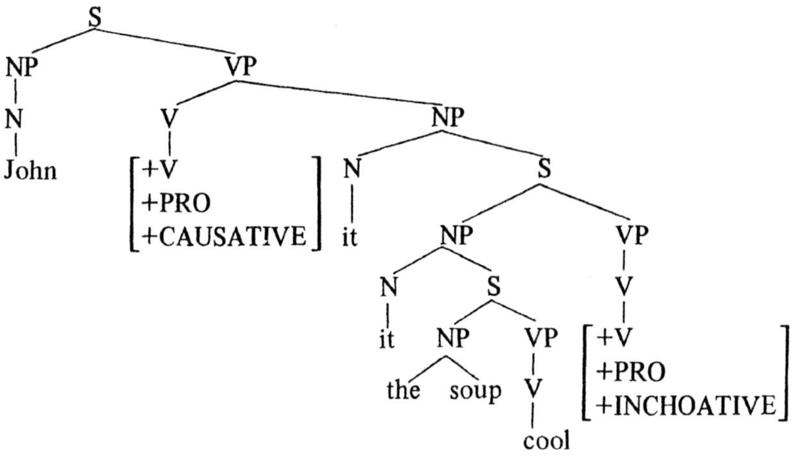

For these deep structures, obligatory transformations will replace the abstract verbs with the real lexical verb from the lower clause, thus reducing the two or three clauses of the deep structure to a single clause in each case. The causative transformation is not limited to cases where the verb has previously undergone the inchoative transformation, however:

(11) a. The window broke.
b. John broke the window.

(12) a. The horse galloped.
b. John galloped the horse.

The (b) example was derived from the (a) example in these cases according to Lakoff's analysis, though *break* and *gallop* have no adjectival, non-inchoative counterparts.

2.1.3. *McCawley's Post-Transformational Lexical Insertion*

As abstract lexical items with semantical significance began to proliferate in deep structures in the later 1960's, Lakoff, James McCawley, J. R. Ross and others began to suggest that the "deepest" level of underlying syntactic structure would turn out to have all the properties formerly attributed to semantic representation – i.e. a "level" of linguistic structure fully representing the meaning of a sentence but not containing words specific to a single natural language. As it was assumed that most "surface" English words would be represented at this deepest level by complex expressions rather than by single elements (indeed, this view was no doubt taken over without question from the decomposition approach of earlier linguists), attention turned to the question of just how individual lexical items of a language came to replace multiple parts of an underlying tree in the course of a derivation. McCawley's (1968) proposal for this problem came to be the most influential one. He used as an example the verb *kill*, and suggested that it be analyzed into components CAUSE, BECOME, NOT and ALIVE in the following way, where the tree represents the underlying structure of *x kills y*:

(13)

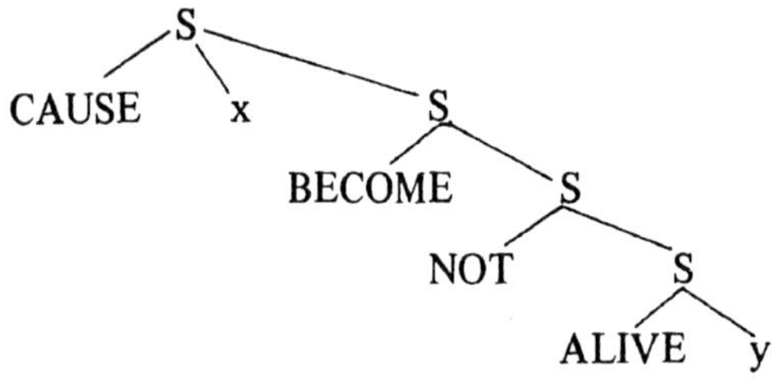

Note that the parts of the treee corresponding to *kill* do not form a constituent (are not dominated by a single node that dominates nothing else). McCawley suggested that transformations would have to rearrange these parts of the tree to form a single constituent before lexical transformation could insert the single word *kill*. This followed the independently motivated principle in transformational grammar that a transformation typically replaces or moves a single constituent rather than parts of different constituents. (Gruber (1965; 1967) proposed a similar theory which did not assume that such elements underlying words had to first be grouped together in this way – the so-called *polycategorial lexical attachment* theory.) McCawley thus postulated a transformation of *Predicate Lifting* (later, *Predicate Raising*) which attaches a predicate (element such as CAUSE, BECOME, NOT, and ALIVE in this tree, though they are not so labeled by McCawley) to the predicate of the next higher sentence. Thus successive stages of the derivation of a surface structure from (13) would be the following:

(14)

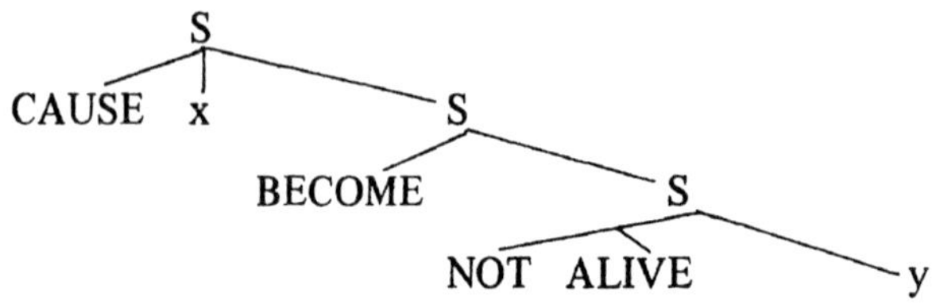

(15)

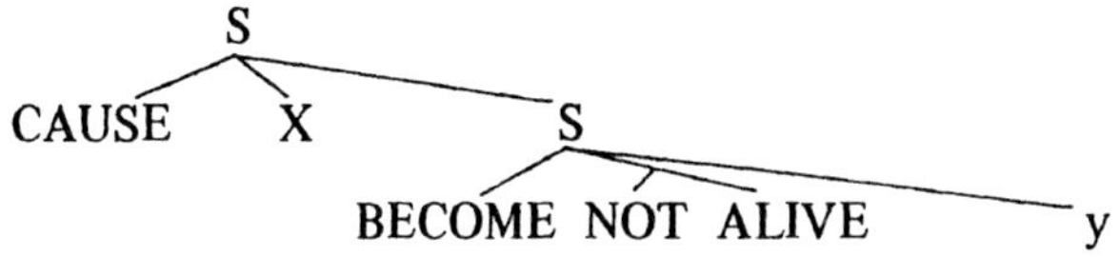

(16)

At this last stage, (16), the elements corresponding to *kill* form a single constituent, and a lexical insertion transformation will replace a sub-tree consisting of just this collection of elements with the word *kill*.

The predicate-raising transformation was to be an optional one at each stage. If it did not apply at all these stages in a derivation from (13), different lexical items would be inserted to replace the different abstract elements or groups of elements that ended up as single constituents. Thus from the same deep structure, other English sentences could also be derived such as *x causes y to become not alive*, *x causes y to become dead*, *x causes y to die*, and *x bring it about that y is dead* (assuming later substitution of noun phrases for the variables).

Also, perfectly well-formed underlying structures might be converted by this transformation into structures for which no existing English words would be appropriate. Suppose the lowest predicate ALIVE in (13) were replaced with a predicate OBNOXIOUS (again, this is an abstract semantic unit, possibly complex itself, not the English word *obnoxious*). If all the same applications of predicate raising took place as in the above derivation, a constituent containing CAUSE-BECOME-NOT-OBNOXIOUS would arise, but there is no English word answering to this meaning. In such cases the derivation "blocks" since not all abstract elements can be replaced with words. This is not a new situation in transformational grammar, since transformations have been used to "filter out" undesired derivations since Chomsky (1965).

2.1.4. *Paradigmatic and Syntagmatic Evidence for Decomposition*

We might now consider the question why this particular analysis of *kill*, as opposed to any other conceivable analysis, should be considered the correct one. Of course, McCawley was only interested here in illustrating the method of lexical insertion, and perhaps did not intend this to be taken too seriously as an analysis of *kill*. Nevertheless, the analysis became a standard one, and there are fairly clear reasons why it would seem motivated, given the traditional linguistic structuralist approach to meaning. Note the similarity of McCawley's analysis to Lakoff's analysis of derived causatives and inchoatives. (Certain differences in the ways the trees are drawn should not be taken too seriously – such as the fact that verbs precede sentential subjects in McCawley's tree but follow them in Lakoff's, or the absence of node labels and feature notation in McCawley's tree.) McCawley's analysis would assign the same relationship among (17a)-(17c) as among (7a)-(7c) (repeated below):

(7) a. The soup is cool.
b. The soup cooled.
c. John cooled the soup.

(17) a. Harry is dead (not alive).
b. Harry died.
c. John killed Harry.

Clearly, the semantic relationship among the three sentences is the same or approximately the same in (7) and (17). Here McCawley has made the analytic leap of going from one case, (7), where certain "units of meaning" are supposedly needed to describe a morphologically-motivated relationship among sentences, to a set of morphologically unrelated cases in (17), where the same semantic relationship seems to obtain, giving it the same analysis as the first case. Why would this be justified? Regardless of what McCawley may have intended, I think subsequent generative semanticists have seen this as a justified (or at least initially plausible) inference because of the assumption that all word meanings are built up out of a single set of fundamental units, and wherever one recognizes the same aspect of meaning, the same unit must be present. If an abstract causative and inchoative predicate are involved in (7), they must be involved in (17) as well. But there is a more basic question now: why, if at all, should the units of meaning contrasting (7a) with (7b) and (7b) with (7c) be basic, rather than some arbitrary combination of more basic units? Of course McCawley and other generative semanticists were careful to point out that these "predicates" might turn out not to be basic, but again they in fact have tended to be taken as basic, and for a methodological reason which became increasingly important in GS, if never explicitly stated. In the causative and inchoative cases we have different syntactic constructions based on the same basic lexical items but with a "unit of meaning" present in one that is not present in the other. As we shall see illustrated later in this chapter, the same "units of meaning" tend to appear over and over as distinguishing other pairs of syntactically related constructions containing the same basic words. The idea seems to have arisen in GS that where this happens, the "unit of meaning" is a primitive element, an "atomic predicate." This is but another way of extending structuralist methodology to semantics – the theory of language is to be justified entirely on the contrasts and patterns evidenced in the language itself. In generative semantics of course, a particular *syntactic* explanation is given to this phenomenon: the meaningful element is present in underlying syntactic structure, and this explains how transformations can be sensitive to it. (I will suggest later, however, that we need not adopt this generative semantics syntactic explanation of such phenomena even though we take them as clues as to how to structure a semantic analysis.)

What is of interest here is that such cases present quite a different kind of evidence for basic semantic units than the paradigmatic considerations illustrated earlier with Hjelmslev's example. There the basic units were thought to be revealed by contrasts in different words of the same distribution, here they are revealed by syntagmatic considerations, differences in meaning that somehow attach to specific syntactic constructions, regardless of the words occurring in them. Such syntagmatic contrasts are far fewer in number than the multitude of possible contrasts among words of an entire vocabulary and are thus easier to investigate thoroughly. A further reason why these syntagmatic contrasts are of greater theoretical interest than the paradigmatic ones is that compositional semantics naturally plays a more basic role in developing a semantic theory than does word semantics (at least in theories such as Montague's, though not of course in traditional linguistic semantics). If such "semantic units" as CAUSE and BECOME are involved in the semantics of syntactic rules in the kinds of sentences discussed by Lakoff, but in a way that cannot be attributed to the basic words occurring in them, then these units are necessarily the concern of compositional semantics as well as word semantics. Most of the evidence to be presented later for postulating certain decomposition analyses is in fact of this syntagmatic variety, though the question of whether the rules involved are syntactic rules proper or a different kind of formation rule will also have to be considered.

2.1.5. *The Place of Lexical Insertion Transformations in a GS Derivation*

Having pointed out that general theoretical considerations led him to hypothesize that at least one transformation – predicate raising – must apply in a derivation before certain lexical items could be transformationally inserted, McCawley raised the question of at just what stages of a derivation lexical insertion might apply. As the matter developed in subsequent research, there are two main ways that this might happen. First, the lexicalization of words with multiple parts to their underlying representations might happen essentially as McCawley illustrated for *kill* – that there is one and only one lexicalization rule involved in deriving this word, a transformation replacing the subtree consisting of the four abstract predicates CAUSE, BECOME, NOT and ALIVE with *kill*. The second possibility is that this lexicalization happens in stages – that after each step of predicate raising, a transformation replaces the newly derived complex predicate of that step by a word of English (if there is a word for that stage). In this second method (though not necessarily in the first method), the lexicalization transformations are cyclical; they apply first to the most deeply embedded clause, then to the next higher clause, and so on. In the case of the derivation of *kill*, the predicate ALIVE is lexicalized as *alive* on the first cycle (most deeply embedded clause). When transformations are then applied to the next higher clause, *alive* is predicate-raised and attached to NOT, yielding the "hybrid" verb [NOT *alive*]$_V$. Then another lexicalization transformation replaces [NOT *alive*]$_V$ with *dead*. At the next higher cycle after this, *dead* is raised and attached to BECOME, yielding [BECOME *dead*]$_V$, and this is then lexicalized as *die*. Finally, on the highest cycle, *die* is raised to give [CAUSE *die*], and this lexicalizes as *kill*. Thus three lexicalization rules are involved in deriving *kill*. (In the first approach on the other hand, the lexicalization rules for *dead, die* and *alive* are quite independent of the rule for *kill* – one such rule replaces [BECOME [NOT ALIVE]] with *die*, another replaces [NOT ALIVE] with *dead*, etc.)

What significant differences are there, if any, between the two approaches? It seems that McCawley's approach, the first approach here, treats the relationship of *kill-die-dead* as the normal relationship to expect among adjectives and the semantically related inchoative and causative verbs. That is, the fact that the three words bear no predictable morphological relationship to each other presents no complication at all, since the rules inserting the three words depend only on their respective "meanings." Under the first approach, the grammar of English would be no more complicated if there were no instances of semantically "nested" groups of words with morphologically related forms (or identical forms, such as *cool* (Adjective) *cool* (intransitive verb) and *cool* (transitive verb)). But in fact, English has literally hundreds of such related words, plus even more cases where two out of the three forms exist but not the third. This first approach leaves such cases of related words as apparent accidents, and thus linguists who adopted it would no doubt feel compelled to postulate some new theoretical device to describe these morphological regularities, something on the order of the *lexical redundancy rules* proposed by Jackendoff (1975).

The second method can obviously accommodate morphologically unrelated words like *dead-die-kill*, but can take into account the morphological form of words as well and thereby capitalize on systematic patterns. Thus instead of a long list of unrelated lexical causative transformations, replacing [CAUSE *cool*] with *cool*, [CAUSE *harden*] with *harden*, [CAUSE *break*] with *break*, etc., we can have a general rule replacing [CAUSE α] with α, where α is an already lexicalized verb.

One particularly striking kind of evidence for the latter kind of lexicalization rule (or perhaps better, *relexicalization* rule) was noticed by Binnick (1971), and independently by Charles Fillmore and David Perlmutter. An (exceptional) causative is *bring*, which is the causative form of *come*. There are numerous idiomatic expressions in English consisting of *come* plus a verb particle or adverb, such as *come down* "become depressed or less euphoric", *come off* "happen successfully (of parties, events, etc.)" *come to* "become conscious", and many others. What these investigators noticed is that for most of these idioms there is a second idiom with *bring* replacing *come* and paraphrasable by prefacing the paraphrase of the original idiom with "cause to." Thus *bring down* can mean "cause to become depressed or less euphoric", *bring off* can mean "cause to happen successfully", etc. It has been assumed in GS that idioms will have underlying structure not predictably related to their surface form, and thus have individual lexicalization rules replacing their semantic representation with a whole phrase. It would now appear quite accidental that the *come* idioms are paralleled by *bring* idioms without the possibility of lexicalization rules of the second type. With this type of rule, we can merely assume a lexicalization rule that replaces [CAUSE *come* α] with *bring* α, where α is an (already lexicalized) particle or adverb. Such a rule correctly predicts that the meaning of *come* α is irrelevant to the lexicalization of the causative form as *bring* α.

There are problems with this account of the *bring* idioms however. If all lexical replacement of multiply complex logical structures is done by the second (relexicalization) method, then we should expect to find idioms with verbs other than *come* to be regularly paralleled by causative forms of those idioms whenever the basic verb of the idiom has a causative form itself (in its literal meaning). But as Binnick notes (1971, p. 260), this is not the case with idioms in *go* and *send* (assuming *send* to be the causative form of *go*), and I am not aware of any other verb whose idioms have the striking number of causative parallels that *come* idioms do. Of course a grammar might contain both kinds of rules – a general relexicalization rule for [CAUSE *come* α], but completely separate rules for lexicalizing *go* and *send* and all idioms in which these morphemes appear. Yet there are still problems. As Binnick notes, there are also quite a few idioms with *come* that are not paralleled by *bring* idioms, such as *come clean* "reveal the full truth," *come by* "get, obtain,", etc. Though such cases might be handled by restricting α in the lexicalization of [CAUSE *come* α],[3] other kinds of cases will be more recalcitrant.

As example (8) illustrated (*The metal was hard, The metal hardened, John hardened the metal*), *hard* is an adjective that has phonologically regular inchoative and causative verbal forms, thus presumably these should be accounted for by a general relexicalization rule. But as Lakoff noted (1965), when *hard* has the meaning "difficult" instead of the meaning "physically rigid or impenetrable", the inchoative and causative forms are not possible:

(18) The problems in this textbook are hard.

(19) a. The problems in this textbook get hard (harder) in the later chapters.
b. *The problems in this textbook harden in the later chapters.

(20) a. The author of the textbook made the problems hard (harder) in the later chapters.
b. *The author of the textbook hardened the problems in the later chapters.

This is the opposite of the Binnick cases – here it is the meaning and not the phonological form that determines whether lexicalization of causative and inchoative takes place. Yet for the other meaning of *hard*, we clearly do want to say that it falls under the phonologically-determined general pattern for English regular causatives and inchoatives, and if the phonological form is all that is at stake for that rule, then there would seem to be no way of excluding the relexicalization rule from applying to *hard* meaning "difficult." I don't know how many cases like *hard* there will be in which morphological and semantic criteria for lexicalization are in conflict,[4] but even a few such cases cast doubt on the claim that all lexicalization rules can be successfully formulated either completely in terms of meaning or else via relexicalization rules. (One could of course reply that there are homonyms *hard*$_1$ and *hard*$_2$ and that only one of these undergoes the general causative and inchoative relexicalization rules. But if a relexicalization rule is sensitive to the distinction between homonyms, then it is unclear that it really describes a generalization stated entirely in terms of the form but not the meaning of a word.)

Of course, relexicalization rules would have to be provided with a means for handling exceptions quite apart from troublesome cases like *hard*. There are many exceptions in English to the causative and inchoative patterns illustrated for *cool* and *hard* (cf. Lakoff, 1965), as there are to the various nominalization patterns. The point of this discussion is merely to establish that the device of post-transformational lexical insertion does not, as is sometimes supposed, unequivocally eliminate the problem of "exceptions" to lexical transformations.

Generative semanticists were not unaware of these problems (cf. Gruber, 1967). McCawley has pointed out (personal communication) that in writing McCawley (1968a) he had in mind "the sort of complex dictionary entry introduced by Gruber, in which specific morphological realizations were indicated for optional adjuncts to a semantic item," and "in addition, there is nothing to prevent general rules for the morphological realization of some of those items (e.g. BECOME → *-en*), with the general rules being overridden by any specific realizations given in particular dictionary entries." (This suggestion, of course, involves a more complicated theory of grammar than I have been describing, since the application of a general lexical insertion transformation would be constrained by properties of certain other, specific lexical insertion transformations that happened to be in the grammar. However, I believe the details of a solution to this problem were not generally agreed upon, nor have they been worked out explicitly since.)

2.2. THE ARISTOTLE-RYLE-KENNY-VENDLER VERB CLASSIFICATION

In this section I will introduce a classification of verbs (or rather, of verb phrases) that developed in the philosophical literature as a result of a distinction made originally by Aristotle. This is not to deny that the distinctions have been recognized at one time or another by various linguists, but attempts at a comprehensive analysis of these classes have been restricted until recently to philosophers (cf. Comrie (1976) for linguistic references). The relevance of the verb classification at this point in the book is that the differences among the various classes will turn out to be explained, to a remarkable degree, by the hypothesis that one verb class differs from another in which of the abstract operators CAUSE, BECOME or other such operators appear in the Logical Structure of all verbs of each class; that is, the classes differ systematically in the way exemplified by the logical structures of the three words *cool* in (7a), (7b) and (7c), or the structures underlying the words *dead, die* and *kill* in McCawley's analyses.

I have earlier referred to this classification (Dowty, 1972) by the term *verb aspect*. This is not a wholly appropriate term, since *aspect* in linguistic terminology is usually understood to refer to different inflectional affixes, tenses, or other syntactic "frames" that verbs can acquire (*aspect markers*), thereby distinguishing "different ways of viewing the internal temporal constituency of a situation" (Comrie, 1976, p. 3). The Slavic languages provide the best-known examples of aspectual affixes for verbs. *Aspect* is distinguished from *tense* from the point of view of semantics in that tenses (like the tense operators of standard tense logics) serve to relate the time of a situation described to the time of speaking (as in past, present and future tenses), whereas *aspect* markers serve to distinguish such things as whether the beginning, middle or end of an event is being referred to, whether the event is a single one or a repeated one, and whether the event is completed or possibly left incomplete. By this use of the term *aspect*, the only instances of pure aspect markers in English are the progressive "tense" and the habitual quasi-auxiliary *used to* (phonetically [ˈyustə]), as in *I used to go to the movies on Saturday*. However, it is recognized that in all languages, semantic differences inherent in the meanings of verbs themselves cause them to have differing interpretations when combined with these aspect markers, and that certain of these kinds of verbs are restricted in the aspect markers and time adverbials they may occur with (Comrie, 1976, Chapter 2). It is because of this intricate interaction between classes of verbs and true aspect markers that the term *aspect* is justified in a wider sense to apply to the problem of understanding these classes of verbs as well, and it turns out to be this same classification of verbs which is the subject of the Aristotelian categorization. If it is necessary to distinguish the two uses of *aspect*, we can (following Johnson, 1977) distinguish the *aspectual class* of a verb (the Aristotelian class to which the basic verb belongs) from the *aspectual form* of the verb (the particular aspect marker or markers it occurs with in a given sentence).

2.2.1. *The Development of the Verb Classification*

It is Aristotle who is generally credited with the observation that the meanings of some verbs necessarily involve an "end" or "result" in a way that other verbs do not. In the *Metaphysics* 1048b, he distinguished between *kineseis* (translated "movements") and *energiai* ("actualities"), a distinction which corresponds roughly to the distinction we shall be making between accomplishments and activities/states. However, Aristotle elsewhere made the distinctions differently and with different terms; couched in metaphysical discussions of the potential and the actual, these contrasts seem barely relevant to natural language semantics and perhaps even contradictory at times. Therefore the reader is referred to Kenny (1963: 173-183) for an exegesis of Aristotle and additional references. (Kenny also claims to have discovered in Aristotle's *De Anima* the distinction between states and activities.)

Despite these problems, several Oxford philosophers of this century have had a go at Aristotle's classes, and in ways that are increasingly relevant for linguistic methodology. The first of these was Gilbert Ryle, who in his book *The Concept of Mind* (Ryle, 1949, p. 149) coined the term *achievements* for the resultative verbs, to be distinguished from the irresultative *activities*. Achievements, such as *win, unearth, find, cure, convince, prove, cheat, unlock*, etc., are properly described as happening at a particular moment, while activites such as *keep (a secret), hold (the enemy at bay), kick, hunt,* and *listen*, may last throughout a long period of time. Ryle also noticed that achievements have a kind of semantic dichotomy that activities do not:

> One big difference between the logical force of a task verb and that of a corresponding achievement verb is that in applying an achievement verb we are asserting that some state of affairs obtains over and above that which consists in the performance, if any, of the subservient task activity. For a runner to win, not only must he run but also his rivals must be at the tape later than he; for a doctor to effect a cure, his patient must both be treated and be well again . . . (Ryle, 1943, p. 150)

However, he also distinguished a sub-class of achievements which lack this dichotomy, "which are prefaced by no task performances." Ryle also supplied a test for these "purely lucky achievements" in the form of a list of adverbs which cannot co-occur with them:

> . . . we can significantly say that someone has aimed in vain or successfully, but not that he has hit the target in vain or successfully; that he has treated his patient assiduously or unassiduously; but not that he has cured him assiduously or unassiduously; that he scanned the hedgerow slowly or rapidly, systematically or haphazardly, but not that he saw the nest slowly or rapidly, systematically or haphazardly. (Ryle, 1949, p. 151)

Additional test adverbs are *attentively, studiously, vigilantly, conscientiously,* and *pertinaciously*.

In *Action, Emotion and Will* (Kenny, 1963, pp. 171-186) Anthony Kenny brought more grammatical and logical criteria to bear on these classifications.

He observed that if ϕ is a *performance verb* (his term for the class that corresponds to Ryle's achievements) "A is (now) ϕing" implies "A has not (yet) ϕed." If a man is building a house, then he has not yet built it. But if ϕ is an activity verb, then "A is (now) ϕing" entails "A has ϕed." If I am living in Rome, then I already have lived in Rome. While Kenny apparently did not appreciate Ryle's distinction between achievements with an associated task and purely lucky achievements,[5] he did on the other hand make precise the distinction between *activities* and *states*. Activities and performances can occur in progressive tenses, states cannot: We say that a man is learning how to swim, but not that he is knowing how to swim. On the other hand, the simple present of activities and performances always has a frequentative or habitual meaning (*John listens to Mary, John builds houses*) in a way that the simple present of states does not; *John knows the answer* is not frequentative. (The rest of Kenny's tests are incorporated below.)

It was Zeno Vendler who first attempted to separate four distinct categories of verbs by their restrictions on time adverbials, tenses, and logical entailments (Vendler, 1967). He distinguished *states, activities, accomplishments* (which are Kenny's performatives, Ryle's "achievements with an associated task"), and *achievements* (which are Ryle's "purely lucky achievements" or "achievements without an associated task"). This terminology will be adopted throughout the present work. Examples of verbs from Vendler's four categories are listed below:

States	*Activities*	*Accomplishments*	*Achievements*
know	run	paint a picture	recognize
believe	walk	make a chair	spot
have	swim	deliver a sermon	find
desire	push a cart	draw a circle	lose
love	drive a car	push a cart	reach
		recover from illness	die

One of the things which seemed to bother Vendler was the question of how the four categories should be grouped together. He considered states and achievements to belong to one "genus" and activities and accomplishments to belong to another, on the basis of the fact that the first two categories lack progressive tenses while the second pair allow them. (We shall see that states and achievements also fail the tests for agency, unlike the other two classes.) Yet he also noticed that achievements and accomplishments share some properties (e.g., they take time adverbials with *in*, such as *in an hour*) which activities and states lack. What we will attempt to do in the analysis that follows is not merely arrive at the most pleasing taxonomy of four or more categories of verbs, but to try to explain by the analysis given just why each of the categories or combinations of categories has the properties it does.

2.2.2. *States and Activities*

The distinction between states and activities (or actually between states on the one hand and activities and accomplishments on the other) is familiar to the linguist as the distinction *stative* vs. *non-stative*[6] drawn by Lakoff in his thesis (Lakoff, 1965) and does not require extensive discussion here. The usual tests are as follows (*know* is a stative, *run* is an activity, and *build* is an accomplishment):

I. Only non-statives occur in the progressive:

(21) a. *John is knowing the answer.
b. John is running.
c. John is building a house.

II. Only non-statives occur as complements of *force* and *persuade*:

(22) a. *John forced Harry to know the answer.
b. John persuaded Harry to run.
c. John forced Harry to build a house.

III. Only non-statives can occur as imperatives:

(23) a. *Know the answer!
b. Run!
c. Build a house!

IV. Only non-statives co-occur with the adverbs *deliberately, carefully*:

(24) a. *John deliberately knew the answer.
b. John ran carefully.
c. John carefully built a house.

V. Only non-statives appear in Pseudo-cleft constructions:

(25) a. *What John did was know the answer.
b. What John did was run.
c. What John did was build a house.

VI. As Kenny noted, when an activity or accomplishment occurs in the simple present tense (or in any non-progressive tense), it has a frequentative (or habitual) interpretation in normal contexts. If (26b) and (26c) are not used in one of a few specialized contexts (e.g. used by an announcer at a sports event, appear as a stage direction, appear in a narrative in the historical present), then they are understood to involve more than one event of reciting a poem or running respectively. But (26a) does not involve more than one occasion of knowing the answer. (The third example is changed from *build a house* to *recite a poem*, because one cannot build the same house more than once, so the frequentative interpretation would be problematic.)

(26) a. John knows the answer.
b. John runs.
c. John recites a poem.

(The behavior of achievements with respect to the stativity tests is complicated and will be discussed below.)

2.2.3. *Activities and Accomplishments*

Activities and accomplishments are distinguished by restrictions on the form of time adverbials they can take and by the entailments they have when various time adverbial phrases are present.

I. Whereas accomplishment verbs take adverbial prepositional phrases with *in* but only very marginally take adverbials with *for*, activity verbs allow only the *for*-phrases:

(27) a. ?John painted a picture for an hour.
b. John painted a picture in an hour.

(28) a. John walked for an hour.
b. (*)John walked in an hour.

II. Almost parallel semantically to the *for-an-hour* sentences and the *in-an-hour* sentences above are (29) and (30):

(29) a. John spent an hour painting a picture.
b. It took John an hour to paint a picture.

(30) a. John spent an hour walking.
b. (*)It took John an hour to walk.

(Though (30b) and perhaps even (28b) have acceptable readings, *an hour* in these readings does not describe the duration of John's action as it does in

(27b) and (29b), but rather seems to give the time that elapsed *before* John actually began to walk. The full explanation of these readings cannot be given until Chapter 7, however.)

III. The entailments of activity verbs with *for*-phrases differ from those of accomplishment verbs under the same conditions. If John walked for an hour, then, at any time during that hour it was true that John walked. But if John painted a picture for an hour, then it is not the case that he painted a picture at any time during that hour. This difference in entailment might be represented as in (31):

(31) If ϕ is an activity verb, then *x ϕed for y time* entails that at any time during *y*, *x ϕed* was true. If ϕ is an accomplishment verb, then *x ϕed for y time* does not entail that *x ϕed* was true during any time within *y* at all.

IV. As Kenny noted, entailments from the progressive to the non-progressive tenses also distinguish activities from accomplishments:

(32) If ϕ is an activity verb, then *x is (now) ϕing* entails that *x has ϕed*. If ϕ is an accomplishment verb, then *x is (now) ϕing* entails that *x has not (yet) ϕed.*

(This last test must be used with caution. It can be true that John is now building a house but also that he has already built a house, namely if he has already built a *different* house from the one he is now building. But the intent of Kenny's test is clear: we must give a "wide scope" reading to any quantifier occurring within ϕ to apply the test appropriately.)

V. A distinction in entailment also shows up if these two kinds of verbs appear as the complement of *stop*:

(33) a. John stopped painting the picture.
b. John stopped walking.

From (33b) we can conclude that John *did walk*, whereas from (33a) we are not entitled to conclude that John *did paint* a picture, but only that he *was painting* a picture (which he may or may not have finished).

VI. Only accomplishment verbs can normally occur as the complement of *finish*:

(34) a. John finished painting a picture.
b. *John finished walking.

VII. The adverb *almost* has different effects on activities and accomplishments:

(35) a. John almost painted a picture.
b. John almost walked.

(35b) entails that John did not, in fact, walk, but (35a) seems to have two readings: (a) John had the intention of painting a picture but changed his mind and did nothing at all, or (b) John did begin work on the picture and he almost but not quite finished it. It is this second reading which is lacking in activity verbs.

Since I have used an intransitive verb *walk* to illustrate the activity class, it might be supposed that the presence or absence of an object accounts for the difference between the two classes. However, there are activity verbs which do take objects. For example, *push a cart* or *drive a car* can be substituted for *walk* in the above examples with the same results.

VIII. Another such difference in possible scope ambiguities between activities and accomplishments has been noticed by generative semanticists, e.g. Binnick (1969). Some accomplishments (specifically, those in which the result brought about is a non-permanent state of affairs) exhibit an ambiguity with *for*-phrases which activities never have:

(36) a. The sheriff of Nottingham jailed Robin Hood for four years.
b. The sheriff of Nottingham rode a white horse for four years.

(36a), an accomplishment, is ambiguous between a repetitive reading (*four years* delimits the time over which the act of jailing repeatedly took place) and a reading in which *four years* delimits the duration of the result-state which the single act of jailing produced. (36b), an activity, has only the repetitive reading.

2.2.4. *Achievements*

Achievement verbs, Vendler's fourth class, can be distinguished by the following tests:

I. Although accomplishments allow both *for*-phrase and *in*-phrase time adverbials with equal success, achievements are generally quite strange with a *for*-phrase.

(37) a. John noticed the painting in a few minutes.
b. ??John noticed the painting for a few minutes.

II. Predictably, the same goes for the *spend-an-hour/take-an-hour* distinction:

(38) a. It took John a few minutes to notice the painting.
b. ??John spent a few minutes noticing the painting.

III. The entailments of achievements also differ from those of accomplishments. If *John painted a picture in an hour* is true, then it is true that John *was painting* a picture during that hour. But from the truth of (37a) it does not follow that John *was noticing* the painting throughout the period of *a few minutes*. Schematically,

(39) If ϕ is an accomplishment verb, then *x ϕed in y time* entails *x was ϕing during y time*.
If ϕ is an achievement verb, then *x ϕed in y time* does not entail *x was ϕing during y time*.

IV. Unlike accomplishment verbs, achievements are generally unacceptable as complements of *finish*:

(40) *John finished noticing the painting.

V. And unlike both accomplishments and activities, achievements are unacceptable as complements of *stop* (except in a habitual reading):

(41) (*)John stopped noticing the painting.

VI. *Almost* does not produce the ambiguity with achievements that it produces with accomplishments; compare (42) with (35):

(42) John almost noticed the painting.

VII. As Ryle observed, there is a class of adverbs which are semantically anomalous with achievement verbs:

(43) ??John { attentively / studiously / vigilantly / conscientiously / obediently / carefully } { discovered the solution / detected an error / found a penny / reached Boston / noticed the painting }.

Since the adverbs *deliberately, carefully* in stativity test IV are a subset of these adverbs, this test distinguishes states as well as achievements from the other categories.

TABLE I

Criterion	States	Activities	Accomplishments	Achievements
1. meets non-stative tests	no	yes	yes	?[7]
2. has habitual interpretation in simple present tense:	no	yes	yes	yes
3. ϕ *for an hour, spend an hour* ϕ*ing*:	OK	OK	OK	bad
4. ϕ *in an hour, take an hour to* ϕ:	bad	bad	OK	OK
5. ϕ *for an hour* entails ϕ *at all times in the hour*:	yes	yes	no	d.n.a.
6. *x is* ϕ*ing* entails *x has* ϕ*ed*:	d.n.a.	yes	no	d.n.a.[8]
7. complement of *stop*:	OK	OK	OK	bad
8. complement of *finish*:	bad	bad	OK	bad
9. ambiguity with *almost*:	no	no	yes	no
10. *x* ϕ*ed in an hour* entails *x was* ϕ*ing during that hour*:	d.n.a.	d.n.a.	yes	no
11. occurs with *studiously, attentively, carefully*, etc.	bad	OK	OK	bad

OK = the sentence is grammatical, semantically normal
bad = the sentence is ungrammatical, semantically anomalous
d.n.a. = the test does not apply to verbs of this class.

These criteria, many of which distinguish subsets of the four categories rather than determining a single category, can be perspicuously summarized in the form of a chart (Table I).

2.2.5. *Lexical Ambiguity*

At this point, a qualification must be made concerning this classification. Activities and accomplishments are supposedly distinguished by criteria 4, 5, 6, 8, and 9, but this is not always the case. Notice first that an activity verb describing movement behaves like an accomplishment verb if it occurs with either a locative of destination (Fillmore's *Goal* case) or with an adverb of extent, as in (44):

(44) John walked { a mile. / to the park. }

Now (44) meets all the requirements for an accomplishment:

(45) a. John walked to the park in an hour.
b. It took John an hour to walk to the park.

(45a) and (45b) are well-formed and have the proper entailments for accomplishments. (46) is also grammatical:

(46) John finished walking to the park.

(47) does not entail that John walked to the park (except on the habitual reading of course):

(47) John was walking to the park.

Furthermore, it can be objected that even when a locative or extent phrase is not present it is possible to assign an accomplishment reading to an "activity" verb in the proper context. Thus if I know (and the addressee knows) that John is in the habit of swimming a specific distance every day (to prepare himself for a swimming race perhaps), then I can assert that today John swam in an hour, or that he finished swimming early, or that on Tuesday he stopped, but did not finish swimming. (The starred sentences (28b), (30b) and (34b) can likewise be grammatical in special contexts.)

This phenomenon is not limited to activity verbs of motion, of course. *Look at*, for example, is normally an activity, but it has a familiar "special sense" in which it is an accomplishment:

(48) I haven't finished looking at your term paper yet, but I'll try to finish it tonight so we can discuss it tomorrow.

In fact, I have not been able to find a single activity verb which cannot have an accomplishment sense in at least some special context. *Look for* (*listen for*, etc.) would seem to be the most inherently irresultative of the activity verbs, but it is easy to find a context in which they are accomplishments: If a library has an established search procedure for books involving a definite number of prescribed steps, then one librarian can tell another that he finished looking for a certain book but never found it.

Furthermore, it may be supposed that those few examples which sound equally felicitous with *for* and *in* adverbials – e.g. Fillmore's (1971) example *He read a book for/in an hour* or *She combed her hair for/in five minutes*, an example pointed out to me by James McCawley – are all cases where a verb phrase can be read ambiguously as an activity or an accomplishment. In other words, *for* phrases may be restricted to activities exclusively, and alleged "marginal" occurrences of *for*-phrases with accomplishments such as (27b) are in fact being read as activities.

If this claim is correct, then Vendler's attempt to classify surface verbs once and for all as activities or accomplishments is somewhat misguided. First, we have seen that not just verbs but in fact whole verb phrases must be taken into account to distinguish activities from accomplishments. (In a certain sense, even whole sentences are involved, as will be seen in the next section.) And second, the possibility of giving accomplishment "interpretations" to activity verbs in special contexts blurs the distinction even further. The problem of distinguishing between lexical verbs which *must* be accomplishments, those which *may* be accomplishments with the right time adverbs, and those which can be accomplishments only under special interpretations is an interesting and difficult one, involving as it does the thorny problems of polysemy versus homophony. These problems will not be completely sorted out until Chapters 6 and 7, but the nature of the distinction and its interaction with tenses and time adverbs can be examined in the meantime anyway. The term "activity verb" will be retained for the present to describe instances of particular verbs in particular sentences when those sentences have the appropriate surface syntactic features (according to the criteria in Table I) and an irresultative meaning when understood in their most typical (or otherwise specified) context.

2.2.6. *The Problem of Indefinite Plurals and Mass Nouns*

There is another, more serious problem for Vendler's classification. Accomplishment verbs which take direct objects unexpectedly behave like activities if an indefinite plural direct object or a mass-noun direct object is substituted for the definite (or indefinite singular) one:

(49) a. John ate the bag of popcorn in an hour.
b. *John ate popcorn in an hour.

(50) a. John built that house in a month.
b. *John built houses in a month.

(51) a. It took an hour for John to eat the bag of popcorn.
b. *It took an hour for John to eat popcorn.

(52) a. It took a month for John to build that house.
b. *It took a month for John to build houses.

(53) a. John finished (eating) the bag of popcorn.
b. *John finished (eating) popcorn.

(54) a. John finishing (building) the house.
b. *John finished building houses.

Unfortunately, this difficulty extends to achievement verbs as well. That is, *discover* and *meet*, achievement verbs, disallow the durative adverbials *for six weeks, all summer* in (55a) and (56a), as they should according to our criteria. But (55b) and (56b), with indefinites or mass nouns, are good:

(55) a. *John discovered the buried treasure in his back yard for six weeks.
b. John discovered {fleas on his dog / crabgrass in his yard} for 6 weeks.

(56) a. *John met an interesting person on the beach all summer.
b. John met interesting people on the beach all summer.

Furthermore, if an indefinite plural occurs even as subject of an achievement, the sentence is acceptable with durative adverbials:

(57) a. *John discovered that quaint little village for years.
b. Tourists discovered that quaint little village for years.

(58) a. *A gallon of water leaked through John's ceiling for six months.
b. Water leaked through John's ceiling for six months.

We can informally state a general principle to cover the cases (55)-(58).

(59) If a sentence with an achievement verb contains a plural indefinite NP or mass noun NP (or if a sentence with an accomplishment verb contains such an NP as object), then it has the properties of a sentence with an activity verb.

How should principle (59) be incorporated into the grammar? Around 1967 most generative-transformational grammarians would probably have agreed how to do this. One would postulate syntactic features such as [± durative] and somehow state selectional restrictions, say, between verbs with these features and time adverbials like *for x time* and *in x time*.

In fact, an excellent and very thorough study of the phenomenon of aspect has already been done from this theoretical point of view (Verkuyl 1972) and it will be useful to consider it at this point. Verkuyl was acutely aware of principle (59) (or at least aware of the data behind it, which is the same in Dutch as in English, and no doubt as in many if not all other languages[9]), and most of his work is devoted to finding a way of generating correctly sentences like (55)-(58). His main thesis is that the notions of durative and perfective aspect are not to be found in any one constituent in surface structure, but arise from the "composition" of certain constituents; hence his title *On the Compositional Nature of the Aspects*. I quote:

> In chapter two the compositional nature of the aspects will be demonstrated with the help of a number of outwardly diverse sentences, all of which allow for the same generalizations regarding the position of durational adverbials. The durative and non-durative aspects in these sentences appear to be composed of a verbal sub-category on the one hand and a configuration of categories of a nominal nature on the other.
>
> (Verkuyl, 1972, p. iv)

This conclusion leads him to propose, for example, that VP nodes should be sub-categorized as *durative* and *non-durative*, the first of which can be expanded as in (60), (61), and (62). Non-durative VPs can be expanded as (63) but not (64); the structure (64), which would correspond to the ungrammatical (49b) or (54), is excluded by the phrase structure rules (Verkuyl, 1972, p. 54):

(60) $[_{VP_{dur.}}$ $[_V$ AGENTIVE$]$ + $[_{NP}$ INDEF. PL.$]]$

(61) $[_{VP_{dur.}}$ $[_V$ NON-AGENTIVE$]$ + $[_{NP}$ INDEF. PL.$]]$

(62) $[_{VP_{dur.}}$ $[_V$ NON-AGENTIVE$]$ + $[_{NP}$ INDEF. SG.$]]$

(63) $[_{VP_{non\text{-}dur.}}$ $[_V$ AGENTIVE$]$ + $[_{NP}$ INDEF. SG.$]]$

(64) $^*[_{VP_{non\text{-}dur.}}$ $[_V$ AGENTIVE$]$ + $[_{NP}$ INDEF. PL.$]]$

Actually Verkuyl later concludes (Verkuyl, 1972, pp. 107ff.) that the subcategorization with respect to aspect must take place at an even higher node than the VP since information outside the VP, e.g. in (57)-(58), must be taken into account.

Verkuyl's solution seems to produce all the good sentences without producing any of the bad ones; yet I think many linguists today would not be totally satisfied with this kind of solution, and for good reasons. In the first place, Verkuyl's analysis does absolutely nothing toward explaining why the structure (64) is ungrammatical while the others are not. Using his formalism and categories, it would be just as simple to write a grammar in which (60) or (61) or (62) would be blocked while (64) would be generated. Yet I doubt that there is any language in which this would be the case.

In the second place, I believe it would be agreed that the distinction between durative and perfective aspect is a semantic notion at least as much as it is a syntactic notion. What all accomplishments (including activity verbs in the "special interpretation" discussed earlier) have in common (as Ryle and Kenny noted) is the notion of a specific goal or task to be accomplished: in some cases it is a specific distance which is traversed or a specific location which the subject (and/or object) ends up at. In other cases it is the creation or destruction of a specific direct object; in still others it is the new state which the object (or subject) comes to be in as a result of the subject's action. If these verbs occur in a simple past tense, then we understand the goal or task to be reached. If these verbs occur in the progressive, then we are not entitled to assume the same task to be accomplished, though we understand that the action the subject performed was the same kind as before. Surely a semantic analysis of these verbs must account for these meanings in terms of the very same notions of time reference, completion of action and definiteness or indefiniteness of object that Verkuyl has neatly explained away as co-occurrence restrictions. The effect of these restrictions would surely have to be reflected in the semantic component, hence duplicated in the grammar.

2.2.7. *Examples of the Four Vendler Categories in Syntactic and Semantic Subcategories*

I believe that a defect of previous studies of the Aristotelian verb classification has been that only a few examples from each category are discussed, possibly giving the reader (not to mention the authors) a somewhat skewed impression of what the full ranges of verb phrases singled out by the given tests actually consist of. To try to rectify this situation, I have inserted here an informal list of different kinds of verbs in each category, subcategorized by both semantic and syntactic properties. The semantic headings should not be taken too seriously; I simply intend these to bring some of the different kinds of verbs in each class to the reader's attention, and I do *not* claim that these are either exhaustive or mutually exclusive categories, and I do not necessarily attach any theoretical significance to them or the way I have arranged them.

Some verbs are aspectually ambiguous in ways that have been alluded to already and will be described further later on.

As the reader may notice, the syntactic tests given for distinguishing the four categories do not give totally consistent results for all examples below. In fact, consideration of some of them will force us to make some revisions in the Vendler-Kenny classification (this revision will be made after interval semantics is introduced in Chapter 3). But for expository purposes, I retain Vendler's four categories here and in the rest of this chapter.

By the term *transitive* as applied to verbs and adjectives, I mean that a second noun phrase essential to the meaning follows the adjective or verb immediately (i.e. semantically a two-place relation is involved). By *two-place phrasal* I mean that a semantically essential noun phrase follows after a preposition. For example, *love* and *like* are transitive in *John loves Mary* and *John is like Mary*, but *listen* and *similar* are two-place phrasal in *John listens to Mary* and *John is similar to Mary*.

I. STATES (STATIVES)

A. Intransitive Adjectives

1. With individuals as subjects: *be tall, big, green, American, quadrilateral.*
2. With propositions as subjects: *be true, false, likely, doubtful.*

B. Intransitive Verbs

1. *exist, stink, itch, burn, live* (as in *Bird lives*).
2. "Pseudo-passives" that have no real active forms, with propositions as subjects: *be rumored, be (widely) believed.*

C. Transitive and Two-place phrasal adjectives

1. *like; similar, identical, related to NP* [These are the symmetric predicates of Lakoff and Peters 1969].
2. *proud, jealous, fond of NP.*

D. Transitive Verbs

1. Animate subjects: *love, hate, dislike, know, have.*
2. Symmetric predicates: *resemble, equal, be.*
3. With propositional object and propositional or human subject: *mean, prove, show, indicate, suggest, imply.*
4. Propositional subject: *involve, concern.*
5. Physical perception verbs [all are achievements as well as states] *see, hear, smell, taste, feel, perceive.*
6. Cognitive verbs with propositional objects [also achievements] *understand, know, believe, doubt, regret.*

7. "Psych-Movement" Verbs [propositional subject, human object; also achievements] *dismay, worry, please, surprise, astonish.*
8. Non-extensional Objects: *need, want, desire, fear.*

E. Two-place phrasal Verbs

1. Locatives
   a. *be in, on, around, under, at NP.*
   b. Pseudo-passives: *be located, be found at, on, around* NP.
   c. *sit, stand, rest, hang, lie, perch, adhere to, on, at, in* NP.
   d. Pseudo-motional locatives, predicated of roads, rivers, etc.: *run, flow, meander* (transitive: *cross*).
2. "Psych-movement" [May be transformational variant of D.7] *be pleased, astonished, dismayed at* NP; *like* NP.

II. ACTIVITIES

A. Adjectives [all adjectival and predicate nominal activities are volitional]

1. Intransitive: *be brave, greedy.*
2. Two-place phrasal: *be rude, nice, polite, obnoxious to* NP.

B. Predicate Nominals: *be a clown, hero, bastard, fool, stick-in-the-mud.*

C. Intransitive Verbs

1. Animate or inanimate subjects: *vibrate, rotate, hum, run, rumble, roll, squeak, roar.*
2. Cosmological: *thunder, rain, snow.*
3. Animate subjects: *cry, smile, walk, run, swim, talk, dance.*
4. Transitive absolute, or "object deletion" verbs: *smoke, eat, drink, play* (*music*).

D. Transitive Verbs of movement: *drive, carry, push* NP.

E. Two-place phrasal [though perhaps the prepositional phrase is a modifier] *sit, write, ride on, in* NP.

F. Non-extensional Object [both transitive and two-place phrasal] *seek, listen for, look for, search for.*

G. Physical Perception Verbs [transitive and two-place phrasal] *listen to, watch, taste, feel, smell* (the last three are also states and achievements).

H. Pseudo-three place idioms: *pay attention to, pay heed to, keep track of* NP.

I. "Aspectual" Complement Verbs: *keep, continue*.

III. ACHIEVEMENTS (May be coextensive with inchoatives)

A. Locatives

1. Transitive verb: *reach, leave, touch* NP (*touch* also stative and active).
2. Two-place phrasal verbs: *arrive at, land on, depart from, fall from* NP.

B. Change of Physical State (Absolute states; cf. 2.3.5 for distinctions between absolute and degree achievements)

1. Intransitives: *melt, freeze, die, be born* (Pseudo-passive), *molt, ignite, explode, collapse*.
2. Two-place phrasal: *turn into a* NOUN, *turn to* NOUN, *become* ADJ.

C. Change of Physical State (Degree state)

1. Intransitive: *darken, warm, cool, sink, improve*.
2. Phrasal: *become* ADJ-*er*.

D. "Aspectual" Complement Verbs

1. Infinitive complement: *begin, start, cease*.
2. Gerundive complement: *stop, resume, begin, start*.
3. With event nominal as subject: *end, stop, resume, start, begin*.

E. Possessive: *acquire, receive, get, lose*.

F. Cognitive (many both achievements and states)

1. Physical perception: *notice, spot, see, catch sight of, hear, taste, smell, feel, lose sight of*.
2. Abstract cognitive: *realize, recognize, understand, detect, find* (also accomplishment), *remember, forget*.

G. Change of State of Consciousness: *awaken, fall asleep*.

IV. ACCOMPLISHMENTS

A. Locatives

1. Transitive verb involving enclosure: *hide, cover, box, uncover, crate, shell* NP.
2. Two-place phrasal: *walk, swim, fly to* NP.
3. Two-place phrasal, can also be stative: *sit, lie, stand on* NP.
4. Pseudo-transitive motion verbs with extent NP – this NP is not a real direct object, as can be seen from absence of passive: **A mile was walked by John: walk a block, swim a mile.*
5. Two-place phrasal derived from activity verbs with locative result state: *drive, carry, push* NP *to* NP.
6. Two-place phrasal not derived from activity verbs: *put, place, set* NP *into* NP.
7. transitive with extent NP: *carry, push, drive* NP *a mile, a block.*

B. Intransitives that are not locatives [may be empty?]: *shape up, grow up* (fig.).

C. Transitive verbs of creation (*accusativus effectivus*)

1. [derived from activities] *draw* (*a picture*), *knit* (*a sweater*), *dig* (*a hole*).
2. [Not derived from activities] *make, build, create, construct, erect.*

D. Transitive Verbs of Destruction: *destroy, obliterate, raze* NP; *melt* (*an icecube*), *erase* (*a word*), *eat* (*a sandwich*).

E. Transitive Change of State: *kill, transmogrify, petrify* NP; *marry* NP *to* NP, *cook* (*a turkey*), *paint* (*a house*), *tan* (*leather*).
[Note that the same verb can be understood to express different semantic relationships to its object and thus belong to IV.D, IV.C, or IV.E accordingly. Cf. *paint a picture* (picture comes into existence) vs. *paint a house* (house undergoes change, but existed already). Also cf. *erase a word* (word ceases to exist) vs. *erase a blackboard* (blackboard undergoes change, but still exists).]

F. Creation of a "Performance Object"

1. Concrete Representation Created: *paint a landscape, photograph a senator, draw a unicorn, record a conversation, transcribe a lecture.* [Here something is created, but not literally

the thing named by the object NP. Rather, a representation of that object is created, and the object itself does not undergo any change. Cf. *draw a picture* vs. *draw a unicorn*. Also, note *paint a picture* (IV.C) vs. *paint a house* (IV.E) vs. *paint a scene* (IV.F.1).]

2. Abstract "Performance Object" Created:
   a. "Agent Performance": *perform a sonata, recite a poem, sing a song, prove a theorem, produce a play*.
   b. "Experiencer Performance": [Here the subject of the sentence does not bring about the performance as in F.2a, but the phrase is an accomplishment by the syntactic tests just the same]. *listen to a symphony, watch a play, attend a course, read a book*. [Note that *listen to the sound of the waterfall* is an activity but *listen to the symphony* is an accomplishment.]
   c. unclassified: *play a game of chess, basketball*.

[It is hard to know whether *prove a theorem* and *sing a song* should be considered ambiguous. If the theorem is being proved or the song sung for the very first time, then the theorem or song is created, just as in *build a house*, though the object is abstract. But if a previously composed song is sung or a theorem in a textbook is proved, there is at most a "re-creation". Yet no strong ambiguity is felt. Also, should *read a poem* be taken as ambiguous between agent and experiencer performances, according as it is read aloud or not? Probably not. Again, these categories are only for expository purposes.]

G. Other syntactic types of accomplishments. [These are not subcategorized semantically, and I have not tried to determine how many of the above semantic types occur in each of these forms.]

1. *That*-complement verbs: *bring about that S*.
2. Infinitive-complement verbs: *make* NP VP, *cause* NP *to* VP.
3. Prepositional Phrase complements: see under Locatives above; also *turn* NP *into a* NOUN, *put* NP *to sleep, drive* NP *to drink, read oneself to sleep*.
4. Factitive (Adjective of Result): *hammer* NP *flat, wipe* NP *clean, wiggle* NP *loose*.
5. Factitive (Nominal of Result): *elect* NP *president, chairman, appoint* NP *chairman*.
6. Verb particle constructions: (i) Transitive: *take* NP *out, chase*

NP *away, turn* NP *off*; (ii): Intransitive: *go out, run away, sit down, dry out*. [As Bolinger (1971) points out, verb-particle constructions are almost invariably accomplishment verbs. In many cases, the particle makes no significant contribution to the meaning of the whole except to indicate unambiguously that an accomplishment is intended (cf. *clean the room* vs. *clean the room up*), so in a sense this particle is the closest thing English has to a marker of perfective aspect.]

2.3. AN ASPECT CALCULUS

2.3.1. *The Goal and Purpose of an Aspect Calculus*

In this section an explanatory hypothesis about the four Vendler categories will be explored (though actually more than four categories will result). This hypothesis is essentially that of Dowty (1972). The idea is that the different aspectual properties of the various kinds of verbs can be explained by postulating a single homogeneous class of predicates – *stative predicates* – plus three or four sentential operators and connectives. English stative verbs are supposed to correspond directly to these stative predicates in logical structure, while verbs of the other categories have logical structures that consist of one or more stative predicates embedded in complex sentences formed with these "aspectual" connectives and operators. These aspectual operators and connectives are treated as logical constants – a standard model-theoretic interpretation is to be given for each – and the stative predicates are non-logical constants.

This hypothesis, then, is essentially a reductionist analysis of the aspectual classes of verbs. The goal is for a puzzling diversity of kinds of verbs to be explained as combinations of an aspectually simple and unproblematic kind of verb – the stative – with an explicitly interpreted operator or operators. The success of this depends not only on the formal interpretation of the operators, but also on the assumption that statives are clearly understood and unproblematic. Intuitively, the notion of a stative predicate will seem clear. Statives can be judged true or false of an individual by reference to the state of the world at only a single movement of time (while other classes of verbs require "information" about more than one point in time and in some cases, from more than one possible world). To make this hypothesis into a substantive claim about possible versus impossible word meanings in a referential framework such as that of UG will require being more specific about "true or false by reference to the state of the world at only a single moment of time", but this problem will be deferred to section 2.4 below.

It seems to me that a goal of this kind can also be seen implicitly in the following passage from Lakoff (1972, pp. 615-616):

> In the analyses offered above [certain lexical decomposition analyses – DRD], certain atomic predicates keep recurring: CAUSE, COME ABOUT, SAY, GOOD, BAD, BELIEVE, INTEND, RESPONSIBLE FOR, etc. These are all sentential operators, that is, predicates that take sentential complements. It seems clear that we would want these, or predicates like these, to function as atomic predicates in natural logic. Since these keep recurring in our analyses, it is quite possible that under the lexical decomposition hypothesis the list would end somewhere. That is, there would be only a finite number of atomic predicates in natural logic taking sentential complements. These would be universal, . . . Moreover, verbs like 'kick' and 'scrub' in [Sam kicked the door open] and [Sam scrubbed the floor clean] could be ruled out as sentential operators since they could be analyzed in terms of already existing operators, as in [Sam caused the door to come to be open, by kicking it] or [Sam caused the floor to come to be clean, by scrubbing it]. This seems to me to be an important claim. Kicking and scrubbing are two out of a potentially infinite number of human activities. Since the number of potential human activities and states is unlimited, natural logic will have to provide an open-ended number of atomic predicates corresponding to these states and activities. Hopefully, this can be limited to atomic predicates that do not take sentential complements . . . It seems to me that under the lexical decomposition hypothesis we have a fighting chance of limiting sentential operators to a finite number, fixed for all natural languages.

(The hypothesis I am considering here differs from Lakoff's in two ways, however. I will suggest that states and activities might be reduced to non-logical predicates of the same sort, and I am not claiming that all words with 'sentential complements' can be analyzed in terms of fixed, language universal operators – I think this claim is probably false – but only that aspectual categories of verbs might possibly be reduced in this way.)

An important methodological assumption of this enterprise is that the appropriate syntactic distribution of these operators in logical structures, as well as the appropriate model-theoretic interpretation of them, can be adduced by careful attention to syntagmatic and paradigmatic contrasts and restrictions evidenced in the language itself. Though this methodology is highly characteristic of GS, I do not think it is one that linguists other than generative semanticists would repudiate; rather, most would merely deny that the conclusions reached in this way applied to a level of *syntactic* (as opposed to semantic) representation. I should be careful to add that I am not presupposing that the structuralist methodology is a wholly reliable one, much less that it is sufficient to discover all we need to know to construct an adequate semantic theory of a natural language (as I think many linguists do assume without question). But I think it is a methodology worthy of further investigation, even in a referential theory like UG.

Ultimately, there will remain some features of the verb classes that cannot be attributed to any structurally-motivated operators I am able to devise (though adequate conditions on model-theoretic interpretations of the verbs involved can be stated precisely anyway). Nevertheless, I think the idea of a structurally motivated natural logic is important enough to justify the presentation of my 1972 aspect calculus before the revisions are introduced. I believe that much can be learned from the attempt to construct such a calculus, no matter whether the resulting analysis is stated entirely in terms of it or not.

In Chapter 4, the possibility of using this aspect calculus to "decompose" verbs via the translation relation will be considered. As I have mentioned that the translation procedure of UG is a theoretically unnecessary step, it may be wondered whether this aspect calculus can have any real significance in such a theory. I think in fact it can be significant. Stated in a way that does not presuppose a translation step, the claim the aspectual calculus makes about the Fregean interpretation $\langle B, G_\gamma, f\rangle_{\gamma \in \Gamma}$ for English (whether induced by translation, directly, or otherwise specified) is merely that there exists a finite set of functions $f_1 \ldots f_n$ (which correspond to the interpretations of aspectual operators) and a set of objects A (which can be interpretations of stative predicates), such that for each verb α of English, the interpretation of α is equivalent to some composite function constructed out of (a finite number of) $f_1 \ldots f_n$ and members of A, and that moreover, this way of specifying the interpretation of α is more economical, elegant, useful, insightful, (or whatever) than any other comparably explicit way of defining the interpretation of α.

2.3.2. *Statives, von Wright's Logic of Change, and BECOME*

Classical propositional and predicate logic is said to deal with "timeless" states of affairs, propositions which are either true or false once and for all. The notion of a state of affairs being true over a certain period of time can, however, be accommodated in a straightforward way. One would need to add to the predicate logic only a set of variables and constants representing points in time, quantifiers for these time variables, and an operator representing the notion of a proposition being true *at* a time. A sentence containing a stative verb and a *for*-phrase time adverbial (e.g. (65)) could be represented logically as in (66), ignoring for the moment the past tense.

(65) John loved Mary for three years.

(66) $(\bigwedge t\colon t \in \textit{three years})$ AT(t, *John love Mary*)

Such formulas could be given a model-theoretic interpretation as follows: An appropriate semantic model for this system would include a set of times $t_i \ldots t_n$ with a transitive, asymmetrical relation defined on them (the "earlier than" relation). Interpretations of non-logical constants would be given relative to each time t, and thus formulas may be true or may be false, depending on which time they are evaluated at. Assuming that time adverbs like *three years* denote (contiguous) sets of these times and that we have some way of identifying the "stretch" of time which an adverb refers to, we can give truth conditions for formulas like (66) very simply: (66) would be true relative to some semantic model if the individuals *John* and *Mary* exist in all of the times in the interval *three years* and the sentence *John loves Mary* is true at all times in the interval. This, in fact, would be the only logical mechanism needed for a "Natural Logic" capable of handling statives and durational adverbials. (Though Montague's intensional logic does not contain variables and constants denoting times directly, evaluation of expressions relative to a time is of course part of the intensional semantics, and we will see later how means of referring to times directly can be introduced easily. Temporally-interpreted languages with expressions denoting times are of course not new in the tense logical literature; one might cite Prior's "B-series logic" (Prior, 1967, p. 38) and Rescher and Urquhart's "R-calculus" (Rescher and Urquhart, 1971, pp. 31-35) as antecedents. For simplicity of exposition, I will continue to assume in this section a simple, predicate-logic-like formal language with temporal interpretation, enlarging this language and its semantic apparatus as the need arises.)

A different solution would be required for events, however, since they are not literally true or false *for* a period of time or even at a point in time. Rather, events somehow "take place" *in* time. Some further logical concepts are therefore necessary to capture this notion.

Georg Henrik von Wright (1963; 1968) observed that an event, such as the closing of a door, is understood to have taken place at a certain time if one state – the state of the door's being open (or being not closed) – is replaced at that time by a second state – the state of the door's being closed. Von Wright claimed that this "change of state" definition of an event was generalizable: that *any* event can be defined as a change of state where the two states are of a particular form. Namely, one of the states is the negation of the other. An event is a change from state p to state q, where $p = \neg q$ (or, to say the same thing, $q = \neg p$).

Von Wright devised a formal calculus of change-of-state which consists of classic propositional logic with the addition of a dyadic operator *T* (called "And Next"). In the T-calculus, all formulas can be reduced to one of four basic types. These are given in (67) along with their intuitive interpretations:

(67) $\neg pTp$ "the state p comes about"
$pT\neg p$ "the state p is destroyed, comes to an end"
pTp "the state p remains, continues to obtain"
$\neg pT\neg p$ "the state $\neg p$ remains" or "the state p fails to come about"

Consider now the relationship between Lakoff and McCawley's abstract verb BECOME (or COME ABOUT) and von Wright's analysis of events. The example *The soup cooled* bears the same relation to *The soup is cool* as *The door closed* bears to *The door is closed*. The first sentence can only be true if the soup's being not-cool was replaced, at the time referred to by that sentence, with the soup's being cool. The same will be true of all sentences analyzed by generative semanticists as containing the operator BECOME.

This observation suggests the possibility of defining BECOME sentences in terms of von Wright's logic of change. Moreover, the atomic predicates END (or STOP or whatever the inverse of BECOME is called) and REMAIN can also be defined in terms of von Wright's formulas:

(68) BECOME (p) $=_{\text{def.}} \neg pTp$
END (p) $=_{\text{def.}} pT\neg p$
REMAIN (p) $=_{\text{def.}} pTp$

Semantically, this claim is simply that one can utter truthfully a sentence like *The soup cooled* when one first observes that the soup is not cool, and thereafter that it is; the meaning of the sentence is that those two states of affairs were true in temporal succession, no more and no less. This analysis makes explicit the temporal relationship among the three pro-verbs and the simple statives.

Furthermore, this analysis would give a semantically correct account of the beginnings and endings of states and of activities such as *It started to rain, John stopped running, Harry just continued eating his ice cream,* etc. That is, the operators in (68) underlie a large number of individually lexicalized "aspectual" verbs like *begin* as well as the "disappearing" operators in *John cooled the soup*:

(69) a. It started to snow.
b. John came to believe that the earth is flat.
c. John went crazy.
d. John got drunk.
e. John sat on the bench. (ambiguous between stative/inchoative)
f. John lay on the sofa. (ambiguous between stative/inchoative)
g. She went t' singing. (some dialects)

Von Wright did not provide a formal semantic treatment of his logic of change, though it is easy enough to construct one. However, there is no need to go through the intermediate step of defining structures with BECOME in terms of the logic of change and then defining truth conditions in terms of von Wright formulas: COME ABOUT, END, and REMAIN can simply be regarded as sentential operators in a "Natural Logic", and truth conditions can be defined directly in terms of these and the same kind of semantic model as was described above. If time is discrete in the model – that is, if for any moment there is a unique moment that most immediately follows it – then we can identify the set of times in the model with the set of positive and negative integers and zero, hence refer to the time immediately preceding a time t as $t-1$, the time immediately following it as $t+1$.

(70) Where ϕ is any formula, and t is any time,
BECOME ϕ is true at t iff ϕ is true at t and false at $t-1$.
END ϕ is true at t iff ϕ is false at t and true at $t-1$.
REMAIN ϕ is true at t iff ϕ is true at t and true at $t-1$.

Alternatively, if time is taken to be dense in the model – if for any two moments no matter how close there is always another moment between the two (and hence an infinite number of moments between any two moments) – then the definitions could be reformulated along the following lines: BECOME ϕ would be true at t iff ϕ is true at t, ϕ is false at t' for some time t' earlier than t, and for all times t'' later than t' but earlier than t ϕ is also false at t''. I presently know of no linguistic reasons why time should be considered dense rather than discrete or vice-versa, so I will leave the matter open here.

It has often been suggested in the literature on presupposition (e.g. Givón, 1972) that the implication of a "negated" earlier state with change-of-state verbs is a presupposition (or conventional implicature) rather than a part of the "assertion" of the verb. This claim is based on the judgment that sentences like (71)-(73) seem to commit the speaker to the view that the gates were closed just before 8 PM:

(71) The gates didn't open at 8 PM.

(72) Did the gates open at 8 PM?

(73) It is possible that the gates opened at 8 PM.

Even more frequently discussed is the implicature of *John has stopped beating his wife* to the effect that John at one time beat his wife. (The aspectual complement verb *stop* would be analyzed on the present view with the operator END above.) If this claim is correct, then these initial state implicatures could be accommodated, I believe, in a treatment of conventional implicature such as that proposed by Karttunen and Peters, with implicatures generated by logical deep structures here rather than by English sentences.

Inchoative verbs derived from adjectives and "aspectual" complement verbs make up a major part of the class of achievement verbs. At this point we will take the further step of suggesting that *all* achievements have a logical structure consisting of BECOME plus an embedded clause.

The BECOME analysis seems to provide an intuitively satisfactory semantic account of the remaining achievement verbs. For example, *realize* (in its inchoative, not its stative sense) seems to be equivalent to "come to know (something which one did not know earlier)." *Forget* is its inverse, just as END is the inverse of COME ABOUT: *forget* is "come to not know (something which one did know earlier)". Likewise, *find* or *discover* is "come to have" or "come to know the location or existence of", with *lose* as the inverse. The locative achievements *arrive at* and *reach* are "come to be at (a place that one was not at just before)". Their inverses are *depart from* and *leave*.

This claim about achievement verbs embodies von Wright's position that all events correspond to a change of state of one form or another. As the analysis of accomplishment verbs suggested below also involves BECOME sentences, these change-of-state entailments are also treated as an essential part of the meaning of accomplishments. This seems to accord with Kenny's view of the essential characteristics of performances (his class that includes both achievements and accomplishments):

> Performances are brought to an end by states. Any performance is describable in the form: "bringing it about that *p*". Washing the dishes is bringing it about that the dishes are clean; learning French is bringing it about that I know French, walking to Rome is bringing it about that I am in Rome. In all of these cases, what is brought about is, by our criteria, a state: "is clean" "knows" "is in Rome" are all static verbs.
>
> (Kenny, 1963, p. 177).

As I mentioned, the beginnings and endings of activities can also be achievements (and for that matter, be involved in accomplishments), so the sentence embedded directly under BECOME will not always contain just a stative verb, but may be an activity or even, as Kenny suggests, another performance:

> A performance may be brought about no less than a state: if the policeman is forcing the prisoner to walk to the police-station, then the policeman is bringing it about that the prisoner is bringing it about that he is in the police-station. Thus in 'bringing it about that *p*", "*p*" may contain a performance verb instead of a static verb. But every performance must be ultimately the bringing about of a state or of an activity; otherwise we could have an action which consisted merely in bringing it about that it was being brought about that it was being brought about that . . . If the description of the action in this form is ever to be completed, it must contain either a perfective verb or an activity-verb. One performance differs from another in accordance with the differences between the states of affairs brought about: performances are specified by their ends.
>
> (Kenny, 1963, pp. 177-178)

The independent syntactic evidence that might be cited for the analysis of achievements in terms of BECOME and an embedded sentence in generative semantics is of two kinds. First, simply the existence of a regular pattern of achievement verbs like *cool, harden*, etc. derived morphologically from stative adjectives might be considered evidence of a sort for this analysis, but acceptance of this pattern as evidence that *all* achievements have this structure depends on one's acceptance of the kind of "analytic leap" mentioned earlier which allows that a unit of meaning that is structurally distinguished in some words should be postulated as an independent part of the meanings of all words with similar overall meanings. Second, it can be argued that certain adverbs must have as their scope the embedded stative clause in an achievement verb, rather than the whole verb (i.e. the BECOME sentence). This second kind of evidence, which also applies to accomplishment verbs, would appear to be more significant than the first, and it will be discussed in detail in 5.6-5.8 below.

2.3.3. *A Semantic Solution to the Problem of Indefinites and Mass Nouns*

Finally, the BECOME analysis can be shown to exclude achievement verbs from the durative constructions (thus explaining the restriction on co-occurrence with *for*-phrases) except in just those cases where an indefinite plural or mass noun occurs in the sentence. This will be demonstrated by considering first what the model-theoretic interpretation of a deviant sentence like (74) would have to be.

(74) *John discovered the buried treasure in his back yard for six weeks.

I again assume that the durative adverbial *for six weeks* is to be represented in terms of a quantified time expression and a two-place AT operator; that is "for all times t such that t is a member of the period *six weeks*, it was true at t that p." (We shall ignore the past tense once again.) Proposition p in this case is that expressed by the sentence "John discovered the buried treasure in his back yard." This embedded sentence, in turn, will be a BECOME sentence, and embedded in this will be a stative sentence to the effect that "John knows the existence of the buried treasure in his back yard." (This sentence does not have to be further analyzed for our present purposes.) This logical form is roughly represented in (75):

(75) ($\bigwedge t$:$t \in$ *six weeks*) AT(t, BECOME [*John knows that . . .*])

Now consider how the truth conditions for this logical structure would have to be satisfied in a model. The temporal quantifier entitles us to pick any arbitrary moment within the time period denoted by *six weeks*, say t_i, and it is asserted by the AT operator that the embedded sentence is true. This embedded sentence in turn is another tensed sentence, which asserts that one state of affairs, expressed by the sentence ϕ is true now (i.e. at t), and its negation, $\neg\phi$ was true at the previous moment, which in this instance is t_{i-1}. Let us represent the truth conditions in the model graphically by writing a horizontal series of t's representing successive moments in time proceeding from left to right, all within the bounds of *six weeks*. Under each t we will list the sentences true at that time.

(76) $\ldots t_{i-3}, t_{i-2}, t_{i-1}, t_i, \quad t_{i+1}, t_{i+2}, t_{i+3}, \ldots$

$\qquad\qquad\qquad\qquad \neg\phi \quad \phi$

This is all well and good so far, but suppose we now pick t_{i-1} as the arbitrary moment. Because this is still part of *six weeks*, the embedded BECOME sentence must also be true then, namely, ϕ at t_{i-1} and $\neg\phi$ at t_{i-2}. Thus we have arrived at a contradiction: both ϕ and $\neg\phi$ are true simultaneously at t_{i-1}. In fact, if we compute the truth conditions for all t's in the interval *six weeks*, the contradiction will be present at each moment in the interval except the very last one. The graphic representation would look something like (76′).

$$(76')\qquad \begin{array}{ccccccc} \ldots t_{i-3}, & t_{i-2}, & t_{i-1}, & t_{i}, & t_{i+1}, & t_{i+2}, & t_{i+3}, \ldots \\ & & & & & \neg\phi & \phi \\ & & & & \neg\phi & \phi & \\ & & & \neg\phi & \phi & & \\ & & \neg\phi & \phi & & & \\ & \neg\phi & \phi & & & & \\ \neg\phi & \phi & & & & & \end{array}$$

Thus this analysis accounts for the semantic anomaly of (74), and I think it accounts for it in an intuitively satisfying way: to say that John has been "discovering" a certain fact (or the existence of a certain object) throughout a period of six weeks would seem to entail that he has repeatedly not known and then come to know the very same fact, which is obviously a contradiction (barring memory loss).

Now consider the cases where there is a plural indefinite or mass noun in a sentence with an achievement verb, e.g., (77)

$$(77)\qquad \text{John discovered} \left\{ \begin{array}{l} \text{fleas on his dog} \\ \text{crabgrass in his yard} \end{array} \right\} \text{for six weeks.}$$

There may be reason to assume that indefinite plurals and mass nouns are to be logically represented as involving variables whose binding existential quantifier lies within the scope of the time quantifier of the surface sentence in which they arise. Notice that (77) can be given the pseudo-logical paraphrase (78a) but not (78b):

(78) a. For six weeks John discovered there to be some x such that x is crabgrass and is in his yard.
b. *There is some x such that x is crabgrass and for six weeks John discovered x to be in his yard.

(77) would have a logical structure like (79):

$$(79)\qquad (\bigwedge t\colon t \in \textit{six weeks})(\bigvee x)[\mathrm{AT}(t, \mathrm{BECOME}\ [\textit{John knows} \ldots x \ldots])]$$

Consider how the truth conditions for (79) might be satisfied in a temporal model. (79) will be true if for each t_i in an interval of six weeks' duration, there is some value for x that makes the BECOME sentence true. Since the existential quantifier binding x is within the scope of the temporal universal quantifier, the value for x may differ from one t to the next and indeed will have to to avoid contradiction. If we let x_i denote some value for x that makes the BECOME sentence in (79) true and let f represent the propositional function "John knows that x is in his yard" at each time, then the conditions under which (79) would be true can be represented schematically as follows:

(80) $$\begin{array}{llllllll} \ldots t_{i-3}, & t_{i-2}, & t_{i-1}, & t_i, & & t_{i+1}, & t_{i+2}, \ldots \\ & & & & \neg f(x_1) & f(x_1) & \\ & & & \neg f(x_2) & f(x_2) & & \\ & & \neg f(x_3) & f(x_3) & & & \\ & & & \text{etc.} & & & \end{array}$$

Again, the analysis makes an intuitively sound claim about (77): if John has been discovering fleas on his dog or crabgrass in his yard for six weeks, then he must have been discovering new patches of crabgrass or new fleas on his dog all the time, not the same one over and over again.

With achievement verbs it does not matter whether the indefinite or mass noun occurs as subject or as object. Since both of these would occur within the scope of BECOME (which is in turn within the scope of the adverb), any indefinite plural or mass noun in the sentence will allow achievements to be used durationally. Accomplishments will be analyzed in such a way that the direct object noun phrase falls within the scope of a BECOME sentence (as in McCawley's analysis of *kill*), hence indefinite plurals and mass terms in the direct object position of accomplishment verbs are predicted to pattern in the same way as the subjects and objects of achievements with respect to durational adverbials. It is therefore not necessary to postulate an elaborate system of syntactic restrictions as Verkuyl (1972) does to account for these distributional restrictions.

Two qualifications must be made about this treatment. First, it may be objected that even the grammatical sentence *John has been discovering crabgrass in his yard for six weeks* does not mean that John has come upon something new at literally every single moment in a six-week period. If we are to use the universal quantifier to represent durational adverbs like *for six weeks* in a natural logic at all, then the moments it quantifies over must be something like "relevant psychological moments" which are both vaguely specified and also contextually determined. Notice that when we utter a sentence like (81) we seldom feel it necessary to qualify it as in (82).

(81) I've done nothing for the past hour except read this damn book.

(82) Well, actually that's not true, there's the two and a half minutes that I went to the bathroom, and the two thirty-second periods I spent looking out the window, and all those fractions of seconds I was blinking . . .

To see that the relevant moments in a durational adverb are contextually determined, note that (83) is not odd in the same way as (84):

(83) John has been working in San Diego for the last five years. He usually spends his weekends at the beach.

(84) ?John has been serving his prison sentence for the last five years. He usually spends his weekends at the beach.

Because of our knowledge of facts about the real world, we know that the relevant moments included in *the last five years* in (83) do not include weekends, vacations, etc., whereas the relevant moments covered by the same quantifier in (84) are much more inclusive. I doubt that anyone would claim that the time adverb itself has a different logical structure in (83) and (84). I realize that "relevant psychological moment" may sound like a vague notion at this point, but it seems that we must either adopt it for the time being or else stop using the universal quantifier to represent durational adverbs. Note that in the analysis presented above the actual number of moments in an interval is not important; as long as there are at least two, then (75) is contradictory.

A second objection to the analysis would be that there are potential counter-examples to it in the form of sentences like (85):

(85) John found his son's tricycle in the driveway for six weeks.

(85) appears to be well-formed, despite the fact that it contains an achievement verb, a durative time adverbial, and no indefinite plural or mass noun.

Part of the solution to this problem is that (85), on its acceptable reading, is understood to be elliptical, in that a second time adverbial of some kind is implicit:

(85′) John found his son's tricycle in the driveway

$$\left\{\begin{array}{l}\text{every day}\\ \text{once a week}\\ \text{frequently}\\ \text{etc.}\end{array}\right\}\quad \text{for six weeks.}$$

That is, the different occasions of "finding" are separated by intervals. (The same observation should perhaps be made about (77), but this is only part of the difference.) I am not sure what the best way of handling this matter is.

A second difference between (85) and (75) is that *discover* in (75) is more likely to mean "come to know the existence of" whereas *find* in (85) is more likely to mean "come to know that NP is at x place at y time." Coming to know the existence of something is a once-and-for-all event (barring memory lapse), whereas an object that reappears in unexpected places presents ever-new "facts" to be discovered. The nouns *buried treasure* and *tricycle* were thus not chosen at random; a buried treasure, once discovered, is not likely to surprise one a second time by reappearing unexpectedly, but a tricycle is just the kind of object that would. The main claim, that one does not discover the same fact more than once, still seems valid, and I think that this way of treating the anomaly of (74) vis-à-vis (77) is viable in spite of the problem of vagueness in durative adverbs.

2.3.4. *Carlson's Treatment of 'Bare Plurals'*

Though the treatment of indefinite plurals and achievements just given (which come from Dowty 1972) seems adequate as far as it goes, it leaves one important question unanswered: if it is correct to analyze an indefinite plural like *fleas* as involving an existential quantifier (i.e. as equivalent to *a flea* or *some fleas*), then just why must this quantifier have narrower scope than the durative adverbial? From what has been said, it might be supposed that the contradictoriness of the wide scope reading with an achievement verb is all that prevents this second reading from being apparent, but this is not so. Examples like (86) and (87) (from Carlson, 1977, p. 27) have stative and activity verbs respectively, yet the (b) sentences only appear to have readings in which this putative existential quantifier has narrower scope than the adverbial, while the (a) sentences with an explicit quantifier *a* or *some* clearly have a reading with the existential quantifier taking wider scope (as well as perhaps a less obvious reading with the quantifier taking narrower scope):

(86) a. {A cat has / Some cats have} been here since the Vikings landed.

b. Cats have been here since the Vikings landed.

(87) a. {A tyrant / Some tyrants} ruled Wallachia for 250 years.

b. Tyrants ruled Wallachia for 250 years.

This is only the beginning of a long story, however. Carlson (1977) examines a number of quantifier-like constructions (negation, other NP quantifiers, durative and frequentative adverbs, aspectual verbs like *continue*, anaphoric constructions) that might be expected to bring out a scope ambiguity with these indefinite plurals, and in every case the only possible reading is one in which the "existential quantifier" underlying the indefinite plural appears to have narrower scope than the other quantifier or operator.

A further peculiar fact is that indefinite plurals (or what Carlson calls *bare plurals* following Chomsky) elsewhere seem to be interpreted as having a kind of universal, or *generic* quantifier, yet it is hard to find a single sentence (at least in certain tenses) in which the bare plural is truly ambiguous between an existential reading (as in (86b), (87b), and earlier examples) and a generic reading. The sentences of (88), for example, have to be taken as referring to smokers, cats, or elephants in general, not just a particular group of smokers, cats or elephants:

(88) a. Smokers are rude.
b. Cats meow.
c. Elephants are quite easily trained.

Note that in *Tyrants ruled Wallachia for 250 years*, some particular tyrants or other are clearly referred to, not tyrants in general. The same comment applies to the examples of indefinite plurals in the previous section.

Even more striking are cases observed by Carlson (1973; 1977) in which an anaphoric pronoun and its bare plural antecedent differ in whether a generic or "existential" interpretation is given. Consider the examples in (89) and (90):

(89) a. May hates *racoons* because *they* stole her sweet corn.
b. *Racoons* stole May's sweet corn, so now she hates *them* with a passion.

(90) a. I didn't think that *goats*$_i$ actually liked *tin cans*$_j$ until I saw *them*$_i$ eating *them*$_j$.
b. Before I actually saw *goats*$_i$ eating *tin cans*$_j$, I didn't think that *they*$_i$ liked *them*$_j$.

(Anaphorically related pronouns and bare plurals are italicized.) In each case, a bare plural and a pronoun can only be understood in one way, but an existential can be the antecedent of a generic pronoun (as in (89b) and (90b)) or a generic can be the antecedent of an existential pronoun (as in (89a) and (90a)). This failure of pronominalization to heed the difference between existential and universal quantification is unheard of elsewhere.

All of these unusual syntactic facts really point unambiguously to one conclusion, but it is so bizarre that it almost escapes notice. This is that first, there is no scope ambiguity with indefinite plurals ("existential" bare plurals) simply because there is no quantifier involved in these noun phrases at all[10] and second, the apparent difference between "generic" and "existential" interpretations is due to the meanings of the verbs they interact with, *not* the meanings of the noun phrases themselves. Inspection of the sentences in (89) and (90) shows, for example, that the bare plural subjects and objects of *steal* and *eat* always have an existential interpretation while those of *like* and *hate* always have generic interpretations. (There is a general class of exceptions to this statement involving generics in subject position; cf. Carlson (1977, pp. 247ff.).) Thus the pronouns and their antecedents in (89) and (90) should be said to have the same meaning in a real sense, though the interaction of the meanings of the verbs with these must somehow obscure this fact.

Though it might at first appear impossible to come up with an explicit semantic analysis of bare plurals that satisfies these syntactic desiderata, Carlson is able to do so by means of some fundamental ontological innovations. Bare plurals, we are told, are the proper names of *kinds*. There are as many kinds as there are bare plurals, so we must note that Carlson's kinds are not just the *natural kinds* of Kripke (1972) and Putnam (1975) but include "unnatural" kinds as well, such as pillows, coffee mugs, and pipe wrenches. A kind cannot, however, be identified with the set of individuals that "make up" the kind or even with the property they all share, but for various reasons must be taken as a basic entity (member of D_e in the UG model) in its own right. A relation *R* is then introduced in the semantic apparatus that specifies what things *realize*, or "make up", a kind; if *a* is a thing and *b* is a kind, then R(*a, b*) asserts that the thing *a* realizes the kind *b*, as for example a particular cat realizes the kind cats.

It is important for Carlson to provide a somewhat parallel ontological treatment of individuals themselves. He distinguishes between *individuals* and what he calls the *stages* of individuals – these might be thought of as "temporal slices" of individuals, their manifestations in space and at individual times. An individual is that "whatever-it-is" that ties stages together and makes them a single unit. This ontology is similar to views of individuals suggested at times by Kaplan (1973), Gabbay and Moravcsik (1973), and Montague (1973), but not quite identical with any of these. It is crucial that the same *R* relation that relates kinds to their members also relate individuals to their stages. (This may seem curious at first, but is justified by the consequences that result.) If *c* is a stage and *d* is an individual then R(*c, d*) asserts at any time that the stage *c* realizes the individual *d* at that time. It is also to be noted that R is transitive, so if stage c realizes individual d at a time and individual d realizes kind b at that same time, then stage c also realizes kind b at that time.

Now it turns out, according to Carlson, that some verbs and adjectives that apparently predicate things of individuals and kinds actually amount to predications about *stages* that realize those individuals or kinds at the current time, while other verbs and adjectives really do predicate things of the individuals (or kinds) themselves. Thus while the relation *loves* is true of individuals x and y at a time just in case the individual x stands in the *love*-relation to the individual y, the relation *eats* is true of individuals x and y just in case there exists some stage x' that realizes x at that time, some stage y' that realizes y at that time, and the stages x' and y' stand in some relation defined on stages, which we may call the *eat'*-relation. For example, *Goats like tin cans* would have the representation (91), but *Goats were eating tin cans* would have roughly the representation (92), ignoring tense. Here, g is the constant denoting the kind goats, t the kind tin cans:[11]

(90) $like(g, t)$

(91) $(\mathrm{V}x)(\mathrm{V}y)[\mathrm{R}(x, g) \wedge \mathrm{R}(y, t) \wedge eat'(x, y)]$

(This is somewhat similar to the way Montague "decomposes" a relation between an individual and a property of properties to an extensional relation between individuals, but the semantic entities involved are here quite different.) In the case of ordinary individuals (i.e., individuals that are not kinds), there is at most one stage that realizes the individual at any given time, so the difference between predicates applying to individuals themselves and predicates applying to their stages is likely to go unnoticed. (However, there may be a few observable syntactic consequences of this difference, some of which will become relevant later in this work.) But with kind names (bare plurals and a few other expressions such as *that kind of animal*), predicates that apply to realizations give rise to an "existential" interpretation, since there will be more than one realization of the kind, and the predicate merely asserts that at least *some* realization has the relevant property. If the predicate applies to kinds themselves rather than stages, then the generic interpretation arises because nothing is being predicated of any realization of the kind, i.e. of any ordinary individuals or stages of them.

I do not have the space here to go into the numerous technical details of Carlson's proposals that are required to make it complete (for example, a three-sorted logic) nor the impressive evidence Carlson amasses for his proposals and against the obvious alternatives to it. Because the proposal may initially sound somewhat implausible, I encourage the reader to refer to Carlson (1977; 1977a) for these details and arguments.

What is important for the present discussion of achievement verbs and durative adverbials is that Carlson's analysis attributes an existential quantifier binding the variable over realizations to the meaning of the verb, not to the meaning of the indefinite plural noun phrase. The indefinite plural noun phrase itself is a proper name wherever it occurs and so it obviously cannot have scope wider than an adverbial quantifier or any other quantifier in the sentence. (Carlson formulated his solution in the PTQ theory, so the "decomposition" of predicates into realization-predicates is accomplished through the translation procedure; when we compare translational decomposition with classical GS decomposition, we will look in detail at ways of insuring in each theory that this existential quantifier necessarily comes from *within* the logical structure of the verb and has narrowest scope. For now, I am assuming that his solution can be accommodated in the generative semantics theory under discussion.) Incorporating Carlson's analysis into the BECOME analysis of achievement sentences like *John discovered fleas on his dog for six weeks* would result in a logical structure roughly represented by (93), where f denotes the kind fleas:

(93)

$(\bigwedge t\colon t \in \textit{six weeks})\mathrm{AT}(t, \mathrm{BECOME}[\textit{John knows that } (\bigvee x[\mathrm{R}(x, f) \wedge$
$x \textit{ is on his dog}])])$

The BECOME analysis here, as before, explains why we understand this example to mean that John did not discover the same fleas over and over (i.e., the same realizations of the kind fleas). If Carlson's analysis is correct, then it is possible to retain the insight from Dowty (1972) that the acceptability of examples like this is to be explained with the BECOME analysis in terms of an existential quantifier with narrow scope but to add the independently motivated account of the narrow scope quantifier that was lacking earlier. Mass terms turn out to have all the same distributional properties as Carlson discovered for bare plurals, and though he does not provide a detailed analysis of mass terms, these parallels suggest that a similar treatment ought to be possible if Carlson's proposal is correct (cf. Carlson, 1977, pp. 462ff., for some suggestions).

2.3.5. *Degree-Achievements*

There are some cases of verbs which would seem to be achievements on some semantic and syntactic grounds but which nevertheless allow durational adverbs (even without indefinite plurals or mass terms):

(94) The soup cooled for ten minutes.

(95) The ship sank for an hour (before going under completely).

(96) John aged forty years during that experience.

These seem to express a change of state like other achievements: *cool* is definitely an inchoative meaning "come to be cool", *sink* here means "come to be not afloat", and *age* is "come to be old." Yet there is no contradiction in (94)-(96), no implication that the same change of state took place over and over.

Upon inspection, it turns out that the class of inchoatives that can occur with durative adverbials are just those which have been called *degree words* by linguists (Sapir, 1949; Bolinger, 1972) and *vague predicates* by philosophers (Lewis, 1970; Kamp, 1975). These involve properties such as *big, wide, good, tall,* etc. of which we cannot definitely say once and for all how to determine what their extension is, but can only say so relative to some agreed-upon standard of comparison or some particular context of use. The most typical vague predicates seem to be adjectives, specifically, those that form the comparative without semantic anomaly. As we have *this is cooler than that*, we also have (94) with the adjective *cool*, but as it is strange to say *Mary is more pregnant than Sue* (on a normal interpretation of *pregnant*), it is strange in the same way to say *Mary got pregnant for a month*.

Recent proposals for a model-theoretic treatment of vague predicates (Lewis, 1970; Ginet, 1973; Kamp, 1975) have all been based in one way or another on an appeal to multiple ways of resolving the vagueness of these predicates by assigning a definite extension to them, i.e. different ways of drawing the "boundary" between cool and non-cool things, big and non-big things, etc. Kamp (1975; pp. 136-137) explains it in this way:

At the present stage of its development – indeed, at any stage – language is vague. The kind of vagueness which interests us here is connected with predicates. The vagueness of a predicate may be resolved by fiat – i.e. by deciding which of the objects which as yet are neither definitely inside nor definitely outside its extension are to be in and which are to be out. However, it may be that not every such decision is acceptable. For there may already be semantical principles which, though they do not determine of any one of a certain group of objects whether it belongs to the extension or not, nevertheless demand that if a certain member of the group is put into the extension, a certain other member must be put into the extension as well. Take for example the adjective *intelligent*. Our present criteria tell us of certain people that they definitely are intelligent, of certain other people that they definitely are not, but there will be a large third category of people about whom they do not tell us either way. Now suppose that we make our standard more specific, e.g., by stipulating that to have an I.Q. over a certain minimum is a necessary and sufficient criterion for being intelligent. Further, suppose that of two persons u_1 and u_2 of the third category u_1 has a higher I.Q. than u_2. Then, whatever we decide this minimum to be, our decision will put u_1 in the extension if it puts u_2 into it. Finally, let us assume for the sake of argument that any way of making the concept of intelligence precise that is compatible with what we already understand that concept to be is equivalent to the adoption of a certain minimum I.Q. Then there will be no completions in the partial model that reflect the present state of affairs and in which u_2 is put into the extension of the predicate but u_1 is not.

This approach leads directly to a way of deriving comparative adjectives from positive (non-comparative) adjectives (rather than deriving the positive form from the comparative, as earlier semantic treatments of comparatives have suggested). That is, *x is taller than y* will in effect count as true if and only if, for all "acceptable" ways of resolving the vagueness of *tall* by separating the tall from the non-tall, if *y* counts as tall then *x* counts as tall also by that method, but not vice versa.

Kamp's proposal is the most detailed that I have seen. He adopts an analysis based on Van Fraassen's supervaluations (Van Fraassen, 1969); that is, the basic interpretation is a partial model that leaves certain predicates undefined (neither true nor false) for certain individuals. Associated with the partial model are a set of (acceptable) completions of that model which fill in the "gaps" in the partial model in various ways – i.e. they assign a truth value for the undefined arguments in the partial model in different ways but otherwise agree with the partial model. In addition to providing a way of treating comparatives, Kamp can also assign a numerical degree of truth (between true and false) to vague sentences like *John is tall* by means of a probability function defined over the acceptable completions. (This method has considerable advantages over attempts to assign degrees of truth to vague sentences by means of multi-valued logics.) The partial model, its completions, and the probability function together form a *vague model* for a language. In a further development, contextual disambiguation of vague sentences is represented by a function from context to models which are less vague than the basic model. Though *John is tall* might be undefined for the basic model, it might well come out true or false (or have greater or lesser degrees of intermediate truth) for certain contexts.

Given such apparatus, an intuitively satisfactory solution to the problem of degree-achievements with durative adverbs begins to emerge. A sentence like *The soup cooled for ten minutes* should be analyzed as saying that for each time t within an interval of ten minutes duration, there is some resolution of the vagueness of the predicate *cool* by which *the soup is cool* is true at t but not true at $t-1$. Conditions on the acceptable resolutions of the predicate *cool* will in effect require that a different, higher threshold of coolness (i.e. a *lower* temperature for the threshold) be chosen for each successive time in the interval; otherwise the soup could not simultaneously count as cool with respect to one time and resolution of vagueness and also count as not cool for the next time and its resolution of vagueness. This seems to accord well with intuitions about how we understand the sentence, and also avoids having to derive *The soup cooled* from the morphologically unmotivated BECOME[*the soup is cooler*] rather than simply BECOME[*the soup is cool*].

What is necessary for this analysis to work is that the way of resolving vagueness must be capable of being chosen differently for each time t within the interval represented by the durational adverb. Just how this is best done is not yet clear to me. If we do not mention resolutions of vagueness at all in the recursive clauses of the semantic truth definition but merely let a complex sentence be true in a context if the context gives a resolution of vagueness for the elementary predicates that makes the whole sentence true, then different resolutions cannot be used for each time covered by a durational adverb. If on the other hand each recursive semantic definition counts a sentence as true if merely some resolution of vagueness makes it true under appropriate conditions, then *The soup cooled for an hour* could be vacuously true though the soup's temperature remained unchanged; there would still be some resolution at such time t which treated the soup as cool and some resolution (a different one) which made it not cool at $t-1$, so BECOME[*The soup is cool*] would be true at each time in the hour. What we must apparently do is this: a sentence BECOME ϕ should be true at t if and only if there is some resolution of vague predicates that makes ϕ true at t but false at $t-1$; then $(\wedge x: x \in$ *an hour*$)\phi$ must be true if and only if for all times t' within the interval *an hour* there is some resolution of vague predicates that makes ϕ true at t'. This effects the right restriction on the "scope" of quantification over times and resolutions. Whether some way will come to light of avoiding this explicit appeal to resolutions in the recursive clauses I do not know, and so I will leave the matter at this point.

2.3.6. *Accomplishments and CAUSE*

The verb *kill*, which appeared as an example in McCawley's influential article on word meaning (McCawley, 1968), is an accomplishment verb. If one examines the large literature on "causatives" in GS, the class of verbs there referred to as causatives seems to be co-extensive with the class of accomplishments, though aspectual syntactic tests like those in 2.2.3. have not been used to define the class. This convergence is not surprising when one recalls that Kenny considered all accomplishments to be describable as "bringing it about that *p*" for some proposition *p*. (This use of *causative* contrasts with the way it is used in traditional linguistics, according to which it refers only to verbs derived by a causative affix, an affix whose meaning is paraphrasable as "cause to", "cause to be" as English *ize* in *randomize*. When it is necessary to distinguish among syntactic and morphological varieties of causatives, generative semanticists generally distinguish among *lexical causatives*, such as *kill*, *derived causatives*, such as *randomize*, and *periphrastic causatives* – phrases containing a general causative verb plus a separate complement verb, such as *make him leave, cause him to leave*.)

In fact, I suggest that in the aspect calculus we construe all accomplishments as having the logical structure [ϕ CAUSE ψ], where ϕ and ψ are sentences. These embedded sentences ϕ and ψ may have various forms, the most common being the case where ϕ is a BECOME sentence or contains an activity predicate, and ψ is a BECOME sentence. For example, an accomplishment sentence like *John killed Bill* would have a logical structure with roughly the form of (97), and that of *John painted a picture* would have roughly the form of (98):

(97) [[*John does something*] CAUSE [BECOME$\neg$[*Bill is alive*]]]

(98) [[*John paints*] CAUSE [BECOME[*a picture exists*]]]

This analysis differs from McCawley's original version in that CAUSE is here treated as a kind of two-place sentential connective, rather than as a relation between individuals and propositions.

This so-called "bisentential analysis" of CAUSE did not originate with Dowty (1972) but had been suggested in various contexts (Vendler, 1967a; Geis, 1970; Fillmore, 1971; J. McCawley, 1971;[12] Lee, 1971; N. A. McCawley, 1973; Rogers, 1972; Givón, 1972). I will not attempt to survey thoroughly the reasons for choosing one or the other analysis in a generative semantics theory, but merely cite a few advantages of the "bisentential" analysis and refer the reader to the above literature, Wojcik (1974; 1976) and Shibatani (1976) for further details.

An obvious motivation for CAUSE as a "subject-complement verb" in generative semantics is Ryle's observation (Ryle, 1949, p. 150) that accomplishments are semantically bipartite in a way that activities are not, that "some state of affairs obtains over and above that which consists in the performance . . . of the subservient activity." Vendler (1967, p. 154) and Geis (1973, p. 211) make essentially the same observation in pointing out that accomplishment sentences like (99) are elliptical; one can conclude (100) and (101) from (99):

(99) John dissolved the Alka Seltzer.

(100) John dissolved the Alka Seltzer by doing something.

(101) John's doing something dissolved the Alka Seltzer.

Geis suggests that (101) is the underlying structure of (100), (100) being derived by a transformation of Agent Creation, a transformation that breaks up the subject complement into an agentive subject and a post-posed *by*-phrase. This transformation may derive some plausibility from the fact that its operation is quite similar to that of the well-motivated Raising (to Subject) transformation, the rule that derives (102a) from (102b) (compare with (101) and (100)):

(102a) John would be unlikely to win the contest.

(102b) John's winning the contest would be unlikely.

For what we may call general causatives like *kill, open* and *make* (in the sense of *create*) the sentential subject analysis might seem unmotivated, since the meaning of these verbs does not seem to specify anything about the kind of activity that is used to bring about the result, but only the result itself. One can kill a person or animal by any number of activities or procedures; one may open a door by pushing, kicking, striking it, by throwing something at it, by setting off an electronic device or maybe even by saying a magic word, and the ways of making a picture are likewise varied. However, many monomorphemic accomplishments do specify this associated activity in more or less detail. In the class of homicidal verbs (always popular as linguistic examples) are examples like *electrocute, strangle, poison, drown, hang*, etc. which give a specific method of bringing about a death (as well as examples like *assassinate* and *execute* which specify a particular motive though not a means[13]), and one can not only make a picture, but can also paint, draw, sketch, etch, carve, or stencil a picture, these activities indirectly giving indications of the kind of picture that results. Thus we want to suppose that the embedded subject sentence of CAUSE in the underlying structure of general causatives like *kill* or *make* contains a quite general activity or event verb, while other accomplishments have a more specific predicate in this place. (Even *act* is not general enough for the causal event of *kill*, since its subject can be an inanimate (so-called "instrumental") subject, as in *The falling tree killed John*; perhaps *do something* is sufficiently general.)

An even more notable motivation for bisentential CAUSE is a kind of accomplishment construction called *factitive* in traditional grammar and *instrumental* in generative semantics (Green, 1970; 1972; McCawley, 1971):

(103) Jesse shot him dead.
She painted the house red.
She hammered the metal flat.
He swept the floor clean.

(104) He drank himself silly.

(The term *instrumental* is really inappropriate since the construction clearly includes examples like *She slammed the door shut, He shook her awake, She pulled it free* in which no "instrument" is involved.) Here, an activity (or accomplishment) verb combines with an adjective and an object noun phrase to give an accomplishment in which the verb describes the causal activity (or accomplishment) and the adjective gives the result state that the direct object comes to be in as a consequence. Given the sentential subject analysis of CAUSE, examples in (103) would have the kind of structure represented in (105):

(105) [[*He sweeps the floor*] CAUSE [BECOME[*the floor is clean*]]]

An interesting feature of the construction is that though the object of the causal clause is usually identical with the subject of the result-clause (cf. (105)), this need not necessarily be the case. In (104) the understood object of the simple verb *drink* is not the person denoted by *himself*, though *himself* clearly functions as object of the "whole phrase" *drink silly*, in the sense that his becoming silly was brought about by his drinking (something). Constructions semantically similar to (103) exist in which a predicate nominal or prepositional phrase replaces the adjective, such as *elect John chairman, cook the steak to a crisp*, as a parallel to (104) is *read oneself to sleep*.

(Sentences like (103), (104) and these last examples will be treated explicitly in 4.7 below.)

Another class of sentences that may motivate a bisentential analysis of CAUSE is a subset of the verb-particle constructions (cf. Fraser, 1965; 1974), those in which the particle expresses a location that the direct object comes to be in as a result of an activity identified by the basic verb, such as *put the book away*. Within the lexical restrictions of English it is often possible to hold the activity constant and vary the result state as in (106), or to hold the result constant and vary the activity as in (107):

(106) throw NP away
throw NP down
throw NP aside
throw NP in
throw NP up

(107) put NP away (aside, etc.)
throw NP away
send NP away
drive NP away
call NP away

The point of these paradigms is to suggest that at least a restricted subset of the verb-particle constructions should not be treated as single lexical units consisting of verb and particle together, but that they are to some real extent compositional accomplishment constructions of activity verb and particle that expresses a result state.

The alternative in GS to deriving *by*-phrases as just proposed is to treat CAUSE as a relation between an individual and a proposition as McCawley originally did and then derive *by*-phrases from yet a different abstract operator. Such an analysis is proposed by McCawley (1971), according to which all of (108)-(110), if not even more sentences, are derived from the structure (111):

(108) He made the metal flat by hammering it.

(109) He flattened the metal by hammering it.

(110) He hammered the metal flat.

(111)

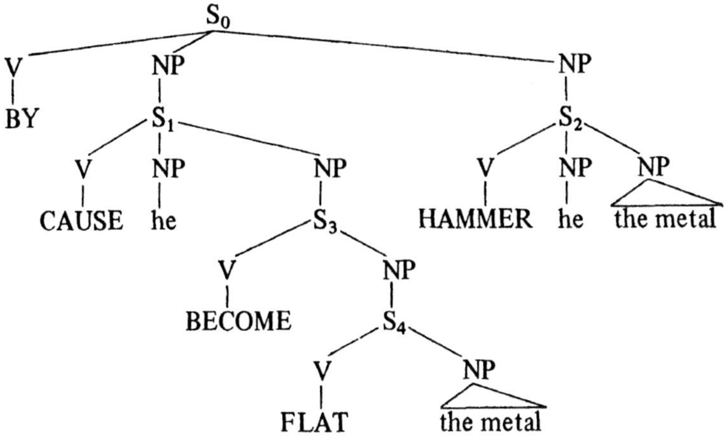

Here, BY is treated as a sentential connective (or in strict GS terms, a "two-place predicate", the NP arguments themselves dominating two S-nodes) in accord with the prevailing GS view that adverbials are derived from sentential operators ("predicates of higher sentences"). The derivation of (108) and (109) from (111) is fairly straightforward, but the derivation of (110) from the same source is somewhat more dubious. McCawley "conjectures" (1971: 31) that after predicate raising has attached BECOME and FLAT to CAUSE in S_1 and *the metal* from S_4 has become the derived direct object of this complex verb (via subject raising?[14]), (i) Equi-NP Deletion deletes the subject of HAMMER in S_2 on the basis of its identity with *he* in S_1 (the same deletion would take place in the derivation of (108) and (109)), then (ii) "a highly suspect transformation deletes the object of HAMMER under God knows what identity condition with S_1", and (iii) predicate raising combines CAUSE-BECOME-FLAT with BY, and then finally (iv) "a transformation hereby christened means-incorporation" combines this derived verb with the remaining verb HAMMER in S_2.

Georgia Green (1972, p. 97) finds that the derivation of (110) works out to her satisfaction if the underlying structure is not (111) but (112):

(112)

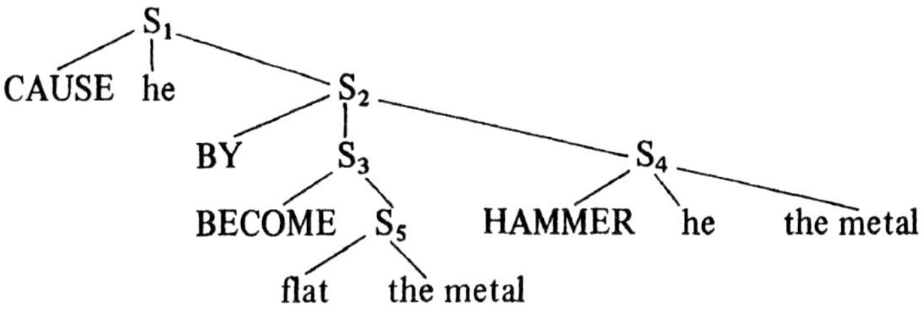

She claims that the derivation of (110) from this structure can be accomplished using only the three rules Subject Raising, Equi-NP Deletion and Subject Formation (a rule that Chomsky-adjoins a subject NP to the left of its verb) – plus lexicalization rules of course – though her derivation in fact involves no less than fourteen applications of transformations in this group and the assumption that transformations apply to their own outputs on the same cycle.

The apparent syntactic simplicity of the derivation I proposed at first might seem to give it an advantage over these two, but given the complexity of accepted GS derivations at that time, this complexity would not likely be taken as a very serious argument. (Needless to say, the proposal of GS derivations of this complexity has given rise in some quarters to the suspicion that potentially any form of surface structure must be derivable from any form of underlying structure whatsoever in a GS grammar, this suspicion then leading to despair over the possibility of ever actually testing whether a GS grammar could generate all and only the well-formed sentences of English or some fragment of English. This is a suspicion I am not unsympathetic with.) The source of all this complexity is of course the unquestioned GS assumption that (110) must have the same underlying syntactic structure as (108) and (109), despite its superficial dissimilarity. If one gave up this assumption, then it would seem much more natural syntactically to derive (108) and (109) from a structure like McCawley's and Green's and to derive (110) from a structure like (105).

Another possible reason for preferring a sentential connective CAUSE over McCawley's CAUSE plus BY is that the intuitive interpretation of BY (ϕ, ψ) seems quite similar to that of $[\phi$ CAUSE $\psi]$, except that the order of arguments is reversed.[15] If BY could be eliminated in favor of CAUSE, a kind of economy could be achieved that is much desired in the GS methodology. A more pragmatic reason for preferring CAUSE as a sentential connective in the present context is that the model-theoretic interpretation of $[\phi$ CAUSE $\psi]$ I want to consider requires that it be a sentential connective (or else that we in effect define McCawley's CAUSE in terms of this sentential connective).

Of the many problems that arise in attempting to analyze accomplishments from an underlying structure containing CAUSE, one deserves discussion here (others will be attended to later). It was noticed at the very first discussion of this kind of analysis that sentences with derived causatives may not be exactly paraphrasable by sentences with the English verb *cause*, though this is sometimes hard to judge. Hall (1965, p. 28) notes that "one argument that probably does not convince anyone who does not already agree is that causing a window to break and breaking a window simply do not mean the same thing," adding examples where she finds a derived causative ungrammatical but the periphrastic causative paraphrase acceptable:

(113) a. A change in molecular structure caused the window to break.
b. *A change in molecular structure broke the window.

(114) a. The low air pressure caused the water to boil.
b. *The low air pressure boiled the water.

(115) a. The angle at which the door was mounted caused it to open whenever it wasn't latched.
b. *The angle at which the door was mounted opened it whenever it wasn't latched.

("Ungrammatical" may be too strong a term for (113b), (114b) and (115b) according to some people – I find them merely a little odd – but there is clearly some kind of difference between the (a) and (b) examples which has to be accounted for.) But as Hall immediately points out, this difference is not automatically evidence against the analysis of causative *break*, etc. in terms of CAUSE. The operator CAUSE is an abstract element and need not be considered identical in meaning with the English "surface verb" *cause*; this surface verb might contain other abstract predicates besides CAUSE in its underlying structure, or it might differ from CAUSE in its presuppositions. This possibility, however, presents the GS theory with a methodological dilemma that potentially all structuralist decomposition analyses are subject to: just how do we decide whether a given decomposition analysis in terms of completely abstract elements adequately represents the meaning of the analyzed word or not, given that the test of a decomposition analysis is not just whether a putative English paraphrase containing the "decomposing" words of the analysis is really synonymous with the analyzed word or not? If we say *kill* is CAUSE BECOME NOT ALIVE but have no independent way of deciding exactly what the meaning of these abstract elements is (once we admit that comparing them to *cause, become, not* and *alive* is no adequate test), then the analysis is in danger of approaching complete vacuity. Even if we were to accept the structuralist's doctrine (which I don't) that we only need to isolate the primitive semantic contrasts of a language, not further analyze these, we still face the problem of knowing whether the theoretical construct CAUSE used to analyze one kind of word is really representing the same meaning as it does when it is used in analyzing another kind of word.

In traditional linguistic analysis, the keen semantic intuitions of the linguist are the only test of whether the significance attached to an abstract element is really constant wherever that element is used, but such judgments are very tricky, especially when each analysis contains more than one abstract element, so that it may be difficult to know just what "part" of the meaning of a real word is being attributed to each abstract element.

In the case of the semantics of causation, further research has magnified rather than diminished the importance of the problem Hall observed. It is now widely assumed that there are at least two kinds of causation evidenced systematically in natural languages, direct (or *manipulative*) causation and indirect (or *directive*) causation (Shibatani, 1976, pp. 31-39) and some writers suggest even more distinctions (Talmy, 1976). Manipulative causation is said to necessarily involve the physical manipulation of the object affected by the agent, while directive causation does not; perhaps the clearest example of the distinction in English is *John stood the child up* (manipulative) vs. *John made the child to stand up* (directive). Shibatani claims that not only in English but in other languages (Korean, Japanese) as well, manipulative causation tends to be expressed by lexical causatives and directive causation by periphrastic causatives (though the generalization is not absolute). But granted that the distinction is well-motivated, the question of how best to analyze the distinction in GS remains open. Should we postulate two causative operators, CAUSE_m and CAUSE_d? Should we assume directive causation is expressed by a primitive causation operator and that manipulative causation is produced by combining this with an adverbial element meaning "by direct manipulation"? Or do we take manipulative causation as basic and posit an adverbial meaning "by indirect means"? Or are there a "general" causation operator and two kinds of specializing adverbials? Are any of these solutions equivalent to any others? (The distinction between kinds of purposeful and non-purposeful causation may possibly be captured by a DO operator introduced below, but this will not help with the kind of difference observed in (113)-(115) above, where no animate subjects are involved.)

The only sure remedy I can see for this problem is to attempt to assign an explicit model-theoretic interpretation to every such abstract element postulated. (Alternatively, one could provide a system of deductive rules which make the entailments derivable with such elements precise, but the model-theoretic method also makes entailments precise and defines meaning in terms of non-linguistic objects as well.) Only in this way will the entailments of a decomposition analysis be really clear, and only in this way can we be sure the same abstract element is used to the same semantic effect in different analyses. The only case where we can satisfactorily make an exception to this rule is the one where one of the elements of a decomposition analysis *can* explicitly be equated with the meaning of an independent English word – for example, in McCawley's decomposition of *kill* it would seem acceptable to take the meaning of the abstract element ALIVE to be that of the adjective *alive*. For when we do this, we can still test the entailments of an analysis precisely in terms of other English sentences, even though these contain non-logical constants that are not given a standard interpretation. For example, if our analysis of *John killed Harry* gives (by virtue of the explicit analysis of CAUSE, BECOME and negation) the formal entailment that *Harry is not alive* is true under just the right conditions, then this serves as an adequate test of the analysis of *kill* even though we leave the stative predicate *alive* unanalyzed.

Accordingly, in the section that follows I will take CAUSE to be a logical operator (rather than as representing the meaning of English *cause* exactly) and attempt to give a model-theoretic interpretation for [ϕ CAUSE ψ]. As this is an ambitious undertaking which remains in the preliminary stages, I therefore do not feel the need to apologize for ignoring the apparent distinctions among the various kinds of direct and indirect causation mentioned in the literature, since I regard what I am doing as a necessary preliminary to exploring these distinctions coherently. In Chapter 6 I will present one way of dealing with unsystematic divergences of derived causatives from their predicted meanings, and I think it could still turn out that no more should or can be said about manipulative (as opposed to directive) causation than this. (Also, see McCawley (1978) for arguments that at least some of the above distinctions in kinds of causation, if not all of them, can be accounted for in terms of conversational implicature.)

2.3.7. *CAUSE and Lewis' Analysis of Causation*

In the long philosophical literature on causation, an intuitive connection between causal statements and counterfactual statements has frequently been observed. For example, G. H. von Wright (1963; 1968) observed that to assert that an agent has brought about an event (as in (116)), the speaker must believe that three kinds of facts obtain, in this case those in (117):

(116) John opened the door.

(117) a. The door was not open just before John acted.
b. The door was open just after John acted.

c. The door would not have become open on that particular occasion if John had not acted and all else had remained the same.

The first two conditions determine that the event of the door's opening took place; these entailments from (116) are accounted for by the truth conditions for the BECOME operator, assuming that $[\phi \text{ CAUSE } [\text{BECOME } \psi]]$ entails BECOME ψ. (117c) is what von Wright calls the "counterfactual element in causation," and the tricky part of it is the phrase "and all else had remained the same." If for example the door in this case had been controlled by some electronic device which happened to open the door on that occasion independently of any of John's actions, then (116) does not truthfully describe the situation, no matter what John did to the door.

Von Wright proposed a simple axiomatic system for this notion of causation. In addition to his "And Next" operator T mentioned earlier, he introduced a two-place operator I, read "Instead of." A formula $((\neg pTp)I\neg p)$ is read "the agent brought it about that $\neg p$ became p instead of remaing $\neg p$. (Von Wright's I-calculus would not be directly adaptable to a counterfactual analysis of causation for our purposes since no explicit reference is made to the agent or to the agent's actions which brought about the result.)

Despite this intuitive connection, attempts to analyze causation in terms of counterfactual statements have not been popular in the literature on causation, no doubt primarily because counterfactuals have traditionally been considered to be as problematic if not more problematic than the idea of causation itself. This situation has changed somewhat with the publication of interesting theories of natural language conditionals (or counterfactual conditionals) by Stalnaker (1968; 1970 with Thomason) and David Lewis (1973). Stalnaker considered the logical properties of the *if . . . then* connective of natural language as it appears in examples like (118) (recall how this would have been taken in the 1968 context of Stalnaker's article when the Vietnam war was still going on):

(118) If the Chinese enter the Vietnam conflict, the United States will use nuclear weapons.

After reviewing the well-known reasons why neither the material implication of standard first-order logic ($p \rightarrow q$) nor stronger kinds of logical connection between antecedent and consequent represent the meaning of (118) adequately, Stalnaker suggests that the way we decide the truth value of an example like this is the following. We take our beliefs, as it were, about the actual world, then somehow "add" to these beliefs the proposition expressed by the antecedent clause *if the Chinese enter the Vietnam conflict*, making "whatever adjustments are required to maintain consistency". Then finally we try to decide whether in this new situation the sentence *the US will use nuclear weapons* is true. If so, then the conditional as a whole is true.

To analyze this notion of beliefs about the actual world "plus some changes," Stalnaker turns to possible worlds semantics. The truth conditions for conditionals are then construed in this way (Stalnaker, 1968, p. 102): "Consider a possible world in which A is true and which otherwise differs minimally from the actual world. *'If A then B' is true (false) just in case B is true (false) in that possible world.*" To formalize this idea we are to add to the semantic apparatus (which will include a set of possible worlds and an interpretation of the language relative to worlds in this set) a *selection function f* which takes a proposition and a possible world as arguments and gives a possible world as value. The world $f(A, \alpha)$ selected for each proposition A and world α is to be one in which A is true and which otherwise differs minimally from α (if it is not in fact identical with α), i.e. it differs in only those ways that are required explicitly or implicitly by A. The truth conditions for the natural language conditional $\Box\!\!\rightarrow$ are formally stated as follows:[16]

(119) $A \Box\!\!\rightarrow B$ is true in α if B is true in $f(A, \alpha)$.
$A \Box\!\!\rightarrow B$ is false in α if B is false in $f(A, \alpha)$.

(For further details cf. Stalnaker, 1968, and for meta-logical results, Stalnaker and Thomason, 1970.)

In Lewis (1973), a number of formal systems of conditional (or as Lewis prefers, *counterfactual*) logic are proposed and studied, most of which differ from Stalnaker's system in one main way. Stalnaker's treatment requires that for each world and proposition there be a unique possible world differing from it minimally in which that proposition is true. But there are reasons to believe this is an unreasonable assumption, these being most obvious in examples like the following pair of conditionals (noted by Stalnaker and Thomason as well as Lewis):

(120) If Bizet and Verdi had been compatriots, Bizet would have been Italian.
If Bizet and Verdi had been compatriots, Verdi would have been French.

Stalnaker's assumption would apparently require that only one of these conditionals can be true (given that in the actual world Bizet was French and Verdi Italian), yet it is implausible that either one is more likely than the other (though we can readily assent to the statement that if Bizet and Verdi had been compatriots, then *either* Bizet would have been Italian *or* Verdi would have been French). To avoid this difficulty, Lewis instead assumes that relative to a given world, the rest of the possible worlds can be partitioned into an ordered set of equivalence classes, each class of which is definitely more similar or less similar to the actual world than all other classes, but within each class of which the worlds are neither more nor less similar to the actual world than the other members of its class. A (counterfactual) conditional $A \mathrel{\Box\!\!\rightarrow} B$ is then true, on Lewis' account, if either (1) there is no world in which A is true, or (2) the "closest" world(s) in which A holds (the world(s) most similar to the actual world in which A holds) and B holds as well is (are) "closer" (more similar to the actual world) than any world in which A holds but B does not. Lewis conceives of the set of more and more similar sets of possible worlds (relative to a given world i) as a set of nested spheres with i as center, each sphere containing possible worlds not contained in the next larger sphere; the smaller the sphere, the more similar to i are the worlds contained within it. Thus we can diagram a situation in which $\phi \mathrel{\Box\!\!\rightarrow} \psi$ is true and $\phi \mathrel{\Box\!\!\rightarrow} \neg\psi$ is false as in (121):

(121)

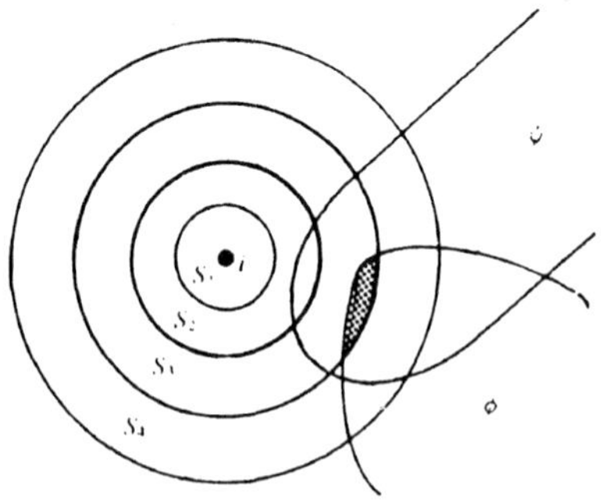

(Here $\phi \mathrel{\Box\!\!\rightarrow} \psi$ is true because some worlds in which ϕ holds – in this case, those in the shaded area – are more similar to i than any worlds in which ϕ holds but ψ does not; the shaded worlds are in S_3, but one has to go to less similar worlds in S_4 to find one in which ϕ is true but ψ is false.)

Though formulated somewhat differently, Stalnaker's system is equivalent to Lewis' under the assumption that in the latter system there is, for each world i and antecedent A entertainable at i, a class of equally-similar

A-worlds containing exactly one member. (There is some slight oversimplification in this; cf. Lewis (1973, pp. 77-83) for exact comparison and some "compromises" between the two.) As is the case with Stalnaker's selection function, Lewis makes no attempt to say just how the similarity relation is to be determined; it is a primitive notion in his theory.

In Dowty (1972a; 1972b) I attempted to give truth conditions for $[\phi \text{ CAUSE } \psi]$ in terms of a counterfactual analysis of causation based on Stalnaker's conditional logic, though I did not make a real attempt to respond to all the traditional philosophical problems in defining causation. Lewis (1973a) presents a more sophisticated attempt at a counterfactual analysis of causation which does attend to these problems, and I will adopt a version of his analysis here.

Though causation is traditionally taken to be a relation between events (whatever these are), to use the counterfactual analysis to define causation Lewis must instead deal with propositions: in place of "event c causes event e" he will have a relation between the propositions $O(e)$ and $O(c)$, where $O(e)$ is the proposition that event e occurs, etc. This is fortunate for our present purposes, since I have treated CAUSE as a sentential connective. Thus I will avoid the problem of constructing expressions denoting events and forming from these event expressions sentences asserting that events occur, since it is only the sentences themselves that are needed as "arguments" for CAUSE (e.g., a BECOME-sentence is one asserting that an event occurs). No further "ontology of events" will be necessary in this book. But in discussing Lewis' theory of causation, I will continue to speak informally of "events e, c" and sentences $O(c)$ and $O(e)$. Moreover, there may well be causal sentences of natural language which we would not want to analyze as relations among events, such as the "stative" causative sentence (122) cited by Fillmore (1971):

(122) Mary's living nearby causes John to prefer this neighborhood.

Finally, English has the "surface" sentential connective *because* which connects two sentences – both those expressing the occurrence of events (*John left because Mary arrived*) and those expressing states (*John prefers this neighborhood because Mary lives nearby*).

Lewis defines the relation of *causal dependence* between events e and c as counterfactual dependence between the propositions that these events occur: *e depends causally on c* if and only if both $O(c) \mathrel{\Box\!\!\rightarrow} O(e)$ and $\neg O(c) \mathrel{\Box\!\!\rightarrow} \neg O(e)$. In the case of two actually occurring events c and e the first conditional is vacuously satisfied[17] (since $O(c) \wedge O(e)$ entails

$O(c) \Box\!\!\rightarrow O(e)$), so we might as well say e depends causally on c if and only if $O(c)$ and $O(e)$ and $\neg O(c) \Box\!\!\rightarrow \neg O(e)$.

For Lewis, causal dependence is not quite the same relation as causation itself: causation is to be a transitive relation, while causal dependence is not. This latter fact already follows because transitivity fails for Lewis' counterfactual connective $\Box\!\!\rightarrow$; it can be true that $\phi \Box\!\!\rightarrow \psi$ and $\psi \Box\!\!\rightarrow \chi$ but at the same time false that $\phi \Box\!\!\rightarrow \chi$, as in the situation represented by the diagram in (123). (cf. Lewis 1973a, p. 563):

(123)

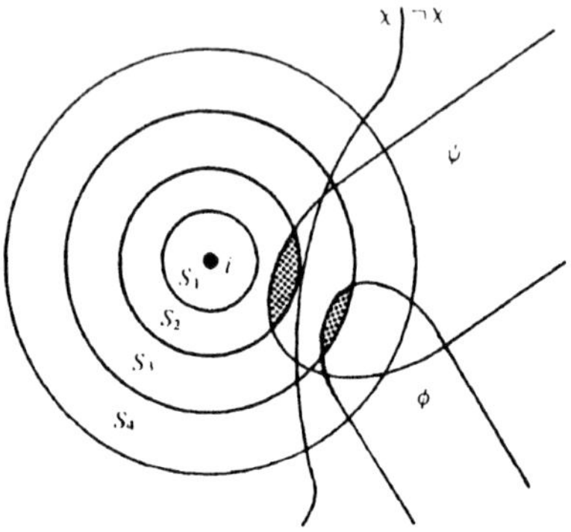

Causation proper is defined by Lewis in terms of causal dependence as follows: Event c *causes* event e just in case there is a series of events c, c_1, $c_2, \ldots, c_n$, e such that c_1 depends causally on c, c_2 depends causally on c_1, and so on throughout the series (for any $n \geqslant 0$, so that a series of only two causally dependent events c and e counts as causation as well as longer "chains" of events). Because of the failure of transitivity for causal dependence, c may cause e even though e does not depend causally on c. (The advantage Lewis sees in this distinction between causation and causal dependence will became clear shortly.)

The first traditional problem Lewis deals with is the problem of the *direction* of causation, i.e. of insuring that the analysis will distinguish between "c causes e" and "e causes c". Presumably, the fact that the barometer has a certain reading depends counterfactually on the fact that the air pressure has a certain strength: if the air pressure had been different, then the barometer reading would have been different. But is it also true that if the barometer reading had been different, then the pressure would have been different? If so, then cause and effect are not distinguished by the counterfactual analysis. But Lewis denies that the second counterfactual is true; perhaps the barometer was merely malfunctioning. The key to the distinction, as Lewis sees it, is in how overall similarity of worlds is understood:

To be sure, there are actual laws and circumstances that imply and explain the actual accuracy of the barometer, but these are no more sacred than the actual laws and circumstances that imply and explain the actual pressure. Less sacred, in fact. When something must give way to permit a higher reading, we find it less of a departure from actuality to hold the pressure fixed and sacrifice the accuracy, rather than vice versa. It is not hard to see why. The barometer, being more localized and more delicate than the weather, is more vulnerable to slight departures from actuality.

(Lewis, 1973a, p. 564f.)

(Lewis distinguishes (1973a, pp. 563-565) between counterfactual dependence and a similar relation which he calls *nomic dependence* which *is* reversible in a certain sense.)

Another problem is that of *epiphenomena*. Suppose (to take an example from Lewis again) that the axe falls (event c), its shadow moves (event d) and the king loses his head (event e). Can we be sure that c, rather than d, causes e? If c had not occurred then d would not have occurred, but it also seems that if d had not occurred then again e would not have occurred. As with the problem of the direction of causation, Lewis here denies the counterfactual that is a problem: it is false that if the shadow had not moved then the kind would not have lost his head. Or in other words, a possible world in which d was absent but e occurred anyway, caused as in actuality by c, is closer on balance to actuality than a world in which d is absent because c is absent and where e is absent as well.

A third problem is the *preemption* of one cause by another. Suppose Colonel Mustard poisons the coffee with poison X and Professor Plum poisons it with poison Y. The victim drinks the coffee and dies. However, it turns out that poison X catalyzes poison Y into an inert substance without losing its lethality, so Colonel Mustard's use of X (event c_1) preempts Professor Plum's use of Y (event c_2) in causing the death (event e). The problem is that neither c_1 nor c_2 may count as causes under the counterfactual analysis, since it is false that if c_1 hadn't occurred then e would not have occurred (the other poison would have done the trick) and it is false that if c_2 hadn't occurred then e wouldn't have occurred (the first poison would have done it). It is at this point that Lewis appeals to the failure of transitivity of causal dependence but not causation itself. There is here a third event (if not more) involved in the causal chain from c_1 to e, namely the victim's ingestion of a lethal dose of X (event d). Here d depends causally on c_1, and e can be said to depend causally on d (because if the victim had not ingested poison X in drinking the coffee then – assuming poison Y had been already decomposed as before – e would not have occurred). So here c_1 still counts as a cause of

e, not because e depends causally on c_1 (which it does not) but because of the chain of causal dependence from e back to d and from d back to c_1; it is in this sort of case that we have causation without causal dependence.

A vexing problem for the counterfactual analysis that Lewis does not attempt to solve is the problem of *overdetermination* of an event by two independently sufficient causes. Suppose that an electrical short starts a fire in one part of a house, and at exactly the same time a cigarette ash starts a fire in another part. The house burns down. Also suppose that in this situation either accident would have led to the destruction of the house if the other had not occurred. Under the counterfactual analysis it seems that neither accident counts as a cause of the destruction of the house, since if one accident had not occurred the house would still have burned down, and if the other accident had not occurred the house would still have burned down.[18] Cf. Lyon (1967) and Loeb (1974, pp. 540-543) for possible ways of resolving this paradox under counterfactual analyses.

Another traditional problem that Lewis does not really attempt to deal with directly is what he calls *causal selection*. As has often been noted, natural language causation statements (accomplishment sentences) ordinarily single out one event as *the cause* of the second, whereas the counterfactual analysis as it stands allows quite a number of events and surrounding circumstances to count as causes. In reply to Lewis it has been pointed out by Kim (1973) and Abbott (1974) that quite a large number of counterfactuals give quite peculiar sentences when converted to causal statements (examples are from Abbott (1974); Kim's examples are similar):

(124) a. If I had not lit John's cigarette, he would not have smoked it.
b. My lighting John's cigarette caused him to smoke it.

(125) a. If Mary had not gotten married, she would have not become a widow.
b. Mary's getting married caused here to become a widow.

(126) a. If I had not been born I would not have come to Amherst.
b. My being born caused me to come to Amherst.

(127) a. If the jewels had not been stolen, the police would not have discovered it.
b. The theft of the jewels caused the police to discover it.

Lewis seems to suggest that this is not an important problem from his point of view. "We may select the abnormal or extraordinary causes, or those under human control, or those we deem good or bad, or just those we want to talk about. I have nothing to say about these principles of invidious discrimination. I am concerned with the prior question of what it is to be one of the causes (unselectively speaking)" (Lewis, 1973a, p. 559). This may be one of the places (cf. below) where philosophical and linguistic desiderata for an analysis of causation differ, since the above examples of causal statements are strikingly abnormal, and as far as I know, almost all accomplishments in English require causal selection in this way. (An exception is the nominalization *cause* of the verb *cause*, where we can speak of *a cause of X, one of the causes of X*.)

Lest it be suggested that Lewis' mention of "those we want to talk about" invites a Gricean analysis (Grice, 1975) of the causal selection problem, note that the counterfactual analysis treats causal statements and counterfactuals as logically equivalent (or to be more exact, "*A* causes *B*" is equivalent to "*A* and *B*, and if *not-A* then *not-B*"). If equivalent, then the two kinds of statements ought to have exactly the same conversational implicatures, according to Grice' definition. Nor does an implication that the causal event mentioned is the most important of several causal factors qualify as a conventional implicature (presupposition) by the usual linguistic tests (cf. Karttunen and Peters, 1974).

It will not help, as Abbott (1974) notes, to try to add to the truth conditions for *c causes e* a clause stating that $\neg O(e) \boxright \neg O(c)$, even though this might seem to solve the selection problem by requiring the causal event to be one that would not have occurred in worlds most similar to the actual world except that the effect did not occur (cf. McCawley, 1976). That is, such a clause would make the asserted cause a kind of sufficient as well as a necessary condition for the result. This seems to pick out the one "causal condition" that most likely would have been otherwise. As Abbott points out, this immediately destroys the assymetry between cause and effect (since both $\neg O(c) \boxright \neg O(e)$ and $\neg O(e) \boxright \neg O(c)$ would be part of the truth conditions) and has other technical problems within Lewis' system as well.

However, there may be another approach to the causal selection problem similar to this but which is less problematic. It does seem that often, if not always, we select as the "cause" of an event that one of the various causal conditions that we can most easily imagine to have been otherwise, that is, one whose "deletion" from the actual course of events would result in the least departure from the actual world. As Abbott points out, it may or may not sound odd to deem a certain causal condition "the" cause, depending on what the other causal conditions were. Though it would normally be odd to say that my lighting John's cigarette caused him to smoke it, this statement might be considered appropriate if at the time I lighted it John was being held down by someone while a cigarette was held in John's mouth and his nostrils were held closed. And though it would be strange to say that Mary's getting married caused her to become a widow if she married her husband as a healthy young man, it might be natural to say this if she married a man on the verge of death. If we had some way of quantifying over all the multiple causes (in Lewis' sense) of an event, then we might identify what we call "the cause" in natural language as that one causal condition whose "deletion" (i.e. its non-occurrence) can be found in worlds more similar to the actual world than can the "deletion" of any of the other causal conditions. The above examples suggest that causal conditions or events happening just prior to the resulting event are "easier to get rid of", as it were, than causal conditions or events that occur further back in the causal chain of events. This would accord with Lewis' suggestion that in determining overall similarity among worlds, "comprehensive and exact similarities of particular fact throughout large spatiotemporal regions seem to have special weight." And if this view of causal selection is right, the fact that we so often label human actions as "the cause" when they appear in a causal chain of events could be explained by the widespread view that the actions of human agents are usually less determined (could more easily have been otherwise) than events involving only inanimate objects. (But see Abbott (1974) for what may be problems for this view.)

Let us relabel Lewis' definition of the causation relation as the *causal factor* relation and approach the truth conditions for [ϕ CAUSE ψ] by the following series of definitions. I will state the definitions in terms of arbitrary sentences ϕ and ψ, leaving it open whether we must eventually restrict these to sentences expressing the occurrence of events or add some other restrictions on them.

(128) ϕ *depends causally on* ψ if and only if ϕ, ψ and $\neg\phi \mathrel{\Box\!\!\rightarrow} \neg\psi$ are all true.

(129) ϕ *is a causal factor for* ψ if and only if there is a series of sentences $\phi, \phi_1, \ldots, \phi_n, \psi$ (for $n \geqslant 0$) such that each member of the series depends causally on the previous member.

(130) [ϕ CAUSE ψ] is true if and only if (i) ϕ is a causal factor for ψ, and (ii) for all other ϕ' such that ϕ' is also a causal factor for ψ, some $\neg\phi$-world is more similar to the actual world than any $\neg\phi'$-world is.

As far as I am aware, this avoids the difficulties we encounter in attempting to add the inverse counterfactual $\neg O(e) \Box\!\!\rightarrow \neg O(c)$ to the definition of causation. Definition (130) requires the assumption that there be a unique "selected" causal factor for each true CAUSE sentence, but perhaps this is too strong. We might instead wish to allow that in some cases two or more causal factors will be equally easy to get rid of (i.e. their absences will be first encountered in equally similar worlds) and can both (all) count as causes, while nevertheless ruling out other, more irreversible causal factors as causes. Thus if a set of equally fortuitous traffic conditions led to an accident we might want to say that all of them caused the accident, while still denying that the driver's having started the car at the beginning of the ill-fated trip also caused the accident. If so, (130) should be changed to (131):

(131) [ϕ CAUSE ψ] is true if and only if (i) ϕ is a causal factor for ψ, and (ii) for all other ϕ' such that ϕ' is also a causal factor for ψ, some $\neg\phi$-world is as similar or more similar to the actual world than any $\neg\phi'$-world is.

Though I will have to leave many aspects of the semantics of causation unresolved, I think I have presented one interesting and promising treatment that gives the reader enough of an idea of the problems and possibilities involved to convince him of the interest in trying to specify the conditions under which CAUSE sentences are true and appropriate. The basic analysis presented here already suggests points at which one might tinker with definitions in order to introduce a distinction between direct and indirect causation, should such a distinction really be needed – for example, restrictions on the number of events in the causal chain, restrictions on the kind of causal event, or on the way causal selection is determined.

The problem of causation itself is a profound and complex one in philosophy, particularly as it pertains to the philosophy of science, and has a much longer history than the study of causative/accomplishment verbs in linguistics. The present discussion does not really do justice to this philosophical literature. I think it is important to leave open the possibility that the best analysis of causation for purposes of the philosophy of science may turn out to be quite different from the best analysisis for causatives in ordinary language. For example, Lewis considers it an important virtue of his treatment that it does not assume a relation of temporal priority between cause and effect and can thus potentially deal with phenomena such as backwards causation and closed causal loops among events, phenomena that are of real concern in some branches of modern physics. Aside from the allowance for contemporaneous cause and effect as in the stative causative example (122), I know of no case where effect fails to be preceded by cause for ordinary language, so I would not consider it a significant defect of a semantic analysis of causation for ordinary language that such extraordinary kinds of causation were automatically excluded. On the other hand, causal verbs are frequently used in ordinary English discourse for relationships that philosophers would be careful to distinguish from true causation:

(132) a. The failure of universal instantiation in line three makes the proof invalid.
b. A kangaroo is a marsupial because it has a pouch.
c. Mary's living nearby causes John to prefer this neighborhood. (= 122)

I am told that the use of causal verbs and connectives for such cases as (132) is characteristic of most natural languages. Thus far from ignoring examples like these, an adequate linguistic analysis of causal discourse should explain just what the connection between (132) and "true" causation is that accounts for this verbal concurrence, if in fact these are not analyzed as the same thing as causation. Perhaps a family of related causal and nomic relationships is called for, some general enough to cover all these cases and some more narrow. Of even greater potential interest to the linguist than the use of causal language in ordinary English discourse are the aspects of the meaning of causative and/or accomplishment verbs shared by *all* natural languages (as such verbs apparently occur in some form in all languages), including the languages spoken by non-literate, non-technological societies whose "philosophical" conception of causation might be quite different from ours.

2.3.8. *DO, Agency and Activity Verbs*

In John Ross' article "Act" (Ross, 1972), he proposed that "every verb of action is embedded in the object complement of a two-place predicate whose phonological realization in English is *do*" (p. 70). A sentence like (133) is claimed by Ross to have an underlying structure something like

(133) Frogs produce croaks.

(134)

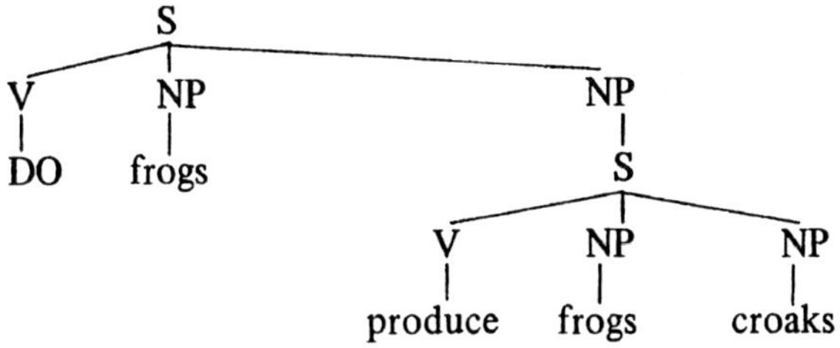

(133) would be derived from (134) via a rule of DO Gobbling, a rule which replaces DO by the verb from the lower sentence. As Ross later observes, however, such a rule as DO Gobbling would be unnecessary in a Generative Semantics theory, where the function of DO Gobbling would be taken over by McCawley's *Predicate Raising*.

This DO would have to be considered a *like-subject verb*, i.e. a complement-taking verb like *try* and *condescend* for which the subject of the embedded clause is (somehow) required to be identical with the subject of the matrix verb. It has been suggested that this requirement be effected by making Equi-NP deletion (which deletes the identical complement subject) obligatory for such verbs (Lakoff, 1965) or by a constraint on well-formed underlying structures (Perlmutter, 1971); cf. Fodor (1974) for discussion of the alternatives. (I will later discuss the possibility of avoiding the like-subject problem altogether by treating DO as a predicate-modifier rather than as a sentential operator, an alternative that generative semanticists did not consider.)

Ross argues that the occurrences of the morpheme *do* (or *did*) in sentences (134) can be accounted for more economically by the grammar if they arise from underlying DO than if they must be introduced transformationally:

(135) a. You've bungled a lot of hands, Goren, but fortunately Jacoby has done {so / it} too.
b. That Bob resigned, which I think I should do, was a good idea.
c. You do one thing right now: apologize.
d. What I did then was call the grocer.
e. Waxing the floors I've always hated to do.
f. Solving English crossword puzzles is impossible to do.
g. Kissing gorillas just isn't done (by debutantes).

Ross argues that the rules of *do-so replacement* (involved in (a)), *Swooping* and *Relativization* (Involved in (b)), *Equative Deletion* (involved in (c)), *Pseudo-Cleft Formation* (involved in (d)), and *Passive* (involved in (g)), would all have to be complicated if the morpheme *do* had to be inserted in these cases. The main complication, of course, is that *do* never occurs in these environments if the verb is stative:

(136) a. *You've known a lot of answers, George, and Harry has done so too.
b. *That John believes me, which everyone should do, is obvious.
c. *John did what I wanted to do: dislike Henrietta.
d. *What I did then was be in Boston.
e. *Knowing how to type I've always hated to do.
f. *Consisting of five members is impossible for the committee to do.
g. *Preferring hot dogs just isn't done (by debutantes).

If the verbs in (136) have no higher DO in their underlying structure, then the ungrammaticality of these examples is predicted by Ross' hypothesis. (For additional complications which the underlying-DO-analysis avoids, see Ross 1972.)

Ross suggests that the case grammarian's notion of *Agent* might be replaced by the notion "possible subject of *do*" (Ross, 1972, p. 105). (Ross' qualms about this suggestion will be discussed below.) The tests which case grammarians usually use for the presence of an agent (cf. Lee, 1971, p. 8) are tests like those in (137):

(137) A sentence contains an *agent* if
(i) it can occur as complement of *persuade, command,* causative *have*.
(ii) it can have an instrumental phrase.
(iii) intentional adverbs can be added to the sentence.
(iv) it can occur as an imperative.

But these tests are of course a subset of the tests Lakoff proposed to distinguish statives from non-statives. Lee, in fact, proposes the useful term "A-tests" to distinguish these agency tests from the other stativity tests (the ability to occur in the progressive and in pseudo-cleft constructions), which he calls "P-tests."

For the purposes of constructing an aspect calculus then, one might hypothesize that the occurrence of an operator DO is what distinguishes a stative sentence from an activity sentence in logical structure. If so, one would also have to suppose that DO may appear in the underlying structure of some (not all) accomplishments but not in that of achievements. Notice that paradigm examples of achievement verbs,[19] exemplified by (138), can never occur in agentive contexts like (139-41):

(138) a. John recognized his long-lost brother in the crowd.
b. John detected a strange odor in the room.

(139) a. *Harry persuaded John to recognize his long lost brother in the crowd.
b. *Harry ordered John to detect a strange odor in the room.

(140) a. *John deliberately recognized his long-lost brother in the crowd.
b. *John carefully detected a strange odor in the room.

(141) a. *Recognize your long-lost brother in the crowd!
b. *Detect a strange odor in the room!

This present conception of DO is somewhat different from that of Ross (1972). Whereas Ross seemed to be supposing that stative verbs and active verbs are disjoint classes of primitive predicates, the latter class differing in that they are required to occur with higher DO in underlying structure, I am supposing that both stative and active verbs are constructed from the some homogeneous class of primitive stative predicates, thus the presence of DO is the *only* thing that distinguishes the meaning of a stative from that of an active verb. From Ross' paper at least one would conclude that no cases exist of the same predicate "surfacing" both with and without its higher DO, and indeed typical activity predicates like *walk, swim, smile, giggle* seem not to have any stative counterparts.

Nevertheless, I think at least three kinds of cases can be observed where the difference between a predicate with and without its higher DO makes itself apparent "on the surface."

In his article 'Three kinds of Physical Perception Verbs', Rogers (1971) distinguishes three classes of verbs described the physical perceptions, the first two of which, *cognitive* and *active*, interest us here:

(142)

	Cognitive	*Active*
	see	look at, watch
	hear	listen to
	feel	feel
	smell	smell
	taste	taste

Rogers observes (1) that the cognitives are syntactically stative[20] (according to Lakoff's tests) whereas the actives are syntactically non-stative: and (2) that an active verb imputes to its subject intention, purpose, and responsibility, while the corresponding cognitive does not. One can see or hear something inadvertently or accidentally, but not watch or listen to something inadvertently or accidentally. Though no morphological difference exists between stative and active forms of *feel, smell* and *taste*, their participation in both kinds of syntactic environments with appropriate meaning differences justifies the distinction here as well.

These differences in grammatical properties suggest that the actives should be analyzed as consisting of the corresponding cognitive (stative) embedded in DO. The structure of *look* and *see* would then be something like (143) and (144):

(143) *look*:

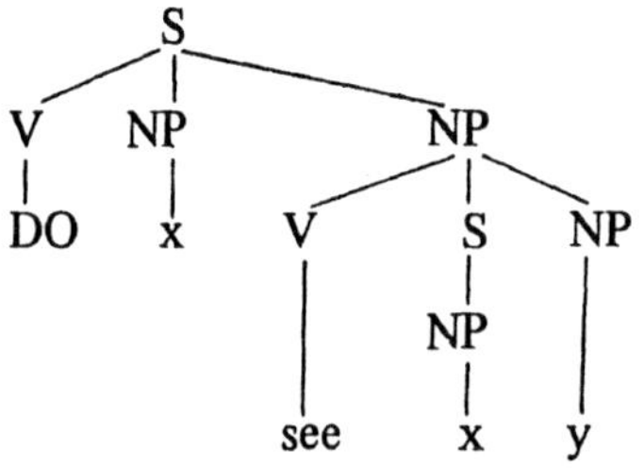

(144) *see*:

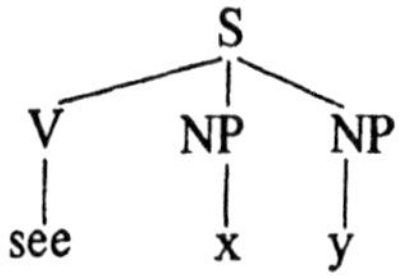

If this is correct, then a semantic factor which DO contributes is roughly the notion of volition (and/or intention), contemporaneous with the act, on the part of the subject. Moreover, there seems to be no other systematic[21] difference between the meaning of the actives and their respective cognitives.

A second case of such stative/active counterparts would be the so-called non-stative adjectives and nouns (*be careful, be a hero*, etc.), which I believe actually have *both* stative and agentive readings. A context like (145) illustrates the agentive reading, (146) and (147) illustrate the stative:

(145) John is being { polite. / careful. / a hero. / an obnoxious bastard. }

(146) John is { polite. / careful. / a hero. / an obnoxious bastard. }

(147) I consider John { polite. / careful. / a hero. / an obnoxious bastard. }

The difference here is a fine one. In (146) and (147), a more or less permanent property is ascribed to an individual, a property which one believes an individual to have because of one's total experience with the individual, even though the individual is not evidencing the property at the moment. In (145), on the other hand, a property currently in evidence is being described. Moreover, it seems to be a kind of activity which is in some sense under the control of the individual. If John is being rude (polite, a bastard, etc.) and someone points this out to him, he can if he wishes stop doing it at once, assuming he agrees that this is a correct description of his behavior. On the other hand, a person cannot immediately alter his stative properties (*tall, erudite*, etc. and – I would maintain – the kind of property expressed in (146)) simply by willing them away.

Under the "higher DO" hypothesis, it could be claimed that the "extra" auxiliary *be* in (145) that does not appear in (146) is the surface manifestation of DO (cf. the "active *be*" postulated by Partee (1977) for these examples). That is, an underlying DO will either (1) lexicalize as *be* when it precedes a surface adjective as in (145), (2) lexicalize as *do* when its complement has been deleted upon identity with a verb phrase elsewhere in the sentence as in Ross' examples (134a)-(134g), or (3) is otherwise "gobbled" – or in GS is predicate raised before it and its complement are together lexicalized as an active verb.

A somewhat different case involving DO is discussed in Quang (1971). The pairs of examples in (148) and (149) are supposedly related by Lakoff and Peters' *Conjunct Movement* transformation (Lakoff and Peters, 1969). But whereas (148a) and (148b) are synonymous, (149a) and (149b) are almost but not quite synonymous:

(148) a. John and Mary are similar.
b. John is similar to Mary.

(149) a. John and Mary kissed.
b. John kissed Mary.

As Quang observed, the difference in meaning seems to be that responsibility for the action is attributed to both individuals in (149a) but only to one of them in (149b), despite the fact that the same basic physical relationship between the two individuals can obtain in both cases. Parallel differences in meaning result when one constructs examples like (149) with the verbs *fuck* (Quang's example) and its synonyms, *commit adultery* (*with*), *hold hands* (*with*), *rub noses* (*with*), *neck* (*with*), *pet*, *play footsie* (*with*) and also *agree with* (in non-stative sense), *argue* (*with*), *communicate* (*with*), *quarrel* (*with*), *fight* (*with*), *meet*, etc.

Quang proposed that (149a) and (149b) be derived from underlying structures (150a) and (150b) respectively:

(150) a.

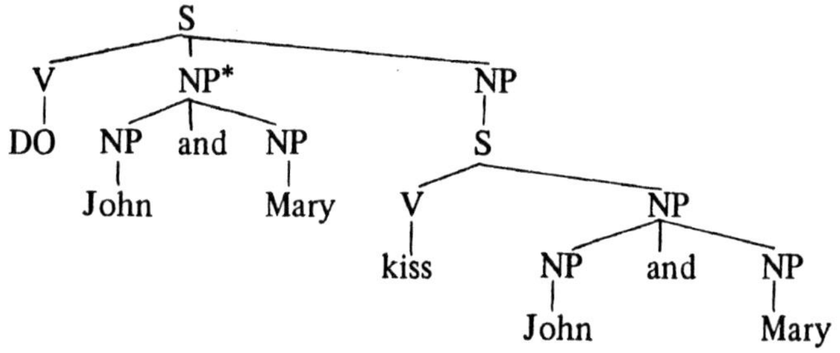

b.

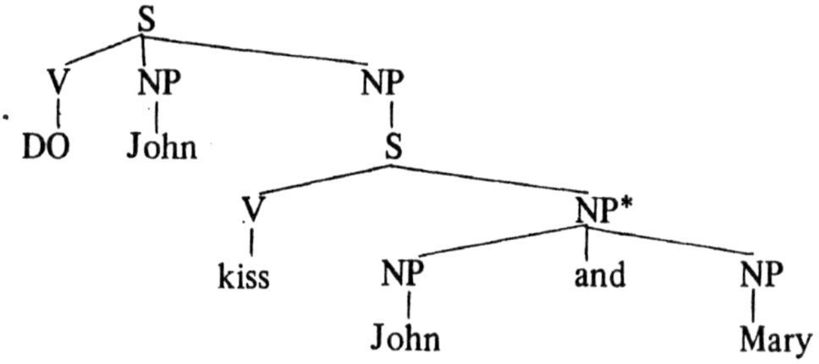

Here, the difference in meaning between (150a) and (150b) is to be accounted for by whether *both* subjects of the lower sentence appear as subject of DO or whether only one of them is subject of DO: this treatment would mesh precisely with the semantic notion of DO developed above. The difference in meaning between such pairs of sentences is just whether one or both individuals are asserted to be voluntary participants in the act. This distinction in logical form would likewise explain the unnaturalness of (151b) as opposed to (151a). (The examples are attributed to Chomsky):

(151) a. The drunk embraced the lamppost.
b. *The drunk and the lamppost embraced.

The semantic anomaly of (151b) under the higher-verb-DO analysis is due to the fact that it ascribes agency to a non-sentient being.

In the derivation of the surface structure (149b) from (150b), Conjunct Movement first separates the noun phrase *Mary* from the conjoined subject, making *Mary* a derived object. Then Equi-NP deletion would be able to apply on the higher cycle, deleting the lower noun phrase *John* on identity with the higher noun phrase. (Though Conjunct Movement is an optional transformation, if it did not apply here, Equi could not apply and the derivation would therefore be blocked, assuming that Equi has to apply in *all* successful derivations where DO occurs.) The successful derivation of a surface structure from (150a) would depend on Conjunct Movement's *not* applying on the lower cycle, since only in this way can Equi apply, deleting the whole lower conjoined noun phrase. (A troublesome point that Quang does not comment on is the question of what prevents conjunct movement from applying in the *higher* sentence in (150a).)

2.3.9. *The Semantics of DO*

Having now seen three cases where the semantic effect of DO can presumably be isolated, we can turn to the question of what semantics should be given to this operator. It should first be noted that DO does not necessarily connote action in the usual sense, because of examples like *John is being quiet, John is ignoring Mary, What John did was not eat anything for 3 days* (Cruse, 1973) which seem to entail merely deliberate avoidance of action of a certain kind. Thus on this view of DO, those (stative) predicates that become activities when combined with DO are distinguished from stative predicates which cannot be activities in that the former are states a person can put himself in by "act of the will" so to speak, and are states that he remains in only so long as he wills to. Thus while *seeking the answer, being polite*, and perhaps *driving (toward Chicago)* are activities, *being in Chicago, being blond*, and *knowing the answer* are not (Cf. **John is being in Chicago*, **Mary is being blond*, **John is knowing the answer*), apparently because one cannot be in Chicago or cease to be in Chicago (or be blond, etc.) simply by deciding that that's what one wants to do (though one can of course bring it about by a causal chain of activities and accomplishments that one is in Chicago, is blond, etc.).

It is almost but not quite possible to equate the meaning of DO with the notion of intentionality or volition (though I have had to use these terms in talking about DO for want of better ones). Note that examples like *John* *is being obnoxious, John is being a fool* do not really entail that John is intending to be obnoxious or intending to be a fool, but they nevertheless entail that some property under his control qualifies him as obnoxious or a fool, something or other that he could avoid doing as soon as he really chose to. It is this which distinguishes these examples from ungrammatical cases like **John is being six feet tall* and stative sentences like *John is a fool*. A low I.Q. may be sufficient reason to assert that John is a fool, but that alone can never be sufficient for asserting that he is *being* a fool. Thus "state under the unmediated control of the agent" may be the best phrase for describing the DO that our syntactic contrasts seem to isolate.[22] The meaning of adverbs like *deliberately, willingly* and *intentionally* is more complex than this in that they require not only that the predicate they combine with denote a controllable property but they entail also that the agent intend that the property denoted by this predicate be one he has, rather than some other controllable property. *John is deliberately being obnoxious* is a stronger statement than *John is being obnoxious*, and there is no contradiction in saying *John is unintentionally being obnoxious*.

Thus whatever the interpretation given to DO (α, ϕ), where α is an individual term and ϕ a sentence), it should satisfy something like the following condition in all models:

(152) $\Box[\mathrm{DO}(\alpha, \phi) \leftrightarrow \phi \wedge u.t.u.c.o.a.\ (\phi)]$

In (152) the abbreviation stands for "is under the unmediated control of the agent (individual denoted by α)" and this is of course a blatant fudge since I have no way of giving a standard (explicit model-theoretic) interpretation for this notion. The second conjunct on the right side of (152) should, in any case, be relegated to the status of a conventional implicature, since the notion of controllability which DO requires must also be satisfied in contexts that test for implicature, e.g. **John isn't being six feet tall*, **It's possible that John is knowing the answer* are just as anomalous as the examples discussed above. Thus in Karttunen's (1970) terms, DO would have to be an implicative verb like *manage*; DO (α, ϕ) entails ϕ and $\sim\mathrm{DO}(\alpha, \phi)$ entails $\sim\phi$. The contribution to meaning that DO makes is entirely in its conventional implicature.

The troublesome like-subject constraint could be eliminated for DO (as it could for all like-subject sentential complement verbs) by treating DO as a predicate modifier (expression of type $\langle\langle s, \langle e, t\rangle\rangle, \langle e, t\rangle\rangle$) instead, just as Montague did with *try*. This alternative is never considered in generative semantics because of the belief that there are no "verb-phrase complements" in logical structure, only sentence complements. (The semantic advantages of predicate modifiers have been shown by Stalnaker and Thomason (1973) and, for passive examples like *John was willingly sacrificed by the natives*, by Partee (1975).)

It would even be possible to give a trivial kind of standard interpretation to DO by designating some proper subset of the properties of individuals (i.e. some subset of $(\{0, 1\}^{D_e})^{I \times J}$ in the PTQ model) as the potentially "controllable" ones, introducing a sorted logic in which these controllable properties belong to a separate sort, and making $DO(\hat{}\delta)(\alpha)$ well-defined only where $\hat{}\delta$ denotes a property of the proper sort. (Note that potentially controllable properties are not always actually controlled. Cf. the contrast between (145) and (146) – so $\delta(\alpha)$ is well-formed (without DO) even if $\hat{}\delta$ is controllable.) However, this still leaves the notion of controllable property as primitive as before, and I can see no useful purpose that is served by the technical maneuver.

In spite of the structural semantic arguments from English for postulating DO, the evidence for DO is less persuasive than that arguing for CAUSE and BECOME, and the role played by DO in the aspect calculus is less significant than that played by CAUSE and BECOME. There is no productive word formation process "adding" a DO to a verb in English (much less in other languages[23] I know of) as there is in the case of CAUSE and BECOME in a large number of languages, and the only case of a large number of systematically contrasting sentences with and without DO is the *John is polite/John is being polite* pattern. While CAUSE and BECOME (and the progressive BE of the next chapter) are like modal and tense operators in that their semantics involves other times and/or other possible worlds, DO at most maps an extensional predicate into another extensional predicate. In this respect, decomposition in terms of DO is much more like the Katzian decomposition of extensional predicates in terms of features like [human], [animate], etc. than decomposition with CAUSE and BECOME. Postulating BECOME turns out to allow us to describe certain scope ambiguities that could not be accounted for otherwise (cf. Chapter 5), but no such ambiguities with DO seem to be attested (with the exception of one rather dubious case mentioned in the next section). Finally, data to be considered in connection with interval semantics in Chapter 3 makes it doubtful that DO can really distinguish all activities from statives, after all. (Alternatives to postulating higher DO can be found for treating the *be being a hero* cases (cf. Partee (1977)), Ross' cases (cf. Chapter 3, note 13), and Quang's cases (cf. Chapter 7, note 17).) Thus though the evidence of this section shows that "Agency" is an important semantic distinction in English from certain points of view, DO turns out to be relatively unimportant for the remainder of this book.

2.3.10. *DO in Accomplishments*

Accomplishments in many cases have the same agentive properties that are associated with higher DO in activities; they occur as imperatives, complements of *force* and *persuade*, etc. The hypothesis of the aspect calculus then leads us to postulate a DO somewhere in the logical structure of these.

It has been argued (by Lakoff, 1970a) that certain accomplishments are ambiguous between an intentional and unintentional reading. For example, *John cut his arm* might describe either an accidental or a purposeful, masochistic action.

In view of this apparent ambiguity, I suggested in my earlier treatment that the ambiguity should be accounted for in terms of the position or positions of the operator DO in the logical structure of accomplishments. In the accidental reading of *John cut his arm* the subject was presumably engaged in some intentional activity or other involving the use of a knife, though he did not intend that this result in injury to his arm. In the other reading, the bringing about of this result was intentional as well. I suggested that the first case, which I called a *non-intentional agentive accomplishment*, have a logical form of (152) while the second case, an *intentional agentive accomplishment*, had the logical structure (153), in which the CAUSE sentence is within the scope of a second, higher DO.

(152)

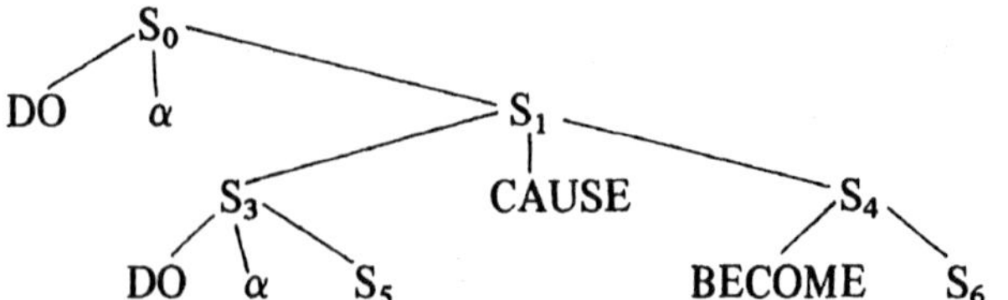

(153)

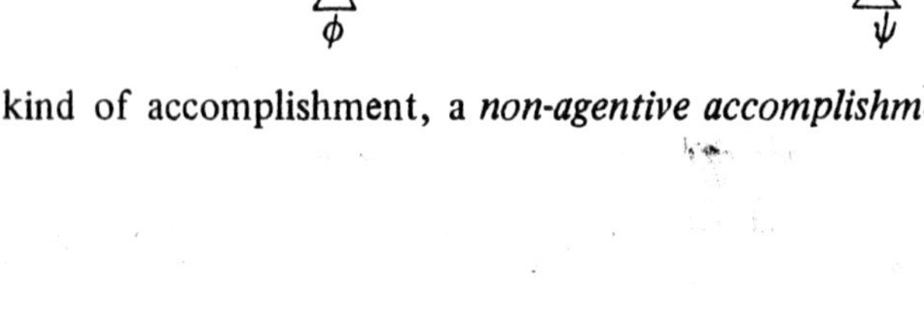

A third kind of accomplishment, a *non-agentive accomplishment*, would be one in which no intentional action at all is asserted, hence no DO. For example, *John hit the wall* might be ambiguous between all three readings: the intentional agentive (hitting the wall was just what he intended to do), non-intentional agentive (he aimed at Bill and missed), and non-agentive or "instrumental" (someone pushed John against the wall). One kind of non-agentive structure would be (154):

(154)

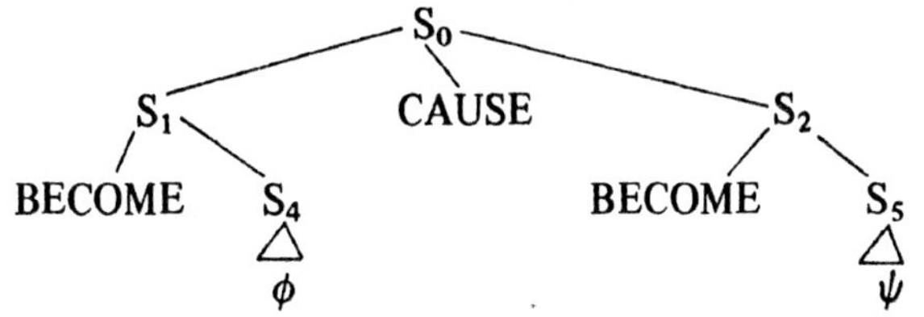

I presented several kinds of possible syntactic motivation for (152) and (153) in my earlier treatment (cf. Dowty, 1972a, pp. 104-108, 1972b, pp. 66-67), but I will not review these here. I am now not sure of the viability of (153) in a GS grammar for several reasons. First, Lakoff's claim that the distinction between intentional and non-intentional causation is a true ambiguity has been called into question by Catlin and Catlin (1972); this issue is discussed at length in Zwicky and Sadock (1975) in the context of the reliability of the linguist's heuristic tests for ambiguity/vagueness (or ambiguity/generality), and they conclude that syntactic data given so far can not conclusively decide whether a true ambiguity is involved in this case. Second, if the semantic "content" of DO is not really intentionality but rather something like unmediated controllability, then it is questionable whether DO can legitimately be claimed to distinguish intentional from non-intentional accomplishments. Can we consistently claim that **John is being in Chicago* and **Mary is being blond* are unacceptable because the states of being in Chicago and being blond are not subject to unmediated control, yet at the same time claim that in the "intentional" reading of *John caused a disturbance by walking out* the state of being such that one of one's actions causes something else is unmediately controllable? Perhaps one can appeal to a kind of transitivity of controllability – if an activity like walking is controllable, then the causation of another event by that action is controllable. But even if this is consistent, the notion of immediate controllability is not intuitively the same thing as the intentional/non-intentional distinction that Lakoff claims to observe.

Finally, there are problems with the syntactic arguments that I cited in 1972 for (153), though I will forego discussion of these here.

2.3.11. *Summary of the Aspect Calculus*

The aspect calculus, as developed provisionally so far, is like a first-order logic except that it contains a number of non-standard tense and modal operators; it is thus to be a kind of *pragmatic language* in the sense of Montague (1968). Its vocabulary consists of a set of individual variables, a set of individual constants, a set of n-place predicate constants (stative predicates) π_n for various natural numbers n, all the logical symbols of standard first-order logic, plus at least the symbols AT, BECOME, CAUSE and DO. (The last operator is included for completeness, in spite of my qualms about it.) It might be advantageous to suppose it is a two-sorted logic, having variables $t_1, t_2, \ldots, t_n$ and constants ranging over times as well as variables $x_1, x_2, \ldots, x_n$ and constants ranging over ordinary individuals. The formation rules are the usual rules for first-order logic plus the following:

(155) a. If ϕ is a formula, then BECOME ϕ is a formula.
b. If ϕ and ψ are formulas, then [ϕ CAUSE ψ] is a formula.
c. If ϕ is a formula and α is a term denoting an individual, then DO(α, ϕ) is a formula. [This must be subject to the like-subject constraint. Alternatively, we assume the language allows predicate modifiers and treat DO as a predicate modifier.]
d. If ϕ is a formula and τ is a term (variable or constant) denoting a time, then [AT(τ, ϕ)] is a formula.

(Other sentential operators might eventually be added,[24] such as the progressive BE discussed in the next chapter.) The semantic interpretation of this language has already been given somewhat informally in the preceding sections and will not be repeated. A more explicit treatment of a revised aspect calculus follows later.

The linguistic hypothesis embodied in such a formal language is that it is a fragment of a *Natural Logic*. Any formula of this language is claimed to be potentially the logical structure of some English sentence, subject to the restrictions of actually occurring lexical items that determine whether it can be fully lexicalized or not. We might then define *possible lexical item*, as any configuration of predicates and operators that can be collected under one node by Predicate Raising in a legitimate derivation from one of these formulas. (By *legitimate derivation* is meant a derivation in accord with the various global and other constraints on transformations that are claimed to be motivated independently in a GS theory.) Alternatively, possible lexical items might naturally be restricted in terms of an explicitly defined subset of the formulas of the aspect calculus. It seems, for instance, that the possible underlying structures of verbs should be restricted to formulas using only clauses (a)-(c) of the recursive clauses, i.e., formulas not involving the AT operator. This is because verbs in natural languages apparently never by themselves have truth conditions depending on states or changes of states happening at specific times independent of the time of the use of the verb (which is what the AT operator would permit) but always have their temporal references determined indexically. (This point will be elaborated upon in section 2.4 below.) Adverbial phrases, on the other hand, do fix time reference "eternally" (for instance, *during the summer of 1945, on May 12, 1977*) as well as indexically (*during last week, tomorrow*), and the AT operator was included in the aspect calculus for the purpose of illustrating how these can be accommodated. The *actual lexical items* of a given language, in turn, are some finite proper subset of these possible lexical items.

The aspect calculus as it stands is still inadequate in several respects, but nevertheless, I think it comes close enough to being viable to illustrate what I consider to be the kind of semantic explicitness that any structural semantic analysis of the linguist's familiar sort must be expected to achieve if we are to be able to test its adequacy to any real extent in a referential semantic theory. If we are to do "structural semantics" of the GS sort (or any other kind, really) in Montague Grammar, then this is how it has to be carried out. The inadequacies of the present calculus could be due either to my own inability to see the right linguistic generalizations about the distribution of "atomic predicates" in logical structure and to give the appropriate semantics for these basic operators, or else the inadequacies arise because no consistent referentially interpreted lexical decomposition analysis will ever be possible for English. Unless we examine such analyses with the requisite detail, we will never really test the status of the "Natural Logic" hypothesis.

Below are the main representative kinds of formulas predicted by the calculus in each of Vendler's four categories. Here, α_i and β_i will stand for arbitrary individual terms, π_n and ρ_n stand for arbitrary n-place (stative) predicates, and ϕ and ψ are arbitrary formulas, either atomic or complex. Surface English examples are given for each kind of sentence.

A. *Statives*

1. Simple statives: $\pi_n(\alpha_1, \ldots, \alpha_n)$. (*John knows the answer.*)

2. Stative causatives: $[\pi_m(\alpha_1, \ldots, \alpha_m)$ CAUSE $\rho_n(\beta_1, \ldots, \beta_n)]$. (*John's living nearby causes Mary to prefer this neighborhood.*)

B. *Activities*

1. Simple activities: DO$(\alpha_1, [\pi_n(\alpha_1, \ldots, \alpha_n)])$. (*John is walking.*)
2. Agentive Stative Causatives (?): [DO $(\alpha_1, [\pi_m(\alpha_1, \ldots, \alpha_m)])$ CAUSE $\rho_n(\beta_1, \ldots, \beta_n)]$. (The existence of this class was suggested to me by Harmon Boertien and would include examples like *He is housing his antique car collection in an old barn*, which are agentive and presumably causative but do not entail any change of state. However, these might be analyzed as [DO$(\alpha_1, [\pi_m(\alpha_1, \ldots, \alpha_m)])$ CAUSE $\neg$ BECOME $\neg$ $\rho_n(\beta_1, \ldots, \beta_n)]$ instead, since this latter formula would account for the durative character of these examples just as well.)

C. *Achievements*

1. Simple Achievements: BECOME$[\pi_n(\alpha_1, \ldots, \alpha_n)]$. (*John discovered the solution.*)
2. Inchoation of Activity: BECOME[DO$(\alpha_1, [\pi_n(\alpha_1, \ldots, \alpha_n)])$]. (Such forms apparently do not lexicalize in English as single verbs or do so only marginally; the only possible unambiguous example I have noticed is *germinate*, which might be analyzed as BECOME plus *grow*, where *grow* is in turn an activity. Otherwise, complex sentences like *John began to walk* represent this class.)
3. Inchoation of accomplishments: BECOME ϕ, where ϕ has one of the forms in D1-D3 below. (Again, no single verbs seem to lexicalize this form, though complex sentences like *John began to build a house* represent the class.)

D. *Accomplishments*

1. Non-agentive Accomplishments: [[BECOME ϕ]CAUSE[BECOME ψ]], where ϕ and ψ are stative sentences (i.e. of the form $\pi_n(\alpha_1, \ldots, \alpha_n)$, as in *The door's opening causes the lamp to fall down*), or are more complex sentences. (*The beginning of the construction of a new highway causes the interruption of many residents' remodeling projects.*)
2. (Non-Intentional) Agentive Accomplishments: [[DO$(\alpha_1, [\pi_n(\alpha_1, \ldots, \alpha_n)])$]CAUSE[BECOME$[\rho_m(\beta_1, \ldots, \beta_m)]$]]. (*John broke the window.*)
3. Agentive Accomplishments with Secondary Agent: [[DO$(\alpha_1, [\pi_n(\alpha_1, \ldots, \alpha_n)])$] CAUSE [DO$(\beta_1, [\rho_m(\beta_1, \ldots, \beta_m)])$]]. (*John forced*

Bill to speak;[25] This is the class Talmy (1976: 112) calls *caused agency*. Also, the result clause can be an accomplishment: *John forced Bill to build a house*.)

4. Intentional Agentive Accomplishments (?): $DO(\alpha_1, [DO(\alpha_1, \pi_n(\alpha_1, \ldots, \alpha_n)) CAUSE\ \phi])$, where ϕ may be any non-stative sentence (*John murdered Bill*).

A possible logical structure that does not fit exactly into any of Vendler's four categories is $DO(\alpha_1, BECOME[\pi_n(\alpha_1, \ldots, \alpha_n)])$; these would be *basic actions*, events under the unmediated control of an agent that are not brought about by any subsidiary activity. Plausible candidates would be *John opened his eyes* and *John raised his arm*, where no conscious causal activity is apparent. The only linguistic evidence I know of that pertains to such cases is that *John tried to open his eyes but wasn't able to do it* seems to entail that John somehow did something that he hoped would bring his eyes to open, perhaps he performed an unobservable "act of the will". This might be taken to indicate that these examples are not basic actions. Perhaps then the only basic actions are acts of the will. But this is scanty evidence with which to try to decide issues that have been the subject of philosophical controversy since Descartes.

Of course, more complex formulas than these would certain underlie many complex English sentences, but I believe that the above table covers most if not all the cases that can be claimed to lexicalize as single verbs in English.

2.4. THE ASPECT CALCULUS AS RESTRICTING POSSIBLE WORD MEANINGS

Though I have suggested that the aspect calculus embodies a hypothesis about possible versus impossible word meanings of English, it is still in a certain sense a vacuous hypothesis within the framework of model-theoretic semantics. The reason for this is that we have not yet put any limitations on the interpretations of stative predicates. Until we do so, the intension of a primitive (stative) one-place predicate can be any function in $(\{0, 1\}^{D_e})^{I \times J}$ whatsoever, and the interpretation is similarly general for two and n-place predicates. To then say that a possible sentence meaning is any proposition expressible by a sentence formed out of stative predicates plus aspectual operators CAUSE, BECOME, DO, etc. is not really to exclude any proposition (set of indices) as impossible, nor is it to exclude any function in $(\{0, 1\}^{D_e})^{I \times J}$ as an impossible intransitive-verb meaning, etc. For that matter, even without the aspectual operators no real limitation is being made by such a language as long as we do not limit the interpretation of the primitive (stative) predicates.

The intuition behind the aspect calculus is of course that stative predicates are somehow simpler or more limited in their interpretation than other kinds of verbs, hence it is an interesting enterprise to try to figure out how non-statives can be constructed out of statives in a tightly-constrained way. The problem is to come up with some initial narrow constraint on the interpretation of statives that makes this a non-vacuous undertaking.

My suggestion as to how to approach this problem is tentative and programmatic, but I hope it will suggest promising ways of proceeding. The meanings of many or perhaps most stative predicates are tied to physical properties of some sort – location in space, size, weight, texture, physical composition, color, etc. The suggestion is to add enough physical structure to the definition of a model to make stative predicates (or at least an interestingly large subclass of them) directly definable in terms of this physical structure.

As an example of the way that increasing the "structure" of a model leads to interesting analyses of word meaning, see the model-theoretic interpretations of various senses of English spatial prepositions in Cresswell (1978) where not only location in space but also the "path" of an object moving through space over time is set-theoretically defined. (The account of locative and change-of-location prepositions given in Chapter 4 differs from Cresswell's in interesting ways in semantics and especially in syntax.)

To carry out this plan I will employ van Fraassen's notion of *logical space* (an idea whose use in this context was suggested to me by Thomason's (1974b) semantic treatment of some English sentences about weight and location). There will be as many axes of logical space as there are kinds of measurement; if the measurables were only weight, color and hardness, for example, a point in logical space would be a triple representing a possible outcome of measurements of weight, color and hardness respectively. Each axis might have a different mathematical structure according to the discriminations that can appropriately be made in each case. For example, tests for hardness give only a linear ordering – we can say that one thing is harder than another but not twice as hard – but in the case of weight, we can say that one thing weighs twice as much as another. Values on the space-axis would represent places, which would themselves be regions in Euclidian or some other sort of space. It is not necessary at this stage to commit ourselves as to just what axes are to be included in logical space nor just what the mathematical structure of each axis is to be, as long as there are only a finite number of axes. A model for a language is then to include – in addition to a set of individuals, a set of worlds and a set of times – a function assigning to each individual at each index a value in logical space. Of course, certain individuals may lack values for certain axes at certain indices – for example, some things are colorless – and this situation might best be handled by including a "null position" on various axes.

We than constrain the interpretation of (physical) stative predicates by requiring that *for each stative predicate there is a region of logical space such that at each index, an individual is in the extension of that predicate at the index if and only if the individual is assigned to a point within that region of space.*

Perhaps other limitations might be added. Most stative predicates seem to depend on only one axis of logical space (color, weight, etc.), so these predicates have as their determining region a "slice" of logical space not varying along the other axes. Also, many if not most predicates correspond to a continuous rather than a discontinuous region of values along their appropriate axis. Basic color terms, for example, denote objects reflecting light within certain continuous segments of the spectrum but not, apparently, disjoint parts of the spectrum (though there are counterexamples like *mottled*).[26] Pursuit of such constraints would quickly lead us into very specific and detailed questions of lexicography that might or might not turn out to have any general interest for theoretical semantics at this point, but we can ignore these questions here. Even with the very general constraint given above, it is now possible to see that certain interpretations of stative predicates are ruled out, relative to a given logical-space assignment. This is because the logical-space conditions for predicates, whatever their complexity may have to be, are required to be the same for all moments of time in the model. (Of course, individuals do change their logical-space values over times, so this requirement by no means entails that the denotations of stative predicates are constant over time, only that the logical-space conditions for whether or not an individual is in the denotation remain constant.)

What kinds of interpretations are ruled out by this condition? One "impossible" word would be Nelson Goodman's famous hypothetical adjective *grue*. An object is *grue*, according to Goodman (1955), just in case it is green up to a given time t and blue thereafter. I think this is a correct result for a theory of word meaning in natural language. Though one can intelligibly define such a special invented predicate, this seems to me to be just the kind of predicate that does not occur naturally in human languages.

With this restriction, the effect of the aspect calculus becomes non-trivial. With its help, we can construct from stative predicates like *green* and *blue* possible verbs meaning "become green", "cease to be green", "cause to become green," even "change from green to blue" (i.e. become not-green and at the same time become blue), etc. but never, as far as I can see, anything like Nelson's *grue*. (It is important to note that subformulas of the form AT(t, ϕ) must be excluded from the class of formulas claimed to underlie single verbs, else *grue* could be constructed.) In general then, the effect of the constraints on the aspect calculus is to exclude predicates whose interpretation depends on the state of the world at more than one time (or in more than one possible world) in any way other than in the ways explicitly allowed for by the tense and modal operators of the calculus. I expect that a good deal of work would be required to show formally just what class of word meanings is excluded by this condition for some specific version of an aspect calculus, but I hope the idea is clear enough. Though formulas of great complexity could be constructed in the aspect calculus which almost surely do not correspond to any verb of a natural language, it seems safe to suggest that the likelihood of occurrence of a verb with the meaning of a very complex formula would be inversely proportional to the length of the formula, so that formulas with more than a small number of connectives and operators (say, eight) could be excluded as candidates for single word meanings altogether. But all *short* formulas of the aspect calculus now seem to be acceptable candidates for possible word meanings.

It is perhaps doubtful whether this method can be extended to *all* stative predicates. Are there really physical criteria for "subjective" stative predicates like *beautiful* or *pleasant*? Even more questionable than these are relations among sentient individuals, as in *x likes y, y knows z*. An extreme materialist would of course readily assent to the position that such predicates must have truth conditions definable ultimately in physical terms, insofar are there any really consistent truth conditions for them at all. But regardless of what metaphysical position one wants to adopt for external reasons it seems that a semantic theory should not presuppose any particular metaphysics of this sort.

Even if it turns out that some natural language words can neither be given a physical criterion nor defined with the aid of novel modal operators in terms of predicates having physical criteria, it may nonetheless be of interest to show how hypotheses of possible and impossible word meanings can be formulated which apply to some large subclass of words. It is interesting in this connection to note that the class of words, as isolated by various syntactic tests, that Carlson (1977) believes to be predicates of "stages" of individuals (rather than predicates of individuals or of kinds) are those for which physical criteria seem suitable (e.g. adjectives *alive, drunk*, etc., verbs *hit, find*), while those he believes to be predicates of individuals or of kinds (e.g. *intelligent, fear, hate, admire*) are those for which physical criteria are inappropriate. Perhaps further investigations of Carlson's hypothesis would lead to a more motivated account of a "physical" subclass of stative predicates.

NOTES

[1] As Cresswell points out (1977), this implicit use of negation and conjunction in the 'language' of semantic markerese amounts to the distinction between logical words (the sentential connectives) and non-logical words (the predicates represented by the semantic features) as it is usually drawn in the formal languages of logicians. That is, the analysis of analytic sentences such as *Every bachelor is unmarried* by decomposition with semantic markers implicitly appeals to the logical properties of conjunction and negation, whether or not logical connectives are explicitly mentioned. Cresswell notes that this is somewhat paradoxical in Katz' theory, since Katz claims to reject the distinction between logical and non-logical words (Katz, 1972, pp. xix, 106).

[2] Though Lakoff's analysis of these sentences in his dissertation (Lakoff, 1965) may be cited as the source of the hypothetical causative and inchoative analysis which most influenced the subsequent development of generative semantics, it is difficult to determine the original source of this idea since it is also discussed in both Hall (1965, pp. 26-28) and Chomsky (1965, pp. 189-190), though the last two authors are inclined to reject the analysis.

[3] Heringer (1976) suggests that the distinction between manipulative causation on the one hand and directive causation or causation for conventionalized purpose on the other can be used to predict which *come*-idioms have *bring*-counterparts and which do not: *come*-idioms whose meaning involves manipulative or directive causation for a conventionalized purpose are claimed to allow corresponding *bring*-idioms, *come*-idioms whose meaning involves non-conventionalized directive causation or indirect causation are claimed not to allow *bring*-idioms. Whether or not this is correct (and I find the facts hard to judge), other problems for the relexicalization analysis do not lend themselves to this solution, cf. the *harden* example below and note 4.

[4] A few of the other such cases I have noticed among causatives derived (possibly by way of inchoatives) from adjectives are *toughen* (loses the meaning "difficult" – *toughen* can mean only "make resistent to tearing", not "make difficult"), *dirty* loses the meaning "obscene", cf. **He dirtied his jokes when the hostess left*), *straighten* (loses the meanings "socially conforming", "heterosexual"), *dry* (loses meaning "boring"). From these examples, it might seem that figurative or slang meanings never carry over to derived causatives while literal meanings do. This is not always the case, since *deaden* has the figurative meanings of its adjective root ("not capable of perceiving sensation", etc.) but lacks the literal meaning completely ("not alive"). Some deadjectival verbs do retain the figurative as well as the literal meaning of the adjective, cf. *That soured his mood, This muddies the issue*. For further proposals about the manner and point at which lexical insertion takes places in a GS derivation, see McCawley (1971) and Newmeyer (1974).

[5] Kenny thought Ryle's achievements fell into all three of his categories (Kenny, 1963, p. 185). I find this inconsistent and think the disagreement hinges only on the misclassification of one or two borderline examples by Ryle.

[6] In addition to verbs, adjectives and nouns also split into stative and non-stative categories, according to whether the progressive can be used when they appear as predicate adjectives and predicate nominals. Cf. *John is being careful* vs. **John is being tall, John is being a hero* vs. **John is being a grandfather*. Non-stative adjectives are first discussed in 2.3.8 below.

[7] Achievements are like statives according to some stativity tests (**John persuaded Bill to notice a stranger in the room*) but not others (cf. note 8): this difference can be accounted for in part by postulating agentive achievements (or *basic actions*, cf. 2.3.11) as well as non-agentive achievements and in part by the revised verb classification suggested in Chapter 3 within an interval-based temporal semantics.

[8] The "does not apply" indication appears here because the (present) progressive tense is somewhat strange with most examples of achievements. That is, ?(*At this moment*) *John is noticing a stranger in the room* is presumably strange for the same reason as ?*John noticed a stranger in the room for a few minutes* – achievements like *noticing* do not in Vendler's view take up time but happen virtually instantly, and the progressive, like durative time adverbials, suggests duration. But in fact, the progressive does not really sound so bad with many achievements (cf. *John is dying, John is arriving*), and this is one of the observations that will lead us to a revision of the aspect analysis in Chapter 3.

[9] The same kind of observations (for English, this time) were made independently by Mittwoch (1971).

[10] It occurred to me at one time (and independently to Carlson (1973)) that one might account for this scope restriction on indefinite plurals by treating them as free variables in logical structure, but this idea had to be abandoned for want of a satisfactory semantic account of how the free variable would be interpreted. On the standard Tarski definitions of truth and satisfaction, a formula with a free variable counts as true just in case the universal closure of the formula is true, but this is of course the wrong result for indefinite plurals.

[11] I have here represented the translations of bare plurals as individuals constants – *goats* translates into *g*, etc. – but in English such bare plurals are obviously derived from singular common nouns. Carlson initially uses this same method for expository purposes, but also shows (Carlson, 1977, pp. 213-219) the syntactic and semantic method for deriving kind-denoting term phrases ("bare plurals") from plural, "ordinary" common nouns (e.g., *goats* as in *I saw two goats*), which are in turn derived from singular "ordinary" common nouns.

[12] McCawley also considered both the possibility that the subject of CAUSE is an agent and that it is an event; cf. McCawley (1973, pp. 34ff).

[13] The usual GS assumption about the analysis of such verbs as *assassinate* whose meaning involves a particular motivation or kind of intention is that this aspect of the meaning comes from a higher adverbial clause in logical structure; cf. McCawley (1973, p. 24).

[14] For convenience I have used a slightly simpler example, (111), than the one McCawley was actually discussing in this context (which was *John hammered the dent out of the fender*), but I believe the comments I have quoted here apply to (111) in exactly the same way.

[15] As is reflected in an observation by Kim (1973), we must be careful to get the right descriptions of the events involved if we analyze *by*-phrases in terms of causation: he notes that if I open the window by turning the knob, "my turning the knob does not cause my opening the window (though it does cause the window's being open)"; see 4.9 for a treatment of this problem.

[16] I use the symbol "$\Box\!\!\rightarrow$" throughout my discussion of conditional (or counterfactual) logic, though Stalnaker used ">" instead of (Lewis') "$\Box\!\!\rightarrow$".

[17] In other words, causative verbs are invariably *If-verbs* in the sense of Karttunen (1970), complement-taking verbs for which the following pattern of inferences holds: "x Vs S" entails S, and "It is not the case that x Vs S" entails neither S nor not-S. It seems to me in fact that all *if*-verbs are causatives.

[18] A "conjunctive" causal statement of the form $[[O(c_1) \wedge O(c_2)]$ CAUSE $O(e)]$ does not help in this situation, because the counterfactual associated with this is $\neg[O(c_1) \wedge O(c_2)] \Box\!\!\rightarrow \neg O(e)$, and this in turn is equivalent to $[\neg O(c_1) \vee \neg O(c_2)] \Box\!\!\rightarrow \neg O(e)$, i.e. nearest worlds in which e occurs but either c_1 does not occur or in which c_2 does not occur are closer than nearest worlds in which e does not occur. This is false in a situation of causal overdetermination. On the other hand, the "disjunctive" causal statement $[O(c_1) \vee O(c_2)]$ would seem to correctly describe this situation since its counterfactual is equivalent to $[\neg O(c_1) \wedge \neg O(c_2)] \Box\!\!\rightarrow \neg O(e)$. This is true in the causal overdetermination situation in Figure 2 below.

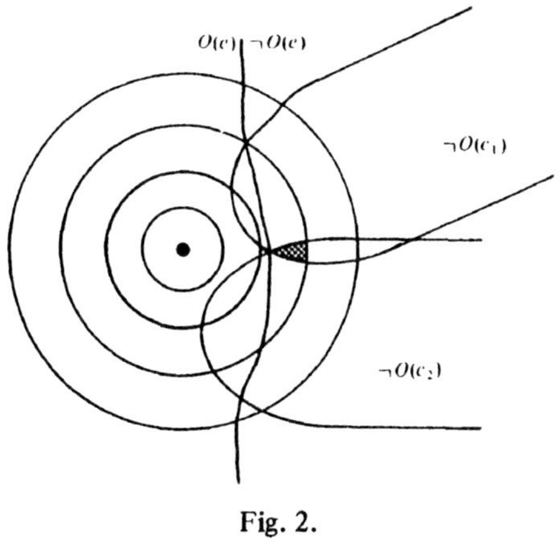

Fig. 2.

However, all obvious ways of rendering such a disjunctive causal statement in ordinary English – such as *Either the electrical short or the cigarette ash caused the destruction of the house* – sound wrong; we take them as $[O(c_1)$ CAUSE $O(e)] \vee [O(c_2)$ CAUSE $O(e)]$ instead, and this last formula has the wrong truth conditions. Philosophers would apparently prefer to shun "disjunctive events" altogether – cf. Loeb's (1974, p. 531) discussion of J. L. Mackie's "trilemma" of causal overdetermination. In any case, the relationship between a "disjunctive event" and the disjunction of two sentences asserting that events occur is obscure to me.

[19] Other verbs which would appear to be achievements by some tests do occur in agentive contexts; these will be treated in Chapter 3.

[20] Like other stative verbs (cf. note 5), *see, hear* and *feel* have an inchoative reading which is really as common as the stative reading.

The distinction between the inchoative and stative readings of these verbs explains (as Vendler noted) Aristotle's puzzlement that one can say *I have seen it* as soon as one can say *I see it*. The *see* in *I have seen it* is inchoative (an achievement), while the *see* in *I see it* is stative. Ryle noticed the strange fact that for the physical perception verbs, the stative reading of *see* etc. (but not the inchoative) is equivalently expressed by *can see*, etc.

[21] See Rogers (1971) for a discussion of some unsystematic differences in this paradigm. There seem to be two apparently distinct senses of *watch* and *look*. If *look* means "see on purpose", *look* entails *see*. (This is the sense under discussion in the text.) But sometimes *look* is paraphrasable as "direct one's eyes toward." In this sense, blind men can look at things and one can "look right at it but not see it." The fact that this second sense does not extend to the other members of the physical perception paradigm (*listen, feel*, etc.) Rogers attributes – correctly, I believe – to the fact that man's organs of sight are directional in a way that his other sensory organs are not.

[22] The phrase *controllability* has sometimes appeared in the literature to describe agentive contexts (e.g. Berman (ms), Givón (1975)), but I do not believe the distinction between controllability and intentionality has been clearly drawn.

[23] Though as far as I know there has been little study of the cross-linguistic evidence for DO, the results from Japanese (Inoue, 1973) are not wholly encouraging. Though there is evidence in Japanese quite parallel to Ross' evidence for DO, Inoue shows that the semantic properties of such a Japanese DO would have to be somewhat different from those attributed to DO in English.

[24] Though I mentioned END and REMAIN earlier as operators, these are really unnecessary as they are definable in terms of BECOME and negation: END ϕ is defined as BECOME $\neg\phi$, and REMAIN ϕ as $\neg$BECOME $\neg\phi$. Similarly, the logical structure underlying the verb *prevent* will involve formulas of the form [ϕ CAUSE$\neg$BECOME ψ] and (at least one sense of) *allow* as $\neg$[ϕ CAUSE $\neg$BECOME ψ].

[25] The verb *force* which occurs with an adjective complement and means "bring about by physical effort exertion against resistance", as in *force the door open*, should not be confused with the *force* that takes an infinitive complement and means "compel to do", which is the verb cited in this example. It is only the latter which is "subcategorized" for a secondary agent – note that **John forced the door to open* is anomalous.

[26] The treatment of vague predicates discussed earlier (section 2.3.5) can also be accommodated here. In fact, the logical-space restriction might form a basis for some of the "semantical principles" mentioned by Kamp that determine how "legal" resolutions of vague predicates can be made. For example, the vague predicate *heavy* can be resolved in any way as long as we assign to it *all* individuals whose value on the weight axis lies above some particular point; no "discontinuous" portion of the weight axis may correspond to the extension of *heavy*.

CHAPTER 3

INTERVAL SEMANTICS AND THE PROGRESSIVE TENSE

3.1. THE IMPERFECTIVE PARADOX

One of the tests used to distinguish activities from accomplishments in 2.2 was the test of entailment from a sentence in a progressive tense to the same sentence in a simple tense. Thus *draw a circle* counts as an accomplishment verb phrase because (1) does not entail (2), while *push a cart* counts as an activity because (3) does seem to entail (4):

(1) John was drawing a circle.

(2) John drew a circle.

(3) John was pushing a cart.

(4) John pushed a cart.

In this chapter I turn to the task of constructing an analysis of the progressive that will complete the account of the semantics of (1)–(4). As we observed, following Kenny (1963), the meaning of an accomplishment verb phrase invariably involves the coming about of a particular state of affairs. For example, *drawing a circle* involves the coming into existence of a circle (or in any case, a *representation* of a circle, cf. *draw a unicorn*), *kicking the door open* involves the door's coming to be open, and *driving the car into the garage* involves the car's coming to be in the garage. The analysis of accomplishments in terms of BECOME-sentences was motivated (on the semantic side) by the need to capture such entailments. Yet it is just this entailment that such a result-state comes about that fails when the accomplishment verb phrase appears in a progressive tense. In other words, the problem is to give an account of how (1) entails that John was engaged in a bringing-a-circle-into-existence activity but does not entail that he brought a circle into existence. This is the 'imperfective paradox'. Notice, furthermore, that to say that John was drawing a circle is not the same as saying that John was drawing a triangle, the difference between the two activities obviously having to do with the difference between a circle and a triangle. Yet if neither activity necessarily involves the existence of such a figure, just how are the two to be distinguished?

I regard the resolution of this paradox as an absolute sine qua non for the theory presented in the previous chapter of the distinction between activities and accomplishments/achievements in terms of BECOME sentences, since inperfective sentences would otherwise provide strong counterexamples to it. (Moreover, the move to interval semantics which is motivated by this problem will lead to a significantly deeper understanding of the verb classification.) But conversely, I think that no analysis of the English progressive should be deemed satisfactory unless it can be shown to be compatible with some analysis or other of the verb classification, given the differing semantic effects that the progressive has on verbs of various classes.

One immediate answer to these questions is that accomplishments must be defined in terms of the intention of an agent to bring about a particular result state. But this condition fails in two ways. Consider a ninety-year-old composer who undertakes the composition of a symphony. He may not believe that he will live to complete the symphony nor seriously intend to try to complete it before his death, but he can still truly describe his activity as *writing a symphony* (and not merely as *writing a part of a symphony*). In the second place, there are instances of accomplishments that have no sentient agent who can have such an intention. Consider examples such as *The rains are destroying the crops, but perhaps they will stop before the crops are destroyed*, or *The river was cutting a new channel to the sea, but men with sandbags succeeded in stopping it from doing so.*

In the GS literature it has been argued that tenses (McCawley, 1971) as well as auxiliaries (Ross, 1969) are "predicates of higher sentences" in logical structure. If we make the usual allowance for reading the phrase "higher predicate" in such a way as to preserve type-theoretic well-formedness, we may interpret this as a claim that tenses appear as sentence operators in logical structure, despite their surface appearance as verb affixes or auxiliary verbs. This claim then meshes precisely with the usual treatment of tenses in tense logic. In accord with this now "standard" (in some quarters) view of tenses, I will assume the logical structure of the example (1) consists of the logical structure of the tenseless sentence underlying *John draws a circle*, prefixed by a sentence operator PROG (for "progressive"), with this in turn prefixed by a sentence operator PAST. (In Chapter 7, however, we shall see that the semantic account of PROG in the present chapter is also compatible with a syntactic treatment of English in which the progressive originates within the verb phrase.) The logical structure of (2) consists of the structure underlying *John draws a circle*, prefixed only by PAST. Since I know of absolutely no evidence from English syntax that the progressive tense in accomplishments such as (1) is a different tense operator from the progressive in activities such as (3), I assume that an adequate analysis must employ the same PROG operator in both kinds of sentences. Thus the solution to this problem lies not only in finding the correct truth conditions for [PROG ϕ], but also in determining how these truth conditions interact differently with the semantic analyses given to accomplishments versus that given to activities.

For accomplishment sentences, we will be concerned essentially with the properties of formulas of the form of (5) versus (6),

(5) [ϕ CAUSE [BECOME ψ]]

(6) PROG[ϕ CAUSE [BECOME ψ]]

since the PAST operator is not crucially involved in the problem, nor is the internal structure of the sentences ϕ and ψ. (In omitting the past tense from discussion of the analysis but not the English examples, I am making a certain simplifying and I hope not too dubious assumption about English progressive and non-progressive tenses. It is well-known that the simple present tense of non-stative verbs, e.g. *John draws a circle*, has a rather specialized role in the English tense system. It is by and large restricted to habitual, or "generic", assertions, and only in special contexts can be used to assert the occurrence of a single event at the present time (such contexts involve the sports announcer's running description of events as they transpire, in stage directions, etc., cf. Braroe (1976)). For this reason, the entailment test exhibited in (1)–(4) cannot be carried out directly with the present progressive and simple present tenses. However, the test does work quite consistently with all the other tenses of English – i.e. past vs. past progressive, perfect vs. perfect progressive, past perfect vs. past perfect progressive, future vs. future progressive and future perfect vs. future perfect progressive. Thus in a framework in which the simple present is taken to be the "tenseless" form from which all other tenses are derived, it seems best to assume that whatever properties of the simple-versus-progressive opposition are responsible for distinguishing activities from accomplishments in these other tenses are also fundamentally inherent in the simple present versus present progressive, even though the preemption of the simple present with non-statives for a special purpose makes it impossible to observe this directly. Such an assumption makes it incumbent on me to try to give a satisfactory account of this "special" behavior of the non-stative simple present sooner or later that meshes with the account of the progressive and simple tenses developed here – cf. Section 3.8.2 for discussion.)

In my 1972 treatment of this problem I suggested that the truth conditions for the progressive be given in such a way that from (6) one could infer ϕ but not infer [BECOME ψ], whereas from (5) both ϕ and [BECOME ψ] could be inferred. Rather, one should be able to draw from (6) only the weaker inference that [BECOME ψ] is possible. Thus from (1) one should be able to conclude that some activity of drawing took place and that the existence of a circle was a possible but perhaps not actual outcome of this activity. This observation was, I still believe, correct as far as it went, but much remained to be said about how the analysis could be carried out formally.

Though I did not attempt to formalize the required conditions for [PROG ϕ], Tedeschi (1973) took up this task, and it became clear to me from his article that truth conditions for [PROG ϕ] in line with my suggestions are impossible to give in terms of an arbitrary sentence ϕ, but only for the special case where ϕ is a formula of the form [ψ CAUSE [BECOME χ]]. To see this, recall that PROG[ψ CAUSE [BECOME χ]] must entail ψ but not entail [BECOME χ], even though [ψ CAUSE [BECOME χ]] entails both ψ and [BECOME χ]. The only obvious way to satisfy both these requirements simultaneously is to write a semantic rule for PROG[ψ CAUSE [BECOME χ]] which explicitly makes reference to both ψ and [BECOME χ], and this is what Tedeschi does. His rule (which I simplify here) states roughly that PROG[ψ CAUSE [BECOME χ]] is true if and only if ψ is true and [ψ CAUSE [BECOME χ]] is possible. But this rule violates the dictum that a semantic theory must specify the meaning of a sentence as a function of the meanings of its immediate parts and the syntactic rule used to form it, for we have now stated the meaning of a sentence [PROG ϕ] not strictly in terms of the meaning of ϕ (which would be identified with the set of possible worlds in which ϕ is true, under our semantic theory), but rather in terms of the meanings of certain syntactic subparts of ϕ. And even if this violation of compositional semantics were admitted, it would be necessary to supply a further truth condition for [PROG ϕ] for those cases where ϕ does *not* have the form [ψ CAUSE [BECOME χ]], i.e., for those cases where ϕ is an activity sentence. But then it would be quite unclear how we would have captured the idea that the progressive tense of an accomplishment sentence such as (1) is the *same* as the progressive tense of an activity sentence such as (3).

A further difficulty arises with achievement verbs. Though I had earlier assumed that achievement verbs could never occur in the progressive (just as they do not naturally occur with durative adverbials), there are at least some occasional acceptable examples of achievements with progressives, and these exhibit the same failure of inference from progressive to simple tense as do accomplishments:

(7) John was falling asleep.

(8) John fell asleep.

(9) John was dying.

(10) John died.

To see that the inferences in question do not hold, consider *John was falling asleep when Mary shook him*, or *John was dying when the operation was performed that saved his life*. The parallel between these cases and the accomplishment cases suggests that under the aspect-calculus-hypothesis, the solution to the 'imperfective paradox' lies in correctly formulating the truth conditions for [PROG ϕ] and [BECOME ϕ] (since the BECOME operator is what these two classes of verbs are alleged to share in their logical structure) and does not, as Tedeschi and I had supposed, directly involve the truth conditions for [ϕ CAUSE ψ]. In fact, the analysis I will propose below turns out not to require the assumption that the meanings of accomplishments and achievements are exactly "decomposable" in terms of operators like CAUSE and BECOME at all, but merely that these two classes of verbs logically entail BECOME-sentences (or other formulas with equivalent semantic properties).

In fact, this failure to distinguish the entailments of the progressive tenses of accomplishments/achievements from those of progressive is symptomatic of a fundamental limitation of the aspect calculus as developed so far, a limitation it shares with virtually all previous formal treatments of tense and time reference. This limitation lies in taking the notion of the truth of an atomic sentence at a *moment* of time as basic, rather than the truth of a sentence over an *interval* of time. One can of course express in a certain sense the fact that a sentence is true over a certain interval by means of the AT operator and quantification over time, as we did in writing formulas such as $\bigwedge t\ [t \in \mathit{six\ weeks} \rightarrow \mathrm{AT}(t, \phi)]$ (this formula also presumes we have a means for naming sets of times). The tense logician's operators G and H (where $G\phi$ is defined as $\neg$FUTURE$\neg\phi$ and read as "it will always be the case that ϕ" and $H\phi$ as $\neg$PAST$\neg\phi$) express a truth-over-an-interval in the same way as do Kamp's connectives SINCE and UNTIL (cf. Kamp, 1966; Prior, 1967, pp. 108 ff), and various other tense operators. But in all these cases an "interval" sentence counts as true just in case some one of its embedded atomic sentences is true at all moments during that interval. Though this seems adequate for stative predicates with durative adverbials, such as *John lived in Boston for three years*, Kenny and Vendler explicitly observed that this is exactly the condition that is *not* met when an accomplishment or achievement sentence is true of an interval greater than a moment. When we say *It took John an hour to draw that circle*, we clearly do not mean that the tenseless atomic sentence *John draws that circle* was true at all moments during some interval of one hour's duration; on the contrary, the tenseless sentence is clearly not true of any interval of *less* than one hour's duration. It is this "independence" of the truth of a tensed sentence at an interval from the truth of its constituent sentence(s) at all moments within the interval that traditional tense logic is not equipped to deal with.

3.2. TRUTH CONDITIONS RELATIVE TO INTERVALS, NOT MOMENTS

To remedy this situation, Bennett and Partee (MS.) made the fundamental revision of taking the truth of an atomic sentence at an *interval* as basic.[1] That is, in an intensional semantics such as Montague's (1970b; 1973) an *index* would be taken to be an ordered pair consisting of a possible world and an interval, and an interpretation function would assign to each constant a function from the set of all such indices to an appropriate extension. I will adopt their proposal here. (Ultimately, this step results in a system that is really too powerful for natural language semantics. Intuitively, the truth conditions for an accomplishment like *John draws a circle* do somehow or other boil down to conditions that the world must meet at certain points of time before, during and/or after the interval of time it took to accomplish the deed. We will eventually want to try to restrict the ways that a sentence can be true "independently" of the times within the interval in a linguistically interesting way, but it is nonetheless necessary to have the notion of truth relative to an interval as a basis for the recursive semantic clauses of our formal language.)

The truth conditions given earlier for BECOME-sentences were likewise limited in an unnatural way by a moment-based semantics. We were forced to define BECOME ϕ as a change from $\neg\phi$ at one moment to ϕ at the next. While those conditions seem adequate for verbs involving typically instantaneous changes of state – such as the "mental" achievements *recognize that S*, *discover that S*, and *realize that S* – such an instantaneous change is impossible in the change-of-state entailed by accomplishments like building a house or crossing the desert. With an interval based semantics, we can define

BECOME sentences (and other, complex change-of-state sentences) as true of an interval, no matter what its size, if the interval is bounded at one end by one particular state of affairs and at the other end by another particular state.

There may be some additional motivation from activity sentences for taking truth-at-an-interval as basic. As has occasionally been observed (e.g. Rescher and Urquhart, 1971, p. 160), it seems that one can truthfully be said to have spent an hour at activities such as reading, working on a mathematical problem or playing the piano, even though one did not engage in the activity at literally every moment within that hour. There are two positions one could take with respect to this discrepancy. One could maintain that ordinary language is simply inaccurate at this point; that it is, strictly speaking, false to assert that one spent an hour at an activity if there were really 'pauses' within that hour. Hence for the purposes of a formal theory of semantics, an activity sentence should count as true of an interval just in case it is true of all moments in that interval. Alternatively, one could accept the situation at face value and allow an interpretation of English to assign a truth value to an activity sentence at times within an interval quite independently of the truth value of the sentence for the whole interval. Perhaps some additional conditions should be added, e.g., if an activity sentence is true at all times during an interval, then it must be true for the interval itself. (I will return to the temporal restrictions on activities in 3.8.1 below.) If the second position is adopted, then this is a reason for moving to interval-based semantics that is independent of accomplishments and achievements.

3.3. REVISED TRUTH CONDITIONS FOR *BECOME*

In order to give the revised truth conditions for BECOME, I will have to introduce definitions for intervals and related notions. I adopt them in the form found in Bennett and Partee (ms.), which I believe is a fairly standard form.

Let T, which we will intuitively regard as the set of moments of time, be the set of real numbers. Let $\leqslant$ be the standard dense linear ordering of T. I is an *interval* iff $I \subset T$ and for all moments t_1, t_2, t_3, if $t_1, t_3 \in I$, and $t_1 \leqslant t_2 \leqslant t_3$, then $t_2 \in I$. (Intervals have no internal gaps.) The following notation will be used for intervals:

> $[t_1, t_2]$ (a *closed interval*) abbreviates $\{t : t_1 \leqslant t \leqslant t_2\}$ (i.e. end points are included).

(t_1, t_2) (a *bounded interval*) abbreviates $\{t : t_1 < t < t_2\}$ (i.e., end points are excluded).

$[t]$ (a *moment*) abbreviates $[t, t]$, which is $\{t\}$.

I is a *subinterval* of J iff $I \subseteq J$, where I and J are intervals. I is a *proper subinterval* of J iff $I \subset J$. I is an *initial subinterval* of J iff I is a subinterval of J and there is no $t \in (J - I)$ for which there is $t' \in I$ such that $t \leqslant t'$. *Final subinterval* is defined similarly. t is an *initial bound* for I iff $t \notin I$ and $[t]$ is an initial subinterval for $\{t\} \cup I$ (i.e., t is the latest moment just before I). *Final bound* is defined similarly. To Bennett and Partee's definitions I will add two more: I is an *initial boundary interval* for J iff I and J are disjoint, $I \cup J$ is an interval, and I is an initial subinterval for the interval $I \cup J$ (i.e., I is an interval immediately preceding J). I is a *final boundary interval* for J iff I and J are disjoint, $J \cup I$ is an interval and I is a final subinterval for the interval $J \cup I$ (i.e., I is an interval immediately following J).

The truth conditions for [BECOME ϕ] relative to an interval I are now as follows:[2]

(11) [BECOME ϕ] is true at I iff there is an interval J containing the initial bound of I such that $\neg\phi$ is true at J and there is an interval K containing the final bound of I such that ϕ is true at K.

In terms of the usual linear diagram for time, [BECOME ϕ] will be true in the following situation:

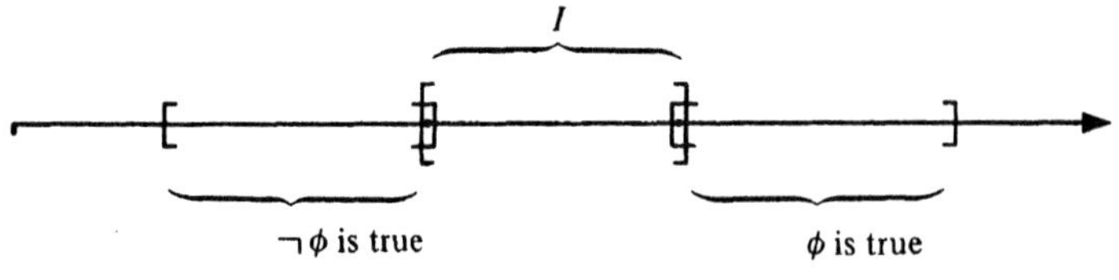

Notice that (11) does not put any requirements on the truth value of ϕ at I itself, nor at times within I. This will have the following undesirable consequence: Suppose that $\neg\phi$ is the case throughout a large interval, and that this is followed by a large interval throughout which ϕ is the case. According to (11), [BECOME ϕ] would be the same in such a situation at a number of successively larger intervals, I, I', I'', etc., as in the following:

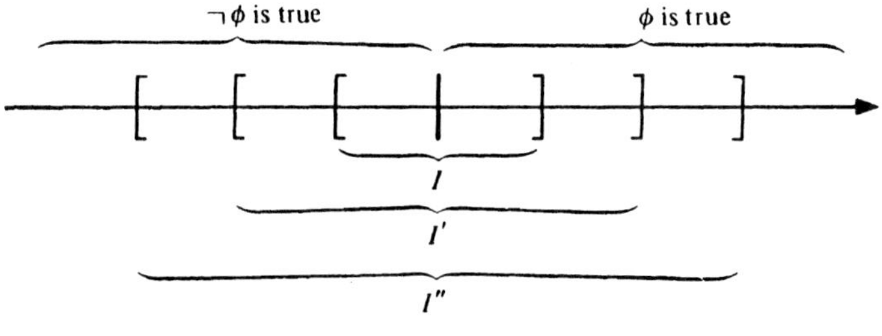

But this is surely counterintuitive. If a door is closed for a long period, then suddenly comes to be open and remains so for another long period, it would be very odd to claim that the sentence *the door opens* is true of any interval whatsoever within this whole period, as long as the interval contains the first moment that the door was open. Rather, we would want the truth of *The door opens* to be limited to the smallest interval over which the change of state has clearly taken place. One way to remedy this problem would be to add to (11) a third clause to give (11′):

(11′) [BECOME ϕ] is true at I iff (1) there is an interval J containing the initial bound of I such that $\neg\phi$ is true at J, (2) there is an interval K containing the final bound of I such that ϕ is true at K, and (3) there is no non-empty interval I' such that $I' \subset I$ and conditions (1) and (2) hold for I' as well as I.

This is a very strong requirement: As long as ϕ is bivalent, then [BECOME ϕ] can only be true at an interval containing just two moments under (11′) (if time is discrete). (Perhaps we will want to allow for truth value gaps in this situation, of course. It does not seem totally implausible to maintain that during the building of a house there is a period of time when it is no longer false that a house exists on the building site but when it is not yet true either. However, I don't want to commit myself on this issue.)

A different way to attack the problem would be to claim that the third clause of (11′) is not a part of the truth conditions for [BECOME ϕ] but is rather to be interpreted as a felicity condition on assertions which follows from some Gricean conversational maxim. If we take this position, then we do not have to appeal to a truth value gap to justify every sentence which asserts that a change of state took place over an interval longer than two moments. Rather, it may be that because of the limits of our knowledge we cannot narrow down precisely the interval at which the change actually took place (or it may be that it would be irrelevant to our interlocutor to know this).

But there is another matter which bears even more directly on the status of (11′). Up to this point I have been considering only changes of state in which the initial state is specified by a proposition which is the negation of the proposition specifying the final state; e.g., *opening* is a transition from 'not open' to 'open', *dying* is a transition from 'not dead' to 'dead'. But there are accomplishment and achievement sentences which do not fit this pattern, the most obvious examples being those involving changes of location. Traveling from place A to place B is not merely changing from being at A to not being at A, nor is it changing from not being at B to being at B, but is apparently the conjunction of these two state changes. Imagine that (12) is true of a (past) interval I:

(12) John walked from the Post Office to the Bank.

If we let P represent *John is at the Post Office* and B represent *John is at the Bank*, then the state-changes of (12) will be representable as follows:

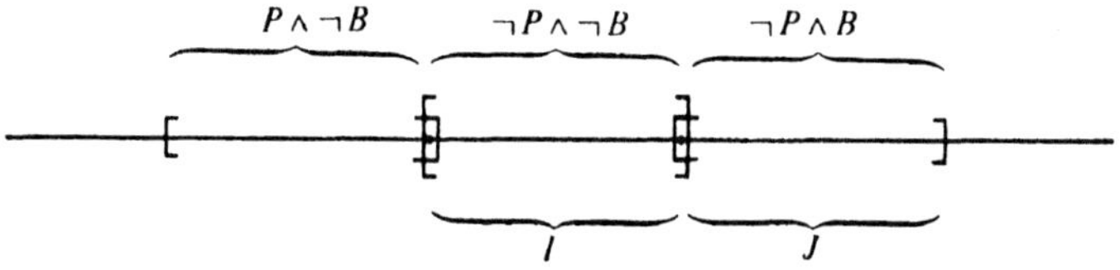

Obviously, during the interval I itself both $\neg P$ and $\neg B$ are the case; no truth-value gaps are involved. But what form of change-of-state sentence does (12) entail? It cannot, under my analysis, be (13):

(13) $\text{BECOME}[\neg P \wedge B]$

since the truth conditions for BECOME (according to (11)) would make (13) true for any subinterval of I containing the last moment of I. (It would be immediately followed by an interval in which $\neg P \wedge B$ is true and immediately preceded by an interval in which $\neg[\neg P \wedge B]$ is true.) According to the strong condition (11′), (13) would be true only at the very *last* moments of I (and at the *first* moments of J). But this is intuitively wrong for (12). (12) must rather entail a sentence of the form (14):

(14) $[\text{BECOME}\,\neg P] \wedge [\text{BECOME}\,B]$

There is clearly no interval smaller than I in this situation at which (14) can be true. (I am assuming that the truth conditions for '∧' and the other truth functional connections are temporally 'straightforward'; that is, that $[\phi \wedge \psi]$ is true at an interval I iff ϕ is true at I and ψ is true at I, etc.) If the requirement in the third clause of (11′) is interpreted as a felicity condition on whole sentences, it would seem to give the right results for (14). But if we take (11′) as the truth condition for BECOME, we are in serious trouble. If John took more than one moment to move between the Post Office and the Bank, there would be no interval whatsoever at which (14) would be true according to (11′), since each of the conjuncts could only be true at different, non-overlapping intervals (actually, moments). This would be a persuasive reason for demoting the third clause of (11′) to the status of a conversational principle.

Another option is offered by M. J. Cresswell's (1977) suggested analysis of natural language *and* in an interval-based semantics. He observes that in natural languages one frequently finds sentences or 'reduced' sentences conjoined by *and* even in cases where there is no particular moment or interval at which both the conjuncts are true. This might seem to be explained by the fact that certain time adverbials apparently naming intervals, such as *yesterday*, really assert that a sentence is true at an unspecified time during the interval – in this case "at some time during yesterday". So (15)-

(15) Yesterday John came and went.

could be analyzed as (16)-

(16) Yesterday John came and yesterday John went.

thus explaining how the time of coming and the time of going can be different. However, this is not all that needs to be said, since (17)-

(17) One day last week John came and went.

cannot be analyzed as (18)-

(18) One day last week John came and one day last week John went.

because (18) allows the comings and goings to be on different days and (17) does not, even though (17) does allow the times of the event to be different within some one day. Cresswell solves this problem by allowing sentences conjoined with *and* to be true at the smallest interval that contains subintervals at which each of the conjuncts is true:

(19) $[\phi \text{ AND } \psi]$ is true at an interval I iff (1) there exist intervals J, K which are subintervals (though possibly not proper subintervals) of I such that ϕ is true at J and ψ is true at K, and (2) there is no smaller subinterval of I meeting condition (1).

(Condition (2) should perhaps be a conventional implicature, not part of the truth conditions for AND.) With this AND, we can retain the stronger condition of BECOME (that in (11′)) and give (12) the form (20):

(20) $[[\text{BECOME} \neg P] \text{ AND } [\text{BECOME } B]]$

(I am not sure whether Cresswell's AND can serve as a satisfactory substitute for the standard 'uni-temporal' connective '$\wedge$' in all situations in which the latter is needed, so I will continue to distinguish the two by writing AND when Cresswell's definition is intended, '$\wedge$' otherwise.) There is obviously a trade-off here between the analysis of BECOME and that of AND as to which of the two we allow to have the flexibility to cover the case where two changes of state that make up an accomplishment happen at different times. As Cresswell's AND seems to be motivated independently of accomplishments (namely, in cases where AND appears as an independent surface conjunction, as in (17)), it seems slightly preferable to appeal to it rather than BECOME for this flexibility.

There is one additional alternative which I will mention briefly. Instead of the one-place operator BECOME we might analyze (12) in terms of a two-place temporal connective much like von Wright's "And Next" operator T (von Wright, 1968). In an interval-based semantics such an operator would be defined as in (21):

(21) $[\phi \text{ T } \psi]$ is true at an interval I iff (1) there is an interval J containing the lower bound of I such that ϕ is true at J and ψ is false at J, (2) there is an interval K containing the upper bound of I such that ψ is true at K and ϕ is false at K, and (3) there is no non-empty interval I' such that $I' \subset I$ and such that (1) and (2) hold for I' as well as for I.

The BECOME operator is definable in terms of T:

(22) $[\text{BECOME } \phi] =_{\text{def}} [\neg\phi \text{T} \phi]$

Although the strong condition corresponding to (11′) is included in (21), the problem with (12) disappears since it can be represented as $[P\text{T}B]$ rather than a conjunction $[P\text{T}\neg P] \wedge [\neg B\text{T}B]$.

Nonetheless, I am less than enthusiastic about (21), since I am here interested in investigating the GS idea of a 'Natural Logic , a formal language in which the set of logical constants is empirically motivated from natural languages. There seems to me to be abundant linguistic evidence for a one-place operator BECOME as such a universal 'atomic predicate' (cf. 2.3.2) but little evidence for giving the two-place operator T such status.[3] However, I know of no process of word formation which combines *two* stative roots X and Y to form a word meaning *change from being X to being Y*, or other such motivation for T. Though there are certain 'two-place' change-of-state verb phrases such as English *move from X to Y* and *change from X into Y*, I believe these can be generated satisfactorily from more basic 'one-place' change-of-state expessions in a semantically compositional way and thus provide little evidence for the two-place connective T as an operator of 'Natural Logic'. If one believes, however, that T can be linguistically motivated, or if one is not interested in the empirical linguistic significance of such operators but regards them as merely a technical convenience for stating truth conditions for 'surface' English, then there is of course no objection to replacing BECOME with T, or to using both operators for that matter. (Explicit rules for producing sentences like (12) from the inverted GS point of view appear in 4.5.)

3.4. TRUTH CONDITIONS FOR THE PROGRESSIVE

My semantic analysis of the progressive tense will be similar to that of Bennett and Partee (ms.), which in turn bears some similarity to earlier analyses by Scott (1970) and by Montague (1968). However, there will be an important difference in the present analysis.

Bennett and Partee's truth condition for the progressive stipulates that [PROG ϕ] is true at I iff there exists an interval I' such that $I \subset I'$, I is not a final subinterval of I', and ϕ is true at I'.[4]

This formal analysis can be seen to have as predecessor one (or perhaps more) of the non-formal theories of the progressive proposed by linguists, in particular Jespersen's so-called "time-frame theory". Jespersen held that "the action or state denoted by the expanded tense is thought of as a temporal frame encompassing something" (1973, pp. IV–178). Thus in *he was writing when I entered*, the activity of his writing is said to form the temporal frame within which the shorter event of my entering is placed. Bennett and Partee's analysis seems to me to capture this idea precisely. Theories of the progressive which stress *duration* as the primary meaning of the progressive are clearly related to this idea; cf. Scheffer (1975, pp. 17-42) for an extensive discussion of Jespersen's and other traditional ideas about the English progressive.[5]

Montague's and Scott's analyses were like Bennett and Partee's except for failing to take the idea of truth relative to an interval as primitive. Instead,

Montague (1968) took PROG ϕ to be true at t just in case there exists an open interval I around t such that ϕ is true at all times t' within I. As I noted, this is impossible as an analysis of the progressive of accomplishment sentences (*John is building a house*), though it might seem adequate if we restricted our attention (as perhaps Montague did) to activities alone (*John is walking*).

While I believe the Bennett–Partee idea of interval semantics is a crucial insight needed to analyze the progressive correctly, it still runs afoul of the imperfective paradox as it stands. That is, it still licenses the inference from an accomplishment sentence in a progressive tense to the same sentence in some simple tense. Actually, the inference from the past progressive to the simple past does fail in their analysis, but for an irrelevant reason. It could turn out that (1) is true and (2) false because the only interval for which *John draws a circle* is true is one beginning in the past but including the present.

(1) John was drawing a circle.

(2) John drew a circle.

Nevertheless, the inference from (1) to (23) would be valid (given a standard tense-logical analysis of the future perfect), as would the inference from *John is drawing a circle* to (23) and the inference from *John will be drawing a circle* to (23).

(23) John will have drawn a circle.

But intuitively, all these inferences should fail and they should fail for the same reason: to say that John was, is, or will be drawing a circle is not to commit oneself to the coming into existence of (a representation of) a circle at any time. On the other hand, to assert that John drew, draws, or will draw a circle is to postulate the existence of a circle at some time or other.

As I pointed out earlier, however, one should be able to conclude from (1) no more than that the existence of a circle was (or will be) a *possible* outcome of John's activity. This observation suggests that the progressive is not simply a temporal operator, but a kind of mixed modal-temporal operator. A natural proposal would be the following truth condition, in which a truth value is now assigned to a sentence relative to an index of an interval I and to a possible world w out of a given set of possible worlds W:

(24) [PROG ϕ] is true at $\langle I, w\rangle$ iff there is an interval I' such that $I \subset I'$ and I is not a final subinterval for I' and there is a world w' for which ϕ is true at $\langle I', w'\rangle$, and w is exactly like w' at all times preceding and including I.

(The idea of one possible world being exactly like another up to a certain time is of course the crucial notion here. I take it that it is intuitively clear enough to the reader what this ought to mean. I will return to the problem of formalizing this notion shortly.)

Consider now the special case of [PROG ϕ] in which ϕ has the form [BECOME ψ], i.e., [PROG[BECOME ψ]]. According to (11) and (24), this kind of sentence will be true in the following situation:

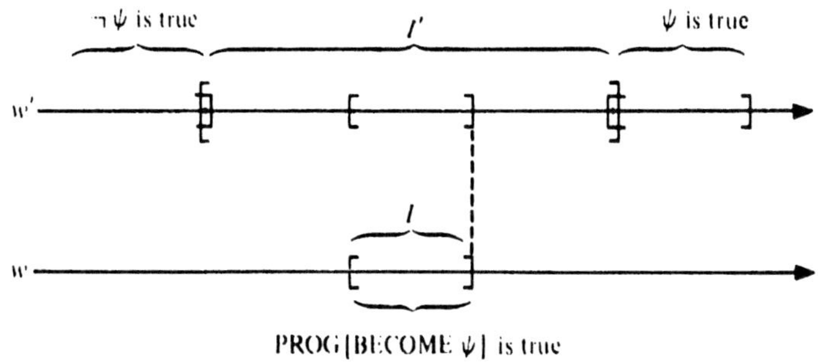

In this diagram the two lines labeled w and w' represent, respectively, the course of time in the actual world and in some possible world perhaps distinct from it, and the dotted line indicates the point up to which w and w' are exactly alike. Note that this analysis does not require that ψ be true at any time in the actual world w (though it does not exclude this possibility), but it does require that some initial subinterval of the coming about of ψ, namely, that part of I' up to and including I, is 'actualized'. It also requires that there be a time in the past in the actual world at which $\neg\psi$ was the case.

One further refinement of (24) is necessary. As it stands, this condition has an undesirable consequence called to my attention by Richmond Thomason. Suppose that a coin is being flipped but has not yet landed. (To make the illustration clear, let us add that the coin has not been tampered with and that nothing else about the situation predetermines how it will land.) Clearly, we would want to say in this situation that there is a possible world just like the actual world up to the present in which the coin comes up heads, as well as one in which it comes up tails. Here (24) requires that the sentences *The coin is coming up heads* and *the coin is coming up tails* should both be true, but this is a counterintuitive result. Perhaps in this example it is hard to distinguish the present progressive from the progressive used as a future tense (the latter use will be examined in 3.7 below). But there are other problematic examples where this is not so. Suppose John has begun making a drawing but has not yet decided whether it is to be a drawing of a horse or a drawing of a unicorn. My analysis appears to predict that both *John is drawing a horse* and *John is drawing a unicorn* should be true here, but again this is clearly wrong for English.

These considerations suggest that the truth conditions for PROG ϕ must require the truth of ϕ (at some superinterval) not just in *some* possible world like the actual world up to the given time, but rather its truth in all of some *set* of worlds that meet certain conditions. Just what set of worlds will this be? David Lewis has suggested to me that this should be the set of worlds in which the "natural course of events" takes place. That is, to say that John was building a house when such-and-such happened is to say that in all worlds like the actual one at that time in which nothing out of the ordinary or unexpected happened, he eventually brought a house into existence. In the case where a coin is being flipped, the relevant set of worlds would include both worlds in which it comes up heads and in which it comes up tails, so *the coin is coming up heads* cannot count as true.

Can "natural course of events" be defined in terms of a more basic notion or one needed independently for a model theory of natural language? The notion seems not to be definable in terms of probability. There are occasions on which we can look back into the past and say truthfully (at least with the benefit of hindsight) that a certain accomplishment or achievement *was occurring* at that time, even though the probability of its completion was very small. Nor can the required notion be defined in terms of Lewis' similarity relation among worlds, used in the analysis of causation in the last chapter, because Lewis requires (for good reasons) that the actual world be as similar or more similar to itself than any other world is. To then say that PROG ϕ is true just in case ϕ is true (at a superinterval) in all worlds having at least such-and-such a degree of similarity to the actual world is to require that ϕ always be true in the actual world itself whenever PROG ϕ is true – just the condition we want to avoid to account for the imperfective paradox.

Thus I reluctantly conclude that we must add to the definition of a model a new primitive function which assigns to each index, consisting of a world and an interval of time, a set of worlds which might be called *inertia worlds* – these are to be thought of as worlds which are exactly like the given world up to the time in question and in which the future course of events after this time develops in ways most compatible with the past course of events. If we call this function *Inr*, then the definition of the progressive operator will read as follows:

(25) [PROG ϕ] is true at $\langle I, w\rangle$ iff for some interval I' such that $I \subset I'$ and I is not a final subinterval for I', and for all w' such that $w' \in Inr(\langle I, w\rangle)$, ϕ is true at $\langle I', w'\rangle$.

It might be useful to consider one more example to help motivate this condition. Suppose the following claim is made among a group of Jones' colleagues at an academic convention:

(26) Jones is ruining his academic reputation by publishing all those crackpot papers on politeness rules in Pre-Indo-European.

Not all the participants in the discussion agree. How does one decide the truth of such a claim? Note that we cannot decide it merely by going into the future (somehow) and seeing whether we eventually reach a time at which Jones' reputation is in a shambles (assuming, for the sake of argument, that our participants could agree whether *that* proposition was true). All might readily assent that if Jones stops publishing the crackpot papers and instead writes up and publishes his really profound ideas on Austronesian morphophonemics, his reputation will be secured. Moreover, they might agree that it is quite likely that somebody or other will eventually persuade Jones to do this before it's too late. Rather, what is at issue is what is happening *now*, what is the outcome of events as they could be expected to transpire without such interference. Clearly, the relevant worlds needed for the evaluation of this particular sentence are those in which Jones continues to publish nutty articles and does not publish the important ideas.

Though the beliefs of an individual are clearly involved in his deciding what worlds count as inertia worlds, we must of course resist the temptation to make the meaning of progressive sentences a function of the speaker of the sentence (i.e., a function of his particular beliefs) or the hearer or of any other particular person. We couldn't resolve the dispute in question simply by interrogating the person who uttered the sentence. While there are severely subjective differences among individual's beliefs as to how the world would "turn out" if left uninterfered with, agreement on the truth of progressive sentences, to the extent that such agreement obtains at all, presupposes that such beliefs are held in common. It's for just this reason that sentences like (26) provoke disagreement, while judgment is straightforward for examples like *John is washing his car* – where the intention of an agent is clearly in evidence – or *The lamp is falling off the table* – where laws of nature suggest an obvious outcome. Once again, the program of truth conditional semantics requires that the *meaning* of expressions of a language not be treated as a part of the private experience or beliefs of individuals, but rather as the common property of all users of the language, even though the actual *use* of these meanings may sometimes involve beliefs which do vary from one individual to the next.

3.5. MOTIVATING THE PROGRESSIVE ANALYSIS INDEPENDENTLY OF ACCOMPLISHMENT SENTENCES

As I indicated earlier, I believe this modal treatment of the progressive (as opposed to the non-modal analysis) can be motivated from non-accomplishment cases. On the face of it, this would not seem to be so. Sentence (27) certainly seems to entail that the time of John's watching television (which is an irresultative activity) actually extended at least a few moments beyond the time that Bill entered the room:

(27) John was watching television when Bill entered the room.

However, I think it is only an 'invited inference' (due to conversational rules) that the activity continued. To see this, compare (27) and (28) (where *John* is the antecedent of *he*):

(28) John was watching television when he fell asleep.

(28) clearly does not require us to suppose that the period of John's watching television extended beyond the time of his falling asleep, but Bennett and Partee's analysis of the progressive, like Scott's and Montague's, would require that it did (if *when* is given a straightforward analysis as 'at the time at which'). The real entailment that I believe both (27) and (28) share is that it was *possible* that John's activity continued beyond the time specified by the *when*-clause. These facts about (27) and (28) would follow exactly from the truth conditions in (24), hence (28) provides independent motivation for (24). The condition (24) would also explain why we take (28) to suggest also the counter-factual "if John had not fallen asleep at that particular time, he would have continued watching television at least a few moments longer".

3.6. ON THE NOTION OF 'LIKENESS' AMONG POSSIBLE WORLDS

Though I have mentioned why I considered the idea of a possible world continuing only in 'predictable' ways not to be definable in terms of other notions needed in semantics, it might seem that the first part of the definition of *inertia worlds* – "identical to the given world up to a time *t*" – might be defined in terms of information already available in the interpretation relative to a model. This I believe not to be the case, for reasons discussed in Dowty (1977, pp. 61-62). Since the revised definition of the progressive in terms of inertia worlds (an idea that was not used in my earlier article) requires a primitive function *Inr* anyway, the point is no longer so important, and I will not discuss it here.

There is however another way of formulating the idea of possible worlds being alike up to certain times and diverging thereafter. This is to consider time itself to be branching rather than linear: for any given point in time there may be not just a single future course of time, but multiple possible futures. Rather than alternative possible worlds, we can now deal with alternative possible futures in stating the conditions for the progressive, and this simplifies the matter somewhat. The idea is that PROG ϕ is to be true at I if and only if there is an interval I' including I (and thus extending into some but perhaps not all possible future(s) of I) at which ϕ is true. In terms of the usual branching tree diagram for this model of time, PROG ϕ would be true at I in the following kind of situation:

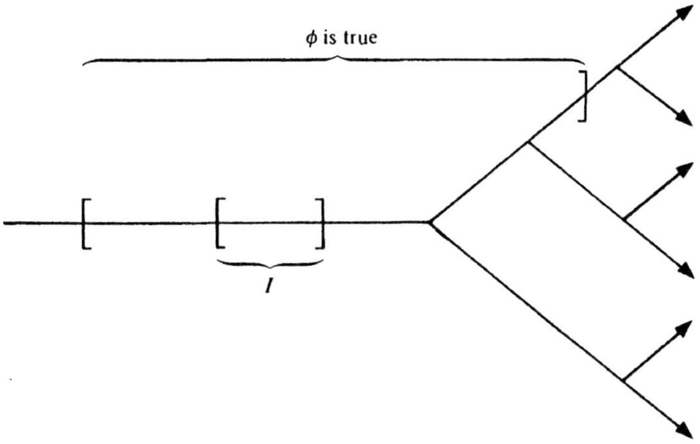

With branching time it would still be necessary to modify the definition of the progressive to make reference to inertia worlds, though they would be called 'inertia futures' here. We would have to include in the model a primitive function which gives for each time some proper subset of the set of possible futures of that time. A sentence PROG ϕ would then be true at a time just in case for each of the inertia futures of that time there is an interval including the basic time and stretching into the inertia future such that ϕ is true for this interval.

The required definitions, with respect to interval semantics, can be constructed as follows. Assume, as before, that T is the set of times, but $<$ is not a total linear ordering of T as before, but merely a transitive relation on T which is treelike, having the property of backwards linearity. That is, for all $t_1, t_2, t_3 \in T$, if $t_1 < t_3$ and $t_2 < t_3$, then either $t_1 < t_2$ or $t_2 < t_1$ or $t_2 = t_1$. A *history* (a *maximal chain*) on T is a subset h of T such that (1) for all $t_1, t_2 \in h$, if $t_1 \neq t_2$, then $t_1 < t_2$ or $t_2 < t_1$, and (2) if g is any subset of T meeting condition (1), then $g = h$ if $h \subseteq g$. (That is, all the times within a history are linearly ordered with respect to each other by $<$, and a history cannot be made longer by the addition of more times – thus it is a maximal linear pathway through the time structure.) An *interval* is a subset I of T such that (1) I is a proper subset of some history h in T, and (2) for all $t_1, t_2, t_3 \in h$, if $t_1, t_3 \in I$ and $t_1 < t_2 < t_3$, then $t_2 \in I$. The function *Inr* assigns to each interval I a proper subset of the histories containing I – these are thought of as representing the inertia futures of I. An *interpretation function* assigns a denotation (of the appropriate sort) to each non-logical constant relative to each interval in T.

We now define PROG ϕ as true at I if and only if for each history h in *Inr*(I), there is an interval I' such that $I' \subset h$ and $I \subset I'$ and ϕ is true at I'.

The use of a branching-future model may have wider applications in natural language semantics. For example, Thomason (1970) shows how the "traditionally popular" view that certain future tense statements may be neither true nor false (cf. Aristotle's discussion of the sea battle tomorrow) can be treated naturally using branching time. Such treatments usually have the consequence that certain formulas (such as [FUTURE $\phi \vee$ FUTURE$\neg\phi$]) which are valid in linear time (and intuitively *ought* to be valid) turn out not to be valid. But by applying van Fraassen's idea of a supervaluation to "branching" tense logic, Thomason is able to avoid this undesirable consequence. Elsewhere (Thomason ms.) he has used branching time in the analysis of 'conditional obligation' in deontic logic. It is sometimes suggested that counterfactuals and modal operators be analyzed in terms of branching time, letting histories play the role that possible worlds play in the usual semantics for modal logic. On this view, to say that *it might have been the case that* ϕ is analyzed as true just in case ϕ is true at a time in some possible history which has split off at an earlier time from the histories containing our present time. And *if* ϕ *were the case, then* ψ *would be the case* would be analyzed as true just in case the history or histories in which ϕ became true which split off most recently from the histories containing our present time are all histories in which ψ also became true. (The parallel between this and Lewis' analysis of counterfactuals in terms of similarity of worlds is apparent, given the assumption that similarity among worlds (i.e. histories) could partly or completely be determined in terms of the length of time that the two histories remained the same before splitting apart. Cf. the discussion of deterministic laws in Lewis (1973, pp. 73-77).)

Despite any conceptual advantages to thinking of modal notations in terms of branching time, this way of using branching time is almost equivalent to a system based on world-time indices in which it is specified which worlds are exactly like which other worlds up to which times. This can perhaps best be appreciated by thinking of a diagram of a branching time system as derived from a diagram of a world-time index system (e.g. the diagram on p. 147) by simply "compressing" together the possible world lines of "like" worlds up until times where the worlds cease to be alike. What were formerly distinct indices in identical segments of two such worlds with the same time co-ordinate are now thought of as a single "time" which has various possible futures. A possible history now takes over the role of a possible world, as it provides the only way of distinguishing possible "worlds" along stretches of time where two "worlds" are the same.

The only difference in the two systems is that in branching time, times which lie on different branches are not temporally ordered with respect to each other by $<$ (or in any other way). Thus we would encounter problems in treating modal and counterfactual statements such as *If I were in New York right now I would do such-and-such*, or *John might have arrived on Thursday, but he also might arrive tomorrow*. Thomason (1974a) suggests circumventing this problem by taking advantage of the metric properties of time and comparing the time shown by clocks (or dates shown by calendars) in different histories to determine which of two times on different branches is the earlier or whether they are the same. But the effect of Thomason's clocks is simply to partition the entire set of moments of time in the branching structure into equivalence classes, each of which contains the moments of various possible histories that are cotemporal from a 'meta-historical' point of view. Since these equivalence classes are in effect ordered with respect to each other (since at least one member in each is ordered by $<$ with respect to at least one member in each of the others), a linear time structure has been imposed over the branching time structure, so the two systems are now completely equivalent in the "information" contained in them. Hence ultimately no significance attaches to the choice between the two ways of formalizing the system.

3.7. EXTENDING THE ANALYSIS TO THE "FUTURATE PROGRESSIVE"

The present progressive tense of English, in addition to its use in describing an action currently in progress, can be used as a special kind of future tense, as in (29):

(29) John is leaving town tomorrow.

For (29) to be true it is apparently not required that we have already entered the smallest interval of time of which it may later be true that *John leaves town*, so the analysis proposed so far will not accommodate it.

However, there may appear to be a certain intuitive but vague connection between the imperfective progressive and the so-called "futurate progressive" of (29). Consider first that an imperfective sentence such as *John is drawing a circle* may be truly uttered on certain occasions when no portion of a circle exists yet on paper, but when John is merely observed to be making *preparations* to draw (assembling compass and paper, etc.) and his intentions are known. Perhaps this use is merely 'speaking loosely', but it suggests at least a psychological tendency of humans to extend the temporal 'duration' of an accomplishment (in Vendler's sense) backward in time to include the preparations for the accomplishment proper, i.e., the direct bringing about of a result. At its extreme, this 'temporal extension' will go all the way back to the agent's decision (if there is an agent) to attempt to bring about the result. Thus there is a certain sense in which the composition of a symphony 'begins' with the composer's decision to undertake the project, and a sense in which a murder 'begins' with the initial premeditation to commit the crime. As it has been argued (as I will explain below) that the futurate progressive of (29) semantically involves some notion of planning, it might seem that the event of leaving described in (29) may, after all, be 'in progress' in this loose sense. Though this line of thinking may have merit, to pursue it would quickly lead us into the fascinating but very difficult questions of how humans conceive of events as grouped together into causally and temporally related 'meta-events' involving intentions as well as actions, and I question whether such investigations would lead us to productive results in model-theoretic semantics anytime soon. Fortunately, there appears to be a somewhat more direct approach to the analysis of (29).

There are actually (at least) three syntactic means of expressing futurity in English; these are exhibited by (30) (the *regular future*) and (31) (which I will call the *tenseless future*) as well as the *futurate progressive* of (29):

(30) John will leave town tomorrow.

(31) John leaves town tomorrow.

The semantic differences among these three forms have been the subject of a series of recent papers by generative transformational linguists (including Vetter, 1973; Prince, 1973; and Goodman, 1973), as well as by linguists outside this school (cf. Scheffer, 1975; Wekker, 1976, for extensive discussion and further references), and the linguistic facts are now fairly well understood, though no formal semantic treatment has been attempted.[6] Vetter, responding to an observation by George Lakoff about the differences among (32a-f), argues that the notion of *planning* crucially distinguishes the tenseless future and futurate progressive from the regular future (and not mere certainty, on the part of the speaker, as Lakoff had claimed).

(32) a. Tomorrow, the Yankees will play the Red Sox.
b. Tomorrow, the Yankees play the Red Sox.
c. Tomorrow, the Yankees are playing the Red Sox.
d. Tomorrow, the Yankees will play well.
e. ?Tomorrow, the Yankees play well.
f. ?Tomorrow, the Yankees are playing well.

(32e-f) are quite odd, except in the unlikely event that the speaker knows that the game has been rigged. The subject of the sentence need not be the agent who does the planning, as can be observed in (33). Note that the event in (33) is naturally understood as planned, though no agent is immediately involved, whereas the event in (34) cannot be naturally construed as planned or scheduled:

(33) a. The bomb will go off at 2 PM.
b. The bomb goes off at 2 PM.
c. The bomb is going off at 2 PM.

(34) a. The telephone in my office will (undoubtedly) ring tomorrow.
b. ?The telephone in my office (undoubtedly) rings tomorrow.
c. ?The telephone in my office is (undoubtedly) ringing tomorrow.

That certainty on the part of the subject or speaker is not the correct criterion for the tenseless future can also be seen from (35), cited by Wekker (1976, p. 35):

(35) I'm not sure whether I get my paycheck tomorrow.

It is still clearly entailed or implicated by (35) that the question of when the speaker gets the paycheck has been subject to planning, though the speaker himself does not know the details of the plan.

Leech (1971, p. 59) and Goodman (1973) observe that the notion of 'planning' is not quite general enough, but should be replaced by a notion something like 'predetermined on the basis of past events' because of examples like (36), in which planning by a human agent cannot be involved.

(36) The sun sets tomorrow at 6:57 PM.

(See Goodman (1973) for discussions of two further semantic entailments of the tenseless future which I will not mention here or attempt to incorporate in my analysis, though they in fact present no problem for it.) Though Vetter had assumed that the futurate progressive had the same semantic properties as the tenseless future, Prince notes that this is not so. The tenseless future implies a greater degree of certainty of predetermination than the futurate progressive, as can be seen from the contrast in acceptability between (38a) and (38b), despite the fact that both sentences in (37) are acceptable. (Examples are taken from Prince (1973), where they are attributed to Jeff Kaplan.)

(37) a. The Rosenbergs die tomorrow.
b. The Rosenbergs are dying tomorrow.

(38) a. *The Rosenbergs die tomorrow, although the President may grant them a pardon.
b. The Rosenbergs are dying tomorrow, although the President may grant them a pardon.

Consider also the contrast between (39) and (40):

(39) a. I am leaving next Thursday at 4:30 PM.
b. I am tentatively leaving next Thursday at 4:30 PM.

(40) a. I leave next Thursday at 4:30 PM.
b. ?*I tentatively leave next Thursday at 4:30 PM.

(Though Prince marks (40b) with '?*', I think (40b) is in fact acceptable, but only in a situation where a plan or schedule of some sort has been arranged. What is tentative is whether the plan will be carried out or changed. With (40b), the speaker's leaving need not depend on any arrangements which have already been made. His departure may depend only upon his making up his mind when to go.) Though (41a) is normal, (41b) is somewhat strange, presumably because the time of the sun's setting, whenever it is, is about as fixed as events can be:

(41) a. The sun sets tomorrow at 6:57 PM.
b. *The sun is setting tomorrow at 6:57 PM.

Lauri Karttunen has suggested (personal communication) that the futurate progressive might be handled by the *same* tense operator as the imperfective progressive if an analysis such as mine were modified to allow [PROG ϕ] to be true at an interval I if and only if ϕ is true at some interval I' which includes *I or else is later than I* (in some appropriate possible history containing I). However, this move would not allow us to account for the semantic differences between the imperfective progressive and the futurate progressive that Prince and Wekker observe. These differences can be clearly seen in another way in (42), which, as Prince points out, is ambiguous between an imperfective progressive reading and a futurate progressive reading. (This ambiguity was also observed by Wekker.)

(42) Lee was going to Radcliffe until she was accepted by Parsons.

The imperfective reading, which Prince paraphrases as "Lee's going to Radcliffe was in progress until she was accepted by Parsons", entails that Lee did go to Radcliffe (since *go to Radcliffe* – in the sense of *attend Radcliffe*, the only sense relevant here – is naturally interpreted as an activity). The futurate progressive reading, paraphrased as "Lee's going to Radcliffe (at some future date) was the plan until she was accepted by Parsons", does not have that same entailment, but on the contrary, conversationally implicates that Lee did *not* go to Radcliffe.[7] One should bear in mind that the futurate progressive consistently involves the notion of plan or predetermination, though the imperfective progressive does not. Compare, for example (34c) with *The telephone in my office is ringing (now)*.

I wish to suggest that if we give the tenseless future the semantic analysis suggested by Goodman and others, the facts about the futurate progressive will follow automatically from the analysis of the 'imperfective' progressive I have already proposed. All we need to do is treat the 'futurate progressive' as an imperfective progressive combined in a purely compositional way with a sentence in the tenseless future. This will enable us to treat 'futurate progressives' without any syntactic and semantic rules except those needed for other kinds of sentences.

Henceforth, I will not attempt to give rigorous model-theoretic definitions but will rather indicate truth conditions informally. To avoid having to develop the syntax and semantics for a full range of time adverbials, I will simply illustrate the semantic rule for the tenseless future by a truth condition for a sentence with future time adverbial *tomorrow*:

(43) [*tomorrow* ϕ] is true at I iff (1) ϕ is true (in all histories containing I) at some interval I' such that I' is included within the day following the day that includes I, and (2) the truth of ϕ at I' is planned or predetermined by facts or events true at some time $t \leqslant I$.[8]

The vague notion in this definition is of course "planned or predetermined by facts or events", and at present I have no idea how to make this notion more precise in model-theoretic terms. Nonetheless, the interaction of (43) with my more exact analysis of the imperfective progressive should be sufficiently clear for present purposes.

Schematically, [*tomorrow* ϕ] will be true at I in the following situation:

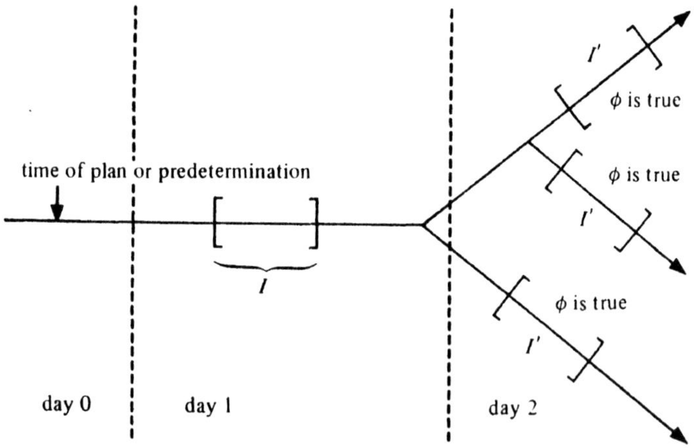

A futurate progressive will thus have the logical form [PROG[*tomorrow* ϕ]], and such a sentence would be true at an interval I_0 if there is an interval $I_1 \supset I_0$ such that [*tomorrow* ϕ] is true at I_1 in all inertia histories containing I_0. And by (43), [*tomorrow* ϕ] would then be true at I_1 if ϕ is true at a future interval I_2 in all histories containing I_1, and ϕ is planned or predetermined at some time at or preceding the lower bound of I_1. Such a situation would be represented as follows, assuming h_1 and h_2 are the only members of $Inr(I_1)$:

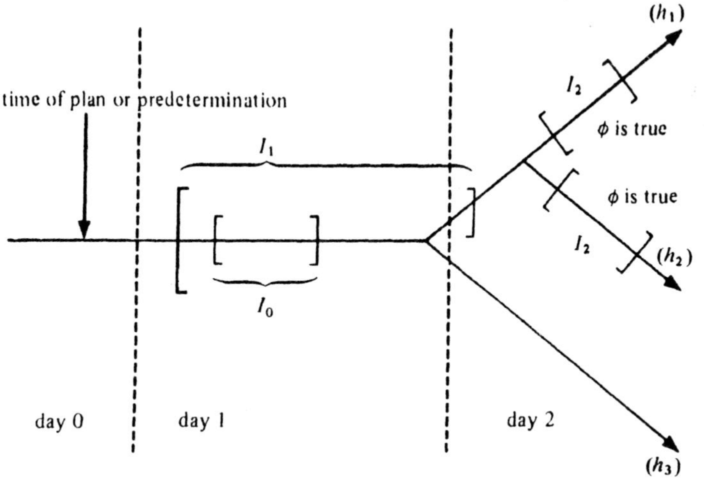

Note that ϕ will not have to be true in all futures containing I_0, but only in all futures containing I_1. This will account for Prince's observation that the futurate progressive is "less certain" than the tenseless future, and it will also distinguish the futurate progressive from the 'regular' progressive, since the planning or predetermination of ϕ must have (actually) occurred with the futurate progressive.

If a straightforward analysis of the regular future is given (or Thomason's analysis, mentioned earlier), then we can distinguish among the three English futures neatly, and, according to the literature, accurately: The regular future will imply (a greater or lesser degree of) certainty but not planning; the tenseless future will imply both planning and certainty; and the futurate progressive will imply planning but not certainty. (I here ignore the important problem of whether 'certainty' should be associated with epistemic necessity or logical necessity or perhaps some other notion, and the problem of just what *degree* of certainty is required for regular future and tenseless future.)

Of course, futurate progressives do not always have an explicit future time adverbial: recall that sentences like (42) or *John is leaving town* have futurate as well as regular progressive interpretations. It is thus of interest to inquire whether there are also sentences which are interpreted semantically as 'tenseless futures' but have no explicit future time adverb (i.e., sentences having present tense and no time adverb which are interpreted as describing a future event planned or predetermined by past events). For if such sentences exist, then the analysis of the futurate progressive that I have proposed already predicts that sentences such as *John is leaving town* can be interpreted as futurate progressives, since it should be possible to derive a futurate progressive sentence from any tenseless future sentence whatsoever, including a tenseless future with no adverb. And in fact, tenseless futures with no explicit adverb can be found, though they may not be too common. Consider the dialogue in (44)

(44) A: Which of the contestants do you suppose you will ultimately select as the winner?
B: Oh, number five wins the competition. His performance was unquestionably better than the others.

Notice how the tenseless future of B's response (as opposed to *He will win the competition* or *He is winning the competition*) suggests that the outcome of the matter has already been determined and does not really depend on any active deliberation by the judge or judges.

I also think that a special use of past tense sentences which was observed by Charles Fillmore (Fillmore, 1971) and which might be called the "restaurant-order past tense" also involves a tenseless future without any explicit future adverbial, the difference being that the sentence is here further embedded in a past tense operator. Such a sentence would be (45), when addressed to a waitress contemplating a table full of customers and a tray full of orders, trying to figure out which order goes with which customer:

(45) I had the cheeseburger with onions.

In contrast to the normal use of (45), this special use does not entail that the speaker has ever been in possession of the cheeseburger in question, but rather conversationally implicates that he has not yet acquired it. If (45) is analyzed as the past of a tenseless future (with an indefinite future time adverbial that is not phonologically realized but semantically plays the same role as *tomorrow* in (43)), then (45) would be interpreted as entailing that at some time in the past (namely, after the customer had placed his order with the waitress) it was planned or predetermined that at some indefinite future time the sentence *I have the cheeseburger with onions* would be true. This seems to me to be a correct account of this special use of (45).

Wekker (1976) offers a somewhat different account of the distinction between the tenseless future (which he calls the *simple future present*) and the futurate progressive (*progressive future present* in his terms). Following Leech (1971), he argues that the main condition on the use of the progressive is that the future event or action must be felt to have been planned or arranged by someone (1976, p. 106) and must involve the intention or initiation of the plan by a human agent (1976, p. 109, 110), whereas his explanation of the tenseless future is Leech's and Goodman's – there must be complete plan or predetermination by past or present events. Thus he would explain the oddness of (41b) (**The sun is setting tomorrow at 6:57*) as opposed to (41a) (*The sun sets tomorrow at 6:57*) as due to the fact that the setting of the sun cannot be determined by human planning.

In support of Wekker's position, I must agree that all clear examples of the future progressive I have observed do seem to involve human planning. But I believe this does not necessarily argue against the analysis I have given. First, the fact that the futurate progressive seems restricted to events involving human intention need not go completely unexplained in my account. The treatment of the futurate progressive as a PROG operator applied to a tenseless future sentence requires that when such sentences are true, in each inertia-history there is an interval I' encompassing our present interval for which the embedded sentence is true in the future of I' and determined by events prior to I'. This is a weaker assertion than a tenseless future sentence, so by Grice's maxim of quantity, we should not use a futurate progressive sentence where we know a tenseless future sentence would be true. The difference between the two is that a futurate progressive should (on my account) assert only that in all worlds which continue in a predictable and unexceptional way are we within an interval for which it is true that the future event is predetermined by past events. By Grice's maxim, we should only use the futurate progressive when it can still somehow fail to be true that past action has predetermined the future event. Under what circumstances can this be so?

When a person makes a decision to do something at a future time and then does it as he intended, two things are involved: the initial decision to perform the action at a later date, and moreover, a failure to change his mind between the time he makes the decision and the time he carries it out. If the person changes his mind and is not otherwise bound to carry out the action, then his decision did not really predetermine the event. If a person has made such a decision, then clearly, in all the inertia histories containing the time of the decision, he carried it out. The inertia worlds for a time t should quite clearly be worlds in which nobody changes his mind after t. The ways that physical events predetermine future events (e.g. the time of the sun's rising) are different. Whatever events or circumstances it is that predetermine such future events, these things happen "once and for all" setting causal chains of events into effect. The same is true when schedules are fixed by persons, are put in writing, and thereby become more-or-less irrevocable without some degree of effort. Even though these are initiated by human intentions, they "go into effect" and become permanent in a way that private personal decisions to perform future actions do not. It thus seems to me that human actions that are predetermined *solely* by private decision can be argued to fall more naturally into the semantic "slot" provided by my analysis of the futurate progressive than do any other sorts of predetermination. (Since human intention is ultimately involved in even scheduled events – those for which the tenseless future *is* used – Wekker still owes us an account of why *those* events are not described in the future progressive as well.) Of course, pre-scheduled events sometimes do fail to come off as scheduled, so I must claim a dictinction between the *overriding* of a predetermining event by some other event (e.g., the train fails to arrive on schedule) from the failure to follow through on a decision to act (my failure to do what I intend but for no external reason). Thus in effect, *I'm doing such and such tonight* should amount on my account to saying that I will do it only if I don't change my mind, but saying *I do such and such tonight* is saying in effect that something else besides my intention leads me to do it. *I will do such and such* makes a more neutral prediction about the future.

In the second place, there are theoretical reasons for preferring an account like mine to Wekker's and Leech's, even if the two are roughly comparable in semantic adequacy. My account explains this tense form in terms of two tense constructions needed anyway in the language, tense forms whose outward characteristics (i.e. *be* + *ing* and a future time adverb) both appear in this form and whose meanings I can claim to be the same as is exhibited elsewhere. According to Wekker's analysis, the meaning of the futurate progressive (planning by decision of human agent) is not obviously related to the meaning of the progressive as it appears elsewhere, so this meaning is idiosyncratic to this construction. Moreover, both the tenseless future and the progressive combine systematically with other tenses (we have, e.g. past present and future progressives, and past as well as present "tenseless futures" – cf. (45)), so an explicit systematic account of English tenses might well *predict* the combination of progressive with tenseless future as part of the complete paradigm of English tense forms. In this case, Wekker's and Leech's approach would have to account for a suspicious gap in this paradigm whose place is taken by a familiar-looking form with an unpredictable meaning.

Finally, we can account for the curious combination of past and future adverbials that Prince and Wekker observe in some sentences. The example from the title of Prince's paper ("Yesterday morning I was leaving tomorrow on the Midnight Special") would have the logical form (46), where a tenseless future is embedded in a progressive embedded in a past:[9]

(46) [PAST + yesterday morning [PROG[tomorrow[I leave on the Midnight Special]]]]

Similarly, we can associate Prince's ambiguous example (42) with the two logical forms (47) and (48). The imperfective reading is (47), and the futurate reading is (48), in which 'indef. fut.' is the phonologically unrealized future time adverbial corresponding to *tomorrow* in (43):

(47) [PAST + until she was . . . [PROG[Lee go to Radcliffe]]]

(48) [PAST + until she was . . . [PROG[(indef. fut.) [Lee go to Radcliffe]]]]

I leave it to the reader to confirm that the conditions for PROG and the tenseless future when applied to (47) and (48) do account for Prince's observations.

3.8. ANOTHER LOOK AT THE VENDLER CLASSIFICATION IN AN INTERVAL-BASED SEMANTICS

As mentioned above, a temporal semantics based on intervals in the way suggested by Bennett and Partee offers richer possibilities in analyzing natural language semantics than does a semantics based on moments alone. Moreover, I believe it will offer a more natural picture of the kind of classification Vendler, Kenny and others were trying to achieve. Before turning to a revision of this classification, we will look in more detail at the activity class (3.8.1) and the progressive test (3.8.2).

3.8.1. *The Non-Homogeneity of the Activity Class*

From the discussion of activities in Chapter four or from Ryle's, Vendler's or Kenny's discussion of this class, it would seem that all activity verbs are agentive (or "controllable") and conversely, that all controllable verbs are activities (or accomplishments), according to the syntactic tests given. It is natural enough that this assumption arose, because the standard examples of activities discussed in the literature on these verb classes are the activities that people engage in – *walking, running, speaking, swimming, smiling,* etc. But a slightly broader perusal of English examples turns up a large number of verb phrases with inanimate subjects that would appear to be activities or accomplishments (they occur in the progressive and in all of Ross' *do*-constructions), yet are not agentive in the usual sense because they do not occur as complements of *force* or *persuade*, in imperatives, or with adverbs like *deliberately*:

(48) a. The rock is rolling down the path.
b. What the rock did was roll down the path.
c. *John persuaded the rock to roll down the path.

(49) a. The motor is making noise.
b. The motor made a loud noise, which I had expected it would do.
c. *The motor is deliberately making noise.

(50) a. The leaves are turning brown.
b. The maple leaves have turned brown, but the oak leaves haven't done so yet.
c. *Turn brown!

Moreover, this turns out to be a point at which verbs and adjectives part company in their syntactic behavior. The examples in (51), noticed by Barbara Partee (1977), nicely illustrate the contrast:

(51) a. The machine makes noise.
b. The machine is noisy.
c. The machine is making noise.
d. *The machine is being noisy.

It seems that only among verbs do we find non-stative predicates that are non-agentive. Non-stative adjectives, in contrast, must apparently always be true agentives even when they are exactly paraphrasable by verbs which need not be, as in (51c) and (51d). That it is agency that is crucial here rather than a mere selectional restriction for animate or human subject can be seen from the contrast in (52), which is exactly parallel to (51):

(52) a. John slept.
b. John was asleep.
c. John was sleeping.
d. *John was being asleep.

For speakers who accept the various kinds of *do*-sentences with agentive adjectives (for example, *What I did then was be as polite to Mary as possible*), the *do*-test distinguishes between non-agentive non-stative verbs and non-stative adjectives:

(53) a. What the machine did was make noise.
b. *What the machine did was be noisy.

It seems that these exceptional non-agentive non-stative verbs can readily be distinguished on semantic grounds: though they have no "agent", they all involve activity in a physical sense – either a change of position or else an internal movement that has visual, audible or tactile consequences (e.g. *the refrigerator is running, the stereo is blaring*). In fact, we might be tempted to suggest that our formulation of the crucial semantic criterion for activity verbs in terms of agency or controllability was wrong and should be replaced by this "movement" criterion. However, recall that this will not do for cases like *John is ignoring Mary, John is refraining from saying anything rude*, which seem to qualify as activities only in that they involve a controllable decision *not* to act (and I would be very reluctant to postulate a "mental" movement or change just to escape from this uncomfortable situation). Moreover, the "controllability" criterion gives just exactly the right results for adjectives and nouns. Within the structuralist linguistic methodology we seem to have no choice at this point but to postulate two distinct elementary semantic units to describe the situation. This is indeed just what D. A. Cruse (1973) was led to do upon independently noticing this heterogeneity in what had been called "agency". Cruse takes the solution to be a matter of positing two semantic features, [volitive] (which corresponds roughly to our notion of "controllability") and [agentive]. (Actually, he postulates three different features that contrast with volitive – [agentive], [effective] and [initiative], – but I find the linguistic evidence he uses to distinguish among these three concepts much less compelling than that which distinguishes them all from volitivity.) In a GS theory one would presumably conclude that two distinct atomic predicates are in evidence here. One of these would have to do with controllability and would be solely responsible for governing the use of progressive *be* with adjectives, but could also lexicalize as *do* in the position of a surface verb whose complement has been deleted or moved. The other would semantically represent something about motion or change and would also lexicalize as *do* under the same circumstances as the first, though it would not lexicalize as *be* with adjectives (nor appear as *do* when its complement is a surface adjective – cf. (53b)).

If we once again go beyond structural semantics and try to work out a real formal interpretation for this second operator of "motional" activity, things look a little less simple. In the first place, note that all the cases we observed where the same predicate might be claimed to be found in surface structure both with and without its higher DO, (e.g. *I consider John careful* vs. *John is being careful*) have a DO of controllability, not a "DO" of motion/change. Thus we apparently have no minimally contrasting pairs of expressions on which an investigation of the meaning of this second "DO" can be based. In other words, we have only paradigmatic data, not syntagmatic data, on which to base an investigation of this second operator.

Nevertheless, there remains much that can be said concerning the referential semantics of "motional" activities, particularly the special way their truth conditions depend on time and states of affairs in the world.

Barry Taylor (1977) presents an account of the English progressive and its application to the various Aristotelian classes of verbs that is like Bennett and Partee's account and the account given above in taking truth relative to intervals of time as basic, rather than relative to moments. It differs from these in assuming a Davidsonian "extensional" semantics (and is thus in principle unable to accommodate the modal treatment of the progressive I have proposed, and does not present any solution to the imperfective paradox).[10] Taylor does not provide a decomposition analysis of each class of verbs, as I have done, but instead gives postulates that specify the logical characteristics of each class. The basic versions of Taylor's postulates (which he revises somewhat, later on) are (54)–(57). (I have rephrased Taylor's definitions here to minimize terminological differences, but I trust his views are not misrepresented.)

(54) If α is a *stative* predicate, then $\alpha(x)$ is true at an interval I just in case $\alpha(x)$ is true at all moments within I.

(55) If α is an *activity* verb ("E-Verb", for *energia*) or an *accomplishment/achievement* verb ("K-Verb", for *kinesis*), then $\alpha(x)$ is only true at an interval larger than a moment.

(56) If α is an *accomplishment/achievement verb*, then if $\alpha(x)$ is true at I, then $\alpha(x)$ is false at all subintervals of I.

(57) If α is an *activity* verb, then if $\alpha(x)$ is true at I, then $\alpha(x)$ is true for all subintervals of I which are larger than a moment.[11]

Taylor's principle (54) is implicit in my earlier discussion of statives, and I will explicitly incorporate it later. His principle (56) would follow for verbs analyzed with BECOME from the "minimal subinterval" condition in the truth definition for BECOME in (11′). Principle (55), however, is not related to any observation made so far. (Postulates such as Taylor's are of course appealing to those who prefer to dabble in word semantics as little as possible, since they allow one to differentiate the behavior of these verbs in combination with tense without committing oneself to any claims about the entailments of these verbs beyond an absolute minimum. But it is of course a primary thesis of this book that a deeper explanation of these differences lies in understanding the change-of-state entailments that are or are not present in the different classes; a description such as Taylor's leave it an apparent accident that the class of verbs that have definite change-of-state entailments and the class of verbs that seem to obey (56) is exactly the same.) He suggests that (54) and (55), together with the interval-contained-within-a-superinterval analysis of the progressive, provide an explanation of why statives and non-statives take the non-progressive and progressive present tense respectively (Taylor, 1977, p. 206). The progressive tense is construed as functioning to indicate a time which, "*though not itself a time of application of the tensed verb*, occurs within a more inclusive time which *is* a period of the verb's application". (By time of *application of a verb* α, Taylor means the time at which the atomic sentence $\alpha(x)$ is true, as opposed to the time at which the tensed sentence is true.) If the "time of utterance" of a normal sentence is always a moment,[12] as seems plausible, then it should be impossible to truthfully utter a simple present sentence with a non-stative (activity or accomplishment/achievement) verb, if Taylor's principle (55) is correct. If truth-relative-to-an-interval is still the basis for the recursive semantic clauses, including those for tense operators, then past and simple future sentences with non-stative verbs nevertheless ought to be acceptable in non-progressive form – as in fact they are – since they can have a moment as time of *utterance*, though the time at which their *embedded* sentence is true has to be an interval. In contrast to non-stative sentences, statives *can* be true at a moment in virtue of (54), so they can occur with the simple present. Taylor then explains the absence of progressive sentences with statives by a kind of Gricean principle of economy (1977, p. 206): "every time within a period of application of [a stative] verb itself being a time of its applications, there is no place for tenses designed to register the existence of times of non-application of the verb within broader periods of its application". Clever and appealing though this explanation is, it is not quite the whole story, because there are also some sentences that are semantically stative but nevertheless take the progressive; these are discussed in 3.8.2 below. However, I believe that (55) leads to an important insight about activity verbs, as I will now explain.

Taylor does not go beyond the statement of postulate (55) to ask *why* non-stative verbs should only be true at intervals larger than a moment, but an intuitive explanation of (55) is readily apparent for non-statives of the "motional" sort. To see this, consider a segment of a motion picture film showing a ball rolling down an inclined plane. A single frame of this film does not in itself offer us the evidence to say that the ball is really in motion, assuming that the film does not show any blurs, but any two frames (adjacent or not) showing the ball in slightly different locations do provide evidence of movement. (Wittgenstein made a similar observation in his *Philosophical Investigations* (Wittgenstein 1958).) If we attempted to tie the truth conditions for basic predicates to physical properties represented in the model by "logical space" as we did in the previous chapter, then quite clearly the truth conditions for "motional" predicates and others denoting a change in physical properties of some sort would require access to information about the physical state of the world at at least two moments in time.

Activities, of the motional sort at least, are characterized by a change in physical properties over time. But we also characterized accomplishments and achievements by a change of state over time, so what is the difference in the two classes? It would seem to be the difference between a "definite" and an "indefinite" change of state. The activity *the ball moves* is true of any interval in which the ball changes its location to any degree at all, and thus may be simultaneously true of an interval and various subintervals of that interval. The accomplishments *the ball moves six feet, the ball moves to the bottom of the slope* are true when a change of location of a particular specified location has taken place, and thus are true of a single interval, but not of any subintervals or superinterval of that interval. We might then try to elaborate on Taylor's postulate for activities along the following lines:

(58) *Activity postulate*
If α is an activity verb, then if $\alpha(x)$ is true at an interval I, there is some physically definable property P such that the individual denoted by x lacks P at the lower bound of I and has P at the upper bound of I.

Intuitively, we would like to strengthen this somewhat. Postulate (58) requires only that for each interval at which an activity verb is true there is *some* physical property which x comes to have during that interval, but would allow this to be a different property for each interval, perhaps a totally "unrelated" property. This is much too weak, for given a particular activity verb, it seems that the same *kind* of property must be acquired for each interval of which that verb is true of an individual.

This problem is easiest to illustrate if we first focus on a maximally simple paradigm example of an activity verb, the simple motion verb *move* (i.e., the intransitive verb *move*, not the causative transitive verb *move*). Let p be a variable ranging over *places* (sets of points in three-dimensional space). Assume that the model for our language includes a function *Loc* that assigns a place to each individual at each moment in time. Then it is possible to describe the truth conditions for *move* (x) informally as follows (for convenience, I am temporarily ignoring the question of whether *move* should be decomposed, and I overlook the distinction between the symbols p and x and their denotations):

(59) "*move*(x)" is true at interval I iff there is a place p such that (1) $Loc(x) = p$ at the lower bound of I and $Loc(x) \neq p$ at the upper bound of I.

It can now be made clear what is meant by an indefinite as opposed to a definite change of state: it is the narrow scope existential quantification over places in this definition that is responsible for the indefiniteness. Note that nothing in this definition excludes the possibility that x undergoes a change to some other locations besides p during this interval t, nor does it exclude the possibility that x also undergoes other changes of location before or after I. Hence x *moves* can be true of subintervals of I as well as I itself, and can likewise be true of superintervals of I. Note that the definition of *move* in (59) makes this verb meet the condition (55) in all models (activities can only be true at intervals larger than a moment), because an interval of only a moment's duration would have the same moment as upper and lower bound. (If the movement is always "continuous", then *move* would satisfy (57) as well.) For comparison, let us write a parallel truth definition (again ignoring the decomposition issue) for a maximally simple change-of-state verb *reach* (or equivalently *move-to* or *arrive-at*), which is a two-place predicate.

(60) "*reach*(x,p)" is true at I iff $Loc(x) \neq p$ at the lower bound of I and $Loc(x) = p$ at the upper bound of I, and there is no interval I' contained within I that meets these two conditions.

To illustrate a change of state verb involving two specified locations, we may write a truth definition for a three-place predicate representing "x moves from p to q".

(61) "*move-from-to*(x, p, q)" is true at t iff $Loc(x) = p$ at the lower bound of I, $p \neq q$, and $Loc(x) = q$ at the upper bound of I, and there is no interval I' contained within I that meets these two conditions.

The verbs in (60) and (61), in contrast to (59), will clearly not be true of any proper subinterval of an interval at which they are true (in fact, (60) requires a "two-moment" interval), nor will they be true of any superinterval of such an interval (though of course they may be true of adjacent, non-overlapping intervals, as when an object oscillates between positions p and q). The reason, obviously, is that there is no existential quantification within these truth definitions as there is in (59). Note that it is not simply the involvement of a change of state that distinguishes activities from accomplishments and achievements (i.e. a BECOME operator could readily be used to decompose all of the verbs in (59)–(61)), but also the effect of the existential quantifier. This situation should be compared with that of the problem with indefinite plurals and mass terms discussed in 2.3.3, where the presence of an existential quantifier in the analysis of a verb likewise led to "activity-like" behavior of a verb otherwise classed as an accomplishment or achievement.

Though the truth conditions of a few motional activity verbs will differ from those in (59) in a rather straightforward way (e.g. *rise* and *fall* require an addition only that the new position acquired be above or below the old position, respectively), complications multiply rapidly. (59) makes reference to only the position (set of points in space) occupied by the object as a whole, but as M. J. Cresswell has pointed out, it would be necessary to make reference to positions occupied by parts of an object as well if we are to include under our definition of movement the case of a perfect sphere rotating in space but not coming to occupy any new previously unoccupied space. The case of an object that moves in a circular path presents another kind of problem – at the end of an interval of movement the object may occupy exactly the same position as at the beginning. Perhaps a recursive definition would be needed for this case: (59) would act as the base clause, then in addition, we could say that "*x moves*" is true at t if t is the union of two or more other intervals at which *x moves* is true.

The motional activities characteristic of humans (*walking, swimming, running, dancing,* etc.) involve even more complex patterns of change of position, changes not just with respect to overall location but changes with respect to positions of parts of the organism. Taylor refers to such activities as *heterogeneous activities*; these require a modification of his postulate (57), because not every minimal subinterval (i.e. one consisting of more than a moment) of such activities is also an interval of that activity. E.g., small subintervals of the time of which *x chuckles* is true may not be times of chuckling themselves (though perhaps intervals of x's producing a glottal stop, etc.). Even particular *sequences* of more simple changes of position can be required for some activities. To take just one special sort of problem, there may be a sequential series of simpler activities required to characterize a certain complex activity, though no particular member of the sequence need occur first. Consider the case of *waltzing*; what minimal conditions must an interval meet for *x waltzes* to be true of that interval? Now since the waltz involves sequences of three steps, I believe it is reasonable to maintain that any interval at which x takes less than three steps is not an interval at which *x waltzes* is true (consider again what one could determine from inspection of a limited number of adjacent frames of a motion picture film), but merely an interval at which x makes certain movements with his or her feet. Nevertheless, we might be willing to count any of the intervals indicated below as intervals of waltzing (where 1, 2 and 3 indicate the steps in their canonical order), despite the difference in the particular cyclic permutation chosen:

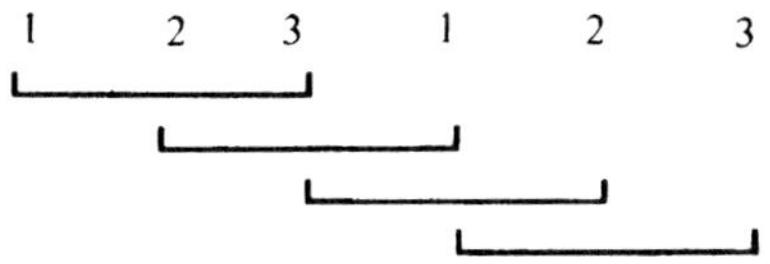

No doubt, a variety of other problematic cases would be uncovered by an investigation of other sorts of activities.

Now it seems plausible that with enough time and patience, one could describe necessary and sufficient truth conditions for most if not all common English verbs of motional activity, making use of only the model-theoretic specification of the position occupied by a body (and/or parts thereof) at each moment in time, with the aid of quantification over positions and times, at least up to the limits of exactness that the words have in their ordinary language use. And it likewise seems plausible that in each case we would be able to note an existential quantifier somewhere or other in the truth definition, thus explaining the semantic behavior of the verb as an activity (i.e. subinterval verb) rather than as an accomplishment or achievement (a non-subinterval verb). But it is not obvious to me at all how one could systematize these analyses by postulating a single operator of "motional activity" that could be combined with a stative predicate or predicates to produce the logical structure of an activity verb in a way that can be used as the basis of the proper model-theoretic interpretation for those verbs. Thus it is not clear that any further linguistic generalization would be revealed by pursuit of such truth-definitions.

Here for the first time we have arrived at a reasonably clear model-theoretic characterization of a "natural linguistic class" of verbs that explains just why this class behaves as it does, yet I am unable to supply an "atomic predicate" or other variety of semantic component (much less a syntagmatically justified one) that can play a key role in interpreting this class of predicates.[13] Assuming I have not just overlooked the right analysis, one can only say in this particular case "so much for the usefulness of structuralist analysis in model-theoretic semantics", but it is also only fair to point out that we would probably have never reached this stage of understanding of this class of verbs without the prior work of numerous structural semanticists of the GS variety as well as from other schools of linguistics.

A difficulty that arises with the view of activities developed here is that the often-cited characteristic entailment from "*x* is V-ing" to "*x* has V-ed" is not validated. That is, PROGϕ (where ϕ is an activity sentence) can be true at a time *t* even though PASTϕ is false, because *t* might fall within the very first "minimal" subinterval of which ϕ is true, hence, there would be no past interval of ϕ's truth. Taylor notes this problem (which arises in exactly the same way in his treatment of activities) but points out, quite correctly I believe, that "there is no cause for undue concern, provided the natural assumption be made that the minimal periods of chuckling within a piece of normal-rate chuckling are the least times of chuckling so discernible by normal empirical criteria. For them it will at least remain true that no speaker will be in a position *warrantably to assert* that *x* is chuckling until, some minimal period of chuckling having passed and been recognized, it is true that *x* has chuckled; so although on the present view it must be denied that there is a genuine entailment from '*x* is V-ing' to '*x* has V-ed' for heterogeneous E-verbs [activities], at least it is clear why it should have seemed plausible for theorists to have held that there is" (Taylor, 1977, p. 214). (Contrast the epistemic position of the utterer of an activity sentence in the progressive with that of the utterer of an imperfective accomplishment discussed above, such as *John is washing the car* or *The lamp is falling to the floor.*)

Thus the more closely we have examined the accomplishment/achievement vs. activity distinction, the more ephemeral it has become, though hopefully it is clear that it has not vanished altogether. Whereas we can distinguish homogeneous activities from the class containing non-homogeneous activities and accomplishments (e.g. by Taylor's (57)), there seems to be a sense in which non-homogeneous activities are always defined in terms of more primitive accomplishments/achievements. There may or may not be a verb of English corresponding to this more primitive accomplishment (or series of them), of course. The definition of *walk* (an activity) would, should we desire to spell it out, seem to involve the accomplishment of "taking a step". But apparently because there is an English expression *take a step*, we do not normally refer to instances of taking a single step as "walking", but rather reserve this activity verb for instances of taking two or more steps. On the other hand, the verb *blink* seems to serve both as an activity (opening and closing ones eyes an indefinite number of times) as well as the primitive accomplishment in terms of which the activity is defined (closing and then reopening one's eyes exactly once). Yet there seem to be no expressions at all describing the minimal accomplishment which defines *chuckling* (Taylor's example) or *laughing*. But by speaking of an activity sense of a verb such as *blink*, we immediately risk involving ourselves in yet another problem, that of iterative aspect (e.g., the most likely reading of *John rode the bus to work for three years*), since iterative aspect, whatever its exact nature, is like activities and states in being "simultaneously" true of an interval and of subintervals and superintervals of that interval. I do not know how to tell whether *John blinked for ten minutes* is correctly analyzed as an activity sentence with a durative adverb, or rather an accomplishment sentence in "iterative aspect". As iterative aspect is one of the problems that I have had to exclude from this study for lack of space (but see the following section), this seems an appropriate point at which to end our discussion of the nature of the activity/non-activity distinction and turn to other matters.

3.8.2. *"Stative" Verbs in the Progressive Tense*

A class of sentences in the progressive tense that has not been mentioned up to this point is exemplified by (62a)–(62d):

(62) a. The socks are lying under the bed.
b. Your glass is sitting near the edge of the table.
c. The long box is standing on end.
d. One corner of the piano is resting on the bottom step.

These examples (and others that can be constructed with verbs like *sit, stand, lie, perch, sprawl,* etc.) are paradoxical in view of what has been said about the English progressive so far, since they involve neither agency (of the "volitional" sort) – they have inanimate subjects – nor is there any apparent movement or other definite or indefinite change of state entailed by these examples. In contrast to the inanimate "motion" examples discussed in the previous section, the "*do*-tests" (Ross, 1972a) do not give the same results as the progressive tests:

(62′) a. *What the socks did was lie under the bed.
b. *The glass is sitting near the edge, and the pitcher is doing so too.
c. *The box is standing on end, which I thought it might do.
d. *The piano did what the crate had done: rest on the bottom step.

And "pronominalization" of the progressive with *at it* (Ross, 1972b) – generally acceptable with agentive activities and somewhat marginal with non-agentive "motion" activities – is totally impossible with these examples:

(63) John was reading a book an hour ago and he's still at it.

(64) It was raining an hour ago and it's still at it.

(65) ?The engine was running an hour ago and it's still at it.

(66) *The socks were lying under the bed this morning and they're still at it if no one has picked them up.

Nevertheless, this kind of progressive is subject to a certain semantic restriction, as can be seen by comparing the progressive examples in (67a)–(67d) with those in (62):

(67) a. New Orleans lies at the mouth of the Mississippi River.
a′. ??New Orleans is lying at the mouth of the Mississippi River.
b. John's house sits at the top of a hill.
b′. ??John's house is sitting at the top of a hill.
c. The new building stands at the corner of First Avenue and Main Street.
c′. ??The new building is standing at the corner of First Avenue and Main Street.
d. That argument rests on an invalid assumption.
d′. ??That argument is resting on an invalid assumption.

Consideration of many such examples leads to the conclusion that the progressive is acceptable with these verbs just to the degree that the subject denotes a moveable object, or to be more exact, an object that has recently moved, might be expected to move in the near future, or might possibly have moved in a slightly different situation. Thus the acceptability of the progressive can depend on the context as well as the subject and verb; compare (68a), which is strange in isolation, with (68b):

(68) a. ??Two trees were standing in the field.
b. After the forest fire, only two trees were still standing.

In a narrative context, progressives of these verbs can be used in describing stationary objects that momentarily come into the observer's view:

(69) When you enter the gate to the park there will be a statue standing on your right, and a small pond will be lying directly in front of you.

Perhaps the explanation of examples like (69) is that the position of the moving observer is somehow taken as the "fixed" point of orientation of the narrative, the locations of the stationary objects thus being "temporary" with respect to this moving point of orientation.

When motion verbs such as *flow, run* and *enter* are used as locatives (i.e., as entailing no literal motion at all), they are likewise excluded from the progressive when they describe a relatively permanent state (cf. Binnick, 1968):

(70) a. The river flows through the center of town.
b. (?)The river is flowing through the center of town.

(71) a. The highway runs past the farm.
b. (?)The highway is running past the farm.

Whereas (70a) is a natural description of a fact of geography, (70b) can only describe a flood in progress, and (71b) can only describe a highway planned or under construction (i.e. it is understood as a futurate progressive), not an existing highway.

This class of examples apparently presents a problem for Taylor's explanation of why stative verbs do not occur in the present tense (i.e., that statives are true at moments and non-statives are only true at intervals, whereas the function of the progressive is to indicate that a certain moment falls within an interval at which the verb is true, though the verb is not true of that moment itself). There is no obvious reason why these particular verbs should not give sentences true at a single moment, since no movement is involved. I can think of three possible explanations of this discrepancy.

First, it might be significant that (as G. A. Miller pointed out to me) all the verbs of this class (*sit, stand, lie,* etc.) are primarily used to denote positions of the human body (or at least of animal bodies in general, cf. *perch*). Now in at least some cases, namely "volitional" adjectives and predicate nominals such as *be polite, be a hero,* the progressive seems to signal only intentionality, not necessarily movement (as noted in 2.3.9, p. 118). Thus it is possible that the correct statement of the semantic distribution of the progressive is disjunctive – that is, it would be appropriate if *either* volitional control *or* (definite or indefinite) change were entailed by the verb. When predicated of humans, verbs such as *sit, stand,* etc. are typically volitionally controlled. Thus it may be that in their "primary" use with animate subjects, the progressive was "triggered" by intentionality and that their use with inanimate subjects is in some way a metaphorical derivative of this primary use, the occurrence with the progressive in such cases being an "accidental" carry-over from the basic use. That is, these progressives might be an exceptional fact about English grammar that has only a historical explanation.

Another possibility is that Taylor's idea about the distribution of the progressive is really correct and applies to these cases as well as all others. Despite the fact that these verbs entail no change, it could be argued that their truth conditions necessarily involve an interval anyway. Consider again the information that can be gleaned from a single frame of a motion picture film. A frame showing a book on the surface of a table does not really tell us whether the book is remaining stationary on that table or is sliding across the table, possibly on its way to sliding off onto the floor. Yet it may be that *The book is lying on the table* is only true if the book remains stationary for at least a short period, and a similar observation may hold for the other verbs *sit, stand,* etc. In support of this claim, suppose that a book is being slid across a series of carefully juxtaposed tables of absolutely equal height. If I am standing in front of one of these tables in the middle of the series, it seems that I can truthfully utter *The book is on this table* at any time that the book is wholly over the surface of the table in question (assuming, perhaps contrary to the fact, that I can utter the sentence very, very quickly!). But if my intuitions serve me correctly, I cannot truthfully say *The book is lying* (*sitting,* etc.) *on this table* at any time at all as long as the book is in motion. If this distinction is a real one (and the judgment is admittedly subtle), then the truth conditions for these verbs do require that the object of which they are predicated remain stationary in over-all position[14] for more than one moment, hence they could plausibly be supposed to be true only at intervals, not moments.

An especially intriguing explanation of the lack of progressives with statives is suggested by Carlson (1977, section 5.2.4.4). He notices that the classic examples of statives (e.g. *know, love, like, believe, hate,* etc.) all turn out to be predicates over *objects*, not predicates over *stages* (cf. discussion of this distinction in 2.3.4). (If Carlson's theory about the intimate connection between "universal" readings of bare plurals and "habitual" (or iterative) readings with definite noun phrases is correct, then the fact that statives are not basically stage-level predicates is shown on the one hand by the fact that *John liked radishes* does not have the single event/multiple event ambiguity that *John ate radishes* has, and on the other hand by the fact that *Dinosaurs liked kelp* does not have the universal/existential ambiguity in the interpretation of *dinosaurs* that *Dinosaurs ate kelp* has.) Since Carlson needs to treat object-level and kind-level predicates as a distinct syntactic category from stage-level predicates anyway, he opts for blocking the progressive from occurring with statives by syntactically restricting the progressive to the stage-level predicate category.

If Carlson's supposition is correct, the fact that we can say *The book is lying on the table* means *lie* is a stage-level predicate. This seems plausible enough, since locative predicates always turn out to be stage-level predicates in his analysis. But then how do we explain the fact that verbs of the *sit-stand-lie* class occur both in the simple and in progressive tenses with the only apparent semantic difference having to do with temporary vs. permanent states? I believe that Carlson's theory leads to an explanation of this fact as well. Carlson explains the "habitual" reading of examples like *John eats radishes* by postulating an abstract operator (actually a non-logical constant) that converts a stage-level predicate into an object-level predicate. He describes the workings of this operator, called G, as follows (1977, pp. 274-275):

The basic intuition behind G is this. If someone makes the claim that Bill smokes cigarettes, that person in some not clearly understood way is saying something about what Bill does on given occasions, what sort of activity Bill-stages participate in. It is clear that Bill-stages actually smoking serve as the basis for such a statement, and that the truth or falsity of the statement is verified in the end only by examination of Bill-stages. Bill in the act of smoking serves as evidence for the knowledge that Bill smokes. It is as if the human mind reasons in the following sort of way. Let us take ϕ as a predicate that applies to stages, and small letters from the middle of the alphabet represent stages. If $\phi(n)$, $\phi(m)$, $\phi(l)$, . . . , $\phi(r)$ is true for enough times, and $n, m, l, \ldots, r$ are stages of b, then we consider $G(\hat{}\phi)(b)$ to hold. Let us call this process 'generalization', thus the choice of G for the means of representing this predicate. This is a cognitive process, and will not be entirely represented in the grammar. In particular, there is no mention made of a necessary and sufficient number of times for some stage-level predicate ϕ to hold of stages to say $G(\hat{}\phi)(x)$.

What I am suggesting is that examples like *New Orleans lies at the mouth of the Mississippi River* involve an object-level predicate *lie* derived from the stage-level predicate *lie* (which is found in *The book is lying on the table*) by means of Carlson's operator G. In other words, the simple-present sentence about New Orleans is true if we have found a "suitable" number of instances of New-Orleans-stages in the appropriate location. Since a "suitable number" depends on pragmatic knowledge (and Carlson argues that the number varies from case to case), it seems natural for normally stationary objects like cities to require a larger number of such instances – no doubt *all* (relatively recent) past instances – than the number needed to make *John lies on the couch* true, given that John is not a stationary object.[15] But now why should the sentence ??*New Orleans is lying at the mouth of the Mississippi River* be so strange? It certainly ought to be true enough. But given that the means for expressing the object-level generalized predication as well as the stage-level predication exists in the language, and given that the object-level statement in effect pragmatically "entails" that the stage-level sentence is also true in this case (because of the assumption that cities are stationary), the object-level statement is stronger and is the more expected statement in the case of such stationary objects. By Grice's maxim of quantity, it seems that the weaker stage-level statement ought to be used by a speaker only if the stronger statement is known to be false or at least not comfortably assumed to be true. And in fact this is just what the progressive sentence seems to convey.

One troubling question which Carlson's claims about the progressive pose is just why progressives should be restricted to stage-level predicates, for there is no obvious explanation for this restriction that arises directly from his analysis.[16] But this leads us to observe that Taylor's explanation of why the progressive does not occur with statives is really only incompatible with Carlson's account in minor details, if at all. Possibly by attempting to combine Taylor's view with the account of the progressive/non-progressive use of the *sit-stand-lie* class that I have derived from Carlson's analysis, we can arrive at an explanation of the situation that is stronger than either in isolation. As was pointed out at the end of the previous chapter (section 2.4), Carlson's stage-level predicates all seem to have truth conditions that are dependent on the state of the world at the current moment (or at the "current" interval) in a relatively straightforward way. We have found in this chapter what I believe are good reasons for believing that not only activities and definite change-of-state verbs but also the *sit-stand-lie* class should depend on an interval, rather than a moment. And given Taylor's view of the function of the progressive, it is clear why the progressive should be needed for using all these verbs in the present tense (though it is not necessary for the past or future tenses). (By the way, this leaves only non-verbal copular predicates like *be on the table, be awake* as the only stage-predicates that can be literally true at a moment.) Generic (or "habitual") predicates are, on Carlson's view of them, quite a different matter. Even when we predicate them of an individual at a particular time, it is really not a property that individual's current stage has at that moment that makes them true, but our "total experience" with previous stages of that individual, cf. Carlson's discussion of *John smokes*. But note that classic stative predicates like *know* and *love* are like this as well. Though these are not derived from stage-level predicates of the language as are "habitual" predicates, it is here again our total experience with prior stages of an individual that somehow makes them true. *John knows French* is made true not by John's doing anything at that moment, but by past occasions of John-stages having stage-properties of speaking French, and *John loves Mary* is somehow or other made true by past (and presumably future) instances of John-stages bearing certain relations to Mary-stages. To the extent that an interval of time could be said to be "the" interval of their truth, it would seem to be (in most cases) only a large and vaguely defined interval including a vague number of past instances of the truth of certain stage-predicates, and presumably including a vague number of future instances of certain stage-predicates. (An exception would be the corresponding inchoative predicates such as *discover, realize,* and *forget*, which serve to mark the transition to such an interval.) Therefore it seems not surprising that our language should treat them as true of an individual (as opposed to its stages) at any moment within this vague interval, rather than make us somehow try to indicate the large interval we have in mind. As Quine might say, both habituals and statives like *know* and *love* express "dispositions". The usefulness of such predicates as *know, like, believe, intelligent, soluble, fragile* (as pointed out in the case of the last two by Quine (1960, pp. 222 ff.)) in language is that they indicate a *potential* for having stage-properties of a certain kind at some future or hypothetical time. And this potential exists at any one moment during the whole interval of their truth as much as at any other moment. The intervals at which stage predicates are true, by contrast, are shorter, have distinct boundaries, and may have truth conditions that differentiate among parts of the interval, so it is perhaps not surprising that our language has a means for locating the present (or some past or future event) at a time within such an interval for stage-predicates but not for object-predicates. Of course it is not *necessary* for a natural language to indicate containment-within-an-interval in just this way; many, maybe most natural languages get by without a progressive tense at all, and no other language besides English that I know of uses its progressive in exactly the way that English does.

In summary, I suggest we distinguish among three classes of statives: *interval statives* (the *sit-stand-lie* class, which are stage predicates), *momentary stage-predicates* (e.g. *be on the table, be asleep*), and *object-level statives* (e.g. *know, like, be intelligent,* etc). The last two classes can be true at moments and are true at an interval if and only if they are true at all moments within that interval (i.e., they obey Taylor's postulate (54)). Unlike Carlson, I do not (yet) want to restrict the progressive to stage-level predicates syntactically, because inchoatives of object-level predicates can occur with the progressive under the right circumstances (e.g. *John is discovering all the clues, John is gradually realizing that you are right, John is forgetting everything he has learned*), and I suspect these are best treated as object-level predicates too; it seems unnatural to suppose that BECOME converts an object-level predicate into a stage-level predicate, though it can clearly convert a momentary predicate into an interval predicate. (In the fragment in Chapter 7 I do not distinguish between syntactic categories of stage-level and object-level predicates as Carlson does.) But I am not sure either that we need to make it a semantic entailment from the truth of PROGϕ at t to the falsity of ϕ at t (as Taylor does, cf. p. 202); perhaps it is merely conversationally inappropriate to use PROGϕ at t when ϕ itself is true at t, or perhaps it is a conventional implicature of PROGϕ at t that ϕ should not be true at t; in either case we have a reason why the progressive should not be used with momentary statives, object-level statives and generics.

3.8.3. *A Revised Verb Classification*

In Chapter 2 we distinguished accomplishments from achievements, following Vendler, by the fact that achievements did not occur happily with the progressive or with durative time adverbials (cf. the strangeness of ??*John noticed the painting for a few minutes,* ??*John is realizing that he forgot to lock the door*) and by the fact that *finish* is anomalous with achievements (cf. ??*John finished finding a penny*) as well as by the fact that achievements did not occur in agentive contexts (?*John persuaded Bill to notice that yesterday was Tuesday*). But we observed at the beginning of this chapter that at least some achievements do occur in the progressive in at least some circumstances (*John is dying, John is falling asleep*). Now that we have developed an interval semantics and an interval analysis of the progressive, we can see that Vendler's accomplishment/achievement distinction should be reanalyzed as four separate distinctions which often, but not always, intersect in his two classes.

First, there is the distinction between change-of-state verbs that normally happen at a nearly minimal interval (i.e. containing the two moments mentioned in the BECOME condition) (e.g. *reach the finish line, remember a person's name* (inchoative reading), *notice a misprint*) and those that occur over a large interval (e.g. *walk from the post-office to the bank*). This is not a completely clear-cut distinction. What may be a relatively instantaneous change in most cases may be viewed as having duration in other cases (e.g. *dying*). Sentences with *take x time to do y* obscure this difference, since *It took John an hour to close the door* normally does not mean that the act of closing the door lasted this long, but more likely that what took an hour was deciding or remembering to act, the actual act of closing the door happening only at the very end of this hour. Thus in *It took John an hour to fall alseep*, it is not clear whether the transition from wakefulness to sleep is being viewed as happening gradually over the hour, over some final subinterval or the hour, or at the very last moment.

Closely related to this distinction is the question whether a change-of-state can be considered to consist in two or more temporally consecutive subsidiary changes. This seems to be what determines whether *finish* occurs naturally with a predicate. That is, the oddness of ??*John finished finding a penny on the sidewalk* and ??*John finished recalling Bill's nickname* seems to lie in the fact that it is hard to imagine that finding a penny or recalling a person's nickname can happen in two distinct steps – hard, but perhaps not impossible. On the other hand, it is easy to imagine multiple temporally successive steps for building a house or eating a sandwich. The verb *finish* seems to indicate that the last of such a sequence of stages takes place at the time the *finish*-sentence is true. I believe that the semantics of *finish* can be rather accurately described in Montague's intensional logic by the meaning postulate (72):

(72) $$\bigwedge P \bigwedge x \Box [\mathbf{finish}'(P)(x) \leftrightarrow \bigvee Q_1 \bigvee Q_2 [\Box [P\{x\} \leftrightarrow [Q_1\{x\} \text{AND } Q_2\{x\}]] \wedge [Q_1 \neq Q_2 \wedge Q_2\{x\} \wedge \text{PAST} Q_1\{x\}]]]$$

Here, P, Q_1 and Q_2 are variables ranging over properties of individuals, AND is Cresswell's "interval" conjunction operator (i.e. $[\phi \text{ AND } \psi]$ is true at the smallest interval within which there are intervals where ϕ and ψ are true, respectively, cf. 3.3), and *finish* is a verb-phrase operator (of type $\langle\langle s, \langle e, t\rangle\rangle, \langle e, t\rangle\rangle$). Thus this asserts that x finishes doing P just in case there are two properties Q_1 and Q_2 which doing P is equivalent to and, moreover, x now does Q_2 and has already done Q_1. The use of Cresswell's AND is crucial here, for note that there are certain accomplishments which happen in successive steps on some occasions but all at once on others. For example, one can eat a cookie in two (or more) successive bites, or one can gulp it down all at once. Thus if P is the property of eating a certain cookie, Q_1 is the property of eating 2/3 of that cookie, and Q_2 is the property of eating the remaining 1/3 of that cookie, the logical equivalence of $P\{x\}$ with $[Q_1\{x\}\text{AND } Q_2\{x\}]$ is not jeopardized by situations in which x eats the whole cookie at one bite (possibly in an instant), because in these situations it can be maintained that $Q_1\{x\}$ and $Q_2\{x\}$ are both true, though true simultaneously; the operator AND indiscriminately allows its two conjuncts to be true at non-overlapping intervals, overlapping intervals or at the same interval. Of course, situations of this last sort are not situations in which *x finishes eating the cookie* are true, according to (72), thanks to the last part of the postulate. It is important to realize that in (72) it is not required that Q_1 and Q_2 be properties actually expressible in the language (though they often may be), and for any given property P, there may be an indefinitely large if not infinite number of pairs of properties that P may be "split" into in ways that satisfy this postulate. Also, note that Q_1 (or Q_2 for that matter) could be the "conjunctive" property of doing two or more actions that we think of as distinct steps in performing an accomplishment. Thus (72) does not have to be complicated to deal with the situation in which one finishes an accomplishment by performing the last of a number of "steps". A possible refinement of (72) would be to restrict P to agentive properties, at least for those speakers who find it odd to say ?*The building finished collapsing*, ?*The sun finished setting* (but note quasi-teleological cases like *the tomatoes finished ripening*). Perhaps this restriction would be sufficient to restrict *finish* from activities (e.g. *John finished walking*) except where the agent has in mind a specific duration or extent of activity in mind (hence the activity is a kind of accomplishment) or perhaps some further restriction is needed. In a theory in which conventional implicature is distinguished from assertion, the implicature of *finish* should include the "definability" of P in terms of Q_1 and Q_2 and also PAST $Q_1\{x\}$, while $Q_2\{x\}$ should be the assertion.

This distinction in "finishability" and the previous one do not give hard and fast categories into which we can split verbs once and for all, but rather depend highly on how we typically understand certain changes in the world to transpire and also how we understand that they can, in unusual circumstances, transpire differently. *The old man finally finished dying* may be an unusual and slightly inaccurate (not to mention irreverent) statement, but I think it is now clear why such things are occasionally said.

The third distinction underlying Vendler's accomplishment/achievement division is between agentive and non-agentive actions. While most of Vendler's examples of achievements were non-agentive (e.g. *die, lose, notice*), there are examples of relatively instantaneous (and typically non-finishable) verbs that can be deliberately brought about (e.g. *reach the finish line, arrive in Boston*), hence these are things which one can do deliberately, etc., can be persuaded or forced to do.

Fourth and closely related to the previous distinction is the distinction between verbs that entail that a subsidiary event or activity brought about the change (e.g. *build a house, shoot someone dead*) and those that do not (e.g. *reach the age of 21, awaken*). While most of the former class are agentive, not all of them are (cf. *the collision mashed the fender flat*), and there may be agentive verbs that do not entail a subsidiary causal activity (e.g. *open one's eyes*). This presence or absence of a causal event seemed to be the most salient distinction between the accomplishment and achievement class for Vendler (and is for me), so I will use *accomplishment verb (phrase)* from this point on to denote "definite interval" predicates which entail this subsidiary activity or event, and *achievement verb (phrase)* to refer to those that do not, irrespective of agency or multi-part change of state.

If we categorize verbs primarily by their temporal properties in an interval semantics and also by agency, we arrive at a classification like that in Table II. Here the cases comprising Vendler's accomplishment and achievement categories have been reorganized into the four categories 5, 6, 7 and 8; all these together might be referred to as *definite change of state predicates* or *non-subinterval predicates*. If *accomplishment* and *achievement* are used in the special sense introduced above (rather than Vendler's more loose use), then both accomplishments and achievements can be found in each of the four categories, whereas Vendler's examples of accomplishments were typically from 6, 7, 8, and his achievements mainly from 5.

The syntactic tests we have used at various times can now be seen to be indicative of five partially cross-classifying semantic distinctions, which are summarized below and correlated with the numbered regions of the chart they distinguish:

TABLE II

	Non-Agentive	Agentive
States	1a. *be asleep, be in the garden* (stage-level); *love, know* (object-level) 1b. interval statives: *sit, stand, lie*	2a. possibly *be polite, be a hero*, etc. belong here, or in 4. 2b. interval statives: *sit, stand, lie* (with human subject)
Activities	3. *make noise, roll, rain*	4. *walk, laugh, dance* (cf. 2a)
Single change of state	5. *notice, realize; ignite*	6. *kill, point out* (*something to someone*)
Complex change of state	7. *flow from x to y dissolve*	8. *build* (*a house*), *walk from x to y, walk a mile*

I. *Momentary* (1a and 'habituals" in all classes) vs. *interval* predicates (1b, 2b, 3–8). Syntactic test: ability to occur in the progressive. (Note: 6 and especially 5 appear less readily in the progressive than other interval predicates.)

II. Predicates entailing *definite or indefinite change* (3–8) vs. those entailing *no change* (1 and 2). Syntactic test: ability to occur in *do* constructions (pseudo-clefts, *do so* reduction, etc.).

III. *Definite change of state* predicates (5–8) vs. *activity* predicates or indefinite change of state predicates (3 and 4). Syntactic test: Does *x was V-ing* (pragmatically) entail *x has V-ed*?

IV. *Singulary change* predicates (5–6) vs. *complex change* predicates (7–8). Syntactic test: Is *x finished V-ing* acceptable?

V. *Agentive* (2, 4, 6, 8) vs. *non-agentive* (1, 3, 5, 7) predicates. Syntactic test: ability to occur in agentive contexts like imperatives, *persuade x to V, do V deliberately*, etc.

The reader will hardly need to be reminded at this point of the many ways in which this classification is "fuzzy". We have noted the syntactic means by which an activity verb can be converted to an accomplishment (addition of a "goal" prepositional phrase or extent phrase) and how an accomplishment can be converted into an activity (by the presence of a "bare plural"). We have just seen how the distinction between 5–6 and 7–8 is fuzzy, not because of syntax, but because of differing expectations about the way changes will happen over time. Similarly, the agentive/non-agentive distinction depends on one's imagination for the kinds of properties that are or could be under voluntary immediate control of a rational being, as well as one's imagination for what entities can be rational, acting beings. Thus not only is this not a categorization of verbs, it is not a categorization of sentences, but rather of the propositions conveyed by utterances, given particular background assumptions by speaker and/or hearer about the nature of the situations under discussion. Despite this "fuzziness", it is the way these distinctions are ensconced in the syntactic structure of the English language that gives them their interest and significance.

The only class I am still uncomfortable about is that consisting of agentive adjectives and predicate nominals (*be a hero, be polite*). It was noted that these at least sometimes denote no action at all, but a conscious abstinence from action, hence are like statives in at least these situations. Yet on the other hand they take the progressive and are fairly natural in *do*-constructions (*What I did then was be as polite as possible*). If we accordingly analyze these in terms of an abstract DO of agency which is *not* necessarily associated with any (indefinite) change of state, then the distribution of the *do*-constructions (and possibly that of the progressive as well) must be stated disjunctively: it is (or they are) appropriate if *either* the verb entails a change *or* is agentive (i.e. controllable). But if it could be argued that the meaning of the agentive *be* here (whether we call it DO or ACT or something else) entails indefinite change as well as controllability, then it would follow from principles I and II as already stated that this class occurs in *do*-constructions and in the progressive. To maintain this position we would have to argue that *John is being a hero by standing still and refusing to budge* entails that some invisible events or other are nevertheless going on, such as John's repeatedly deciding not to run away just yet. Perhaps this is right, and the simplicity of the correlations in I and II that results from this position is certainly appealing, but one would like further evidence to decide such a question. Note, finally, that if we adopt the second position just outlined, then the syntactic evidence for an abstract DO in a GS theory is weakened almost to vacuity, since we have made the distribution of surface *do*-constructions dependent on change entailments, not agency (cf. note 11), and we saw that it did not seem possible to create an operator DO which would compositonally produce a class of predicates with the desired indefinite change entailments from more basic predicates.

3.8.4. *Accomplishments with Event-Objects*

Aside from the question of distinguishing activities from other classes by a DO operator, can we now maintain that it is really true that all other state-change entailments of the classes 5–8 are expressible with an interval semantics by formulas involving the CAUSE[17] and BECOME operators? As previous discussion and especially the next chapter should indicate, this can be done in a fairly straightforward way for a very large subset of the predicates in 5–8, since the changes brought about are one or two in number and are usually states describable either by expressions found independently in English or by simple model-theoretic definitions. For all these cases it really seems to be true, as Kenny maintained, that "performances are specified by their ends" (Kenny, 1963, p. 178). Note that this is the case even for complex accomplishments like *build a house*, since *A house exists* is a reasonable test of the completion of the accomplishment. (Though *John has built a house* is of course vague as to just what *degree* of completion has been achieved, *A house exists* is vague in exactly the same way.)

An exception to this claim is the class I called (in section 2.2.7) *creation of a performance object*, exemplified by *produce a play, perform a sonata, listen to a symphony* and *read a book*, which clearly belong to categories 7 and 8 by the aspectual tests. Yet what result-state defines the completion of these accomplishments and achievements? It is of course true that the state of having reached the end of the performance of a sonata does in a sense define the successful completion of *perform a sonata*, but this is hardly enlightening as an analysis of this accomplishment (in the same way as I believe it is enlightening to point out that the coming into existence of a letter is a crucial part of the truth conditions of *write a letter*). The performance of a musical composition (or the complete hearing of one) can of course be said to consist in a particular temporal succession of the beginnings and endings of certain musical notes, and such a succession could no doubt be described by complex formulas involving stative predicates, BECOME, a temporal succession operator like von Wright's AND NEXT, and perhaps a means for indicating measurement of temporal intervals. Plays, lectures, academic courses of instruction and the reading of books seems likewise amenable in principle to analysis in terms of successions of simple states and/or activities. But formulas expressing such successions would be exceedingly long. Even as simple a melody as "Twinkle, twinkle little star" has (in the version I am acquainted with) fifty-six notes, and symphonies and plays have a much higher number of notes to be performed and lines to be spoken, respectively. Now many generative semanticists might not balk at all at analyzing *John whistled "Twinkle, twinkle little star"* as derived from a logical structure involving more than fifty-six atomic sentences, but while one may not be able to object in principle to such a program of analysis as this, it seems reasonable to say that a theory with such logic-to-surface derivations would have little practical testability. While I have very little to suggest about this class of cases, it might nevertheless be important to point out that these cases are always or almost always overtly characterized by the fact that they have a direct object (or subject, in the case of some achievements) that names an abstract event (e.g. *play, sonata, lecture*), rather than the concrete object that appears in all accomplishments that are amenable to "result-state" analysis (e.g. in *build a house, open a door, paint a room*). An exception may be *a book* in *read a book*, but even here the concrete object that is a book is intimately connected with a particular abstract event (the successive understanding of a sequence of sentences) in a way that distinguishes this case from, e.g. *build a house*. Perhaps it can even be argued that *a book* in *read a book* should be analyzed as denoting an abstract object ("sequence of codified hypothetical utterances" or the like), rather than the concrete object it denotes in *put a book on the table*. All this is to suggest that these exceptional cases which are problems for the result-state analysis may form a natural class that is best analyzed in a quite different method, perhaps in terms of an abstract predicate of events, such as TRANSPIRE or OCCUR (so that *John performs a sonata* might be usefully treated as having the logical form [[*John acts*] CAUSE TRANSPIRE(*a sonata*)]. But this possibility will have to remain a mere speculation here.

NOTES

[1] This innovation was independently made by Barry Taylor (1977) with essentially the same motivation; his work is discussed below. See M. Bennett (to appear) for a revision of his and Partee's ideas.

[2] In an earlier version of this analysis (Dowty, 1977) I formulated this condition in a slightly different way: BECOME ϕ was to be true at an interval I iff $\neg\phi$ was true at an interval *immediately preceding I* and ϕ was true at an interval *immediately following I.*

In other words, the moments at which $\neg\phi$ and ϕ were true were formerly placed "just outside" the upper and lower boundaries of *I* respectively, while now I have placed them "just inside" these boundaries. The differences in the two formulations are for most purposes inconsequential. The former version allowed me a slight simplification in the truth definition for PROGϕ, but the revision allows me to make an important generalization later about the semantics of activities and accomplishments/achievements as a single class.

[3] However, James McCawley has pointed out to me that the Japanese conjunction *to* has a use that is very much like von Wright's T.

[4] Actually, Bennett and Partee (though not Taylor) allow PROGϕ to be true at *I* only when *I* is a moment, but I think this is probably a mistake because of the existence of examples like *John was wearing sunglasses when I had lunch with him*. It will turn out that sentences in the *present* progressive are normally required to be true at a moment, however, because I require for independent reasons (cf. 3.8.2) that the "moment of utterance" for normal conversational purposes must be a moment, not a larger inverval.

[5] I believe that Scheffer's putative counterexamples to the time-frame theory (Scheffer, 1975, pp. 74-75) arise from a failure to distinguish a habitual or "iterative" reading (what Carlson (1977) calls a "generic reading"; see 3.8.2 below) from a non-habital reading; habitual readings occur with progressive as well as non-progressive sentences.

[6] The futurate progressive (*John is leaving town tomorrow*) must not be confused, on the other hand, with the more familiar *future progressive* (*John will be leaving town tomorrow*). The latter construction is the perfectly predictable combination of a future tense (with future time adverb) and a sentence in the imperfective progressive.

[7] Since I fear it may be objected that Prince's example could involve merely a lexical ambiguity in *go to Radcliffe*, I will supply an ambiguous example of my own which does not have this problem:

(i) Rob was working on the research project until he got the job offer from U. of M.

The futurate progressive reading, which conversationally implicates that Rob will not and perhaps never did work on the project, would be a reply to the question "What is Rob planning to do next fall?" The imperfective progressive reading, which entails that he did work on the project and implicates that he no longer does, would be an answer to the question "What was Rob doing last year?"

[8] It is natural to ask whether part of this condition should be relegated to conventional implicature. A sentence like *It's possible that John leaves tomorrow* does seem to me to commit the speaker to the view that the question whether John will leave and when is subject to some already arranged plan or schedule. However, it doesn't implicate that John definitely *will* leave (at some time or other), since the plan might require that John not leave at all. Note that it will not do to test for implicature with an *if*-clause here, since *will* is routinely absent from *if*-clauses involving future time; hence what I am calling the tenseless future construction cannot be syntactically distinguished in an *if*-clause from a statement about future time that neither entails nor implicates anything at all about planning. As noted by Partee (1964), the use of *will* in an *if*-clause seems to be largely restricted to the 'willing-to' sense of *will*: cf. *If John meets Bill at the party tomorrow*... vs. *If John will meet Bill at the party tomorrow*... and also **If the telephone will ring tomorrow*... (but see Wekker (1976, pp. 70-73) for some counterexamples to this

principle). Wekker's example (35) also can be taken to indicate an implicature, since direct and indirect questions allow implicatures to "filter through".

[9] The "+" in this formula is meant to indicate informally that this normal combination of time adverbial and tense (i.e., past adverb with past tense and future adverb with future tense, but not the tenseless future adverb) is not the compositional combination of two tense operators, one within the scope of the other, but is the syncategorematic use of tense and time adverb together as if they were a single operator; this construction is treated in detail in 7.1 and 7.2.

[10] Taylor's reply to this problem appears in his footnote 9 (p. 210). In an example like *John was crossing the Atlantic in a balloon at time* t *when a storm arose and forced him to turn back*, his position is to deny that John was really crossing the Atlantic at *t* (since *t* did not fall within a period *of* his crossing the Atlantic); rather according to Taylor, he was merely doing something at *t* that *would have been* crossing the Atlantic had the storm not come up. I am not sure how Taylor means this, but I believe we must construe him as saying either (1) examples like this one, which appear frequently in ordinary conversation, are always false when we regard them as true, in spite of the fact that people communicate successfully with them, (2) though false, we take them as a kind of figure of speech, (3) there is a syntactic rule which deletes a subjunctive conditional connective and turns the sentence into a progressive-and-*when*-clause structure under mysterious circumstances, or (4) the semantics of *when*-clauses works in mysterious ways to block entailments in certain cases that go through in all other cases. None of these positions seems tenable as a linguistic analysis of English to me, given the fact that cases where the entailment goes through and cases where it doesn't are syntactically indistinguishable and semantically "the same" construction according to intuitions of native speakers. Moreover, Taylor's subjunctive paraphrase seems far from a correct rendering of the meaning of the progressive to me. Finally, Taylor owes us an analysis of the subjunctive conditional, which is a serious difficulty within the extensionalist framework he advocates. There are obvious parallels between Lewis' (1973) analysis of counterfactuals (though Taylor wouldn't accept this presumably) and my analysis of the progressive, but there are also clear and important differences in detail, and these differences suggest that it would be of dubious value to try to *derive* the progressive construction syntactically from a counterfactual construction. Though I can't accept Taylor's paraphrase of the progressive, I think the analysis I have given makes it clear why a counterfactual comes *close* to paraphrasing the progressive in these cases.

[11] Taylor (1977, p. 208) also requires, in his version of this postulate, that the interval *I* of which an activity verb ("E-verb") is true be an *open-fronted* interval (i.e. a *bounded* interval, as defined on p. 140). The motivation for this is said to go back to Aristotle, but it still seems dubious to me. (See also Bennett (to appear) for a theory exploiting the bounded/closed distinction.) Also, Taylor later refines his view of activities to take account of *heterogeneous activities*, as discussed below.

[12] As pointed out at the beginning of this chapter, special contexts such as sports announcers' jargon, stage directions and the historical present are exceptional in that they allow the simple present to have non-habitual readings with non-statives. Thus the requirement that the time of utterance be a moment must be relaxed for these situations. Perhaps the right way to view these situations, as has often been suggested, is that they somehow view time as "compressed", in that the distinction between moments and

intervals larger than a moment is obscured (in this one respect), as contrasted with "real time" descriptions of actions.

Susan Schmerling has pointed out to me that in order to make this account of simple versus progressive tense choice complete, one ought to explain from this point of view why performative sentences require the simple present rather than the present progressive. This is apparently a problem for my account, because performatives clearly aren't statives; this is apparent from their semantics and is confirmed by the fact that when we describe the present performance of a speech act by another person, the progressive is required – e.g., *He is pronouncing them man and wife* but not (except in sports announcer or stage direction register) *He pronounces them man and wife*. Though my intuitions are that the performance of a speech act is in some obscure sense a "momentary" occurrence in spite of the time it takes to utter the requisite sentence (perhaps the relevant moment is the final moment of the utterance and/or the first moment the audience can have comprehended the utterance), I am unable to explain why this should be so. If I am wrong, then note in any case that the substitution of the progressive for the present in a performative (e.g. *I am pronouncing you man and wife*) does seem to suggest that the performance of the act in question is somehow of longer duration than the utterance of this one sentence itself (as would be in accord with the semantics of PROG if "speech time" equals sentence-utterance time), and this is perhaps why such a sentence suggests that the pronouncement of marriage is being accomplished by some means other than by the utterance of this sentence alone. It may be, then, that simply because of this inappropriateness of the present progressive, the simple present by default becomes the appropriate form for a performative sentence, in spite of this violation of the prohibition against "speech times" longer than a moment that otherwise obtains in normal register.

[13] If this view of activities is correct, then we cannot explain the distribution of *do* in Ross' *do*-constructions by appeal to an underlying DO. Though this presents a dilemma for the GS theory, I do not believe it does for the "Upside-Down generative semantics" theory. In such a theory it is probably best to treat **do so**$_n$ as a variable over properties of individuals (analogous to Montague's **he**$_n$, but of different type) for independent reasons involving the so-called "sloppy identity" problem (cf. Klein, ms.: Edmundson, 1976). A sentence like **John left and Mary did so too** would then be derived by quantifying with **leave** over **John did so**$_3$ **and Mary did so**$_3$ **too.** It could then be made an entailment (or more accurately, a conventional implicature) of the pro-form **do so**$_n$ that the predicate filling in its value has the appropriate semantic property or properties. As I point out below, the notion of "definite or indefinite change" may turn out to characterize *exactly* those predicates that accept *do so*, regardless of whether agency is also a necessary concomitant or not. If so, then the implicature for **do so** verbs might be described by (perhaps among other methods) the method of using a higher-order property **action**′, where this property is restricted by roughly the following meaning postulate:

$$\wedge P\Box[\mathbf{action}'(P) \leftrightarrow \vee Q \wedge x \wedge t \Box[\mathrm{AT}(t, P\{x\}) \rightarrow \vee t_1 \vee t_2 [t_1 \subseteq t \wedge t_2 \subseteq t \wedge \mathrm{AT}(t_1, Q\{x\}) \wedge \mathrm{AT}(t_2, \neg Q\{x\})]]]$$

To avoid vacuity, the value of Q in this postulate must be restricted somehow to *physically definable* property, in the sense explained earlier in 2.4. Though such a postulate is not a *sufficient* condition to capture our intuitive notion of *activity*, for the reasons just pointed out, it is nonetheless a *necessary* condition for activities and also turns out to characterize accomplishments and achievements defined in terms of BECOME, thus it correctly distinguishes predicates that occur with **do so** from those that don't.

[14] I say "overall position" to exclude movement of sub-parts of the individual which do not affect its overall location. Thus *John is sitting* may be true even though he is moving his arms about, and *The clock is sitting on the shelf* may be true even if it is ticking and moving its gears.

[15] If it is correct that *New Orleans lies at the mouth of the Mississippi river* is derived with Carlson's G, then there are further problems that need to be explained. Carlson has pointed out to me that this hypothesis requires us to explain (1) why there is apparently no "opaque" reading in such cases (cf. Carlson (1977, section 2.2.1) for explanation of this sense of "opacity") and (2) why only the "existential" readings of indefinite plurals and the determiner *a*(*n*) appear in, e.g. *Small cities lie along the bank of the Thames* and *A large city lies at the base of Mt. Adams*. One would hope that these facts could somehow be explained in terms of special features of the semantics of locative verbs that distinguish them from other cases where G appears, but I do not feel aware enough of all the implications of Carlson's hypotheses to speculate on such possibilities. Cf. section 7.4 of Carlson (1977) for discussion of problems related to this.

[16] Carlson gives a discussion on pp. 424–432 which largely duplicates my explanation that follows, but differs in various details. For example, he thinks (though I do not) that *all* stage predicates are true only of intervals larger than a moment, and he speculates that this is because stages, though not necessarily events, somehow "occupy" stretches of time. In contrast, I would suppose that the truth conditions of all stage predicates ultimately amount to conditions on stages at one or more moment, yet events "take" time because of their temporally complex truth conditions.

[17] I have so far said nothing about the way the truth conditions for [ϕ CAUSE ψ] depend on the intervals at which ϕ and ψ are true respectively (among the other conditions for causation). This is a complex problem (cf. Thomson, 1971; Cresswell ms.). The likely possibilities are (1) [ϕ CAUSE ψ] is true (among other conditions) at the interval at which ϕ is true, (2) [ϕ CAUSE ψ] is true (among other conditions) at the smallest interval containing the intervals at which ϕ and ψ are true, (3) [ϕ CAUSE ψ] is true at the interval at which ψ is true (among other conditions). Note first of all that examples in which ϕ and ψ each have explicit definite time specifications will not tell us anything, since these are then "eternally true sentences" and allow [ϕ CAUSE ψ] to be true no matter how we state its temporal conditions. Thus examples like *John left on Thursday because Mary arrived on Friday* are of no help for this problem. Thus we must apparently decide the matter simply by consulting our intuitions about sentences in which causal activity and coming-about of result are easily imagined as happening over different intervals, even though no separate adverbs indicate these two events. (So examples like *John built a house* are also not useful to choose among these three possibilities, because while the building activity may last a long time, the coming-into-existence of a house overlaps with this almost exactly.) Unfortunately, this test does not give clear results. Consider case I: Terrorists plant a bomb in a car on Saturday and the bomb explodes the next day, destroying the car. When is the sentence *The terrorists destroy the car* true? (Imagine this as a historical present sentence.) My intuitions favor the time of the explosion (i.e. solution (3)), though I can't definitely rule out the interval from the planting of the bomb up through the time of explosion (solution (2)). But consider

case II: Kidnappers call John on Sunday and demand that he withdraw $10,000 ransom from the bank on Monday, else his kidnapped daughter will be harmed. On Monday he does this. So it is true that *The kidnappers force John to withdraw money from the bank*, but when is it true? Here I am inclined to the time of the phone call (solution (1)), but perhaps again the whole stretch from the phone call to the withdrawal of money could instead be correct. All in all, it seems that (2) is the best compromise solution for these and also even more clearly for all of the various examples discussed by Thomson (1971) (though this is not her position), though clearly more study is needed. Note also the phenomenon, discussed at the beginning of 3.7, of "extending" the time of an accomplishment to include preparations for the accomplishment proper. Cresswell's (ms.) discussion is clouded, in my view, by the fact that he uses as his prime example *x sends y to z* but does not observe that this example is not an accomplishment at all parallel to *x takes y to z* (in the sense that arrival of *y* at *z* is the result) and thus also not parallel to *x kills y*. That is, *John sent the package to Boston but it never arrived there* is not at all contradictory, but both *John took the package to Boston but the package never came to be in Boston*, or *John killed Bill but Bill never died* are obviously contradictions. Clearly, *send* has to be analyzed along the lines of "do something intended to cause *y* to come to be at *z*"; it *is* an accomplishment, but the result-stage is merely "*y* is in a situation intended to eventually result in *y*'s coming to *z*". The fact that Cresswell opts for what would appear to be solution (1) here is not surprising but also probably not generalizable to $[\phi \text{ CAUSE } \psi]$. (There are of course some situations in which we do infer *y arrives at z* from *x sends y to z*, but I believe this inference is conversational, not semantic, and is parallel to the conversational inference of *y did z* from *x persuaded y to do z*, or *x did y* from *x was able to do y*.)

CHAPTER 4

LEXICAL DECOMPOSITION IN MONTAGUE GRAMMAR

In this chapter we will see how the lexical decomposition analyses developed in the previous two chapters can be formulated within the UG framework according to the "upside-down generative semantics" theory sketched in Chapter 1. One of the general points that I hope this section will establish is that because "surface" English syntax is here taken as the starting point and because of the overall explicitness of the UG theory, it will be possible to explore details of English syntax and their interaction with decomposition analyses to a degree that seems to have rarely been approached in GS literature. Because accomplishment/achievement predicates exhibit the greatest variety of syntactic forms in English, attention will largely be restricted to these classes. Explicit comparison of the relative merits of the classical generative semantics method and the "upside down generative semantics" method will be the subject of the following chapter. But first, we will take a brief look at "lexical decomposition" as it already exists in PTQ.

Linguists, especially, should be very careful to note the differences between what I am calling "lexical decomposition" in PTQ and the various meanings which this term has had in certain linguistic theories (cf., e.g. Fodor, Fodor and Garrett (1975)).

4.1. EXISTING "LEXICAL DECOMPOSITION" IN THE PTQ FRAGMENT

In discussing the PTQ fragment in this chapter and in the remainder of the book, I will assume all the definitions and notations of PTQ exactly as Montague gave them, with one exception: following Bennett (1974), Thomason (1976), Dowty (1978c) and Wall, Peters and Dowty (to appear), I have simplified PTQ slightly in eliminating individual concepts in favor of individuals simpliciter as the members of the extensions of CN and IV. That is, the basic syntactic categories are t, CN and IV, and the recursive rule for other categories specifies that if A and B are categories, then so are A/B and A//B. The rule mapping categories of English into types of intensional logic is then the following: $f(\mathrm{t}) = t, f(\mathrm{CN}) = f(\mathrm{IV}) = \langle e, t\rangle$, and for all A, B, $f(\mathrm{A/B}) = f(\mathrm{A//B}) = \langle\langle s, f(\mathrm{B})\rangle, f(\mathrm{A})\rangle$. I use x, y and z as variables over individuals (not individual concepts), and translations otherwise look exactly like their counterparts in the original PTQ, expressions of type $\langle s, e\rangle$ being systematically replaced by expressions of type e. Thus the distinction between, e.g. **walk**$'(x)$ and **walk**$'_*(u)$ disappears, the former formula already being an extensional first-order formula. (The only purpose which individual concepts served in PTQ anyway was to treat the single example **The temperature is ninety and is rising**, and it now appears that Montague's solution to the problem presented by this example is problematic in various ways anyway (cf. Wall, Peters and Dowty (to appear)).) I also adopt henceforth Montague's convention of citing English examples generated by PTQ (or by the fragment developed in this book) in boldface type; the occasional English expressions cited hereafter that are of a form not produced by these fragments will be given in italic type.

The PTQ fragment contains a variety of instances of what can be termed "decomposition" of the meanings of words; these are carried out in different ways.

The words **be** and **necessarily** are given a complex translation by the function g, which assigns a translation to each basic expression of English, as are all proper names and the subscripted pronouns **he**$_n$ for each n. (These translations are modified slightly, as indicated above.)

(1) **be** translates into: $\lambda\mathscr{P}\lambda x\mathscr{P}\{\hat{y}[x = y]\}$
necessarily translates into: $\lambda p[\Box{}^{\vee}p]$
John, **Mary**, etc., translate into:[1] $\lambda P[P\{j\}]$, $\lambda P[P\{m\}]$, etc. respectively
he$_n$ translates into: $\lambda P[P\{x_n\}]$

The determiners **every**, **the** and **a(n)** are also decomposed by the translation process, though this is somewhat obscured by the fact that in PTQ Montague introduced these three words syncategorematically, i.e. by three separate syntactic operations, rather than treating them as independent basic expressions in their own right. Thus their decompositions into complex formulas of intensional logic is accomplished by the three translation rules corresponding to these operations, rather than as values of the function g. (The values of g for the remaining basic expressions of the English fragment are to be simply some constant of intensional logic of the appropriate type, each such value designated by a primed variant of the corresponding English word.) But a syntactically and semantically equivalent fragment is obtained if we introduce a new category of determiners (defined categorially as T/CN) containing the three basic expressions **every**, **the**, **a(n)**, together with a functional application rule for combining T/CN with CN to give T. This treatment is frequently adopted instead of the PTQ treatment of determiners; cf. Dowty, Peters and Wall (to appear) and Cooper and Parsons (1976). By this method, the definition of g would include the following special values as well as those in (1):

(2) **every** translates into: $\lambda P \lambda Q \bigwedge x [P\{x\} \rightarrow Q\{x\}]$
the translates into: $\lambda P \lambda Q \bigvee y [\bigwedge x [P\{x\} \leftrightarrow x = y] \wedge Q\{y\}]$
a(n) translates into: $\lambda P \lambda Q \bigvee x [P\{x\} \wedge Q\{x\}]$

The translations of **be, necessarily** and the determiners have the effect of fixing the interpretations of these expressions once and for all (i.e., of giving them a *standard interpretation*); that is, no matter which particular intensional model may be chosen for interpreting English, the denotations of these expressions will be determined exactly the same way. This is because these translations consist entirely of expressions of intensional logic that are themselves given a fixed interpretation by the semantic rules of intensional logic (and also include bound variables, whose interpretation is likewise fixed by the semantic rules). By contrast, the translations for the proper names each contain a non-logical constant (j, m, etc., of type e), whose interpretation will differ according to the model chosen. The effect here is to drastically limit the possible interpretations of **John, Mary**, etc. (in comparison to what it could be if these words translated into arbitrary constants of intensional logic denoting a set of properties of individuals, most of which would not single out an individual at all) though the exact denotation may still vary. Specifically, **John** will denote the set of properties that jointly characterize some particular individual at each index in each possible model (i.e. **John** denotes the *individual sublimation*, or *individual character*, of that individual), though this individual may vary from model to model, as the denotation assigned to the non-logical constant j varies. Thus we may describe this as a *partial decomposition* of an English word. Its advantage is that it allows us to capture a class of entailments that are clearly desirable (namely, those connected with the fact that names like **John** intuitively "denote" exactly one particular entity) without having to commit ourselves to more specific entailments which we are not so interested in and which would be a nuisance to have to deal with constantly (here, the question of just *which* particular individual **John** denotes).

Obviously, the complex translations for names and determiners are artifacts of the decision to systematize the English category Noun Phrase (or P_T) by having all expressions of this category denote sets of properties, while introducing by purely semantic means the desired distinction between names and quantifiers. Such "decompositions" would have no counterpart in theories (like GS) in which names and quantifier phrases are syntactically heterogeneous.

Another kind of decomposition in PTQ consists in reducing the higher-order relations denoted by certain transitive verbs to first-order relations. While the category transitive verb must correspond basically to a higher-order relation (in order to accommodate the fact that one can stand in the **seek**-relation to a "non-specific unicorn" or a "non-specific friend" without standing in any first-order relation to a particular unicorn or friend), ordinary "extensional" transitive verbs such as **find** disallow this possibility. Montague captured this fact about such verbs as **find** not by decomposing them via the translation function itself, but rather by translating **find** into a higher-order non-logical constant **find**′ of the same type as the intensional **seek**′ and by then restricting the possible models for English to those in which **find**′ is in effect equivalent to a first-order extensional relation. This is done by fiat: all models in which the interpretation assigned to **find**′ does not meet this requirement are declared "illegal"; that is, the only models to be considered "admissible" as interpretations for English are ones in which the following principle (or *meaning postulate*) obtains:

(3) $$\bigwedge \mathscr{P} \bigwedge x \Box [\mathbf{find}'(x, \mathscr{P}) \leftrightarrow \mathscr{P}\{\hat{y}[\mathbf{find}'_*(x, y)]\}]$$

This also provides a partial rather than a complete decomposition, as it does not completely fix the interpretation of **find**′ but only specifies that it is definable in terms of a certain first-order relation among individuals (here denoted by $\mathbf{find}'_*$), though which *particular* first-order relation this is is left unspecified and so varies from one possible model to another.

Despite the apparent difference in the two methods of decomposition, it must be emphasized that the semantic effect is of the same kind. Since the semantic interpretation assigned to a fragment is ultimately nothing other than the (class of) admissible model-theoretic interpretations determined by the translation procedure together with any other means of restricting these interpretations, it makes no difference that some translations may "look" different under the two methods. One must not make the mistake of confusing the form of the translation with the model-theoretic interpretation(s) it stands for.

Nor is there really any technical reason why a meaning postulate is needed in one place rather than a complex translation, or conversely. Rather than assign **be**, **necessarily**, and **John** the complex translations in (1), for example, we could let these translations be the non-logical constants **be**′, **necessarily**′ and **John**′ respectively, and then achieve the same semantic effect as before by restricting interpretations with the following postulates:

(4) $\bigwedge \mathscr{P} \bigwedge x \Box [\mathbf{be}'(x, \mathscr{P}) \leftrightarrow \mathscr{P}\{\hat{y}[x = y]\}]$
$\bigwedge p \Box [\mathbf{necessarily}'(p) \leftrightarrow \Box {}^{\vee}p]$
$\Box [\mathbf{John}' = \lambda P[P\{j\}]]$

Conversely, we could dispense with the meaning postulate for transitive verbs by assigning **find** (similarly for other extensional verbs) a complex translation as in (5):

(5) **find** translates into: $\lambda \mathscr{P} \lambda x \mathscr{P}\{\hat{y}[\mathbf{find}'_*(x, y)]\}$

(Technically speaking, we could now no longer define the notation δ_* as Montague did, since δ_* is defined in terms of δ, and this would be circular if we adopt (5); rather, $\mathbf{find}'_*$ and other instances of δ_* would now simply denote arbitrary first-order relations (of type $\langle e, \langle e, t \rangle\rangle$) and would be so-named simply because they appeared in the translation of the respective δ.) That Montague himself did not attach any great significance to the choice of methods is indicated by the fact that **be** was "decomposed" by a meaning postulate in the English fragment in UG but by a complex translation in the otherwise similar fragment in PTQ.

The meaning postulate method does afford a certain flexibility that complex translations do not; given a certain completely specified translation procedure and a set of meaning postulates, we may alternatively consider either the class of possible models in which the meaning postulates are all satisfied, or the larger class of models that also include models in which these postulates are not satisfied. As *entailment* is defined in terms of the class of possible models, we get two correspondingly different definitions of possible models. (In UG, Montague refers to the former as K'_1*-entailment* and the latter as K_1*-entailment*.) But once a complex translation has been assigned for a word, we cannot alternate so readily between classes of models which do and don't adhere to this decomposition.[2] However, I can see no useful purpose which the larger class of models and its definition of entailment serve. Perhaps Montague felt that the decompositions he treated by complex translations were more certain or immutable than those he treated by meaning postulate. But I must agree with Cresswell (1978a) that once one crosses the boundary from pure compositional semantics into word semantics, one is hard pressed to find a clear and justifiable criterion for separating the "logical words" from "non-logical" words of a natural language (aside from mere tradition). From the linguistic semanticist's point of view, the question of which words to subject to further analysis and which words to leave as non-logical constants is entirely a question of one's interests and the heuristics of research strategy. From this point of view it clearly *is* advisable to start with the traditional "logical words" since their semantics is simpler and, of course, they may play a more pervasive role in deduction in natural language. But as we progress beyond these, the question of which kinds of words to analyze next is a matter of deciding which classes of words will probably reveal the most interesting generalizations about natural language and are at the same time the most tractable in terms of the model-theoretic tools currently available.

Yet a third variety of decomposition in PTQ is exemplified by the meaning postulate that defines **seek** in terms of **try to find**:

(6) $\bigwedge \mathscr{P} \bigwedge x \Box [\mathbf{seek}'(x, \mathscr{P}) \leftrightarrow \mathbf{try\text{-}to}'(x, \hat{}[\mathbf{find}'(\mathscr{P})])]$

This neither assigns a completely fixed interpretation to **seek** nor reduces the interpretation of a higher-order constant to that of first-order constants, but rather specifies that a certain equivalence will hold among the specified non-logical constants, without otherwise fixing the interpretation of any of them. It does render certain entailments among English sentences logically valid that would not be valid otherwise. For example, (7) is equivalent to (8) (on parallel syntactic analyses) by virtue of this postulate:

(7) **Every unicorn seeks a friend.**

(8) **Every unicorn tries to find a friend.**

Probably Montague's reason for including this postulate in PTQ was to emphasize that his treatment of the referential opacity problem with **seek** was compatible with the claim that **seek** is equivalent to **try to find**, even though it does not really depend on their being equivalent (as do other familiar analyses of this problem); postulate (6) could be dispensed with (thereby cancelling the automatic equivalence of (7) and (8)) without affecting his solution to the **seek** problem, and Montague thought it was significant that other examples of intensional verbs such as **imagine, conceive of** and **worship** offered no such ready English paraphrase as **seek** does.

It should perhaps also be emphasized that the *form* a particular postulate or postulates take should not be considered a "linguistic analysis" of a word in the same sense that "semantic representations" of words are usually viewed in linguistic semantics, i.e., in which each detail of the representation embodies a deliberate claim about the structure of natural languages. Rather, the model-theoretic effect of the postulate *within the system as a whole* is the only thing that really matters. For example, nothing of importance would change in the PTQ system if we replaced the meaning postulate (6) above with (6′) or (6″):

(6′) $\bigwedge \mathscr{P} \bigwedge x \Box[\mathbf{seek}'(x, \mathscr{P}) \leftrightarrow \mathbf{try\text{-}to}'(x, \hat{y}[\mathbf{find}'(y, \mathscr{P})])]$

(6″) $\bigwedge \mathscr{P} \bigwedge x \Box[\mathbf{seek}'(x, \mathscr{P}) \leftrightarrow \mathbf{try\text{-}to}'(x, \hat{y}[\mathscr{P}\{\hat{z}[\mathbf{find}'_*(y, z)]\}])]$

The formula (6) is trivially equivalent to (6′) according to a principle of lambda conversion. Though (6″) is not equivalent to (6′) – because it specifies, in addition, that the **find′** relation in (6) is really a first-order relation – this additional specification is already accomplished elsewhere by the postulate for extensional transitive verbs, including **find**. Such "redundancy" in postulates could not be taken to be of any significance, nor could any trade-off accomplished by switching part of the "work" from one postulate to another. In other words, justifying a particular "lexical decomposition" was for Montague never a goal of linguistic analysis in the same way as it has been for linguists, but was merely a means for describing the intended class of possible model-theoretic interpretations of English (and thus the definition of truth and entailment) more conveniently.

This point is all the more important because in what follows, I will be employing lexical decompositions not only for Montague's purpose of describing entailments conveniently, but also for the further purpose of exploring in this framework the traditional linguistic hypothesis that such treatments can also be taken as making significant linguistic generalizations about word meaning in natural language. Yet here again, it is not necessarily the form of a particular complex translation or meaning postulate that is literally significant, but the more subtle claim that word meanings of certain kinds are always logically equivalent to polynomial semantic operations constructable out of a certain fixed set of primitive semantic operations (here represented by the interpretations of operators such as CAUSE and BECOME) and stative properties. As mentioned in Chapter 1, the use of the translation procedure involving these particular formulas may turn out to be only one of several trivially different ways of formalizing this hypothesis with a satisfactory degree of precision.

4.2. THE GENERAL FORM OF DECOMPOSITIONAL TRANSLATIONS: LAMBDA-ABSTRACTION VS. PREDICATE-RAISING

It will be recalled that McCawley's (1969) scheme of lexical insertion in generative semantics (cf. the discussion in 2.1.3) required not only a lexical insertion transformation that replaced a "large chunk" of logical structure involving operators and/or abstract predicates with a single "surface" English word, but that it also required one or more applications of pre-lexical transformations (such as Predicate Raising) whose purpose was to re-arrange logical structure so that the elements underlying the eventual surface verb could be made into a single constituent, separate from other elements of logical structure that might originally appear interspersed with them. For example, the structure underlying *John dies* would be (9),

(9)

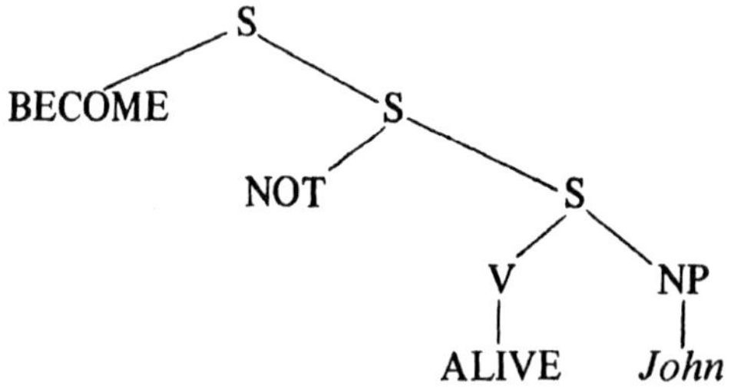

yet the NP *John* occurs embedded within the group of predicates that must be turned into *die*. Successive applications of Predicate Raising (two, to be exact) convert (9) into (9′), in which BECOME, NOT and ALIVE form a constituent and meet the structural description for the lexicalization transformation inserting *die*:

(9′)

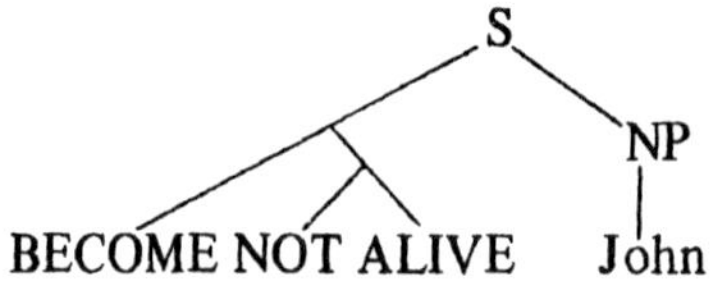

Similarly, (10) must be converted to (10′) by three applications of Predicate Raising, in order to form CAUSE, BECOME, NOT and ALIVE into a constituent separate from *John* and *Bill*, so that *John kills Bill* can be derived:

(10)

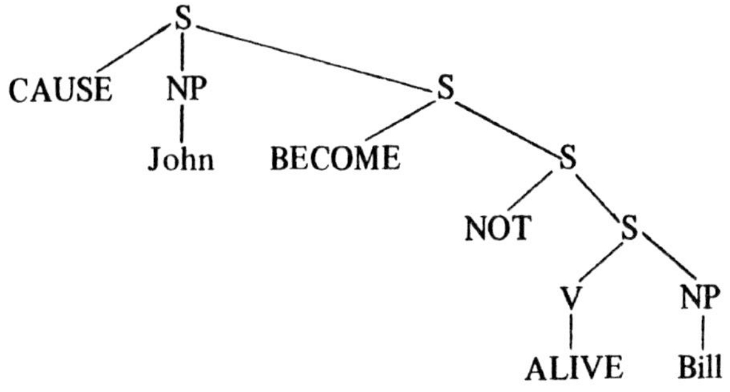

(10′)

In doing decomposition "interpretively" by the translation function, however, such manipulations are not necessary (nor would they be compatible with the notion of a translation procedure as Montague described it) because their purpose can, in effect, be served by the use of lambda-abstraction in writing the formulas of intensional logic that serve as the translations of these words. Instead, we can simply translate the intransitive verb **die** by the translation rule (11)

(11) **die** translates into: $\lambda x[\text{BECOME}\neg\textbf{alive}'(x)]$

(Since I am here assuming that the operators of the Aspect Calculus are incorporated into the formal language of intensional logic developed by Montague, I substitute **alive**′ for ALIVE, to indicate that it is a non-logical (stative predicate) constant (translating **alive**[3]), rather than an operator with a fixed interpretation, like BECOME: thus this is a *partial decomposition* as defined above.) Thus **John dies** will be given the translation (12) by the translation rules, and this is logically equivalent to (12′) in intensional logic:

(12) $\lambda P[P\{j\}](\hat{x}[\text{BECOME}\neg\textbf{alive}'(x)])$

(12′) $\text{BECOME}\neg\textbf{alive}'(j)$

It must be stressed that there is no necessary notion of a "derivation" linking (12) with (12′) in this theoretical framework, as there is a crucial derivational link between (9) and (9′) in the GS theory. Though we may use principles of logical equivalence of intensional logic to *prove*, by a series of intermediate steps, that (12) is equivalent to (12′), (12) "already" has a model-theoretic interpretation equivalent to that of (12′) by the semantic interpretation rules of intensional logic – the "proof" merely gives an additional and convenient way of demonstrating that fact. The process of reducing a translation to its simplest equivalent formula is, here and elsewhere in this book, a matter of convenience for the persons using the theory, not in any way an essential aspect of the theory itself.

When we turn to transitive verbs, the procedure is essentially the same. In treating CAUSE as a sentential connective, I will accommodate the claim that causative verbs such as **kill** have an "unspecified activity verb" in their causal clause by using existential quantification over properties – using the property variable P of type $\langle s, \langle e,t \rangle\rangle$ – to represent the "unspecified predicate" that was represented by a triangle in the analysis of accomplishments in Chapter 2:[4]

(13) **kill** translates into:
$\lambda \mathscr{P} \lambda x \mathscr{P}\{\hat{y}\,[\bigvee P[P\{x\}\text{ CAUSE BECOME } \neg \textbf{alive}'(y)]]\}$

To understand that (13) nevertheless gives us the desired interpretation for **kill**, it is best to consider an English example and amplify it in stages. Suppose we combine **kill** with the term phrase **Bill** by the verb-object rule of PTQ. Then the resulting IV-phrase **kill Bill** translates into (14) by the PTQ translation rules:

(14) $\lambda \mathscr{P} \lambda x \mathscr{P}\{\hat{y}\,[\bigvee P[P\{x\}\text{ CAUSE BECOME } \neg \textbf{alive}'(y)]]\}(\hat{P}P\{b\})$

By lambda-conversion (substituting for $\mathscr{P}$) and ˇ ˆ-cancellation (cf. Dowty, Wall and Peters (to appear)), (14) converts to (15) (with extra square brackets added for perspicuity):

(15) $\lambda x\,[\lambda P P\{b\}(\hat{y}\,[\bigvee P[P\{x\}\text{ CAUSE BECOME } \neg \textbf{alive}'(y)]])]$

By lambda-conversion (this time substituting for P) and ˇ ˆ-cancellation again, (15) converts to (16):

(16) $\lambda x\,[\lambda y\,[\bigvee P[P\{x\}\text{ CAUSE BECOME } \neg \textbf{alive}'(y)]]\,(b)]$

and by one more application of lambda-conversion (substituting for y), (16) is equivalent to (17):

(17) $\lambda x\,[\bigvee P[P\{x\}\text{ CAUSE BECOME } \neg \textbf{alive}'(b)]]$

With this simplified translation of **kill Bill**, we can proceed to translate the sentence **John kills Bill** produced by the subject-predicate rule:

(18) $\lambda P P\{j\}(\hat{x}\,[\bigvee P[P\{x\}\text{ CAUSE BECOME } \neg \textbf{alive}'(b)]])$

And by a more familiar simplification, this reduces to (19):

(19) $\bigvee P[P\{j\}$ CAUSE BECOME $\neg$**alive**$'(b)]$

This is clearly the kind of decomposition specified for accomplishments in Chapter 2, asserting that the fact that John does something (i.e., that he has some property P) causes it to come to be the case that Bill is not alive. The steps of simplication (14)–(19), by the way, are exactly the same as for the translation of a sentence using the transitive verb **be** in Montague's PTQ, in which **be** has the translation $\lambda\mathscr{P}\lambda x\mathscr{P}\{\hat{y}[x = y]\}$, and the reader may wish to compare the simplification of **John is Bill** with that of **John kills Bill** as given here.

As was the case with the decompositions in PTQ, we could equivalently translate **die** and **kill** into the non-logical constants **die**$'$ and **kill**$'$ respectively and instead capture the desired semantic effect by meaning postulates:

(20) $\bigwedge x\Box[$**die**$'(x) \leftrightarrow$ BECOME $\neg$**alive**$'(x)]$

(21) $\bigwedge\mathscr{P}\bigwedge x\Box[$**kill**$'(x,\mathscr{P}) \leftrightarrow \mathscr{P}\{\hat{y}[\bigvee P[P\{x\}$ CAUSE BECOME $\neg$**alive**$'(y)]]\}]$

However, one possibility that the meaning postulate method offers that the complex translation method does not is the possibility of weakening the biconditional to a conditional:

(20$'$) $\bigwedge x\Box[$**die**$'(x) \rightarrow$ BECOME $\neg$**alive**$'(x)]$

(21$'$) $\bigwedge\mathscr{P}\bigwedge x\Box[$**kill**$'(x,\mathscr{P}) \rightarrow \mathscr{P}\{\hat{y}[\bigvee P[P\{x\}$ CAUSE BECOME $\neg$**alive**$'(y)]]\}]$

This is of interest because of the frequent objection to decomposition analyses that the meaning of the analyzed word is more specific than the decomposed paraphrase – e.g. **kill** is more specific than **cause to become not alive**. For those who find such objections a compelling obstacle to the program of analysis undertaken here, such postulates would enable us to formally capture all the entailments of accomplishment and achievement verbs that the decomposition method makes possible, yet without commiting ourselves to the unwelcome claim that **kill**, etc. mean *exactly* what the decomposition analysis specifies. (However, we will note, in the next chapter, one reason for requiring that accomplishments and achievements must be equivalent to some decomposed paraphrase, rather than merely entailing it.)

With these two examples of accomplishment and achievement verbs I will leave syntactically simple verbs and turn to the syntactically more interesting cases; the decomposition analyses of most other simple accomplishment verbs will be exactly parallel to these two, differing only in the particular stative predicate occurring in the innermost position and/or in having a particular kind of activity predicate (cf. note 4) replacing the property variable *P* (cf. **kill** vs. **drown**, **electrocute**, etc.); the reader should have no difficulty in constructing analyses of other members of this class from this pattern. However, I might indicate with a general schema how a GS decomposition analysis of arbitrary complexity of a transitive or intransitive verb might be converted to a PTQ "interpretive" decomposition. Suppose (22) is the logical structure underlying a sentence with an intransitive verb, which is converted to (22′) by n applications of Predicate Raising (where $OP_1 \ldots OP_n$ are "atomic predicates" of generative semantics) before lexical insertion replaces the accumulation of predicates with the English word $Verb_i$:

(22)

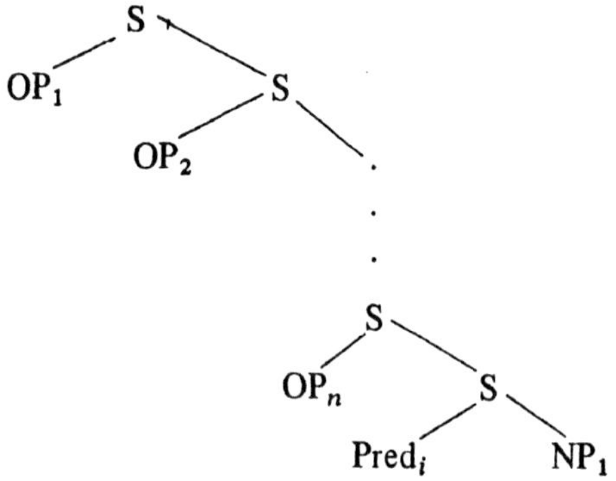

(22′)

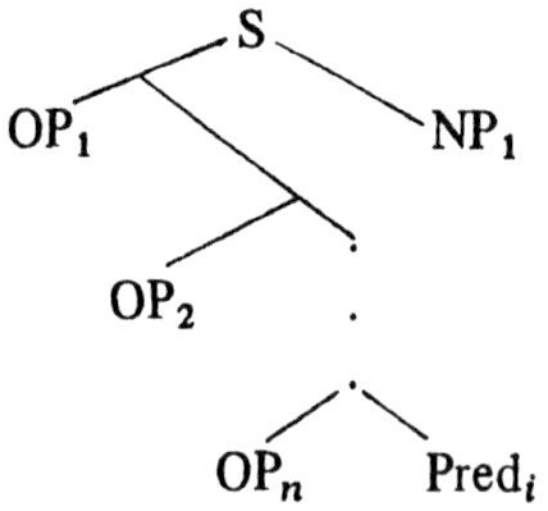

In the corresponding PTQ treatment, $Verb_i$ will be given a translation rule of the form of (22″):

(22″) $Verb_i$ translates into: $\lambda x [OP_1 \ldots OP_n [Pred_i(x) \ldots]]$

Of course, the success of this procedure will depend on whether (a) care is taken that the operators $OP_1 \ldots OP_n$ and $Pred_i$ are assigned to the appropriate logical types such that the formula in (22″) is a well-formed expression of intensional logic and of the appropriate type to serve as the translation of an intransitive verb, namely $\langle e, t \rangle$, and (b) appropriate truth conditions for these operators and predicate can be stated relative to the intensional model in such a way that all the entailments can be accounted for that motivated the decomposition analysis (22) in the first place.

Suppose (23) is the logical structure underlying a sentence with a transitive verb and that (23) is converted to (23′) by Predicate Raising before $Verb_j$ is inserted:

(23)

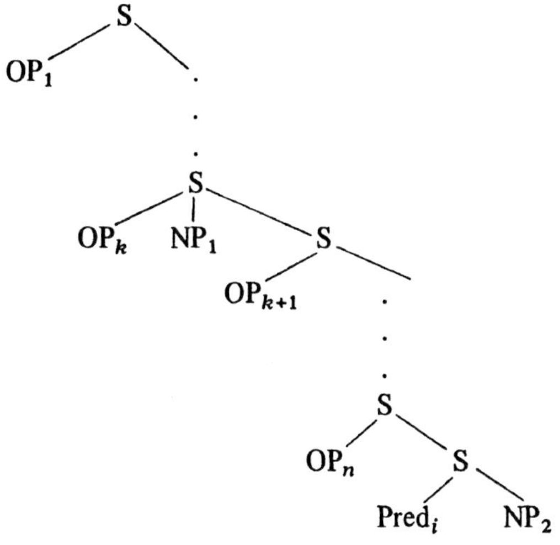

(23′)

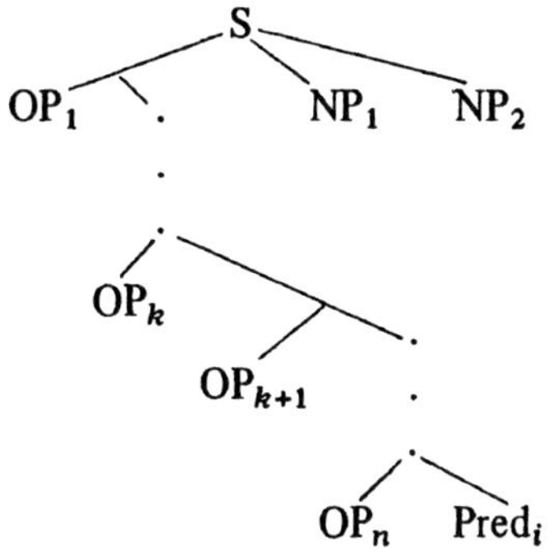

Then in the PTQ treatment $Verb_j$ will be translated by (23″)

(23″) $Verb_j$ translates into:[5]
$\lambda \mathscr{P} \lambda x \mathscr{P}\{\hat{y}\,[\mathrm{OP}_1 \ldots \mathrm{OP}_k(x, \mathrm{OP}_{k+1} \ldots \mathrm{OP}_n\,[\mathrm{Pred}_i(y)]\ \ldots) \ldots]\}$

4.3. MORPHOLOGICALLY DERIVED CAUSATIVES AND INCHOATIVES

Inchoative verbs which are derived from stative adjectives (like **cool** from **cool, sweeten** from **sweet**) can be related to their adjective sources by a rule which changes the category of a word from ADJ (which I assume to be categorially defined as t///e, cf. note 3) to IV, sometimes adding the suffix **-en**, sometimes leaving the form of the word unaltered. This choice of forms seems to be governed fairly regularly by phonological properties of the adjective; the principle seems to be that if the adjective ends in a non-nasal obstruent, **-en** is added (cf. **dampen, cheapen, shorten, brighten, gladden, harden, blacken, weaken, roughen, stiffen, loosen, lessen, freshen**), but no suffix is added if the adjective ends in a nasal (**slim, tame, thin, clean, wrong**), **l** (**cool, dull**), **r** (**near, clear**), or a vowel (**free, blue, slow, steady, yellow** (cf. Jesperson, 1931, 6.20.55)). Exceptions exist (e.g. **wet** instead of ***wetten**) but are few in number. The rule S23 produces this effect, and its translation rule T23 adds the inchoative meaning:

S23. If $\alpha \in P_{ADJ}$, then $F_{23}(\alpha) \in P_{IV}$, where $F_{23}(\alpha) = \alpha$ **en** if α ends in a non-nasal obstruent, $F_{23}(\alpha) = \alpha$ otherwise.[6]

T23. $F_{23}(\alpha)$ translates into: $\lambda x[\text{BECOME } \alpha'(x)]$

Using this rule, **the soup cools** will be derived with the analysis tree (24) and will have a translation which reduces to (24′):

(24)

the soup cools, t, 4
- **the soup**, T, 1
  - **soup**, CN
- **cool**, IV, 23
  - **cool**, ADJ

(24′) $\bigvee x[\bigwedge y[\textbf{soup}'(y) \leftrightarrow x = y] \wedge \text{BECOME } \textbf{cool}'(x)]$

Causative transitive accomplishment verbs in English are often phonologically identical with the corresponding intransitive noncausative verb. As such pairs of related homophonous verbs include those not derived from a stative adjective (cf. **John broke the window** vs. **the window broke** and similar pairs with **bend, boil, freeze, run, move, dissolve**, etc.) as well as verbs derived from an adjective (cf. **John cooled the soup** and examples with de-adjectival verbs in the previous list), it seems best to subsume both these classes under a single rule turning an intransitive verb into a transitive causative, assuming that the verbs in examples like **John cooled the soup** have undergone both S23 and *then* the causative rule S24:

S24. If $\alpha \in P_{IV}$, then $F_{24}(\alpha) \in P_{TV}$, where $F_{24}(\alpha) = \alpha$.

T24. $F_{24}(\alpha)$ translates into: $\lambda\mathscr{P}\lambda x\mathscr{P}\{\hat{y}\bigvee P[P\{x\}\text{ CAUSE }\alpha'(y)]\}$

The combination of both rules is illustrated in the tree (25) and its translation (25′); note that the constant **cool′** that appears in this translation is thus the constant that translates the *adjective* **cool**:

(25) **John cools the soup**, t, 4
  John, T
  cool the soup, IV, 5
    cool, TV, 24
      cool, IV, 23
        cool, ADJ
    the soup, T, 1
      soup, CN

(25′) $\bigvee x[\bigwedge y[\mathbf{soup}'(y) \leftrightarrow x = y] \wedge \bigvee P[P\{j\}\text{ CAUSE BECOME }\mathbf{cool}'(x)]]$

As was noted in Chapter 2, there are many exceptions to this rule, both in its applicability to certain verbs (there is no causative transitive **disappear**, parallel to intransitive **disappear**) and in the semantics of the resulting verb when the rule does apply. These properties will lead us in Chapter 6 to revise our view of the *status* of these two rules in a grammar of English, though the *form* of the rules and their translation rules will remain exactly as presented here.

4.4. PREPOSITIONAL PHRASE ACCOMPLISHMENTS

It was noted in Chapter 2 that an activity verb can apparently be turned into an accomplishment verb by the addition of a syntactically optional prepositional phrase, typically a locative one expressing what is called *Goal* in case grammar. For example, the intransitive activity **walk** in (26a) becomes an accomplishment (i.e. has a natural end point or completion) in (26b), and the transitive activity verb **move** in (27a) becomes an accomplishment in (27b).

(26) a. **John walked.**
b. **John walked to Chicago.**

(27) a. **John moved a rock.**
b. **John moved a rock to the fence.**

If the suggested structures of activity and accomplishment are to differentiate each of these pairs in Logical Structure in a GS analysis, prelexical transformations will have to separate CAUSE and the BECOME sentence from the activity verb embedded within the structure, since here the activity apparently lexicalizes as a separate verb while the remainder of the accomplishment structure is turned into the preposition **to**. As far as I know, no completely explicit treatment of such derivations has been advanced, though hints can be found in Binnick (1968; 1969) and elsewhere. Of course, one should perhaps not conclude from the absence of an explicit treatment in the GS literature that it would be impossible to give one. Part of the problem is that a number of pre-lexical transformational cycles are involved, and one might have to exhibit a complete grammar with all cyclical rules as well as lexicalization rules present in order to know whether exactly these surface structures would be produced without giving rise to ill-formed surface structures as well. An explicit formulation of this kind of sentence will thus require a formalization of a large part of the GS theory, and this has never been undertaken.

In the "upside-down" GS method, on the other hand, we begin with the surface structure directly and so have no trouble seeing what will and won't be produced. It turns out to be best to treat the optional prepositional phrase **to Chicago** as an expression of category IV/IV (verb-phrase modifier) in (26b) but as an expression of TV/TV (i.e. a transitive verb modifier) in (27b). This postulation of double category membership might at first seem unnecessary; there is clearly no *syntactic* problem in treating the phrase as a member of IV/IV in (27b) as well, since **move a rock** forms an expression of category IV in (27b) just as **walk** does in (26b). But note that the entailment is crucially different in (27b) from that in (26b). In (26b) it is the referent of the *subject* of the sentence that is understood to come to be in Chicago, while in (27b) it is the referent of the *direct object* that changes location.[7] (That it can be only the object[8] that moves is even clearer from examples like **John threw the letter into the wastebasket** and **John pushed the rock over the cliff.**) Entailments involving the direct object are more directly producible if the modifier responsible for the entailment is treated as TV/TV (i.e. its meaning applies to a function of two arguments to give a new function of two arguments, one of which will be the direct object) than if the modifier is treated as IV/IV (its meaning applies to a function of one argument, namely the subject of the sentence).

To be sure, there are certain examples where the real-world facts about transportation make it difficult if not impossible to determine which sort of entailment is essentially present, since one referent normally changes location if and only if the other does in certain situations. For example, it is hard to say whether **John drove his car to Chicago** should be analyzed as basically asserting that John came to be in Chicago as a result of driving his car, or rather that John caused his car to come to be in Chicago by driving it, since both John and his car would normally be understood to end up in Chicago in either case. The sentence may well be syntactically (and semantically) ambiguous, though the two readings are indiscernible for pragmatic reasons.

Let us consider the "intransitive" case (26) first. It might seem obvious that a causal relation between John's walking and his coming to be in Chicago is entailed by (26b). However, it is known (Schmerling, 1975) that causal relationships are often conveyed by conversational implicature rather than by direct entailment in natural languages – cf. for example *The alarm clock went off and John awoke with a start*. In view of this possibility it is significant to note the existence of examples like (28) and (29), cited by Fillmore (1974) and attributed to Leonard Talmy:

(28) Mary wore a green dress to the party.

(29) John $\left\{\begin{array}{l}\text{read a newspaper}\\ \text{slept}\end{array}\right\}$ all the way to Chicago.

Clearly, no causal relation between activity (or state) and change-of-location is required by such sentences, which seem syntactically parallel to (26b). Rather, the change of state seems merely to be concurrent with the activity or state described by the verb. To decide whether the alleged implicature in (26b) is "cancellable" and thus presumably conversational in origin, we would consider situations in which John walks around in the back of a truck or up and down the aisle of a plane while being conveyed to Chicago, and decide if (26b) is still appropriate here as well. To me this use of (26b) seems to be quite awkward, though possible, but this awkwardness may be merely the result of violating additional conversational principles (such as the maxim of quantity), so that (26b) would be a misleading understatement in this unusual situation. In view of this indeterminacy and the undeniable existence of (28) and (29), Ockham's Razor leads me to propose that the meaning of **to** is the same in both instances, and that the causative inference is here conversational. (If I am wrong, this simply means that the connective "$\wedge$" in each translation in (32) below should be replaced with "CAUSE", and some other way of deriving (28) and (29) must be devised.) On the other hand, I believe that the causal relation between activity and change of position is actually entailed in the transitive-modifier case of (27b). I am able to find no examples parallel to (28) and (29) in which the object alone changes location but in which there is clearly no inference that the activity caused the change of position. And all attempts to "cancel" the causative inference that I have been able to construct seem truly contradictory:

(30) John moved the rock to the fence, but his moving it was not a cause of its coming to be at the fence.

(31) John threw the letter into the wastebasket, but his throwing the letter was not a cause of its coming to be in the wastebasket.

The desired semantic effect of the "intransitive" prepositions (which are of category IAV/T, i.e. (IV/IV)/T) is produced by translating them as follows:

(32) **to** translates into: $\lambda\mathscr{P}\lambda P\lambda x\mathscr{P}\{\hat{y}[P\{x\} \wedge \text{BECOME}[\mathbf{be\text{-}at}'(x,y)]]\}$
into translates into:
$\lambda\mathscr{P}\lambda P\lambda x\mathscr{P}\{\hat{y}[P\{x\} \wedge \text{BECOME}[\mathbf{be\text{-}in}'(x,y)]]\}$
onto translates into:
$\lambda\mathscr{P}\lambda P\lambda x\mathscr{P}\{\hat{y}[P\{x\} \wedge \text{BECOME}[\mathbf{be\text{-}on}'(x,y)]]\}$
away from translates into:
$\lambda\mathscr{P}\lambda P\lambda x\mathscr{P}\{\hat{y}[P\{x\} \wedge \text{BECOME}[\neg\mathbf{be\text{-}at}'(x,y)]]\}$
out of translates into:
$\lambda\mathscr{P}\lambda P\lambda x\mathscr{P}\{\hat{y}[P\{x\} \wedge \text{BECOME}[\neg\mathbf{be\text{-}in}'(x,y)]]\}$
off of translates into:
$\lambda\mathscr{P}\lambda P\lambda x\mathscr{P}\{\hat{y}[P\{x\} \wedge \text{BECOME}[\neg\mathbf{be\text{-}on}'(x,y)]]\}$

For convenience, I use **be-at**′, **be-on**′ and **be-in**′ as constants of type $\langle e, \langle e, t\rangle\rangle$ in these translations (i.e., two-place extensional predicates), though they are not literally the constants translating English **at**, **on** and **in**, which would deserve the symbolization **at**′, **on**′ and **in**′. This latter group of constants would rather be of type $\langle\langle s, f(\mathrm{T})\rangle, \langle\langle e, t\rangle, \langle e, t\rangle\rangle\rangle$, and though it would be possible to translate **to, into**, etc. in terms of them, it would be less perspicuous to do so; the interpretation of **be-at**′, etc. is more intuitively obvious. Alternatively, we could adopt a richer model in which positions are assigned to individuals by a function *Loc* for each index in each model, and then **be-at**, etc. could be given an explicit standard interpretation in such a model with the aid of supplementary notions like adjacency of one region of space to another (for **at**), containment of one region within another (for **in**), and location adjacent to but above a horizontal surface (for **on**). However, this would take us too far afield here, and I refer the reader to Cresswell (1978) for suggestions on this kind of undertaking. To be sure, there are many other English change-of-position prepositions which present a variety of interesting problems (cf. Bennett, 1975 and Cresswell, 1978) as well as non-locative uses of "change" prepositions (as in *He re-wrote the novel into a screenplay*), but those above will have to serve as representative examples for our present purposes.

The example (26b) (omitting now the past tense) will now be produced by the analysis tree (26b′) and have a translation reducible to (26b″).

(26b′)

```
            John walks to Chicago, t, 4
           /                \
     John, T            walk to Chicago, IV, 7
                          /                 \
          to Chicago, IV/IV, 5            walk, IV
             /             \
       to, IAV/T         Chicago, T
```

(26b″) $\mathbf{walk}'(j) \wedge \text{BECOME}\ [\mathbf{be\text{-}at}'(j, c)]$

It is often supposed that directional prepositional phrases such as these should be syntactically restricted to cooccurrence with verbs of motion, since ?*John slept to the door* and similar examples are anomalous. But I agree with Bennett (1970, p. 112) that "verb of motion" is a hard notion to pin down in just the right way to account for this anomaly (are *nod* and *twitch* verbs of motion?). The syntactic rules will be left unrestricted, and the strangeness of *John slept* (*twitched, sniffed*) *to the door* is best viewed as pragmatic/semantic rather than as syntactic.

The most straightforward way to accommodate the transitive-verb-modifying prepositional phrases would be to postulate systematic "homonyms" of **into**, **to**, etc. in category (TV/TV)/T. Thus for example, **to** in (TV/TV)/T could be given the translation in (33), which incorporates the causative relation between activity and the change of position that the referent of the object term phrase undergoes:

(33) **to** translates into:

$$\lambda\mathscr{P}\lambda\mathscr{R}\lambda\mathscr{Q}\lambda x\mathscr{Q}\{\hat{y}\mathscr{P}\{\hat{z}[\,{}^{\vee}\mathscr{R}(x, \hat{P}P\{y\})\ \text{CAUSE}\ \text{BECOME}\ [\mathbf{be\text{-}at}'(y, z)]]\}\}$$

In this rule, $\mathscr{P}$ and $\mathscr{Q}$ are both to be variables of type $\langle s, f(\text{T})\rangle$ (ranging over the intensions of translations of terms), and $\mathscr{R}$ is a variable of type $\langle s, f(\text{TV})\rangle$

(ranging over intensions of translations of transitive verbs). In reading this complicated expression, it may be helpful to note that $\mathscr{P}$(and later z) fills the position of the object of the preposition, $\mathscr{Q}$(later y) fills the position of the direct object, x fills the position of the subject, and $\mathscr{R}$ fills the position of the verb. Thus (27b) would be produced as in (27b′) and would have a translation equivalent to (27b″).

(27b′) **John pushes a rock to the fence**, t, 4
- **John**, T
- **push a rock to the fence**, IV, 5
  - **a rock**, T, 2
  - **push to the fence**, TV, 7
    - **to the fence**, TV/TV, 5
      - **to**, (TV/TV)/T
      - **the fence**, T, 1
        - **fence**, CN
    - **push**, TV

(27b″) $\bigvee x[\mathbf{rock}'(x) \wedge \bigvee y[\bigwedge z[\mathbf{fence}'(z) \leftrightarrow y = z] \wedge$
$\mathbf{push}'_{*}(j, x)$ CAUSE BECOME $[\mathbf{be\text{-}at}'(x, y)]]]$

This syntactic derivation requires two additional functional application rules, one for combining TV/TV with TV to give TV (using the operation F_7), and another for combining (TV/TV)/T with T to give TV/TV (using F_5). More important, this derivation requires a modification of the operation F_5 as it is used to combine the TV **push to the fence** with **a rock** to give **push a rock to the fence**, since the existing PTQ F_5 would give ***push to the fence a rock** instead. However, it turns out that there will be a variety of instances in a Montague Grammar of English in which an expression of category TV containing more than one word is combined with a direct object term, and in each such instance the object needs to be placed after the first basic expression within the TV; such cases first appear in Thomason (1976) and are discussed extensively in Dowty (1978) and Bach (1977). Thus I will henceforth assume that F_5 has been modified accordingly.

But postulating such a large set of homophonous lexical prepositions with systematically similar meanings seems undesirable. Fortunately, it is possible to derive the TV-modifying prepositions from the IV-modifying prepositions by a general rule with semantically adequate results. Such a rule is S25:

S25. If $\alpha \in P_{\text{IAV/T}}$, then $F_{25}(\alpha) \in P_{\text{(TV/TV)/T}}$, where $F_{25}(\alpha) = \alpha$.

T25. If α translates into α', $F_{25}(\alpha)$ translates into:
$\lambda\mathscr{P}\lambda\mathscr{R}\lambda\mathscr{Q}\lambda x\mathscr{Q}\{\hat{y}\mathscr{P}\{\hat{z}[\check{\ }\mathscr{R}(x, \hat{P}P\{y\})$ CAUSE $[\alpha'(\hat{P}P\{z\})(\hat{x}[x = x])(y)]]\}\}$

Example (27b) can now be produced by the analysis tree (34), which makes use of the same basic "intransitive" preposition **to** as (26b′):

(34)

- **John pushes a rock to the fence**, t, 4
  - **John**, T
  - **push a rock to the fence**, IV, 5
    - **a rock**, T, 2
      - **rock**, CN
    - **push to the fence**, TV, 7
      - **to the fence**, TV/TV, 5
        - **to**, (TV/TV)/T, 25
          - **to**, IAV/T
        - **the fence**, T, 1
          - **fence**, CN
      - **push**, TV

The translation of this analysis tree is nevertheless logically equivalent to (27b″). To understand exactly how T25 accomplishes this equivalence, note first that the interpretation of an IV-modifier is a function applying to a property of individuals. However, there will be no such appropriate property for it to apply to in the interpretation of (34), so T25 fills this argument position with the "dummy property" $\hat{x}[x = x]$, which is of course a real enough property but one that all individuals necessarily always have. Thus when the translation of F_{25}(**to**) is simplified to (35) by lambda conversion,

(35) $\lambda\mathscr{P}\lambda\mathscr{R}\lambda\mathscr{Q}\lambda x\mathscr{Q}\{\hat{y}\mathscr{P}\{\hat{z}[\check{\ }\mathscr{R}(x, \hat{P}P\{y\})$ CAUSE $[y = y \wedge$
BECOME [**be-at**$'(y, z)$]]]}}

the tautology $y = y$ appears conjoined with a BECOME sentence. By a familiar principle of propositional logic, the conjunction of any sentence with a tautology is logically equivalent to that sentence itself, so this conjunct in effect "disappears", leaving exactly the same translation for **to** as given in (33). Otherwise, the analysis trees and their translations are identical. (The simplication of F_{25}(**to**) to (35) is rather complicated, involving six lambda conversations, and I trust the reader will take my word for it that (35) does in fact result or else will work it out for himself as an exercise.)

4.5. ACCOMPLISHMENTS WITH TWO PREPOSITIONAL PHRASES

One important class of examples of change of state over an interval discussed in Chapter 3 involved movements whose origin and destination are both specified by prepositional phrases; such sentences are the intransitive (36) and transitive (37) (assuming (37) does in fact have a transitive modifier analysis).

(36) **John walked from Boston to Detroit.**

(37) **John drove a car from Boston to Detroit.**

If we confine our attention to the intransitive examples for a moment, it seems that the **from**-phrase is a modifier independent of the **to**-phrase, as we have (38) as well as (36) and (26b) (**John walked to Chicago**):

(38) **John walked from Boston.**

However, it is now apparent that (26b) and (38) are both semantically "elliptical": (38) implies an unmentioned destination (which would normally be implicit in the context of utterance), just as (26b) implies an unmentioned point of origin.[9] The prepositions **from** and **to** would be more accurately translated as in (39):

(39) **to** translates into:
$\lambda\mathscr{P}\lambda P\lambda x\mathscr{P}\{\hat{y}[P\{x\}$ AND $\bigvee z[$BECOME $\neg$**be-at**$'(x,z)]$ AND BECOME **be-at**$'(x,y)]\}$
from translates into:
$\lambda\mathscr{P}\lambda P\lambda x\mathscr{P}\{\hat{y}[P\{x\}$ AND BECOME $\neg$**be-at**$'(x,y)$ AND $\bigvee z[$BECOME **be-at**$'(x,z)]]\}$

With these translations, (26b) (**John walked to Chicago**) would receive the translation (26b‴) and (38) (**John walked from Boston**) would receive the translation (38′) (again omitting the past tense)

(26b‴) [**walk**$'(j)$ AND $\bigvee z[$BECOME $\neg$**be-at**$'(j,z)]$ AND BECOME **be-at**$'(j,c)]$

(38′) [**walk**$'(j)$ AND BECOME $\neg$**be-at**$'(j,b)$ AND $\bigvee z[$BECOME **be-at**$'(j,z)]]$

The example (36) with two modifiers would now receive the translation (36″) on the analysis (36′). The two existentially quantified conjuncts are logically redundant, however, and (36″) is actually equivalent to the shorter (36‴):

(36′)

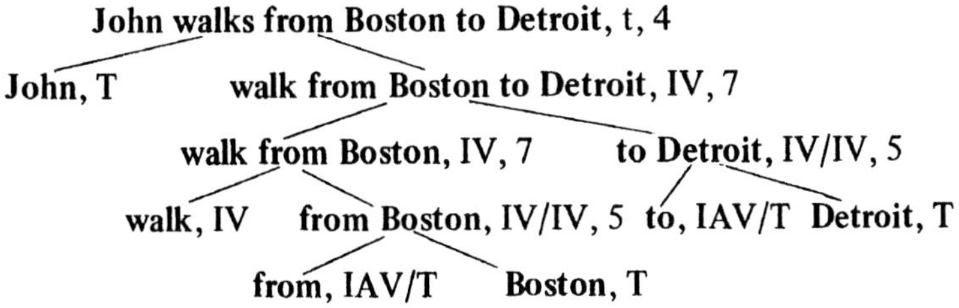

(36″) [walk′(j) AND BECOME ¬be-at′(j, b) AND
$\vee z$[BECOME be-at′(j, z)] AND $\vee z$[BECOME ¬be-at′(j, z)] AND
BECOME be-at′(j, d)]

(36‴) [walk′(j) AND BECOME ¬be-at′(j, b) AND BECOME be-at′(j, d)]

As always, the truth-conditions for BECOME sentences developed in Chapter 3 should be borne in mind when reading such formulas as these. For example, the formula in (36‴) (and therefore the English sentence (36)) will be true of an interval I just in case the following is true of I: (1) I is an interval during which John walks, (2) I is bounded at the lower end by a moment at which John is at Boston, though this ceases to be true after the beginning of I, and (3) I is bounded at its upper end by a moment at which John is at Detroit, though this is not true just before the end of I, and (4) there is no smaller interval for which all three conditions hold.

When we turn to the transitive sentence (37), a problem arises if we attempt to use the obvious syntactic analysis in which the prepositional phrases are "nested" modifiers as they were in the intransitive case:

(37′)

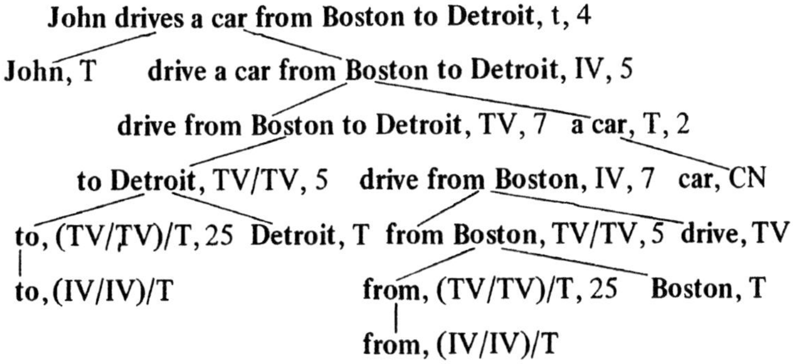

This is because the causative entailment involved in TV/TV modification would also be nested, i.e. (37) would assert that John's causing the car to be no longer in Boston (by driving it) causes the car to come to be in Detroit, which is almost surely an incorrect entailment. An alternative is to treat the **from**-phrase as modifying the **to**-phrase; this may be syntactically justified by the observation that certain syntactic tests for constituent structure (Zwicky, 1978) seem to suggest that **from Chicago to Detroit** forms a constituent (*It was from Chicago to Detroit that he drove his car; Where did he drive his car? From Chicago to Detroit*; for comparison, **It was to Chicago on Thursday that John drove his car from Boston*).[10] The preposition **from** would now also be entered in the basic category ((TV/TV)/(TV/TV))/T, and the analysis tree would be (37″).

(37″) **John drives a car from Boston to Detroit**, t, 4

John, T **drive a car from Boston to Detroit**, IV, 5

drive from Boston to Detroit, TV, 7 **a car**, T, 2

from Boston to Detroit, TV/TV, 6 **drive**, TV **car**, CN

from Boston, (TV/TV)/(TV/TV), 5 **to Detroit**, TV/TV, 5

from, ((TV/TV)/(TV/TV))/T **Boston**, T **to**, (TV/TV)/T, 30 **Detroit**, T

to, (IV/IV)/T

To achieve the translation (37‴), this new **from** would be translated as in (38), in which $\mathscr{G}$ is a variable of type $\langle s, f(\mathrm{TV/TV})\rangle$:

(38) **from** translates into:

$$\lambda\mathscr{P}\lambda\mathscr{G}\lambda\mathscr{R}\lambda\mathscr{Q}\lambda x\mathscr{P}\{\hat{y}\mathscr{Q}\{\hat{z}[{}^{\vee}\mathscr{G}(\mathscr{R})(\hat{P}P\{z\})(x) \text{ AND } [{}^{\vee}\mathscr{R}(\hat{P}P\{z\})(x) \text{ CAUSE BECOME } \neg \mathbf{be\ at}'(z,y)]]\}\}$$

(37‴) $\bigvee x[\mathbf{car}'(x) \text{ AND } [\mathbf{drive}'(j,x) \text{ CAUSE BECOME } \neg\mathbf{be\text{-}at}'(x,b)] \text{ AND } [\mathbf{drive}'(j,x) \text{ CAUSE BECOME } \mathbf{be\text{-}at}'(x,d)]]$

4.6. PREPOSITIONAL PHRASE ADJUNCTS VS. PREPOSITIONAL PHRASE COMPLEMENTS

Though the verbs discussed so far in this section may occur equally happily with or without the prepositional phrase that turns them into an accomplishment, there are other verbs, such as **put**, **set** and **lay**, which require a "goal" adverbial:

(39) **John** {**put** / **set** / **laid**} **a book into a box.**

(40) ***John** $\left\{\begin{array}{l}\textbf{put}\\ \textbf{set}\\ \textbf{laid}\end{array}\right\}$ **a book.**

In transformational grammar, such verbs would be described as *obligatorily subcategorized* for a directional locative adverbial, while the activity verbs considered earlier would only be *optionally subcategorized* for such a complement. In more traditional terminology, the prepositional phrases are *complements* in (39), *adjuncts* in the earlier examples. In a Montague grammar, the obvious way to capture this obligatory co-occurrence is to place these verbs in a category of functors that combine with adverbials to form transitive verbs (whereas in the previous cases the adverbial was a functor applying to the verb instead). That is, **put, set** and **lay** would be categorized as TV/(IV/IV) or as TV/(TV/TV), the choice depending on whether we want these verbs to combine with "intransitive" directional modifiers or "transitive" directional modifiers. Though possibly an analysis could be made to work with either category, the latter category seems to me to be less problematic. As a (somewhat rough) approximation of the meaning of the verb **put** with this latter method, I suggest (41):

(41) **put** ($\in P_{TV/(TV/TV)}$) translates into:
$\lambda\mathscr{G}\lambda\mathscr{P}\lambda x\bigvee\mathscr{R}\,[\,{}^{\vee}\mathscr{G}(\mathscr{R})(\mathscr{P})(x)]$

Here, $\mathscr{G}$ is a variable of type $\langle s, f(\mathrm{TV/TV})\rangle$, i.e., senses of transitive verb modifiers. Then **John puts a book into a box** would have the analysis tree (39′):

(39′)

John puts a book into a box, t, 4
- **John**, T
- **put a book into a box**, IV, 5
  - **put into a box**, TV, 7
    - **put**, TV/(TV/TV)
    - **into a box**, TV/TV, 5
      - **into**, (TV/TV)/T, 30
        - **into**, (IV/IV)/T
      - **a box**, T, 2
        - **box**, CN
  - **a book**, T, 2
    - **book**, CN

The translation of **into a box** (after lambda conversions) is (42):

(42) $\lambda\mathscr{R}\lambda\mathscr{Q}\lambda x\mathscr{Q}\{\hat{y}\,[\bigvee z\,[\mathbf{box}'(z) \wedge {}^{\vee}\mathscr{R}(x, \hat{P}P\{y\})$ CAUSE BECOME $\mathbf{be\text{-}in}'(y, z)]]\}$

Combining this with the translation of **put** and reducing the result gives (43):

(43) $\lambda\mathscr{P}\lambda x \bigvee \mathscr{R}\mathscr{P}\{\hat{y}\,[\bigvee z\,[\mathbf{box}'(z) \wedge [\,{}^{\vee}\mathscr{R}\,(x, \hat{P}P\{y\})\ \text{CAUSE}$
$\text{BECOME}\ \mathbf{be\text{-}in}'(y, z)]]]\}$

Therefore the translation of the whole sentence turns out to be (39″):

(39″) $\bigvee\mathscr{R}\bigvee x\,[\mathbf{book}'(x) \wedge \bigvee z\,[\mathbf{box}'(z) \wedge$
$[\,{}^{\vee}\mathscr{R}(j, \hat{P}P\{x\})\ \text{CAUSE BECOME}\ \mathbf{be\text{-}in}'(x, z)]]]$

Thus the sentence is analyzed as asserting that for some book and some box, there is a relation John stands in to the book (i.e. "something John does with the book") that causes it to come to be in the box. Homing in more precisely on the meaning of **put** would be a matter of putting further restrictions on the existentially quantified relation variable $\mathscr{R}$ to the effect that the action is intentional or involves direct manipulation, or something of the sort. Also, we would eventually want to be able to distinguish **put** from **set** and **lay**; this distinction (though surprisingly subtle, as the three sentences in (39) are all but synonymous) seems to involve entailments involving the orientation of the object (cf. **lay**) or the manner of manipulation. Nevertheless, the most important entailments of the sentence are already captured in (39″).

Also note that modifiers other than prepositional phrases will no doubt appear in the category TV/TV and thus are predicted to occur with **put**. In some cases this is as it should be, for just as we have **John walks away (down, in, aside)**, we also have **John puts the book away (down, over, aside,** etc.). I am not sure whether other kinds of adverbs like **slowly, deliberately, with a knife,** etc. present an additional problem or not, because it is unclear to me whether the anomaly of ***John put the book slowly** can be claimed to follow from the semantics of **put** as it stands, whether these adverbs for some reason occur in IV/IV but not in TV/TV, or whether there may be independent reasons for putting them even in a separate subcategory of intransitive modifiers from directionals (a multiple slash variant of IV/IV), and thus preventing them from occurring with **put**.

Transitive verbal constructions with adverb complements (**John put the book away**) are of course more commonly discussed under the heading of verb-particle constructions. As this construction is traditionally defined by the ability of the adverb complement to occur either before or after the direct object (**John put the book away** vs. **John put away the book**), it includes not only the directional constructions which I have here treated as being formed by compositional syntactic rules but also the more or less frozen combinations of a verb plus directional adverb whose meaning is clearly not compositional (e.g. **John cleaned the room up, They egged him on, Will you cut the noise out**?), since these likewise allow both positions for the "particle". As I assume these "idiomatic" verb particle combinations will have to be considered single basic expressions (unlike the cases where the meaning is directional) to get the right semantic results, these cases illustrate the importance of letting the notion *word* be distinct from the notion of *basic expression* in a Montague grammar (cf. section 6.3.). In particular, non-compositional verb particle combinations will be basic expressions consisting of more than one word (as will idioms in general), and thus will be treated just like the syntactically 'complex' combinations by principles of word order. I am not sure what the best means of accounting for the second ordering possibility will be. It was already noted by Ross (1967) that this case seems to be one instance of a more general syntactic phenomenon in English, which is a tendency to order the direct object either before or after the complement of a transitive verb (or perhaps even after adverbial adjuncts as well) according to the relative "heaviness" (roughly, the length) of the two constituents, the heavier constituent going last. E.g. a particle is "lighter" than a pronoun (***He looked up it** vs. **He looked it up**) but as heavy as an ordinary noun phrase (**He looked up the number** and **He looked the number up**); a prepositional phrase or adjective complement (see next section) is heavier than an ordinary noun phrase (?**He hammered flat the metal**, vs. **He hammered the metal flat**) but not heavier than a noun phrase with relative clause attached (?**He hammered the metal which he has not been able to bend by hand flat** vs. **He hammered flat the metal which he had not been able to bend by hand**). Perhaps these cases will be best treated by a series of transformations (as in the most familiar transformational treatment), a single transformation, or maybe even by directly altering the operation F_5 for combining transitive verb (phrases) with their objects to allow this operation to be sensitive to this sort of distinction.

4.7. FACTITIVE CONSTRUCTIONS

Another class of accomplishment sentences that played a part in Chapter 2 and has been discussed in the GS literature (Green, 1970; 1972; McCawley, 1971) is sentences consisting of an activity verb followed by an object and then an adjective expressing the result-state that the object comes to be in as a result of the activity:

(44) a. **John hammered the metal** $\left\{\begin{array}{l}\textbf{flat.}\\\textbf{smooth.}\\\textbf{shiny.}\end{array}\right\}$

b. **John wiped the surface** $\left\{\begin{array}{l}\textbf{clean.}\\ \textbf{dry.}\\ \textbf{smooth.}\end{array}\right\}$

c. **Mary wrenched the stick** $\left\{\begin{array}{l}\textbf{free.}\\ \textbf{loose.}\end{array}\right\}$

d. **Mary shot him dead.**

I adopt the traditional term *factitive* for this construction. Much of the concern in the GS literature (especially Green, 1972) has been with the question of why certain combinations of this form sound natural while other apparently parallel constructions such as (45) do not:

(45) a. **?John hammered the metal** $\left\{\begin{array}{l}\textbf{beautiful.}\\ \textbf{safe.}\\ \textbf{tubular.}\end{array}\right\}$

b. **?John wiped the surface** $\left\{\begin{array}{l}\textbf{damp.}\\ \textbf{dirty.}\\ \textbf{stained.}\end{array}\right\}$

c. **?Mary shot him** $\left\{\begin{array}{l}\textbf{lame.}\\ \textbf{wounded.}\end{array}\right\}$

I will not deal with this problem of exceptionality in this section, but I will return to it in Chapter 6. It should also be noted at this point that not all constructions of this syntactic pattern have the same semantic entailments as the examples in (44). There are other sentences (e.g. **Mary found John alone**) where the final adjective expresses a property the object possesses temporarily at the time of the event described by the verb, as well as sentences in which the adjective expresses a property believed by the subject to be possessed by the object (e.g. **Mary considers John obnoxious**), a kind of "propositional attitude" construction. I will not treat these last two classes of sentences here.

Examples like (44) can be produced by a rule which combines a transitive verb with an adjective to produce a new transitive verb, the translation rule introducing the causative relationship that is understood to obtain:[11]

S26. If $\delta \in P_{TV}$ and $\alpha \in P_{ADJ}$, then $F_{26}(\delta, \alpha) \in P_{TV}$, where $F_{26}(\delta, \alpha) = \delta\alpha$.

T26. $F_{26}(\delta, \alpha)$ translates into:
$\lambda\mathscr{P}\lambda x\mathscr{P}\{\hat{y}[\delta'(x, \hat{P}P\{y\})\ \text{CAUSE BECOME}\ \alpha'(y)]\}$

The sentence **Mary shakes John awake** will then have the analysis (46) and a translation that reduces to (46′)

(46)

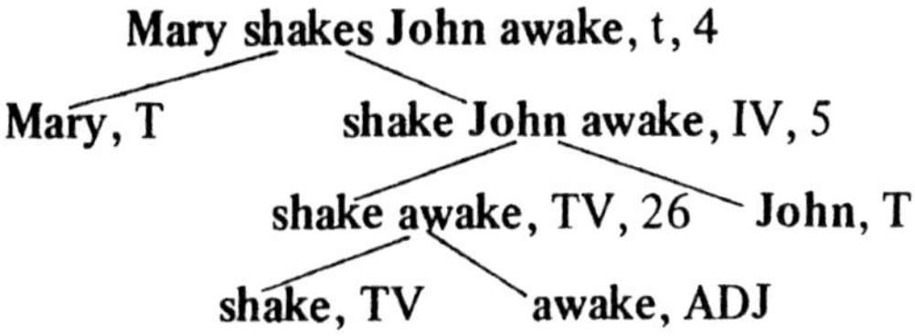

(46′) $[\text{shake}'_*(m, j)$ CAUSE BECOME $\text{awake}'(j)]$

In all these examples the term phrase following the verb behaves semantically as the direct object of the basic transitive verb, as well as the subject of the adjective. That is, (47a) entails (47b), as well as entailing that the metal became flat.

(47) a. **John hammered the metal flat.**
b. **John hammered the metal.**

Both these entailments are in fact accounted for by the translation rule T26, given the semantic interpretation assigned to CAUSE. But as noted in 2.3.6, the superficially similar example (48a) does not entail (48b); though it does still entail that an act of drinking caused John to be silly.

(48) a. **John drank himself silly.**
b. **John drank himself.**

Moreover, there are similar examples in which the verb in isolation is always intransitive, so the parallel sentence that should be entailed is not even grammatical:

(49) a. **John slept himself sober.**
b. ***John slept himself.**

Significantly, all the examples like (48) that I have discovered involve a verb that can be used intransitively as well as transitively (cf. **John drank, John drank a glass of beer**), so it seems best to derive both (48a) and (49a) by a rule similar to S26 except that it combines an intransitive verb with an adjective to form a derived factitive verb:

S27. If $\delta \in P_{IV}$ and $\alpha \in P_{ADJ}$, then $F_{27}(\delta, \alpha) \in P_{TV}$, where $F_{27}(\delta, \alpha) = \delta\alpha$.

T27. $F_{27}(\delta, \alpha)$ translates into:
$\lambda\mathscr{P}\lambda x\mathscr{P}\{\hat{y}[\delta'(x)$ CAUSE BECOME $\alpha'(y)]\}$

The existence of sentences such as (48), by the way, provides an argument against the familiar transformational analysis in which transitive absolute verbs, as in **John drank**, are always derived from underlying transitives (**John drank something**) by an Unspecified Object Deletion transformation. For under this analysis, the semantically plausible source for (48) would be ***John drank something himself sober**, which is not only ungrammatical (Herbert, 1975) but of a general form (NP Verb NP NP Adjective) not found in English at all. An alternative way of relating transitive to transitive absolute verbs that does not present this problem is given in chapter six.

In view of the necessity of having S27 as well as S26, it might now be wondered whether S26 is really necessary. Could it not be the case that **John hammered the metal flat** is really produced by S27 and entails only that John hammered something or other, it being only by virtue of conversational implicature that we infer that the metal was in fact the object he hammered? In fact, there are several reasons to suppose this is not the case. First, there are certain factitives in which the basic verb cannot be used intransitively, e.g. **Mary slammed the door shut** but not ***Mary slammed, Mary wrenched the stick free** but not ***Mary wrenched**. Second, the putative conversational implicature does not seem to be cancellable. Though we can maintain that John drank himself silly, not really by drinking himself but by drinking something else, it seems truly contradictory to maintain that Mary shot Bill dead not by shooting Bill, but by shooting his favorite pet canary, which caused Bill to die of a heart attack on the spot. Third, the intransitive verb most readily available as a source for some examples would be the "wrong" verb. For example, the intransitive verb **shake** that immediately comes to mind is not the transitive absolute form of transitive **shake** but rather a still more basic verb of which transitive **shake** is the causative form: **Mary shook** does not normally mean that she shook something or other but that she herself trembled. Yet **Mary shook John awake** cannot mean that Mary trembled to such an extent that John (who was sleeping in the same bed) was thereby awakened.

Of course, the postulation of both rules predicts that if a basic verb is both transitive and intransitive, then a factitive construction derived from that verb is likewise potentially ambiguous, and as this last example shows, this is not always the case (nor is it the case even most of the time). The reason why this ambiguity fails to occur systematically will be discussed in chapter six. However, there are at least some ambiguous constructions; Barbara Partee has suggested to me the example **The carpenters were pounding me deaf**, which is equally interpretable as entailing that my deafness was being brought on by their pounding on me or by their pounding on something else. This ambiguity is thus a fourth reason for believing that S26 and S27 are distinct.

There is also a kind of transitive construction based on intransitive or transitive absolute verbs in which the result state is expressed by a prepositional phrase rather than an adjective:

(50) a. John read himself to sleep.
b. The king ate himself to death.
c. He drank the officers under the table.
d. He ate his father out of house and home.
e. John bowed her into an arm chair.
f. He studied himself into a pale white ghost.

(Example (e) is cited in Jespersen (1924, p. 311); (f) was brought to my attention by Christopher Smeall.) These examples are highly restricted (what can be substituted for **sleep** and **death** in (a, b)?), often metaphorical (c, d), and/or clearly literary in flavor (e, f). For this reason I cannot justify any one particular path of derivation for them, though the entailments are of the same general class as the earlier examples. Possibly they should be produced by a rule involving TV/TV prepositional phrases, or possibly through a rule using adjectives, since many prepositional phrases largely overlap in distribution with predicative adjectives, in addition to their adverbial function.

Just as there are verbs taking directional adverbs as complements (**put**, **set**, **lay**), so there is at least one factitive construction in which the verb does not occur independently of the result adjective; this is factitive **make** as in **John made Bill happy**, **Mary made the project successful**. To be sure, there is a transitive accomplishment verb **make**, but this means "cause to exist" (**John made a sandcastle**, **Mary made a statement**). Thus deriving factitive **make** from this transitive **make** would give the incorrect result that **John made Bill happy** entailed that John caused Bill to exist and that this act caused Bill to become happy. Instead, factitive **make** is better treated as a separate lexeme of category TV/ADJ with the translation (51):

(51) **make** ($\in P_{TV/ADJ}$) translates into:
$\lambda P \lambda \mathscr{P} \lambda x \mathscr{P}\{\hat{y}[\forall Q[Q\{x\} \text{ CAUSE BECOME } P\{y\}]]\}$

In other words, factitive **make** is a "semantically neutral" factitive causative verb, just as **put** is a "neutral" prepositional phrase complement causative and (as we shall see later) **cause** is a "neutral" infinitive complement causative. With none of these verbs is a particular kind of causative activity entailed, but only a particular result state (thanks to the complement). With this translation for factitive **make**, **John made Bill happy** would have the translation $\bigvee P[P\{j\}$ CAUSE BECOME **happy**$'(b)]$.

A final class of accomplishment constructions that are traditionally called factitives are those in which the result-state is expressed by a noun rather than by an adjective or a preposition:

(52) a. **Mary appointed Bill chairman.**
b. **They elected John president.**
c. **John named Mary representative to the council.**
d. **They made him king.**

As the number of basic verbs that occur in this construction is quite limited, I am inclined to propose that they be categorized as TV/CN, rather than derived by a rule combining a TV with a CN to form a new TV. It is true that at least **elect** and **appoint** also occur as simple transitive verbs without the CN complement (**Mary appointed Bill, They elected John**), but such cases are semantically elliptical; it is understood that there is some particular position to which the person was elected or appointed nevertheless. It thus seems to me more appropriate to derive this use as TV by a "relation reduction" operation (as described in Chapter 6) from the TV/CN occurrence, rather than conversely. However, I can at this point offer no real argument that the derivation must go in this direction rather than the other way. One mysterious question about this construction is whether the sentence-final CN is really a T (cf. **they made him their king** but ?**They elected him the president**); see Hankamer (1973) and Ard (to appear) for discussion. Another mystery is the relationship of this construction to the very similar "naming" construction in which a true name appears (**They named their son John**) and in which this name is *mentioned*, not *used*. An approximate translation rule for **appoint** is (53), which would result in the translation (52a$'$) for (52a). Here p is a variable over propositions and **say**$'$ is of type $\langle\langle s, t\rangle, \langle e, t\rangle\rangle$. This translation reflects the fact that the causal activity for this class of verbs is a speech act, though of course it is really a much more restricted kind of speech act than this translation indicates.

(53) **appoint** translates into:
$\lambda P \lambda \mathscr{P} \lambda x \mathscr{P}\{\hat{y}[\bigvee p[\mathbf{say}'(x, p) \text{ CAUSE BECOME } P\{y\}]]\}$

(52a$'$) $\bigvee p[\mathbf{say}'(m, p) \text{ CAUSE BECOME } \mathbf{chairman}'(b)]$

4.8. PERIPHRASTIC CAUSATIVES

In this section I will discuss syntactic constructions having a verbal complement and the "neutral" causative verbs **make, have** and **cause**, which entail no particular kind of causal activity. My division between factitives and periphrastic causatives is merely for convenience and may be somewhat arbitrary; it is not necessary that any such natural division exist.

The transitive verbs **have** and **make** occur with an IV complement:

(54) **Mary had John wash the car.**

(55) **Mary made John wash the car.**

Along with the physical perception verb complements (**John saw Mary leave the room, John heard Mary leave the room**), these cases form the only instances of the pattern NP verb NP VP in English, the pattern in which the VP complement is preceded by the infinitive marker **to** being much more common than this (**Mary forced John to leave the room, Mary expected John to leave the room**). It is sometimes suggested that the "bare IV" complement is derived from an infinitive complement by a late rule of **to**-deletion, because the **to** is said to appear even in these sentences in their passive forms (**John was made to wash the clothes, Mary was seen to leave the room**). However, these passives are stylistically much more formal than both the "bare-IV" active forms and other passives, probably do not occur at all in the speech of some speakers of English, and have been shown not to be synonymous with their actives (Kirsner, 1977). Whatever the source of the passives, I prefer for the moment to treat the "bare IV" active as a separate basic construction. Thus **make** and **have** will be placed in the category TV/IV, which combines by the operation of simple concatenation with IV to give TV. I assume we have a separate category of infinitives, INF, which is formed from IV-phrases by a rule prefixing **to** to the IV-phrase, though this rule does not alter the meaning of the IV; **force, cause**, etc. will be placed in the category TV/INF rather than in TV/IV. The translation for **make** is (56), and (55) has the translation (55′).

(56) **make** translates into:
$\lambda P \lambda \mathscr{P} \lambda x \mathscr{P}\{\hat{y}[\bigvee Q[Q\{x\} \text{ CAUSE } P\{y\}]]\}$

(55′) $\bigvee x[\bigwedge y[\mathbf{car}'(y) \leftrightarrow x = y] \wedge \bigvee Q[Q\{m\} \text{ CAUSE } \mathbf{wash}'_*(j, x)]]$

The causative **have** occurs not only with a tenseless IV complement as in (54) but also with adjectival, prepositional phrase and apparently "progressive" and past participle complements (cf. Baron, 1974, p. 308):

(57) a. **The cook had the soup hot in a jiffy.**
b. **The dean had the students out of his office in ten minutes.**
c. **The actress had her director eating out of her hand.**
d. **John had the suit cleaned.**

However, there is a subtle difference in meaning between **have** with tenseless complement and the other constructions, as can be observed by comparing (58) with (59) (brought to my attention by Tadeusz Daniliewicz):

(58) **Mary had John visit her every day.**

(59) **Mary had John visiting her every day.**

The "progressiveness" of (59) is something of a red herring, however, since there is another difference here as well. Note that (59) suggests a much more indirect form of coercion on the part of Mary than does (58). I believe the essential difference here is that **have** with "bare IV" complement is restricted to what Talmy (1976) calls *directive causation*, while **have** with the other complements is not. Thus (58) is really only appropriate if Mary *instructed* John to visit her; presumably the inference felt from (59) that Mary brought about John's visit by a less direct means than this is due to a conversational implicature stemming from the fact that (58) would be a more informative sentence if the causation were in fact directive, hence ought to be used in that case instead of (59). The claim that this is a distinction involved predicts that the direct object with the bare IV complement must be a secondary agent (as defined in Chapter 5), hence a sentient being. And in fact this is so; **John had the motor running again in an hour** is normal, but ?**John had the motor run again in an hour** is strange. There is a similar contrast between **John had the soup hot in a jiffy** and ?**John had the soup be hot in a jiffy** or ?**John had the soup warm up in a jiffy**; similarly **John had the letter at the Post Office by 3 P.M.** but ?**John had the letter be at the Post Office by 3 P.M.**/?**John had the letter arrive at the Post Office by 3 P.M.**[12] As is usual elsewhere with tests for agency, computers and intelligent animals that can be instructed to act seem to qualify as agents here: **John had the computer print out the information** is fairly natural, and **John had the bear walk across the stage** is appropriate if the bear was trained to do this on a command or signal though not if the bear were untrained and John brought this about simply by frightening it. (But **John had the bear walking across the stage** is appropriate no matter how John got the bear to do it.) I suspect the reason that adjectives, prepositional phrases and progressive and passive participles all pattern alike in this construction is that these three kinds of expressions can all be used to modify common nouns, hence form a natural syntactic class of some kind; for convenience I will assume this class is the category ADJ, though perhaps some more general syntactic category should be postulated.

The two **have** causatives can be distinguished by the following translations:

(60) **have** ($\in P_{TV/IV}$) translates into:
$\lambda P \lambda \mathscr{P} \lambda x \mathscr{P}\{\hat{y}[\mathbf{direct}'_*(x,y) \text{ CAUSE } P\{y\}]\}$

(61) **have** ($\in P_{TV/ADJ}$) translates into:
$\lambda P \lambda \mathscr{P} \lambda x \mathscr{P}\{\hat{y}[\vee Q[Q\{x\} \text{ CAUSE BECOME } P\{y\}]]\}$

(Of course, appealing to $\mathbf{direct}'_*$ is a stopgap measure here and is not intended to be taken too seriously; I can think of no single existing English verb whose meaning fits exactly what is needed here.)

The causatives **cause** and **get** in TV/INF can be given the same translation as in (61); what subtle differences in meaning there are among these three verbs will have to remain unanalyzed here.

4.9. *BY*-PHRASES IN ACCOMPLISHMENT SENTENCES

One kind of accomplishment sentence discussed in Chapter 2 was one in which the causal activity is expressed through a phrase introduced by **by**, as in (62a). (62a) seems to entail (62b), though as we saw there has traditionally been a problem with deriving (62a) and (62b) from the same underlying structure in GS and a similar problem with explaining the relationship between (63a) and (63b):

(62) a. **John awakened Mary by shouting.**
b. **John's shouting awakened Mary.**

(63) a. **John flattened the metal by hammering it.**
b. **John hammered the metal flat.**

Though my comments about such examples will be somewhat tentative, it does seem possible to account for the entailment relationships among these examples in one way or another. One's first inclination might be to give a translation for **by** that introduces CAUSE, asserting that the event mentioned in the **by**-phrase causes the event mentioned by the main verb. The obvious way to try to do this is (64):

(64) **by** ($\in P_{(TV/TV)/GER}$) translates into:
$\lambda P \lambda \mathscr{R} \lambda \mathscr{P} \lambda x \mathscr{P}\{\hat{y}[P\{x\} \text{ CAUSE } [{}^{\vee}\mathscr{R}(\hat{P}P\{y\})(x)]]\}$

For simplicity, I assume the gerund phrases **shouting, hammering it** appear in a category GER (for gerund) and have the same translations there as the corresponding IV phrase **shout, hammer it**; I do not know what the best syntactic treatment of these will turn out to be in the long run.

However, (64) has the rather bizarre effect of analyzing (62a) (for example) as asserting that John's shouting caused John's awakening of Mary. That is, (if **awaken** itself is given a causative analysis), (62a) would have the translation (62a′)

(62a′) $[\mathbf{shout}'(j)\ \text{CAUSE}\ \vee P[P\{j\}\ \text{CAUSE BECOME}\ \mathbf{awake}'(m)]]$

Philosophers writing about causation (e.g. Kim, 1973; Thompson, 1971) have frequently asserted, without feeling the need for any further discussion, that such an analysis cannot possibly be correct: John's shouting does not cause his awakening of Mary, though it very well may cause Mary to awaken. While I completely agree with this intuition, I am hard-pressed to show, under the counterfactual analysis of causation, exactly what is wrong with this analysis. For if CAUSE is interpreted as suggested, (62a′) would merely seem to assert that in the most similar worlds in which John does not shout, he does not cause Mary to awaken, and it is unclear to me just what is incorrect about this, if anything. This matter clearly involves the much deeper issue of the individuation of the events mentioned by the two sentences. In this case, is the event of John's shouting the same as or different from the event of John's awakening Mary? If the two events are the same, then we have the strange result that here an event causes itself, but on the other hand it seems equally peculiar to say that there are two distinct events here which stand in a causal relationship. I do not have anything to add to this difficult problem here (see Cresswell (ms.) for a recent discussion of events within the possible worlds framework). I think I cannot rule out the possibility that (62a′) could be defended, particularly if (as was recommended in 2.3.7) CAUSE is taken to represent a somewhat more encompassing relation than causation is usually taken to be by philosophers and/or if events are given an analysis that ties them more closely to the propositions asserting that they occur than is often assumed (e.g. Montague's (1969) analysis treating events as properties of times and the discussion by Cresswell (ms.)). But I will suggest instead a less problematic way of accounting for the entailments of **by**, which is to treat it as an expression of category (IV/IV)/T and its translation **by**′ as a non-logical constant restricted by the following meaning postulate:

(65) $\bigwedge p \bigwedge P \bigwedge Q \bigwedge x \Box[\mathbf{by}'(P)(\hat{y}[Q\{y\}\ \text{CAUSE}\ {}^{\vee}p])(x) \rightarrow$
$[P\{x\}\ \text{CAUSE}\ {}^{\vee}p]]$

This specifies that if by doing Px does something (Q) that causes some proposition p to obtain, then in this situation x's doing P causes p to obtain. This postulate leaves open the question of just how the events involved are to be individuated; it does not require that the event which P is the property of being "involved in" (however this notion is to be defined) is the same as the event which Q is the property of being involved in, because it does not even require that P and Q be the same property. This is as it should be, since if John hammers the metal flat by pounding it with a pipe wrench, we do not wish to say that the *property* of hammering the metal is the same as the property of pounding it with a pipewrench, though the extension of these two properties may be the same in the actual and/or most relatively similar worlds.[13] Under this analysis (62a) would have the translation (62a″), and this entails (66) (which ought to be the translation of (62b), though I will not try to give syntactic rules for producing (62b)) in view of the meaning postulate (65):

(62a″) $[\mathbf{by}'({}^\wedge\mathbf{shout}')(\hat{x}[\bigvee Q[Q\{x\} \text{ CAUSE BECOME } \mathbf{awake}'(m)]])(j)]$

(66) $[\mathbf{shout}'(j) \text{ CAUSE BECOME } \mathbf{awake}'(m)]$

Likewise, the translation (63a′) of (63a) will entail (63b′), which is the translation of (63b):

(63a′) $\bigvee x[\bigwedge y[\mathbf{metal}(y) \leftrightarrow x = y] \wedge$
$\mathbf{by}'({}^\wedge\mathbf{hammer}'(\hat{P}P\{x\}))(\hat{z}[\bigvee Q[Q\{z\} \text{ CAUSE}$
$\text{BECOME } \mathbf{flat}'(x)]])(j)]$

(63b′) $\bigvee x[\bigwedge y[\mathbf{metal}'(y) \leftrightarrow x = y] \wedge [\mathbf{hammer}'_*(j, x) \text{ CAUSE}$
$\text{BECOME } \mathbf{flat}'(x)]]$

4.10. CAUSATIVE CONSTRUCTIONS IN OTHER LANGUAGES

Though the variety of causative and factitive constructions of English discussed in this chapter may seem great, these possibilities are in fact restricted when compared with other languages. While English can convert an intransitive verb to a causative transitive by a fairly regular process (**The window broke** vs. **John broke the window**), it cannot convert a transitive verb to a causative three-place verb, nor a three-place verb to a causative four-place verb. Where such causative counterparts exist at all in English, they are completely different lexical items: it has been suggested (cf. Baron, 1974, p. 303 and references cited there) that **feed** is, semantically, the causative counterpart of **eat, give** of **have, show** of **see**, etc. But other languages regularly derive causative verbs from these other categories of verbs as well.

In an interesting cross-linguistic study of causative constructions in a large number of languages, Comrie (1976) investigates the syntactic patterns of causatives derived from intransitive, transitive and three-place verbs. Comrie conceived of the problem in transformational terms; that is, he assumed that the underlying structure of all such derived causatives consists of a sentence with a noncausative verb embedded in a higher sentence with a possibly abstract verb CAUSE, whose subject denotes the agent or instigator of causation. In the surface structure the causative element and embedded verb are fused into a single verb (either a verb with causative affix or a compound verb), and the subject of the higher CAUSE in underlying structure becomes the surface structure subject. The problem, then, is to describe what each language does with the subject of the embedded sentence which is necessarily "displaced" from subject position by this operation, as for example, the underlying subject in **The window broke** is displaced by the agent and becomes an object in **John broke the window.** As a background against which to solve this problem for the various types of verbs, Comrie sets up what he calls the *paradigm case*, to which few languages correspond exactly but from which all languages differ minimally. This paradigm is summarized in (67):

(67)	*Embedded verb is*:	*And thus originally has these arguments*:	*Old subject becomes new*:
(a)	intransitive	subject	direct object
(b)	transitive	subject, direct object	indirect object
(c)	three-place	subject, direct object, indirect object	oblique object or prepositional object

The paradigm case can be described as a general principle by reference to the Keenan–Comrie *accessibility hierarchy* – the ranking (1) *subject* (2) *direct object* (3) *indirect object* (4) *oblique object* – which is claimed to be reflected in universal principles of relative clause formation and other syntactic universals (Keenan and Comrie, 1977). That is, the paradigm case simply prescribes that in forming a derived causative, the embedded subject merely "moves down" the accessibility hierarchy to the first "vacant" position on the hierarchy, according to the complement of arguments the verb originally had. (Comrie devotes the bulk of his article to discussion of the various deviations from the paradigm case that sometimes occur, but I will only be concerned with the description of the unexceptional paradigm case causatives here.)

In order to accommodate the additional kinds of verbs, I propose to treat three-place verbs as members of the category TV/T (i.e. expressions that will combine with a term by a functional application rule to produce expressions of the category TV) and four-place verbs as members of the category (TV/T)/T, which is an analogous extension. This permits us to define the "grammatical relations" of the Keenan–Comrie hierarchy and their natural ordering in the following way:

(68)

Term bearing the grammatical relation:	*Is defined as*:
Subject	Any term (P_T) that is combined with an IV-phrase to form a sentence
Direct Object	Any term that is combined with a TV-phrase to form an IV-phrase
Indirect Object	Any term that is combined with a TV/T-phrase to form a TV-phrase
Oblique Object	Any term that is combined with a (TV/T)/T-phase to form a TV/T-phrase

This account of "grammatical relations" is like that given by the theory of Relational Grammar (Perlmutter and Postal, to appear), by the way, in defining these relations in a way that is independent of the linear ordering of terms or phrase-structure configurations that realize these relations in particular languages; note that the definitions above are independent of the form of the syntactic operations associated with each functional application rule alluded to, and these operations may differ from one language to another. (For further discussion and a treatment of "relation changing rules" see Dowty, 1978.)

The rules for paradigm case causatives are (69)–(71); in particular languages the causative-forming syntactic operation that I have represented as F_{C1}, F_{C2}, etc. might leave the form of the verb unchanged (as in English), add a causative affix (as in Turkish), or concatenate the verb with a verb otherwise meaning "cause" (as in French causatives with *faire*).

(69) SC1. (Transitive causative verbs from intransitive verbs)
If $\alpha \in P_{IV}$, then $F_{C1}(\alpha) \in P_{TV}$.

TC1. $F_{C1}(\alpha)$ translates into:
$\lambda\mathscr{P}\lambda x \mathscr{P}\{\hat{y}[\mathrm{V}P[P\{x\}\ \mathrm{CAUSE}\ \alpha'(y)]]\}$

(70) SC2. (Three-place causative verbs from transitive verbs)
If $\alpha \in P_{TV}$ then $F_{C2}(\alpha) \in P_{TV/T}$.
TC2. $F_{C2}(\alpha)$ translates into:
$\lambda\mathscr{Q}\lambda\mathscr{P}\lambda x\mathscr{Q}\{\hat{y}[VP[P\{x\}\ \text{CAUSE}\ \alpha'(\mathscr{P})(y)]]\}$

(71) SC3. (Four-place causative verbs from three-place verbs)
If $\alpha \in P_{TV/T}$ then $F_{C3}(\alpha) \in P_{(TV/T)/T}$.
TC3. $F_{C3}(\alpha)$ translates into:
$\lambda\mathscr{S}\lambda\mathscr{Q}\lambda\mathscr{P}\lambda x\,\mathscr{S}\{\hat{y}[VP[P\{x\}\ \text{CAUSE}\ \alpha'(\mathscr{Q})(\mathscr{P})(y)]]\}$

In these translations, $\mathscr{P}$, $\mathscr{Q}$ and $\mathscr{S}$ are all variables of type $\langle s, f(T)\rangle$, and to make the translations somewhat easier to decipher, I have consistently used $\mathscr{P}$ in the position of the direct object, $\mathscr{Q}$ in the position of the indirect object, and $\mathscr{S}$ in the position of the oblique object. An important difference to note between this treatment and the kind of analysis assumed by Comrie (and most transformationalists, e.g. Aissen, 1974) is that here causativization is an operation on verbs themselves, rather than an operation on complex sentences containing these verbs. This difference will turn out to have important consequences in Chapter 5.

NOTES

[1] Actually, **John**, **Mary**, etc. are translated into j^*, m^*, etc. respectively in PTQ, where the notation α^* is then defined as $\lambda P[P\{\alpha\}]$. But the intermediate notation α^* seems to me to serve no useful function, so I bypass it here.

[2] In section 4.2 below we will take note of another kind of flexibility offered by meaning postulates but not by direct decomposition.

[3] Thus I assume that adjectives such as **alive** translate into predicates (of type $\langle e, t\rangle$) rather than into predicate modifiers (of type $\langle\langle s, \langle e, t\rangle\rangle, \langle e, t\rangle\rangle$) as adjectives like **former** do: cf. Siegel (1976a, 1976b) for arguments that both categories of adjectives are required in Russian and in English.

[4] It may be desirable to restrict the property variable P in this formula to make it range only over agentive activities, and this could be done in various ways: by inserting a specification that P has the higher-order property of being an activity (replacing $P\{x\}$ with $[\textbf{activity}'(P) \wedge P\{x\}]$), by making use of a DO operator of type $\langle\langle s, \langle e, t\rangle\rangle, \langle e, t\rangle\rangle$ (replacing $P\{x\}$ with $[DO(P)](x)$), or perhaps by conventional implicature by the method described in Karttunen and Peters (1975; 1978). I will not pursue any of these options here however.

[5] Other variants of this translation would be possible in which the sub-part of the formula . . . $\mathscr{P}\{\hat{y}$ . . . is placed differently. The reasons for this choice of position in (13′) and elsewhere will be made clear in the next chapter.

[6] A technical difficulty with this rule (and others that follow) in the UG system is that the requirements of *disambiguated language* would not literally allow any syntactic

operation ever to give exactly the same expression as output that it takes as input. Thus it would be necessary to invent some trivial difference or other between the adjective **cool** and the verb **cool** produced by this rule, say a subscript or prime on the latter, though we could have the ambiguating relation *R* remove this difference if we like. A solution which is in keeping with the principle of transformational syntax (and generative phonology for that matter (Chomsky and Halle, 1968)) is to treat expressions as not simply strings but bracketed expressions (or equivalently, trees) labeled with the syntactic category to which they belong. Thus each syntactic rule would always add outer brackets labeled with the category of the output, and this would suffice to differentiate the inputs and outputs of rules such as S23 (and S24 below) which may not otherwise alter their inputs. E.g. the adjective **cool** would be identified with the expression $[\textbf{cool}]_{ADJ}$ and the intransitive verb derived from it would be $[[\textbf{cool}]_{ADJ}]_{IV}$. The transitive verb derived in turn from this by S24 would be $[[[\textbf{cool}]_{ADJ}]_{IV}]_{TV}$, and so on.

[7] Actually, the analyses given predict that the two examples cited here, as well as (27b), should be ambiguous, since there is nothing to prohibit the IV-modifier **into the wastebasket** from combining with the IV **throw the letter.** In other words, **John threw the letter into the wastebasket** should also be interpretable as saying that John somehow ended up in the wastebasket, tossing the letter as this happened. As far as I can tell, this is an acceptable result, though such a reading is highly unlikely for pragmatic reasons. Likewise, (30) and (31) below should have a non-contradictory reading as well as a contradictory one when the possibility of reading the prepositional phrases as IV-modifiers is taken into account.

[8] Here and elsewhere it will be convenient to indulge in a minor use-mention confusion to avoid a pedantic verbosity: I will often say "the direct object" when I mean "the entity denoted by the direct object", etc., but no confusion should arise.

[9] James McCawley has pointed out to me that **walk from Boston** is "more elliptical" than **walk to Chicago,** in that (i) allows the various walks to have different starting points, while (ii) seems to require that all walks have the same goal:

(i) **John walks to Chicago several times a year.**
(ii) **John walks from Chicago several times a year.**

I am not sure that this is a semantic restriction, however. The preference for the suggested reading of (ii) might arise purely from expectations about the common real-world situations in which (ii) is likely to be used. If the restriction *is* semantic in origin, I suspect it is best handled by treating **from Chicago** as an indexical; I do not see how to rig the scope restrictions within the fragment of chapter seven so that the existential quantifier binding the "destination" that appears in my translation of **from** must have wider scope that the adverbial **several times a year.**

[10] Susan Schmerling has pointed out that these tests also seem to show that **from Chicago to Detroit** can be a constituent even in intransitive sentences – cf. *It was from Chicago to Detroit that John walked*. Thus **from Chicago** should perhaps also occur in the category IAV/IAV, even though I do not (so far) see the semantic motivation for treating it as a modifier of IV-modifiers that would parallel the motivation we have just seen in the transitive case. Of course, **from Chicago** might well occur in IAV (as I have treated it in (36')) as well as in IAV/IAV and in (TV/TV)/(TV/TV).

[11] Since this not only takes TV as input but also gives TV as output, it could potentially iterate, e.g. combining a derived TV **hammer flat** with **smooth** to give ***hammer flat smooth**, and this must be prohibited in one way or another. This difficulty is partially alleviated by the classification of S26 as a lexical rather than as a syntactic rule (in Chapter 6), though this treatment still suggests that ***hammer flat smooth** is a potential if not yet actual lexical phrase of English.

[12] It seems to me that this last example might be acceptable if it is understood that John directed someone else to cause the letter to arrive at 3 P.M. If so, I am not sure what sort of modification of the translation of **have** this observation suggests, since the other examples given here do not seem to allow the interpolation of an intermediary agent. All of these examples are of course acceptable (if unusual) if **have** is read as the so-called "experiential *have*", describing an unwelcome incident that befalls the person denoted by the subject (as in the natural reading of *John had his car stolen yesterday*). This *have* must of course be treated differently from the causative **have** under discussion.

[13] Note the interconnection between this point and the matter of causal selection discussed in Chapter 2. If the truth conditions (or possibly even the conventional implicature) of CAUSE were somehow restricted to always require a unique cause for each result, P and Q could not be distinct.

CHAPTER 5

LINGUISTIC EVIDENCE FOR THE TWO STRATEGIES OF LEXICAL DECOMPOSITION

It is not merely for semantic reasons that the classical GS theory postulates a level of underlying structure at which words are decomposed, but also because it is explicitly argued that these decomposed structures are of the same general form as English syntactic structures and that the same set of operations, namely transformations (or "derivational constraints" if preferred), is responsible for successive stages of the deep-to-surface mapping before as well as after lexical insertion. In this chapter I will examine the arguments that have been presented for this position, determine what modifications must be made in the "inverted generative semantics" model of decomposition to accommodate the data on which these arguments are based, and evaluate the overall success with which this data is treated in the two methods under consideration. I will first consider briefly four kinds of putative syntactic arguments for decomposition found in the literature that I do not find to be serious contenders for persuasive arguments at all, then turn to arguments of a more compelling nature.

5.1. ARGUMENTS THAT CONSTRAINTS ON SYNTACTIC RULES RULE OUT "IMPOSSIBLE" LEXICAL ITEMS

There is now a large body of evidence (of which Ross (1967) was the first major source) that syntactic transformations are quite generally prohibited from extracting material from certain types of syntactic configurations. For example, the *Complex NP Constraint* provides that expressions cannot be extracted from relative clauses, thus there is no question (1b) corresponding to the structure (1a) except that *something* has been extracted by WH-movement:

(1) a. John knows a man who told Mary something.
b. *What does John know a man who told Mary?

Similarly, it is known that noun phrases cannot in general be extracted from conjoined structures, so there is no question corresponding to (2a) except that *something* has been questioned:

(2) a. John left all his money to Bill and someone.
b. *Who did John leave all his money to Bill and?

It has been pointed out (McCawley, 1971; 1973; Morgan, 1969) that if prelexical transformations such as Predicate Raising are subject to these same constraints (as they should be,[1] under the GS hypothesis), certain logical structures are thereby ruled out as candidates for words of English. For example, McCawley (1971) asserts that there could be no possible English verb **flimp* under this hypothesis whose meaning is such that (3a) is a paraphrase of (3b):

(3) a. *Bert flimped coconuts.
b. Bert kissed a girl who is allergic to coconuts.

This is because the Predicate Raising transformation would have to combine elements from within a complex NP (namely those underlying *allergic to*) with elements outside the complex NP (namely, *kiss*) in order for a lexicalization transformation to insert **flimp*, and such movement would be prohibited by the Complex NP Constraint. Similarly, McCawley (1973) observes that there would be no verb **thork* whose meaning made (4a) a paraphrase of (4b), because its pre-lexical derivation would violate the Coordinate Structure Constraint:

(4) a. *John thorked Harry 5000 yen.
b. John lent his uncle and Harry 5000 yen.

And, the argument goes, there are in fact no words on record whose meaning violates these constraints. Thus the generative semantics decomposition hypothesis correctly rules out a number of impossible lexical items and so offers a (partial) theoretical characterization of "possible lexical items".

While I must agree that this is in principle an argument in favor of the syntactic decomposition hypothesis, in practice it seems all but totally untestable. Note that under this hypothesis there will still be quite a number of possible lexical items that are nevertheless not actual ones, so no list of ungrammatical examples such as (3a) and (4a), no matter how long, really provides any direct evidence for the hypothesis at all, since all these might merely be "accidental lexical gaps" (cf. the previously cited possible but non-occurring word that would mean "cause to become not obnoxious") whether or not the restriction is a real one. Instead, one would presumably have to examine the entire vocabulary of English and show that the correct decomposition analysis of every occurring word falls within the limits prescribed by the hypothesis. This monumental undertaking has not been begun.

McCawley (1973) actually interprets this claim somewhat differently: he asserts that as native speakers of English, we have *intuitions* that words like *flimp* are not merely non-occurring words but impossible words – intuitions parallel to the frequently cited phonological intuition of native speakers; that *blick* is a phonologically possible but non-occurring word of English, while **ftick* is an impossible word of English (due to the prohibition against [ft] as an initial consonant cluster in English). But I at least have no such strong intuition about the meanings of **flimp* and **thork*. In all fairness, it must be pointed out that McCawley's rather fanciful meanings for **flimp* and **thork* could hardly be imagined as meanings of words of English quite aside from the question of whether their form would violate Ross' constraints; we are all implicitly aware that the lexical items which a language contains are in part conditioned by aspects of the culture of its speakers which create a need for names of certain classes of objects, states or actions that are important to those speakers, and it seems hard to separate one's intuitions about the cultural unlikelihood of a word for kissing girls with certain allergies from intuitions about the form of such meanings.

Moreover, in many cases more than one obvious paraphrase of a word is available, some of which may appear to violate a syntactic constraint as a putative underlying structure and some of which do not. Supporting the hypothesis in such cases is a matter of arguing on independent grounds that only the syntactically "legal" paraphrases could be the correct source, and this may be hard to do. Consider for example the verb *cuckold*. One obvious paraphrase of a sentence with this verb, (5a), is (5b):

(5) a. John cuckolded Bill.
b. John had sexual intercourse with the woman who is married to Bill.

But if (5a) is derived from an underlying structure with the approximate form of (5b), the complex NP constrain is violated. But, it may be objected, (5b) is the wrong paraphrase; the verb *cuckold* should perhaps be derived from the noun *cuckold* (in accord with its historical origin), so that the verb *cuckold* means "cause to be a cuckold," where the noun *cuckold* is derived from "a man whose wife has committed adultery." But then the point is, how do we know that **flimp* is really impossible, for it might likewise be analyzed as "cause to be a flimp", where the noun *flimp* means "a foodstuff that some girl who has been kissed is allergic to"? The two analyses make slightly different predictions in each case. If the verb *cuckold* really means "cause to be a cuckold," then one could presumably cuckold a man simply by compelling some third party to have sexual intercourse with his wife. That is "coreference" between the subject of *cause* and the lower verb would not be required by this analysis. Unfortunately, the verb *cuckold* is not part of my active vocabulary, so I am unable to decide on the basis of my own intuitions whether this analysis accurately represents the meaning of *cuckold* or not (though all citations for *cuckold* in the OED seem to involve "direct" cuckolding, not the "indirect" act allowed for by this analysis). Again, the point is that claims about the non-occurrence of words like **flimp* must be carefully hedged in a parallel way.

To cite just one other worry, Borkin (1972), following Paul Postal, suggests that a deletion transformation is responsible for removing the head noun and part of the relative clause structure in (6a) to give something like (6b), the resulting abbreviated NP being called a *beheaded* NP.

(6) a. All the people who live in the apartment house have hepatitis.
b. The whole apartment house has hepatitis.

But if instead the correct analysis of (6b) were that the prelexical material underlying *all the people who live in the apartment house* were raised by predicate raising onto a single node before *the whole apartment house* was inserted by a lexical transformation, then the Complex NP Constraint would be violated here by a pre-lexical transformation. Conversely, the violation of the Complex NP Constraint in the derivation of **flimp* could be avoided if one could argue for an analysis that merely deleted material from within the complex NP *girl who is allergic to coconuts*, rather than raising it out of this structure by Predicate Raising. This discussion of *cuckold* and beheaded NPs is not intended to suggest that the Complex NP Constraint actually *is* violated in these cases, but merely to point out the extreme difficulty in determining whether there are any counterexamples to McCawley's claim or not. As far as I know, the evidence we have about the details of pre-lexical stages of such derivations remains very sketchy; for example, evidence for deletion vis-à-vis raising at the prelexical level is hard to come by. Hence the impact of McCawley's argument is very weak for the time being.

5.2. ARGUMENTS THAT FAMILIAR TRANSFORMATIONS ALSO APPLY PRELEXICALLY

McCawley (1973) claims that a number of familiar transformations can be observed to apply in the pre-lexical derivation of English words. For example reflexivization is said to apply in the derivation of *suicide* (which presumably comes from *x kills x*, by way of *x kill's x's self*), Equi-NP Deletion is said to apply in *Ernest is looking for a lion* (which would come from a structure of the form *Ernest tries* [*Ernest finds a lion*]), Passive is said to apply in the phrase *under study* and in German *polizeilich verboten*. If we are to take these cases as evidence for prelexical syntactic manipulation (rather than merely corollaries which follow when this hypothesis is established independently), then the argument must rest on two assumptions which are questionable in the present context: (1) that any operation whose effect seems to resemble that of a familiar well-motivated transformation should be attributed to that transformation itself rather than merely one which is similar to it, and (2) we are not permitted to appeal to semantic principles to account for entailments but should expect them to be "laid out" in underlying logical structure (as for example when we postulate an underlying embedded subject in *John tried to walk* because the sentence intuitively involves John's walking rather than just anyone's walking). This first argument in fact appears even earlier in the transformational literature in Chapin (1967), where, for example, it is assumed that the reflexive transformation applies in the derivation of *self-addressed envelope* (because the reflexive transformation, after all, is known to introduce the morpheme *self*) and that the passive transformation applies in the derivation of *washable* in *this shirt is washable* (because the same change of direct object into subject is observed here as in *This shirt was washed*). This assumption, while perhaps unquestioned in the earliest days of transformational research, has become progressively weaker as a rule of thumb as it has become necessary to postulate more and more instances of similar but yet not identical transformations (cf. the discussion of reflexive pronouns in Ross (1970) which do not originate by "ordinary" reflexivization and also the special reflexives in *picture of himself*, for example), and I think it is fair to say that hardly any linguist would feel confident today in arguing that the *same* transformation must be postulated in such a case without good evidence to that effect. The second assumption, while still frequently encountered in generative semantics literature, is, as we have noted, not compelling at all as soon as we realize that no "logical form" of a sentence can literally represent *all* the semantic entailments of that sentence without recourse to further semantic principles. Moreover, we will note below that Newmeyer (1976) has shown that serious problems arise from the assumption that familiar cyclic transformations such as *there*-insertion are free to apply pre-lexically.

5.3. PRONOMINALIZATION OF PARTS OF LEXICAL ITEMS

One of the earliest arguments for abstract stages of a syntactic derivation came from a kind of example cited by Lakoff (1965; 1970), where it can be observed that a pronoun sometimes seems to have as its antecedent a part of the meaning of a lexical item (perhaps along with other parts of the sentence), though not the meaning of the "whole" word. For example, italicized *it* in (7) seems to refer to the sentence *the glass melted* rather than *Floyd melted the glass*:

(7) Floyd melted the glass though it surprised me that he was able to bring *it* about.

Similarly, *do so* in (8) seems to stand for the intransitive verb *melt*, not the causative transitive *melt* in the first clause:

(8) Floyd melted the glass though it surprised me that it would *do so*.

If we assume that the pro-forms *it* and *do so* in these two sentences are introduced by a syntactic transformation contingent upon a syntactically identical antecedent being present earlier in the same sentence, these examples provide an argument that transitive *melt* in the first clause of each example should be derived from a complex structure *cause the glass to melt* (if not a more complex structure).

However, Fodor (1970) observed that the same argument does not extend to monomorphemic lexical causatives. For if an earlier syntactic stage of the derivation of *kill* involves a structure of the form *cause to die* (or some more complex structure), then we should expect *do so* in (9) to refer felicitously to *die*, just as it does in (10):

(9) *John killed Mary, and it surprised me that she *did so*.

(10) John caused Mary to die, and it surprised me that she *did so*.

It was shown by Postal (1969) that this "blockage" of anaphoric relationships between a pronoun and a sub-part of a monomorphemic lexical item is in fact quite general, as Postal provides dozens of cases parallel to (9) and (10); that is, monomorphemic lexical items are quite generally "anaphoric islands". Postal himself did not consider this data to be evidence against the syntactic derivation of words from more complex sources, but rather tried to turn the argument around and show that his evidence really supported the generative semantics theory by pointing to a number of subtle and idiosyncratic parallel restrictions between sublexical anaphoric possibilities and "super-lexical" anaphoric possibilities. But Postal's conclusion from his data is open to question for various reasons. First, the importance of the subtle, alleged parallels between the constraints on the two kinds of anaphora is a matter of the linguist's subjective judgment of their importance, given the highly incomplete knowledge we presently have of the total restrictions involved in a complete grammar of English. Also, one cannot rule out the possibility that these parallels are due to as yet unknown factors which would equally affect sub-lexical and syntactic anaphoric possibilities. But most important, the cases of "syntactic" constructions Postal discusses (in particular *proper pseudo-adjectives*, as in "the *American* attack on Columbia") are just those constructions for which it is no longer clear that a syntactic derivation – rather than a lexical – is advisable. Thus the data Postal cites seems to me on the whole to disconfirm rather than to confirm the GS syntactic lexical decomposition hypothesis, in that the differences between sub-lexical and super-lexical anaphoric possibilities seem to greatly outweigh the similarities.

5.4. SCOPE AMBIGUITIES WITH *ALMOST*

Morgan (1969) was the first to claim that scope ambiguities appearing with certain adverbs argue for a lexical decomposition analysis. One such case is the adverb *almost* (and its synonyms *nearly*, etc.; adverbs like *only* and *even* produce parallel examples). He suggested that (11) is at least three ways ambiguous, these different readings being brought out by the paraphrases (12a), (12b) and (12c) respectively:

(11) John almost killed Harry.

(12) a. What John almost did was kill Harry.
b. What John did was almost kill Harry.
c. What John did to Harry was almost kill him.

Following up on Morgan's claims, McCawley (1973) proposes that the logical structures (13a), (13b) and (13c) respectively underlie the three readings paraphrased in (12a)-(12c):

(13)

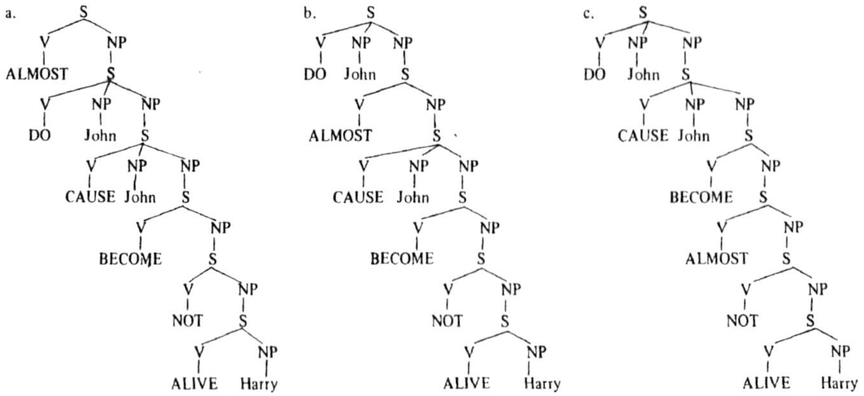

According to Morgan and McCawley, there is a transformation of *Adverb Raising* which may optionally move the adverb *almost* to a higher position in the tree; this then allows Predicate Raising to derive a structure which can lexicalize as *kill* in each case.

Morgan suggests that there is independent motivation for Adverb Raising from examples like (14a) and (14b): (14b) seems to have the reading of (14a) in addition to a second reading, and Morgan suggests that Adverb Raising here also can "raise" the adverb from its position in (14a) to that in (14b):

(14) a. John drank almost all his milk.
b. John almost drank all his milk.

Two things should be noted about this motivation for Adverb Raising, however. If Morgan is correct about the transformational relationship between these two sentences, then they still only provide evidence for a rule moving an adverb from a noun phrase (or determiner) node to a verb phrase node within the same clause, though in the derivation of (13b) and (13c) the transformation would have to raise the adverb from a lower to a higher clause. But transformations (at least, meaning-preserving ones) must generally be prohibited from moving an adverb from a lower to a higher clause; note that (15a) ≠ (15b) ≠ (15c):[2]

(15) a. John claimed that Bill denied that Mary left the country on Thursday in a blue Plymouth.
b. John claimed that Bill denied on Thursday that Mary left the country in a blue Plymouth.

c. John claimed on Thursday that Bill denied that Mary left the country in a blue Plymouth.

Though one might suggest that adverbs like *on Thursday* be prohibited from undergoing Adverb Raising even though *almost* undergoes it, temporal adverbs such as *again* and *for six weeks* also lead to scope ambiguities with accomplishment verbs (as we shall see shortly) but nevertheless cannot be substituted in the sentence patterns (15a)-(15c) with "meaning preserving" results. Though one might contrive even further restrictions on Adverb Raising to achieve just the correct results, the effect of such restrictions would be to abolish all independent motivation for Adverb Raising aside from those cases where it is needed for McCawley's and Morgan's analysis of monomorphemic accomplishments.[3]

Moreover, it is not at all clear that the alleged ambiguities of (11) are in fact structural ambiguities rather than just an instance of vagueness (or generality) among an indefinite number of possibilities. Note that it is not sufficient to be able to imagine a number of distinct situations to which the alleged different readings of (11) could be applied; to base a claim for ambiguity solely on this intuition would be to commit the fallacy discussed by Zwicky and Sadock (1975) of supposing that, for example, *John has a shirt* is ambiguous between a reading "John has a red shirt" and a reading "John has a blue shirt" because one can imagine distinct situations to which the sentence can be applied with equal appropriateness. There might conceivably be only one source and one meaning for *almost* in (11), yet this meaning might be general enough to cover all the situations individuated by (12a)-(12c). If, as Sadock (ms.) suggests, "*x almost VERBs*" means simply "there is a possible world very similar to the actual world in which 'x VERBs' is true", then this meaning might be equally appropriate for situations in which John has the intention of killing Bill but at the last minute decides to do nothing at all (12a), situations in which John's act comes close to causing Harry's death but really affects him not at all (e.g. the bullet misses by an inch) (12b), or situations in which John's action causes an effect in Harry which is near to death (e.g. he is critically wounded but recovers) (12c). Likewise, it can be nearly true that John drinks all his milk either if he has the intention of drinking it all but at the last minute changes his mind and drinks none at all, or if he drinks all but a small part of it. That is, the meaning of *almost* in (14a) might be general enough to cover the case of (14b) as well. To try to test for the alleged ambiguity of (11) by one of the linguistic tests suggested by Sadock and Zwicky (1975), we should examine a case such as (16):

(16) The Vice-President's trip to Lower Glinocovia nearly resulted in tragedy on two occasions. First, an assassin almost killed him – though the Secret Servicemen captured him just before he fired – and so did the case of malaria he contracted.

Here, *so did* must be read as "almost killed him."[4] On the Morgan-McCawley analysis the first clause presumably required the source in which *almost* modifies the highest clause (since the assassin does not act at all) while the second clause requires *almost* to come from a lower clause (since the disease did affect him). Though I find the judgment delicate, and the example is of necessity somewhat awkward, (16) does not seem to me to have the clear anomaly that usually results from such "crossed senses" readings when a proform such as *so do* is incorrectly substituted for a structurally distinct verb phrase, hence (16) suggests that no true ambiguity is present.[5] If there are in fact two distinct readings for (11) (and I find it hard to persuade myself that there could be *more* than two, as McCawley believes), the two readings can probably be accommodated in the manner suggested for adverbs like *again* below.[6]

5.5. SCOPE AMBIGUITIES WITH ADVERBS: *HAVE*-DELETION CASES

One important class of arguments for decomposition from the scope ambiguities of adverbs involves intensional verbs such as *want, need* and *seek*. Though these verbs do not involve the same kind of decomposition analysis as do the accomplishment/achievement verbs which are the focus of this book, the problems are somewhat parallel and turn out to be of great relevance to the decomposition issue at hand. This argument is stated in its most seductive form in McCawley (1974) and Partee (1974), though it also appears elsewhere in various partial forms (cf. Bach, 1968; Quine, 1960).

Verbs like *want* (similarly *need, demand, desire, wish for, promise, expect, hope for* and others, with minor syntactic differences) appear in multiple syntactic configurations, among them one in which there is an object plus infinitival complement (and in which the object is presumably the underlying subject of the infinitive, so that the verb *want* has a sentential complement in underlying structure). An example is (17a). *Want* also occurs without the subject of the infinitive as in (17b) (in which case this subject is assumed in transformational grammar to have been deleted on identity with the subject of the higher clause) and also with a simple NP object as in (17c):

(17) a. John wants Mary to win.
b. Max wants to eat a banana.
c. Max wants a lollipop.

It can also be argued that (17c) has a sentential object in underlying structure. That is, (17c) would be claimed to have as source the sentence underlying (17c′):

(17) c′. Max wants [Max have a lollipop].

The underlying subject in (17c′) has been deleted by Equi-NP Deletion in the same way as in (17b), and a transformation of *have*-deletion would be postulated which deletes *have* and *to* in the structure (17c′) when the verb is one of the class *want*, *need*, *desire*, etc. In the GS theory, *have*-deletion may not really be needed; instead, Predicate Raising could be assumed to apply to raise *have* (or what underlies it) up onto the higher verb *want* prior to lexicalization; the lexicalization rule for *want* specifies that *want* is inserted whether or not the verb complex includes *have* as well.

A certain syntactic economy is achieved by this analysis: verbs of the *want* class can be categorized uniformly for a sentential object in underlying structure (rather than for *either* a sentential object *or* a noun phrase object) and semantic interpretation is presumably somewhat simplified for (17c), since we seem to interpret all such sentences as if there were a lower verb *have* (or at least something very much like this) present.[7]

But there are also syntactic arguments for a sentential-complement source for (17). As McCawley observes, the adverbials in (18) do not describe the "time of the wanting" but rather the "time of having," as is brought out more clearly in (19):

(18) Bill wants your apartment { until June / for 6 months / while you're in Botswana. }

(19) Right now Bill wants your apartment until June, but tomorrow he'll probably want it until October.

In McCawley's view, the adverbials in (18) originated in the lower clause in underlying structure, and (19) contains adverbs from both clauses. Note that verbs which are not of the *want* class do not allow two adverbials specifying distinct times:

(20) a. A week ago Bill wanted your car yesterday.
b. *A week ago Bill painted your car yesterday.

This analysis also explains why the second time adverbial in *want* sentences (i.e., the one allegedly originating from a lower sentence) need not correspond to the tense of the main verb in the way that is usually required for tense-adverb combinations with other verbs:

(21) a. (Yesterday) Bill wanted your bicycle tomorrow.
b. *(Yesterday) Bill painted your bicycle tomorrow.

This distributional fact follows from the fact that the complement sentences of verbs of the *want* class regularly "refer" to a time which is "future" to the time of the main verb (cf. (*Yesterday*) *John wanted to go to Boston tomorrow*).

The next step in the argument consists in the observation that verbs of the *want* class differ from "normal" transitive verbs in that the object NP may have a non-specific (or other *de dicto*) interpretation: (22) may be true even though there is no particular cigarette that John desires, and (23) does not even entail that unicorns exist, much less that there is a particular one that John wants:

(22) John wants a cigarette.

(23) John wants a unicorn.

Now this property is in fact extremely restricted among simple transitive verbs; only a handful of English transitive verbs may have non-specific direct objects and virtually all of these are of the *want*-class (i.e., may take sentential objects as well as NP objects, and may have time adverbials like those in (18)). On the other hand, noun phrases occurring within subordinate complement clauses are quite regularly "referentially opaque", and there are many indirect-context-creating verbs (philosophers would call them *propositional attitude verbs*) besides those of the *want* class (such as *believe, think, say, deny*, etc.). Thus not only is the opacity of transitive *want* predicted by this analysis, but the analysis allows us to entertain the generalization that *all* instances of referential opacity are due to subordinate clauses, thus possibly simplifying the treatment of referential opacity in natural languages greatly.

The final step of the argument involves the verb *seek* and its synonyms and near-synonyms *search for, look for, hunt for, listen for,* etc. This tiny class of verbs (plus a few three-place verbs mentioned later in this chapter) constitutes the only remaining class of transitive verbs whose object position may be referentially opaque:

(24) John is seeking a unicorn.

The *have*-deletion analysis cannot be extended to cover them (we cannot derive (24) from **John is seeking to have a unicorn*, nor *John is looking for a unicorn* from **John is looking for to have a unicorn*). But under the GS decomposition hypothesis, no problem arises. The structure underlying (24) can be claimed to be the same as that underlying (25), which seems to paraphrase (24) exactly, and Predicate Raising can be claimed to collapse the material underlying *try* and *find* prior to the lexicalization rule introducing *seek*:

(25) John is trying to find a unicorn.

In fact both Bach (1968) and Quine (1960) suggest "deriving" (25) from (24) in order to maintain the generalization that referential opacity is restricted to subordinate clauses, though they do not present the intermediate steps of the argument involving the *want* class.

Impressive though this argument may be, Partee (1974) points out in her critique of McCawley that there is one remaining prediction of this analysis which he has failed to test. If the derivation of *seek* is indeed parallel to that of the *want* class, then *seek* ought to show the same possibilities for subordinate clause adverbs that the *want* class uniformly exhibits. But this prediction seems to be false. *Seek* and its (near) synonyms do not allow this kind of adverbial modification.

(26) a. Martha is trying to find an apartment by Saturday.
b. *Martha is looking for (seeking, etc.) an apartment by Saturday.

And though (27a) is ambiguous, since the adverb *before the meeting began* can be understood as modifying either the higher or the lower clause, (27b) is unambiguous, having only the higher clause reading:

(27) a. Fred was trying to find the minutes before the meeting began.
b. Fred was looking for the minutes before the meeting began.

And so Partee suggests that if this were the only evidence relating to the syntactic decomposition hypothesis (or if the evidence were otherwise equal), then we would have to reject that hypothesis; a transformation deleting a lower *have* would be, after all, a relatively uncontroversial addition in a conservative transformational theory, and such a transformation would seem to account for all the actual adverb evidence for an underlying embedded clause.

Moreover, if the decomposition analysis of *seek* were chosen for independent reasons, then the grammar would have to be somehow restricted to exclude adverbs originating in a lower clause when *seek* occurs. This would presumably have to be a restriction on the lexical insertion rule introducing *seek* itself, rather than a general structural restriction (since such adverbs must be allowed in the parallel *want* cases). This is an unprecedented kind of restriction as far as I know, and it is not clear how it could be effected. The insertion of *seek* would have to be blocked only if an adverb from a subordinate clause followed directly (since an adverb from a higher clause or from the same clause is permissible), and it is not clear that such a distinction would be structurally present at the time *seek*-insertion would apply: Predicate Raising might trigger tree-pruning (removal of the S-node that originally dominated the lower clause) and so obliterate all trace of the adverb's lower clause origin. One could always appeal to judicious rule ordering or a global constraint to effect the proper restriction, but it seems highly unlikely that the details of such a restriction could be plausibly motivated by cases independent of these.

Though Partee laments the fact that such important issues as the lexical decomposition hypothesis and the generalization about opaque contexts might have to be decided on the basis of such a small class of words as the *seek* class, the evidence is even less clear-cut than she suggests. From what has been said so far, one might assume that lower-clause adverbs with intensional verbs arise only when the same (or a phonologically identical) verb occurs with a subordinate clause (or at least an infinitive complement). But there is one exception. The verb *owe* has long been recognized as opaque with respect to at least its direct object (i.e. *a horse* in *John owes Bill a horse* can be non-specific), but if my intuitions are correct, a lower-clause adverbial can occur with it:

(28) John owes the bank $1000 by the end of the week.

Though *owe* is historically cognate with *ought*, it seems certain that the two verbs are not identified as the same by present-day speakers of English, and moreover the meaning of *owe* has diverged from that of *ought* so that (29) is no longer semantically appropriate as a source for (28):

(29) John ought to give the bank $1000 by the end of the week.

Thus *owe*, and this verb alone, provides the kind of successful final test of McCawley's predictions that failed with the *seek* class. The existence of one verb that supports McCawley's hypothesis does not make the difficulty with the *seek* class go away, of course, and I must agree with Partee that the data on the whole fails to support the syntactic decomposition of *seek* even though it is not clear that it totally disconfirms it either.

From a broader perspective, I must nevertheless agree that there must be something to the hypothesis that referential opacity is somehow intimately connected with subordinate clauses. I should first digress at this point to note that Montague thought that *worship* was an opaque transitive verb, presumably because *John worships a god* can be true even if there "exists" no god that he worships. But I must agree with Michael Bennett (1974, pp. 95-103) and Partee, following Kripke, that it is wrong to confuse the question of the physical existence of a referent with the matter of the "non-specificity" (as linguists call it) of the object of *seek* and *want* which is the true hallmark of "opaque" transitive verbs. If *worship* were indeed like *seek* and *want*, then just as it can be true that *John wants a cigarette* even though there is no particular cigarette, existing or not, which he wants, then it should also be possible for *John worships a god* to be true even though there is no particular "existing" or "non-existing" god which he is worshipping (neither Zeus nor Baal nor . . .). This I believe is wrong. More troublesome are verbs like *conceive* (*of*) and *imagine*, since it is quite unclear to me whether one can conceive of an arbitrary triangle without conceiving of a particular triangle (existing or not). Perhaps mathematical proofs that use universal instantiation and universal generalization involve us in conceiving of non-specific objects of this sort (e.g. "Let ABC be an arbitrary right triangle. Then ABC has the following properties . . . "). In any case, these verbs seem to be related to subordinate clause structures (*imagine a triangle* seems roughly paraphrasable as *imagine that there is a triangle*). Thus when we put the case of *worship* aside, I can hardly regard it as an accident that of the hundreds of transitive verbs in English, the very few that are referentially opaque are clearly paraphrasable by subordinate clauses (e.g. *seek*), if not arguably related to them syntactically (e.g. *want*). But given that Partee's arguments show that it is probably not desirable to literally derive all such verbs from subordinate clause structures syntactically, it is unclear just what the nature of this intimate connection is. From a cultural point of view, this skewed distribution in the meanings of verbs is perhaps understandable. It is clear why a natural language "needs" to denote extensional relations among pairs or triples of individuals, but it is less clear why relations between individuals and "non-specific" objects are important enough to deserve lexical items. But if we examine the truth conditions for such higher-order relations as *seek*, *want*, etc., reasons become apparent. In each case the relation turns out to be logically equivalent to a relation between an individual and a proposition involving the non-specific object, a proposition that the individual wishes, hopes, fears, etc. to come to be true at a later time. For example, *x seeks y* is true just in case *x* hopes that *x finds y* will come to be true and is trying to bring it about that this will be true. The "non-specific" object of the higher-order relation plays a "specific" role within this future proposition in each case, as in *x finds y*. The "non-specificity" of the object may be attributed to the fact that the proposition need not yet be a true one and can indeed be made true in various ways using various values for *y*. Speaking somewhat loosely, we may think of relations to non-specific objects as always being determined derivatively: we can understand what it means to look for a book only if we understand what it means to find a (specific) book; we understand what it means to want a cigarette only if we have some idea of what it means to have a (specific) cigarette, and so on. It is unclear whether this somewhat vague (but I hope not unintelligible) observation suggests that only such derivatively determined higher-order relations have enough cultural significance to merit their own designating expressions, or whether there might be some psychological sense in which our conception of possible propositions is more fundamental than our conception of nonspecific objects (i.e. semantical objects of type $\langle s, f(\mathrm{T})\rangle$), if indeed either of these possibilities is on the right track. One might also entertain or try to test the hypothesis that opaque transitive verbs originate historically as sentence-complement verbs (the OED records an archaic usage of *seek* with a complement clause; perhaps this survives in the bookish *He sought to persuade us that we were wrong*) or that children might understand sentence-complement verbs before the corresponding opaque transitive verbs. But if any of these hypotheses about the connection between non-specificity and subordinate clauses can be substantiated, this nevertheless does not establish that a synchronic "adult" grammar of English should be prohibited from having transitive verbs denoting a relation between individuals and non-specific objects; Partee's observations suggest that this may be the best-motivated kind of grammar after all, and Montague (in UG and PTQ) has of course shown us how to construct successfully a direct semantics for opaque transitive verbs.

5.6. SCOPE AMBIGUITIES WITH ADVERBS: ACCOMPLISHMENT CASES

Arguments from adverb scope for the lexical decomposition of causatives seem to have been first noticed by Robert I. Binnick, according to Morgan (1969) and McCawley (1971; 1973). Binnick's now familiar example is the ambiguous (30):

(30) The Sheriff of Nottingham jailed Robin Hood for four years.

As Binnick pointed out, (30) has not only the (rather unlikely) *durative reading* (30a) but also the more plausible reading (30b), which for convenience I will refer to as the *internal reading*:

(30) a. [*Durative Reading*]. The Sheriff of Nottingham spent four years bringing it about that Robin Hood was in jail.
b. [*Internal Reading*]. The Sheriff of Nottingham brought it about that for four years Robin Hood was in jail.

Example (30) may have in addition an *iterative reading* ("On multiple occasions throughout a period of four years, the Sheriff of Nottingham jailed Robin Hood"), but the durative/iterative ambiguity seems to occur fairly systematically with all kinds of verbs with durative adverbs, and the distinction between durative and iterative readings will not be the subject of discussion here. Intuitively, the adverbial in its durative reading specifies the time of the *action* denoted by the verb, while the internal reading of the adverbial specifies the time that the *result* of that action obtained. Similar ambiguities arise with adverbials such as *temporarily* and *until Thursday*. Thus under the generative semantics hypothesis, it is natural to assume that the durative reading arises from a logical structure of the general form of (30a′) while the internal reading arises from the kind of structure in (30b′):

(30) a′.

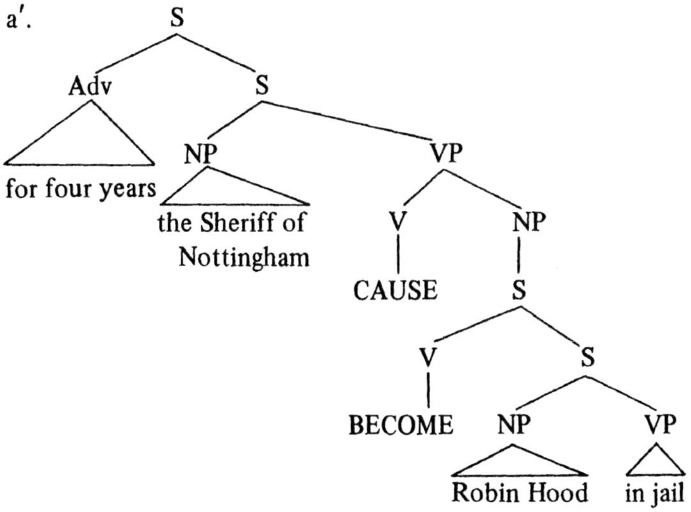

(30) b′.

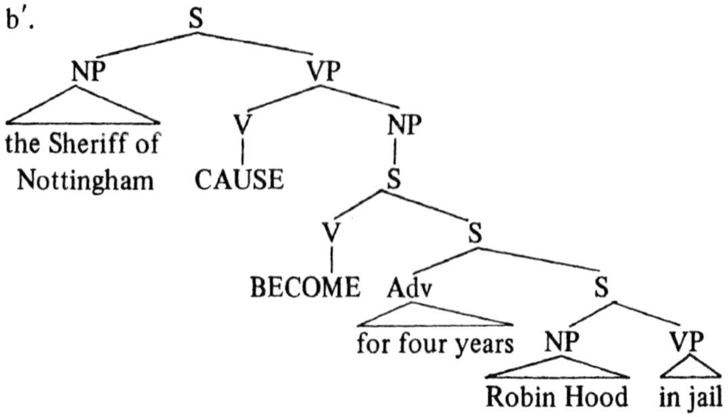

McCawley (1971; 1973) and Morgan (1969) observed that a similar ambiguity arises with *again*, though with *again* the situation is slightly simpler since it is a point-in-time adverb and the durative/iterative ambiguity does not arise. Rather, we can describe the two readings of (31) as the *external reading* (John has performed the action of closing the door at least once before) and the *internal reading* (John has brought it about that the door is again in a closed state, though he need not have closed it on any earlier occasion):

(31) John closed the door again.

A familiar example of an internal reading with *again* is (32),

(32) All the king's horses and all the king's men couldn't put Humpty Dumpty together again.

which is obviously not intended to entail that anyone had put Humpty Dumpty together on an earlier occasion, but merely that Humpty Dumpty had been "together" once before.

Significantly, no such ambiguity is perceived with stative verbs:

(33) a. John stayed in his room until seven o'clock.
b. John slept again.

Particularly telling are examples like (34) (attributed by McCawley to Masaru Kajita) in which a future adverbial appears with a past tense verb, though as we noted earlier, such failure of tense-adverb agreement is unacceptable with other stative verbs (except the *want*-class, of course):

(34) a. John lent his bicycle to Bill until tomorrow.
b. *John stayed at home until tomorrow.

As with the "*have*-deletion" cases, the possibility of this future adverb is predicted by the decomposition analysis, since (34a) would come from approximately the same logical structure as (34a′):

(34) a′. John caused Bill to have possession of his bicycle until tomorrow.

Evidence that the ambiguity is truly structural in nature comes from the fact that the internal reading is only present when the adverbial appears at the end of the sentence, even though the adverb occurs sentence-initially in the external or durative/iterative reading; (35a) and (35b) have only the external, durative or iterative reading, and (35c) is ungrammatical because the durative reading is blocked by the clash of tense and future adverb:[8]

(35) a. Again John closed the door.
b. For four years the Sheriff of Nottingham jailed Robin Hood.
c. *Until tomorrow John lent his bicycle to Bill.

Before leaving this argument one complicating factor involving the durative adverbs should be noticed. Michael Bennett suggested to me that perhaps the internal reading of *for four years* in *The Sheriff of Nottingham jailed Robin Hood for four years* merely describes the length of time that the agent (the Sheriff) intended that the result of his action would last and does not really entail anything at all about how long Robin Hood actually remained in jail. To test this hypothesis directly, consider the following situation. Suppose John places a cake in the oven, with the intention of leaving it there for forty-five minutes then immediately leaves the kitchen. Unknown to him, Mary comes into the kitchen shortly thereafter and removes the cake ten minutes after it was put in the oven. Is (36) then true in this situation?

(36) John put the cake in the oven for forty-five minutes.

Unfortunately, judgments differ. For some speakers (myself included), (36) is clearly and patently false in this situation. To other speakers it is just as clear that (36) is true. (Perhaps there are even speakers for whom (36) is ambiguous.) There are two things to be noted about this. First, the "intentional" analysis cannot in any case be applied to the internal reading of *again*. Suppose John finds the pieces of a new jigsaw puzzle spread across a table, and, believing that someone had previously assembled the pieces and then separated them, puts the puzzle together himself. However, the pieces were in fact fabricated separately and had never been assembled before. Even speakers who accept the intentional internal reading for (36) cannot, to the best of my knowledge, accept (37) as true in this situation:

(37) John put the puzzle together again.

Second, the fact that some speakers accept the intentional reading of the adverbial of (36) does not mean that (36) fails to present evidence for decomposition in their dialect but only means that the analysis of (36) is more complicated for that dialect. To get the correct entailments of (36) for that dialect, the scope of the adverbial must still be taken to be the intended *result* of that action, not the act of putting the cake in the oven. To interpret (36) correctly in that dialect we must still "decompose" *put the cake into the oven* into act and result in the same way as for the other dialect. (As I am not a speaker of this dialect and do not understand its data too well, I will not attempt to give an analysis of it here.)

This brings me to another possible rebuttal to the adverb argument, which is that English treats actions such as that in (36) in a quasi-metaphorical way as extending not just over the time that the agent was physically active but also over the time of the result as well, at least when that result is important or specifically intended by the agent to last for a certain time. If so, then the adverb might be claimed to modify the whole sentence even on this allegedly "internal" reading. But this view can be directly argued against as well: it leaves us absolutely no account of why a future "internal" adverbial with a past tense verb is acceptable for an accomplishment but not for an activity or state. That is, it cannot explain why (38a) is acceptable while (38b) and (38c) are not:

(38) a. John left his bicycle at Bill's house until tomorrow.
b. *John visited Bill until tomorrow.
c. *John stayed in his room until tomorrow.

It is certainly as plausible (and in fact more plausible) that a visit which begins on one day and is intended to extend to the next is treated in English as an act that extends over a two-day period as it is plausible that an act of leaving a bicycle in a certain place on one day with the intention that it remain there until the next be so viewed. But the fact of the matter is that English simply does not allow us to combine a future adverb with a past tense to describe such an action which begins in the past and extends into the future. The *only* cases of the curious combination of past tense and future adverbial that occur are precisely those cases of an accomplishment or achievement verb where the future adverb can be understood as giving the time of the state which results from a past action (plus of course the "*have*-deletion" cases). (Actually, not quite all accomplishments can felicitously take an internal adverb but only those in which the result state is a reversible one; we find it very hard to interpret ?*John killed Bill for three weeks* with an internal reading because we ordinarily assume death to be an irreversible state. But such exceptions as this should clearly not be viewed as evidence against the decomposition hypothesis.)

One other suggestion for avoiding the implications of the adverb argument was made by Charles Fillmore (1974, p. 27), who suggested that apparent internal readings might simply be evidence for a transformation deleting part of a conjoined clause. That is, the internal reading of (38a) might be derived in this way from (38b):

(38) a. John went upstairs for a few minutes.
b. John went upstairs and stayed there for a few minutes.

But such a treatment is really only viable for those accomplishment constructions in which the result state is expressed as a separate word or phrase and where this state is a locative. What is the conjoined source of (39a) (which I believe is an example of Jerry Morgan's)? Is it (39b)? Probably not.

(39) a. John hid the grass until the police left.
b. ?John hid the grass and it stayed there until the police left.

And what about examples where the result state is not a locative? Since the conjoined source for (40a) cannot plausibly have *it stayed there* in its source, perhaps the source would be (40b):

(40) a. John inflated the balloon temporarily to test it.
b. John inflated the balloon to test it and it stayed in that state temporarily.

But now the question is, what is the source of the pro-forms *there* and *that state* in (39b) and (40b)? Clearly, these refer to just the result-states entailed by the respective accomplishment verbs *hide* and *inflate*. Thus we still need a semantic analysis for *hide* and *inflate* which makes their result-states explicit in order to give the semantics for these sentences, and it is not obvious that postulating abstract structures like (39b) and (40b) has simplified this task at all. (As for the hypothesis that the internal adverbs really only refer to "some state semantically entailed by the verb," I will have evidence against this solution later.)

5.7. ARGUMENTS FROM *Re-* AND REVERSATIVE *Un-*

The English derivational prefixes *re-* (as in *recapture*) and reversative *un-* (as in *unwrap*) can be used to make an argument for decomposition that is parallel to the argument from the internal readings of durative adverbials and *again*. In fact, the meaning of *re-* seems to be quite literally the same as that of internal *again*; its meaning is that the result-state of an accomplishment is true for a second time, but not necessarily that the bringing about of this state occurs for the second time. This apparent from examples like (41),

(41) The satellite reentered the earth's atmosphere at 3:47 p.m.

which need not be taken to imply that the satellite had ever entered the earth's atmosphere on an earlier occasion, but simply that it had been within the earth's atmosphere on an earlier occasion. Similarly, to say that the Druids recaptured their homeland from the invaders is not to necessarily say that they had ever captured their homeland from anyone before but merely that they had been in possession of their homeland before. If the "againness" meaning of *re-* were applied compositionally to the "whole meaning" of verbs like *enter* or *capture* or to the sentence containing these verbs, it seems that repetition of the whole action would be entailed, but if *re-* were derived from an adverb meaning "again" occurring just below BECOME in logical structure (just like internal *again*), then only the correct entailment should follow. McCawley has pointed out to me the example *He rearranged the boulders on the hillside*, in which there need not have been any prior act of arranging at all, hence no prior agent.

Comments made by Marchand (1960, pp. 189-190) are in agreement with these observations. He notes that "*re-* does not express mere repetition of an action; it connotes the idea of repetition only with actions connected with an object. And it is with a view to the result of the action performed on an object that *re-* is used."

It is unclear to me whether *re-* should be claimed to be ambiguous in the way that *again* is. We can obviously have no structural evidence of ambiguity as was observed with the initial vs. final position of *again* in a sentence. There are of course instances where the most likely interpretation of a sentence with *re-* is that the agent has in fact performed the same action earlier, as in *he rewrote the letter to his father*. But notice that the internal reading is perfectly consistent with the possibility that the action leading to the result state has been performed before, either by the same agent or a different one (as in *John typed the letter and then the secretary retyped it*; Marchand notes "The agent of the *re*-action may or may not be the same as that of the original action" (1960, p. 190)), and there would be clear pragmatic reasons for assuming that this was the case in many instances. In the case of *John rewrote the letter to his father*, it is unlikely that anyone else would have written the letter to John's father and even less likely that the letter existed in a written state without having been written by anyone at all. Thus instances of apparently "external" *re-* may be attributable to conversational implicature. There may be occasional examples of *re-* with an activity verb (e.g. *reconsider*), for which only the external reading would be possible, but in any case the "internal" reading is by far the dominant one; Marchand notes (p. 190) "The prefix is rare with intransitive or intransitively used verbs . . . there are no **recome, *relie, *resmoke*, and words like *re-arise, rebecome, rego, remeet, respeak* have not gained general currency."

The reversative transitive verb prefix *un-* (as in *unwrap*) must first of all be distinguished from the negative adjective prefix *un-*. It is only by accident of the phonological history of English that the two have come to have the same form:[9] reversative *un-* is from Old English *and-, ond-* (cognate with German *ent-* as in *entladen*, "unload"), while negative *un-* is cognate with German *un-* and Latin *in-*. The negative adjective prefix *un-* provides no evidence for decomposition, since it simply negates a (stative) predicate in a perfectly compositional way – *untrue* is simply "not true" – though as Zimmer (1964) notes, negated adjectives tend to drift in meaning toward contrary negation rather than simply contradictory negation (e.g. *unhappy* is stronger than "not happy"). As the two prefixes have mutually exclusive distributions, the cases of "structurally" ambiguous words in *un-* that one often sees cited in linguistic texts are not purely structural but really depend on the homophony of the two *uns* as well. Thus *The unwrapped books are on the table* can mean either "the books which are not (yet) wrapped are on the table" or "the books which have been removed from their wrappings are on the table." But the former reading of *unwrapped* – i.e. $[un\text{-}[wrap_{TV}\text{-}ed]_{ADJ}]_{ADJ}$ – must contain negative *un-* (which attaches to the adjectival past participle *wrapped*) while the latter must involve reversative *un-*, i.e. $[[un\text{-}wrap_{TV}]_{TV}\text{-}ed]_{ADJ}$. Significantly, reversative *un-* attaches *only* to (transitive)[10] accomplishment verbs, and *all* instances of verbs with *un-* are accomplishment verbs. (This is in contrast to *dis-*, which, though predominately a reversative prefix (as in *disassemble*) also occasionally occurs with stative verbs, and in those cases is thus necessarily negative in meaning rather than reversative, e.g. *dislike, distrust*.) Thus there are not (and *cannot* be) stative verbs with *un-* such as **unknow*, **unlove*, **unbelieve* in English, nor activity verbs **unplay, *unsing, *unswim* (cf. Marchand, 1960, p. 205).

The derivation of a reversative from a negation "inside" the meaning of the word is anticipated by Marchand himself: "At the level of the underlying syntactic structure the analysis [of *untie*] is thus 'cause to be *un-*(= not)*-tied*' " (Marchand, 1960, p. 205). Thus a (McCawley-style) underlying structure for (41) would be (41′):

(41) John uncrated the bicycle.

(41′)

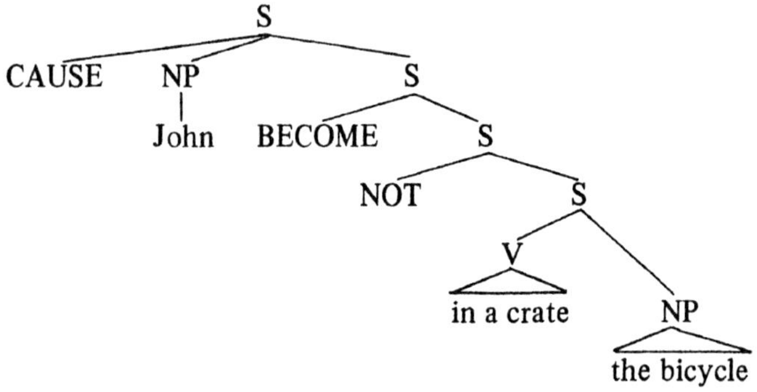

I will not attempt to determine the details of the generative semantics derivation (though I will be giving an explicit Montague grammar treatment later), except to note that an "operator raising" rule will be needed if we wish to claim that *un-* is quite literally the surface representation of the NOT in (41′);[11] that is, the logical structure at the time of lexicalization must be (41″):

(41″)

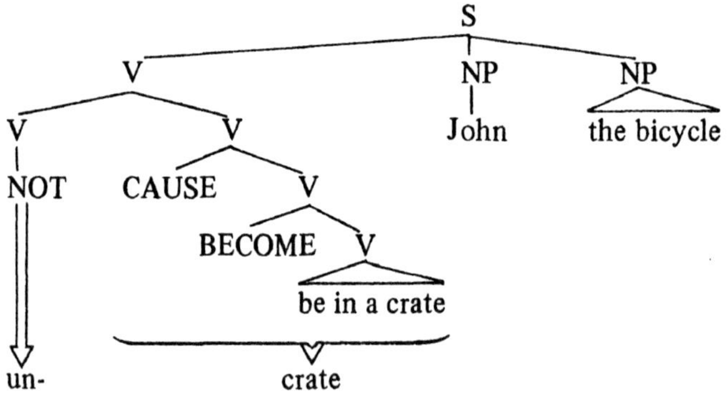

The postulation of such a (presumably cyclic) Operator-Raising transformation again raises questions about other possible readings for (41) predicted by the generative semantics theory. Why can't (41) also have the meanings of (42a) and (42b)?

(42) a. John didn't cause the bicycle to come to be in the crate.
b. John caused the bicycle not to come to be in the crate.

Note also that this raising transformation cannot be the same as the familiar NEG-Raising transformation (cf. Horn, 1978a) because NEG-Raising is governed by (a subset of) a semantically coherent class of verbs (*think, believe, suppose*, etc.) which is disjoint from the accomplishment verbs taking *un-*.

Arguments for decomposition could also be made from reversative *dis-* and what Marchand calls the *ablative* prefix *de-* (e.g. *defrost the window* means roughly "cause the frost to come to be not on the window"), but these would be quite parallel to *un-* and *re-*. Cf. Marchand (1972) for discussion of ablative prefixes.

Despite the syntactic problems with generating the internal readings for *re-*, *un-*, *again* and durative adverbs under the generative semantics hypothesis, I believe that as arguments for a *semantic* analysis of accomplishments into causative-plus-result-state (ignoring for the moment the question of how meaning is related to syntactic form), this group of scope phenomena provide a compelling case when taken together. Though they come from superficially quite different parts of the grammar (interpretation of adverbs and what is traditionally considered to be word formation), note that all these cases argue for an operator originating in exactly the same place in logical structure: just below the BECOME operator. Because they provide evidence for exactly the same "split" in the meaning of a verb, I believe the arguments from derivational prefixes and adverbs reinforce each other. That is, the evidence from the derivational prefixes might be discounted by philosophers particularly because they tend to regard word semantics as vague and not neatly analyzable, and after all, the words of a language are ultimately only finite in number and formulation of compositional principles for the semantics of derived words is not absolutely crucial in the same way as it is for syntactically produced constructions. Certain linguists, on the other hand, might find the derivational prefixes more convincing because word derivation has been more thoroughly studied in linguistics than the compositional semantics of adverbs. Note that the internal readings of adverbs have been attested so far in only one language (English) at only one stage in its historical development (the present), but *re-* and reversative *un-* and, apparently, their internal meanings, have been attested through a long period of the history of English and other Indo-European languages as well (cf. e.g. German *ent-* and Marchand's comment (1960, p. 188) that ancient Latin *re-* had the internal sense, though late Latin (and modern French) acquired the "repetition" (i.e. external) sense as the dominant one). Finally, the paradoxical co-occurrence of *until tomorrow* with past tense verbs provides a kind of argument not paralleled with the derivational prefixes. Together, all these data seem to show conclusively that an adverb or prefix whose "semantic scope" is the result-state of an accomplishment is a very real and widely attested phenomenon in natural language, however it is to be analyzed.

5.8. ACCOMMODATING THE ADVERB SCOPE DATA IN A PTQ GRAMMAR

As the adverb scope arguments are the only arguments for the syntactic decomposition hypothesis that I find truly compelling, I believe we will have satisfactorily replied to the existing evidence for that hypothesis if we can find an adequate way of treating this data in the "upside-down generative semantics" model.

Note first of all that in a Montague grammar there can be no semantic ambiguity without syntactic ambiguity (at the level of the disambiguated language at least) as well. I am aware of two methods by which the internal readings can be accommodated, and these require not just a syntactic ambiguity but a lexical ambiguity (homophony) as well: either the verb (5.8.1) or the adverb (5.8.2) participating in these constructions can be treated as ambiguous.

5.8.1. *Treating the Verb as Ambiguous*

If we are willing to postulate a lexical ambiguity in verbs to account for the internal readings of adverbs, then the way to derive the internal readings of adverbials with transitive verbs is to treat the "second" member of each pair of homonyms as a functor combining with an adverbial (of category $P_{t/t}$) to form a transitive verb, i.e. a member of category TV/(t/t). (Compare this with the way we captured the fact that **put**, **set**, and **lay** are "obligatorily subcategorized" for a locative adverbial by treating them as members of TV/IAV.) The two verbs **open**, for example, would have the respective translations in (43), in which **open′** is the translation of the predicative adjective **open**.

(43) a. **open**$_1$ ($\in P_{TV}$) translates into:
$\lambda\mathscr{P}\lambda x\mathscr{P}\{\hat{y}\bigvee P[P\{x\}\ \text{CAUSE BECOME}\ \mathbf{open}'(y)]\}$

b. **open**$_2$ ($\in P_{TV/(t/t)}$) translates into:
$\lambda S\lambda\mathscr{P}\lambda x\mathscr{P}\{\hat{y}\bigvee P[P\{x\}\ \text{CAUSE BECOME}\ [{}^{\vee}S({}^{\wedge}[\mathbf{open}'(y)])]]\}$
where S is $v_{0,\langle\langle s,t\rangle,t\rangle}$.

Note that it is lambda-abstraction over the variable S in (43b) which will be responsible for "placing" the adverb in the correct internal position. By this method, the internal reading of **John opens a door again** would be produced as in (44) and will have a translation that reduces to (44′)

(44)

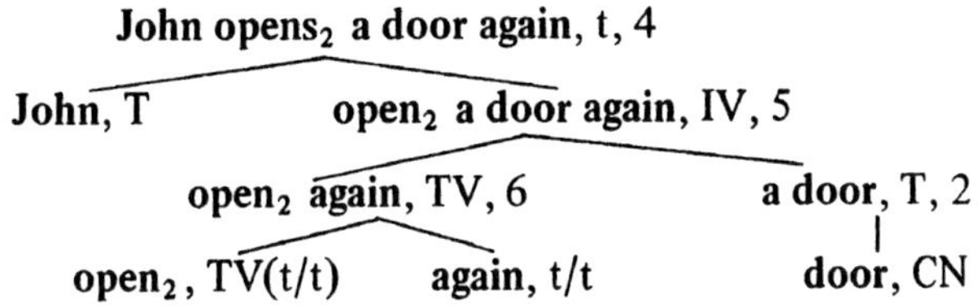

(44′) $\bigvee x[\mathbf{door}'(x) \wedge \bigvee P[P\{j\}\ \text{CAUSE BECOME}\ \mathbf{again}'({}^{\wedge}[\mathbf{open}'(x)])]]$

By comparison, the external reading for this same sentence is produced as in (45) and has a translation equivalent to (45′):

(45)

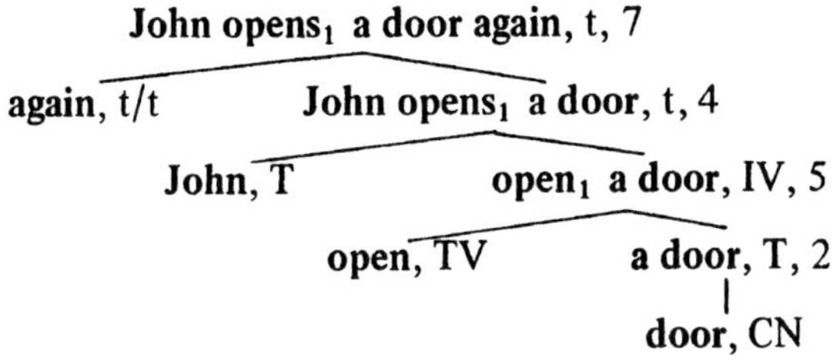

(45′) $\mathbf{again}'({}^{\wedge}[\bigvee x[\mathbf{door}'(x) \wedge \bigvee P[P\{j\}\ \text{CAUSE BECOME}\ \mathbf{open}'(x)]]])$

To complete the account of the entailments of these examples, we need only to fix the interpretation of the sentence modifier **again**. This interpretation seems rather simple (at least if we ignore the distinction between entailment and conventional implicature) and can be captured in terms of the past tense operator of PTQ by the postulate (46) (or equivalently, by a decomposition translation for **again**):

(46) $\bigwedge p\Box[\mathbf{again}'(p) \leftrightarrow [{}^{\vee}p \wedge H[\neg{}^{\vee}p \wedge H{}^{\vee}p]]]$

That is, **again**(p) is true just in case p is now true, there was an earlier time at which p was false, and a still earlier time at which p was true. The intermediate time of p's falseness is needed to distinguish **John is here again** from **John is still here**. This latter sentence also involves p's being true at an earlier time as well as at the present, but unlike the former sentence does not require the intermediate time at which p was false.

Given (46), the internal reading (44) will entail that there was an earlier time at which the door was open, though not necessarily that there was an earlier time at which John (or anyone else) had opened it, but (45′) has the stronger entailment that John opened a door at an earlier time.

It is difficult for me to imagine arguments on independent grounds that would show this method to be the correct way of accounting for the internal readings. Since this treatment requires us to postulate homophony among a large class of lexical items, it would seem to allow the possibility that certain verbs of the same semantic class as **open** might idiosyncratically lack the internal reading. Hence one possible argument for this treatment would be to find certain accomplishment verbs that would be expected to allow the internal reading but which, paradoxically, lacked it. I have noticed a few verbs for which the internal reading does seem very hard to get, though the judgment is very delicate. These are exemplified in (47), along with paraphrases which make the hypothetical internal readings explicit (since it is important not to confuse the internal with the durative readings in these cases).

(47)
- a. John defrosted the TV dinner all afternoon (and then he put it back in the freezer).
- a′. John brought it about that for all afternoon the TV dinner was in a thawed state [i.e. *not* the reading in which it took all afternoon for the TV dinner to thaw].
- b. John melted the paraffin until all the children had dipped their candles.
- b′. John brought it about that [the paraffin was in a liquid state until all of the children had dipped their candles].
- c. John erased the blackboard until the last part of his lecture.
- c′. John brought it about that the blackboard was blank until the last part of his lecture.
- d. John bought a piano for three years (and then he had to sell it).
- d′. John brought it about that he owned a piano for three years.
- e. (*)John sold his car to Mary until next summer (at which time she will sell it back to him).
- e′. John brought it about that Mary will own his car until next summer.

Though I have tried to create example sentences in which the internal reading would be plausible, I cannot be absolutely sure that there are not extraneous pragmatic or semantic considerations that would tend to block the internal reading in these cases. Perhaps significantly, all these questionable examples involve non-locative accomplishments (i.e., in which the result state is not simply one of position), though of course there are at least some non-locatives that do allow internal readings (cf. 39, 40). All locative accomplishments seem to allow internal readings quite freely.

In spite of this apparent evidence that would favor this treatment over the one given below, there are complications with accomplishments whose syntactic form is not simply that of a (monomorphemic) TV. Note that the various other syntactic forms of accomplishments all allow internal readings:

(48) a. John fell asleep during the lecture, but Mary quickly shook him awake again.
b. The book had fallen down, but John put it on the shelf again.
c. John swam to our side of the pool temporarily.

Since these examples do not involve simply a basic TV, a somewhat different treatment of the ambiguity will be required, in fact a different treatment in each case. If "ordinary" **put** is treated as a member of TV/IAV (as suggested in the previous chapter), the second **put** which leads to the internal reading must be placed in some new category such as (TV/IAV)/(t/t). If factitives such as **shake awake** are formed by a syntactic rule combining a transitive verb and adjective, then it is probably not best to postulate a lexical ambiguity at all but rather an additional syntactic rule combining a transitive verb δ, an adjective α and a sentence adverbial β to form a transitive verb $\delta\alpha\beta$, the result translating as

$$\lambda\mathscr{P}\lambda x\,\mathscr{P}\{\hat{y}\,[\delta'(x, \hat{P}P\{y\})\text{ CAUSE BECOME }\beta'({}^{\wedge}[\alpha'(y)])]\}.$$

Still a different kind of solution is called for in cases such as (48c) where the result state is expressed by a prepositional phrase which is a modifier (adjunct) rather than a complement. Here the only obvious way I see to achieve a parallel semantic solution for the internal reading is to postulate a lexical ambiguity in the preposition **to** (similarly for **into**, **onto**, etc.). The **to** which produces the internal reading would be of category (IAV/T)/(t/t) and would have the translation

$$\lambda S\lambda\mathscr{P}\lambda P\lambda x\,\mathscr{P}\{\hat{y}\,[P\{x\}\text{ CAUSE BECOME }{}^{\vee}S({}^{\wedge}[\textbf{be-at}'(x, y)])]\}.$$

Finally, getting the right reading for derived verbs with the prefixes *re-* and *un-* would require deriving **reenter** from the **enter** in TV/(t/t). The simplest treatment of this sort would be interpreted as applying the meaning of this verb **enter** to the meaning of **again**. This is in itself a bit suspicious because the semantics reverses the functor-argument relationship apparent in the morphology: it treats the verb as the functor and the prefix as the argument semantically, while from the point of view of morphology it is the derivational prefix which is the functor and the verb which is the argument. Moreover, this treatment requires us to assume that the "internal" homonym of a verb must exist before the derived verb with **re-** or **un-** can be formed.

While each of these treatments is in itself perhaps not too undesirable (except the **re-** and **un-** case), there is a suspicious lack of generality in producing the internal readings in such different ways for each syntactic construction. As we shall see, the treatment involving ambiguous adverbs is quite different in this respect, since postulating an "internal" adverb predicts that internal readings will appear with accomplishments of all syntactic forms. Moreover, we shall see in (5.9) below that the postulate predicts correctly a generalization about internal adverb scope that would not follow automatically from the ambiguous verb treatment.

Before leaving this treatment, one further approach to the internal readings for factitives should be mentioned. In Dowty (1976) I suggested that factitives such as **hammer flat** be derived by a rule which combines a transitive verb δ not with an adjective α, but rather with a sentence of the form **he**$_n$ **is** α, giving $\delta\alpha$ as output. This treatment has the virtue that it predicts the internal readings for adverbs with factitives automatically. This is so because sentences of the form **he**$_n$ **is flat again** will qualify as inputs to such a factitive rule. Combining this last sentence with the transitive verb **hammer** will give the factitive transitive verb **hammer flat again**, and this result leads to the proper semantic interpretation for the internal reading of **John hammers the metal flat again**. But this virtue becomes a questionable one as soon as it is realized that absolutely the *only* motivation for this more complicated factitive rule is that it produces the internal reading correctly. Also, this method can be extended to accomplishments with resultative prepositional phrases only at the expense of an even more abstract syntactic analysis (cf. Dowty, 1976, for details), and it offers no analogous analysis for the internal readings of simple monomorphemic accomplishments.

5.8.2. *Treating the Adverb as Ambiguous*

If we attempt to account for the internal readings by treating the adverb as ambiguous, then what category should the second (internal) homonym of the adverb be? Though I see no semantic barrier to treating these internal adverbs as of the same category as the external adverbs ($P_{t/t}$), a category of verb phrase adverbials as well as sentence adverbials is well-motivated for English (cf. Stalnaker and Thomason, 1973; Cresswell, 1973). Moreover, putting the "internal" adverbs in this category affords us a syntactic explanation of why the internal reading does not appear when the adverb is in sentence-initial position. While sentence adverbs are in general equally at home in sentence-initial and sentence-final position, at least most kinds of verb-phrase adverbials do not occur in sentence initial position (cf. ***Easily, he avoided the question**, ***Well he did his work**, cf. Jackendoff, 1972, pp. 49-51). Though the directionals which I treated as members of the verb-phrase modifier category are subject to a certain kind of fronting (as in *Into the room he walked*), this fronting is stylistically marked (connotes in this case a quasi-literary style) in a way that sentence-initial position for sentence adverbs is not.[12] Also, this kind of fronting can trigger subject-verb inversion in some cases (cf. *Into the room walked John*), while sentence-initial position for sentence-adverbials cannot (cf. **On Thursday arrived John*, **Possibly left John*). (This fact and distributional differences among adverbs such as those observed by Jackendoff can be taken as evidence for distinguishing among two or more subcategories of verb-phrase adverbs.)[13]

Producing the internal reading with a verb-phrase adverb cannot, as far as I can tell, be accomplished as directly as it was in the treatment given above, no matter how the adverb is translated. Instead, the internal reading will have to be produced with the aid of the somewhat complicated meaning postulate (49), stating a relationship that holds between the meaning of the verb phrase adverb $\mathbf{again}_2$ and the sentence adverb $\mathbf{again}_1$:

(49) $$\bigwedge x \bigwedge P \bigwedge p \Box [\mathbf{again}_2{}'(\hat{y}[P\{y\} \text{ CAUSE BECOME } {}^{\vee}p])(x) \leftrightarrow [P\{x\} \text{ CAUSE BECOME } \mathbf{again}_1{}'(\dot{p})]]$$

This says, in effect, that an individual x stands in the $\mathbf{again}_2$-relation to the property of bringing it about that p by doing P, if and only if x brings it about that $\mathbf{again}_1$ p by doing P.[14]

A similar postulate would be needed for the other adverbs (**temporarily**, **momentarily**, etc.) that produce an internal reading, but in each case this would be of exactly the same form as (49) with δ_1 and δ_2 substituting for $\mathbf{again}_1$ and $\mathbf{again}_2$ respectively, for each adverb δ. Though there are an infinite number of durative adverbials of the form **for** α and **until** α (because α here represents a syntactically open class of expressions), we would still need to postulate ambiguity only in **for** and **until** themselves, not an infinite number of ambiguities in basic expressions. Though this treatment requires us to postulate a slightly suspicious number of lexical homonyms, the number of adverbs that lead to internal readings is still only a handful and would be far fewer than the number of homonyms required under the "ambiguous verb" treatment. (Thus a final desirable refinement of this treatment would be a rule deriving the internal verb-phrase adverb from its sentence-adverb homonym. Though I would not be surprised that this could be done somehow, I do not presently see how to write the appropriate semantic rule.)

As noted above, a primary advantage of this treatment over the former one is that it automatically accounts for internal readings with all syntactic varieties of accomplishments. That is, no matter how accomplishments may be produced syntactically, they all eventually lead to an expression of category IV, at which point the internal adverb (of category IAV) can be added. At the point where the category IV is reached, each accomplishment will have a meaning logically equivalent to some abstract property $\hat{y}[P\{y\}$ CAUSE BECOME$\check{}p]$ of the form mentioned in meaning postulate (49), hence the correct semantics will result.

Finally, verbs derived with **re-** and reversative **un-** can be treated in a parallel way under this method. We can produce them syntactically by the rules S34 and S35 (this kind of rule will be discussed in greater detail in Chapter 6):

S34. If $\alpha \in P_{TV}$, then $F_{34}(\alpha) \in P_{TV}$, where $F_{34}(\alpha) =$ **re** $+ \alpha$.

T34. $F_{34}(\alpha)$ translates into:
$\lambda\mathscr{P}\lambda x[\mathbf{again}_2{}'(\hat{}\alpha'(\mathscr{P}))(x)]$

S35. If $\alpha \in P_{TV}$, then $F_{35}(\alpha) \in P_{TV}$, where $F_{35}(\alpha) =$ **un** $+ \alpha$.

T35. $F_{35}(\alpha)$ translates into:
$\lambda\mathscr{P}\lambda x[\mathbf{un}'(\hat{}\alpha'(\mathscr{P}))(x)]$

Since the meaning of **re-** is, as mentioned earlier, the same as that of internal **again**, $\mathbf{again}_2{}'$ can be used in the translation of S34. But for reversative **un-**, a new constant **un**$'$ has to be introduced and this must be made subject to meaning postulate (49), i.e., with **un**$'$ replacing $\mathbf{again}_2{}'$ and the ordinary negation operator replacing $\mathbf{again}_1{}'$.

Finally, we can note that if all adverbs that produce internal readings with accomplishment verbs are subject to a meaning postulate of exactly the form of (49) (or, even better, if some way of deriving internal adverbs in IAV from adverbs in t/t can be found), this makes the claim that all such adverbs have the same "semantic" scope (i.e., correspond to a sentence operator occurring just inside the BECOME operator (but never anywhere else)), and as far as I know, this claim is correct.[15]

In summary, the ambiguous adverb treatment seems to offer a more general and simple solution to the internal readings than does the ambiguous verb treatment. I have nevertheless discussed both kinds of treatments because I suspect that not all the relevant evidence pertaining to this problem has been observed yet, and a treatment more like the ambiguous verb analysis could still turn out to be preferable.

I mentioned in the previous chapter the possibility that we do not want to claim that accomplishment predicates are actually logically equivalent to expressions of the form $\lambda x \bigvee P[P\{x\} \text{ CAUSE BECOME } {}^{\vee}p]$ but merely logically entail such expressions. These entailments could then be captured by a meaning postulate with a conditional, rather than a biconditional, connective. It is thus worth considering how the internal readings might be captured if this option is taken. Since meaning postulate (49) will not be effective under this approach, we might try one of the form of (50):

(50) $\bigwedge x \bigwedge P \bigwedge Q \bigwedge p \Box[[\textbf{again}_2{}'(P)(x) \wedge \Box[P\{x\} \rightarrow [Q\{x\} \text{ CAUSE BECOME } {}^{\vee}p]]] \rightarrow [Q\{x\} \text{ CAUSE BECOME } \textbf{again}_1{}'(p)]]$

That is, whenever x stands in the **again**$_2$-relation to some property P, and, moreover, it is a logical truth that doing P entails bringing it about that p, then it is also the case that x brings it about that **again**$_1$ p. Though this would apparently work correctly for adverbials considered so far, Stanley Peters has pointed out to me a kind of case where (50) seems to give unacceptable results. It seems plausible to consider it an analytic truth that being in a hospital implies being in a building or other structure (or for the sake of argument, let us temporarily ignore those "remote" indices at which hospitals are not buildings or other structures). Now let us assume that the accomplishment verb **hospitalize** is analyzed as "cause to be in a hospital" (or if preferred, "cause to be a patient who is in a hospital"). Now consider example (51):

(51) Dr. Jones hospitalized John for the first time.

Though this sentence may have an external reading that means that this was the first occasion on which it was Dr. Jones who was responsible for John's being in the hospital, the reading which is of interest here is the one which entails that this is the first time that John has ever been in a hospital. Given our above assumption about hospitals, causing someone to be in a hospital surely entails causing someone to be in a building or other structure (and this is provable from our semantics for CAUSE and this assumption). But under meaning postulate (50) this "internal" reading of (51) would entail that on this occasion John came to be in a building (or other structure) for the first time. This is clearly wrong. Another example would be the internal reading of *John drew a square around the picture for the first time* and the unwelcome entailment *A rectangle came to be around the picture for the first time*, since causing a square to exist is necessarily causing a rectangle to exist.

The crucial difference between the semantics of **for the first time** and the other adverbials we have been considering can be illustrated by the two arguments in (52):

(52) a. **again**$'(p)$

$\square[{}^\vee p \rightarrow {}^\vee q]$

$\therefore$ **again**$'(q)$

b. **for-the-first-time**$'(p)$

$\square[{}^\vee p \rightarrow {}^\vee q]$

$\therefore$ **for-the-first-time**$'(q)$

The argument form in (52a) is intuitively valid for any propositions p and q: if p is again true and p logically entails q, then q is again true as well. And in fact the validity of (52a) follows from our semantics for **again**. But whatever the exact analysis of **for the first time**, (52b) should clearly not be valid, as the reader can confirm from any number of examples; **for-the-first-time**$'$ is not closed under logical entailment as **again**$'$ is. But meaning postulate (50) unfortunately has the effect of making any internal adverb closed under entailments of the "internal" sentence, while (49) does not. Thus any internal adverb for which (52a) is not valid presents counterarguments to (50).

If Peters' problematic example (and others like it) cannot be discounted on some grounds or other, then we seem to have here a particularly strong reason for treating accomplishments as logically equivalent to some "bring about" formulas, rather than merely as entailing such a formula. This problem, of course, does not depend on any particular syntactic approach to the internal adverb problem, nor can I imagine any semantic variant of the particular decomposition of accomplishments offered here that would allow us to escape it. (Claiming that all accomplishment verbs are logically equivalent to a property $\hat{x}[P\{x\}$ CAUSE BECOME ${}^\vee p]$ does not commit us to the claim that the examples discussed in this and the preceding chapter have to have *exactly* the simple and often only roughly approximate translations I have given; the meaning postulate (49) would still be effective where the "activity" property P and result state proposition p are instantiated by much more specific and detailed translations or constants than I have used, so maintaining (49) still leaves us much "room" to refine the semantic analysis of accomplishments.) Though the main focus of this chapter is the relative merits of syntactic treatments of decomposition, the general phenomenon of internal adverb scope and in particular Peters' problem have turned out to be one of the strongest reasons I know of for advocating a *semantic* decomposition of accomplishments – i.e. for giving them a semantic analysis (by whatever means) as logically equivalent to "bring about" statements.

5.8.3. *Accommodating the "*Have*-Deletion" Cases*

If a transformation deleting the sequence **to have** from examples like (53a) is adopted, then the "internal" adverb in (53b) is of course accounted for automatically, as observed by McCawley and Partee.

(53) a. **John wants to have a car until the end of the week.**
b. **John wants a car until the end of the week.**

But as Partee adds, there are similar cases where "*Have*-deletion" would be inappropriate; instead something like a rule of "*Give*-deletion" would be needed to capture the appropriate paraphrase:

(54) a. **John promised to give Mary the book by the end of the week.**
b. **John promised Mary the book by the end of the week.**

In addition to **promise, offer** and **refuse** pattern the same way.

But even more problematic for a deletion transformation is the case of **owe,** since the correct paraphrase involves a different verb:

(55) a. **John is obliged (obligated?) to give Mary $10 by the end of the week.**
b. **John owes Mary $10 by the end of the week.**

Because of these problems, I am inclined to advocate a treatment of these cases that is like the "ambiguous verb" approach of 5.8.1. rather than a deletion transformation. The translations for examples of the relevant sets of homonyms are given in (56):

(56) a. $\mathbf{want}_1 (\in P_{TV/INF})$ translates into: **want′**
b. $\mathbf{want}_2 (\in P_{TV})$ translates into:
$\lambda\mathscr{P}\lambda x[\mathbf{want}'(\hat{}[\mathbf{have}'(\mathscr{P})])(x)]$

c. $\textbf{want}_3 (\in P_{TV/(t/t)})$ translates into:
$\lambda S \lambda \mathscr{P} \lambda x [\textbf{want}'(\hat{y}[{}^{\vee}S({}^{\wedge}[\textbf{have}'(y, \mathscr{P})])])(x)]$

d. $\textbf{promise}_1 (\in P_{(IV/INF)/T})$ translates into: $\textbf{promise}'$

e. $\textbf{promise}_2 (\in P_{TV/T})$ translates into:[16]
$\lambda \mathscr{P} \lambda \mathscr{Q} \lambda x \mathscr{P}\{\hat{y}[\textbf{promise}'(\hat{P}P\{y\})({}^{\wedge}[\textbf{give}'(\hat{P}P\{y\})(\mathscr{Q})])(x)]\}$

f. $\textbf{promise}_3 (\in P_{(TV/T)/(t/t)})$ translates into:
$\lambda S \lambda \mathscr{P} \lambda \mathscr{Q} \lambda x \mathscr{P}\{\hat{y}[\textbf{promise}'(\hat{P}P\{y\})$
$(\hat{z}[{}^{\vee}S({}^{\wedge}[\textbf{give}'(\hat{P}P\{y\})(\mathscr{Q})(z)])])(x)]\}$

g. $\textbf{owe}_1 (\in P_{TV/T})$ translates into:
$\lambda \mathscr{P} \lambda \mathscr{Q} \lambda x [\textbf{obligated}'({}^{\wedge}[\textbf{give}'(\mathscr{P})(\mathscr{Q})])(x)]$

h. $\textbf{owe}_2 (\in P_{(TV/T)/(t/t)})$ translates into:
$\lambda S \lambda \mathscr{P} \lambda \mathscr{Q} \lambda x [\textbf{obligated}'(\hat{z}[{}^{\vee}S({}^{\wedge}[\textbf{give}'(\mathscr{P})(\mathscr{Q})(z)])])(x)]$

In these translations, **give**′ is a constant of type $f(\mathrm{TV/T})$[17] and **obligated**′ is a constant of type $\langle\langle s, \langle e, t\rangle\rangle, \langle e, t\rangle\rangle$. Using these translations, (53b), (54b) and (55b) would have the respective translations (53b′), (54b′) and (55b′); here the hyphenated expressions indicate translations that have been left unanalyzed for simplicity's sake:

(53b′) $\textbf{need}'(\hat{y}[\textbf{until-the-end-of-the-week}'({}^{\wedge}[\textbf{have}'(y, {}^{\wedge}\textbf{a-car})])])(j)$

(54b′) $\textbf{promise}'(\hat{P}P\{m\})(\hat{z}[\textbf{by-the-end-of-the-week}'$
$({}^{\wedge}[\textbf{give}'_{*}(z, m, {}^{\wedge}\textbf{the-book}')])])(j)$

(55b′) $\textbf{obligated}'(\hat{z}[\textbf{by-the-end-of-the-week}'({}^{\wedge}[\textbf{give}'_{*}(z, m, {}^{\wedge}\$10)])])(j)$

(The relationship among the "homonyms" of these multi-place verbs will be given a more systematic account in Chapter 6.) An alternative approach would be to take the "internal adverb" homonym (δ_3 in each case) as more basic than the δ_2 homonym and write syntactic rules deriving the δ_2 homonym from the δ_3 form; the translation of this operation would in each case involve merely applying the meaning of the verb to an "idempotent" sentence operator (i.e. $\lambda p[{}^{\vee}p]$).

My reasons for preferring an "ambiguous verb" treatment rather than an "ambiguous adverb" treatment for these cases are: (1) we would need additional homonyms of the adverbs *besides* those postulated for the accomplishments and the same meaning postulate would not serve for them; and (2) I am afraid that any meaning postulate general enough in meaning for adverbs to cover both the "give" and "have" cases would be so general as to predict an internal reading for **seek** as well, the reading that Partee showed **seek** not to have. (Thus I consider the cases of accomplishment verbs that do not seem to have a readily perceivable internal reading (examples 47) as relatively "soft" facts which are so far not very compelling, but the absence of an internal reading for **seek** is much clearer, well documented, and thus more persuasive.)

Though the deletion analysis does not seem to be the correct one for a synchronic grammar, the relationship between (53a) and (53b) can hardly be an accidental one. Perhaps some version of syntactic analogy was responsible for creating the "internal" syntactic pattern at some point in the history of English. That is, in the historical linguists' formula,

John needs to have a car : *John needs a car* : : (53a) : *x*

the form (53b) then being innovated to fill in the value of *x* here. However, this is only a speculation at present.

5.9. OVERPREDICTIONS OF THE GENERATIVE SEMANTICS HYPOTHESIS

The GS hypothesis that "pre-lexical" logical structures are of the same nature as "post-lexical" structures and are operated on by the same transformations as the latter makes a number of predictions which turn out not to be met. To evaluate the merits of the two strategies of decomposition, these overpredictions of the generative semantics theory must be weighed against the complications noted in the previous section that were required to treat the adverb scope ambiguities in the "upside down" decomposition theory.

5.9.1. *Newmeyer's and Aissen's Cases: Interaction with Familiar Cyclic Transformations*

In most discussions of Predicate Raising in the GS literature it has been assumed that this transformation is a *cyclic rule*; that is, it and all other cyclic transformations apply to an embedded sentence of a syntactically complex structure before any cyclic rule is applied to the matrix sentence containing that embedded sentence. Thus in any derivation in which Predicate Raising applies to raise the verb of sentence S_j into the higher sentence S_i, the cyclicity hypothesis predicts that known cyclic transformations can potentially apply on the S_j cycle before any rules apply on the S_i cycle, hence they can apply prior to the insertion of the lexical item which is inserted to replace the complex verbal structure created by Predicate Raising on S_i (or higher sentences).

The first linguist to attempt to test this implicit prediction of the GS lexical decomposition hypothesis was Newmeyer (1976).[18] But Newmeyer found that in the case of four cyclic transformations (*There*-Insertion, Passive, *Tough*-Movement and Subject Raising), Predicate Raising and/or subsequent lexicalization must apparently be prohibited from applying where these transformations have applied in the embedded clause. For example, *There*-Insertion (the transformation which forms *There is a unicorn in the garden* from *A unicorn is in the garden, There exists a solution to this problem* from *A solution to this problem exists*) can clearly apply in the embedded sentence in (56a) to give (56b):

(56) a. John causes a furor to exist.
b. John causes there to exist (be) a furor.

But if *make* or *create* is inserted to replace the complex predicate structure [CAUSE *Exist*]$_V$, as would otherwise be assumed in generative semantics, then we would expect (57b) as well as (57a) to be acceptable:

(57) a. John created a furor.
b. *John created there a furor.

That is, there is no reason why Predicate Raising should not apply in a higher cycle after *There*-Insertion has applied, leading to the insertion of *create* and thus to (57b). But in fact, no sentences of the form of (57b) exist in English. Similarly, *Tough*-Movement can apply in the embedded sentence in (58a) to convert it to (58b):

(58) a. The astronomer made it possible for me to see the comet.
b. The astronomer made the comet possible for me to see.

Yet if *enable* can be inserted in the Predicate-Raised structure that would otherwise underlie *cause to be possible*, then (59b) as well as (59a) ought to be produced:

(59) a. The astronomer enabled me to see the comet.
b. *The astronomer enabled the comet (for) me to see.

Of course, the generative semantics theory postulates devices such as global rules which are powerful enough to block the application of Predicate Raising in just those derivations in which one of these transformations (or the others discussed by Newmeyer) has applied. But such a coincidental global restriction on Predicate Raising is highly suspicious and if adopted would seriously detract from the generality and appeal of the pre-lexical syntax theory.

Newmeyer instead suggests that Predicate Raising be classified as a pre-cyclic transformation, i.e. one that is applied (repeatedly to its own output) *before* cyclic transformations have begun to apply to even the most deeply embedded sentence, though the evidence for pre-cyclic transformations is slight and is not accepted by all linguists. In fact, Newmeyer claims that the only other transformation which *can* be argued to be pre-cyclic is Nominalization, a transformation which (like Predicate Raising) would be rejected by more conservative transformationalists who advocate interpretive semantic rules to relate underlying syntactic structure to semantic representations. Thus we are left with a theory in which just those transformations rejected by interpretivists are treated as precyclic and thus prohibited from interacting in any observable way with other transformations. This leads Newmeyer to suspect that the generativist and interpretivist theories cannot really be distinguished by observable evidence, hence are more similar than had been supposed. The "upside down" generative semantics strategy of decomposition developed in this book likewise predicts no interaction between pre-lexical structures and syntactic rules since these prelexical decomposed structures are not "syntactic" structures of English in any sense. But as we shall see shortly, the conclusion that can be reached about the relationship of this treatment to the others is much stronger than the kind Newmeyer draws.

In a study which parallels Newmeyer's, Aissen (1974) investigated the derivation of sentences with productively derived causatives in a number of languages, such as the French example (60) and the Turkish example (61):

(60) J'ai fait partir Jean.
"I made Jean leave"

(61) Hasan ben - i agla - t - ti.
Hasan me-Acc cry-cause-past
"Hasan made me cry"

Aissen assumes that sentences such as this are complex in underlying structure (as in English *I brought it about that Jean left*) but presents clear evidence that in each case the surface structures consist of only one clause. Thus she argues that a raising operation has combined the verb of the lower clause with the (possibly abstract) verb CAUSE of the higher sentence in the derivations of these sentences. Though this operation would be considered identical with Predicate Raising by generative semanticists, Aissen refers to it as *Verb Raising* because there is no direct evidence that it has applied prelexically in her cases (the embedded verb is morphologically intact in surface structure) and Aissen prefers not to commit herself to the existence of pre-lexical transformations. Given the prima facie evidence of an underlying two-clause structure here that did not exist in the cases discussed by Newmeyer, one might expect to find that cyclic transformations in these languages do apply on the lower as well as on the higher cycle. But Aissen examines cyclic transformations such as Passive and Reflexive in these languages (and similar data in Spanish and Sanskrit) and discovers that such "lower cycle" applications lead to ungrammaticality. Like Newmeyer, she concludes that the raising rule under investigation must be pre-cyclic.

But here again, if productive derived causatives were produced in these languages by the kind of rule suggested in (4.10) in the discussion of Comrie's paradigm case, it would also follow that no syntactic rule applying to sentences (i.e. transformation-like rule) could apply to the embedded sentence at all in the syntactic derivation. In view of this observation, it becomes highly pertinent to examine Aissen's reasons for assuming that there *is* a bi-sentential structure at some underlying stage. These reasons (Aissen 1974, 331-332) are: (1) the selectional restrictions of the non-causative verb are matched exactly, *mutatis mutandis*, by those of the causative verb; (2) the "deep grammatical relations" of the non-causative are mirrored, with the same changes of case role as in (1), in the causative sentence; (3) the subcategorization restrictions of the non-causative are reflected in those of the causative (e.g. just as the Turkish verb meaning "put" requires a locative complement, the causative of this verb also requires a locative complement, as well as the additional noun phrase); (4) producing the causative non-transformationally requires a phrase-structure rule not needed in the transformational analysis (e.g. in Turkish the only verbs which take four noun phrase arguments are derived causatives). But reasons (1) and (2) are just the alleged "syntactic" facts of the early transformationalists that have come to be recognized as "semantic" facts in recent years by transformationalists of all schools, and if this kind of fact does indeed follow from the semantic interpretation of a sentence, then the rules for derived causatives given in (4.10) predict them. Aissen's reason (3) is likewise closely bound up with semantics, but it would follow in the syntax too if we consistently adopt this principle that causative rules convert a verb of subcategory X (whatever this may be) to category X/T and follow the pattern of translation rule for derived causatives illustrated in (4.10). As for the last reason, Aissen herself observes that (p. 333) "If the necessity for an additional phrase structure rule were the only complication of a phrase structure analysis, its existence would be no argument for the transformational analysis since that analysis must posit a rule of Verb Raising." Thus it seems preferable on syntactic grounds to assume a single sentence source for Aissen's cases, and the kind of rule illustrated in section 4.10 explicitly accounts for the appropriate semantics as well.[19]

5.9.2. *Adverb Raising/Operator Raising*

The overpredictions connected with the generative semantics account of the internal readings of adverbs have already been discussed and do not need repeating here. The transformation of Adverb Raising needed to get the internal adverb out of the way of Predicate Raising fails to be attested "post-lexically" in any accomplishment sentence, and not only Adverb Raising but the alternative analysis which avoids it (cf. note 3) predict readings which do not occur either in pre-lexical or post-lexical situations. Similarly, Operator Raising (needed to raise the NEG to its initial position in *unwrap, unstop*, etc.) predicts scopes of negation that do not occur.

5.9.3. *Pre-Lexical Quantifier Lowering*

When I first noticed how the semantic effect of a lexical decomposition could be achieved by the translation process of a PTQ-type grammar, I was puzzled as to which of the following translations for an accomplishment verb like transitive **open** should be the correct one:

(62) a. $\lambda\mathscr{P}\lambda x\mathscr{P}\{\hat{y}\bigvee P[P\{x\}\text{ CAUSE BECOME }\mathbf{open}'(y)]\}$
b. $\lambda\mathscr{P}\lambda x\bigvee P\mathscr{P}\{\hat{y}[P\{x\}\text{ CAUSE BECOME }\mathbf{open}'(y)]\}$
c. $\lambda\mathscr{P}\lambda x\bigvee P[P\{x\}\text{ CAUSE }\mathscr{P}\{\hat{y}[\text{BECOME }\mathbf{open}'(y)]\}]$
d. $\lambda\mathscr{P}\lambda x\bigvee P[P\{x\}\text{ CAUSE BECOME }\mathscr{P}\{\hat{y}[\mathbf{open}'(y)]\}]$

I at first thought that it made no difference which form of translation was used; I had been examining decompositions of verbs like **kill** (i.e., with $\neg\mathbf{alive}'(y)$ replacing $\mathbf{open}'(y)$ in the above pattern) using examples like **John killed Bill**, and indeed, all four forms of the translation listed in (62a)-(62d) lead to exactly the same simplified translation for this example. But it later came to my attention (thanks to a comment of Stanley Peters') that the four forms of translation give semantically distinct results where the direct object term phrase is a quantified term phrase rather than a name.[20] In such cases the location of . . . $\mathscr{P}\{\hat{y}[$. . . within the translation of a transitive verb determines the scope that the quantifier binding the term phrase will have in the resulting translation of the sentence. That is, suppose that we have decided to name a particular door or window **Harry**; then (63) will have the translation (63′) no matter which of the four translations for **open** in (62) is used:

(63) **John opened Harry.**

(63′) $\bigvee P[P\{j\}$ CAUSE BECOME **open**$'(h)]$

But (64) will receive one of the four distinct translations in (64a)-(64d) according to which of the four translations (62a)-(62d) is used, respectively:

(64) **John opened every window.**

(64′) a. $\bigwedge y[$**window**$'(y) \rightarrow \bigvee P[P\{j\}$ CAUSE BECOME **open**$'(y)]]$
b. $\bigvee P \bigwedge y[$**window**$'(y) \rightarrow [P\{j\}$ CAUSE BECOME **open**$'(y)]]$
c. $\bigvee P[P\{j\}$ CAUSE $\bigwedge y[$**window**$'(y) \rightarrow$ BECOME **open**$'(y)]]$
d. $\bigvee P[P\{j\}$ CAUSE BECOME $\bigwedge y[$**window**$'(y) \rightarrow$ **open**$'(y)]]$

Because we have assigned all the symbols in (64′a)-(64′d) an explicit formal interpretation, it can be determined exactly what the difference in interpretation among these is.

Consider first (64′d). Suppose we are concerned with the interpretation of this formula in a model at an index at which there are exactly four windows. Among other conditions, (64′d) is true at this index if at the end of the time interval of the index all four windows are open, though it was false that all four were open at the beginning of the interval. Though this condition is met if each of the four changes from being closed to being open during the interval, it will also be met if three of the windows were already open at the beginning of the interval and only the fourth actually became open during this time. But no native speaker of English would consider (64) true under these latter circumstances. Thus (64′d) is defective as a translation of (64).

Consider next (64′c). This translation avoids the problem of the (64d) because the universal quantifier binding y has wider scope than BECOME; (64′c) can only be true where each of the windows undergoes the transition from being closed to being open, as (64) intuitively entails. But (64′c) has another problem. Suppose the index in question is a situation in which the first three windows are controlled by an automatic opening device connected to a foolproof timer which has been set some time in advance and cannot be easily tampered with. Suppose that this timer opens the first three windows at exactly the same time as John opens the fourth. Given our semantics for causation, (64′c) ought to be true in this situation because in the possible worlds most similar to the actual world except that John does not act, the formula $\Lambda y[\mathbf{window}'(y) \rightarrow \text{BECOME } \mathbf{open}'(y)]$ is not true either, i.e., the fourth window does not open in these worlds and this suffices to make this last formula false. But this result is likewise not in accord with our intuitions about the meaning of (64), and so (64′c) should not be used to translate (64) either.

Both (64′a) and (64′b) avoid the problem with (64′c); the quantifier binding y has wider scope than CAUSE in both cases, so it must be the case for *each* appropriate value of y that John causes y to become open. Distinguishing between (64′a) and (64′b) is harder than distinguishing these two translations from the previous two, however. One is at first tempted to suppose that (64′b) requires that the same activity caused all the windows to open, whereas (64′a) allows that a different causal activity might be responsible for the opening of each window. The meaning of (64) seems equally appropriate whether the causal actions were "the same" or "separate", by the way; here one can imagine one of those once-popular luxury cars which has electric powered windows that can be operated by a single switch at the driver's seat as well as by individual switches on each door; (64) may be used no matter which method of opening the windows John chooses. But it is not clear that (64′a) and (64′b) are really distinct in this way because of the extremely general notion of "property" that "$\bigvee P$" quantifies over in this formula. That is, the property of performing four separate activities is just as good a value for the variable "P" in this case as is the property of performing just one activity. (Also note that if the variable P were replaced by a particular activity predicate (as it is, for example, in the translations of factitive sentences), no analogous scope difference in the translation rule could be made since there would be no existential quantifier.) Nevertheless, I am inclined to propose (62a) rather than (62b) as the more appropriate form of translation because of the possibility that we might later wish to restrict the property variable P in some way that would make "conjunctive activities" inadmissible as values, thus creating a real need for permitting the "activity quantifier" to have narrower scope than the direct object quantifier. (For example, P might be restricted to activities of "direct manipulation", as suggested by Shibatani's (1976) observation about the difference between lexical and periphrastic causatives in general.) But whether we choose (62a) or (62b) as the translation for **open**, it is abundantly clear that these and not (62c) or (62d) represent possible meanings for **open**.

What is also interesting about this observation is the consequence it suggests for the analogous situation in the GS theory. The examples one finds in the existing literature on decomposition all seem to have a name in object position. But now it is apparent that the GS analysis of quantifiers (that they arise from higher sentences and are lowered into their surface position by the Quantifier Lowering transformation) predicts interesting interactions with the lexical decomposition hypothesis. Specifically, we are led to ask which of the structures like (65b), (65c) and (65d) are underlying logical structures for (64) in the GS theory:

(65)
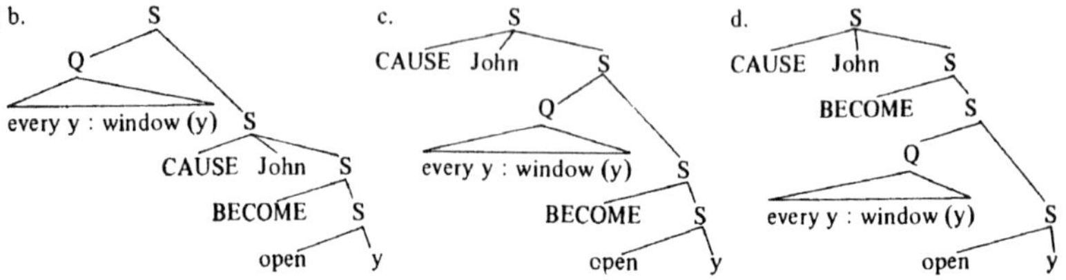

To sidestep unnecessary controversies, I represent universal quantifiers with their restricting noun predicates as "restricted quantifiers" in (65) as McCawley prefers (McCawley, 1978b), rather than by a combination of an unrestricted quantifier and the connective "→". Also, I have omitted all other irrelevant details in (65), choosing the simplest form of decomposition that is found in generative semantics literature. Now just as I have shown that (64c′) and (64d′) were not correct translations of (64), it follows for exactly the same reasons that (65c) and (65d) would be semantically wrong as logical structures for (64), since these two logical structures have the quantifier scopes that were responsible for the incorrectness of (64c′) and (64d′). But how can (65c) and (65d) be ruled out? These structures are not semantically anomalous in themselves, since we have already discussed what they mean. Furthermore, multi-clause sentences can be constructed that do seem to have these readings:

(65′) c. John caused it to be the case that every window opened.
d. John brought it about that every window was open.

Quantifier Lowering has always been assumed to be a cyclic transformation, and there is nothing about (65c) and (65d) that I can imagine that would block it in these cases, nor any relevant syntactic constraint to appeal to.

One should not be too hasty to follow Newmeyer and Aissen's lead and attempt to "segregate" Quantifier Lowering from Predicate Raising by appealing to the cyclic/precyclic distinction. It is true that the tack of claiming Predicate Raising is precyclic while Quantifier Lowering is cyclic offers an explanation of the lack of the (65c) and (65d) readings of **John opens every window**. The presence of the quantifer in (65c) and (65d) at the time Predicate Raising applies could be supposed to block the raising of the predicates **open** and BECOME up into the CAUSE sentence; nevertheless, these predicates would be allowed to lexicalize as separate verbs in (65c′) and (65d′). But this tack has disastrous consequences for McCawley's and Bach's analysis of the opaque reading of **John seeks a unicorn**, which has to come from (something like) (66):

(66)

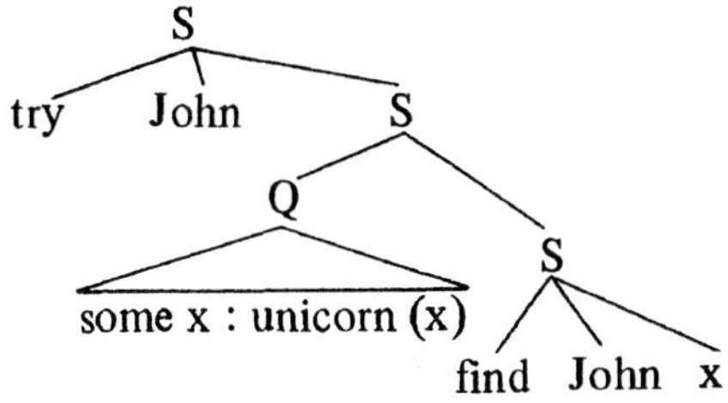

For just as surely as the intervening quantifier would block a precyclic Predicate Raising transformation in (65c) and (65d), so it would by the same token block the raising of *find* up to *try* in the derivation of (66). Rather, for the derivation from (66) to proceed as McCawley and Bach suggest, Quantifier Lowering must apply *before* Predicate Raising. And if it applies before Predicate Raising in at least one derivation, then Predicate Raising cannot be precyclic unless Quantifier Lowering is precyclic as well. But if Quantifier Lowering too were precyclic then we would once again have no way to block (65c′) and (65d′) from reaching the surface in the form of (64). Thus we have an "ordering paradox" of the classical sort that cannot be handled by rule ordering at all. We could appeal to global rules, but such a solution lacks generality completely, since the restriction would depend entirely on the choice of particular lexical items: pre-lexical Quantifier Lowering would be permitted in the case of **seek** (and the **want**-class), prohibited in the case of accomplishments, and "post-lexical" Quantifier Lowering (i.e. lowering over entire lexicalized verbs) would be permitted for all verbs.

Let us consider the predictions about lexical-item-internal scopes of quantifiers made by the "upside down generative semantics" method, i.e. predictions made by the method in general, not just the particular analyses advanced so far. By this method, a transitive verb will necessarily have a translation (or equivalent "meaning postulate" decomposition) of the general form of (67):

(67) $\lambda \mathscr{P} \lambda x [\mathrm{OP}_1 \ldots \mathrm{OP}_j \mathscr{P} \{\hat{y} [\mathrm{OP}_k \ldots \mathrm{OP}_n [\mathrm{Pred}_i(y)] \ldots]\} \ldots]$

Such a translation gives the direct object quantifier a scope narrower than the operators $OP_1 \ldots OP_j$ but wider than $OP_k \ldots OP_n$. Of course, one or the other (or both) of this series of operators may be empty; if the series $OP_1 \ldots OP_j$ is empty (as it in fact is in all the translations of accomplishments I have given), the direct object quantifier has the "whole" meaning of the word as its scope. The point to note, since this is what crucially distinguishes the two theories, is that the quantifier has *exactly one* possible word-internal scope, if that. This situation must be carefully distinguished from the question of possible quantifier scopes which are *wider than* the meaning of the word itself, for in the "upside down" decomposition method in Montague grammar, the quantifier scopes wider than that of the verb are produced by the syntactic quantification rules S14-S16, and there are at least as many of these possibilities as there are sentences, IV-phrases and CN-phrases within which the quantifying term phrase is embedded in "surface" structure. The classical GS theory, by contrast, seems forced to predict (aside from ad-hoc global constraints) either (1) there are as many possible direct-object quantifier scopes as there are embedded sentences in (pre-lexical) logical structure (assuming Quantifier Lowering and Predicate Raising are both cyclic or both precyclic) or else (2) there are no possible word-internal quantifier scopes (assuming Predicate Raising is precyclic while Quantifier Lowering is cyclic or postcyclic). As we have just seen, both these predictions are false. By contrast, the predictions made by the other theory are, to the best of my knowledge, completely borne out. This approach to decomposition is of course in principle falsifiable: it would tend to be falsified if a verb could be found for which the quantifier could be interpreted as having either of two internal scopes (on pain of having to postulate homonyms in that theory that differed only in the scope position assigned) and would be most clearly falsified if a class of verbs could be found for which all scopes theoretically present in the decomposition analysis were really possible scopes for the quantifier. But so far, no such verbs are known.

5.9.4. *Quantifier Lowering and Carlson's Analysis of Bare Plurals*

The difficulty that the GS method of decomposition encountered with pre-lexical quantifier lowering in the case just discussed suggests that other problems might potentially arise with "sub-lexical" quantifiers and their interaction with Quantifier Lowering and the lexicalization process. I am not sure how many, if any, problems of this sort there might be, but such difficulties might be encountered with Carlson's analysis of bare plurals (cf. 2.3.4) if we attempted to incorporate it into a classical GS theory. Recall that Carlson observed that the alleged "existential quantifier" underlying a bare plural never seems to have wider scope than another quantifier, a negative, or a durative adverbial, etc. To cite just one example, (68) has the familiar scope ambiguity involving the two quantifiers, but (69) has only one reading:

(68) Everyone read a book on giraffes.

(69) Everyone read books on giraffes.

While (68) can be used to assert that there was one book read by all individuals (as well as its other reading), (69) cannot be taken to assert that there were particular books which were read by all individuals (cf. Carlson, 1977: section 2.2.2). The two translations which (68) receives in Carlson's system are (roughly) represented by (68′a) and (68′b), while (69) receives the translation (69′):

(68′) a. $\bigwedge x[\mathbf{person}'(x) \rightarrow \bigvee y[\mathbf{book}'(y) \wedge \bigvee w \bigvee z[R(w, x) \wedge R(z, y) \wedge \mathbf{read}^{\dagger}(w, z)]]]$
b. $\bigvee y[\mathbf{book}'(y) \wedge \bigwedge x[\mathbf{person}'(x) \rightarrow \bigvee w \bigvee z[R(w, x) \wedge R(z, y) \wedge \mathbf{read}^{\dagger}(w, z)]]]$

(69′) $\bigwedge x[\mathbf{person}'(x) \rightarrow \bigvee w \bigvee z[R(w, x) \wedge R(z, \mathbf{books}') \wedge \mathbf{read}^{\dagger}(w, z)]]$

Here, R is the "realization relation" which relates kinds and objects to their stages, **read**† is the relation between stages corresponding to the verb **read**, and **books** is the proper name of the kind books (which I have shortened from **books on giraffes** in all three cases). (For simplicity, I ignore the further decomposition of **read**† here.) Now if these three translations were instead to be treated as logical structures in a classical GS theory (and appropriate rules were supplied to convert them to the surface structures in (68) and (69)), the further question arises of how we are to prevent the additional logical structure (69″) (or others equivalent to it) from surfacing as (69):

(69″) $\bigvee z \bigwedge x[\mathbf{person}'(x) \rightarrow \bigvee w[R(w, x) \wedge R(z, \mathbf{books}') \wedge \mathbf{read}^{\dagger}(w, z)]]$

The formula in (69″) of course represents the reading which (69) is observed not to have, yet if Quantifier Lowering removed the part of the underlying structure represented by $\bigwedge x[\mathbf{person}(x) \rightarrow$ in (69″), then it is not at all clear how the lexicalization of **read** and the remainder of the derivation could be blocked. Even if this case could be satisfactorily handled, similar problems will arise with negation, durative adverbials and the other cases discussed by Carlson.

In Carlson's own treatment (in the PTQ theory), this difficulty never arises. The quantifier contributing the "existential" reading of bare plurals always appears in the translation of the verb; e.g. **read** would translate as in (70):

$$(70) \qquad \lambda\mathscr{P}\lambda x\mathscr{P}\{\hat{y}[\bigvee w \bigvee z\,[R(w,x) \wedge R(z,y) \wedge \mathbf{read}^{\dagger}(w,z)]]\}$$

Since other quantifiers, negation, adverbials, etc. must inevitably be added "outside" the translation of this verb in the translation of a whole sentence, it follows that the quantifiers $\bigvee w$ and $\bigvee z$ responsible for "existential" bare plurals must always have narrow scope. This situation is thus on the whole parallel to the one in the previous section.

5.10. CONCLUDING EVALUATION

It is time to take stock of what we have seen about the evidence for decomposition and how well it can be handled in the two decomposition strategies we have considered. First, of all the alleged arguments for decomposition of the *meaning* of a verb into semantic parts, only the arguments from internal scope of adverbs and *re-* and *un-* are persuasive. (Even these only really provide evidence that the meaning of an accomplishment must be factored into BRING ABOUT plus result state, not three or more parts as I have decomposed accomplishments.) Nevertheless, this evidence became more persuasive the more closely it was examined and the more closely were examined the apparent alternative treatments of the data.

Second, the GS account of this phenomenon offered what was at first sight an appealing explanation, since the claim was that this peculiar phenomenon could be explained simply by generalizing a method of analysis (abstract deep syntax) supposedly already required in a linguistic theory on independent grounds. This approach, if correct, suggests the further appealing possibility that what is learned about language from relatively visible phenomena ("superficial" syntax) can be applied to the analysis of relatively inaccessible phenomena (semantics).

The treatment of this data by the "upside down generative semantics" method, by contrast, required one of two apparently ad hoc steps – postulating semantic and categorial ambiguity in lexical items, either verbs or adverbs.

However, the GS theory turns out, on closer inspection, to make overpredictions of three different kinds: (1) it predicts observable syntactic interactions with cyclic transformations (Passive, There-Insertion) which do not occur, (2) Adverb Raising predicts scopes of adverbs that do not occur, (3) it predicts quantifier scopes that do not occur. While the tack of making Predicate Raising precyclic (itself an ad hoc step) would avoid the consequence (1), this tack cannot in fact be used because of the problem it creates with the analysis of **seek** and other opaque verbs. Moreover, in each of these three cases there is not just *one* predicted reading or form that does not occur but two or possibly even more, depending on the number of abstract embedded sentences postulated in logical structure.

Thus on the grounds of a simple count of problems existing and problems solved, the "upside down" treatment of decomposition must be preferred: though the solution in this method requires an ad hoc step, this one step gives exactly the right predictions without further ado; the GS method on the other hand creates a number of potential readings or forms that are not attested, and these must be blocked by even more suspicious ad hoc devices, such as global rules.

But an even more significant point is indicated by these results. The essential claim underlying the GS theory is that prelexical syntax is "just like" postlexical syntax – Predicate Raising, Adverb Raising and Quantifier Lowering being claimed to be transformations of the same sort as the more familiar transformations. Regardless of whether we classify these transformations as cyclic or precyclic, as syntactic transformations they have what can be called a *pseudo-cyclic* property by their very nature. That is, since Quantifier Lowering is an *unbounded movement rule* (moves elements across an indefinite number of clause boundaries), a quantified noun phrase occurring embedded within *n* sentences in logical structure ought to have *n* possible scopes for its quantifier – this after all is what we must conclude from the observed behavior of post-lexical applications of Quantifier Lowering in this theory. And though Adverb Raising may not be unbounded, it must nevertheless apply iteratively to its own output, moving an adverb through an indefinite number of clauses. Thus an adverb in a surface structure that comes from a logical structure with *n* embedded sentences ought to have *n* possible scopes; compare this with the way that Passive and Raising to Object can together raise a noun phrase over an arbitrary number of sentence boundaries. Claiming that Adverb Raising and Quantifier Lowering are ordinary transformations is claiming that in principle they should behave this way. The more this behavior is restricted by global or word-specific constraints, the less substance to the claim that pre-lexical syntax is "just like" post-lexical syntax.

As we have seen, the "upside-down generative semantics" method of handling the decomposition problem predicts that if a verb allows word-internal quantifier scope, then there will be exactly one word-internal scope and not more, and it predicts that if an adverb has word-internal scope then here as well there will be exactly one scope possibility. Both these predictions seem to be met.

The reason that this treatment makes such predictions is that the mapping of words into their semantic analysis is accomplished by a "one-step" translation process (i.e. one translation rule per constituent), not the multi-stage process characteristic of a transformational derivation (i.e. an arbitrary number of operations per clause). In treating the sub-lexical scope problems, the transformational approach with its indefinitely many stages offers no natural way to limit potentially iterative or unbounded processes in the narrow way that is really appropriate for the data, though this "iterativeness" is just what is called for in super-lexical syntax, e.g. WH-movement and cyclic transformations. All the data in this chapter thus suggests a general result:

> Rules of semantic interpretation of lexical items are not of the same nature as those of a transformational derivation.

Not only does this result have consequences for the GS theory, it may have exactly the same consequences for other theories of semantics developed by linguists. Specifically, Katz has claimed (Katz, 1971) that the GS theory is merely a notational variant of his own interpretive semantics, and I believe his view was or is widely accepted in certain circles. Not only does Katz find the GS claim that semantic representations are phrase markers not distinguish his theory from GS, but he finds that the apparent absence of semantic projection rules in the GS theory is not significant either. He writes (p. 322) "Recall that Lakoff claims that projection rules are 'formal operations of a very different sort than grammatical transformations.' This claim is either a falsification, or a misunderstanding." He goes on to conclude (p. 327) that "such collection rules [as Predicate Raising, DRD] are nothing more than backwards versions of type 1 projection rules." But it should be clear from the discussion in this chapter that if the pre-lexical stages of a GS derivation (i.e., a series of phrase markers $P_1, P_2, \ldots P_n$) are matched exactly by stages of Katz' interpretation in reverse order (i.e., a series of readings P_n, $P_{n-1}, \ldots P_1$) these stages being related by rules which are the inverse of Predicate Raising, Adverb Raising, and Quantifier Lowering, then Katz' theory will make exactly the same overpredictions as those of the GS theory discussed above. This suggests the result:

> To the extent that the Interpretive Semantics account of word meaning is a notational variant of the Generative Semantics account, Interpretive Semantics makes wrong predictions about the interpretation of word-internal quantifiers and adverbs.

Of course, this result applies only if the interpretive projection rules in question are really very general rules applying to all the sentence-like constituents of Katz' readings in the recursive, pseudo-cyclic manner described above. It is open to Katz to claim that the work of such putative projection rules should be taken over by rules associated more intimately with the lexical entries of particular verbs, hence they would escape the over-predictions. (And perhaps more recent versions of Katz' theory should be taken in this way.) But this is of course just what we have done in the "upside-down" model of decomposition presented in this book.

Perhaps there is a moral to be gleaned from this study for the notion of "level of linguistic structure" as it is currently used in linguistic syntax and semantics. In the wake of the inconclusive debate between the generative semantics and the interpretive semantics theories about the "direction" of mappings and their properties, linguists of all schools have more and more often come to postulate some "level of linguistic structure" or other which has such-and-such significant properties, without explicitly describing the rules which relate this level to the levels "above" or "below" it (though apparently the notion of a quasi-transformational derivation lurks behind such ideas). One such example might be Chomsky's notion of *logical form*, which hovers somewhere between surface structure and "meaning" (cf. Chomsky, 1975, p. 105). Another example would be Newmeyer's (1976) *middle structure*. If the situation discussed above is any indication of the kind of problems that can be expected to arise when one attempts to flesh out the explicit rules and intermediate stages required by such proposals, then perhaps it is time to conclude that the idea of a "level of linguistic structure" has gotten somewhat out of hand and to declare a moratorium on the postulation of such levels in the absence of rules and explicit examples with which the real consequences of such suggestions can be tested.

NOTES

[1] Susan Schmerling has pointed out that it perhaps should not have been so readily taken for granted that Predicate Raising would be subject to extraction constraints, for Ross (1967) observed that these constraints only apply to rules of certain forms, and it is not obvious that Predicate Raising falls into any of the appropriate categories to which extraction constraints apply.

[2] As McCawley has reminded me, there are at least a few cases where an adverb seems to have been "raised" out of a lower clause:

(i) On Thursday John wants to go to the opera.

(ii) John wants to go to the opera on Thursday.

However, the verb in this example is not of the same semantic class as the verbs at issue here (*kill*), but is rather of the notorious Neg-Raising class, verbs which have semantic/pragmatic properties that "encourage" one to treat an operator as it is commuted with the verb (cf. Horn, 1978a)). But no matter whether Adverb Raising applies in (i) or not, what is relevant to the present issue is to establish independently that Adverb Raising applies in sentences with *accomplishment* verbs. And this is just what we do not find. Note that the adverbs discussed in section 5.6 below (which is a much clearer case of ambiguity than the *almost* cases) do not have the ambiguity in (35a)-(35c) and (30a)-(30b) that Adverb Raising predicts they should have, if these examples behaved parallel to the putative raising in (i) above.

[3] I can think of one way that the proponent of the syntactic decomposition hypothesis could escape this paradox. It might be claimed that it is really unnecessary to postulate a transformation of Adverb Raising at all. While it was traditionally assumed in transformational grammar that adverbs – at least, sentence adverbs – originated in sentence final position and that there is an optional transformation of Adverb Preposing (to account for *On Thursday John left town* as well as *John left town on Thursday*), in the GS theory with its verb-initial hypothesis and the hypothesis that adverbs are of the same kind of category as predicates it is more natural to assume that all sentence adverbs originate in sentence-initial position and that there is instead an optional transformation of Adverb Postposing. The two proposals make roughly equivalent predictions. But now it could be supposed that it is Adverb Postposing which gets the internal adverb "out of the way" to allow Predicate Raising to take place. That is, suppose the derivation of the internal reading of *John closed the door again* has reached the stage (i):

(i)

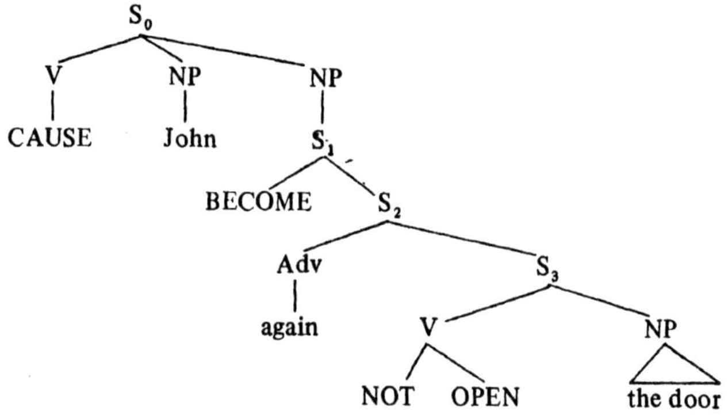

(For the sake of argument, I ignore various questions about details of the tree and various problems that could potentially arise, e.g. with tree pruning.) Then Adverb Postposing would apply on S_2 to give rise to (ii):

(ii)

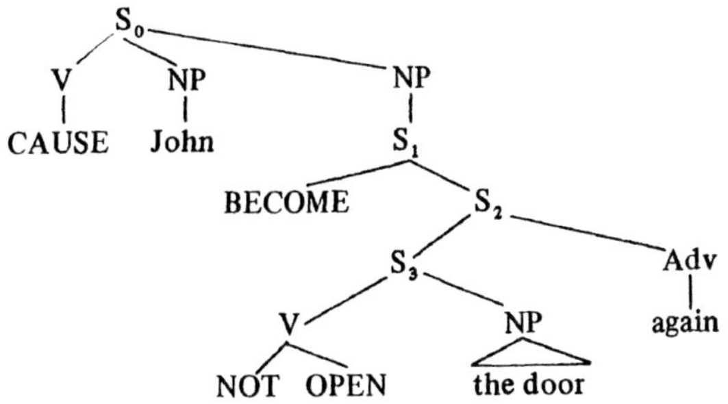

Now the structural description of Predicate Raising (cf. Newmeyer, 1976, p. 113) is apparently met on the S_1 cycle (assuming the intervening S node does not for some reason block the rule), and its application would convert (ii) into (iii), then on the next cycle into (iv) (assuming tree pruning):

(iii)

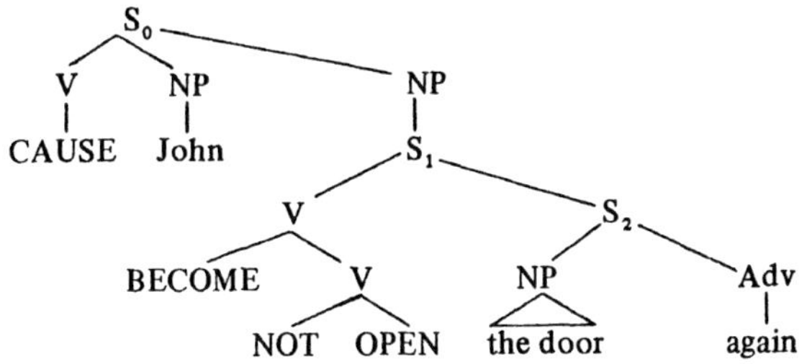

(iv)

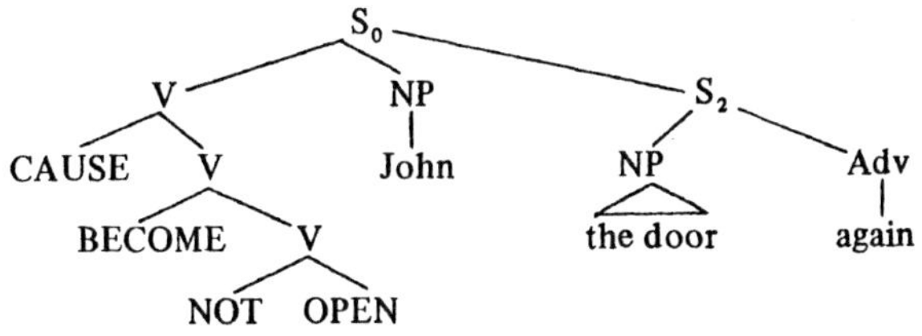

Then after lexicalization of *close* and Subject Formation, an acceptable derived structure would be produced – note that *again* winds up inside the surface "VP" node (i.e. S_2), which is arguably where it should be for this reading, unlike the external reading. Despite the smoothness of this derivation, there are still problems. As McCawley and Morgan observed, there do not seem to be internal readings in which the adverbs originate *below* a negation. For example, *Dr. Frankenstein almost killed the monster* cannot mean "Dr. Frankenstein brought it about that the monster was not almost alive," *Dr. Frankenstein killed the monster again* cannot mean "Dr. Frankenstein brought it about that the monster was not again alive" and *John closed the door again* cannot mean "John brought it about that the door was not again open." They suggest that there is an independently motivated constraint against lifting an adverb out of the scope of a negative, as *John didn't almost leave* cannot mean the same as *John almost didn't leave*. But as I said earlier, there is no really strong evidence that movement of *almost* takes place in the unnegated version of these last two sentences, and moreover there must be at least some cases where the putative constraint on crossing quantifiers and operators over negation is violated, such as one of the readings of *Everyone didn't leave*. Of course, it is possible that what these cases indicate is that it is simply wrong to decompose *kill* as "cause to become not alive" and *close* as "cause to become not open"; rather it might be that *kill* should be "cause to become dead" and *close* should be "cause to become CLOSED" (where the capital letters are supposed to indicate a primitive predicate, not a derived one as English *closed* actually is). Yet there are indications otherwise: *dead* presupposes "having once been alive" and *closed* presupposes "having once been open." Probably this is just one instance of the general problem discussed below of the overpredictions made by the syntactic decomposition model.

But in any case, notice that under the hypothesis that it is Adverb Postposing rather than Adverb Raising which gets the adverb out of the way of Predicate Raising, the adverb is neither crossed over the negation nor removed from its scope in any other straightforward way in the "illegal" derivation just mentioned. That is, Adverb Postposing could convert (iv) to (v) in such a derivation, then Predicate Raising would convert (v) to (vi), then to (vii), etc.

(iv)

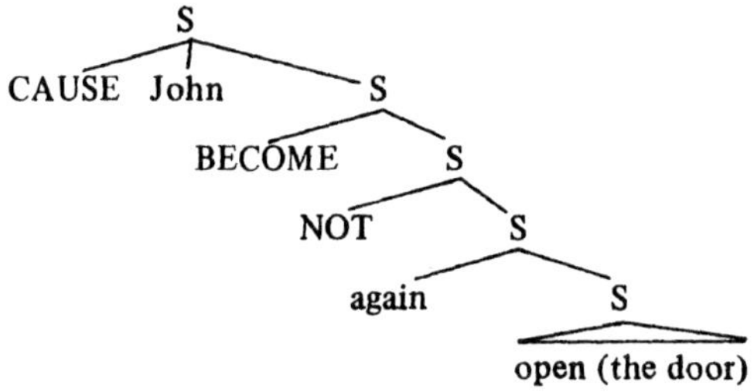

(v)

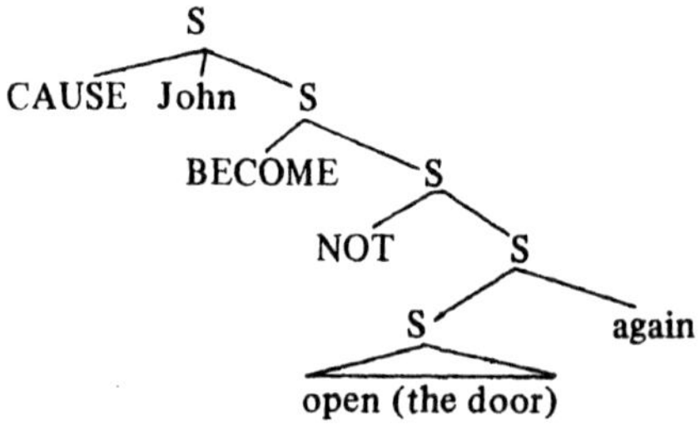

(vi)

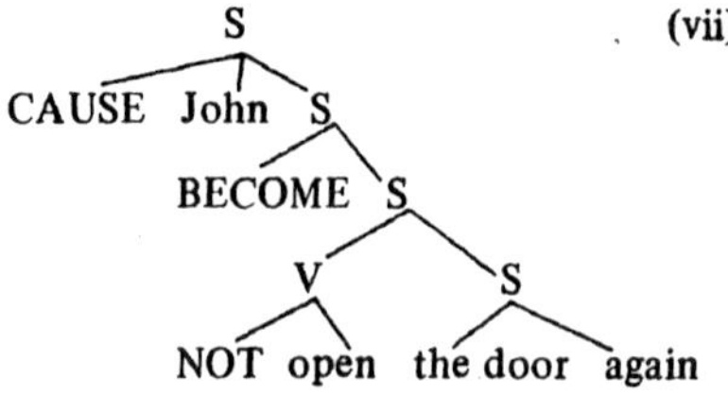

(vii)

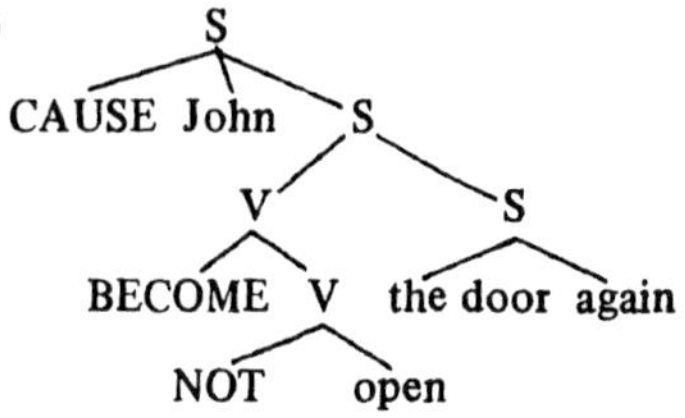

Thus there is no obvious way to appeal to an independently motivated constraint to block this derivation, nor to block a parallel derivation with *almost*.

[4] Note that in order for the ambiguity test to be valid, the phrase *almost did so too* cannot be substituted for *so did* in this example. For if the former phrase was used, then *do so* would not replace the whole phrase that is being tested for structural ambiguity (*almost kill him*) but only a phrase (*kill him*) whose meaning would be the same after the adverb had been extracted, no matter whether it had been the same before this extraction or not. Cf. Sadock and Zwicky (1975) for discussion.

[5] I have noticed (only after writing this) that Kempson (1977, pp. 131-132) performs exactly the same test and likewise concludes that *almost* does not produce a true ambiguity in this kind of example.

[6] Another class of potential adverb arguments might be made from the subtle difference in meaning of adverbs like *carefully* depending on the position in which they occur in a sentence:

(i) John carefully washed the dishes.

(ii) John washed the dishes carefully.

This difference happens to be brought out more clearly by the paraphrases (i') and (ii') respectively:

(i') John was careful to wash the dishes.

(ii') John washed the dishes in a careful manner.

That is, the adverb in (i') seems to characterize the intent of the agent in performing the act at all (e.g. he made a deliberate attempt not to forget to wash the dishes, because some undesirable consequence would result if he did), whereas (ii'), like (ii), describes the manner in which the action was carried out. One might conceivably argue that the meaning of *carefully* in (i) and (i') is outside the scope of an operator of intention DO, while in (ii) and (ii') it is inside this operator. I will not attempt to pursue this argument because (1) it is not clear how the semantics of DO should work, if such an operator is to be postulated at all, and (2) the English data itself seems very hazy to me (e.g. is (i) really ambiguous between the readings (i') and (ii')?). Jackendoff (1972, Chapter 3) contains some discussion of these ambiguities.

[7] As Partee notes, a related class of verbs has a paraphrase with *give* rather than *have* (cf. 5.8.3 below), and for other verbs it is not clear what the "missing" verb is (does *John expects Mary* mean *John expects Mary to arrive*?).

[8] I have encountered some speakers who are able to perceive an internal reading for these adverbs even in initial position. I suspect that this possibility may be due to a process of fronting verb phrase adverbs which operates under restricted circumstances for most speakers; this is discussed in 5.8.2 below.

[9] As Marchand notes (1960: 204), it is probably not completely coincidental that the two homophonous forms exist. Marchand thinks the survival of Old English *and-*, *ond-* was aided by the semantic similarity of reversative and negative *un-*; they both involve "negativity" in a loose sense.

[10] There are to be sure some reversative intransitive accomplishments, such as *unwind*, *uncurl*, *unfold*, etc. However, these are all used transitively as well, and since it can be independently shown that there must be a rule of English deriving non-causative intransitives from causative transitives (i.e. the exact inverse of the rule S24 in Chapter 4)

which derives, e.g., the verbs in *The play sold out in two days, This car drives like a dream*, it might be argued that intransitive *unwind*, etc. are derivative of reversative transitives. In any case, the generalization still holds that all reversatives are transitive or intransitive accomplishments/achievements, never activities or statives.

[11] As far as I know, this is the assumption that is always made; cf. Lakoff (1971) on the *dis-* in *dissuade*. The alternative – which is to let *uncrate* replace [CAUSE[BECOME[NOT[*be-in-a-crate*]]]] with no prior raising of NOT – does not capture the generalization that the morpheme *crate* in *uncrate* has the same meaning as the verb *crate* (because their lexical insertion rules are not the same) nor the generalization that *un-* contributes to the meaning of the verb in the same way wherever it occurs.

One might try to avoid the transformation of "operator raising" by a series of lexicalization steps like the following (suggested to me by McCawley): IN-A-CRATE → *crated*; NOT → *un-*, BECOME → (removal of *-ed*). Even if this is viable semantically (I have doubts, though I do not at present have crucial examples to discredit it), it is morphologically unmotivated: there is no independent evidence that adding BECOME to an adjective (or participle) would cause the suffix *-ed* to be deleted. This derivation also suggests that the *un-* here should be the negative *un-* that attaches to adjectives and participles rather than an independent reversative *un-*, yet inchoatives seem never to be formed from adjectives with negative *un-* otherwise (**The jello unfirmed, *The supply soon unequaled the demand* though we have *The jello firmed* and *The supply soon equaled the demand*).

[12] As mentioned in note 8, I suspect that the existence of this or a similar fronting operation may explain why some individuals perceive an internal reading for the initial adverbs in (35a)-(35c).

[13] Barbara Partee (personal communication) has noticed a fact which may be relevant to the proper syntactic analysis of internal adverbs, though I do not understand its significance at present. When the verb with which *again* appears is a verb-particle construction, the internal reading seems to be present only when the particle follows the direct object (as in (i)), not when the particle precedes the direct object (as in (ii)):

(i) John blew the candle out again.

(ii) John blew out the candle again.

Thus (i) is ambiguous as to the scope of the adverb, while (ii) has only the external reading entailing that John had blown out the candle before. This difference may have something to do with the stress pattern caused by the position of the particle; as McCawley observed (1971), the adverb seems always to be unstressed on the internal reading. Another possibility is that this fact is related to the fact that particle shift is obligatory when the direct object is a pronoun:

(iii) John lit the candle, but the wind quickly {blew it out again. / *blew out it again.}

I think that the cases where the internal reading is intended by and large turn out to be instances where the direct object is anaphoric, as in (iii), so perhaps the internal reading has in this way somehow come to be associated with post-object position of the particle. A final speculation is that the order of constituents *the candle out again* required for the internal reading has something (quite mysterious) to do with the fact that they appear in this order in the entailed sentence *The candle is out again*.

14 This postulate of course leaves it quite open what the meaning of **again**$_2$ (P) is when P is not an accomplishment property (i.e. not equivalent to the bringing about of some state p). Perhaps it should be a conventional implicature of **again**$_2$ that **again**$_2$ (P) is only appropriate when P is an accomplishment property. Alternatively, we could add another postulate specifying that when P is *not* an accomplishment property, the meaning of **again**$_2$ in **again**$_2$ (P) is virtually the same as that of **again**$_1$:

(i) $$\bigwedge x \bigwedge P[\neg \bigvee p \bigvee Q \Box [P = \hat{y}[Q\{y\} \text{ CAUSE BECOME } {}^{\vee}p]] \rightarrow [\mathbf{again}_2{}'(P)(x) \leftrightarrow \mathbf{again}_1{}'({}^{\wedge}[P\{x\}])]]$$

15 Of all the proposals for decomposition analysis that I am aware of, the only counterexample to this claim would be Lakoff's (1971) analysis of *dissuade* as something like (i)

(i) (CAUSE(x, BECOME(*intend*(x, NOT(P(x))))))

Here the negative operator is embedded not just below BECOME but below *intend* as well. However, I think it can be argued that the analysis of *dissuade* should not be (i) but rather (ii):

(ii) CAUSE(x, BECOME(NOT(*intend*(x, P(x)))))

Horn (1978b) cites the frequently-made observation that (iii) does not seem to "presuppose" that Bill had once had the intention of dating many girls, though (iv) does. Yet on Lakoff's analysis, both (iii) and (iv) ought to have the logical structure (i):

(iii) I persuaded Bill not to date many girls.

(iv) I dissuaded Bill from dating many girls.

Nor, Horn observes, is there any obvious explanation for the difference between (iii) and (iv) in McCawley's "Least Effort" Hypothesis (cf. Horn, 1978b). But if (ii) were the right source for *dissuade*, there would be a well-motivated explanation for this "presupposition": all change of state verbs (i.e., any verb analyzed as entailing BECOME ϕ) have an implicature (whether it be conversational or conventional in origin) that the negation of the new state obtained earlier (i.e., $\neg\phi$, which in the case of (ii) would be NOT(NOT(*intend*(x, P(x)))), or *intend*(x, P(x))). This implicature is attested in all other reversative verbs (e.g. *disassemble, disarm*) as well as other kinds of change of state verbs. But now of course the *assertion* of (iv) is weaker than (iii): (iv) would entail a resulting *lack* of intention, not an intention not to act. But a relevant fact here is that *intend* is of the semantic class of potential "Neg-Raising Predicates" (cf. Horn, 1978a), predicates for which the principle $\bigwedge x \bigwedge p \Box [\delta(x, \neg {}^{\vee}p) \leftrightarrow \neg\delta(x, p)]$ is (conversationally) assumed to hold. In the case of *dissuade*, the tendency to infer from $\neg$*intend*(x, p) to *intend*(x, $\neg{}^{\vee}$p) should be even stronger than usual because of the BECOME implicature, since if one had formerly had the intention of doing P and then abandoned that intention, it is certain that one would have given some thought to whether one wanted to do P or not, hence a retreat from *intend*(x, p) would be tantamount to *intend*(x, $\neg{}^{\vee}$p). And the persuader's goal of changing the persuadee's mind is more likely to be bringing him round to intend(x, $\neg{}^{\vee}$p) rather than simply to $\neg$intend(x, p). This strong "suggestion of perlocutionary success" could, furthermore, naturally be attributed to the Horn/McCawley "Least Effort" Hypothesis. Thus I believe it is likely that (ii) is the "source" of *dissuade*, and (iii) differs from (iv) in its literal assertion as well as its "presupposition" though not in the conveyed effect of the assertion.

[16] There actually seem to be two ways to interpret **promise** (and maybe **owe** as well) in the category TV/T; this translation rule gives only one of them. This distinction came to my attention as a result of reading Bach (1977). Though these verbs are apparently three-place relations (e.g. in **John promised Mary a book**), there is a sense in which they are really four-place relations. This can be seen by comparing (i) not just with (ii) but with (iii):

(i) John promised Mary a book.

(ii) John promised to give Mary a book.

(iii) John promised Bill to give Mary a book.

That is, **promise** might involve not only a promiser, a thing promised, and a future recipient of that thing, but also a distinct person to whom the promise is made. I believe that we often take the recipient and the person to whom the promise is made to be one and the same (e.g. **Mary** in (i) and (ii)), though they can be expressly different in the syntactic form (iii). Indeed, it took me a long time to realize that the use of **promise** in (i) need not absolutely entail that they are the same. The enlightening examples, suggested by Bach, include cases like (iv)

(iv) The father of the kidnapped girl promised $1000 to the first person who offers information about the kidnappers.

(Here I use the alternative dative construction because the length of the indirect object noun phrase makes the other form awkward.) Clearly, the indirect object of this sentence does not name the person to whom a promise is verbally made but only the recipient. The question of how one understands **promise** and **owe** in TV/T bears on the opacity or transparency of this third argument position; if **a man** in **I promised a man a horse** names the person to whom the promise is made as well as the recipient, then this position is transparent (since if I made a promise to someone, then there exists such a (particular) person), but if the recipient is not taken to necessarily be the person to whom the promise is made, then this position can be understood as opaque, as shown by the example (iv).

The translation rule (56d) gives the reading in which recipient and promise-ee are the same; for the other way of understanding **promise**, the translation should be:

$$\lambda\mathscr{P}\lambda\mathscr{Q}\lambda x V y[\mathbf{promise}_1'(\hat{P}P\{y\})(^{\wedge}[\mathbf{give}'(\mathscr{P})(\mathscr{Q})])(x)].$$

[17] In Dowty (1978a) the **give** in TV/T (as in **give someone a book**) is further derived from **give** in another category TV//T (as in **give a book to someone**); the constant **give′** in translations here assumes the former **give** in TV/T as basic. The order of arguments in these translations would be different if stated in terms of the translation of **give** in TV//T.

[18] Actually, Newmeyer notes that Gruber (1970) proposed that his lexical incorporation rules should apply before cyclic transformations, though this view was not adopted by generative semanticists in general.

[19] In Dowty (1978a) I have proposed that even rules like Passive and Raising should not be transformations in the usual sense (mappings from (the phrase-markers of) whole

sentences to (those of) sentences) but rather operations on verbs themselves. This reintroduces the possibility that Causative and Passive, etc. might interact, insofar as the category of verb produced by Passive or other such rule is the input category for some causative rule of the language. I have ignored this possibility in this chapter because, from the linguist's point of view, claiming that Passive and other cyclic rules are not transformations is a much more radical step than claiming Predicate Raising is not a transformation, and arguing (on the basis of familiar assumptions) that Predicate Raising is not a transformation seems to me to be a logically prior undertaking. If Causative is a lexical rule in a given language (as treated in Dowty (1978) and in Chapter 6) and the other rules are syntactic in that language, then Causative can only precede these other rules, since all lexical rules are in effect ordered before all syntactic rules. But in languages (such as Turkish) where Causative is clearly a syntactic rule (or for that matter, in languages in which Causative and Passive, etc. are *all* lexical rules, should there by any such languages) such ordering effects cannot be appealed to. Possibly in such languages Passive could be argued to produce a verbal subcategory to which Causative does not apply (as would be the case for the English lexical passive rule in Dowty (1978a)), or there might be morphological constraints against this combination of suffixes (a possibility discussed by Zimmer 1976, pp. 403ff). Despite the restriction against causatives of passives in a large number of languages, it would probably be wrong to seek a language-universal explanation, since at least Eskimo (cf. Newmeyer, 1976: footnote 10) and, marginally, Turkish (Zimmer, 1976, p. 403) allow causatives of passives. See Zimmer (1976) for further discussion of this problem.

[20] In the PTQ assignment of types to categories, quantifiers appearing in subject position will necessarily have wider scope than any operators appearing in the translation of a verb. But if the type assignment of UG is used (where IV would be categorially defined as t/T rather than t/e), such operators could have wider scope than the subject, and the remark that follows in the text would apply to subject quantifiers as well.

CHAPTER 6

THE SYNTAX AND SEMANTICS OF WORD FORMATION: LEXICAL RULES

In traditional grammar, *word formation* is well-established as the study of how new words of a language are produced from old. Typical means of word formation found in English include adding a *derivational affix* (e.g. the verb *blacken* from the noun *black*, noun *decision* from verb *decide*, adjective *washable* from verb *wash*, etc.), *compounding* two existing words to form a third (nouns *blackbird, steamboat* or *pickpocket* from combinations of verb, adjective or noun), and the process of *zero-derivation* (or *conversion*), by which a word changes its grammatical class and meaning but not its form (e.g. noun *walk* from verb *walk*).

In early transformational grammar, such word-formation processes were analyzed as syntactic transformations; cf. the study of English compounding by Lees (1960) and the study of derivational morphology by Chapin (1967). However, such rules seemed to defy precise systematization, and eventually Chomsky (1970) proposed that rules for forming complex words should be excluded from the syntactic component entirely, the regularities among sets of morphologically related words being described by a new kind of rule, a *lexical redundancy rule*. Chomsky's motivation for this new position was three-fold. First, word formation seemed much less systematic than syntax in both the question of just which potential derived words of each pattern turn out to be accepted words of the language and in the morphological details of some derived words of a given pattern. Second, the meaning of a derived word is not always completely predictable from the meanings of its parts. For example, *decision* means "act of deciding" but *delegation* means not just "act of delegating" but also "people to whom something is delegated" and *transmission* means not only "act of transmitting" but also "thing (part of an automobile) that transmits something". *Washable* is "capable of being washed", *breakable* is "capable of being broken", and this semantic pattern holds for most words in *-able*. Yet as Chapin and Chomsky noted, *changeable* more often means "capable of changing" than "capable of being changed", and various derived words of this pattern have subtleties of meaning that go beyond these gross paraphrases: *readable* in its usual sense does not simply mean "capable of being read" but something more like "capable of being read without undue effort". Third, the hypothesis that nominals are syntactically derived from sentences (e.g. *the destruction of the city by the enemy* from *The enemy destroyed the city*) predicts that cyclic transformations can apply prior to nominalization, a prediction which Chomsky found not to be fulfilled in most cases. (Note the similarity between this situation and the Verb Raising case described by Aissen (1974).) Proponents of the Extended Standard Theory have further developed Chomsky's suggestions with respect to the morphological aspects of word formation (cf. Halle, 1973; Jackendoff, 1975; Aronoff, 1976), though the semantic side of word formation has remained rather vague in their work.

Moreover, we noted in 2.4.1 that the GS account of lexical insertion either leaves morphological regularities among simple and derived words unexplained (i.e. takes *kill-die-dead* as the normal case and leaves the similarity among *cool*-(causative)-*cool*(inchoative)-*cool*(adjective) as an accident) or else captures such similarities at the expense of global and probably transderivational lexical insertion rules (cf. the problem with literal and figurative uses of *hard/harden, dead/deaden*, etc.). Thus here too something like a "lexical redundancy rule" seems to be called for. The pervasive fact about word formation which any theory of language must eventually come to grips with (and which generative semantics has *not* come to grips with) is this: on the one hand, it is universally agreed that principles of word formation are real enough principles that must be described in any account of a native speaker's knowledge of his language, yet these principles are everywhere subject to exceptions (at least in a language like English, if perhaps not in some other languages), both in the matter of "productivity" (which potential words are "actual") and in semantics (how the meaning is/isn't determined by the meanings of the parts).

The philosopher of language may be inclined to ignore this kind of problem, leaving its treatment in the hands of his linguistic colleagues. After all, the basic expressions of a language are only finite in number at any one point in the history of a language, whatever the relationships among them may be, and these can always be described by a finite list if necessary. It is the more crucial problem of giving syntactic and semantic rules for the infinite number of syntactically derived expressions that holds the philosopher's interest. But the relevance of word formation to the present study is great: any attempt to elucidate the relationships among accomplishments, activities and states on the basis of the structure of a natural language itself inevitably leads to the data of word formation, for it is in this domain that a language's ways of relating members of one of these classes to corresponding members of another are most clearly revealed. Indeed, several of the processes introduced as "syntactic" rules in chapter four are more properly considered to be lexical rules.

6.1. MONTAGUE'S PROGRAM AND LEXICAL RULES

How should one go about formulating a theory of lexical rules in a Montague framework? One's first inclination might be to distinguish a subset of the rules of the grammar which would derive new basic expressions ("lexical items") from other basic expressions. But it is not at all clear how such rules would fit into the careful algebraic definitions of grammar and semantics in UG without major revisions of these. An expression that is derived from other expressions is, by definition, not a basic expression in this system, and it is not at all clear how to reconcile the failure of compositionality and partial productivity that we want such rules to have with the exceptionless notion of *rule* that the UG theory is based on.

Let us instead approach the construction of a lexical theory by considering how knowledge of lexical rules can be useful to speakers of a language. One revealing fact about derived words is that a speaker cannot only distinguish between *actual* derived words and non-words, but also can distinguish an intermediate class of possible but non-occurring words. Thus native speakers of English readily agree that *beautify* is a word of English whereas *uglify* is not, though it conforms to the same pattern of word formation and would clearly mean "make more ugly" if it were a word, just as *beautify* means "make more beautiful". (On the other hand, **beautiglok* and **burbify* are "impossible" as derived words.) This capability suggests that speakers somehow remember particular derived words that they have heard other speakers use but are in general cautious about using a derived word they have not heard in common usage before, even if it conforms to a familiar pattern. Likewise, the fact that speakers know idiosyncractic details of the meanings of various derived words which are not predictable by rules suggests individual learning. This situation is to be contrasted with that of syntactically complex expressions, since speakers rarely take notice of whether each sentence they use has occurred before but presumably rely on general syntactic rules and compositional semantic rules whenever they utter or understand such phrases. And speakers make no distinction between "actual" sentences and "grammatical but non-occurring" sentences.

From this point of view, a primary purpose (if not the only purpose) that principles of word formation serve for speakers of a language is as an aid in the acquisition of new vocabulary. Knowledge of word formation rules and of semantic rules for these makes it possible for the speaker to know at least the *approximate* meaning of a new derived word upon first hearing it, or to make up a new word which his audience will understand approximately, but the rules do not prevent him from later deciding that the word has a more specialized meaning than that specified by a general rule. These details of its meaning can be inferred by induction on the contexts in which it is used, by hearing an explicit definition, and perhaps in other ways. As Jackendoff (1975) writes, "it makes sense to say that two lexical items are related if knowing one of them makes it easier to learn the other". Also, it is reasonable to suppose that the more or less transparent internal structure of a derived word makes it easier to remember a derived word and its meaning once it has been heard.

These observations suggest the formalization of lexical rules not as a part of the grammar proper, but as a means for *changing* the grammar of a language from time to time by enlarging its stock of basic expressions. In terms of the UG theory, the definition of a *language* (i.e. what linguists would call the syntactic component of a language, not the set of sentences generated) can be left just as it is. We will define a *lexical component W for a language L* as the same kind of formal object as a language in Montague's sense, though a distinct language from the "basic" language. This lexical component will have its own set of "syntactic" rules (i.e. the lexical rules) and its own set of basic expressions, though these will be the same as the basic expressions of the "basic" language. These rules will operate on the basic expressions to produce "syntactically" derived expressions, which will be regarded as the set of *possible derived words* of *L*. We can then define various kinds of *lexical extensions* of the basic language, extensions which consist in adding a new basic expression, which may be one of the possible derived words specified by *W*. The lexical component is interpreted just as any other language is interpreted, so for each lexical rule there is a semantic rule (a translation rule) giving the predicted translation of the derived expressions in terms of the interpretations of their part(s). However, not all lexical extensions need use exactly the interpretation predicted by these rules.

Now it is of course not very intuitive to think of a lexical component as a separate "language" from the basic language to which it is appended. (And lexical components for natural languages will not be very interesting languages from a technical point of view, since they will in most cases lack any significant recursion.) The advantage in setting things up in this way is simply that the formal theory that results will give lexical rules the properties that linguists have traditionally wanted them to have, but at the same time it remains entirely within the existing formal framework of UG.

6.2. A LEXICAL COMPONENT FOR A MONTAGUE GRAMMAR

Somewhat more formally, the definitions of a language, its lexical component and the various kinds of lexical extensions of that language are as follows. These definitions can readily be fully formalized in the UG theory.[1]

I. Montague's definitions of a *language* L and its interpretation has these parts:

(L1) a set of names of syntactic categories (or category indices).

(L2) for each syntactic category, the set of *basic expressions* (if any) in that category.

(L3) a set of syntactic rules.

Together, (L1)–(L3) determine recursively

(L4) the set of well-formed expressions (both basic and derived) in each category of L.

The *interpretation* of L (which may be induced by translation into an interpreted intensional logic) consists of

(L5) an interpretation (translation) for each basic expression of L.

(L6) an interpretation rule (translation rule) corresponding to each syntactic rule in L3).

Together, (L5) and (L6) determine recursively

(L7) an interpretation for each of the well-formed expressions in (L4).

II. A *lexical component* W for L is formally defined as a language independent of L but has certain parts in common with L. W consists of

(W1) a set of names of syntactic categories of W. (W1) = (L1).

(W2) a set of basic expressions for each category. (W2) = (L2).

(W3) a set of *lexical rules*. These are formally defined just as syntactic rules were defined in UG. (W3) $\neq$ (L3) and may be disjoint from (L3).

Together, (W1)–(W3) recursively determine

(W4) the set of *possible derived words of L* for each syntactic category.

The interpretation for *W* consists of

(W5) an interpretation for each basic expression. (W5) = (L5).

(W6) an interpretation rule (translation rule) corresponding to each lexical rule in (W3).

Together, (W5) and (W6) recursively determine:

(W7) the *derivationally predicted interpretations* of all the possible derived words in (W4).

III. A *lexical extension* of an interpreted language L is an interpeted language *L'* exactly like *L* except that *L'* contains one additional basic expression not found in *L*.[2] Relative to some lexical component *W* for *L*, there are three kinds of lexical extensions:

A. *A semantically transparent lexical extension of L* is a lexical extension of *L* in which (1) the new basic expression added is one of the possible derived words of *L* according to *W* and (2) the interpretation assigned to this new expression in *L'* is the interpretation given it by *W*.

B. *A semantically non-transparent lexical extension of L* is a lexical extension of *L* meeting condition (1) in A but not condition (2).

C. *A non-derivational lexical extension of L* is a lexical extension of *L* meeting neither condition (1) nor condition (2) in A.

Finally,

A *lexical semantic shift* in an interpreted language *L* is an interpreted language *L'* exactly like *L* except that the interpretation of some basic expression in *L'* is different from the interpretation of that expression in *L*.

The situation hypothesized above in which a speaker first guesses the approximate meaning of a new derived word through his knowledge of lexical rules and then later refines his understanding of its precise meaning by some other means can be formally reconstructed in this theory as a semantically transparent lexical extension of his language followed by a semantic shift in the resulting language (i.e. with respect to the new expression just added). The net result of this process would of course be the same as that of a semantically non-transparent lexical extension alone, but the two-stage process reflects the semantic role played by word formation rules in a way that the one-step process does not.

We can regard an "adult" grammar with its many derived words as having evolved by a long hypothetical series of lexical extensions in this theory. Alternatively, we may just as well interpret the theory as supplying analyses of many of the basic expressions of a single stage of the "adult" language:

A basic expression of α of a language L is given the *analysis* $\mathscr{T}$ by a lexical component W for L (where we may equate "analysis" with a Montague-type analysis tree, from which the input expressions, their categories, and the rules used are inferable) if and only if $\mathscr{T}$ is an analysis tree in W of which α is the top node. Analysis of this sort may be further classified as sematically transparent or non-transparent, as the interpretation usually given to α in L turns out to match that provided for $\mathscr{T}$ by W.

One other useful definition would be that of a *back-formation*. Given a language L containing a basic expression β but not the expression α, and a lexical component W for L, then α is a *back-formation* from β iff (1) α is not a possible derived word of W, but (2) we can construct an alternative lexical component W' having the same rules as W but having α as an additional basic expression, and (3) β is a possible derived word in W' (i.e., by virtue of α and of some existing rule of W that will derive β from α in W'). For example, let β be the noun *usher* and α be a verb *ush*. Then *ush* is a back-formation from *usher* because *ush* is not a possible derived word of English, yet if *ush* were a verb then the existing lexical rule that derives agentive nouns in *-er* from verbs would be in fact derive *usher* from *ush*. For a *transparent back-formation* of α from β we require that the interpretation given to α be such that the rule-predicted interpretation of β in the hypothetical component W' will match the interpretation actually given to β in L.

As an example of a word-formation rule of English, the rule S^w1 is offered as a rough formulation of the **-able** rule mentioned earlier. (In the translation rule, $\Diamond$ is the possibility operator; $\Diamond\phi$ is definable in the intensional logic of PTQ as $\neg\Box\neg\phi$.)

S^w1. If $\delta \in P_{TV}$, then $F_{w1}(\delta) \in P_{ADJ}$ (where ADJ = t///e), and $F_{w1}(\delta) = \delta +$ **able**.
Translation: $\lambda x \Diamond \bigvee y[\delta'(y, \hat{P}[P\{x\}])]$

For example, if **breakable** is added via a semantically transparent lexical extension with this rule (and we assume a fairly obvious syntax combining a (semantically empty) copula **be** with a t///e to give an IV), then (1) will have a translation equivalent to (1′):

(1) **Every egg is breakable.**

(1′) $\bigwedge x[\mathbf{egg}'(x) \rightarrow \Diamond \bigvee y[\mathbf{break}'_*(y, x)]]$

In keeping with what I take to be Montague's methodology of beginning with a highly general theory of language and only later (if at all) adding constraints which limit the theory specifically to *natural* languages, I will not at this stage propose any other limits on lexical rules nor any other distinctions between these and syntactic rules (though a number of the properties that linguists have suggested to be peculiar to lexical rules can be shown to follow from the unadorned theory as it stands – cf. Dowty 1978a). But a few comments about the relationship of lexical rules to morphology and to syntax are in order.

6.3. LEXICAL RULES AND MORPHOLOGY

So far I have said nothing about the distinction between morphology and syntax, and it might be thought that this distinction should have been taken into account in setting up the basis for a lexical theory. However, taking only partial productivity and semantic unpredictability as the essential properties of lexical rules will have the interesting and I think correct result that the distinction between syntactic and lexical rules may cut across the traditional distinction between morphology and syntax. If we are to introduce a distinction between morphology and syntax (in at least some languages), this should probably be done in the following way.

Barbara Partee (to appear) has proposed that we try to systematize and eventually constrain syntactic operations by trying to isolate and motivate a set of primitive basic operations (such as concatenation, substitution for a variable, etc.), from which the composite syntactic operations of each particular syntactic rule must be built up recursively. I suggest that we distinguish two disjoint classes of such primitive operations, *morphological operations* and *syntactic operations*. We will eventually want to constrain these two classes in different ways. For example, we might require that morphological operations must always give a fixed linear ordering of elements, while syntactic operations need not do so, and we might require that syntactic operations may not interrupt constituents which have been formed by morphological operations, whereas syntactic operations may interrupt and rearrange constituents formed by other syntactic operations. These requirements would then account for such traditional criteria for distinguishing words from syntactic phrases as invariant ordering and uninterruptability.

(No doubt, the implementation of this distinction would involve differentiating the traditional *morpheme boundary* introduced by morphological concatenation from the *word boundary* introduced by syntactic concatenation.[3])

However, both morphological and syntactic operations may be available to be used in either syntactic rules or lexical rules. Thus we have the cross-classification below:

operation used: \ kind of rule:	Syntactic Rules	Lexical Rules
Syntactic Operations:	traditional syntactic rules (PS-like and transformation-like)	Rules forming lexical units of more than one word, e.g. Eng. V-Prt combinations and factitives (*hammer flat*) – Bolinger's 'stereotyping'
Morphological Operations:	1. rules introducing inflectional morphology 2. rules introducing "derivational" morphology when unrestricted and semantically regular (polysynthetic lang.)	rules introducing derivational morphology, zero-derivation, and compounding where partially productive and less than predictable semantically

The upper left and lower right boxes are the traditional classes, the upper right and lower left are more novel. Note that a single syntactic rule may involve *both* a syntactic and a morphological operation – as for example the English subject-predicate rule, which concatenates two expressions syntactically and also uses the morphological operation of verb agreement.

Morphological operations which are used by syntactic rules will correspond to those traditionally classed under inflectional morphology. However, even morphological operations usually classed as derivational should in my view be classed with syntactic rather than lexical rules if these morphological operations are used in a completely productive way and in a completely regular way semantically. The best candidates for this class probably come from polysynthetic languages like Eskimo. Such languages have extremely long constituents that from a morphological point of view seem to count as single words. Yet such "words" present a problem for the traditional single division between syntax on the one hand and morphology/lexicon on the other. The morphology here is wildly productive and amazingly recursive when compared with lexical morphological processes of more English-like languages. Jerry Sadock has pointed out to me that when an object is incorporated into a verb in Eskimo, it may still be modified syntactically by an indefinite number of modifiers (i.e. independent words). Also, words are not in any way "anaphoric islands" as they are in other languages. If, as I strongly suspect, such morphological processes are completely compositional semantically, then these words should be treated as formed by syntactic rules, not lexical rules, though the operations they use may well be classified as morphological.

To take the converse case, I believe that there are instances of lexical rules that combine expressions syntactically, rather than morphologically, so that the derived unit functions as two separate words from the point of view of subsequent syntactic operations. A clear case of this from English is the verb-adjective factitive construction discussed in Chapter 5. We noted there that many verb-adjective combinations clearly strike us as non-English (e.g., *?John hammered the metal shiny, ?John wiped the surface damp, ?She shot him lame*), despite the fact that they are perfectly intelligible and apparently parallel both syntactically and semantically to completely natural examples (cf. *John hammered the metal flat, John wiped the surface clean, She shot him dead*). Research on this problem (Green, 1972) has uncovered no general principle which predicts this difference in acceptability, and I take this as a good indication that this construction is a kind of lexicalized compound verb, though one which typically appears as a discontinuous constituent. As was noted, this construction is syntactically and semantically similar to the verb-particle construction. Both of these constructions have been examined in detail by Bolinger (1971), and he too recognizes these constructions as "lexicalized", but faced with the traditional distinction between morphology and syntax, Bolinger balks at calling the rules forming them "morphological rules" and instead invents the term *stereo-typing* for them. (Once we have specified that the verb-adjective factitive rule uses syntactic rather than morphological concatenation, it follows that the complex expressions it produces are discontinuous in full sentences, given the modification we have made in the verb-object rule S5.[4]) An interesting question which my proposal leaves open for the time being is why morphological operations *tend* to be associated with lexical rules while the looser, syntactic operations are usually associated with syntactic rules. Part of the answer surely lies in Zwicky's (1978) observation that smaller constituents tend to be more tightly bound together (in a number of senses) than larger ones.

Another point of interest is that with morphological operations (as with syntactic ones) we do not need to make a basic distinction between operations of concatenation and more complicated kinds of operations. In traditional terms, operations that take two words and concatenate them are called *compounding*, operations that prefix or suffix new phonological material which does not constitute an independent word itself are called *derivational*, and other more complex operations are those referred to as "process morphemes", such as reduplication or ablaut. (A remnant of a once-prevalent process morpheme of English is the "plural morpheme" in *men, geese, mice,* etc., a morpheme manifested only in the change of an existing vowel, not the addition of a prefix or suffix.) Since operations, not just morphemes, are assigned meaning in a Montague Grammar, there is no need to distinguish a bound morpheme itself (i.e., the phonological material added by a derivational rule, for example *-able* in $S^{w}1$) from the operation of affixing that morpheme. Similarly, there is no reason to prefer an analysis of a so-called process morpheme like reduplication or ablaut in terms of an underlying abstract "reduplicative morpheme" that lurks about somewhere in underlying phonological structure, rather than simply an analysis which associates meaning directly with the reduplication operation itself. In terms of Hockett's (1954) traditional distinctions, this framework allows us to formulate an *item and process grammar*, not just an *item and arrangement grammar*. The notion of a "process" as having meaning is not an unfamiliar one in morphology, and the reasons why it might be preferred in cases like reduplication are obvious. But I would point out that the situation is exactly parallel with syntax: in the Montague framework syntactic rules themselves are always assigned an explicit meaning, while in transformational and generative semantics theories it seems to be only the elements occurring *in* syntactic structures that are seriously thought of as having meaning. Of course, in both syntax and morphology, operations of pure concatenation are more common than "fancier" operations such as inversion in syntax (to indicate questions) or vowel-changing (or reduplication or infixing) in morphology. (What I am calling "concatenation operations" in syntax are those treated as Phrase Structure rules in transformational grammar.) The reason for this is apparent, I think, if we note that it is important in a natural language that a derived expression must reveal in a more-or-less straightforward way the elements and operations that made it up. The operation of concatenation and the operation of adding a prefix or suffix can be iterated to great complexity while still revealing how the resulting expression was formed, while fancier operations (like inversion or infixing) will have a more limited "readability" if iterated. Yet I believe this preference for concatenation-like operations in natural language has obscured for us the fact that these sorts of operations need not be fundamentally different for the task of associating expressions with meaning.

6.4. LEXICAL RULES AND SYNTAX

Though in most Extended Standard Theory treatments of the lexicon (Halle, 1973; Jackendoff, 1975; Aronoff, 1976; Bresnan, 1978), Lexical Rules seem to be formally quite a different sort of rule from syntactic rules (either phrase structure rules or transformations), I have made no such distinction here. Note that the *-able* rule S^w1 above (or for that matter most any of the rules in Chapter 4) would have exactly the same form whether it is considered syntactic or lexical; the difference is rather in the status of the expressions produced by it. In transformational grammar, on the other hand, this same question about the status of the *-able* rule seems usually to be interpreted as a question of whether a transformational operation converts a sentence like *It is possible for someone to read this book* into *This book is readable* (cf. Chapin, 1967) or rather a lexical rule adds *-able* to a verb *read*.

I think this parallel formulation is desirable, not just because it makes the grammar of English look more homogeneous than might have been thought, but for two other reasons. I expect that a common syntactic change in the history of a language is for a process that was formerly syntactic to become a lexical process, or vice-versa. Such a change can now be viewed as merely a change in the function of a rule, not in its form. As a case in point, I think that English has probably reanalyzed its lexical passive rule as a syntactic rule at some point in its history (cf. Dowty, 1978a for discussion).

Also, I suspect that since children have often been observed to "overgenerate" certain lexical processes in the course of language acquisition, they may be acquiring as *syntactic* rules certain rules which are *lexical* rules in the speech of their parents. The rule S^w11 discussed below (which derives verbs like *box*, "put in a box", from the homophonous nouns) is probably such a case, as attested by the multitude of children's overgeneralizations observed by Clark (1978). That the rule S^w3 (discussed earlier as the rule deriving causative *break* from intransitive *break*) is another rule commonly treated as syntactic by children is suggested by the data in Bowerman (1974). Such a strategy would obviously be useful to a child who has a small vocabulary and could get by with only the approximately correct semantics. If this supposition is correct, this need not entail that any change in the form of the rule or its interpretation takes place when the child reclassifies it as lexical, but merely that she or he starts paying attention to individual expressions produced by it, noting for the first time whether each is really used by adult speakers and whether it has idiosyncratic details of meaning not predicted by the rule.

However, the theory of lexical rules given here does predict certain differences in the domain of applicability of lexical versus syntactic rules. Since the domain of lexical rules is the set of basic expressions[5] alone and does not include expressions derived by syntactic values, it is predicted that in any sentence in which both lexical and syntactic rules are in evidence, the lexical rules must have applied *before* any syntactic rules have been used, hence lexical rules are in a sense "intrinsically ordered" before syntactic rules. This would explain why the hypothesis that rules like Predicate Raising and Nominalization are "precyclic" tends to make correct predictions (cf. Newmeyer, 1976, Appendix). Also, this theory turns out to predict semantic limits on what the interpretation rule of a lexical rule can do, and this prediction seems to be borne out by and large (cf. Dowty, 1978a).

Given this possible similarity among the two kinds of rules, I think it behooves us to re-examine the instances of allegedly *lexically governed transformations* such as Dative Shift, Raising to Subject, Raising to Object and Unspecified Object Deletion to decide whether perhaps they too should be considered lexical rules. If these are transformations moving noun phrases around, then there is no possibility that they could be lexical rules, since the number of instances of the rules' application would be infinite and thus the output of these rules could not all be included among the list of basic expressions. If however the rules in question are operations on the verbs themselves, then the number of expressions resulting from these rules is finite, and the resulting recategorized but phonologically unaltered verbs could all be basic. This hypothesis would also explain why it is invariably the *verb* of a sentence that "governs" a transformation such as Dative Shift, rather than, say, the NP moved. Note that the hypothesis that all governed transformations are really lexical rules affecting verbs is not without empirical consequences in this theory, for it must be possible to write a semantic rule accounting for appropriate relationships among sentences to make a lexical analysis work, and in Montague's strictly compositional semantic theory it is demonstrably not possible to dispense with just any transformation in favor of a lexical rule (cf. Dowty, 1978a, for discussion). It now seems reasonable to me to suppose that virtually every instance of an observed governed transformation turns to be analysable as a lexical rule in this theory, whereas ungoverned transformations (e.g. the unbounded movement rules) turn out not to be so analysable by their very nature.

6.5. EXAMPLES OF LEXICAL RULES

Besides the **-able** rule (S^w1) discussed earlier, the following ten rules will serve as illustrative lexical rules. Most of these have already been introduced as syntactic rules, but motivation for considering them to be lexical rules is easily found.

S^w2 (Inchoative Rule; formerly S30). If $\alpha \in P_{ADJ}$, then $F_{W2}(\alpha) \in P_{IV}$, where $F_{W2}(\alpha) = \alpha + \textbf{en}$ if α ends in a non-nasal obstruent, α otherwise.

T^w2. $F_{W2}(\alpha)$ translates into: $\lambda x[\text{BECOME}\, \alpha'(x)]$

S^w3 (Causative Rule; formerly S31). If $\alpha \in P_{IV}$, then $F_{W3}(\alpha) \in P_{TV}$, where $F_{W3}(\alpha) = \alpha$.

T^w3. $F_{W3}(\alpha)$ translates into: $\lambda \mathscr{P} \lambda x \mathscr{P}\{\hat{y} \bigvee P[P\{x\}\ \text{CAUSE}\ \alpha'(y)]\}$

S^w4 (Deadjectival causatives). If $\alpha \in P_{ADJ}$ then $F_{W4}(\alpha) \in P_{TV}$, where $F_{W4}(\alpha) = \alpha + \textbf{ize}$.

T^w4. $F_{W4}(\alpha)$ translates into:
$\lambda \mathscr{P} \lambda x \mathscr{P}\{\hat{y} \bigvee P[P\{x\}\ \text{CAUSE BECOME}\ \alpha'(y)]\}$

S^w5 (Adjective Negative). If $\alpha \in P_{ADJ}$ then $F_{W5}(\alpha) \in P_{ADJ}$, where $F_{W5}(\alpha) = \textbf{un} + \alpha$.

T^w5. $F_{W5}(\alpha)$ translates into: $\lambda x[\neg \alpha'(x)]$

S^w6 (Reversative Verbs). If $\alpha \in P_{TV}$, then $F_{W6}(\alpha) \in P_{TV}$, where $F_{W6}(\alpha) = \textbf{un} + \alpha$.

T^w6. $F_{W6}(\alpha)$ translates into:
$\lambda \mathscr{P} \lambda x[\text{un}'(\hat{\ }\alpha')(\mathscr{P})(x)]$ (cf. postulate (49), Chapter 5)

S^w7 (*Re*- Prefix). If $\alpha \in P_{TV}$ then $F_{W7}(\alpha) \in P_{TV}$, where $F_{W7}(\alpha) =$ **re** $+ \alpha$.

T^w7. $F_{W7}(\alpha)$ translates into:
$\lambda\mathscr{P}\lambda x[\mathbf{again}_2'(\hat{}\alpha')(\mathscr{P})(x)]$ (cf. postulate (49), Chapter 5)

S^w8 (Detransitivization, or "Unspecified Object Deletion"). If $\alpha \in P_{TV}$ then $F_{W8}(\alpha) \in P_{IV}$, where $F_{W8}(\alpha) = \alpha$.

T^w8. $F_{W8}(\alpha)$ translates into:[6] $\lambda x[\alpha'(\hat{P}\bigvee yP\{y\})(x)]$

S^w9 (Factitives from Transitives, formerly S33). If $\delta \in P_{TV}$ and $\alpha \in P_{ADJ}$, then $F_{W9}(\delta, \alpha) \in P_{TV}$, where $F_{W9}(\delta, \alpha) = \delta\ \alpha$.

T^w9. $F_{W9}(\delta, \alpha)$ translates into:
$\lambda\mathscr{P}\lambda x\mathscr{P}\{\hat{y}[\delta'(x, \hat{P}P\{y\})$ CAUSE BECOME $\alpha'(y)]\}$

S^w10 (Factitives from Intransitives, formerly S34). If $\delta \in P_{IV}$ and $\alpha \in P_{ADJ}$, then $F_{W10}(\delta, \alpha) \in P_{TV}$, where $F_{W10}(\delta, \alpha) = \delta\ \alpha$.

T^w10. $F_{W10}(\delta, \alpha)$ translates into:
$\lambda\mathscr{P}\lambda x\mathscr{P}\{\hat{y}[\delta'(x)$ CAUSE BECOME $\alpha'(y)]\}$

Though the inchoative rule is fairly productive, there are isolated exceptions: Marchand (1960, p. 371) notes that many adjectives ending in *-y* lack inchoative forms, e.g. there are no verbs ***happy**, ***sloppy**, ***pretty**. But there is no absolute phonological prohibition at work here, since there do exist the deadjectival verbs **empty**, **ready**, **muddy**, and **dirty**. As Lakoff (1965) pointed out, some verbs lack the inchoative form but have the causative form apparently derived from it (cf. **The cow fattened* vs. *The farmer fattened the cow*, **The sidewalks have wet* vs. *The rain has wet the sidewalks*). There are morphological irregularities (*wet* instead of predicted **wetten*) and also semantic irregularities, as witnessed by the irregular distribution of literal and figurative meanings with *hard/harden, tough/toughen, dead/deaden*, etc., which has been mentioned twice before. The causative rule has exceptions, cf. *The rabbit disappeared* vs. **The magician disappeared the rabbit*. As predicted by the general phenomenon of *blocking* (or *preemption*) observed elsewhere in word formation (Aronoff, 1976), a rule-derived causative is not possible when there is an independent causative in the language that has the same meaning, so a "zero-derived" causative of *come* and *die* is not possible because their meaning is preempted by *bring* and *kill*. (This principle is apparently ignored by young children acquiring language, so we do hear things like *Come that in here* from them, cf. Bowerman (1974); this would follow if they are indeed using these rules as syntactic rules at this stage.) A particularly subtle semantic difference that has been introduced in either the derived causative or the derived factitive (or both) can be seen in the examples in (2)–(4), which were pointed out to me by Christopher Smeall:

(2) a. John squeezed the orange dry.
b. John dried the orange by squeezing it.

(3) a. John scraped the plate clean.
b. John cleaned the plate by scraping it.

(4) a. John painted the house red.
b. ?John reddened the house by painting it.

The contrast in (4) is of course less subtle than (2) and (3); the meaning of *redden* is quite specialized in a way that clearly excludes painting as a means of making red. The verb *dry* seems to suggest a more extreme state of dehydration than the factitive *squeeze dry*, and a similar observation holds for *clean* and *scrape clean*, but not for *redden* and *paint red*. In most cases, however, the two forms yield an almost perfect paraphrase (cf. *John hammered the metal flat, John flattened the metal by hammering it*). Exceptional behavior of the remaining rules listed above is easy to document, so I will not bother to do so here.

6.6. PROBLEMS FOR RESEARCH IN THE PRAGMATICS AND IN THE SEMANTICS OF WORD FORMATION

So far I have said nothing (and I will have nothing to say) about a number of thorny problems traditionally connected with the study of word formation. For example, the simple theory I have advanced makes a two-way distinction between rules that are fully "productive" (syntactic) and those that are not (lexical rules), but natural languages exhibit something more like a continuum between "partially productive" and "fully productive" rules; for example, derivations in **-ity** are relatively unproductive, while derivations in **-ness** and **-able** are so free as to almost allow them to be considered syntactic rules. Aronoff (1976) has pointed out that greater productivity seems to go hand in hand with greater semantic regularity. Even with a single affix, there are "more free" and "less free" formations. For example, Karl Zimmer (personal communication) has pointed out that though we have fairly clear intuitions as to which **-able** derivations are and are not words for very common verbs (e.g. *washable, breakable* and *readable* are actual words, while one has fairly strong feelings that **killable*, **sayable*, and **seeable* are not – the last is pre-empted by *visible*), we are inclined to accept the *-able* derivative with most any uncommon verb (e.g. *weldable*), even though it is highly unlikely that we have remembered hearing all these uncommon forms before. That is, outputs of the same rule are sometimes "lexicalized", at other times are not. Aronoff (1976) offers interesting evidence that there are two (if not three) distinct suffixes *-able*, though I think this does not explain the problem Zimmer has observed but rather poses questions about yet another phemomenon of word formation, which may have in part a historical explanation. There is also a growing body of research indicating that Gricean rules of conversation and other pragmatic factors play an important role in determining what possible words are actual (cf. Horn, 1972; 1978a; 1978b; McCawley, 1978b; if I am correct that governed transformations are lexical rules, then Green, 1976, is relevant here too), as well as determining how the actual meanings of derived words "drift" from their predictable meanings (Zimmer, 1964; Horn, 1972; 1978b). And of course morphological properties of base words place complex restrictions on productivity (Zimmer, 1964; Aronoff, 1976).

However, it is important to realize that all of these problems, important as they ultimately are for a full understanding of language in the broadest sense, can be viewed as problems for a theory of language use and/or language acquisition, not as inadequacies of the formal theory of lexical rules I have developed here. From the point of view of this theory, the "continuum" in productivity merely reveals a difference in our willingness to "change" our language via various lexical rules. It need not bother us that we change our language constantly, as this theory requires, or that some changes may be temporary while others are permament, or that Zimmer's examples suggest that we are more willing to change our language via a given rule if the input to the rule is an uncommon word than if the input is quite common. The abstraction from the complex data of actual language use to the construction of a formal theory of some idealized aspect of that data is of course characteristic of present-day linguistic research, and the idealization of the word formation process represented by this theory should cause no more concern than the convenient fiction that there is such a thing as "the" English language which we all speak. In fact, I think this idealization is a useful one and makes it possible to isolate from these pragmatic problems the important task of investigating the *semantics* of word formation, i.e. the question of just what semantic relationships can and do appear in the semantic *rules* associated with a word-derivation process, as distinct from the idiosyncractic deviations from the rule-predicted meaning which arise for pragmatic reasons in certain derived words. For it is these general principles which are of most relevance to the main issues raised in this book concerning common or universal properties of word meanings.

In contrast to these pragmatic problems, I would now like to turn to some purely *semantic* problems of word formation that are of more immediate concern to the goals of this book.

One inherent difficulty in this program is that any one example of a derived word we happen upon may be one of the words which deviates in its actual meaning from the "rule-predicted" meaning, so it is necessary to ask just what strategy we should use to determine what the semantic rule itself prescribes in the light of the exceptional nature of the data. For the time being I think an acceptable strategy consists in looking at a suitably large number of words produced by a given rule and using informal induction over such a corpus to decide what semantic rule gives the "closest fit" to the data. A hope that lies behind the application of such an explicit semantic framework as Montague's to this problem is that we will eventually be able to see just exactly how much of the meaning of derived words *is* rule-governed and how much is adduced by other means. Sooner or later, the induction-over-a-large-corpus strategy may need to be supplemented by other methods of investigation. Wolfgang Dressler has pointed out to me that even in cases of spontaneously produced new derived words in normal conversational contexts, the context itself may clue in the audience to details the speaker intends to convey by the novel word, details which go beyond what the rule predicts. Dressler suggests that the semantics of word formation processes might profitably be studied by investigating special situations (where this contextual determination does not occur to such a great degree) such as overgeneralization by children, utterances of certain types of aphasics (who rely extensively on general principles of word formation because they are not able to retrieve from memory many quite ordinary words), and the creative exploitation of word formation processes by poets for aesthetic effect (Dressler, 1976; 1978). (See also Clark and Clark (to appear).)

A second common problem that will arise in this undertaking is determining whether one is dealing with two (or more) grammatically "indistinguishable" word formation rules with two (or more) corresponding distinct and specific associated semantic rules, or whether there is really only one rule associating a very general meaning with the process, the apparent "ambiguity" arising out of pragmatic conditions that tend to force the actually occurring meanings into apparently discrete semantic patterns. One example of such a problematic situation is the rule (or rules) forming locative accomplishments by zero-derivation from nouns denoting containers or other kinds of locations. This rule gives us verbs such as **box, crate, cage, bottle, file, beach, ground, table, tree**, etc. In each of these cases the derived verb is roughly paraphrasable as "cause to be in a(n) α" or "cause to be on a(n) α", where α is the noun from which the verb is formed. We might formulate such a lexical rule as S^w11 with translation T^w11:

S^w11. If $\alpha \in P_{CN}$, then $F_{W11}(\alpha) \in P_{TV}$, where $F_{W11}(\alpha) = \alpha$.

T^w11. $F_{W11}(\alpha)$ translates into:[7]
$\lambda\mathscr{P}\lambda x\mathscr{P}\{\hat{y}\bigvee P\bigvee z[\alpha'(z) \wedge P\{x\}$ CAUSE BECOME $[IN(y, z)]]\}$

(Here I intend *IN* to represent a two-place locative predicate that is general enough in meaning to encompass that of both **on** and **in** in English; such a predicate is easy to define for a model which includes an assignment of objects to points in space, where space has the usual three-dimensional Cartesian structure.) Some members of this class have of course become quite specialized in meaning, cf. **tree** (where the direct object must normally be an animal that climbs trees to escape predators) and **table** (whose meaning is only metaphorically related to the predicted one).

On the other hand, there is a class of denominal verbs for which the paraphrase is not "cause to be in a(n) α" but rather "cause to be not in a(n) α", i.e. "remove from a(n) α"; these include **shell (the shrimp), skin (an animal) husk (the corn)** and **peel (the apple)**. These would require as a translation rule $\lambda\mathscr{P}\lambda x\mathscr{P}\{\hat{y}\bigvee P\bigvee z[\alpha'(z) \wedge [P\{x\}$ CAUSE BECOME $[\neg IN(y, z)]]]\}$. At this point, it seems that we are dealing with two fairly regular semantic patterns, though it may be a little surprising that one is the opposite of the other.

But there are still other apparent patterns. In cases such as **milk (the cow), fish (the stream), gut (the fish), pit (the cherry), weed (the garden)** and **worm (the dog)**, the paraphrase is not "remove from a(n) α" but rather "remove a(n)/some α from", i.e. the appropriate translation rule is
$\lambda\mathscr{P}\lambda x\mathscr{P}\{\hat{y}\bigvee P\bigvee z[\alpha'(z) \wedge [P\{x\}$ CAUSE BECOME $[\neg IN(z, y)]]]\}$.

At this point we might revise our view of these last two cases. Perhaps it is wrong to consider them to be separate rules, rather, the pattern might simply be "separate from α", the question of which object is removed from which in each case being attributable to our pragmatic knowledge of the world rather than the existence of two distinct principles of word formation. That is, the differences in meaning of the actual words are real enough, but perhaps we can attribute them to easily-recognized deviations from (or if preferred, "specializations" of) the predicted meaning. (Of course, we are now bound to ask whether there is a fourth pattern that corresponds to the first in just the same way as the third pattern corresponds to the second: are there denominal verbs paraphrasable as "cause a(n) α to be in (on)"? In fact, cases like **flavor (the soup)**, **frost (the cake)**, **muzzle (the dog)**, **mask (the bandit)**, and **tar (the roof)** fill this category, so we should collapse the first with this fourth pattern if we collapse the second with the third.)

But now that we have brought pragmatic knowledge about the world into the picture, an even more disturbing relationship becomes apparent. Both of the classes of ablative (perhaps better, "separative") denominal verbs involve associations of covering/location with an object that is found in that association in nature (e.g. **shell/shrimp**, **peel/apple** on the one hand and **milk/cow**, **fish/stream** on the other), while all of the allative (or "converging") verbs involve associations which do not arise naturally but are often brought about by some causal force (e.g. **book/box**, **animal/cage** on the one hand and **flavor/soup**, **muzzle/dog** on the other). Thus it seems that whether a verb is of (one of the two) allative type(s) or else of (one of the two) ablative type(s) is also predictable with a high degree of accuracy from common knowledge about the world. In other words, this observation compels us to consider the possibility that all a speaker of English really knows about the meaning of a denominal verb α *as a consequence of his knowledge of word formation principles alone* is that it means "cause to become either spatially associated with or spatially disassociated from a(n) α", all else being supplied by general knowledge, which is sufficient to "disambiguate" the intended one of the four meanings. (There are still other denominal zero-derivation processes besides these in English of course, e.g. the pattern "act as a(n) α", exemplified in **mother**, **nurse**, **pilot**, **referee**, **usher**, and "make into a(n) α", as in **arch**, **group**, **cash**, **pool**; the most extensive list of patterns I know of is in Clark and Clark (to appear).)

We might take as an indication of genuine ambiguity the fact that certain denominal verbs are ambiguous between two of the four patterns. For example *dust* in *dust the furniture* means "remove dust from", but in *dust the crops* it means "put dust on" (an example from Rose, 1973). But once we realize that derived words often have two or more distinct senses even when it is not plausible that two distinct patterns of word formation could be responsible for them (cf. the two senses of **loop** discussed above), this argument is seen to have no force.

Like Rose (1973), (who also wrestles with the ambiguity/vagueness problem for this process), I am inclined to suppose that distinct semantic patterns of denominal verb derivation are in evidence in the locative cases, rather than only one very general one. But this is based purely on the observation that natural languages like English elsewhere exhibit words or phrases expressing one of the four meanings (cf. prepositions like **into, out of**) but do not to my knowledge have expressions that are vague among two or four of these senses. Yet if we are to use the semantics of word formation to shed more light on word semantics in general, this reasoning is ultimately circular, and we would like to find an independent reason for making the decision in the case of denominal verbs. So far, I am not sure where such evidence might be found. (Clark and Clark (to appear), which did not come to my attention until after this section had been written, discuss these and several other patterns of zero-derived denominal verbs and document in great detail the role played by context in their interpretation. But even from this impressive study it does not clearly emerge whether ambiguity or vagueness characterizes the word formation process(es) itself (themselves), as distinct from the contextual contribution to the meaning of actual instances of words produced.)

The most notorious and well-studied problem of this kind in linguistic literature is the case of noun-noun compounds such as **steam boat, garden party**, and **flea bite**. Both the position that a small number of discrete semantic patterns "underlie" such compounds and the position that potentially any semantic relationship whatsoever can be represented by such a compound have been defended by linguists at one time or another, the latter position apparently at least as old as Bradley (1906) (according to Zimmer, 1972). The former position has been more commonly taken in recent linguistic research, most notably by Lees (1960; 1970) and by Levi (1975). Levi proposes that one of exactly seven abstract predicates is deleted in the formation of such compounds, as indicated in (5) below.

Within the present framework, the "null hypothesis" of Bradley (1906) (the claim that any relationship between the two nouns whatsoever is possible in such a compound) can be interpreted as the position that the only principle of word formation behind these compounds is S^w12/T^w12 (where R is a variable of type $\langle s, \langle e, \langle e, t\rangle\rangle\rangle$).[9]

S^w12. If $\alpha \in P_{CN}$, $\beta \in P_{CN}$, then $F_{W12}(\alpha, \beta) \in P_{CN}$, where $F_{W12}(\alpha, \beta) = \alpha\,\beta$.

T^w12. $F_{W12}(\alpha, \beta)$ translates into: $\lambda x[\beta'(x) \wedge \bigvee R \bigvee y[\alpha'(y) \wedge {}^{\vee}R(y, x)]]$

(5) Levi's sources for noun-noun compounds[8]

Deleted Abstract Predicate	Examples (N_1 N_2)
1. CAUSE ("active participle", i.e. "N_2 which causes N_1")	disease germ tear gas concussion force
CAUSE ("passive participle", i.e. "N_2 which is caused by N_1")	future shock vapor lock pot high
2. HAVE ("active participle")	vertebrate animals picture book apple cake
HAVE ("passive participle")	student power lemon peel pole height
3. MAKE ("active participle")	silk worm honey bee
MAKE ("passive participle")	daisy chains root system youth corps
4. BE	sand dunes heart design girlfriend
5. USE	hand brake radio communication shock treatment
6. IN	spring flowers night flight desert rat
7. FOR	sanitation engineer boiler shop arms budget

Levi's hypothesis, on the other hand, would be interpreted as the claim that there are ten distinct rules (i.e. one for each abstract predicate plus the three "passive forms") with translations of the form of T^w12', T^w12'', etc.:

T^w12'. $\lambda x[\beta'(x) \wedge \bigvee y \bigvee P[P\{x\}$ CAUSE BECOME exist$'(y)]]$

T^w12''. $\lambda x[\beta'(x) \wedge \bigvee y \bigvee P[P\{x\}$ CAUSE BECOME exist$'(x)]]$

etc.

An intermediate position between these two extremes is represented by recent work of Zimmer (1971; 1972) and Pamela Downing (1977). While agreeing that the types described by Levi (and similar sets of types proposed by various other linguists) are the most *common* relationships attested in noun-noun compounds, Downing argues that no finite set of relationships will characterize all existing, much less all possible compounds. She notes, for example, the difficulty in fitting examples like **thalidomide parent**, **cranberry morpheme** (a linguist's term for the kind of morpheme exemplified by **cran** in **cranberry** which ought to be a free morpheme but isn't), **pancake-stomach** ('a stomach full of pancakes') and **plate-length** ('what your hair is when it drags in your food') into one of Levi's categories. On the other hand, she and Zimmer (1972) have demonstrated by a series of experimental tests involving subjects' interpretation of novel compounds that certain kinds of relationships clearly *cannot* characterize a possible compound, e.g. **house tree** could not refer to 'tree standing between two houses' nor could **cousin-chair** refer to 'chair reserved for non-cousins'. The suggestion is rather that something like Zimmer's (1972) criterion of being "appropriately classificatory" constrains the relations that may be involved, where this notion has rather complex pragmatic and cultural correlates (see Downing (1977) for an enlightening discussion). If a higher-order predicate **appropriately-classificatory**$'$ (denoting sets of relations-in-intension) can be elucidated with enough clarity to be useful, then Downing's position can be described as claiming that $T^{w}12'''$ is the sole semantic principle of noun-noun compound derivation:

$$T^{w}12'''.\ \lambda x[\beta'(x) \wedge \bigvee R \bigvee y[\alpha'(y) \wedge \textbf{appropriately-classificatory}'(R) \wedge {}^{\vee}R(x,y)]]$$

This is not the place to review the multitude of evidence that has been cited for and against positions such as Levi's and Downing's, much less to argue the issue of the existence of a finite set of potential compound relations. Rather, my point is to suggest that the issue cannot be resolved until the semantic claims involved can be given a much more precise statement than they have been given to date, and that Montague's semantic theory, in the form of the theory of lexical rules given here, may provide a convenient and suitably precise framework in which to pursue these hypotheses. For example, Levi's postulation of seven abstract but very general relations has the chronic defect of linguistic semantics that it is all but impossible to know whether a putative counterexample or misclassification really is that or not, since Levi gives us no specification of just what the meanings of CAUSE,

USE, FOR, etc. are supposed to be. Levi herself finds it hard to put some compounds in a definite category (e.g. is **chocolate bar** "bar that is chocolate" or "bar made of chocolate"?), and Downing notes such paradoxical classifications in Levi's list as the fact that both **headache pills** and **fertility pills** supposedly involve the abstract predicate FOR, "though **headache pills** are designed to eliminate headaches while **fertility pills** are intended to enhance fertility" (p. 814). It seems to me that only when all of Levi's abstract predicates can either be given an explicit model-theoretic interpretation or at least partially limited by meaning postulates can we determine (1) if examples like those are real problems for Levi's theory at all and (2) to what degree the seven abstract predicates account for all and only the relations that occur in compounds. Also, Levi's underlying "logical structures" are quite inexplicit; what we are given is the kind of structure in (6), which is presumably a relative clause (i.e. "rash which diaper(s) cause"), though no variables or quantifiers are included to show how these "predicates" represented by the nouns are related.

(6) $[_{NP}\text{rash } [_{S}\text{ CAUSE}_{V}\ [\text{diaper}]_{NP}\ [\text{rash}]_{NP}\ {}_{S}]\ {}_{NP}]$

As soon as we begin to supply the variables and quantifiers (as I have done in the translations $T^{w}12$–$T^{w}12'''$ above), questions arise about the choice of quantifier and scope (e.g. is *drug death* "death caused by a (certain) drug" or "death caused by any drug"). Also, it is clear that some modal or tense operator is called for in this/these translations; for example, a fruit tree need not be a tree that currently has fruit but only one that has had, or will have, or maybe even can have fruit, and silkworms similarly need not be making silk at the moment that they are so described. In the translation which represents Downing's theory, should the "appropriately classificatory" relation be a relation between two individuals having the properties denoted by the two respective nouns (as I have given it), or rather a relation between the two properties themselves? The correct choice is unclear. An intriguing possibility is that it should be neither, but rather a relation involving the *kinds* (in the sense of Carlson (1977)) associated with the two nouns. It is questions such as these which have not yet been asked in the literature on compounds.

A final significant feature of the noun-noun compound construction that is relevant here is that it illustrates very clearly the virtue in distinguishing between the actual meaning of a derived word and the meaning which is given by a word formation rule. Over the past few years it has gradually become apparent to linguists that the noun-noun compound construction (like nominalizations in general) is not merely, in Vendler's (1967) famous phrase, "a means of packing a sentence into a bundle that fits into another sentence", (p. 125). That is, it is wrong to assume the sentential paraphrase that naturally associates itself (by whatever means) with a compound really gives the exact meaning of the compound. As noted already by Gleitman and Gleitman (1970, p. 96) "not every man who removes the garbage is a garbage man. Only a man who occupationally, customarily, eternally removes the garbage is a garbage man". Nor, one can add, is every blue flower that resembles a bonnet a Blue Bonnet, nor is every friend who is a girl a girl friend, nor is just any man wearing a red cap called a red cap, etc. I believe this implicit possible disparity is an essential part of the way compounding is used in a language. On the other hand, the acquisition of a compound like *garbage man* by a speaker of English necessarily involves the realization that garbage-men are so-called because they bear some more-or-less specific relationship to garbage, but on the other hand, I doubt that it is a common mistake (if one that occurs at all) to assume that any man who takes out the garbage is a garbage man. The "sentential paraphrases" which are associated with compounds are implicitly recognized as giving a convenient mnemonic and "stereotypical" property by which the actual extension of a new derived noun can be remembered and, with a varying amount of success, recognized, but not a necessary and sufficient condition for being in the extension. (I believe this is essentially the position of Downing and Zimmer as well; cf. also the discussion of Putnam's "stereotypes" in Chapter 8.) The psychological pressure to associate such a paraphrase with a compound seems quite strong; when encountering a new compound we feel there must be *some* reason why the class of things was given that name rather than another one. It does not matter very much that we sometimes make the wrong association. Richard Warner has suggested to me that many people today assume that bull dogs are so-called because their ferocious appearance suggests a bull, though in fact it seems that the breed received this name because it was used in bull-baiting (cf. the OED). However, this "error" has no important consequence for the way the compound is correctly or incorrectly used. The standard examples of folk etymologies (words corrupted in form in order to give them the structure of a plausible derived word), which are typically compounds, illustrate this pressure. But note here as well that a disparity in meaning was implicit; the person or persons who corrupted *crevisse* into *creyfish* was probably not really under the impression that the creature was a kind of fish, but only that this was a plausible mnemonic name for an aquatic creature (and, of course, sounded like *crevisse*). Similarly, the corruption of *primerole* to *primrose* was no doubt aided by the semantic association of *rose* with flowers in general, though this need not suggest that the corrupter thought the flower in question really was a rose. (Though I cannot take the space to argue the point here, I believe that this disparity is far greater for derived nouns than for derived verbs, and this fact is related to the general difference in the way nouns and verbs function in natural language, which is ultimately a pragmatic difference. Thus rules corresponding to semantically transparent derived verbs give something much closer to necessary and sufficient conditions for the extension than those for most derived nouns.)

Perhaps then a translation for a compounding rule that more accurately represents what a speaker of English really assumes about an arbitrary novel compound would be T^w12'''':

$$T^w12''''.\ \lambda x \bigvee P[P\{x\} \wedge \bigvee R\,[\textbf{appropriately-classificatory}'(R) \wedge \bigwedge y[P\{x\} \rightarrow [\beta'(y) \wedge \textbf{typically}'(\hat{}\bigvee z\,[\alpha'(z) \wedge \check{}\, R(y,z)])]]]]$$

That is, a novel compound $\alpha\beta$ denotes some set (exactly which one we do not know) such that all members of this set are β's and are typically associated by some appropriately classificatory relation to an α. Needless to say, this represents only a rough approximation of a compounding rule (though in itself it is precise, relative to the two constants), but I believe something like this must be the starting point for more exact research.

NOTES

[1] The formal definitions based on UG are as follows:

1. Assume L is a *language* (as defined in UG) and $L = \langle\langle A, F_\gamma, X_\delta, S, \delta_0\rangle_{\gamma\in\Gamma,\delta\in\Delta}, R\rangle$. Assume $\mathscr{B}$ is a *Fregean interpretation* for L (as defined in UG) and $\mathscr{B} = \langle B, G_\gamma, f\rangle_{\gamma\in\Gamma}$. Then an *Interpreted Lexical Component* $\mathscr{W}$ for L is an ordered pair $\langle L^w, \mathscr{B}^w\rangle$ such that (1) L^w is a disambiguated language and $L^w = \langle A^w, F^w_\gamma, X^w_\delta, S^w, \delta^w_0\rangle_{\gamma\in\Gamma^w,\delta\in\Delta^w}$, (2) $\mathscr{B}^w$ is a Fregean interpretation for L^w and $\mathscr{B}^w = \langle B^w, G^w_\gamma, f^w\rangle_{\gamma\in\Gamma^w}$, and (3) $\Delta^w = \Delta$, $X^w_\delta = X_\delta$ for each $\delta \in \Delta$, $\delta^w_0 = \delta_0$, $f^w = f$, and the type assignment for L^w is the same as that for L. The family of syntactic categories C^w generated by L^w is the set of possible derived words for L.
2. A *lexical extension of an interpreted Language* L is a pair $\langle L', \mathscr{B}'\rangle$ such that (1) L' $(= \langle\langle A', F'_\gamma, X'_\delta, S', \delta'\rangle_{\gamma\in\Gamma',\delta\in\Delta'}, R'\rangle)$ is a language exactly like L except that for some $\delta \in \Delta'$, X'_δ contains exactly one more member than X_δ; and (2) $\mathscr{B}'$ $(= \langle B', G'_\gamma, f'\rangle_{\gamma\in\Gamma'})$ is exactly like $\mathscr{B}$ except that f' assigns an interpretation also to the new member of X'_δ.
3. We distinguish three kinds of lexical extensions:

   a. A *semantically transparent lexical extension* of L relative to $\mathscr{B}$ and $\mathscr{W}$ is a pair $\langle L', \mathscr{B}'\rangle$ such that (1) for some $\delta \in \Delta$, X'_δ contains the new basic expression α not found in X_δ and $\alpha \in C^w_\delta$; and (2) if g^w is the meaning assignment for L^w determined by $\mathscr{B}^w$, then $f'(\alpha) = g^w(\alpha)$.

b. A *semantically non-transparent lexical extension* of L relative to $\mathscr{B}$ and $\mathscr{W}$ is a lexical extension of L meeting condition (1) but not condition (2) in (3a) above.

c. A *non-derivational lexical extension* of L relative to $\mathscr{B}$ and $\mathscr{W}$ is a lexical extension of L meeting neither condition (1) nor condition (2) in (3a) above.

[2] After a language has been "extended" by the addition of a new lexical item, then the original lexical component must likewise be revised to include the new actual word as a basic expression (whereas it was formerly a derived expression in the lexical component), in order for it to meet the definition of a lexical component for the extended language; this is because the lexical component must contain as basic expressions all the basic expressions of the "basic" language. Whereas this creates no important problem that I can see, it does create the minor technical problem in UG that the same expression would be both a basic and a derived expression in the same language (i.e. in the lexical component), and this is not allowed in UG (because a language is a free algebra). This difficulty can be circumvented by adding (or deleting) some trivial marker – a parenthesis or subscript – when "transferring" a derived expression of the lexical component to a basic category in the basic language; this marker, like other such markers that may be needed to satisfy the disambiguation requirement literally (cf. note 6 of Chapter 4) can be assumed to be deleted by the ambiguating relation R. Another consequence of these definitions is that when a non-transparent extension is made (or a transparent extension is followed by a semantic shift), the rule-predicted meaning still remains as a potential meaning for a derived word. This I believe is a correct result. For example, I noted that *changeable* actually means "capable of changing" rather than the predicted "capable of being changed", but I think this predicted meaning is still possible in a suitable context just like other newly-derived **-able** words are possible; suppose a stereo repairman says "I am afraid you'll have to replace the whole motor in this turntable; the part that's burned out just isn't changeable in this model".

[3] More than two distinct kinds of boundaries may have to be postulated. For various phonological reasons, it is sometimes argued that one derivational affix should be separated from the root by a phonologically "weak" boundary (a morpheme boundary), another by a "stronger" boundary which is normally assumed to be a word boundary. For example, Aronoff (1976) argues that there are two distinct **-able** suffixes, one involving a morpheme boundary and the other a word boundary. Yet even the latter derivations cannot be interrupted in the way that syntactic phrases usually are (*__This shirt is wash, I think, -able; *This shirt is wash in cold water -able__), so its boundary must probably be kept distinct from "true" word boundaries.

Though the treatment of morphology outlined in the text would seem to be adequate for cases of agglutinative morphology (i.e., in which each affix is a distinguishable sequence of phonemes) and for many cases of fusional morphology as well (i.e. in which some combinations of two or more affixes are realized as a special sequence of phomenes not linearly segmentable into morphemes), I would not rule out the possibility that extreme cases of fusional morphology might be more elegantly treated by another method. Perhaps in such cases syntactic rules should not introduce "surface" inflectional morphology directly but should instead insert "abstract" morphemes, it then being left to a special morphophonemic component to "spell out" particular collections of root and abstract markers as phonological forms. A treatment of this sort has been proposed for a Montague grammar fragment of Serbo-Croatian in unpublished work by Sarah G. Thomason and Richmond Thomason.

[4] As mentioned in section 4.6, a complication arises with verb-particle constructions, where the "phrasal" transitive verb may optionally precede the object entirely (cf. **clean up the room**) as well as "wrap around" the object (**clean the room up**).

[5] Actually, the domain of a lexical rule in this theory is not just the actual basic expressions but rather the set of all possible derived words (of the appropriate category). One apparent generalization that the theory given here does not directly account for is that a multiply-complex potential derived word only seems to become a "serious" candidate for a new word when the word from which it can be derived in one step is an actual word, e.g. **marginalizational** would probably only be introduced if **marginalization** were already in use. I am not sure whether this generalization holds up, nor whether it calls for a modification of the theory if it does hold.

[6] In an earlier article (Dowty, 1978a) I gave this translation as $\lambda x \vee y[\alpha'(\hat{P}P\{y\})(x)]$, but T. M. V. Janssen has pointed out to me that this translation predicts that an intensional verb used intransitively (e.g. **John seeks**) would necessarily have a de re reading (e.g. "there is some particular thing that John seeks"). Though I can think of no intensional verb that *is* regularly used intransitively, this nevertheless seems to be an incorrect result. The revised rule would give only a de dicto reading for intensional verbs used intransitively, though it results in the same extensional reading for extensional verbs as before, thanks to the meaning postulate for extensionality of transitive verbs.

[7] Note that in this translation the direct object is given wider scope than the quantifier for the object denoted by the base noun; this is because **John boxed every hat** does not entail that there is a particular box into which he put every hat.

[8] Levi (1975) also treats other kinds of nominal compounds besides these, as well as the compound-like "non-predicating adjective" constructions (*malarial mosquitoes, tidal wave, musical comedy*, etc.), which she argues to have a similar derivation to that of compounds. My comments here would apply equally to these other constructions.

[9] Since the variable R in $T^{W}12$ ranges over relations-in-intension in the very general set-theoretic sense, its role in this translation rule is all but vacuous; as long as the extension of α' is non-empty, there is trivially some relation that any individual in the extension of β' will stand in to something in the extension of α'; a more reasonable formalization of the "null hypothesis" position would be to restrict R to "relations-in-intension expressible in the language", or something like this, though the restriction should not be as narrow as that in $T^{W}12'''$ below. Alternatively, it might be suggested that there are general cognitive constraints (though not specifically linguistic ones) on values for R here.

CHAPTER 7

THE SYNTAX AND SEMANTICS OF TENSE AND TIME ADVERBIALS IN ENGLISH: AN ENGLISH FRAGMENT

In this chapter I present an English fragment within the UG framework that contains enough tense and time adverbial apparatus to explicitly generate the example sentences, involving durative/non-durative adverbials and progressive/non-progressive tenses, that were appealed to in chapters two and three to classify verbs aspectually. This is followed by a "lexicon" of words analyzed in this book, together with their translations and/or relevant meaning postulates.

Since the syntax and semantics of tenses and time adverbials is not the subject of this book, I have deliberately not tried to incorporate all results of the (vast and exciting) recent research on tense and time reference in English, nor have I attempted to motivate all details of the analysis linguistically as in earlier chapters. Rather, I have tried to keep the fragment straightforward and easy to follow. As a consequence, its treatment of tense will be obviously ad hoc at points, and there are problems I have had to ignore entirely (most notably, the problems of *sequence of tense* (cf. Costa, 1972; Smith, 1978), time reference "across" clause boundaries (Partee, 1973) and problems of tense and intensionality (Ladusaw, 1977)). My goal is simply to demonstrate how the analyses of verbal constructions developed in previous chapters can be embedded successfully in a fragment that generates a variety of complete English sentences. As I pointed out in the Forward to this book, I believe that the perspective to be gained from actually seeing analyses of word meanings placed within a complete fragment is much needed in current research. As is frequently pointed out but cannot be overemphasized, an important goal of formalization in linguistics is to enable subsequent researchers to see the defects of an analysis as clearly as its merits; only then can progress be made efficiently.

A secondary and related purpose of this chapter is to expose a number of difficult problems that arise when one attempts to combine tenses with time adverbials in a formalized fragment, problems the complexity of which I think has been seriously underestimated. Though tense logicians and formally-minded linguists have recently turned their attention to the problems of English tenses (especially the progressive and perfect) with ever-more sophisticated tools (e.g. Clifford (1975), Kamp (1971), Gabbay (1974), Åqvist

(1976), Taylor (1977), Saarinen (1978) and many others), the examples treated are almost always sentences *without* time adverbials. But I hope to show why tenses in English are primarily parasitic on time adverbials (as has already been suggested by linguists, e.g. McCawley (1971b), Partee (1973)) and cannot be properly understood without an understanding of their interaction with time adverbials. Though somewhat rudimentary, I believe the analyses presented here are novel in important ways that may lead to useful further developments. No comparably explicit treatment of these problems in English is to be found in the literature, though, ironically, a detailed Montague fragment (Johnson, 1977) exists for Kikuyu, a Bantu language with a very complex tense and aspect system.

7.1. THE SYNCATEGOREMATIC NATURE OF TENSE-TIME ADVERBIAL INTERACTION

A basic point to be established first is that the "ordinary" combination of tense and time adverbial, as in (1) (where this is *not* read as a "tenseless future" implying predetermination),

(1) **John left yesterday.**

cannot be treated as the compositional result of separate rules, parallel, for example, to the way tense and adverb are successfully treated by separate rules in producing **John will walk slowly** in PTQ. The reason for this is that either the tense would come within the scope of a time adverbial or vice versa, and either arrangement gives incorrect results. That is if [**yesterday**$'\phi$] is interpreted as true at a time t iff ϕ is true on the day before t, and if Hϕ is interpreted as in PTQ (where "H" was the past tense operator), then (1′) does not represent the meaning of (1) correctly, because this is true (now) if there is a time t' on the day before today such that there is another time t'' *still earlier than* t' at which "John leaves" is true.

(1′) **yesterday**′[H[**leave**′(j)]]

Thus (1′) is true if John left two days, or a month, or a year ago. But (1″) suffers exactly the same defect as (1′).

(1″) H[**yesterday**′[**leave**′(j)]]

Instead, (1) ought to assert that **John leaves** was true yesterday, and it redundantly adds the information that **John leaves** was true at some time or other in the past. With the exception of one method to be discussed below, the only way I know to avoid this problem is to have a *single* rule that introduces a time adverbial in a sentence as it tenses the verb.

At first I thought that the solution to this problem would involve syntactically subcategorizing time adverbials into past, present and future categories, each of which would then be inserted along with the appropriate tense. We somehow want to block ***John will leave yesterday**, of course; we don't want to produce it with the interpretation that **John leaves** was true yesterday and also true at some future time or other. But syntactic subcategorization is inadvisable (if for no other reason) because there are adverbs like **today, this week, this morning, this year** which function equally well as past, present and future time adverbials:

(2) a. **John is in Boston today (this week,** etc.)
b. **John was in Boston today (this week,** etc.)
c. **John will be in Boston today (this week,** etc.)

The key to these examples lies in making the observation (which holds just as well for **yesterday, tomorrow, last week, next week,** etc.) that the adverbials here only superficially *appear* to associate a sentence with the time interval mentioned; **today** as it is used in (2a)–(2c) really asserts that the sentence is true at some unspecified interval *within* the (twelve or twenty-four hour) interval denoted by **today**. Since adverbials like today (but *not* **yesterday**) involve an interval *surrounding* the present, they function equally well with past, present, or future tenses; these tenses then limit the choice of appropriate subintervals within **today** etc. in (2a)–(2c). Thus (2b) in effect asserts that John is in Boston at some unspecified time earlier today, while (2c) involves an unspecified time later today.

At this point life will become simpler if we eschew sentential tense operators like "H" or "W" in favor of (1) variables and quantifiers over time, (2) the "AT" operator from chapter two (i.e. $\mathrm{AT}(t_1, \phi)$ is true at any time t iff ϕ is true at the time denoted by t_1) and (3) predicates of times PAST, PRES and FUT (i.e. $\mathrm{PAST}(t_1)$ is true at any time t iff (the time denoted by) $t_1 < t$; $\mathrm{PRES}(t_1)$ is true at t iff $t_1 = t$, and $\mathrm{FUT}(t_1)$ is true iff $t < t_1$). I would not go so far as to deny that what is done in this chapter *cannot* be accomplished with (one or two-place) tense operators and without time variables, but I believe it will be more perspicuous to employ variables. (Nor do I have any structural linguistic motivation for variables and AT, as I did for BECOME and CAUSE.) Thus we will want to associate (1) with a translation equivalent to (1‴) and (2a)–(2c) with (2a′)–(2c′) respectively:[1]

(1‴) $\bigvee t[\mathrm{PAST}(t) \wedge t \subseteq$ **yesterday**$' \wedge \mathrm{AT}(t,$ **leave**$'(j))]$

(2′) a. $\bigvee t[\mathrm{PRES}(t) \wedge t \subseteq$ **today**$' \wedge \mathrm{AT}(t,$ **be-in-Boston**$'(j))]$
b. $\bigvee t[\mathrm{PAST}(t) \wedge t \subseteq$ **today**$' \wedge \mathrm{AT}(t,$ **be-in-Boston**$'(j))]$
c. $\bigvee t[\mathrm{FUT}(t) \wedge t \subseteq$ **today**$' \wedge \mathrm{AT}(t,$ **be-in-Boston**$'(j))]$

(Here of course t and t_1 and the constants **today**′, etc. are understood as taking *intervals* of time as values, and the (meta-language and object language) expression "$t < t_1$" must be taken as asserting that every moment within t is earlier than any moment within t_1.) The expressions in (1‴) and (2′) are almost but not quite adequate as representations of the meaning of (1) and (2). The subformulas PAST(t), PRES(t) and FUT(t) should more properly be taken as conventional implicatures (or presuppositions) of (1) and (2a)–(2c), while the rest of the expressions must represent the "assertion" of the English sentences. This is because we want ***John will not leave yesterday** to come out as deviant in some way (i.e. inappropriate), not true, and likewise ***John will leave yesterday** should be inappropriate, not simply false. The system developed by Karttunen and Peters (1975, to appear) offers the means to incorporate this distinction formally in a Montague Grammar,[2] but as a formal treatment of conventional implicature is one of the desirable features that I will have to omit from the fragment for the sake of simplicity, I will ignore this refinement here and in what follows, merely making note informally of what parts of translations should eventually be relegated to conventional implicature.

7.2. RULES FOR "MAIN TENSE" ADVERBIALS

To actually incorporate translations like (1‴) and (2′) into the UG framework, we will have to make some "housekeeping" modifications. Neither PTQ nor UG allows expressions to denote times (i.e., members of the set J in PTQ) directly, though of course times are involved in the definition of a model in crucial ways and are the second members of the pairs (i.e. indices) which are the arguments of functions denoted by expressions of type $\langle s, a\rangle$ for any type a. I know of three ways that we might modify Montague's intensional logic to be able to refer to times directly: (1) We might include times among the entities in the domain of basic individuals (entities) D_e. This would require us to use a *sorted* intensional logic, by which method we can have a special set of variables than range only over a proper subset of D_e, namely the times. Precedents for this exist in Cooper (1975) and Carlson (1977), and Waldo (to appear) gives a general development of sorted intensional logic.

But the primary motivation for sorting is to allow certain variables and constants to range over the *whole* domain of entities, as well as allowing other variables to range over only a part of it. This flexibility will not be needed here, as I will not need to let any one expression take indifferently as value either a time or a (concrete) entity (as Carlson and Cooper need to do for their sorts). (2) Another possibility (pointed out to me by Barbara Partee) is to let certain propositions play the role of times. That is, the proposition which is true at just the time t in every possible world can "represent" the time t. This does less violence to Montague's IL than the first option, since expressions denoting propositions are present already. But here again we would need to resort to sorting to use formulas like (1‴) successfully (or else introduce an object-language predicate-of-propositions **is-a-time′** and use this predicate to restrict the values of propositional variables in each and every translation in which we "refer" to times, and this would be highly cumbersome). (3) An option which is apparently more drastic but nevertheless turns out to be the simplest and most satisfactory of the three for our purposes is to introduce a new primitive type into the type hierarchy: the type i of expressions denoting intervals of times. That is, the primitive types will be e, t, and i, and the recursive type definition will then give types $\langle a, b\rangle$ and $\langle s, a\rangle$ for any types a and b. With this option (or with the other two as well) we will want to redefine an index as an ordered pair $\langle w, i\rangle$, where w is a possible world and i is an interval of time. As notational conventions, I will let t, t_1, t_2 etc. be variables of type i; for variables over *properties of times* (i.e. expressions of type $\langle s, \langle i, t\rangle\rangle$) I will merely subscript a t to the symbols used for properties of individuals, e.g. P_t, Q_t, etc. The symbols $\mathscr{P}_t$ and $\mathscr{Q}_t$ will denote properties of properties of times. The intensionality present in these higher types is needed not because temporal expressions might denote different intervals in different possible worlds but because they sometimes denote different intervals when used at different times, e.g. expressions like **yesterday**, **tomorrow**, etc. are indexical or "deictic" expressions. With these minor changes, we are ready to proceed to the formation and translation of English sentences.

Some temporal expressions of English clearly involve quantification over times rather than just reference to single (intervals of) time (cf. **John drinks whenever Mary does, John sings at certain times, Mary sings frequently**), so it will be useful to have a category of English expressions Tm that denote sets of properties of times. This step is taken for essentially the same reasons as Montague used the category T to denote sets of properties of individuals: in this way we can subsume quantification over times and reference to individual times in the same syntactic category. I will let expressions like **Thursday**, **Christmas** and **midnight** be basic expressions in category Tm. It is useful to distinguish Tm from a category of temporal adverbials, TmAV, because expressions like **Thursday** are used with prepositions when they function as adverbs (e.g. **John left on Thursday**), while other expressions like **yesterday** and **tomorrow** are not (cf. ***John left on yesterday**). Hence **yesterday**, etc. will be basic expressions in category TmAV, and temporal prepositions like **on** will combine with expressions in Tm to give expressions in TmAV. (Since even some expressions in Tm can also occur adverbially without prepositions – cf. **John left Thursday** – these expressions can apparently be shifted directly to TmAV without benefit of preposition, though this doesn't always work: cf. ***John left noon**. The conditions governing this "shift" of category are obscure to me.[3]) But TmAV will have the same type as Tm, and in fact **Thursday** (in TmAV) and **on Thursday** will turn out to have the same translation.

We are now ready to give some sample rules for tense and what I will call *Main Tense Adverbials*. For conciseness, I will state the syntactic rules of the fragment in the format specified in UG rather than in the way they are described in PTQ. In UG, a *syntactic rule* is a sequence $\langle F_\gamma, \langle \delta_\xi \rangle_{\xi < \beta}, \epsilon \rangle$, where F_γ is a β-plate syntactic operation, $\langle \delta_\xi \rangle_{\xi<\beta}$ is a β-place sequence of syntactic categories (the categories of the inputs to the rule), and ϵ is a syntactic category (the category of the output of the rule). I will follow each rule with a description of just what the structural operation mentioned in the rule does, e.g. "$F_n(\alpha, \beta) = \ldots$" Note that the meta-language variables in "$F_n(\alpha, \beta)$" after the rule will be understood to appear in the same order as the order of input categories mentioned in the rule itself; for example, the sequence of input categories in S36 below is ⟨TmAv, t⟩, so in the description "$F_{36}(\alpha, \phi) = \ldots$" that follows, α is understood to be an expression of category TmAV and ϕ is understood to be an expression of category t (a sentence). To describe the translation rule corresponding to each syntactic rule, I use the notation "$k(F_n(\alpha, \beta)) = \ldots$", as Montague used k in UG to represent the translation function. In spelling out the values of the translation of $k(F_n(\alpha, \beta))$, I use α' and β', etc., to represent the translations of the inputs α and β respectively (as Montague did in PTQ).

S36. $\langle F_{36}, \langle \text{TmAv, t} \rangle, t \rangle$ (*Past Tense Adverb Rule*); $F_{36}(\alpha, \beta) = \phi'\alpha$, where ϕ' is the result of changing the main verb in ϕ to past tense. $k(F_{36}(\alpha, \beta)) = \alpha'(\hat{t}\,[\text{PAST}(t) \wedge \text{AT}(t, \phi')])$.

S37. $\langle F_{37}, \langle \text{TmAV}, \text{t}\rangle, \text{t}\rangle$ (*Present Tense Adverb Rule*); $F_{37}(\alpha, \phi) = \phi\,\alpha$.
$k(F_{37}(\alpha, \phi)) = \alpha'(\hat{t}\,[\text{PRES}(t) \wedge \text{AT}(t, \phi')])$.

S38. $\langle F_{38}, \langle \text{TmAV}, \text{t}\rangle, \text{t}\rangle$ (*Future Tense Adverb Rule*); $F_{38}(\alpha, \phi) = \phi'\,\alpha$, where ϕ' is the result of inserting **will** before the main verb of ϕ.
$k(F_{38}(\alpha, \phi)) = \alpha'(\hat{t}\,[\text{FUT}(t) \wedge \text{AT}(t, \phi)])$.

Let us now introduce some translations for temporal adverbs; for simplicity, I will treat **at-noon** as a basic expression here, though it should really be derived syntactically: **today**$'$, **yesterday**$'$, and **noon**$'$ are (indexical) constants denoting intervals.

(3) **today** ($\in B_{\text{TmAV}}$) translates into: $\lambda P_t \bigvee t[t \subseteq \textbf{today}' \wedge P_t\{t\}]$
yesterday ($\in B_{\text{TmAV}}$) translates into:
$\lambda P_t \bigvee t[t \subseteq \textbf{yesterday}' \wedge P_t\{t\}]$
at-noon ($\in B_{\text{TmAV}}$) translates into:[4] $\lambda P_t[P_t\{\textbf{noon}'\}]$

Assuming the fragment contains the syntactic rules from PTQ, we can now generate some example sentences:

(4) **John left today**, t, 36
  today, TmAV **John leaves**, t, 4
    John, T **leave**, IV

(5) **John will leave**[5] **at noon**, t, 38
  at-noon, TmAV **John leaves**, t, 4
    John, T **leave**, IV

The translation of (4) given directly by the translation rules is (4$'$), but with lambda-conversions and other simplifications (including relettering of variables to avoid variable collision where necessary), it reduces to (4$''$), and the reduced translation of (5) is (5$'$):

(4$'$) $\lambda P_t \bigvee t[t \subseteq \textbf{today}' \wedge P_t\{t\}](\hat{t}\,[\text{PAST}(t) \wedge \text{AT}(t, [\lambda P P\{j\}(\hat{}\,\textbf{leave}')])])$

(4$''$) $\bigvee t[t \subseteq \textbf{today}' \wedge \text{PAST}(t) \wedge \text{AT}(t, \textbf{leave}'(j))]$

(5$'$) $[\text{FUT}(\textbf{noon}') \wedge \text{AT}(\textbf{noon}', \textbf{leave}'(j))]$

In actuality, English allows a sentence to have any number of "Main Tense Adverbials", as is shown by examples like (6):

(6) **I first met John Smith at two-o'clock in the afternoon on a Thursday in the first week of June in 1942.**

However, such examples cannot be successfully produced by iterations of rules like S36–S38. Examples like (6) clearly "work" (while examples like ***John will leave on Thursday on Friday** do not) because there can be a single time of John's leaving which simultaneously satisfies all four of the time specifications in (6). When operators with the semantic properties of AT are iterated, all but the innermost operator is vacuous. That is, $AT(t_1, [AT(t_2, \phi)])$ is true at any time t if and only if ϕ is true at t_2, regardless of what time t_1 denotes and regardless of the state of things at t_1; relative to a fixed time t, $AT(t, \phi)$ is an "eternal sentence" and is not affected in truth value by affixing any further tense operator. Thus ***John left on Thursday on Friday** would be generated by such iteration with the perfectly normal interpretation that John left on Thursday, or on Friday, according to which adverbial was innermost. I will thus forego treatment of examples like (6) in this fragment and restrict rules like S36–S38 to at most one application per sentence. (Alternatively, we could have separate rules introducing one, two, three, etc. time adverbials at once, each with a separate translation, but this is a stopgap method too.)

I will briefly mention one possible way of avoiding this problem (though I will not adopt it in the fragment for simplicity's sake and because of certain problems), a method which would also allow tense and time adverbials to be introduced by separate rules. This was discovered by Johnson (1977), and involves the use of "double-indexing", a formal technique used by Kamp (1971) and other tense logicians for quite different purposes. Truth relative to a time is defined by means of the intermediate notion of *truth relative to a pair of times* $\langle i, j \rangle$. An atomic sentence ϕ (i.e., one with no time reference) is defined as true relative to $\langle i, j \rangle$ (call this *true'*) iff the appropriate conditions are met at i, for any j whatsoever (no matter what obtains at j). A sentence formed by adding a time adverbial α to ϕ is *true'* at $\langle i, j \rangle$ iff it is both the case that ϕ is true at $\langle i, j \rangle$ and that i is a time having the properties specified by α. (This rule may be iterated at will.) A sentence formed by adding a tense to ϕ is *true'* at $\langle i, j \rangle$, on the other hand, iff it is both the case that ϕ is *true'* at $\langle i, j \rangle$ and that i stands in an appropriate relation to j (in the case of the past tense, that i is earlier than j). Finally, the desired definition of truth relative to a (single) time (i.e. *true* unprimed) is given by stating that ϕ is *true* relative to a time j iff there is some time i such that ϕ is *true'* relative to $\langle i, j \rangle$. A little reflection should convince one that a past tense sentence with a number of time adverbials can be true (or in a refined theory, have consistent conventional implicatures) just in case there is at least one past time appropriate to all the adverbs and at which the untensed sentence is true. There is an apparent similarity between this use of two indices and Reichenbach's (1947) famous distinction between *speech time* and *reference time*, as i in this method is analogous to reference time and j is analogous to speech time. But it would be a mistake to think of this as a formal *theory* of Reichenbach's notion, at least it is a mistake if we think of these Reichenbachian notions as most linguists apparently do (e.g. Smith, 1978, and possibly Johnson herself) as somehow an essential aspect of the notion of "meaning of a sentence" that the theory gives us. (Note that in Smith (1978) we seem to be required to take these Reichenbachian notions as a kind of semantic primitive.) For this double-indexing is clearly just a technical trick to get the restrictions on adverb reference to come out right, and the second time index i ultimately plays no role in the interpretation of the sentence. In this respect it is exactly like the assignment of values to variables that appears in Tarski's intermediate definition of *satisfaction* (or *truth relative to an assignment of values to variables*), which is introduced to get quantifier interpretation to work out properly, though the choice of variable assignment plays no role in the ultimate definition of truth. (I will have more to say about the Reichenbach notions below.) Nevertheless, Johnson's technique appears promising as a way of getting a more syntactically natural account of tenses and multiple adverbials.

Of course, tensed sentences occur without adverbials as well as with them. We could treat these by postulating a "phonologically null" time adverbial, meaning "at some time", which would play the role of α in S36–S38, but a better solution might be to add one-place syntactic tensing rules S39 and S40:

S39. $\langle F_{39}, \langle \mathrm{t} \rangle, \mathrm{t} \rangle$ (*Past Tense Rule*); $F_{39}(\phi)$ is the result of replacing the main verb of ϕ with its past tense form. $k(F_{39}(\phi)) = \bigvee t[\mathrm{PAST}(t) \wedge \mathrm{AT}(t, \phi')]$

S40. $\langle F_{40}, \langle \mathrm{t} \rangle, \mathrm{t} \rangle$ (*Future Tense Rules*); $F_{40}(\phi)$ is the result of inserting **will** before the main verb of ϕ. $k(F_{40}(\phi)) = \bigvee t[\mathrm{FUT}(t) \wedge \mathrm{AT}(t, \phi')]$

Another possibility, suggested by Partee (1973) explicitly (and implied elsewhere) is that the past tense is indexical in its time reference. Considering the example *I didn't turn off the stove*, Partee comments (p. 602),

> When uttered, for instance, halfway down the turnpike, such a sentence clearly does not mean either that there exists some time in the past at which I did not turn off the stove or that there exists no time in the past at which I turned off the stove. The sentence clearly refers to a particular time – not a particular instant, most likely, but a definite interval whose identity is generally clear from the extra-linguistic context.

If Partee is correct about this, then the way to interpret the time reference of the past tense is not with an existential quantifier but with an indexical constant that would be interpreted as one of the contextual parameters, just as indexicals like **I**, **you**, demonstrative **this**, etc. would be interpreted. Thus we would be introducing a second time index not just for the purpose of doing semantics of adverbs efficiently (as in Johnson's proposal for time adverbs) but also of doing pragmatics. This may in fact be one of the ways (though not the only way) that the present perfect differs from the simple past; the past time referred to by the present perfect may differ from that of the simple past in that it is *not* a definite contextually-determined time. As Clifford suggests (1975, p. 49) "In the case of {have + N} [the present perfect – DRD], like that of *some*, no claim is made that the speaker could indicate the time more precisely while the {-D} form [the simple past] does seem to require this".

This brings us to Reichenbach's famous and popular account of the difference between the simple past and the present perfect, which lies in the distinction between *speech time*, *event time*, and *reference time*. Reichenbach's theory was (roughly) that the present perfect has its reference time (*R*) at the same time as the speech time (*S*), with event time (*E*) earlier than these, while the simple past has the reference time at the same time as event time, with both earlier than speech time, as in the familiar diagram below:

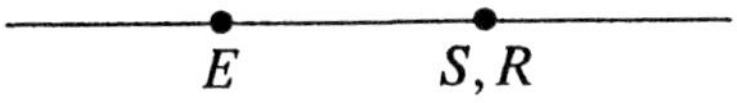

Present Perfect

Simple Past

As frequently pointed out in connection with this theory (cf. McCoard, 1978, p. 88) and "present-of-a-past" theories of the present perfect (McCoard, 1978, p. 195), this approach fails completely as a *semantic* account of the difference between the two tenses (as it stands, at least) because it gives the two forms exactly the same truth conditions. (It is thus surprising to see Reichenbach's reference point crop up in purely truth-conditional accounts of semantics, e.g. Taylor (1977).) But if viewed as a theory of a *pragmatic* difference between the two forms (i.e. as indicating in at least some cases the degree to which the speaker expects his audience to be able to identify the indefinite past time he does not explicitly mention, on the basis of contextual information that includes previous discourse), it may be significant. I suspect that Reichenbach's *reference time* really has its proper place in a theory of narration, i.e. of the way indefinitely identified times in a sequence of sentences in a narrative are understood to be ordered, perhaps with the aid of common information not included in the sentences themselves. Insights such as those of Smith (1978a; 1978b) will, I believe, receive their proper formalization within such a theory. I expect it will be necessary to distinguish the (pragmatic) interpretation of simple past sentences (without adverbs) in a "narrative mode" from their interpretation in a "non-narrative" mode, and only in the narrative mode is contextual identifiability conventionally implicated by the simple past; it is clearly not always the case that the simple past is deictic (cf. McCoard, 1978, Chapter 3), and when it is not deictic, its interpretation is bound to be that of S39, no matter what technique is used to achieve this interpretation.

7.3. ASPECTUAL ADVERBIALS: **FOR AN HOUR** AND **IN AN HOUR**

Ideally, one should first attempt to write a fragment in which all time adverbials are of the same syntactic category, attempting to account for their differential behavior by a proper understanding of the differences in their meanings and only resorting to syntactic subcategorization if and when it fails. But in fact the only way I see at present of constructing an adequate fragment requires me to put adverbials such as **for an hour, in an hour,** and **frequently** in the category IV/IV rather than in TmAV.[6] The semantic difference between these and the adverbials discussed previously is that the former class (e.g. **today, yesterday**) are like tenses in locating the time of the verb's truth with respect to the speech time, while the latter class does not do this but rather functions in much the same way as aspectual operators like the progressive. These *aspectual adverbs*, as I will call them, do not create the problem with iteration that the tense adverbs did; on the contrary, they can be iterated in a perfectly compositional way and in fact produce significantly different meanings when understood as being in different scope relationships. This is clearly brought out in the (preferred reading) of (7) versus that of (8):

(7) **John slept in his office frequently for six weeks.**

(8) **John slept in his office for an hour frequently.**

That is, (7) can place the frequent times of sleeping within a six week period, while (8) is more likely to assert that one-hour periods of sleeping were frequent.

I will treat phrases like **an hour** and **six weeks** as basic expressions denoting sets of intervals; that is, **six weeks** denotes, at any index,[7] the set of intervals that have exactly six weeks' duration. Thus temporal **for** and temporal **in** will be of category (IV/IV)/(t/i), as they combine with an expression denoting an interval property to form a verb phrase adverbial. (I assume a functional application rule combining **in** in (IV/IV)/(t/i) with **an hour** in (t/i).) In writing the translations of aspectual adverbs, it will be useful (though not necessary) to employ an indexical constant n (for "now"), which denotes at any index the time coordinate of that index:

(9) At any index $\langle w, i \rangle$, the denotation of n is i.

The constant n is thus not the "non-shifting" *now* of Kamp (1971) that always denotes the speech time (which is presumably the way English *now* usually works) but a fully indexical constant; if n occurs in the scope of $AT(t, \phi)$ (and not embedded in any further tense operators), n denotes t.

An approximate translation for **for** is thus (10):

(10) **for** ($\in P_{(IV/IV)/(t/i)}$) translates into:
$$\lambda P_t \lambda P \lambda x [P_t\{n\} \wedge \bigwedge t [t \subseteq n \rightarrow AT(t, P\{x\})]]$$

With this translation, (11) receives the translation (11′) (with relettering of variables to avoid collision):

(11) **John slept for an-hour**, t, 36
  |
 John sleeps for an-hour, t, 4
 John, T **sleep for an-hour**, IV, 7
  for an-hour, IV/IV **sleep**, IV
   for, (IV/IV)/(t/i) **an-hour**, (t/i)

(11′) $$\bigvee t_1 [\mathrm{PAST}(t_1) \wedge AT(t_1, [\text{an-hour}'(n) \wedge \bigwedge t_2 [t_2 \subseteq n \rightarrow AT(t_2, \text{sleep}'(j))]])]$$

By the semantic principle of the interpretation of n just referred to (I'll call this *n-elimination*), (11′) can be simplified to (11″):

(11″) $$\bigvee t_1 [\mathrm{PAST}(t_1) \wedge AT(t_1, [\text{an-hour}'(t_1) \wedge \bigwedge t_2 [t_2 \subseteq t_1 \rightarrow AT(t_2, \text{sleep}'(j))]])]$$

And if **an-hour′** is a rigid designator (at least with respect to different times in the same possible world), (11′) is equivalently written (by *AT-elimination*)[8] as (11‴):

(11‴) $\bigvee t_1\,[\text{PAST}(t_1) \wedge \textbf{an-hour}'(t_1) \wedge \bigwedge t_2\,[t_2 \subseteq t_1 \rightarrow \text{AT}(t_2, \textbf{sleep}'(j))]]$

The actual meaning of English **for** differs from that given in (10) in several respects. First, to allow **for**-adverbials to be used with heterogeneous activities (as well as homogeneous activities and states), (10) should not make reference to literally *all* subintervals of the measured intervals but merely all subintervals large enough to be minimal intervals for the activity in question; how to do this is unclear. Second, even this would apparently be too strong in view of examples mentioned in chapter two such as **John worked in New York for four years but he usually spent his weekends at the beach.** But this kind of example may involve a generic reading, as discussed in Carlson (1977), and this may account for the apparent discrepancy here. Third, the duration specified by the **for**-adverbial may be the duration of the union of several non-contiguous intervals: **John served on that committee for four years** can be true if he served four non-consecutive one-year terms. Perhaps the best view of **for** α is that it asserts that something is the case at each one of some set S of possibly non-contiguous intervals of times, the total duration of which is α. though the exact choice of members of S is left to contextual interpretation. But for simplicity, I will leave (10) as it stands.

As a first translation for **in**, we might try (12):

(12) **in** ($\in P_{(IV/IV)/(t/i)}$) translates into:
$\lambda P_t \lambda P \lambda x\,[P_t\{n\} \wedge \bigvee t\,[t \subseteq n \wedge \text{AT}(t, P\{x\})]]$

This rule specifies only that the time of the verb's truth is some subset of the interval mentioned, though not necessarily a proper subset; I believe it is for purely Gricean reasons that we usually take the t in this definition to be *equal* to n in the case of the multiple-change accomplishments, as in **John washed the dishes in an hour**. But if the verb is a singulary change verb and/or if the time we normally expect that kind of verb to take is much shorter than the duration specified by the adverbial, we normally understand the verb to have been true at a final proper subinterval of the indicated interval, as in **John closed the door in an hour**. If I say that John will close the door in an hour and he in fact closes within five minutes, I do not believe that I have spoken falsely, only that a more restricted statement would have been more appropriate to this situation. (**It will take him an hour**, by contrast, asserts that the interval is at least an hour long but may conversationally implicate that it is not longer.) Of course, there must also be a conversationally implicit way of determining the *start* of the measured interval in the case where the verb is true at only a final subinterval (i.e. an hour from *when*?), but I believe that this point too is determined only conversationally.

However, the translation (12) does not explain why **in**-adverbials do not naturally occur with stative verbs. As we noted in chapter two, ?**John slept in an hour** is not too natural in the first place, and the only way we *can* interpret it is as asserting that John *fell asleep* within an hour (i.e. **sleep** is taken as an inchoative, not as a stative), not as asserting that he slept during some subinterval of an hour. To remedy this, we must make the translation for **in** require that the verb is true at a *unique* subinterval (though still not necessarily a proper subinterval) of the measured interval:

(12′) **in** translates into: $\lambda P_t \lambda P \lambda x [P_t\{n\} \wedge \bigvee t_1 [t_1 \subseteq n \wedge \mathrm{AT}(t_1, P\{x\}) \wedge \bigwedge t_2 [[t_2 \subseteq n \wedge \mathrm{AT}(t_2, P\{x\})] \rightarrow t_2 = t_1]]]$

(The requirement of the uniqueness of t_1 here should actually be a conventional implicature, not part of the assertion.) As an example, (12) will be produced with the translation (12′), and after eliminating n and an AT, this becomes (12″)

(12) **John awakened in an hour.**

(12′) $\bigvee t_1 [\mathrm{PAST}(t_1) \wedge \mathrm{AT}(t_1, [\textbf{an-hour}'(n) \wedge \bigvee t_2 [t_2 \subseteq n \wedge \mathrm{AT}(t_2, [\mathrm{BECOME}\ \textbf{awake}'(j)]) \wedge \bigwedge t_3 [[t_3 \subseteq n \wedge \mathrm{AT}(t_3, [\mathrm{BECOME}\ \textbf{awake}'(j)])] \rightarrow t_2 = t_3]]])]$

(12″) $\bigvee t_1 [\mathrm{PAST}(t_1) \wedge \textbf{an-hour}'(t_1) \wedge \bigvee t_2 [t_2 \subseteq t_1 \wedge \mathrm{AT}(t_2, [\mathrm{BECOME}\ \textbf{awake}'(j)]) \wedge \bigwedge t_3 [[t_3 \subseteq t_2 \wedge \mathrm{AT}(t_3, [\mathrm{BECOME}\ \textbf{awake}'(j)])] \rightarrow t_2 = t_3]]]$

It is not clear to me whether the inchoative reading just mentioned for **John slept in an hour** requires that we treat **sleep** as ambiguous between a (stative) interpretation **sleep**′ and the interpretation $\lambda x[\mathrm{BECOME}\ \textbf{sleep}'(x)]$. For suppose that the stative interpretation of **sleep** were used and we pick the interval of one hour's duration so that the very last moment of this interval is a time at which **John sleeps** is true, though it is true at no earlier time in this interval. Then indeed there is a unique interval within the hour at which **John sleeps** is true (though there would not be if there are *two* moments of John's sleeping within the hour), and the interpretation of **in an hour** can be satisfied.

If we continue to require that the time of utterance be no larger than a moment, then we have the (correct) result that **John is in Boston for six weeks** cannot really have the reading that the rules given so far would give it (since the present would have to be an interval), and in fact the only reading it does have is a tenseless future reading, a reading in which it describes a previously *scheduled* event. I think there are pragmatic (though not semantic) reasons why **John arrives in Boston in an hour** appears to have only a tenseless future reading (cf. note 1).

Thus the semantics given here for **for**-adverbials and **in**-adverbials explain why **for**-adverbials are appropriate for states and activities (i.e., both these classes of predicates are true of most or all subintervals of an interval of the predicate's truth) but not for accomplishments and achievements (since these are "non-subinterval predicates") and, conversely, why **in**-adverbials are appropriate for accomplishments and achievements (since they can satisfy the "uniqueness" requirements in the semantics of **in**) but not for activities and states (except with the inchoative reading just mentioned). Thus we have accounted for the observation of Chapter 2 that **for** and **in** adverbials are, in many cases, a diagnostic for separating activities and statives from accomplishments and achievements, or, in other cases, can disambiguate a verb phrase that can have either a "perfective" or an "imperfective" interpretation (as in **He read a book in an hour/he read a book for an hour**).

7.4. THE SYNTACTIC STRUCTURE OF THE AUXILIARY

In the syntactic treatment of auxiliaries given in the fragment, expressions such as **sleep, be sleeping, have slept** and **have been sleeping** are all treated as members of the category IV. On the other hand, **can sleep, (can be sleeping,** etc.) is treated not as an IV but as an expression of category t/T, a functor that combines with a term phrase (the subject) as its argument to form a sentence; modals such as **can, may** etc. are thus treated as members of a category (t/T)/IV.[9]

Though I am not sure this treatment is really the most preferable one, I adopt it here because it simultaneously captures what appear to be syntactic and semantic generalizations about English, and I think it deserves to have attention drawn to it for this reason.

On the syntactic side, the generalization to be captured assumes that infinitive complements (such as **to win** in **John tried to win**) can be derived directly from IV's (as Montague derived them) rather than derived from complete sentences by Equi-NP deletion (as in traditional transformational grammar[10]). A vexing problem for the traditional transformational treatment (though one that is so familiar as to be frequently overlooked) is that modal auxiliaries never appear in infinitive complements, though all other auxiliaries do:

(13) **John prefers to sleep**
John prefers to be sleeping
John prefers to have slept
John prefers to have been sleeping
***John prefers to can sleep**
***John prefers to can be sleeping**
etc.

If however a "verb phrase" with a modal is of a different category than the other cases of verb phrase auxiliaries, then this problem is automatically solved. (It has sometimes been suggested by linguists that in **John could have been sleeping**, each of the phrases **have been sleeping, been sleeping**, and **sleeping** is a verb phrase; cf. J. Geis (1970), Ross (1967).) To be sure, a different subject-predicate rule will be required for **John can win** from that used in **John has won, John is winning**, etc. But thanks to a quirk of the history of English, this is not really a disadvantage at all, for modal verb phrases differ from all others in that they do not undergo subject-verb agreement (the addition of the suffix **-s** for third person singular, etc.), and distinguishing the two kinds of verb phrases by category simplifies the account of this difference.

On the semantic side, the PTQ grammar captures an interesting generalization about the distribution of de dicto term phrases in English. While such "opaque" term phrases can appear in direct object position (**John is seeking a unicorn**), in object-of-preposition position (**A unicorn** in **John is talking about a unicorn** is opaque, in Montague's view at least) and perhaps in other non-subject positions, opaque terms in subject position only appear under restricted circumstances: (1) when there is a modal auxiliary (**Some student must collect the papers**), (2) when there is a future tense (**A Republican will win the election**), (3) when the sentence is embedded as object of a propositional attitude verb, or (4) in sentences in which the "surface" subject is treated in transformational grammar as being derived from non-subject position (**A girl with green eyes and black hair was needed by the casting director**) or from embedded subject position (**A unicorn seems to be approaching**). If we continue to use transformations for the cases in (4), then this syntactic treatment of auxiliaries preserves this generalization about opaque positions by treating "verb phrases" with modals, but not other verb phrases, as functors applying to subjects, i.e. it puts subjects *within* the scope of modal verb phrases.

Whether this semantic generalization will hold up is of course not completely clear. If Thomason's (1976) non-transformational treatment of Passive and Raising ultimately turns out to be preferable, then the type of at least verbs like **seem** and **be certain** (and for the sake of generality, probably *all* IV's) must be raised by shifting their category from IV (as t/e) to t/T, in which case there will be no type distinction between modal and non-modal verb phrases. (In that case, each of the translations for non-modal auxiliaries given below can be easily modified for this new type assignment, e.g. the translation of the progressive rule below would be changed from $\lambda x[\text{PROG}\,\alpha'(x)]$ to $\lambda\mathscr{P}[\text{PROG}\,\alpha'(\mathscr{P})]$.[11]) Also, it is not clear whether auxiliaries other than modals can be claimed to always have narrower scope than the subject quantifier (as my treatment requires). In support of the view that the subject quantifier should have *wider* scope that the progressive, note that (14) cannot truthfully be used in a situation where each of two (or more) Republican candidates is clearly going to beat each of the non-Republican candidates but in which it is not yet clear *which* Republican will win:

(14) **A Republican is winning the election.**

(By contrast, note that **A Republican will win the election** or **A Republican is certain to win** can be used here, with **A Republican** understood opaquely.) On the other hand, Cresswell (1977) argues that the progressive must have wider scope than the subject in some cases, though I am not yet sure what to make of his argument.

The analysis of the tenseless future and futurate progressive in chapter three requires us to suppose that the tenseless future comes inside the scope of the progressive. Thus the maximally complex "compositional structure" of tenses and auxiliaries that a sentence can have in the fragment is indicated schematically in (15):

(15) (*Tense* + TmAV(*Modal*(*Subject*(have + TmAV(PROG(TF + TmAV(IV)))))))

Here, the "+" indicates two elements inserted by the same rule. (I will show below why the perfect has its own adverb in TmAV.) Since the tenseless future rule (here indicated by "TF", a "tense" having no morphological manifestation) must provide an input to the progressive rule, it too must form an IV-phrase from an IV-phrase. Thus three rules – the tenseless future, the perfect rule and the progressive rule – must form IV's from IV's. As these three rules apparently apply only in this particular order, I assume here that they must be syntactically prevented from applying in any other order or applying to their own output: i.e., the tenseless future operation will be a partial function that is undefined for arguments which are themselves outputs of the tenseless future, progressive or perfect rule; the progressive is undefined for arguments that are outputs of the progressive or perfect rule, and the perfect rule is undefined for arguments that are its own outputs. (A near-equivalent treatment would be to split the category IV into three distinct subcategories allowing **have**, **be**, or no auxiliaries, respectively; see Akmajian, Steele and Wasow (1979) for arguments for this approach.) Hopefully, this syntactic treatment can be better motivated, or else the non-occurring combinations and iterations of auxiliaries can be excluded on semantic/pragmatic grounds.[12] Note also that the aspectual adverbs are predicted by this analysis to have potential scope ambiguities with auxiliaries (since I have treated these adverbs as IV-modifiers), but it is not clear whether this option is required (for complicated reasons to be explained in the next section).

The reader will no doubt note that several syntactic variants of this treatment of tenses and adverbials are possible which achieve the same overall semantic effect. If all verb phrases are assigned to the "higher type" category t/T (rather than just modal verb phrases), it would for example be possible to introduce Main Tense Adverbials and tenses via operations on t/T, rather than via operations on sentences, while still allowing the subject term phrase to be within the scope of the tense and adverbial; this achieves a certain syntactic naturalness because the verb phrase is after all the place where the tense marker appears. In syntactic analyses which distinguish between the two categories S and $\bar{S}$, it would on the other hand be possible to introduce tenses and time adverbials via the rule which converts S to $\bar{S}$ by adding a complementizer (**that**, **for**, etc.); this would prohibit undesired iteration of the tense rules in a straightforward way.

7.5. THE PRESENT PERFECT

Aside from the progressive, no English tense has received more attention from linguists and yet eluded a convincing analysis so completely as the present perfect. The history of these attempts is well-documented in McCoard (1978). One of the most popular theories of the meaning of the present perfect is Jespersen's *current relevance* theory – the theory that the present perfect is used to describe an event which has more present relevance than events described by the simple past. McCoard (1978, Chapter 2) examines a number of attempts that have been made to pin down just exactly what is meant by "current relevance" and finds that there are counterexamples for each of these positions. In particular, counterexamples to the generalizations drawn by Chomsky (1970) and by McCawley (1971) from the famous examples **Einstein has visited Princeton** and **Princeton has been visited by Einstein** are not hard to find. McCoard takes this demonstration to show that "current relevance" has nothing to do with the *meaning* of the present perfect, but I believe this conclusion is not quite warranted. What McCoard has *not* ruled out, it seems to me, is the possibility that the perfect has as part of its meaning (or to be more exact, as part of its conventional implicature) a very, very general notion of "current relevance", more general than any one of the particular theories he examines would allow (say roughly, "the event described has some relevance or other to the present context, the nature of which is to be inferred entirely from contextual factors"). If so, this "current relevance" implicature, however it is to be stated, could no doubt be added to the perfect rule given below, but I will not have anything to add here about this aspect of the perfect's meaning.

We have already discussed a second of McCoard's classes of "perfect theories", the *indefinite past theory*. This is the view that the present perfect makes a less definite assertion about the past time of the verb's truth than the simple past does, and I have explained why I think this aspect of the present perfect's meaning is to be captured in a theory of the pragmatics of discourse.

Fortunately, there is yet another way that the present perfect distinguishes itself from the simple past, a way which is far more concrete than "present relevance" but which has been ignored in formal analyses that I am acquainted with. This is the difference in the time adverbials that are allowed by the two tenses. As McCoard reminds us, there are adverbials like **yesterday** which occur with the simple past (or maybe the past perfect as well) but not with the present perfect, adverbials such as **for six weeks** which occur with either simple past or present perfect, and other adverbials such as **since Thursday** and **now**, which occur with the present perfect but not with the past:

(16) a. **John left yesterday.**
b. ***John has left yesterday.**

(17) a. **John lived in Boston for six years.**
b. **John has lived in Boston for six years.**

(18) a. ***John lived in Boston since 1971 (now).**[13]
b. **John has lived in Boston since 1971 (now).**

McCoard gives a list of adverbials he finds to belong in each of these three classes (p. 135):

(19)

Occur with simple past but not with perfect:	*Occur with either simple past or with perfect*:	*Occur with perfect but not with simple past*:
long ago	long since	at present
five years ago	in the past	up till now
once [= formerly]	once [= one time]	so far
the other day	today	as yet
those days	in my life	during these last five years
last night	for three years	herewith
in 1900	recently	lately
at 3:00	just now	since the war
after the war	often	before now
no longer	always	[by now – DRD]
	never	
	already	
	before	

It might seem that this overlapping distribution could be accounted for by the theory that the present perfect is a past tense embedded within a present tense (cf. Bach, 1967; McCawley, 1971; McCoard, 1978, Chapter 5), i.e. the adverbs in the first and second columns could be associated with the "embedded" tense, those in the second and third could be associated with the "higher" tense. But this will not work (or at least, it is not the whole story) because only some of the adverbials in the third column (and none in the second) can be successfully used with the present tense itself, cf. ***John is here since yesterday**, ***John is here during these past five years.** (Compare this with modern German, which has no semantically corresponding perfect tense and uses the present for these adverbials: *Hans ist seit gestern hier.*)

I will base the treatment I give here on McCoard's favored theory of the present, the *extended now theory*. This is the view that the perfect serves to locate an event within a period of time that began in the past and extends up to the present moment, while the simple past specifies that an event occurred at a past time that is separated from the present by some interval (though it may be a very tiny one, cf. **I saw it just a second ago**). (Though McCoard and his primary source for this theory (Bryan, 1936) argue that this is the *only* asserted meaning of the perfect, I have already indicated that I am disinclined to believe this.) To incorporate this approach, we will modify the definition of the predicate PAST and add a new predicate of times, XN (McCoard's abbreviation for "Extended Now"):

(20) PAST(t) is true at $\langle w, i \rangle$ iff there exists an interval i' such that (the time denoted by) $t < i' < i$.

(21) XN(t) is true at $\langle w, i \rangle$ iff i is a final subinterval of the interval denoted by t.

(If time is dense, we must specify that the i' mentioned in (20) has some minimal duration in order to escape vacuity.) The rule for the perfect (where it occurs without any associated time adverbial of its own) can now be stated as S41.[14]

S41. $\langle F_{41}, \langle \mathrm{IV} \rangle, \mathrm{IV} \rangle$ if $\alpha \neq F_{41}(\beta)$, for some β, then $F_{41}(\alpha) =$ **have** α', where α' is the result of replacing the first verb in α by its past participle form. $k(F_{41}(\alpha)) = \lambda x \bigvee t_1 [\mathrm{XN}(t_1) \wedge \bigvee t_2 [t_2 \subseteq t_1 \wedge \mathrm{AT}(t_2, \alpha'(x))]]$

With the rules now given, we can produce examples like (22) (in which **now** is introduced as a present tense adverbial) and also (23), that is, the treatment of (23) is like the "embedded past" account just mentioned.

(22) **John has left now**, t, 37

now, TmAV **John has left**, IV, 4

John, T **have left**, IV, 41

leave, IV

(23) **John has slept for an hour now**, t, 37

now, TmAV **John has slept for an hour**, t, 4

John **have slept for an hour**, IV, 41

sleep for an hour, IV, 7

for an hour, IV/IV **sleep**, IV

for, (IV/IV)/(t/i) **an-hour**, t/i

Sentences (22) and (23) will have translations equivalent to (22′) and (23′) respectively:

(22′) $[\mathbf{PRES}(\mathbf{now}') \wedge \mathrm{AT}(\mathbf{now}', \bigvee t_1 [\mathrm{XN}(t_1) \wedge \bigvee t_2 [t_2 \subseteq t_1 \wedge \mathrm{AT}(t_2, \mathbf{leave}'(j))]])]$

(23′) $[\mathbf{PRES}(\mathbf{now}') \wedge \mathrm{AT}(\mathbf{now}', \bigvee t_1 [\mathrm{XN}(t_1) \wedge \bigvee t_2 [t_2 \subseteq t_1 \wedge \mathbf{an\text{-}hour}'(t_2) \wedge \bigwedge t_3 [t_3 \subseteq t_2 \rightarrow \mathrm{AT}(t_3, \mathbf{sleep}'(j))]]])]$

It may be doubted, however, whether (23′) is a correct interpretation for (23). The interpretation of (23) which first comes to mind is stronger than (23′), for (23), without any contextual information, is most naturally taken as asserting that the one-hour period of John's sleeping is an interval which began exactly an hour ago and extends up to the present moment. Yet (23′) would allow not only this possibility but also the possibility than the hour of sleeping lay at some distance in the past. But in fact (23) allows this interpretation as well; it could for example also be used to describe the present state of a sleep experiment at which John is sitting wide awake in front of us, having slept an hour in some previous part of the experiment and now being ready to undergo further sleeping tests. Similarly, **John has lived in Boston for four years** is first interpreted out of context as implying that he still lives there, but it could also be used to introduce John, a former Boston resident, to someone who wants to know more about the city. Perhaps then it is only the result of conversational principles that we first take perfects with **for**-adverbials to imply that the t_2 mentioned in S41 is *equal* to t_1, rather than being a proper subset of it; after all, the simple past (**John lived in Boston for 4 years**), would be available in this situation to assert unambiguously that the interval of the verb's truth is separated from the present.

Perhaps, indeed, this is the only explanation of the preference for the interpretation that puts the last moment of the **for**-interval at the present. Yet there may be reasons to believe otherwise. Note the peculiar and striking fact that when the **for**-adverbial is preposed, the interpretation in which the **for**-interval extends up to the present is the *only* interpretation possible:

(24) **For four years, John has lived in Boston.**

This I take to be a strong indication of a true syntactic ambiguity; if we are to account for the difference in preposability, then there must be *some* syntactic difference in the two readings. (Cf. the way that internal readings of adverbs were observed in Chapter 5 to vanish when these adverbs occurred in initial position.) Moreover, we still have not accounted for adverbials like

since Thursday in **John has been here since Thursday**; **since Thursday** should probably not be an IV adverbial, else we will generate ***John was here since Thursday** (but see below), and **since Thursday** cannot be the Main Tense Adverb of a present, else we would get ***John is here since Thursday.** A natural explanation of this restricted distribution of **since Thursday, during these past five years, up to now** and "preposable" **for four years** is that these adverbials denote the "extended now" interval mentioned in the perfect rule: note that what these adverbs that appear *only* with the perfect tense all have in common is that they denote a stretch of time including the past but also the present. To complete the syntactic side of the account of (23) vs. (24), we need only suppose that TmAV's, though not IV/IV's, can occur in sentence initial position. In fact, the suggestion that time adverbials with the present perfect identify the "Extended Now" was already made in Bennett and Partee (1972). (Whether initial position of the TmAV is brought about by an Adverb Fronting transformation or some other means does not matter here.) Thus we will add a second perfect rule S42 which adds a temporal adverb (expression in TmAV) as it forms the perfect IV-phrase. Translations for **since** (in TmAV/Tm) and **for** (in TmAV/(t/i)) are given in (25):

S42. $\langle F_{42}, \langle \mathrm{TmAV}, \mathrm{IV}\rangle, \mathrm{IV}\rangle$ If $\beta \neq F_{41}(\delta)$ or $F_{42}(\delta, \gamma)$, for some δ, γ, then $F_{42}(\alpha, \beta) =$ **have** $\beta'\ \alpha$, where β' is the result of changing the first verb in β to past participle form. $k(F_{42}(\alpha, \beta)) = \lambda x[\alpha'(\hat{t}[\mathrm{XN}(t) \wedge \mathrm{AT}(t, \beta'(x))])]$

(25) **since** ($\in B_{\mathrm{TmAV/Tm}}$) translates into:
$\lambda \mathscr{P}_t \lambda P_t \mathscr{P}_t\{\hat{t}_1[\bigwedge t_2[[t_1 < t_2 \wedge \mathrm{XN}(t_2)] \rightarrow P_t\{t_2\}]]\}$
for ($\in B_{\mathrm{TmAV/(t/i)}}$) translates into:
$\lambda P_t \lambda Q_t \bigvee t_1[\mathrm{XN}(t_1) \wedge P_t\{t_1\} \wedge \bigwedge t_2[[t_2 \subseteq t_1 \wedge \mathrm{XN}(t_2)] \rightarrow Q_t\{t_2\}]]$

The restricting clauses "$[t_1 < t_2 \wedge \mathrm{XN}(t_2)]$" and "$[t_2 \subseteq t_1 \wedge \mathrm{XN}(t_2)]$" in these last two translations have the effect of letting t_2, the time of the verb's truth, range over all final subintervals of the "measured" interval of the adverbial. Where statives and homogeneous activities are involved (ignoring the heterogeneous activity problem here), this is tantamount to requiring that the verb be true at *all* subintervals of the measured interval. However, we could not use instead the simpler restricting clauses "$[t_1 < t_2 \leqslant n]$" and "$[t_2 \subseteq t_1]$" in place of the clauses given, because the translation of the **have** rule S42 will add the additional assertion that t_2 here is an Extended Now, and this would be contradictory. It cannot be the case that *all* subintervals of an interval can be Extended Nows, though all *final* subintervals can. Reduced translations of (26) and (27), as these are produced using S42, are given in (26′) and (27′) respectively:

(26) **John has slept since midnight**, t, 4

  John, T **have slept since midnight**, IV, 42

    since midnight, TmAV **sleep**, IV

      since, TmAV/Tm **midnight**, Tm

(27) **John has slept for an hour**, t, 4

  John, T **have slept for an hour**, IV, 42

    for an hour, TmAV **sleep**, IV

      for, TmAV/(t/i) **an-hour**, t/i

(26′) $\bigwedge t_2 [[\mathbf{midnight}' < t_2 \wedge \mathrm{XN}(t_2)] \rightarrow [\mathrm{XN}(t_2) \wedge \mathrm{AT}(t_2, \mathbf{sleep}'(j))]]$

(27′) $\bigvee t_1 [\mathrm{XN}(t_1) \wedge \mathbf{an\text{-}hour}'(t_1) \wedge \bigwedge t_2 [[t_2 \subseteq t_1 \wedge \mathrm{XN}(t_2)] \rightarrow [\mathrm{XN}(t_2) \wedge \mathrm{AT}(t_2, \mathbf{sleep}'(j)]]]$

In these translations the last occurrence of "$\mathrm{XN}(t_2)$", which derives from S42, is of course otiose. But we cannot delete this clause from S42, since it is what gives ***John has left yesterday** contradictory entailments (or ultimately, contradictory conventional implicatures), i.e., no time during yesterday can be an Extended Now.[15] Note also that ***John left since yesterday** is given contradictory entailments because **since yesterday** denotes all times in an Extended Now, which the simple past tense excludes.

We should also be able to get a correct interpretation for sentences in the past perfect such as **When I visited John, he had been sick since Thursday** (though **when**-clauses are not actually included in the fragment). Past perfects will be produced syntactically by the obvious method of applying the past tense rule to a sentence in the present perfect. When this happens, the translation of the present perfect and its associated time adverbial (**since Thursday**) are placed within the scope of the Main Tense Adverbial (**when I visited John**). In this context, the predicate XN denotes intervals whose final bound is the past time denoted by the Main Tense Adverbial, not intervals whose final bound is the time of utterance.

The tactic of appealing to a double categorization of **for**-adverbials admittedly looks rather ad hoc. But let it be noted that this tactic (or an equivalent one) is needed for other adverbials as well. Example (16) is ambiguous:

(16) **John was solving the puzzle in five minutes.**

First, imagine that John has been timing himself to see how quickly he could solve a certain kind of puzzle, and that when we last saw him, he almost had the puzzle solved and the timer read just over four minutes. In this situation (16) is naturally interpreted as having **solve the puzzle in five minutes** within the scope of the progressive; i.e., some past time was within an interval of which the natural outcome was **John solves the puzzle in five minutes.** Second, imagine a situation in which I know that John is a fanatical puzzle-solver and that I invite him over, having conspicuously placed an intriguing puzzle on my coffee table. Sure enough, within a few minutes of his arrival he has picked up the puzzle and gone to work on it. When used in this situation, (16) would be interpreted as having **be solving the puzzle** within the scope of **in five minutes**: within an interval of five minutes' duration there was a time (a moment here) contained within a larger possible interval of John's solving the puzzle. Now in fact this ambiguity is already predicted, since the IV/IV **in five minutes** could combine with its IV argument either before or after the progressive is added. But note here again what happens if the adverbial is preposed:

(17) **In five minutes, John was solving the puzzle.**

Now the only reading present is the one in which **in five minutes** has wider scope. But if **in five minutes** can also be a TmAV and if TmAV's but not IV/IV's occur in initial position, this fact about (17) vs. (16) is now accounted for. A translation of **in** in TmAV/(t/i) would be (18):

(18) **in** ($\in B_{TmAV/(t/i)}$) translates into:
$\lambda P_t \lambda Q_t \bigvee t_1 [P_t\{t_1\} \wedge \bigvee t_2 [t_2 \subseteq t_1 \wedge Q_t\{t_2\} \wedge \bigwedge t_3 [[Q_t\{t_3\} \wedge t_3 \subseteq t_1] \rightarrow t_3 = t_2]]]$

To complete the translation of (16) and (17), we need only the progressive rule itself, which is straightforward:

S43. $\langle F_{43}, \langle IV \rangle, IV \rangle$ If $\alpha \neq F_{41}(\beta)$, $F_{42}(\beta, \delta)$ or $F_{43}(\beta)$, for some β, δ, then $F_{43}(\alpha) =$ **be** α', where α' is the result of suffixing **-ing** to the first verb in α. $k(F_{43}(\alpha)) = \lambda x [\text{PROG}\ \alpha'(x)]$

With these rules, (17) will have the translation (17′), while (16) may have the translation (16′) as well as (17′). To aid in comprehension, I indicate below each translation the temporal relationships required by it.

(16′) $\bigvee t[\text{PAST}(t) \wedge \text{AT}(t, \text{PROG}[\textbf{5-minutes}'(n) \wedge \bigvee t_1 [t_1 \subseteq n \wedge \text{AT}(t_1, \textbf{solve-the-puzzle}'(j)) \wedge \bigwedge t_2 [[t_2 \subseteq n \wedge \text{AT}(t_2, \textbf{solve-the-puzzle}'(j))] \rightarrow t_2 = t_1]]])]$

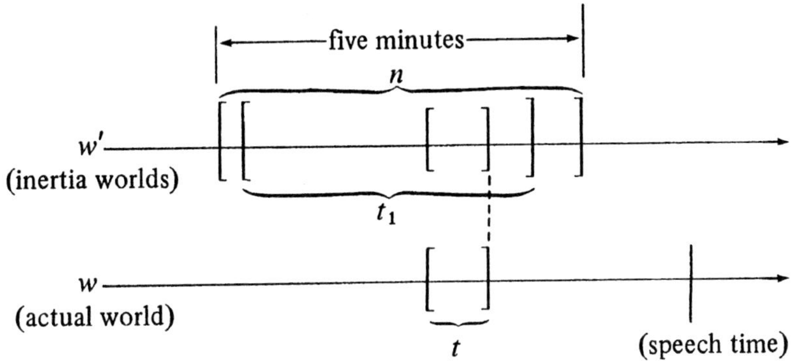

(17′) $\bigvee t_1 [\textbf{5-minutes}'(t_1) \wedge \bigvee t_2 [t_2 \subseteq t_1 \wedge \text{PAST}(t_2) \wedge \text{AT}(t_2, \text{PROG}[\textbf{solve-the-puzzle}'(j)]) \wedge \bigwedge t_3 [[t_3 \subseteq t_1 \wedge \text{PAST}(t_3) \wedge \text{AT}(t_3, \text{PROG}[\textbf{solve-the-puzzle}'(j)])] \rightarrow t_3 = t_2]]]$

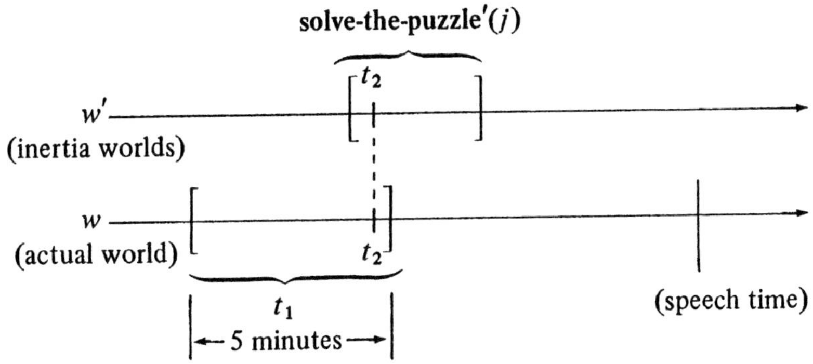

There are still some unresolved problems with this treatment. For most speakers (though apparently not quite all), **since** α has an interpretation (parallel to the IV/IV interpretation of **for** α) that need not entail that its sentence has been true at all times since α, but only at some time since α. That is, **John has been in Boston since 1971**, when used in the right context, need not entail that he is still there now. But just as was the case with **for** α, this possibility vanishes when the adverbial is preposed (for most, though not quite all speakers, though all report the same phenomenon for **for** α), cf. **Since 1971, John has been in Chicago.** We cannot capture this possibility by changing the translation of **since** in TmAV/Tm, though we could by postulating a second **since** in (IV/IV)/Tm. I find this a little suspicious, however, since **since** α is one of the adverbials that locates the time of the verb with respect to the time of speech, i.e. it is not an aspectual adverbial. Another problem is that the only readings available in this treatment for **John has been here today** are one in which **today** is a present tense adverbial (this allows John to have been here yesterday or earlier) and one in which it is an Extended Now adverbial (and requires that John still be here). But intuitively this sentence means that John was here at some earlier time today (not yesterday), though he need not still be here now.

I would be the first to admit that this treatment of the perfect appears ad hoc in a number of respects. But I have not been able to find any other treatment which makes as many correct predictions about adverbials and time reference with the perfect as this does, though I have investigated a dozen alternatives to it (including eliminating the XN predicate in some rules or dispensing with it altogether, dispensing with the distinction between IV/IV and TmAV adverbials, inserting a subinterval specification like that in S41 into one or more translations, etc.). My hope is merely that I have exposed the problems of time adverbials in the perfect tense clearly and that this treatment may serve as a springboard to a more elegant and adequate analysis.

7.6. NEGATION

The category of modals, (t/T)/IV will contain as basic expressions not only **can, will, must,** etc. but also **can't (cannot), mustn't (must not), won't,** etc. The reason for this is that these negated modals are idiosyncratic in meaning. In most cases, the negation is understood as occurring outside the modal (e.g. **John can't go** = it is not the case that John can go), but with **must** the negation goes inside the modal: **John mustn't (must not) go** means "It is required that John not go", not "It is not required that John go". (It is for this reason that English speakers have trouble with German *muss nicht*, which translates as "doesn't have to", not "must not".) Thus (basic) **can't** translates into $\lambda P \lambda \mathscr{P}[\neg \mathbf{can}'(P)(\mathscr{P})]$, while (basic) **mustn't** translates into $\lambda P \lambda \mathscr{P}[\mathbf{must}'(\hat{x}[\neg P\{x\}])(\mathscr{P})]$. A second negation that goes inside the scope of the modal is introduced by S44 in the fragment, as discussed below.

This "IV negation", with emphatic stress, shows up in sentences like *You can nót go to the party* ("You have the option of not going to the party") and *You can't nót go to the party* ("You have no choice but to go to the party"). I use the contracted forms as basic expressions in the fragment to emphasize Horn's (1972, p. 399) observation that only the "external" negative can be contracted: *You can not go* is ambiguous, but *You can't go* is not.

The rule that negates an IV is S46:

S46. $\langle F_{44}, \langle \mathrm{IV} \rangle, \mathrm{IV} \rangle, F_{44}(\alpha) = \mathbf{not}\ \alpha.\ k(F_{44}(\alpha)) = \lambda x[\neg\alpha'(x)]$

This rule is needed for two reasons besides the second modal negation just cited. Since we are deriving infinitives from IV's, not from whole sentences, it is needed to produce **John tried not to sleep** (or **John tried to not sleep**), as no "sentence negation" rule will do this. Second, it is needed to produce the (relatively rare) examples (28b) and (29b) in addition to (28a) and (29a):

(28) a. **John has not been watering the plants.**
b. **John has been not watering the plants.**

(29) a. **John could not be watering the plants.** (actually ambiguous)
b. **John could be not watering the plants.**

Though presumably the (b) examples are logically equivalent to the (a) examples, they convey different implicatures somehow; the (b) examples suggest a deliberate avoidance of action (He's afraid he had been giving them too much water), or they could be used as a reproach if it were John's responsibility to water the plants (Maybe that's why they're wilting), and though unlikely, two, perhaps three negatives are possible:

(30) **John has not been not watering the plants.**

(31) **John can't have (not) been not watering the plants.**

By the way, these examples, like **You can't not go to the party**, are counterexamples to the claim found in textbook transformational grammar that there can be only one negative per Aux node. Having the rule S46 necessitates a modification in the subject-predicate rule S4 to make it perform "NEG-Placement" and "DO-support":

S4. $\langle F_4, \langle \mathrm{T}, \mathrm{IV} \rangle, \mathrm{t} \rangle$ (1) If $\beta =$ **not be** γ or **not have** γ, $F_4(\alpha, \beta) =$ α **is not** γ or α **has not** γ, respectively; (2) If $\beta =$ **not** γ but not **not be** γ or **not have** γ, then $F_4(\alpha, \beta) = \alpha$ **does not** γ; (3) otherwise, $F_4(\alpha, \beta) = \alpha\,\beta'$, where β' is the result of replacing the first verb of β with its third person singular form.

Though having negation introduced in the IV may be useful for the reasons given, we still need a "sentence negation" rule for the reading of **Everyone didn't leave** in which negation has wider scope than the quantifier:

S45. $\langle F_{45}, \langle T, IV \rangle, t \rangle$ (1) If $\beta =$ **be** γ or **have** γ, then $F_{45}(\alpha, \beta) = \alpha$ **is not** γ or α **has not** γ, respectively; (2) otherwise, $F_{45}(\alpha, \beta) = \alpha$ **does not** β. $k(F_{45}(\alpha, \beta)) = \neg\alpha'({}^\wedge\beta')$

An alternative worth exploring is to omit S45 and add instead a basic "modal" **doesn't**, translating as $\lambda P \lambda \mathscr{P}[\neg \mathscr{P}\{P\}]$.

(Gregory Stump pointed out to me, just before this book went to press, that this fragment has the apparent flaw of giving past and future tenses wider scope than negation. Thus **John didn't return the lawnmower** can receive only the interpretation "There is some past time at which it is not true that John returns the lawnmower" rather than the interpretation it is customarily assumed to have, "There is no past time at which it is true that John returns the lawnmower". While the possibility cannot be ruled out that perhaps *all* simple tenses can be interpreted indexically according to Partee's suggestion, given an appropriate theory of contextual interpretation (so that the question of scope of the simple past vis-à-vis sentence negation would become moot, allowing the fragment to remain essentially as it is), it might on the other hand turn out to be necessary to revise the syntactic analysis to insure that negation receives wider scope than tense. If so, I presently see no syntactically natural way of introducing tenses and negation via independent syntactic rules in a way that achieves this scope relation, so we might be forced to revert to a treatment like Montague's PTQ analysis, which introduces the combination of a negation with tense via a single operation, distinct from the operation introducing the unnegated tense (i.e. by operations which translate roughly as $H\phi$, $\neg H\phi$, $W\phi$, and $\neg W\phi$, respectively).)

7.7. AN ENGLISH FRAGMENT

Several desirable refinements for which this book or other work has laid the groundwork are omitted from this fragment for the sake of brevity; these include (1) a distinction between asserted meaning and conventionally implicated meaning (cf. Karttunen and Peters, 1975), (2) an assignment of individuals to points in "Logical Space", in terms of which locative predicates and other physical predicates could be interpreted explicitly (cf. 2.4), and (3) the ontology of Carlson (1977), which distinguishes between stages of objects, objects and kinds (cf. 2.3.4). It should be clear how these refinements can be added, however.

The usual format for defining the syntax and model theory of a formal language (which Montague followed) is to give all syntactic definitions first and all semantic definitions (or translations) afterwards. But I found it much more perspicuous to follow each syntactic rule with its corresponding semantic rule (or translation rule). Accordingly, I will begin with model-theoretic definitions (7.6.1), followed by paired syntactic and semantic rules for the *translation language*, an expanded version of Montague's intensional logic (7.6.2), followed by paired syntactic and translation rules for English (7.6.3), Lexical rules (7.6.4), and a "Lexicon" of basic expressions and their associated translations and/or meaning postulates (7.6.5).

7.7.1. *Basic Model-Theoretic Definitions*

The set of *types* is the smallest set T such that (1) e, t, and i are in T (regarded as the types of *entities*, *truth values* and *intervals of time*, respectively), (2) if $a, b \in T$, then $\langle a, b\rangle \in T$, and (3) if $a \in T$, then $\langle s, a\rangle \in T$.

An *intensional model* $\mathfrak{A}$ for the translation language is an ordered octuple

$$\langle E, W, M, <, R, Inr, \$, F\rangle$$

defined as follows:

(1) E is a non-empty set (the set of basic *entities*).

(2) W is a non-empty set (the set of *possible worlds*).

(3) M is a non-empty set (the set of *moments of time*).

(4) $<$ is a strict linear ordering of M.

(5) The set of *intervals of time* I is the set of all subsets i of M such that if $i \in I$, then for all $m_1, m_2, m_3 \in M$, if $m_1, m_3 \in i$ and $m_1 < m_2 < m_3$, then $m_2 \in i$. *Initial bound*, *final bound*, *initial subinterval*, and *final subinterval* are defined as in Chapter 3, pp. 140.

(6) Let "$i_1 \preccurlyeq i_2$" abbreviate "for all $m_1 \in i_1$ there exists $m_2 \in i_2$ such that $m_1 < m_2$" (i.e., either i_1 completely precedes i_2, i_1 is contained within i_2 but is not a final subinterval of i_2, or i_1 and i_2 partially overlap with some part of i_2 later than i_1). Then R is a three-place relation in $W \times W \times I$ such that (a) if $\langle w_1, w_2, i\rangle \in R$ then for all $i' \in I$ such that $i' \preccurlyeq i$, $\langle w_1, w_2, i'\rangle \in R$, and (b) where R' is that two-place relation such that $\langle w_1, w_2\rangle \in R'$ iff for some i, $\langle w_1, w_2, i\rangle \in R$, R' is transitive, reflexive and symmetric. ("$\langle w_1, w_2, i\rangle \in R$" is read "world w_1 is exactly like world w_2 at all times up to and including i".)

(7) *Inr* is a function from $W \times I$ into subsets of W such that if $w_1 \in Inr(\langle w_2, i \rangle)$, then $\langle w_1, w_2, i \rangle \in R$, for all $w_1, w_2 \in W$, $i \in I$. (I.e., the "inertia worlds" for a given index $\langle w, i \rangle$ are always a subset of the worlds that are exactly like w up to i, according to R.)

(8) \$ is a function that assigns to each $w_i \in W$ a *set of sets of members of W*, designated $\$_{w_i}$, such that (a) $\$_{w_i}$ is centered on w_i, (b) $\$_{w_i}$ is *nested,* (c) $\$_w$ is *closed under unions*, and (d) $\$_{w_i}$ is closed under *non-empty intersections*. (I.e., each set in $\$_{w_i}$ is a set of worlds that are all equally similar to w_i; cf. Lewis (1973a, p. 14), from which these definitions are taken.)

(9) For each type $a \in T$, the set D_a of *possible denotations of type a*, is defined recursively as follows: (a) $D_e = E$, (b) $D_t = \{0, 1\}$ (the truth values "false" and "true", respectively), (c) $D_i = I$, (d) $D_{\langle a,b \rangle} = D_b^{D_a}$, and $D_{\langle s,a \rangle} = D_a^{W \times I}$. The set of *senses* of type a, denoted S_a, is $D_{\langle s,a \rangle}$.

(10) F (the *interpretation function*) assigns to each constant of the translation language of type a a member of S_a.

A *value assignment* g is a function that assigns to each variable of type a a value in D_a.

7.7.2. *The Syntax and Interpretation of the Translation Language*

The set of *basic expressions* of the translation language consists of a set Con_a, of *constants of type a*, and a denumberably infinite set Var_a, of *variables of type a*, for each $a \in T$.

The set of *meaningful expressions of the translation language of type a*, ME_a, is defined recursively as follows, together with the recursive definition of *the denotation of a meaningful expression α with respect to an interpretation* $\mathfrak{A}$, *world w, interval of time i* and *value assignment g*, denoted $[\![\alpha]\!]_{\mathfrak{A},w,i,g}$.

1. If $\alpha \in Con_a$, then $\alpha \in ME_a$, and $[\![\alpha]\!]_{\mathfrak{A},w,i,g} = F(\alpha)(\langle w, i \rangle)$.
2. If $u \in Var_a$, then $u \in ME_a$, and $[\![u]\!]_{\mathfrak{A},w,i,g} = g(u)$.
3. If $\alpha \in ME_{\langle a,b \rangle}$ and $\beta \in ME_a$ then $\alpha(\beta) \in ME_b$, and $[\![\alpha(\beta)]\!]_{\mathfrak{A},w,i,g} = [\![\alpha]\!]_{\mathfrak{A},w,i,g}([\![\beta]\!]_{\mathfrak{A},w,i,g})$.
4. If $\alpha \in ME_a$, and $u \in Var_b$, then $\lambda u \alpha \in ME_{\langle b,a \rangle}$, and $[\![\lambda u \alpha]\!]_{\mathfrak{A},w,i,g}$ is that function h with domain D_b that gives for each argument x the value $[\![\alpha]\!]_{\mathfrak{A},w,i,g'}$ where g' is that assignment exactly like g except for the (possible) difference that $g(u) = x$.
5. If $\alpha, \beta \in ME_a$, then $[\alpha = \beta] \in ME_t$, and $[\![[\alpha = \beta]]\!]_{\mathfrak{A},w,i,g} = 1$ iff $[\![\alpha]\!]_{\mathfrak{A},w,i,g}$ is $[\![\beta]\!]_{\mathfrak{A},w,i,g}$.

6. If $\phi \in ME_t$, then $\neg\phi \in ME_t$, and $[\![\neg\phi]\!]_{\mathfrak{A},w,i,g} = 1$ iff $[\![\phi]\!]_{\mathfrak{A},w,i,g} = 0$. (Similarly for $\wedge, \vee, \rightarrow$, and $\leftrightarrow$.)

7. If $\phi \in ME_t$ and $u \in Var_a$, then $\bigvee u\phi \in ME_t$, and $[\![\bigvee u\phi]\!]_{\mathfrak{A},w,i,g} = 1$ iff there exists x such that $[\![\phi]\!]_{\mathfrak{A},w,i,g'} = 1$, where g' is as in 4. (Similarly for $\bigwedge u\phi$.)

8. If $\phi \in ME_t$ then $\Box\phi \in ME_t$, and $[\![\Box\phi]\!]_{\mathfrak{A},w,i,g} = 1$ iff $[\![\phi]\!]_{\mathfrak{A},w',i',g} = 1$, for all $w' \in W$ and $i' \in I$.

9. If $\alpha \in ME_a$ then $\hat{}\alpha \in ME_{\langle s,a \rangle}$, and $[\![\hat{}\alpha]\!]_{\mathfrak{A},w,i,g}$ is that function h with domain WXI such that for each $\langle w', i' \rangle \in WXI$, $h(\langle w', i' \rangle) = [\![\alpha]\!]_{\mathfrak{A},w',i',g}$.

10. If $\alpha \in ME_{\langle s,a \rangle}$, then $\check{}\alpha \in ME_a$, and $[\![\check{}\alpha]\!]_{\mathfrak{A},w,i,g} = [\![\alpha]\!]_{\mathfrak{A},w,i,g}(\langle w, i \rangle)$.

11. If $\phi \in ME_t$ then BECOME $\phi \in ME_t$, and $[\![\text{BECOME } \phi]\!]_{\mathfrak{A},w,i,g} = 1$, iff (1) for some $j \in I$ containing the lower bound of i, $[\![\phi]\!]_{\mathfrak{A},w,i,g} = 0$; (2) for some $k \in I$ containing the upper bound of i, $[\![\phi]\!]_{\mathfrak{A},w,k,g} = 1$; and (3) there is no $i' \subset i$ such that (1) and (2) hold for i' as well as i.

12. If ϕ, $\psi \in ME_t$ then $[\phi \text{ AND } \psi] \in ME_t$, and $[\![[\phi \text{ AND } \psi]]\!]_{\mathfrak{A},w,i,g} = 1$ iff (1) for some $j \subseteq i$, $[\![\phi]\!]_{\mathfrak{A},w,j,g} = 1$; (2) for some $k \subseteq i$, $[\![\psi]\!]_{\mathfrak{A},w,k,g} = 1$; and (3) there is no $i' \subset i$ such that (1) and (2) hold for i'.

13. If $\phi \in ME_t$ then PROG $\phi \in ME_t$, and $[\![\text{PROG } \phi]\!]_{\mathfrak{A},w,i,g} = 1$ iff there is some i' such that $i \subset i'$, i is not a final subinterval for i', and for all $w' \in Inr(\langle w, i \rangle)$, $[\![\phi]\!]_{\mathfrak{A},w',i',g} = 1$.

14. If ϕ, $\psi \in ME_t$, then $[\phi \,\Box\!\!\rightarrow \psi] \in ME_t$, and $[\![[\phi \,\Box\!\!\rightarrow \psi]]\!]_{\mathfrak{A},w,i,g} = 1$ iff either (1) there is no set $S \in \$_w$ for which there is $w' \in S$ such that $[\![\phi]\!]_{\mathfrak{A},w',i,g} = 1$, or else (2) there is some set $S \in \$_w$ such that $[\![\phi]\!]_{\mathfrak{A},w',i,g} = 1$ for some $w' \in S$, and for all $w'' \in S$, $[\![[\phi \rightarrow \psi]]\!]_{\mathfrak{A},w'',i,g} = 1$. (Cf. Lewis (1973a, p. 16).)

15. If ϕ, $\psi \in ME_t$ then $[\phi \text{ CAUSE } \psi] \in ME_t$, and $[\![[\phi \text{ CAUSE } \psi]]\!]_{\mathfrak{A},w,i,g} = 1$ iff (1) there is some $i_1 \subseteq i$ such that $[\![\phi]\!]_{\mathfrak{A},w,i_1,g} = 1$, (2) there is some $i_2 \subseteq i$ such that $[\![\psi]\!]_{\mathfrak{A},w,i_2,g} = 1$, (3) there is no $i' \subseteq i$ meeting (1) and (2), and (4) there is a sequence of formulas $\chi_1, \chi_2, \ldots \chi_n$, where $\phi = \chi_1$ and $\psi = \chi_n$ such that $[\![[\neg\chi_k \rightarrow \neg\chi_{k+1}]]\!]_{\mathfrak{A},w,j,g} = 1$, where $1 \leqslant k < n$ and $j \subseteq i$.

16. If $\phi \in ME_t$, $\zeta \in ME_i$, then $AT(\zeta, \phi) \in ME_t$, and $[\![AT(\zeta, \phi)]\!]_{\mathfrak{A},w,i,g} = 1$ iff $[\![\phi]\!]_{\mathfrak{A},w,i',g} = 1$, where $i' = [\![\zeta]\!]_{\mathfrak{A},w,i,g}$.

17. If $\zeta \in ME_i$ then $PAST(\zeta) \in ME_t$, and $[\![PAST(\zeta)]\!]_{\mathfrak{A},w,i,g} = 1$ iff there is some non-empty $i' \in I$ such that $[\![\zeta]\!]_{\mathfrak{A},w,i,g} < i' < i$.

18. If $\zeta \in ME_i$, then $XN(\zeta) \in ME_t$ and $[\![XN(\zeta)]\!]_{\mathfrak{A},w,i,g} = 1$ iff i is a final subinterval for $[\![\zeta]\!]_{\mathfrak{A},w,i,g}$.

19. If $\zeta \in ME_i$, $PRES(\zeta) \in ME_t$, and $[\![PRES(\zeta)]\!]_{\mathfrak{A},w,i,g} = 1$ iff $[\![\zeta]\!]_{\mathfrak{A},w,i,g} = i$. (Similarly for $FUT(\zeta)$.)

20. If ζ, $\xi \in ME_i$ then $[\zeta \subseteq \xi]$ and $[\zeta < \xi] \in ME_t$, and $[\![[\zeta \subseteq \xi]]\!]_{\mathfrak{A},w,i,g} = 1$

iff $\mathfrak{A}\ [\![\zeta]\!]_{\mathfrak{A},w,i,g} \subseteq [\![\xi]\!]_{\mathfrak{A},w,i,g}$, and $[\![[\zeta < \xi]]\!]_{\mathfrak{A},w,i,g} = 1$ iff for all $m_1 \in [\![\zeta]\!]_{\mathfrak{A},w,i,g}$ and all $m_2 \in [\![\xi]\!]_{\mathfrak{A},w,i,g}$, $m_1 < m_2$.

If ϕ is a formula (member of ME_t), ϕ is *true* with respect to $\mathfrak{A}$ and $\langle w, i\rangle$ iff $[\phi]_{\mathfrak{A},w,i,g'} = 1$ for all g'.

If $w \in W$ and $i \in I$, then $\langle w, i\rangle$ is an *index of possible utterance* iff i contains exactly one moment.

The following abbreviations are employed: $\alpha(\beta, \gamma)$ is $\alpha(\gamma)(\beta)$; $\alpha\{\beta\}$ is $[{}^{\vee}\alpha](\beta)$; where $\phi \in ME_t$, $\hat{u}\phi$ is ${}^{\wedge}[\lambda u \phi]$.

7.7.3. *The Syntax and Translation of English*

The set of possible syntactic categories of English is the smallest set Cat such that (1) t, CN, IV, ADJ, INF, GER and t/i are members of Cat,[16] and (2) If A, B $\in$ Cat, then A/B and A//B $\in$ Cat. The categories used in this fragment are the following:

Symbol	*Categorial Definition*	*Name of Category*
t		Sentence
IV		Intransitive Verb Phrase
ADJ		Adjective
INF		Infinitive
GER		Gerund
CN		Common Noun Phrase
T	t/IV	Term
DET	T/CN	Determiner
IV/t		Sentence-Complement Verb
IV/ADJ		Copula
IV/INF		Infinitive-Complement Verb
IV/GER		Gerund-Complement Verb
(IV/INF)/T		Term-Infinitive-Complement Verb
TV	IV/T	Transitive Verb Phrase
TV/IV		IV-Complement TV
TV/ADJ		Adjective-Complement TV
TV/GER		Gerund-Complement TV
TV/CN		Noun-Complement TV
TV/(TV/TV)		TV/TV-Complement TV
TV/T		Three-place Verb
t/t		Sentence Modifier
IAV	IV/IV	Intransitive Modifier
IAV/GER		Gerund Preposition (**by**)
IAV/T		IV-Preposition

Symbol	*Categorial Definition*	*Name of Category*
TV/TV		TV-Modifier
(TV/TV)/T		TV-Preposition
(TV/TV)/(TV/TV)		TV/TV-Modifier
((TV/TV)/(TV/TV))/T		TV/TV-Preposition (**from**)
t/i		Temporal Measure Phrase
Tm	t/(t/i)	Temporal Phrase
TmAV	t//(t/i)	Temporal Adverbial
TmAV/Tm		Temporal Preposition
TmAV/(t/i)		Temporal Measure Preposition
TV/TmAV		TmAV-Complement TV
(TV/T)/TmAV		TmAV-Complement TV/T
(IV/IV)/(t/i)		Aspectual Measure Preposition
(IV/IV)/TmAV		Aspectual Temporal Preposition
t/T		Modal Verb Phrase
(t/T)/IV		Modal Auxiliary

The *type assignment* f for English categories is defined as follows: (1) $f(\mathrm{t}) = t$, (2) $f(\mathrm{CN}) = f(\mathrm{IV}) = f(\mathrm{INF}) = f(\mathrm{ADJ}) = f(\mathrm{GER}) = \langle e, t \rangle$, (3) $f(\mathrm{t/i}) = \langle i, t \rangle$, (4) for all categories A/B, $f(\mathrm{A/B}) = \langle\langle s, f(\mathrm{B})\rangle, f(\mathrm{A})\rangle$.

The syntactic rules are stated in the UG format; see pp. 327 for explanation of this format and the format of the translation rules.

The typographical conventions for commonly-used variables of the translation language that appear in these translation rules are as follows:

Variable Symbols used	Type of Variable
$x, y, z, x_1, x_2, \ldots$	e
$P, Q, P_1, P_2, \ldots$	$\langle s, \langle e, t\rangle\rangle$
$p, q, p_1, p_2, \ldots$	$\langle s, t\rangle$
R	$\langle s, \langle e, \langle e, t\rangle\rangle\rangle$
$\mathscr{P}, \mathscr{Q}, \mathscr{P}_1, \mathscr{Q}_2, \ldots$	$\langle s, f(\mathrm{T})\rangle$
$\mathscr{R}$	$\langle s, f(\mathrm{TV})\rangle$
$\mathscr{G}$	$\langle s, f(\mathrm{TV/TV})\rangle$
$t, t_1, t_2, \ldots$	i
$P_{\mathrm{t}}, Q_{\mathrm{t}}$	$\langle s, \langle i, t\rangle\rangle$
$\mathscr{P}_{\mathrm{t}}, \mathscr{Q}_{\mathrm{t}}$	$\langle s, f(\mathrm{Tm})\rangle$

For conciseness, I will describe only once at the beginning those kinds of syntactic operations that appear repeatedly and assign them mnemonic

If $\alpha =$ **not** β, $F_{19}(\alpha) =$ **not to** β, otherwise $F_{19}(\alpha) =$ **to** α.
$k(F_{19}(\alpha)) = \alpha'$.

S20. $\langle F_{20}, \langle \mathrm{IV} \rangle, \mathrm{GER} \rangle$ (*Gerund Formation*, cf. p. 228).
$F_{20}(\alpha) =$ the result of suffixing **-ing** to the first verb in α.
$k(F_{20}(\alpha)) = \alpha'$.

S21. $\langle F_{21}^{\mathrm{LC}}, \langle \mathrm{TV/TV}, \mathrm{TV} \rangle, \mathrm{TV} \rangle$ (*TV-modifier*, cf. p. 208).

S22. $\langle F_{22}^{\mathrm{RCA}}, \langle (\mathrm{TV/TV})/\mathrm{T}, \mathrm{T} \rangle, (\mathrm{TV/TV}) \rangle$ (*TV-Preposition-Object*, cf. p. 211).

S23. (See Lexical Rule $\mathrm{S}^{\mathrm{w}}2$)

S24. (See Lexical Rule $\mathrm{S}^{\mathrm{w}}3$)

S25. $\langle F_{25}^{\mathrm{I}}, \langle \mathrm{IAV/T} \rangle, (\mathrm{TV/TV})/\mathrm{T} \rangle$ (*Preposition Shift*, cf. p. 212).
$k(F_{25}^{\mathrm{I}}(\alpha)) = \lambda\mathscr{P}\lambda\mathscr{R}\lambda\mathscr{Q}\lambda x \mathscr{Q}\{\hat{y}\mathscr{P}\{\hat{z}[\,{}^{\vee}\mathscr{R}(x, \hat{P}P\{y\})$ CAUSE $[\alpha'(\hat{P}P\{z\})(\hat{x}[x = x])(y)]]\}\}$.

S26. (See Lexical Rule $\mathrm{S}^{\mathrm{w}}9$)

S27. $\langle F_{27}^{\mathrm{LC}}, \langle (\mathrm{TV/TV})/(\mathrm{TV/TV}), \mathrm{TV/TV} \rangle, \mathrm{TV/TV} \rangle$ (*Prepositional Phrase Modifier*, cf. p. 216).

S28. $\langle F_{28}^{\mathrm{RCA}}, \langle ((\mathrm{TV/TV})/(\mathrm{TV/TV}))/\mathrm{T}, \mathrm{T} \rangle, (\mathrm{TV/TV})/(\mathrm{TV/TV}) \rangle$ (*Preposition-Object*, cf. p. 216).

S29. $\langle F_{29}^{\mathrm{RC}}, \langle \mathrm{TV}/(\mathrm{TV/TV}), (\mathrm{TV/TV}) \rangle, \mathrm{TV} \rangle$ (*Verb-TV/TV Complement*, e.g. **put**, cf. p. 217).

S30. $\langle F_{30}^{\mathrm{RC}}, \langle \mathrm{TV/ADJ}, \mathrm{ADJ} \rangle, \mathrm{TV} \rangle$ (*Verb-ADJ Complement*, cf. p. 220).

S31. $\langle F_{31}^{\mathrm{RC}}, \langle \mathrm{TV/CN}, \mathrm{CN} \rangle, \mathrm{TV} \rangle$ (*Verb-CN Complement*, cf. p. 224).

S32. $\langle F_{32}^{\mathrm{RC}}, \langle \mathrm{TV/IV}, \mathrm{IV} \rangle, \mathrm{TV} \rangle$ (*Verb-IV Complement*, cf. p. 225).

S33. $\langle F_{27}^{\mathrm{RC}}, \langle \mathrm{TV/INF}, \mathrm{INF} \rangle, \mathrm{TV} \rangle$ (*Verb-INF Complement*, cf. p. 227).

S34. $\langle F_{34}^{\mathrm{RC}}, \langle (\mathrm{IV/IV})/\mathrm{GER}, \mathrm{GER} \rangle, \mathrm{IV/IV} \rangle$ (**by**-phrase formation, cf. p. 227).

S35. $\langle F_{35}^{\mathrm{RC}}, \langle \mathrm{IV/GER}, \mathrm{GER} \rangle, \mathrm{IV} \rangle$ (**finish**-Complement)

Rules for Tense and Time Adverbials:

S36. $\langle F_{36}, \langle \mathrm{TmAV}, \mathrm{t} \rangle, \mathrm{t} \rangle$ (*Past Tense & Adv*). If $\phi \neq F_{36\text{–}38}(\beta, \psi)$ or $F_{39\text{–}40}(\psi)$ for some β, ψ, then $F_{36}(\alpha, \phi) = \phi'\,\alpha$, where ϕ' comes from ϕ by changing the first verb[17] in ϕ to past tense.
$k(F_{36}(\alpha, \phi)) = \alpha'(\hat{t}\,[\mathrm{PAST}(t) \wedge \mathrm{AT}(t, \phi')])$.

or **him**$_n$ in ϕ by **he/she/it** or **him/her/it** respectively, according to the gender of the first basic CN in α. $k(F_{3,n}(\alpha, \phi)) = \lambda x_n [\alpha'(x_n) \wedge \phi']$.

S4. $\langle F_4 \langle \mathrm{T, IV} \rangle, \mathrm{t} \rangle$ (*Subject-Predicate*). (1) If $\beta =$ **not be** γ or **not have** γ, $F_4(\alpha, \beta) = \alpha$ **is not** γ or α **has not** γ, respectively; (2) If $\beta =$ **not** γ but not **not be** γ or **not have** γ, then $F_4(\alpha, \beta) = \alpha$ **does not** γ; (3) otherwise, $F_4(\alpha, \beta) = \alpha \beta'$, where β' is the result of replacing the first verb of β by its 3rd person singular form.

S5. $\langle F_5^{\mathrm{RW}}, \langle \mathrm{TV, T} \rangle, \mathrm{IV} \rangle$ (*Verb-Object*).

S6. $\langle F_6^{\mathrm{RCA}}, \langle \mathrm{IAV/T, T} \rangle, \mathrm{IAV} \rangle$ (*Preposition-Object*).

S7. $\langle F_7^{\mathrm{RC}}, \langle \mathrm{IV/t, t} \rangle, \mathrm{IV} \rangle$ (*Sentence Complement*).

S8. $\langle F_8^{\mathrm{RC}}, \langle \mathrm{IV/INF, INF} \rangle, \mathrm{IV} \rangle$ (*Infinitive Complement*).

S9. $\langle F_9^{\mathrm{RC}}, \langle \mathrm{t/t, t} \rangle, \mathrm{t} \rangle$ (*Sentence Modifier*).

S10. $\langle F_{10}^{\mathrm{LC}}, \langle \mathrm{IAV, IV} \rangle, \mathrm{IV} \rangle$ (*IV-Modifier*).

S11. $\langle F_{11}, \langle \mathrm{t, t} \rangle, \mathrm{t} \rangle$ (*Sentence Conjunction*). $F_{11}(\phi, \psi) = \phi$ **and** ψ.
$k(F_{11}(\phi, \psi)) = [\phi' \text{ AND } \psi']$.

S12. $\langle F_{12}, \langle \mathrm{IV, IV} \rangle, \mathrm{IV} \rangle$ (*IV-Conjunction*). $F_{12}(\alpha, \beta) = \alpha$ **and** β.
$k(F_{12}(\alpha, \beta)) = \lambda x [\alpha'(x) \text{ AND } \beta'(x)]$.

S13. $\langle F_{13}, \langle \mathrm{T, T} \rangle, \mathrm{T} \rangle$ (*T-Disjunction*). $F_{13}(\alpha, \beta) = \alpha$ **or** β.
$k(F_{13}(\alpha, \beta)) = \lambda P[\alpha'(P) \vee \beta'(P)]$.

S14. $\langle F_{14,n}^{\mathrm{Q}}, \langle \mathrm{T, t} \rangle, \mathrm{t} \rangle$ (*Quantification over Sentences*).
$k(F_{14,n}^{\mathrm{Q}}(\alpha, \phi)) = \alpha'(\hat{x}_n [\phi'])$.

S15. $\langle F_{15,n}^{\mathrm{Q}}, \langle \mathrm{T, CN} \rangle, \mathrm{CN} \rangle$ (*Quantification over CN*).
$k(F_{15,n}^{\mathrm{Q}}(\alpha, \beta)) = \lambda y [\alpha'(\hat{x}_n [\beta'(y)])]$.

S16. $\langle F_{16,n}^{\mathrm{Q}}, \langle \mathrm{T, IV} \rangle, \mathrm{IV} \rangle$ (*Quantification over IV*).
$k(F_{16,n}^{\mathrm{Q}}(\alpha, \beta)) = \lambda y [\alpha'(\hat{x}_n [\beta'(y)])]$.

S17. (The role of this PTQ rule is taken over by S36–S45.)

New Rules from Chapter 4:

S18. $\langle F_{18}^{\mathrm{RC}}, \langle \mathrm{IV/ADJ, ADJ} \rangle, \mathrm{IV} \rangle$ (*Copula-Adjective*).

S19. $\langle F_{19}, \langle \mathrm{IV} \rangle, \mathrm{INF} \rangle$ (*Infinitive Formation* cf. p. 225).

superscripts; all other syntactic operations (i.e. without superscripts) will be described following the rule in which they are used. For ease of reference, each syntactic operation will also be assigned a numerical subscript that is the same as the syntactic rule in which it appears; this subscript also helps achieve the UG requirement of keeping all operations distinct even when the "same" operation is used in more than one rule. These numerical indices will also appear in analysis trees where the operation in question has been used.

Commonly used operations:

$F_n^{\mathrm{I}}(\alpha) = \alpha$ (*Identity operation*)

$F_n^{\mathrm{RC}}(\alpha, \beta) = \alpha\,\beta$ (*Right Concatenation*; argument is placed to *right* of functor)

$F_n^{\mathrm{LC}}(\alpha, \beta) = \beta\,\alpha$ (*Left Concatenation*; argument is placed to *left* of functor)

$F_n^{\mathrm{RCA}}(\alpha, \beta) = \alpha$ **him**$_m$ if $\beta =$ **he**$_m$; otherwise $\alpha\,\beta$. (*Right Concatenation* with *accusative* case marking)

$F_n^{\mathrm{RW}}(\alpha, \beta) =$ the result of inserting β' after the first word in α, where β' is **him**$_m$ if $\beta =$ **he**$_m$, $\beta' = \beta$ otherwise. (*Right Wrap*, cf. Bach 1977)

$F_{n,m}^{\mathrm{Q}}(\alpha, \phi) =$ the result of replacing the first occurrence of **he**$_m$ or **him**$_m$ in ϕ with α and replacing all subsequent occurrences of **he**$_m$ or **him**$_m$ in ϕ with **he/she/it** or **him/her/it** respectively, according to the gender of the first basic CN or T in α. (*Quantification*)

If no translation rule is given following a syntactic rule, it is to be understood that the rule is a *rule of functional application*, and all such rules have the translation rule $k(F_n(\alpha, \beta)) = \alpha'(\hat{}\beta')$.

Rules from PTQ:

S1. $\mathrm{B_A} \subseteq \mathrm{P_A}$.

S2. $\langle F_2^{\mathrm{RC}}, \langle \mathrm{DET}, \mathrm{CN}\rangle, \mathrm{T}\rangle$ (*Determiner-Noun*).

S3. $\langle F_{3,n}\, \langle \mathrm{CN}, \mathrm{t}\rangle, \mathrm{CN}\rangle$ (*Relative Clause*). $F_{3,n}(\alpha, \phi) = \alpha$ **such that** ϕ', where ϕ' comes from ϕ by replacing each occurrence of **he**$_n$

S37. $\langle F_{37}, \langle \mathrm{TmAV, t}\rangle, \mathrm{t}\rangle$ (*Present Tense & Adv*, cf. p. 328). If $\phi \neq F_{36-38}(\beta, \psi)$ or $F_{39-40}(\psi)$ for some β, ψ, then $F_{37}(\alpha, \phi) = \phi\alpha$. $k(F_{37}(\alpha, \phi)) = \alpha'(\hat{t}\,[\mathrm{PRES}(t) \wedge \mathrm{AT}(t, \phi')])$.

S38. $\langle F_{38}, \langle \mathrm{TmAV, t}\rangle, \mathrm{t}\rangle$ (*Future Tense & Adv*, cf. p. 328). If $\phi \neq F_{36-38}(\beta, \psi)$ or $F_{39-40}(\psi)$ for some β, ψ, then $F_{38}(\alpha, \phi) = \phi'\,\alpha$, where ϕ' = the result of inserting **will** before the first verb in ϕ. $k(F_{38}(\alpha, \phi)) = \alpha'(\hat{t}\,[\mathrm{PAST}(t) \wedge \mathrm{AT}(t, \phi')])$.

S39. $\langle F_{39}, \langle \mathrm{t}\rangle, \mathrm{t}\rangle$ (*Past Tense*, cf. p. 330). If $\phi \neq F_{36-38}(\beta, \psi)$ or $F_{39-40}(\psi)$ for some β, ψ, then $F_{39}(\phi)$ = the result of changing the first verb in ϕ to past tense. $k(F_{39}(\phi)) = \bigvee t\,[\mathrm{PAST}(t) \wedge \mathrm{AT}(t, \phi)]$.

S40. $\langle F_{40}, \langle \mathrm{t}\rangle, \mathrm{t}\rangle$ (*Future Tense*, cf. p. 330). If $\phi \neq F_{36-38}(\beta, \psi)$ or $F_{39-40}(\psi)$ for some β, ψ, then $F_{40}(\phi)$ = the result of inserting **will** before the first verb of ϕ. $k(F_{40}(\phi)) = \bigvee t\,[\mathrm{FUT}(t) \wedge \mathrm{AT}(t, \phi')]$.

S41. $\langle F_{41}, \langle \mathrm{IV}\rangle, \mathrm{IV}\rangle$ (*Perfect*, cf. p. 342). If $\alpha \neq F_{41-42}(\beta[, \gamma])$, for some β, γ, then $F_{41}(\alpha)$ = **have** α', where α' is the result of changing the first verb in α to past participle form. $k(F_{41}(\alpha)) = \lambda x \bigvee t_1\,[\mathrm{XN}(t_1) \wedge \bigvee t_2\,[t_2 \subseteq t_1 \wedge \mathrm{AT}(t_2, \alpha'(x))]]$.

S42. $\langle F_{42}, \langle \mathrm{TmAV, IV}\rangle, \mathrm{IV}\rangle$ (*Perfect & Adv*, cf. p. 344). If $\beta \neq F_{41-42}(\delta[, \gamma])$ for some δ, γ, then $F_{42}(\alpha, \beta)$ = **have** $\beta'\,\alpha$, where β' is the result of changing the first verb in β to past participle form. $k(F_{42}(\alpha, \beta)) = \lambda x \alpha'(\hat{t}\,[\mathrm{XN}(t) \wedge \mathrm{AT}(t, \beta'(x))])$.

S43. $\langle F_{43}, \langle \mathrm{IV}\rangle, \mathrm{IV}\rangle$ (*Progressive Rule*, cf. p. 346). If $\alpha \neq F_{41-43}(\beta[, \gamma])$. then $F_{43}(\alpha)$ = **be** α', where α' comes from α by suffixing **-ing** to the first verb in α. $k(F_{43}(\alpha)) = \lambda x\,[\mathrm{PROG}\,\alpha'(x)]$.

S44. $\langle F_{44}, \langle \mathrm{TmAV, IV}\rangle, \mathrm{IV}\rangle$ (*Tenseless Future & Adv*). If $\beta \neq F_{41-45}(\delta[, \gamma])$ for some δ, γ, then $F_{44}(\alpha, \beta) = \beta\,\alpha$. $k(F_{44}(\alpha, \beta)) = \lambda x \bigvee t_1\,[\mathrm{PAST}(t_1) \wedge \mathrm{AT}(t_1, [\mathbf{predetermined}'(\hat{}\,[\alpha'(\hat{t}_2\,[\mathrm{FUT}(t_2) \wedge \mathrm{AT}(t_2, \beta'(x))])])])]$.

S45. $\langle F_{45}, \langle \mathrm{IV}\rangle, \mathrm{IV}\rangle$ (*Tenseless Future*). If $\alpha \neq F_{41-45}(\beta[, \gamma])$ for some β, γ, then $F_{45}(\alpha) = \alpha$. $k(F_{45}(\alpha)) = \lambda x \bigvee t_1\,[\mathrm{PAST}(t_1) \wedge \mathrm{AT}(t_1, [\mathbf{predetermined}'(\hat{}\bigvee t_2\,[\mathrm{FUT}(t_2) \wedge \mathrm{AT}(t_2, \alpha'(x))])])]$.

S46. $\langle F_{46}, \langle \mathrm{IV}\rangle, \mathrm{IV}\rangle$ (*IV-Negation*, cf. p. 349). $F_{46}(\alpha)$ = **not** α. $k(F_{46}(\alpha)) = \lambda x\,[\neg\alpha'(x)]$.

S47. $\langle F_{47}, \langle \mathrm{T}, \mathrm{IV}\rangle, \mathrm{t}\rangle$ (*Sentence Negation*, cf. p. 350). If $\beta =$ **be** γ or **have** γ, then $F_{47}(\alpha, \beta) = \alpha$ **is not** γ or α **has not** γ, respectively; otherwise $F_{47}(\alpha, \beta) = \alpha$ **does not** β. $k(F_{47}(\alpha, \beta) = \neg\alpha'(\hat{}\beta')$.

S48. $\langle F^{\mathrm{RC}}_{48}, \langle \mathrm{TmAV/Tm}, \mathrm{Tm}\rangle, \mathrm{TmAV}\rangle$ (forms **since Thursday**).

S49. $\langle F^{\mathrm{RC}}_{49}, \langle \mathrm{TmAV/(t/i)}, \mathrm{(t/i)}\rangle, \mathrm{TmAV}\rangle$ (forms **for six weeks** $\in P_{\mathrm{TmAV}}$).

S50. $\langle F^{\mathrm{RC}}_{50}, \langle \mathrm{(IV/IV)/(t/i)}, \mathrm{(t/i)}\rangle, \mathrm{(IV/IV)}\rangle$ (forms **for six weeks** $\in P_{\mathrm{IV/IV}}$).

S51. $\langle F^{\mathrm{RC}}_{51}, \langle \mathrm{(t/T)/IV}, \mathrm{IV}\rangle\ \mathrm{(t/T)}\rangle$ (*Modal Verb Phrase*).

S52. $\langle F^{\mathrm{LC}}_{52}, \langle \mathrm{(t/T)}, \mathrm{T}\rangle, \mathrm{t}\rangle$ (*Subject-Modal Predicate*, cf. p. 336).

S53. $\langle F^{\mathrm{RC}}_{53}, \langle \mathrm{(IV/IV)/TmAV}, \mathrm{TmAV}\rangle, \mathrm{IV/IV}\rangle$ (forms **until tomorrow** $\in P_{\mathrm{IV/IV}}$).

S54. $\langle F^{\mathrm{RC}}_{54}, \langle \mathrm{TV/TmAV}, \mathrm{TmAV}\rangle, \mathrm{TV}\rangle$.

S55. $\langle F^{\mathrm{RC}}_{55}, \langle \mathrm{(TV/T)/TmAV}, \mathrm{TmAV}\rangle, \mathrm{TV/T}\rangle$.

S56. $\langle F^{\mathrm{RC}}_{56}, \langle \mathrm{TV/GER}, \mathrm{GER}\rangle, \mathrm{TV}\rangle$.

S57. $\langle F^{\mathrm{RCA}}_{57}, \langle \mathrm{(IV/INF)/T}, \mathrm{T}\rangle, \mathrm{IV/INF}\rangle$ (forms **promise Mary** $\in P_{\mathrm{IV/INF}}$).

S58. $\langle F^{\mathrm{RCA}}_{58}, \langle \mathrm{TV/T}, \mathrm{T}\rangle, \mathrm{TV}\rangle$.

7.7.4. *Lexical Rules* (*cf. Chapter 6*)

$\mathrm{S^{w}1}$. $\langle F_{\mathrm{W1}}, \langle \mathrm{TV}\rangle, \mathrm{ADJ}\rangle$ (**-able** Rule). $F_{\mathrm{W1}}(\alpha) = \alpha +$ **able**. $k(F_{\mathrm{W1}}(\alpha)) = \lambda x \neg\Box\neg\bigvee y[\alpha'(\hat{P}P\{x\})(y)]$.

$\mathrm{S^{w}2}$. $\langle F_{\mathrm{W2}}, \langle \mathrm{ADJ}\rangle, \mathrm{IV}\rangle$ (*Inchoative*). $F_{\mathrm{W2}}(\alpha) = \alpha +$ **en** if α ends in a non-nasal obstruent, α otherwise. $k(F_{\mathrm{W2}}(\alpha)) = \lambda x[\mathrm{BECOME}\ \alpha'(x)]$.

$\mathrm{S^{w}3}$. $\langle F^{\mathrm{I}}_{\mathrm{W3}}, \langle \mathrm{IV}\rangle, \mathrm{TV}\rangle$ (*Causative*). $k(F_{\mathrm{W3}}(\alpha)) = \lambda\mathscr{P}\lambda x\mathscr{P}\{\hat{y}\bigvee P[P\{x\}\ \mathrm{CAUSE}\ \alpha'(y)]\}$.

$\mathrm{S^{w}4}$. $\langle F_{\mathrm{W4}}, \langle \mathrm{ADJ}\rangle, \mathrm{TV}\rangle$ (**-ize** *Causative*). $F_{\mathrm{W4}}(\alpha) = \alpha +$ **ize**.
$k(F_{\mathrm{W4}}(\alpha)) = \lambda\mathscr{P}\lambda x\mathscr{P}\{\hat{y}\bigvee P[P\{x\}\ \mathrm{CAUSE\ BECOME}\ \alpha'(y)]\}$.

$\mathrm{S^{w}5}$. $\langle F_{\mathrm{W5}}, \langle \mathrm{ADJ}\rangle, \mathrm{ADJ}\rangle$ (*Adjective Negation*). $F_{\mathrm{W4}}(\alpha) =$ **un** $+ \alpha$.
$k(F_{\mathrm{W5}}(\alpha)) = \lambda x[\neg\alpha'(x)]$.

$\mathrm{S^{w}6}$. $\langle F_{\mathrm{W6}}, \langle \mathrm{TV}\rangle, \mathrm{TV}\rangle$ (*Reversative Verb*). $F_{\mathrm{W6}}(\alpha) =$ **un** $+ \alpha$.
$k(F_{\mathrm{W6}}(\alpha)) = \lambda\mathscr{P}\lambda x[\mathrm{un}'\hat{}(\alpha')(\mathscr{P})(x)]$.

S^w7. $\langle F_{W7}, \langle TV \rangle, TV \rangle$ (Re-Prefix). $F_{W7}(\alpha) = \mathbf{re} + \alpha$. $k(F_{W7}(\alpha)) = \lambda \mathscr{P} \lambda x [\mathbf{again_2}'\hat{\ }(\alpha')(\mathscr{P})(x)]$.

S^w8. $\langle F^{I}_{W8}, \langle TV \rangle, IV \rangle$ (*Detransitivization*). $k(F_{W8}(\alpha)) = \lambda x [\alpha'(\hat{P} \bigvee y P\{y\})(x)]$.

S^w9. $\langle F^{RC}_{W9}, \langle TV, ADJ \rangle, TV \rangle$ (*Factitives from TV*). $k(F^{RC}_{W9}(\alpha, \beta)) = \lambda \mathscr{P} \lambda x \mathscr{P}\{\hat{y}[\alpha'(x, \hat{P}P\{y\})$ CAUSE BECOME $\beta'(y)]\}$.

S^w10. $\langle F^{RC}_{W10}, \langle IV, ADJ \rangle, TV \rangle$ (*Factitives from IV*). $k(F^{RC}_{W10}(\alpha, \beta)) = \lambda \mathscr{P} \lambda x \mathscr{P}\{\hat{y}[\alpha'(x)$ CAUSE BECOME $\beta'(y)]\}$.

S^w11. $\langle F^{I}_{W11}, \langle CN \rangle, TV \rangle$ (*Denominal Locative*; this may be one of a set of four or more rules, cf. pp. 311–313). $k(F_{W11}(\alpha)) = \lambda \mathscr{P} \lambda x \mathscr{P}\{\hat{y} \bigvee z \bigvee P[\alpha'\{z\} \wedge P\{x\}$ CAUSE BECOME $\mathbf{be\text{-}in}'(y, z)]\}$.

S^w12. $\langle F^{RC}_{W12}, \langle CN, CN \rangle, CN \rangle$ (*Noun-Noun Compounds*, cf. pp. 314–319). $k(F^{RC}_{W12}(\alpha, \beta)) = \lambda x \bigvee P[P\{x\} \wedge \bigvee R[\mathbf{appropriately\text{-}classificatory}'(R) \wedge \bigwedge y[P\{y\} \rightarrow [\beta'(y) \wedge \mathbf{typically}'(\hat{\ }\bigvee z[\alpha'(z) \wedge \check{\ }R(y, z)])]]]]$

S^w13. $\langle F^{I}_{W13}, \langle TV \rangle, \overline{IV} \rangle$ (Relates **Mary kissed John** to **John and Mary kissed**; not really a rule in this fragment[18]). $k(F^{I}_{W13}(\alpha)) = \lambda X \bigwedge x[X(x) \rightarrow \bigvee y[X(y) \wedge \alpha'_*(x, y) \wedge \alpha'_*(y, x)]]$.

7.7.5. *Lexicon*

The meaning postulates, which limit the possible interpretations of certain non-logical constants in all admissible models, are stated first. Each is assigned a number, a descriptive name and sometimes an abbreviated name. In the list of basic expressions which follows this list, the number (or abbreviated name) of a postulate is listed following the translation of each basic expression to which that meaning postulate is to apply. In this way, the list of basic expressions *designates* the value which the meta-variable δ may take in each postulate.

MP1. (*Stative Verbs*; *Stat.*)

$\bigwedge x \Box[\delta(x) \leftrightarrow \bigwedge t[t \subseteq n \rightarrow AT(t, \delta(x))]]$, where δ translates a designated member of B_{IV} or *any* member of B_{CN} or B_{ADJ}.

$\bigwedge x \bigwedge \mathscr{P} \Box[\delta(x, \mathscr{P}) \leftrightarrow \bigwedge t[t \subseteq n \rightarrow AT(t, \delta(x, \mathscr{P}))]]$, where δ translates a designated member of B_{TV}.

MP2. (*Inchoative*, or *Singulary Change Verbs*; *Inch*. These postulates are automatically satisfied by verbs translated with a single BECOME not in the scope of an existential quantifier.)

$\bigvee P \bigwedge x \Box [\delta(x) \leftrightarrow \text{BECOME } P\{x\}]$, where δ translates a designated member of B_{IV}.

$\bigvee P \bigvee Q \bigwedge x \bigwedge \mathscr{P} \Box [\delta(x, \mathscr{P}) \leftrightarrow \mathscr{P}\{\hat{y}[P\{x\} \text{ CAUSE BECOME } Q\{y\}]\}]$, where δ translates a designated member of B_{TV}.

MP3. (*Activity Verbs*; *Act.*)

$\bigvee Q \bigwedge x \Box [\delta(x) \rightarrow [Q\{x\} \text{ AND} \neg Q\{x\}]]$, where δ translates a designated member of B_{IV}.

$\bigvee Q \bigwedge x \bigwedge \mathscr{P} \Box [\delta(x, \mathscr{P}) \rightarrow [Q\{x\} \text{ AND} \neg Q\{x\}]]$, where δ translates a designated member of B_{TV}.

MP4. (*Complex Accomplishments*; *CmAc*; this is automatically satisfied by IV-phrases translated by two or more BECOME operators not in the scope of an existential quantifier. The ellipses in this postulate must be understood to indicate that for each value of δ there is to be a particular finite number of quantifiers and conjuncts for which the postulate holds, though perhaps different numbers for different values of δ.)

$\bigvee Q_1 \bigvee Q_2 \ldots \bigvee Q_n \bigwedge x \bigwedge y \Box [\delta(x, \hat{P}P\{y\}) \leftrightarrow [P\{x\} \text{ CAUSE BECOME } [Q_1\{y\} \text{ AND } Q_2\{y\} \text{ AND} \ldots \text{ AND } Q_n\{y\}]]]$, where δ translates a designated member of B_{TV}.

MP5. (*Extensionality*; *Ext*. This is automatically satisfied by most verbs given a complex translation.)

$\bigvee R \bigwedge \mathscr{P} \bigwedge x \Box [\delta(x, \mathscr{P}) \leftrightarrow \mathscr{P}\{\hat{y}\, {}^{\vee}R(x, y)\}]$, where δ translates a designated member of B_{TV}.

MP6. (*Rigidity* for names; *rgd.*)

$\bigvee x \Box [\delta = x]$, where $\lambda P P\{\delta\}$ translates a designated member of B_T.

MP7. (*Rigidity* for temporal meaning phrases; *rgd.*)

$\bigvee T \Box [\delta = T]$, where T is a variable of type $\langle i, t \rangle$ and δ translates any member of $B_{t/i}$.

MP8. (Interpretation of n, "now".) $\Box[\text{PRES}(n)]$, $n \in Con_i$.

MP9. $\bigwedge P \bigwedge x \Box[\textbf{finish}'(P)(x) \leftrightarrow \bigvee Q_1 \bigvee Q_2 [\Box[P\{x\} \leftrightarrow [Q_1\{x\} \text{ AND } Q_2\{x\}]] \wedge Q_1 \neq Q_2 \wedge Q_2\{x\} \wedge \bigvee t[t < n \wedge \text{AT}(t, Q_1\{x\})]]]$

MP10. $\bigwedge p \bigwedge P \bigwedge Q \bigwedge x \Box[\textbf{by}'(P)(\hat{y}[Q\{y\} \text{ CAUSE } {}^{\vee}p])(x) \rightarrow [P\{x\} \text{ CAUSE } {}^{\vee}p]]$

MP11. (*Internal Adverbs*)

$\bigwedge x \bigwedge P \bigwedge p \Box[\delta_2(\hat{y}[P\{y\} \text{ CAUSE BECOME } {}^{\vee}p])(x) \leftrightarrow [P\{x\} \text{ CAUSE BECOME } \delta_1({}^{\wedge}P\{x\})]]$, where either (1) $\delta_2 = \textbf{again}^2$ and δ_1 translates **again** in t/t, or (2) $\delta_2 = \textbf{un}'$ and δ_1 is $\lambda p[\neg {}^{\vee}p]$.

$\bigwedge x \bigwedge P \bigwedge p \Box[\delta_2(\hat{y}[P\{y\} \text{ CAUSE BECOME } {}^{\vee}p])(x) \leftrightarrow [P\{x\} \text{ CAUSE BECOME } \delta_1(\hat{t}[\text{AT}(t, {}^{\vee}p)])]]$, where either (1) $\delta_2 = \textbf{until}^2 \alpha$ and $\delta_1 = \beta\, \alpha$, where α translates any member of P_{TmAV}[19] and β translates **until** in TmAV/Tm, or (2) $\delta_2 = \textbf{for}^2 \alpha$ and $\delta_1 = \beta\, \alpha$, where α translates any member of $P_{t/i}$ and β translates **for** in TmAV/(t/i).

For convenience, I have listed all basic expressions alphabetically. The order of items in the entries is (1) phonological (or here orthographic) form of the expression, (2) syntactic category, (3) translation, (4) applicable meaning postulate(s) (in case the translation is or contains a non-logical constant), (5) reference to pages of the text where the analysis of this expression is discussed. In the case of lexically derived words, I list instead of a translation the number of the lexical rule by which the transparent reading of the expression is derived (though as noted earlier, most of these derived words do not have *exactly* the meaning specified by the rule). This list thus serves as an index to the words analyzed in this book. Since phonologically "identical" expressions often appear in more than one category, it is useful for purposes of the UG theory to think of a basic expression as an ordered pair consisting of the form of a word and its category (or in the case of "homonyms" of the same category, a form, a category and an index). Such a pair (or triple) would then correspond closely to the linguistic notion of a *lexeme*, (Lyons, 1968, p. 197), while the form alone corresponds to Lyons' *grammatical word*. But I have made no attempt to capture the linguists' distinction between *polysemy* (identical forms with different but "related" senses) and *homophony* (identical forms with "unrelated" senses), and for purposes of model-theoretic semantics, I believe this distinction is not (at present) a useful one anyway (though it may be for purposes of a psychological theory of semantics).

a(n), DET, $\lambda P \lambda Q \bigvee x [P\{x\} \wedge Q\{x\}]$ (PTQ).

again, IV/IV, **again**^{2}, MP11, cf. p. 265.

again, t/t, $\lambda p \bigvee t_1 \bigvee t_2 [\,{}^{\vee}p \wedge t_1 < n \wedge \mathrm{AT}(t_1, \neg {}^{\vee}p) \wedge t_2 < t_1 \wedge \mathrm{AT}(t_2, {}^{\vee}p)]$, cf. p. 261.

an-hour, t/i, **an-hour**$'$, MP7, cf. p. 333.

appoint, TV/CN, $\lambda P \lambda \mathscr{P} \lambda x \mathscr{P}\{\hat{y} \bigvee p [\mathrm{say}'(x, p)$ CAUSE BECOME $P\{y\}]\}$, cf. p. 333.

at, IAV/T, $\lambda \mathscr{P} \lambda P \lambda x \mathscr{P}\{\hat{y} [P\{x\} \wedge \mathbf{be\text{-}at}'(x, y)]\}$.

at-noon, TmAV, $\lambda P_t [P_t\{\mathbf{noon}'\}]$, cf. p. 333.

away from, IAV/T, $\lambda \mathscr{P} \lambda P \lambda x \mathscr{P}\{\hat{y} [P\{x\}$ AND BECOME $[\neg \mathbf{be\text{-}at}'(x, y)])\}$, cf. p. 210.

be$_1$, IV/ADJ, $\lambda P \lambda x [P\{x\}]$. (This is the semantically "vacuous" **be** that appears before predicative adjectives.)

be$_2$, IV/ADJ, **act**$'$. (This is the "active" **be** that appears in **John is being polite**; alternatively, this could be translated as the "agentive" DO of chapters two and three; cf. pp. 115, 185.)

be, TV, $\lambda \mathscr{P} \lambda x \mathscr{P}\{\hat{y} [x = y]\}$ (PTQ).

Bill, T, $\lambda P[P\{b\}]$, *rgd.* (PTQ).

book, CN, **book**$'$.

box, CN, **box**$'$.

box, TV, from S^w11.

break, IV, **break**$'$, *Inch*.

break, TV, from S^w3.

breakable, ADJ, from S^w1.

by, (IV/IV)/GER, **by**$'$, MP10.

can, (t/T)/IV, **can**$'$.

can't, (t/T)/IV, $\lambda P \lambda \mathscr{P}[\neg \mathbf{can}'(P)(\mathscr{P})]$, cf. p. 348.

changeable, ADJ, λx[**typically**$^\wedge$(**change**$'(x)$)] (i.e. *not* derived by S^w1).

Christmas, Tm, $\lambda P_t[P_t\{$**Xmas**$'\}]$.

Christmas, TmAV, $\lambda P_t[P_t\{$**Xmas**$'\}]$.

cool, ADJ, **cool**$'$.

cool, IV, from S^w2.

cool, TV, from S^w3.

die, IV, λx[BECOME$\neg$**alive**$'(x)$], cf. p. 201.

drink silly, TV, from S^w10.

eat, IV, from S^w8, *Ext. ComplAcc.*

every, DET, $\lambda P\lambda Q\bigwedge x[P\{x\} \to Q\{x\}]$ (PTQ).

find, TV, *Ext. Inch.* (Approximate meanings seem to be $\lambda\mathscr{P}\lambda x\mathscr{P}\{\hat{y}\bigvee z$[**place**$'(z)$ $\wedge$ BECOME [**know**$'(x, {}^\wedge$[**be-at**$'(y,z)$])]]} and $\lambda\mathscr{P}\lambda x\mathscr{P}\{\hat{y}$[BECOME [**know**$'(x, {}^\wedge$[**exist**$'(y)$])]]}, the former exhibited in **John found his book**, the latter in **John found a solution to the problem**.)

finish, IV/GER, **finish**$'$, MP9.

for$_1$, (IV/IV)/(t/i), $\lambda P_t\lambda P\lambda x[P_t\{n\} \wedge \bigwedge t[t \subseteq n \to \mathrm{AT}(t, P\{x\})]]$, cf. p. 333.

for$_2$, (IV/IV)/(t/i), **for**^{2}, MP11, cf. p. 363.

for, TmAV/(t/i), $\lambda P_t\lambda Q_t\bigvee t_1[\mathrm{XN}(t_1) \wedge P_t\{t_1\} \wedge \bigwedge t_2[[t_2 \subseteq t_1 \wedge \mathrm{XN}(t_2)] \to Q_t\{t_2\}]]$, cf. p. 344.

from, IAV/T, $\lambda\mathscr{P}\lambda P\lambda x\mathscr{P}\{\hat{y}[P\{x\}$ AND BECOME $\neg$**be-at**$'(x,y)]\}$, cf. p. 214.

from, ((TV/TV)/(TV/TV))/T, $\lambda\mathscr{P}\lambda\mathscr{G}\lambda\mathscr{R}\lambda\mathscr{Q}\lambda x\mathscr{P}\{\hat{y}\mathscr{Q}\{\hat{z}[{}^\vee\mathscr{G}(\mathscr{R})(\hat{P}P\{z\})(x)$ AND $[{}^\vee\mathscr{R}(\hat{P}P\{z\})(x)$ CAUSE BECOME $\neg$**be-at**$'(z,y)]]\}\}$, cf. p. 216.

give, TV/T, **give**$'$.

hammer flat, TV, from S^w9, p. 219–221.

have, TV/ADJ, $\lambda P\lambda\mathscr{P}\lambda x\mathscr{P}\{\hat{y}\bigvee Q[Q\{x\}$ CAUSE BECOME $P\{y\}]\}$, cf. p. 227.

have, TV/IV, $\lambda P\lambda\mathscr{P}\lambda x\mathscr{P}\{\hat{y}$[**direct**$'_*(x,y)$ CAUSE $P\{y\}]\}$, cf. p. 227.

have, TV/GER, $\lambda P\lambda\mathscr{P}\lambda x\mathscr{P}\{\hat{y}\bigvee Q[Q\{x\}$ CAUSE PROG $P\{y\}]\}$, cf. p. 227.

in, IAV/T, $\lambda\mathscr{P}\lambda P\lambda x\mathscr{P}\{\hat{y}[P\{x\} \wedge$ **be-in**$'(x,y)]\}$.

in, (IV/IV)/(t/i), $\lambda P_t \lambda P \lambda x [P_t\{n\} \wedge \bigvee t_1 [t_1 \subseteq n \wedge \mathrm{AT}(t_1, P\{x\}) \wedge \bigwedge t_2 [[t_2 \subseteq n \wedge \mathrm{AT}(t_2, P\{x\})] \rightarrow t_2 = t_1]]]$, cf. p. 335.

in, TmAV/(t/i), $\lambda P_t \lambda Q_t t_1 [P_t\{t_1\} \wedge \bigvee t_2 [t_2 \subseteq t_1 \wedge Q_t\{t_2\} \wedge \bigwedge t_3 [[t_3 \subseteq t_1 \wedge Q_t\{t_3\}] \rightarrow t_3 = t_2]]]$, cf. p. 346.

into, IAV/T, $\lambda \mathscr{P} \lambda P \lambda x \mathscr{P}\{\hat{y} [P\{x\}$ AND BECOME **be-in**$'(x, y)]\}$, cf. p. 210.

John, T, $\lambda P[P\{j\}]$, *rgd.* (PTQ).

kill, TV, $\lambda \mathscr{P} \lambda x \mathscr{P}\{\hat{y} \bigvee P[P\{x\}$ CAUSE BECOME $\neg$**alive**$'(y)]\}$, cf. p. 202.

leave, IV, *Inch.*

love, TV, **love**$'$, *Ext. Stat.*

make, TV, $\lambda \mathscr{P} \lambda x \mathscr{P}\{\hat{y} \bigvee P[P\{x\}$ CAUSE **exist**$'(y)]\}$, cf. p. 223.

make, TV/ADJ, $\lambda P \lambda \mathscr{P} \lambda x \mathscr{P}\{\hat{y} \bigvee Q[Q\{x\}$ CAUSE BECOME $P\{y\}]\}$, cf. p. 223.

make, TV/IV, $\lambda P \lambda \mathscr{P} \lambda x \mathscr{P}\{\hat{y} \bigvee Q[Q\{x\}$ CAUSE $P\{y\}]\}$, cf. p. 225.

Mary, T, $\lambda P[P\{m\}]$, *rgd.* (PTQ).

must, (t/T)/IV, **must**$'$.

mustn't, (t/T)/IV, $\lambda P \lambda \mathscr{P}[$**must**$'(\hat{x} \neg P\{x\})(\mathscr{P})]$, cf. p. 348.

necessarily, t/t, $\lambda p \Box {}^{\vee}p$ (PTQ).

now, TmAV, $\lambda P_t [P_t\{n\}]$, MP8.

off-of, IAV/T, $\lambda \mathscr{P} \lambda P \lambda x \mathscr{P}\{\hat{y} [P\{x\}$ AND BECOME $\neg$**be-on**$'(x,y)]\}$, cf. p. 210.

on, IAV/T, $\lambda \mathscr{P} \lambda P \lambda x \mathscr{P}\{\hat{y} [P\{x\} \wedge$ **be-on**$'(x, y)]\}$.

on, TmAV/Tm, $\lambda \mathscr{P}_t \lambda P_t \mathscr{P}_t\{\hat{t}_1 \bigvee t_2 [t_2 \subseteq t_1 \wedge P_t\{t_2\}]\}$.

open, ADJ, **open**$'$.

open, IV, from S^w2.

open, TV, from S^w3.

out-of, IAV/T, $\lambda \mathscr{P} \lambda P \lambda x \mathscr{P}\{\hat{y} [P\{x\}$ AND BECOME $\neg$**be-in**$'(x, y)]\}$, cf. p. 210.

owe, TV/T, $\lambda \mathscr{P} \lambda \mathscr{Q} \lambda x$ **obligated**$'({}^{\wedge}[$**give**$'(\mathscr{P})(\mathscr{Q})])(x)$, where **obligated**$' \in \mathrm{ME}_{\langle f(\mathrm{IV/IV}) \rangle}$.

owe, (TV/T)/TmAV, $\lambda \mathscr{P}_t \lambda \mathscr{P} \lambda \mathscr{Q} \lambda x [$**obligated**$'(\hat{z} \mathscr{P}_t\{\hat{t}\, \mathrm{AT}(t,$ **give**$'(\mathscr{P})(\mathscr{Q})(z))\})(x)]$ where **obligated**$' \in \mathrm{ME}_{\langle f(\mathrm{IV/IV}) \rangle}$, cf. p. 270.

promise, (IV/INF)/T, **promise**′.

promise, TV/T, $\lambda\mathcal{P}\lambda\mathcal{Q}\lambda x\mathcal{P}\{\hat{y}\,\mathbf{promise}'(\hat{P}P\{y\})({}^{\wedge}\mathbf{give}'(\hat{P}P\{y\})(\mathcal{Q}))(x)\}$.

promise, (TV/T)/TmAV, $\lambda\mathcal{P}_t\lambda\mathcal{P}\lambda\mathcal{Q}\lambda x\mathcal{P}\{\hat{y}\,\mathbf{promise}'(\hat{P}P\{y\})(\hat{z}\,\mathcal{P}_t\{\hat{t}\,\mathrm{AT}(t, \mathbf{give}'(\hat{P}P\{y\})(\mathcal{Q})(z))\})(x)\}$.

put, TV/(TV/TV), $\lambda\mathcal{G}\lambda\mathcal{P}\lambda x\bigvee\mathcal{R}\,[\mathcal{G}\,(\mathcal{R})(\mathcal{P})(x)]$, cf. p. 217.

randomize, TV, S^w4.

readable, AD̀J, from S^w1, though not quite a transparent extension, cf. p. 305.

seek, TV, $\lambda\mathcal{P}\lambda x\,[\mathbf{try}'({}^{\wedge}[\mathbf{find}'(\mathcal{P})])(x)]$ (PTQ).

send, TV/(TV/TV), $\lambda\mathcal{G}\lambda\mathcal{P}\lambda x\bigvee p\bigvee P[[P\{x\}\ \mathrm{CAUSE}\ {}^{\vee}p] \wedge \mathbf{intend}'(x, {}^{\wedge}\bigvee y\bigvee\mathcal{R}[{}^{\vee}p\ \mathrm{CAUSE}\ {}^{\vee}\mathcal{G}\,(\mathcal{R})(\mathcal{P})(y)])]$, cf. p. 192. (Here **intend**′ translates **intend** in IV/t, not **intend** in IV/INF.)

shake awake, TV, from S^w9.

shoot dead, TV, from S^w9.

since, TmAV/Tm, $\lambda\mathcal{P}_t\lambda P_t\mathcal{P}_t\{\hat{t}\bigwedge t_2\,[[t_1 < t_2 \wedge \mathrm{XN}(t_2)] \rightarrow P_t\{t_2\}]\}$, cf. p. 344.

six-weeks, t/i, **six-weeks**′, MP7, cf. p. 333.

the, DET, $\lambda P\lambda Q\bigvee x\,[\bigwedge y\ [P\{y\} \leftrightarrow x = y] \wedge Q\{x\}]$ (PTQ).

Thursday, Tm, $\lambda P_t\,[P_t\{\mathbf{Thursday}'\}]$.

Thursday, TmAV, $\lambda P_t\bigvee t\,[t \subseteq \mathbf{Thursday}' \wedge P_t\{t\}]$.

to, IAV/T, $\lambda\mathcal{P}\lambda P\lambda x\mathcal{P}\{\hat{y}\,[P\{x\}\ \mathrm{AND\ BECOME}\ \mathbf{be\text{-}at}'(x, y)]\}$, cf. p. 210.

today, TmAV, $\lambda P_t\bigvee t\,[t \subseteq \mathbf{today}' \wedge P_t\{t\}]$, cf. p. 328.

unhappy, ADJ, from S^w5.

until$_2$, (IV/IV)/TmAV, **until**^{2}, MP11.

until, TmAV/Tm, $\lambda\mathcal{P}_t\lambda P_t\mathcal{P}_t\{\hat{t}_1\bigwedge t_2\,[n \leqslant t_2 < t_1 \rightarrow P_t\{t_2\}]\}$.

want, IV/INF, **want**′.[20]

want, TV, $\lambda\mathcal{P}\lambda x\,[\mathbf{want}'({}^{\wedge}[\mathbf{have}'(\mathcal{P})])(x)]$, cf. p. 269.

want, TV/TmAV, $\lambda\mathcal{P}_t\lambda\mathcal{P}\lambda x\,[\mathbf{want}'(\hat{y}\,\mathcal{P}_t\{\hat{t}\,\mathrm{AT}(t, \mathbf{have}'(y, \mathcal{P}))\})(x)]$.

washable, ADJ, from S^w1.

will, (t/T)/IV, **is-willing-to′**, cf. p. 372, note 9.

won't, (t/T)/IV, $\lambda P \lambda \mathscr{P} \neg$**is-willing-to′**$(P)(\mathscr{P})$.

wipe clean, TV, from $S^{w}9$.

yesterday, TmAV, $\lambda P_t \vee t\,[t \subseteq$ **yesterday′** $\wedge\, P_t\{t\}]$, cf. p. 328.

7.7.6. *Examples*

As examples of sentences of the fragment have already been introduced for syntactically complex accomplishments (Chapter 4) and tense and time adverbials (Section 7.2–7.5), I include only three examples here: two which illustrate the combination of the internal readings of adverbs discussed in chapter five with the explicit semantics of adverbials from this chapter, and one example which illustrates the futurate progressive. The reader may wish to construct additional examples and translations from the fragment for other more complex tenses (e.g. past perfect, future perfect, past and future perfect progressive, etc.) with various kinds of verb phrases, but I believe these examples will all be routine and will receive the expected semantics.

(32) **John put a book into a box until$_2$ Christmas yesterday**, t, 36

yesterday, TmAV **John puts a book into a box until$_2$ Christmas**, t, 4

John, T **put a book into a box until$_2$ Christmas**, IV, 10

until$_2$ Christmas, IV/IV, 53 **put a book into a box**, IV, 5

until$_2$, (IV/IV)/TmAV **Christmas**, TmAV **put into a box**, TV, 29 **a book**, T, 2

put, TV/(TV/TV) **into a box**, TV/TV, 28 **book**, CN

into, (TV/TV)/T, 25 **a box**, T, 2

into, (IV/IV)/T **box**, CN

For clarity, I give the translation of (32) in stages:

k(**into a box**) =

$$\lambda \mathscr{R} \lambda \mathscr{P} \lambda x \mathscr{P}\{\hat{y} \vee z\,[\textbf{box}'(z) \wedge [\,{}^{\vee}\mathscr{R}(x, \hat{P}P\{y\}) \text{ CAUSE BECOME } \textbf{be-in}'(y, z)]]\}\cdot$$

k(**put a book into a box**) =

$$\lambda x \vee \mathscr{R}[\vee y\,[\textbf{book}'(y) \wedge \vee z\,[\textbf{box}'(z) \wedge [\,{}^{\vee}\mathscr{R}(x, \hat{P}P\{y\}) \text{ CAUSE BECOME } \textbf{be-in}'(y, z)]]]]$$

k(**until$_2$ Christmas**) = $\mathbf{until}^2(\hat{P}P\{\mathbf{Xmas}'\})$

By MP11, k(**put a book into a box until$_2$ Christmas**) is logically equivalent to:

$$\lambda x \bigvee y[\mathbf{book}'(y) \wedge \bigvee \mathscr{R} \bigvee z[\mathbf{box}'(z) \wedge [\,{}^{\vee}\mathscr{R}(x, \hat{P}P\{y\})\ \mathrm{CAUSE}\ \mathrm{BECOME}\ k(\mathbf{until\ Christmas})(\hat{t}\,[\mathrm{AT}(t, \mathbf{be\text{-}in}'(y, z))])]]]$$

The expression **until Christmas**, whose translation is referred to in this formula, is the phrase of category TmAV that corresponds to the homophonous expression in IV/IV according to MP11. Since k(**until Christmas**) = $\lambda P_t \bigwedge t[n \leqslant t < \mathbf{Xmas}' \rightarrow \mathrm{AT}(t, P_t\{t\})]$, the above formula is further spelled out, with lambda conversion and AT-elimination, as

$$\lambda x \bigvee \mathscr{R} \bigvee y[\mathbf{book}'(y) \wedge \bigvee z[\mathbf{box}'(z) \wedge [\,{}^{\vee}\mathscr{R}(x, \hat{P}P\{y\})\ \mathrm{CAUSE}\ \mathrm{BECOME}\ \bigwedge t[n \leqslant t < \mathbf{Xmas}' \rightarrow \mathrm{AT}(t, \mathbf{be\text{-}in}'(y, z))]])]]]$$

Finally, $k(32)$ =

$$\bigvee t_1\,[t_1 \subseteq \mathbf{yesterday}' \wedge \mathrm{PAST}(t_1) \wedge \mathrm{AT}(t_1, \bigvee \mathscr{R} \bigvee y[\mathbf{book}'(y) \wedge \bigvee z[\mathbf{box}'(z) \wedge [\,{}^{\vee}\mathscr{R}(j, \hat{P}P\{y\})\ \mathrm{CAUSE}\ \mathrm{BECOME}\ \bigwedge t_2\,[n \leqslant t_2 < \mathbf{Xmas}' \rightarrow \mathrm{AT}(t_2', \mathbf{be\text{-}in}'(y, z))]]]]])]$$

This translation should be examined carefully to see that it does in fact represent the internal reading of the adverb in the correct way. Note that the indexical constant n is within the scope of BECOME. Since the BECOME-sentence will be true at the interval at which its embedded sentence changes from being false to being true, this interval must contain the first moment at which n takes as value a time at which the book is in the box. Though this embedded sentence is also true at intervals at which n includes later moments in its value, the requirement that a BECOME sentence must only be true at the *smallest* appropriate interval rules these possibilities out. Thus the CAUSE sentence will be true at the smallest interval stretching from the time of John's action to the first moment at which the book is in the box. This explains how the CAUSE sentence itself can be true at a past time, even though the time that its result-state lasts, as indicated by the internal adverb, extends into the future.

Example (33) will have an analysis tree similar to (32) and will have (33′) as its (reduced) translation:

(33) **John put a book into a box for six weeks yesterday**

(33′) $\bigvee t_1\,[t_1 \subseteq \mathbf{yesterday}' \wedge \mathrm{PAST}(t_1) \wedge \mathrm{AT}(t_1, \bigvee \mathscr{R} \bigvee y[\mathbf{book}'(y) \wedge \bigvee z[\mathbf{box}'(z) \wedge [\,{}^{\vee}\mathscr{R}(j, \hat{P}P\{y\})\ \mathrm{CAUSE}\ \mathrm{BECOME}\ \bigvee t_2\,[\mathrm{XN}(t_2) \wedge \mathbf{six\text{-}weeks}'(t_2) \wedge \bigwedge t_3\,[[t_3 \subseteq t_2 \wedge \mathrm{XN}(t_3)] \rightarrow \mathbf{be\text{-}in}'(y, z)]]]]])]$

Here again, note that the two XN predicates are within the scope of BECOME. It turns out here that the only appropriate value for t_2 will be exactly the first six-week interval throughout which the book remains in the box. Moreover, this interval must also be the interval at which the whole sentence just within the scope of BECOME is taken to be true (call this interval k). (The definition of XN allows an interval to be an Extended Now for itself, which is the case here.) Though this embedded sentence itself could also be made true by selecting a proper final subinterval for t_2 as the value for k, the "minimal interval" condition on BECOME rules this out: to make this sentence within the scope of BECOME false, we must go back to an interval containing a time at which the book was not in the box, for only then is there no satisfactory value of t_2 that is an Extended Now. But now the BECOME sentence itself is true at an interval stretching from the last moment of book-not-in-box to the first moment of our chosen k. To reduce the size of the interval for the BECOME sentence maximally, we must select k as equal to t_2. Also, if the book remained in the box longer than six weeks (a possibility which is only conversationally ruled out by (33)), we cannot select some later six-week period as the value for t_2 because of the minimal interval condition on BECOME. Because of the second XN predicate, the only appropriate value for t_3 will also be equal to t_2 and to k, but this is acceptable because **be-in** is a stative predicate and will have to be true at all moments within t_2 if it is true at t_2 anyway. (Needless to say, all this could be made much simpler if some other way of treating preposable **for**-phrases successfully could be found.)

Example (34) illustrates the futurate progressive (combination of the progressive with the tenseless future):

(34) **John was leaving on Thursday yesterday**, t, 36

- **yesterday**, TmAV
- **John is leaving on Thursday**, t, 4
  - **John**, T
  - **be leaving on Thursday**, IV, 43
    - **leave on Thursday**, IV, 44
      - **on Thursday**, TmAV, 48
        - **on**, TmAV/Tm
        - **Thursday**, Tm
      - **leave**, IV

(34′) $k(34) = \bigvee t_1\,[\mathrm{PAST}(t_1) \wedge t_1 \subseteq \mathbf{yesterday}' \wedge \mathrm{AT}(t_1,$
$\mathrm{PROG}[\bigvee t_2\,[\mathrm{PAST}(t_2) \wedge \mathrm{AT}(t_2, \mathbf{predetermined}'(\hat{}\bigvee t_3\,[t_3 \subseteq$
$\mathbf{Thursday}' \wedge \mathrm{FUT}(t_3) \wedge \mathrm{AT}(t_3, \mathbf{leave}'(j))]))]])]$

The intuitive significance of this kind of translation and the distinction between it and the translation of **John left on Thursday yesterday** was discussed on pp. 157–163. (A potential problem that I will not attempt to deal with here is the reference of indexical temporal adverbs that appear as internal adverbs. For example, we want **tomorrow** in **Yesterday John was leaving tomorrow** to refer to a time during the day after the speech time, not the day after yesterday. The desired reading could be produced by a quantifying-in rule for TmAV, but ultimately the better solution might be given by the method described in Kamp (1971).)

NOTES

[1] A peculiar consequence of this treatment is that **John is here now, John is here today, John is here this week,** etc. will all come out logically equivalent, since there is exactly one present moment that satisfies each of these adverbials (or any other present adverbial). But I don't think this is necessarily a bad result. Rather, I think because of this equivalence we do not even notice the "ordinary" readings that would be produced by S37 (given below) for these sentences (in which the adverbial is totally redundant) but notice only some "extraordinary" reading: either a historical present reading, a tenseless future reading (e.g. John's being here this week is part of his schedule) or possibly a "generic" reading as described in Carlson (1977) (e.g. John-stages seem to be here at enough times within this week to make it "generically" true that he is here all week, even if he is not here at this moment). I have no idea how to treat temporal adverbials for generic readings (if there are such), but the tenseless future readings of these sentences are produced by the fragment.

[2] Actually, there is a defect in the Karttunen–Peters system which would become quite significant in the treatment of tense given below. The Karttunen–Peters system does not allow a quantifier to bind the "same" variable in both the "assertion" and the implicature of an expression (cf. appendix to Karttunen and Peters (to appear)), yet this possibility is apparently needed for the proper treatment of conventional implicature in the rules I give, as well as for other cases. Though I believe an adequate solution to this problem can be found, I am not yet prepared to demonstrate exactly how this is to be done.

[3] Even with this category distinction, there are still details that cannot be captured: no matter how items are assigned to categories, there is no way to produce both **until noon** and **until tomorrow** without also producing ***until at noon, *until on Thursday,** etc. Perhaps the best means for handling these problems will turn out not to involve a category distinction between Tm and TmAV at all. There are other syntactic problems with these expressions that I cannot go into here. For example, how does one capture the fact that days require **on** as their temporal preposition (**on Thursday**, **on the day after Christmas**) but both shorter and longer intervals require **in** (**in the afternoon, in the first week of June, in July, in 1942**), given that there is no apparent semantic distinction in the way **in** and **on** function here?

[4] Expressions like **noon′** and **Thursday′** are of course indexical names, not rigid designators. This can be seen in **John frequently arrived on Thursday**, one reading of which involves different Thursdays.

[5] A detail which I will ignore is that the present tense ending must be removed when the future **will** is inserted. An alternative would be to dispense with the regular subject-predicate rule (S4 in PTQ) entirely and make all tense-inserting rules rules which combine the subject with predicate as they insert tense (and time adverbial). See also footnote 9 on **will**.

[6] Though this would appear to contradict the claim made in Chapter 5 that the "ordinary" durative reading (but not the interval reading) of **for an hour** arises when **for an hour** is a sentence adverbial, it later turns out to be necessary to postulate another **for**-adverbial in TmAV; this adverb in TmAV but not the one in IV/IV is preposable, and this analysis is consistent with Chapter 5.

[7] Perhaps measure phrases like **six weeks**, **one hour**, etc. should be rigid designators, denoting the same set of intervals at all times in all possible worlds, as Kripke (1972, pp. 273–276) argues for the measure phrases **one meter** and **100° Centigrade**. But note that **day** and **year** are sometimes used indexically by astronomers, e.g. "earth days" or "Mars days" depending on the planet under discussion.

[8] Logical equivalences for a simple system of tense logic having the equivalent of my AT and n are discussed by Rescher and Urquhart (1971, pp. 31–35).

[9] This means we will not capture the generalization that the **will** inserted by the future tense rule behaves just like a modal auxiliary. However, there appears to be a second **will** in English (whose meaning is "willing to") that will be treated as a modal. As noted in Chapter 3, note 7, the only syntactic environment that reliably distinguishes the two **will**'s seems to be *if*-clauses, where only the "willing" **will** occurs.

Another difficulty is that my rules will not be able to account for a Main Tense Adverbial within an infinitive (e.g. **Today John prefers to leave tomorrow**), since Main Tense Adverbials are inserted in sentences, not in IVs. Should no better solution come to light, such examples can be treated by adding a rule that forms a tensed infinitive from an IV α and a TmAV β (e.g. **to leave tomorrow** from **leave** and **tomorrow**), which would have the translation $\lambda x \beta'(\hat{t}[\mathrm{AT}(t, \alpha'(x))])$.

[10] Some linguists have also argued against the derivation of (subjectless) infinitive complements from complete sentences recently, cf. Brame (1976), Bresnan (1978).

[11] Yet another possible translation for the progressive rule in the system that uses t/T for verb phrases is $\lambda \mathscr{P} \mathscr{P}\{\hat{x}[\mathrm{PROG}\, \alpha'(\hat{P}[P\{x\}])]\}$; this would allow non-progressive verb phrases to have de dicto readings for their subjects but make progressive IV's always extensional. This might in fact be correct (though I find the judgments very difficult), because **A Republican is seeming (more and more) certain to win** seems much more likely to be extensional than **A Republican seems certain to win**, and likewise **A midget is being sought by the casting director** seems "more" extensional than **A midget is sought (needed) by the casting director.**

[12] We would have to argue along the following lines. Suppose, for example, (*)**John is having solved the problem** is really grammatical but is not used for semantic/pragmatic reasons. Why might this be the case? By Taylor's principle (the progressive should be used only when the embedded phrase is true at an interval containing the current moment but not at the current moment itself), this sentence should not be used if **John has solved the problem** is already true. If (*)**John is having solved the problem** is nevertheless

true, then this leaves us with only the possibilities that John is still solving the problem or that he has not yet started (though he will eventually solve it in all inertia worlds). If the speaker knows that **John is solving the problem** is true, then he should of course say this rather than the longer sentence. But if he doesn't know that this is the case (or believes that John will later start and finish the problem in all inertia worlds), I am at a loss to see exactly why the "ungrammatical" sentence should not occur. It is easier to see why (*)**John is being solving the problem** should not occur, since it follows semantically that if PROG[PROG ϕ] is true, then PROG ϕ is also true, and this violates Taylor's principle. On the other hand, ***John has had solved the problem** would be no more informative than **John has solved the problem** and could be ruled out for this reason; the "past of a past" is only informative when a relevant intermediate past point can be identified (or at least conventionally implied to exist), and only by using the past perfect (i.e. the past of a perfect) can this be done, not by the iteration of the perfect.

[13] Informants I have questioned do not judge this to be as bad as (16b), though they still maintain they would not say it; some report having heard such examples and associate it with a colloquial or slightly non-standard dialect.

[14] Note that this treatment literally validates Vendler's (1967) claim that one can say **I have seen it** as soon as one can say **I see it**. I am not inclined to place too much emphasis on this fact, however, because reacting to a visual stimulus and then uttering a sentence take at least a bit of time, so one might argue that for this reason alone one is only in a position to warrantably assert **I see it** at a time at which it is also true that **I have seen it**. The Extended Now theory of the perfect also predicts that **I have seen it** should be true at least one moment sooner than **I saw it**. Suppose someone at a party asks you **Have you seen John**? and at the very moment you have comprehended the question, you spot John for the first time behind the speaker's back. The Extended Now theory predicts that you can truthfully answer "yes", though you would not have been able to answer "yes" if the question had been **Did you see John**? (with no "indexical" past time intended). This may in fact be correct, though I find it hard to say.

[15] As McCoard (1978, pp. 135–136) notes, "past" adverbs like **yesterday** do occur with the present perfect when they are conjoined with other adverbs, cf. *I have tried to call him yesterday, last night, and today, but with no success*. I suspect that the explanation of this fact involves something like Cresswell's (1977) AND. That is, the adverbs when conjoined together denote an interval stretching at least from the earliest to the latest time mentioned by the individual adverbs, and this interval somehow qualifies as an Extended Now.

[16] As mentioned earlier, I have dispensed with Montague's awkward use of individual concepts as members of the extensions of IV and CN in favor of individuals.

[17] Here "Verb" must be taken to include not only the members of B_{IV}, B_{TV}, $B_{IV/t}$, $B_{IV/ADJ}$, etc. but also modals (members of $B_{(t/T)/IV}$) and the auxiliary verbs **have** and **be** introduced syncategorematically by the tense rules. In a more linguistically adequate but more complex fragment, syntactic categories could be treated as ordered pairs consisting of a morphological category (Verb, Noun, Adjective or Particle) and a logical type, or perhaps the first member of the pair would instead be a complex of syntactic features (as in *Aspects* (Chomsky, 1965), or in "X-Bar" Notation (Jackendoff, 1977); see also Bach, 1977). Basic expressions could then be treated as "labeled" with their appropriate category, and syncategorematically introduced material like **have** and

be could likewise be given such labels. Informal notions such as "Verb" that appear in the rules here could then be replaced with an explicit and systematic reference to expressions with any one of a certain set of these labels.

[18] This cannot be a rule in this fragment because it turns a TV into a predicate of sets, a category which I have symbolized $\overline{\text{IV}}$ (cf. Bennett, 1974), though it does not appear in this fragment. The translation (which uses X as a variable over sets) gives a predicate that is true of a set just in case every member of the set is symmetrically related to some other member of the set by the original TV α. This rule can thus have the effect of turning an asymmetric predicate into (a kind of) symmetric one, and this accounts for the difference in meaning between **John kissed Mary** and **John and Mary kissed**. That this rule should not say anything specifically about "agency" specifically is shown by the fact that a semantic asymmetry shows up between **The truck collided with the lamppost** and **The truck and the lamppost collided** just as with **kiss**, though here the entailment that becomes "symmetric" in the second sentence is that the individual is in motion (thus the second sentence entails that the lamppost as well as the truck was in motion). The rule S^W13 treats **kiss** and **collide** exactly alike. The observation about **collide** does not mean that the data involving **kiss** fails to be structuralist linguistic evidence for the notion of "agency", but it does show that there is a more general phenomenon at work here (namely S^W13) than the analysis of the **kiss** data in chapter two would imply.

[19] This postulate violates the traditional form of Montague's meaning postulates since α is here allowed to range over *phrases* over a certain category, rather than merely basic expressions. The postulate can be cast in the official form if separate postulates are given for **for** and **until**.

[20] In a more complete fragment, the verb **want** in IV/INF should be derived from an even more basic verb **want** in TV/INF; see Dowty (1978a) for the rule that accomplishes this.

CHAPTER 8

INTENSIONS AND PSYCHOLOGICAL REALITY

Contemporary linguists, unlike many contemporary philosophers of language, almost invariably profess to be concerned with the "psychological reality" of the theoretical concepts they postulate in semantic analysis. One linguist, Charles Fillmore, has gone so far as to propose (1974) that "issues in semantics that have no conceivable application to the process of comprehension cannot be very important for semantic theory", and he suggests this as a "relevance test" for evaluating research in semantics. Now that a class of analyses of word meanings has been proposed for the purpose of capturing a large and important class of entailments of these words (and, motivated to a greater or less extent, to describe "structural" linguistic relations among words as well), it is time to turn to the question of what the model-theoretic notion of *intension* in general has to do with "psychological reality", and what if anything these analyses in particular have to do with this notion.

To get to the point right away, let me confess that I believe that the model-theoretic intension of a word has in principle *nothing whatsoever* to do with what goes on in a person's head when he uses that word. But I will nevertheless try to show why this notion of intension is just as fundamental and indispensible a concept from the point of view of "psychological semantics" as it is from any other reasonable view of what the goal of natural language semantics is supposed to be.

The traditional justification for the model-theoretic treatment of a proposition (set of possible worlds) as the meaning of a sentence is always something more or less like the following discussion from Cresswell (1973, p. 23).

> If we think for a moment of the job a proposition has to do we see that it must be something which can be true or false, not only in the actual world but in each possible world. Suppose for the moment that we could 'shew' a person all possible worlds in turn. This of course is impossible, but try to imagine it anyway. We want to know whether two people are thinking of the same proposition. So we ask them, as we shew them each (complete) possible world, 'Would the proposition you are thinking of be true if that was the way things were?' If their answers agree for every possible world there is at least the temptation to suppose that they have the same proposition in mind. Or to put it in another way, if the set of worlds to which *A* says 'yes' is the same as the set of worlds to which *B* says 'yes' we can say that *A* and *B* have the same proposition in mind. So why not simply identify the proposition with the set of worlds in question? As a first approximation therefore we shall say that a proposition is a set of possible worlds.[1]

(Similar "tests" could be constructed for determining whether two individuals have the same property, individual concept, relation-in-intension, etc. in mind.)

Now even if it were true that understanding a sentence gives one the ability to carry out this task appropriately (though I will argue in a moment that it probably does not in most cases), this view tells us nothing whatsoever about *how* a person is able to distinguish the proposition in question. It seems abundantly clear that a person does not in any sense "visualize" or "imagine" a set of possible worlds (an enormously large if not infinite one) whenever he understands or utters a sentence, and one may reasonably doubt whether sets of possible worlds have anything at all to do with the psychological process of sentence comprehension. I believe there is no sense in which a person mentally has access to "all the possible worlds that there are", as would be required by this view in the case where a logically true proposition is comprehended.

The most reasonable answer to this dilemma is, I believe, the one given by Hilary Putnam in a series of recent articles, particularly in the chapter "Reference and Understanding" in Putnam (1978). The problem, according to Putnam, is that the task of giving an account of *language understanding* has been confused with the task of giving an account of what he calls *language success*. Explaining what goes on in people's heads is of course what Putnam means by a theory of language understanding, and a theory of truth and reference is what Putnam says explains language success, or to be more exact, "not the success or failure of our linguistic behaviour, but rather the *contribution* of our linguistic behavior to the success of our total behavior" (Putnam, 1978, p. 101). What Putnam means by *success* can perhaps best be appreciated by the following story. Suppose earth is visited by a group of intelligent, non-human anthropologists from outer space who are bent on studying the human inhabitants of this planet. Suppose also that they have no language but instead communicate by mental telepathy (or better yet, that because of their telepathic abilities they have a kind of collective consciousness, so that the whole notion of "communication" between distinct sentient beings is foreign to them). What do they notice about us? A most striking characteristic of humans from their point of view is the way that the noises humans make with their vocal tracts play a role in the way they interact with their environment and with each other. It seems that these noises are crucially involved in the way that humans enable each other to benefit from their individual experiences and the way they organize themselves to do things like build bridges, grow crops, form social organizations and so on. An explanation of the remarkable success with which they do this is, from the alien anthropologists' point of view, the novel theory that there is a systematic correspondence between particular utterances on the one hand and particular objects and situations on the other, a correspondence which is reflected in the utterances of all members of a speech community. Whatever it is that goes on in people's heads when they speak, it relies on and exploits the correspondence in order to "work" to their benefit.

Explaining natural language understanding is quite a different matter in Putnam's view. The account he discusses (which he attributes to Carnap and Reichenbach) involves a model of a speaker/hearer as possessing an inductive logic, a deductive logic, a preference ordering, and a rule of action (e.g. 'maximize the estimated utility'), but it does not involve any correspondence between language and the world or other definition of *truth*. Putnam's main point is that *both* a theory of correspondence and a theory of understanding will be needed to explain the whole phenomenon of what is usually called "meaning" in natural language; either by itself is only part of the story. (See Putnam (1978) for further elaboration of this idea.)

If Putnam's view of these issues is correct, then possible worlds semantics on the one hand and most linguistic theories of semantics on the other (which seem to be conceived as theories of understanding in Putnam's sense) should not be taken as *competing* explanations of the same phenomenon but rather as *complementary* theories of distinct though related phenomena. (Possibly the most useful research in the theory of understanding will turn out to be experimental work by computer scientists, cf. e.g. Woods, 1970; Winograd, 1972; Charniak and Wilks, 1976; Cooper, 1978).

Perhaps it will be useful to try to visualize the relationship between these two complementary theories in terms of a triangular diagram:

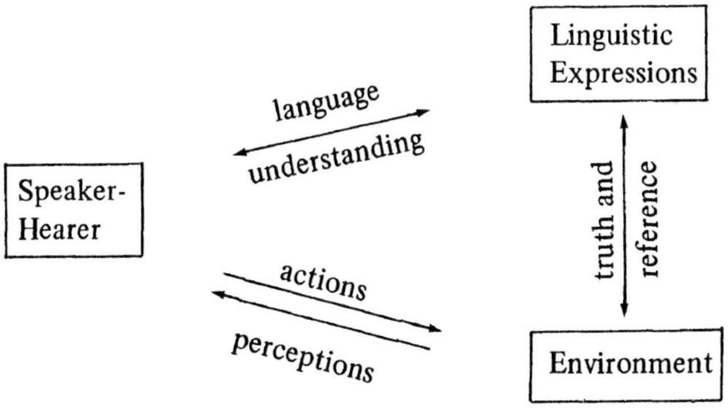

It does seem to be the case that if one had an adequate and complete theory of language understanding and an adequate and complete theory of human action and perception as well, one would seem to have indirectly determined the third side of the triangle already. That is, if we think of the speaker–hearer as an automaton (following Carnap–Reichenbach–Putnam) and suppose that we have (1) a description of how each "input" expression affects the internal state of the automaton and what internal stages prompt the automaton to "output" any expression, and (2) how non-linguistic input (i.e. non-linguistic perceptions) affect the internal stage of the automaton and how the internal state of the automaton prompts it to perform (non-linguistic) actions, then we would seem to have indirectly determined the relationships between expressions and the environment that is given by the theory of truth and reference. However, we will shortly see reasons to believe that the account of truth and reference for a language used by a community of speakers is more general and complete than what is determined by the understanding, perception and action of any one individual alone. Another important point is that such adequate theories of understanding, perception and action will no doubt be much more difficult to develop and lie further in the future than a theory of truth and reference; hence a theory of truth and reference will be an important check upon (and possibly a guide to) the development of theories of understanding and perception and action. And of course the fact that there *is* such a correspondence between language and the world directly (in addition to a correspondence between language and whatever "mental representation" of the world we may find it desirable to build into our theory of a speaker's understanding) cannot be circumvented without losing an account of what language is "good for", in Putnam's view. (Putnam goes on to point out how the distinction between reference and understanding enables one to give a causal explanation of the reliability of learning even though the definition of language use itself does not mention the correspondence between language and the world; cf. Putnam (1978, pp. 103–107). Also, the distinction enables one to escape certain objections raised against verificationism in the 19th century (pp. 110–111).)

To see the role of linguistic behavior in "successful" behavior more clearly, we need to include at least two speaker–hearers: the point here is that the use of a language enables the first speaker–hearer to take advantage of the interactions with the environment that the second speaker–hearer has experienced but the first has not; the reception of a (true) linguistic expression from another speaker–hearer is a kind of short-cut direct interaction with the environment (thanks to the underlying language-environment correspondence

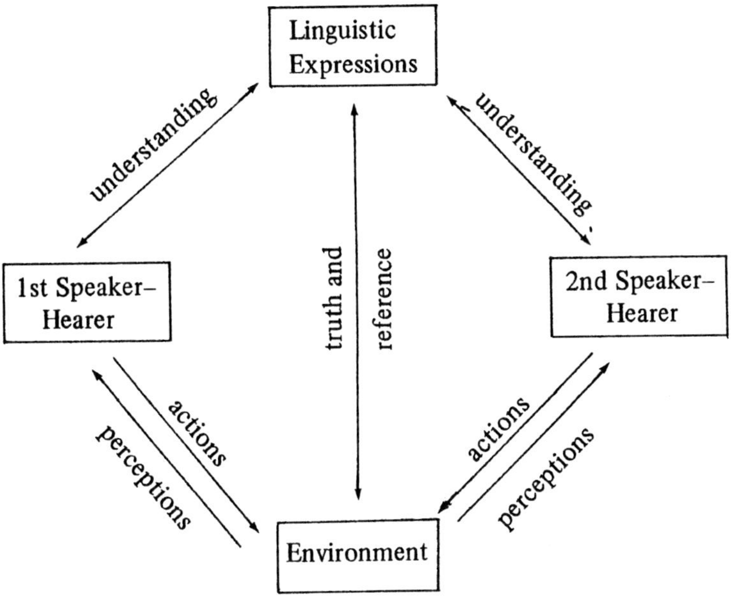

and the assumption that speakers ordinarily utter only true sentences). And furthermore, the use of language enables the two speaker–hearers to coordinate their future interactions with the environment in a more sophisticated and profitable way than would be possible otherwise.

A highly ironic observation about so-called "mentalistic" theories of semantics as exemplified by Katz (1966; 1972) and most work in linguistic semantics is that such theories would inevitably seem to fail in explaining what ought to be, ultimately, one of the most important facts about language according to the stated goals of some of these workers. Many linguists repeatedly emphasize that language is a psychological, hence neurological and biological phenomenon (cf. Chomsky, 1968) and involves some degree of innate ability. But surely the "ultimate" biological fact about natural language that has to be explained is why the ability to use (and the predisposition to acquire) a natural language confers a selectional advantage over an otherwise genetically identical population that has no such ability. (Though the degree of complexity of this "innate ability" is of course a subject of extreme controversy, I take it that it is universally agreed that homo sapiens has at least *some* genetically initiated linguistic capability that sets it apart from other species; even the recent research on teaching "language" to apes has not given us reason to doubt the weaker forms of this hypothesis.) Putnam's view of the theory of reference as a theory of "the contribution of our linguistic behavior to the success of our total behavior" shows how the theory of reference can be a central part of this explanation of biological advantage, together with a theory of language use based on that theory of reference (e.g. Lewis' "Convention of Truthfulness and Trust in *L*", (Lewis, 1969)). For example, the ability to utter and respond appropriately to sentences such as *There is a good source of food and water over here* or *There is a dangerous animal over there* in exactly those situations in which the actual world *is* a member of the proposition expressed by such sentences clearly aids the survival of the individuals who are genetically predisposed to learn to do this. On the other hand, the theory that meaning in natural language is to be completely analyzed in terms of the ability to pass abstract "semantic representations" from one individual to another does not offer any explanation at all of what language is good for, in this crude biological sense, since semantic representations are deliberately defined in such a way as to have no connection with the external environment of an individual whatsoever. Of course, a theory of semantic representations might well be a part of a theory of the psychological processes that enable an organism to "match up" sentences and situations in the environment in the same way as its cohorts do, but this is in accord with the Putnam view of meaning.

Now it may be readily admitted that correspondence to the *actual* world and reference to *actual* objects in it is an important part of explaining language success, while at the same time it is doubted whether correspondence to various *possible* worlds and reference to subjects in those worlds has anything to do with such success. After all, language-speaking humans live their lives entirely "in" the actual world, and their survival depends entirely on what they do there. (It should be noted that Putnam himself does not discuss possible worlds semantics in this connection.) But I believe the extension of "language success" to possible worlds semantics is not only straightforward but inevitable. All we need to do is consider how sentences with future tenses, modals, conditionals and other indirect contexts contribute to language success. It is important here to bear in mind the model of communication that goes along with possible worlds semantics: though speakers of a language do not know exactly *which* possible world is the actual one (else they would be omniscient), they know that it is a member of a certain set of worlds (namely a member of the intersection of all those sets which are the propositions they know to be true),[2] and the communication of new factual information from one speaker to another consists in enabling others to "narrow down" the candidates for the actual world by "ruling out" worlds not included in the true propositions expressed by their utterances. In view of the incomplete epistemic state of the speakers of a language, modal and other indirect context expressions enable speakers to communicate important relationships about various alternative states of affairs that the actual environment might *or might not* belong to, at times where the relevant properties of the actual state of the environment are not known. To take just one example, consider (1):

(1) Go into the next room. There may be a large red book on the table. If so, the information you want can be found on page 37. If the book is not on the table, it may be on top of the bookcase.

Now consider two situations in which this utterance is used. In the first, the addressee hears the utterance, goes into the next room, finds a book on the table, and gets the information he wants. In the second situation, the addressee hears the utterance, goes into the next room, does not find the book on the table but finds it on the bookcase, and gets the information he wants anyway. In both situations, communication "succeeded" in the sense that it enables the addressee to interact with the environment in a useful way. But how can the "correspondence" account of this success be reconciled with the two conflicting situations in which the same utterances were used? The only way I know to do this in a systematic fashion lies in the theory that the relevant correspondence involves not only sentences and the actual state of affairs but also sentences and each of a range of alternative states of affairs. In the case of the first modal clause, the theory that there is *some* kind of correspondence is needed to explain the success of the addressee's behavior in the situation where the book was in fact on the table; the fact that the correspondence need not be between the sentence and the *actual* state of affairs is needed to explain that the addressee did not feel he had been misled in the situation where there was no book on the table. More sophisticated examples than this can surely be constructed as well. The "survival advantage" that a language with possible worlds semantics confers upon its users is thus the ability to cooperatively make preparations for future events which may or may not come about, to anticipate dangers and by using counterfactuals, to discuss hypothetical but non-actual past states of their environment, thus understanding causation more clearly and being able to manipulate their environment more effectively in the future. (Cf. Lewis, 1973.)

Of course, one of the most striking achievements of Montague's was to demonstrate how the theory of reference could be generalized to include even expressions of natural language that have been traditionally assumed (by linguists at least, cf. Lyons (1968, p. 425)) to correspond to nothing whatsoever in the "non-linguistic" world, e.g. the abstract noun *sincerity* in (2) and the "non-specific" interpretation of *a unicorn* in (3):

(2) John admires sincerity.

(3) John is seeking a unicorn.

Of course the entities referred to by these phrases are treated as abstract set-theoretic "semantical objects" (assuming *sincerity* in (2) denotes that property which has as its extension at each index the set of sincere individuals, though no existing fragment I know of actually treats such abstract nouns), but they are nevertheless "semantical objects" whose definition in terms of concrete entities and indices is made completely explicit. The justification for a treatment postulating such abstract entities lies in (A) the adequacy of the account of the entailments of such sentences that results, and (B) the overall generality with which reference is assigned in the language as a whole. If this method of analysis using abstract "semantical objects" turns out to be satisfactory on the grounds (A) and (B) for all such expressions of natural language, then on methodological grounds it is to be preferred to other kinds of accounts (e.g. non-referential ones) because it makes possible the very general claim that *all* expressions of natural languages have some kind of correlation with the environment that explains their "success value" in Putnam's sense in a fundamentally uniform way. To me, this is the most exciting prospect that Montague's work offers to linguistics.

Thus there are three reasons why "possible worlds" semantics is important to linguistic theory in spite of its non-psychological nature. First, the theory of truth and reference is an integral part of explaining the total phenomenon of natural language, and it is possible to define the all-important notion of *entailment* among sentences entirely within such a theory (and likewise the related notions of *logical equivalence*, *logical validity*, *contradiction*, etc.). Second, to be able to really evaluate a theory of language understanding for adequacy (when we have such a theory), we must be able to show, perhaps in conjunction with theories of other aspects of human behavior such as visual perception, just how it is that the collective linguistic behavior of humans conspires to make the utterance of and reaction to such sentences "fit" a uniform theory of truth and reference for these sentences, and to do this, we must know exactly what an appropriate theory of truth and reference for a natural language is. To use a current phrase, showing how the theory of understanding and the theory of reference match up must be the "bottom line" in any overall explanation of "meaning" in natural language.

But third, I believe it is fair to say that the theory of truth and reference is, at present, far better developed than theories of understanding in at least one very important way, that of showing exactly how the sense and reference of a complex expression is built up out of the sense and reference of its parts. In the particular versions of Montague Grammar in use today, it is possible to show that certain ways of putting a sentence together syntactically are *not* compatible with the task of getting the sense and reference of the whole sentence correctly. Now it is of course conceivable that the appropriate way of putting the parts of a sentence together for the purposes of a theory of understanding could turn out to be different from the appropriate way of putting the parts of a sentence together for the purpose of a theory of truth and reference. But in view of the fact that such a correlation between expressions and "meaning" must be specified for an infinite number of sentences in both cases, I suspect that it is quite likely that the two analyses of the "compositional structure" of a sentence will have to be isomorphic for all sentences (or at least, our first hypothesis should reasonably be that they are isomorphic). Hence we may tentatively adopt the *thesis of parallel structure of reference and understanding*:

> If certain ways of deriving the meaning of English sentences compositionally from the meanings of their parts can be shown to be necessary in a theory of truth and reference, then it may be concluded that the same compositional analysis is necessary in a theory of language understanding.

If this hypothesis is a serviceable one, then this is yet another contribution that the study of reference has to make to the study of language understanding.

Of course one would hope that there will turn out to be some more direct relationships between model-theory and language comprehension after all than the rather bleak picture I have painted so far would suggest. It may turn out that the best theory of comprehension of certain kinds of sentences involves a "mental representation" or "mental picture" of the world that has many properties of the formal models we construct in a theory of reference. One instance where this is probably the case is in the comprehension of a description of a route from one place to another or a description of the floor plan of a building, where it seems intuitively that one does construct a two- or three-dimensional mental "map" that would be somewhat like a model which has enough structure to interpret locatives directly in terms of Cartesian coordinates in space. But a theory of understanding might also under certain circumstances treat the meanings of such sentences (and other, non-locative sentences) as stored and processed in terms of symbolic representations in an abstract formal language that look more like the "semantic representations" of some linguistic theories than anything in familiar model theory. The meaning of a word might in some cases be treated as an algorithm for recognizing the extension in terms of perceptions, in other cases as a finite list of ordered pairs, in still other cases as a combination of the two, or just in terms of "meaning postulates" for computing deductions. My point is simply that a conclusion about the best way of treating an intension in a theory of reference does not *automatically* indicate anything at all about the best way of treating the corresponding concept in a theory of understanding (for example, treating a sentence meaning as a list of possible worlds is undoubtedly not appropriate in a theory of understanding; cf. note 2), but at most, indicates a useful place to start in developing such a treatment.

Assuming that this picture of the bipartite[3] nature of the study of semantics is fundamentally correct, we now turn specifically to the matter of lexical semantics. First, a point of terminology. I will continue to use *intension of a word* in the model-theoretic definition used elsewhere, e.g. that function which determines the extension of that word at every index. For the corresponding notion in the theory of understanding (i.e. whatever it is in a person's head that determines how he uses and understands the word), I will use the term *concept of a word*. (This caveat is important because in some discussions the terms *intension* and *sense* are sometimes contrasted with *extension* and *reference* in that the former two are used for psychological notions while only the latter are used for referential notions, e.g. in Putnam's writings.)

First we will consider stative predicates (i.e. stative verbs and all adjectives and common nouns) and then turn to words involving "operators" later (i.e. both traditional logical words like negation and quantifiers and also verbs analyzed in terms of BECOME and CAUSE). A first point to note is that Putnam (in 'The Meaning of Meaning', (Putnam, 1975)) has argued persuasively that, contrary to the traditional wisdom that each person's concept of a word determines the intension of the word (or as Putnam would say, determines its reference), a person's concept of a word often grossly underdetermines its intension. Putnam's main examples of this underdetermination are *natural kind* terms, e.g. names of biological species like *tiger*, or names of chemical elements or compounds, like *water*. Putnam argues that such terms are typically first used by speakers who have no idea of the real necessary and sufficient conditions for being in the extension of such terms, but rather are used to "dub" a particular instance or member of a natural kind, with the implicit assumption that there are as yet unknown conditions which differentiate examples of this kind from other things and that future examples of this kind distinguished by these same characteristics are likely to be found. It can later be discovered empirically what these necessary and sufficient conditions are, e.g. it was at some point discovered that water is H_2O. In this way even a necessary truth (*water is* H_2O) can be a posteriori (cf. also Kripke, 1972). (While I believe this view is correct and essential to the understanding of the progress of scientific knowledge, I believe it is important to realize that not all predicates work this way – see below.)

Another reason that the concepts of words we possess underdetermines their intension is what Putnam calls the *division of linguistic labor* (or the *socio-linguistic hypothesis*). This is the claim that not all speakers of a language need know all the relevant "connections" between a word and its intension (i.e. how to recognize its extension, all semantic entailments and true empirical facts involving the word) that account for its successful use, because many speakers' successful use of a word is parasitic on the knowledge of other "experts" in the speech community who do have the appropriate knowledge. The ordinary individual's successful use of *gold*, for example, does not depend on his being able to distinguish gold from non-gold reliably, or to know the important chemical and physical properties of gold, etc., because of the way we interact linguistically with a community of individuals that includes people who do have the relevant abilities. When we say to a television repairman *The horizontal hold control on this set needs to be repaired*, the success of our utterance in getting the job done fortunately does not depend on our having the acquaintance with the intension of *horizontal hold control* that is crucially involved in actually fixing it. On the other hand, it is impossible to imagine that our use of such words as *gold* would be anything like what it is if there were not at least *some* individuals in our speech community that could reliably determine its extension in many situations. The more one thinks about this matter, the more apparent it becomes that our acquaintance with the intensions of many words we consider ourselves to understand perfectly well is remarkably scanty. As a speaker of English, I would hardly consider myself to have failed to "understand" the words *beech* and *elm* in the hundreds of times I have heard them, but like Putnam, I can't really tell a beech from an elm at all and know nothing about them except that they are two kinds of common deciduous trees.[4]

Putnam suggests that what we *do* expect the normal speaker of a language to know about the meanings of the words he "understands" is a certain more or less standard set of entailments, though these do not suffice to delimit the intension correctly and may even be inaccurate. This he calls the *stereotype* of a word. (For example, English speakers are supposedly expected to know that tigers are large feline animals that are yellow with black stripes.)[5] This may in fact be the case, but I am pessimistic about the chances of fixing a stereotype for each word once and for all. It is a commonplace of socio-linguistics that the boundaries of various technical jargons with "non-technical" English are hard if not impossible to draw, and the nature of the expected stereotype will vary according to the degree to which a word is treated as a technical term in each context. Probably an important part of a speaker's "communicative competence" lies in continually making estimates of the inferences one's audience will or won't draw from each word and choosing one's vocabulary accordingly.

When we think for a moment about the kinds of criteria and psychological abilities that can be involved in using a word, it is not hard to come up with quite a diverse list. The way natural kind terms are used is one way word concepts work (i.e. we know a few characteristics by which examples of a kind can be more or less reliably recognized but expect there to be other more precise criteria which may not yet be known). Another common criterion is what may be called a *functional* criterion – how an object, especially a human artifact, is used in our culture. For example, I do not expect that we treat *chair* like natural kind terms but rather call things chairs merely on the grounds of how they are used. If in the twenty-first century (or in a science-fiction story) ordinary chairs are replaced by local anti-gravity devices which suspend a person in mid-air in a sitting position, I believe these devices will deserve and receive the designation *chair*, despite the fact that they share no physical properties with present-day chairs. In other cases, a finite list is the principal or only criterion actually used to recognize the extension of a term (e.g. *state of the U.S.A.*), and I expect that children often learn words by first acquiring a finite list of things in the extension (e.g. Daddy is a man, Uncle Henry is a man, Mr. Brown is a man, etc.) and use this as a basis for an inductive generalization to some criterion or other. For words denoting classes recognizable by an elementary sensory stimulus (most notably color terms), I believe that personal perception of such a stimulus is the most common and relevant factor involved in using the term. Of course, different individuals may employ different sorts of abilities in using the same word. A color-blind individual, for example, may distinguish a red traffic light from a green traffic light by its position in the standard vertical arrangement of three lights rather than by its color, and one individual may rely on different abilities or knowledge in using the same word in different situations. In view of this diversity, does it really make sense to postulate a uniform and structured theoretical entity (its semantic representation) that is identified with the concept of a word and has the same "psychological reality" for all speakers? Presumably, a mentalistic linguist would say that it does, but I am pessimistic. Rather, I think the lesson to be drawn from Putnam's observations about the "linguistic division of labor" in word meaning is that *it does not matter* that different individuals use quite different concepts of the same word. As long as these differing concepts do not lead individuals' behavior to determine *conflicting* intensions for the word in very many situations, it is unimportant that these concepts *underdetermine* the intensions in different ways. In fact, it may be a significant property of natural language that this diversity *can* exist. From this point of view, it becomes even more dramatically evident how important the non-psychological notion of an intension is; it is the underlying "glue" that implicitly ties psychologically divergent word concepts together into a useful system.[6]

A color-blind person may use color terms with success in a remarkable number of situations, despite his roundabout way of compensating for his deficient concepts for these terms. The most remarkable example of this sort was of course Helen Keller, whose writings are strikingly "normal" in spite of her deficiencies in the perceptual abilities that for most of us are intimately involved in the ways we acquire and use language.

Of course, the employment of different criteria in word meaning does lead to overtly conflicting determination of its intension in some cases. For example, I once heard *weed* defined (by a botanist, I think) as "any plant that is growing where it is not wanted". Aware of the hidden indexicality of this word, he has pointed to a functional criterion for its use. But for most individuals, I believe *weed* is more like a kind term and is a rigid designator. I doubt that most people would be inclined to revise the opinion that "Crabgrass is a weed" upon encountering a patch of crabgrass cultivated and neatly labelled in a botanical exhibit. A converse case is provided by *fruit* (as opposed to *vegetable*). For the botanist, fruit is a natural kind, a part of a plant that has common botanical characteristics in each species which can be discovered empirically. But in the everyday use, this word has a functional criterion, i.e. a part of a plant that is eaten as a dessert or snack. I was amused to learn recently (*Scientific American*, August, 1978, p. 78) that the question of whether the tomato is a fruit or a vegetable has been decided by no less austere a body than the Supreme Court of the United States (in 1893).[7] Alas for Kripke and Putnam, the Supreme Court ruled against them in this case. Associate Justice Horace Grey wrote the opinion that:

Botanically speaking, tomatoes are the fruit of a vine, just as are cucumbers, squashes, beans, and peas. But in the common language of the people, whether sellers or consumers of provisions, all these are vegetables which are grown in kitchen gardens, and which, whether eaten cooked or raw, are, like potatoes, parsnips, turnips, beets, cauliflower, cabbage, celery, and lettuce, usually served at dinner in, with, or after the soup, fish, or meats which constitute the principal part of the repast, and not, like fruits generally, as dessert.

But while there sometimes fails to be a single intension that is consistent with all speakers' concepts of a word in a few cases, it is exactly in these cases that communication potentially breaks down. Though the notion of an intension is an idealization in this respect, it nevertheless provides us with a theory of how language works *when it does work*. In this way it is exactly like the convenient fiction that all members of a speech community speak "the same" language, even though it must at the same time be acknowledged that the language of any one person differs in subtle phonetic, phonological, morphological and syntactic details from that of all others, and these details can likewise lead to a breakdown of communication on occasion.[8]

Given this view of the bipartite nature of "word meaning", what is the status of structurally-motivated lexical decomposition analyses? Note first of all that while the thesis of parallel structure of reference and understanding gives us plausible reason to "transfer" results about the referentially-motivated analysis of a *sentence* to the "conceptual structure" of the meaning of a sentence (i.e., the way in which the brain puts word concepts together in the appropriate way to produce the concept of the sentence as a whole, whatever these "concepts" are), there is no corresponding reason to transfer any particular model-theoretically motivated analysis of a *word*'s meaning, such as those given in this book, to a claim about the "structure" of a word's concept. This is so, first, because there will be numerous semantically equivalent ways of achieving such an analysis (at least in the system used in this book) – by one or more different "decomposing" translations, by one or more meaning postulates or other restrictions on possible models, or by various combinations of these. Second, my comments about the underdetermination and diversity of word concepts, as opposed to their intensions, gives even more reason not to make such an automatic transfer. Third, the basic expressions of a language are finite in number, and we do not need to appeal to further analysis of them to account for language learnability (as we do in the case of sentences). This leaves us with only a psychological version of the structuralist "analytic leap" mentioned in chapter two (the view that semantic contrasts evidenced repeatedly in a language *must* be attributed to the same basic "cognitive unit" wherever they occur) to motivate decomposition, and while I have advocated structuralist decomposition as a heuristic strategy in word semantics, I am not prepared to extend claims of psychological reality to analyses justified by this methodology alone.

If on the other hand, we had some psychological evidence for believing in the "psychological reality" of certain analyses but not others, these might reasonably be seen as predicting certain referential consequences in some cases. For illustration, consider the hypothesis found in early linguistic decomposition that there is a fixed finite and perhaps language-univeral set of semantic primitives in the form of (first order) predicates such as MALE, FEMALE, ADULT, ANIMATE, CONCRETE, etc. Many (though probably not all) linguists have seen this as a hypothesis about the structure of word concepts, i.e. as a claim of the psychological reality of these predicates. (In this respect it is not a completely implausible hypothesis, given the observation that the mind is finite and that word concepts, whatever they are, are probably constructed out of *some* kind of more primitive units.) But in Putnam's bipartite view of meaning, this hypothesis is naturally seen as entailing limits on the intensions of words (and other expressions) as well. That is, the propositions expressed by MALE(x), FEMALE(x), etc. are propositions expressible in natural language, as are Boolean operations over these propositions (e.g. MALE(x) $\wedge$ ADULT(x), etc.), relative to some value for x. And the claim that this is a closed system of semantic primitives means that (to the extent that intensions are determined by concepts, at least) no two possible worlds which are indistinguishable by Boolean operations over these primitive propositions can be distinguished by an expression of natural language. Seen from this point of view, the hypothesis seems somewhat less plausible (It is really the case that there are pairs of possible worlds that cannot be distinguished by an expression of any *possible* human language?), but I think that this indicates the direction in which further rigorous investigation of theories of structural semantics should proceed.

When we turn from predicates to operators, the case for psychological correlates of model-theoretic notions may become somewhat stronger. It is hard for me to imagine that the concepts that correspond to the truth functional operations negation, conjunction, etc. in any significant way "underdetermine" the intension, as do the concepts corresponding to the intensions of natural kind terms. What for example could be the Putnamian stereotype that corresponds to conjunction but does not amount to the same thing? For tense and modal operators and operators like BECOME, PROG and CAUSE, the situation is slightly less clear, but here too I find it hard to suppose that the concept underdetermines the intension or varies significantly from speaker to speaker. Likewise, I find it hard to believe that a person could leave anything like an acceptable "stereotype" for an accomplishment like *build* or *kill* without having awareness that these verbs have the kind of entailments characteristic of accomplishments in general. (Recall also the discussion in 2.4 of how the temporal and modal aspects of word meanings, as opposed to the truth conditions for extensional predicates, might turn out to be limited by an "aspect calculus" or some such theory.)

This brings me to the difficult question of what the psychological process of "comprehending a sentence" can be said to consist in. Psycholinguists have often implicitly demanded that semantic representations be psychologically real in the sense that "given appropriate idealizations, understanding a sentence requires the recovery of its semantic representation" (Fodor, Fodor and Garrett, 1975, p. 515).[9] What I would like to suggest instead is that the process of "comprehending" a sentence is highly variable across different instances of comprehending the same sentence (by the same speaker–hearer), and depends greatly on the context and purpose for which the sentence is used.

In this respect I believe I differ slightly with the view expressed in Partee's 'Montague Grammar, Mental Representations and Reality' (Partee, to appear b), an article which makes many of the same points as this chapter (and other important points as well). Partee points out the problems Putnam observed in taking the intension of a word as determined by its concept but suggests that compositional semantics is different from lexical semantics in this way. She seems to imply that model-theoretic possible worlds semantics (as it appears in Montague Grammar) is appropriate to the traditional goals of linguistics in the realm of compositional semantics of sentences in a way that it is not appropriate in the realm of lexical semantics. To the extent of advocating the Parallel Structure hypothesis mentioned earlier, I agree. But if compositional model theoretic semantics is being viewed as somehow an acceptable model of the process of comprehending a sentence in other ways besides this isomorphism, I am suspicious. I suggest that what is usually meant by comprehending a sentence involves, perhaps among other things, the "on-line computation" of some very few of the many inferences that the proposition expressed by the sentence potentially allows in conjunction with the common ground of the conversational context in which it is uttered.

For example, one relevant aspect of "comprehending" the sentence *Every state has exactly two senators* may in one context involve "computing" the inference *Rhode Island has exactly two senators*, in another context *South Dakota has at least one senator*, in still another context *No state has three senators*, and so on. In other words, the problem that I foresee in taking model-theoretic semantics too literally as a theory of sentence comprehension is that it makes no distinction at all among the huge if not infinite number of entailments prescribed by the definition of entailment that modal theory gives us. Thus even when the deficiencies of one's knowledge of intensions of the words of a sentence are taken into account, the "partially specified" proposition that literally results from the full definition of entailment in a given context is still far too much "information" to correspond to what happens when we initially "grasp" a sentence. Note that when one reads a particularly profound or complex passage, the process of "understanding" it (i.e. computing more and more inferences) may go on for some time after one has finished reading it, perhaps for days or weeks. Exactly what the "initial grasp" of a sentence's "meaning" consists in, I obviously do not know (beyond the point that it must be grasping *something* which is isomorphic to its analysis tree), but I believe the formal definition of entailment provides only the extreme outer limits of what this can involve.

The relevance of all this discussion for the lexical decomposition analyses presented in this book can now be made clear. I believe these analyses provide a description of what kind of inferences *can* be drawn by a speaker in "comprehending" a sentence involving these words, but do not in any way describe what he *must* "cognitively compute". Consequently, these analyses are not psychologically real by the above "comprehension" criterion. Consider two narratives in which the sentence *John killed Bill* may occur. If the story is one in which John is a major character and Bill is an insignificant one, the comprehension of this sentence that the author expects of the reader may involve the inferences that John has committed a morally reprehensible act of the severest sort, that the police are likely to arrest John, that John may flee the country, etc., but inferences involving Bill may be ignored (though of course they *can* be retrieved later). But if Bill is the main character and John is insignificant, the relevant inferences may be that Bill is no longer alive at this time, that he will not be able to rescue the heroine after all, that the heroine will be distraught, etc., but no inferences involving John.

To the extent that there is any direct psychological evidence as to what one necessarily "computes" in understanding a word like *kill* or other accomplishment, the evidence seems to support this kind of view. Most notably, experiments have been designed to try to test whether one computes *become not alive* when "grasping" the meaning of a sentence with *kill* (Fodor, Fodor and Garrett, 1975; Kintsch, 1974). It turns out that computing inferences from a sentence with an overt negative (such as *not*), and to a lesser extent sentences with a morphological negative marker like *un-*, requires a measurably longer reaction time than computing similar inferences from the corresponding unnegated sentences. However, inferences from sentences in which a word occurs that is typically given a decomposition that involves a negative (e.g. *kill* as *cause to become not alive* or *bachelor* as *unmarried man*) were found by these investigators not to require the tell-tale delay in reaction time. If such experiments are methodologically sound, then this is at least prima facie evidence against the view that "decomposition" is a necessary cognitive step in comprehension of word meaning (though alternative interpretations of these results may still be possible).

But this conclusion also does not mean that cognitive concepts which would correspond closely to the intension of operators like BECOME and CAUSE are psychologically *un*real either. After all, we have to account for the fact that *sometimes* speakers do (and always can) infer from *John killed Bill* to *Bill is not alive*. If deductions involving steps corresponding to the semantics of BECOME and CAUSE are more common than other kinds of deductions involving words of natural language and, if, as I suggested earlier, there is no "gap" between a speaker's stereotype of these notions and their intensions as there is with predicates, then perhaps it is more than wishful thinking to suppose there is something psychologically special about concepts corresponding to BECOME and CAUSE. That is, these might be fundamental concepts that can be called into play in some inferences, if not every time we use or understand an accomplishment verb. After all, the experiments cited above give clear evidence that at least *one* semantic operation is psychologically real in some instances (namely negation), so why shouldn't there be others as well?

Finally, there may be yet a broader way in which the linguist's traditional search for structural "semantic primitives" and his belief in the explanatory power of such primitives as ANIMATE, HUMAN, CAUSE, BECOME, DO, etc. can be related to modern referential semantics. While I believe that, in general, linguistic semantics has suffered rather than profited from constructing its theories too closely on the model of phonology, at this point I think an analogy between phonology and semantics becomes relevant. In the earlier days of phonological distinctive feature theory, there was some dispute as to whether the set of distinctive phonological features should be defined essentially in terms of acoustic properties of speech signals or in terms of physiological properties of the production of these speech signals; phonologists tended to come up with slightly differing views of what the "universal" set of basic phonological contrasts (features) should be, depending on which aspect of phonetics was taken as fundamental. The more usual current view (expressed for example by Peter Ladefoged in his 1978 presidential address to the Linguistic Society of America) is that the set of phonological contrasts which are most typically exploited by languages to distinguish one class of phonemes from another is best understood as a *compromise* between (1) the phonetic distinctions most easily and consistently produced by the human vocal apparatus and (2) the acoustic distinctions most easily perceived by the ear. Human language achieves efficiency in its phonological systems by maximizing both these parameters simultaneously.

The bipartite (or tripartite) division of semantics suggested in this chapter offers a parallel view of "structurally primitive" semantic contrasts represented by CAUSE, BECOME, etc. If we are searching for an explanation, in the broadest sense, of why so many verbs have meanings that are given *approximately* correct interpretations by formulas of the aspect calculus, then this explanation is not to be found solely in the extent to which such formulas systematize truth conditions for these verbs. Rather, we should also seek part of the explanation of this "convergence" around the aspect calculus by paying attention to two other matters: to the psychology of language understanding perhaps, but as a more tangible concern, to the kinds of situations in the environment and the kinds of interactions of humans with the environment and with each other that it is *useful* to communicate about. When what can be called the teleology of human communication is considered, then obviously not just certain states of things are going to be important, but also the changes from one state to another (cf. BECOME) and the causation of one state or change by another (cf. CAUSE) are going to be ubiquitous and fundamental. On the level of interaction with the environment, changes initiated by a human agent will be of special importance (cf. DO), as these behave quite differently within chains of causation from the ways non-agentive events behave in such chains (cf. the notion of *secondary agent* in the aspect calculus, for example). It is noteworthy that von Wright's work, which provided the original incentive for my work on verb semantics, was not undertaken as a linguistic analysis at all, but as a general theory of human action. I suggest that it is no accident that the same operators that provide the most general utility in a theory of action turn out to have a close correspondence with some of the structural linguist's "semantic primitives" that have reappeared widely in word semantics.

Thus just as the most typical structural contrasts to be found in phoneme systems of natural language are best understood as resulting from the intersection of two kinds of constraints, the structural semantic contrasts in verbs that appear most repeatedly (across sets of monomorphemic verbs, in the semantics of word formation rules, and in the analysis of "internal" scopes of adverbs with verbs) are ultimately to be understood as resulting from the interaction of two if not three requirements which a human semiotic system is subject to: (1) features of the environment (possible and actual) which the language is used to talk about (e.g., the structure of time and space, and ontology of individuals, kinds and other entities), (2) the kinds of states and changes in the environment and of human interactions with it that are *useful* to talk about and are perceivable by the human sensory apparatus, and (3) the psychological limitations on encoding, decoding and processing information via a human language. This book has of course been concerned only with the referential correlates of the linguist's traditional semantic units (and we have at points been forced to go beyond these few units in developing an adequate interpretation for English). If further understanding of the significance of these units can be found, I suspect it will have to come from the theory of human action and possibly from the psychology of language understanding, not from referential semantics.

In spite of these hopeful speculations about psychological reality, I must remind the reader that the important motivation I presently see in the kind of decomposition analysis pursued in this book lies in getting a broader explicit definition of entailment for classes of words for which no such definitions were formerly available. I believe that expanding the class of entailments of various words of natural language that can be treated formally is one of the most important tasks facing the analysis of meaning in natural language today. Though the study of natural language understanding can and surely will proceed parallel to the study of referential semantics, the theory of understanding cannot ultimately progress very far if the study of referential semantics lags behind.

NOTES

[1] To be fair to Cresswell, I must add that it is clear both from other passages in his book, e.g. pp. 48–51 and from conversations that I have had with him that he is perfectly aware of the problems with this view that I discuss below.

[2] A somewhat paradoxical aspect of this view is that it seems to require us to suppose that we somehow have acquaintance with large *sets* of worlds but not with any of the individual possible worlds that make them up. This paradoxical air can partially be

removed by bearing in mind that it is often profitable in model-theory to treat what is intuitively a vague notion as represented formally by a set of specific things of the same sort: the "vagueness" in the meaning of a sentence is captured by letting it be represented by a set of "completely specified" possible worlds which differ among themselves in certain ways; likewise, it was discussed in 2.3.5 how Kamp (1975) handles the vagueness of predicates like *tall* by appealing to a set of completely specific but conflicting interpretations for such predicates. Thus the conceptual counterpart of the proposition expressed by a sentence may be much more like a "single but vague" possible world (perhaps a "mental picture" of such a world in some cases) than like a set of totally specified possible worlds.

[3] Actually, semantics should be at least tripartite, since we of course want to distinguish pragmatics (speech acts, conversational implicature, etc.) from truth-conditional semantics. But pragmatics itself can be studied from both a referential and a cognitive point of view, and perhaps even more distinctions within pragmatics should be recognized for various purposes. It is perhaps one of the most important advances of this decade that we have realized that our formerly monolithic theories of semantics are best broken up into a number of subtheories in this way, each of which may best be investigated with a different methodology.

[4] As Partee (to appear) observes, this distinction between our concept of a word and its full intension may hold the key to the traditional problems with treating propositions (sets of worlds) as the object of belief, namely, the theory seems to require that if we believe a proposition we believe all propositions logically equivalent to it, and if we believe one logical truth, we believe them all. But if our knowledge of word-intensions is less than complete, then discovering a mathematical truth need not be viewed as discovering a new proposition that one had not encountered before but rather as discovering something new about the intensions of the words that express the logical truth – namely, that when put together in the appropriate way, these intensions yield the (familiar) necessary proposition.

[5] This discussion should be elaborated somewhat by Carlson's (1977) distinction between kind-properties and properties of all the objects that make them up, but I think my general points remain valid.

[6] Dahlgren (1978) provides some very interesting examples of how a complex give-and-take between the intension of a word and its concept must be recognized in order to explain how the meanings of certain words of English have changed during the history of the English language; see also Partee (to appear b) for further commentary on Dahlgren's examples.

[7] The reason that such an issue came before the Supreme Court was that a customs official had been collecting a duty on imported tomatoes, though the relevant tariff act specifically applied only to vegetables, not fruits.

[8] One formal means for dealing with this linguistic inconsistency is provided by Cresswell's (1973, p. 59) definition of a *communication class*.

[9] Fodor, Fodor and Garrett (1975) in fact criticize this requirement. For discussion of recent work on the problem of sentence comprehension, see Miller and Johnson-Laird (1976).

REFERENCES

Abbott, Barbara (1974) 'Some Problems in Giving an Adequate Model-Theoretic Account of CAUSE', in Charles Fillmore, George Lakoff, and Robin Lakoff (eds.), *Berkeley Studies in Syntax and Semantics* **1** pp. I, 1–14.

Aissen, Judith (1974) 'Verb Raising', *Linguistic Inquiry* **5.3**, 325–366.

Akmajian, Adrian, Susan M. Steele and Thomas Wasow (1979) 'The Category AUX in Universal Grammar', *Linguistic Inquiry* **10.1**, 1–64.

Åqvist, Lennart (1976) 'Fundamentals of a Theory of Aspect and Events within the Setting of an Improved Tense Logic', in F. Guenther and C. Rohrer (eds.), *Studies in Formal Semantics*, North-Holland, Amsterdam.

Ard, William Josh (to appear) 'Diachronic Evidence for Non-Uniqueness in Montague Grammar', to appear in M. Mithun and S. Davis (eds.), *Proceedings from the 1977 Albany Conference on Montague Grammar, Philosophy and Linguistics*, University of Texas Press, Austin.

Aronoff, Mark (1976) *Word Formation in Generative Grammar*, The MIT Press, Cambridge, Massachusetts.

Bach, Emmon (1967) '*Have* and *Be* in English Syntax', *Language* **43**, 462–485.

Bach, Emmon (1968) 'Nouns and Noun Phrases', in Emmon Bach and Robert T. Harms (eds.), *Universals in Linguistic Theory*, Holt, Rinehart and Winston, New York, 90–122.

Bach, Emmon (1977) 'Control in Montague Grammar', Paper presented to the Symposium on Montague Grammar at the 1977 Annual Meeting of the Linguistic Society of America.

Baron, Naomi S. (1974) 'The Structure of English Causatives', *Lingua* **33**, 299–342.

Bennett, David C. (1970) *Spatial and Temporal Uses of English Prepositions*, unpublished doctoral dissertation, Yale University.

Bennett, David C. (1975) *Spatial and Temporal Uses of English Prepositions: An Essay in Stratificational Semantics*, Longman, London.

Bennett, Michael (1974) *Some Extensions of a Montague Fragment of English*, University of California dissertation.

Bennett, Michael (to appear) 'Of Tense and Aspect: One Analysis', in the proceedings of the Symposium on Tense and Aspect at Brown University, Academic Press, New York.

Bennett, Michael and Barbara H. Partee (1972) 'Toward the Logic of Tense and Aspect in English', System Development Corporation, Santa Monica, California (also distributed by Indiana University Linguistics Club).

Berman, Arlene (ms) 'Agent, Experience and Controllability'. (Unpublished paper, Harvard University, no date.)

Bever, Thomas (1970) 'The Cognitive Basis for Linguistic Structures', in R. Hayes (ed.), *Cognition and Development*, Wiley and Sons, New York, pp. 277–360.

Binnick, Robert (1968) 'On the Nature of the "Lexical Item",' *CLS* **4**, 1–13.

Binnick, Robert (1969) *Studies in the Derivation of Predicative Structures*, doctoral dissertation, University of Chicago.

Binnick, Robert (1971) '*Bring* and *Come*', *Linguistic Inquiry* **2.2**, 260–265.

Bolinger, Dwight (1971) *The Phrasal Verb in English*, Harvard University Press, Cambridge, Massachusetts.

Bolinger, Dwight (1972) *Degree Words* (*Janua Linguarum, Series Major*, 53), Mouton, the Hague.

Borkin, Ann (1971) 'Coreference and Beheaded NP's', *Papers in Linguistics* **5**, 28–45.

Bowerman, M. (1974) 'Learning the Structure of Causative Verbs: A Study in the Relationship of Cognitive, Semantic, and Syntactic Development', in E. Clark (ed.), *Papers and Reports on Child Language Development No. 8*, Stanford University Committee on Linguistics, pp. 142–178.

Bradley, Henry (1906) *The Making of English*, Macmillan, London.

Brame, Michael K. (1976) *Conjectures and Refutations in Syntax and Semantics*, North-Holland Publishing Co., Amsterdam.

Braroe, Eva (1974) *The Syntax and Semantics of English Tense Markers*. (*Monographs from the Institute of Linguistics*, University of Stockholm, 1.)

Bresnan, Joan (1978) 'A Realistic Transformational Grammar', in Morris Halle, Joan Bresnan, and George A. Miller (eds.), *Linguistic Theory and Psychological Reality*, The MIT Press, Cambridge, Massachusetts, 1–59.

Bryan, W. (1936) 'The Preterite and the Perfect Tense in Present-Day-English', *Journal of English and Germanic Philology* **35**, 363–382.

Burling, Robbins (1964) 'Cognition and Componential Analysis: God's Truth or Hocus-pocus?' *American Anthropologist* **66**, 20–28.

Carlson, Gregory N. (1973) *Superficially Unquantified Plural Count Noun Phrases in English*, M.A. Thesis, University of Iowa.

Carlson, Gregory N. (1977) *Reference to Kinds in English*, doctoral dissertation, University of Massachusetts.

Carlson, Gregory, N. (1977a) 'A Unified Analysis of the English Bare Plural', *Linguistics and Philosophy* **1.3**, 413–456.

Catlin, J.-C. and J. Catlin (1972) 'Intentionality: A Source of Ambiguity in English?' *Linguistic Inquiry* **3**, 504–508.

Chapin, P. (1967) *On the Syntax of Word Derivation in English*, MIT dissertation.

Charniak, E. and Y. Wilks, eds. (1976) *Computational Semantics: An Introduction to Artificial Intelligence and Natural Language Processing*, North-Holland, Amsterdam.

Chomsky, N. (1955) 'Logical Syntax and Semantics: Their Linguistic Relevance', *Language* **31.1**, 36–45.

Chomsky, N. (1965) *Aspects of the Theory of Syntax*, The MIT Press, Cambridge, Massachusetts.

Chomsky, Noam (1968) *Language and Mind*, Harcourt, Brace, and World, New York.

Chomsky, Noam (1970) 'Deep Structure, Surface Structure, and Semantic Interpretation', in R. Jakobson and S. Kawamoto (eds.), *Studies in General and Oriental Linguistics*, TEC Corporation, Tokyo.

Chomsky, Noam (1975) *Reflections on Language*, Pantheon Books, New York.

Chomsky, Noam (1977) *Essays on Form and Interpretation*, American Elsevier, New York.

Chomsky, Noam, and Morris Halle (1968) *The Sound Pattern of English*, Harper and Row, New York.

Clark, Eve V. (1978) 'Discovering What Words Can Do', to appear in *Papers from the Parasession on the Lexicon*, Chicago Linguistic Society, Chicago.

Clark, Eve V. and Herbert H. Clark (to appear) 'When Nouns Surface as Verbs', to appear in *Language*.

Clifford, John E. (1975) *Tense and Tense Logic*, (*Janua Linguarium, Series Minor*, 215), Mouton, The Hague.

Comrie, Bernard (1976) 'The Syntax of Causative Constructions: Cross-language Similarities and Divergences', in M. Shibatani (ed.), *Syntax and Semantics VI: The Grammar of Causative Constructions*, Academic Press, New York.

Cooper, Robin (1975) *Montague's Semantic Framework and Transformational Syntax*, doctoral dissertation, University of Massachusetts.

Cooper, Robin and Terence Parsons (1976) 'Montague Grammar, Generative Semantics and Interpretive Semantics', in B. Partee (ed.), *Montague Grammar*, Academic Press, New York, pp. 311–362.

Cooper, William S. (1978) *Foundations of Logico-Linguistics* (*Synthese Language Library*), D. Reidel, Dordrecht.

Costa, Rachel (1972) 'Sequence of Tense in *That*-Clauses', *CLS* **8**, 41–51.

Cresswell, M. J. (1973) *Logics and Languages*, Methuen & Co., London.

Cresswell, M. J. (1977) 'Interval Semantics and Logical Words', in C. Rohrer (ed.), *On the Logical Analysis of Tense and Aspect*, TBL Verlag Gunter Narr, Tübingen, pp. 7–30.

Cresswell, M. J. (1978) 'Prepositions and Points of View', *Linguistics and Philosophy* **2.1**, 1–41.

Cresswell, M. J. (ms) 'Interval Semantics for Some Event Expressions'.

Cresswell, M. J. (to appear) Review of Montague (1974), to appear in *Philosophia*.

Cresswell, M. J. (1978a) 'Semantic Competence', in M. Guenthner–Reutter and F. Guenthner (eds.), *Meaning and Translation*, Duckworth, London, pp. 9–28.

Cruse, D. A. (1973) 'Some Thoughts on Agentivity', *Journal of Linguistics* **9**, 11–23.

Dahlgren, K. (1978) 'The Nature of Linguistic Stereotypes', *Papers from the Parasession on the Lexicon*, Chicago Linguistic Society, Chicago.

Dillon, George L. (1975) 'Some Postulates Characterizing Volitive NP's', *Journal of Linguistics* **10**, 221–233.

Dillon, George L. (1977) *Introduction to Linguistic Semantics*, Prentice-Hall, Englewood Cliffs, NJ.

Downing, Pamela (1977) 'On the Creation and Use of English Compound Nouns', *Language* **53.4**, 810–842.

Dowty, David (1972a) 'On the Syntax and Semantics of the Atomic Predicate CAUSE', *CLS* **8**, 62–74.

Dowty, David (1972b) *Studies in the Logic of Verb Aspect and Time Reference in English*, (*Studies in Linguistics*) Department of Linguistics, University of Texas, Austin.

Dowty, David R. (1976) 'Montague Grammar and the Lexical Decomposition of Causative Verbs', in B. Partee (ed.), *Montague Grammar*, Academic Press, New York, pp. 201–246.

Dowty, David R. (1977) 'Toward a Semantic Analysis of Verb Aspect and the English 'Imperfective' Progressive', *Linguistics and Philosophy* **1.1**, 45–78.

Dowty, David R. (1978a) 'Lexically Governed Transformations as Lexical Rules in a Montague Grammar', *Linguistic Inquiry* **9.3**, 393–426.

Dowty, David R. (1978b) 'Applying Montague's Views on Linguistic Metatheory to the Structure of the Lexicon', *Papers from the Parasession on the Lexicon*, Chicago Linguistic Society, Chicago.

Dressler, Wolfgang (1976) 'Wortbildung bei Sprachverfall', Unpublished paper, University of Vienna.

Dressler, Wolfgang (1978) 'On Poetic License in Word Formation', (Lecture presented at Ohio State University, March 1978.)

Edmundson, Jerold A. (1976) 'Strict and Sloppy Identity in λ-Categorical Grammar', Indiana University Linguistics Club, Bloomington.

Fillmore, Charles (1971) *Lectures on Deixis*, (Lectures delivered to the 1971 Santa Cruz Linguistics Institute; distributed by the Indiana University Linguistics Club, Bloomington.)

Fillmore, Charles (1974) 'The Future of Semantics', Charles Fillmore, George Lakoff and Robin Lakoff (eds.), *Berkeley Studies in Syntax and Semantics* **1**, pp. IV, 1–38.

Fodor, J. A. (1970) 'Three Reasons for Not Deriving "Kill" from "Cause to Die",' *Linguistic Inquiry* **1**, 429–438.

Fodor, J. A., J. G. Bever and M. Garrett (1974) *The Psychology of Language*, McGraw-Hill, New York.

Fodor, Janet Dean (1974) 'Like Subject Verbs and Causal Clauses in English', *Journal of Lingustics* **10**, 95–110.

Fodor, J. D., J. A. Fodor, and M. F. Garrett (1975) 'The Psychological Unreality of Semantic Representations', *Linguistic Inquiry* **6.4**, 515–532.

Fraser, Bruce (1965) *An Examination of the Verb-Particle Construction in English*, MIT, Doctoral dissertation, Cambridge, Massachusetts.

Fraser, Bruce (1976) *The Verb-Particle Combination in English*, Academic Press, New York.

Gabbay, Dov, and J. M. E. Moravcsik (1973) 'Sameness and Individuation', *Journal of Philosophy* **70**, 513–26.

Gazdar, Gerald (1977) *Implicature, Presupposition and Logical Form*, Indiana University Linguistics Club, Bloomington.

Geis, Jonnie E. (1970) *Some Aspects of Verb Phrase Adverbials in English*, Unpublished dissertation, University of Illinois.

Geis, Jonnie E. (1973) 'Subject Complementation with Causative Verbs', in B. Kachru, Robert B. Lees, Yakov Malkiel, Angelina Pietrangeli, and Sol Saporta (eds.), *Issues in Linguistics: Papers in Honor of Henry and Renee Kahane*, University of Illinois Press, Urbana, pp. 210–230.

Ginet, Susan (1973) 'Semantic Structure of Comparative Constructions', Paper presented at the 1973 Summer Meeting of the Linguistic Society of America.

Givon, Talmy (1972) 'Forward Implications, Backward Presuppositions and Time Axis Verbs', in J. Kimball (ed.), *Linguistic Symposia*, Vol. I, Seminar Press.

Givon, Talmy (1975) 'Cause and Control: On the Semantics of Inter-personal Manipulation', in J. Kimball (ed.), *Syntax and Semantics IV*, Academic Press, New York.

Gleitman, Lila F. and Henry Gleitman (1970) *Phrase and Paraphrase: Some Innovative Uses of Language*, Norton, New York.

Goodman, Fred (1973) 'On the Semantics of Futurate Sentences', *Ohio State University Working Papers in Linguistics No. 16*.

Goodman, Fred (1976) *A λ-Categorical Transformational Grammar*, Unpublished M.A. Thesis, Department of Linguistics, the Ohio State University.

Goodman, Nelson (1955) *Fact, Fiction, and Forecast*, Third Edition, Bobbs-Merrill, New York.

Green, Georgia M. (1970) 'How Abstract is Surface Structure?' *CLS* **6**, 270–281.

Green, Georgia M. (1972) 'Some Observations on the Syntax and Semantics of Instrumental Verbs', *CLS* **8**, 83–97.

Green, Georgia M. (1974) *Semantics and Syntactic Regularity*, Indiana University Press, Bloomington.

Green, Georgia M. (1976) 'On the Notion of Rule Government', in *Problems in Linguistic Metatheory: 1976 Conference Proceedings*, 28–72.

Grice, H. P. (1975) 'Logic and Conversation', in D. Davidson and Gilbert Harman (eds.), *The Logic of Grammar*, Dickenson Publishing Co., Encino, CA, 64–74.

Gruber, J. S. (1965) *Studies in Lexical Relations*, MIT doctoral dissertation. (Distributed by Indiana University of Linguistics Club.)

Gruber, J. S. (1967) *Functions of the Lexicon in Formal Descriptive Grammars*, System Development Corporation Report, Santa Monica, CA.

Gruber, Jeffrey S. (1976) *Lexical Structures in Syntax and Semantics*, North-Holland, Amsterdam.

Hall, Barbara (1965) *Subject and Object in English*, MIT doctoral dissertation.

Halle, Morris (1973) 'Prolegomena to a Theory of Word-Formation', *Linguistic Inquiry* **4.1**, 3–16.

Halvorsen, Per-Kristian and William Ladusaw (1977) 'Montague's Universal Grammar: An Introduction for the Linguist', *Texas Linguistic Forum* **6**, 51–88. (Also to appear in *Linguistics and Philosophy*.)

Hankamer, J. (1973) 'Unacceptable Ambiguity', *Linguistic Inquiry* **4.1**, 17.

Harman, Gilbert (1972) 'Deep Structure as Logical Form', in Donald Davidson and Gilbert Harman (eds.), *Semantics of Natural Language*, Reidel, Dordrecht, pp. 25–47.

Heidrich, Carl H. (1975) 'Should Generative Semantics be Related to Intensional Logic?' in E. L. Keenan (ed.), *Formal Semantics of Natural Language*, Cambridge University Press, Cambridge, pp. 188–204.

Herbert, Robert K. (1975) 'Observations on a Class of Instrumental Causatives', *CLS* **11**, 260–71.

Heringer, James T. (1976) 'Idioms and Lexicalization in English', in M. Shibatani (ed.), *Syntax and Semantics VI: The Grammar of Causative Constructions*, Academic Press, New York, pp. 205–216.

Hjelmslev, Louis (1943) *Prolegomena to a Theory of Language*, (translated from the Danish 1943) Indiana University Press, Bloomington, (1953).

Hockett, Charles (1954) 'Two Models of Grammatical Description', *Word* **10**, 210–231.

Horn, Lawrence (1972) *On the Semantic Properties of Logical Operators in English*, University of California, dissertation.

Horn, Lawrence (1978a) 'Remarks on Neg-Raising', in Peter Cole (ed.), *Syntax and Semantics 9: Pragmatics*, pp. 129–220.

Horn, Lawrence (1978b) 'Lexical Incorporation, Implicature and the Least Effort Principle', *Papers from the Parasession on the Lexicon*, Chicago Linguistic Society, Chicago, pp. 196–209.

Inoue, Kyoko (1973) 'What does DO do in Japanese?', *University of Michigan Papers in Linguistics* **1.2**, 69–78.

Jackendoff, Ray (1972) *Semantic Interpretation In Generative Grammar*, MIT Press, Cambridge, Massachusetts.

Jackendoff, Ray (1975) 'Morphological and Semantic Regularities in the Lexicon', *Language* **51.3**, 639–671.

Jackendoff, Ray (1977) *X-bar Syntax: A Study of Phrase Structure* (*Linguistic Inquiry Monograph Series 2*), MIT Press, Cambridge, Massachusetts.

Jakobson, Roman (1936) 'Beitrag zur allgemeinen Kasuslehre', *Travaux de Cercle Linguistique de Prague* **6**, 240–288.

Jakobson, Roman (1971) *Selected Writings*, Vol. 2: *Word and Language*, Mouton, the Hague.

Jesperson, Otto (1924) *The Philosophy of Grammar*, George Allen & Unwin, London.

Jesperson, Otto (1931) *A Modern English Grammar on Historical Principles, Part IV, Syntax*, George Allen & Unwin, London, (Reprinted 1965).

Johnson, Marion R. (1977) *The Syntax and Semantics of Kikuyu Tense and Aspect*, Unpublished doctoral dissertation, the Ohio State University.

Kamp, J. A. W. (1971) 'Formal Properties of "Now",' *Theoria* **37**, 227–273.

Kamp, J. A. W. (1968) *Tense Logic and the Theory of Linear Order*, doctoral dissertation, University of California, Los Angeles.

Kamp. J. A. W. (1975) 'Two Theories about Adjectives', in Edward L. Keenan (ed.), *Formal Semantics of Natural Language*, Cambridge University Press, Cambridge, MA, pp. 123–155.

Kaplan, David (1972) 'Bob and Carol and Ted and Alice', in K. J. J. Hintikka, J. E. Moravcsik, and P. Suppes (eds.), (1973) *Approaches to Natural Language: Proceedings of the 1970 Stanford Workshop on Grammar and Semantics*, Reidel, Dordrecht.

Karttunen, Lauri (1970) 'On the Semantics of Complement Sentences', *CLS* **6**, 328–339.

Karttunen, Lauri, and Stanley Peters (1975) 'Conventional Implicature in Montague Grammar', in *BLS I: Proceedings of the First Annual Meeting of the Berkeley Linguistics Society*, Berkeley, CA.

Karttunen, Lauri, and Stanley Peters (1978) 'Conventional Implicature', in C.-K. Oh (ed.) *Syntax and Semantics XI: Presupposition*, Academic Press, New York.

Katz, Jerrold, and Jerry A. Fodor (1963) 'The Structure of a Semantic Theory', *Language* **39**, 170–210.

Katz, Jerrold (1966) *The Philosophy of Language*, Harper and Row, New York.

Katz, Jerrold (1970) 'Generative Semantics Versus Interpretive Semantics', *Foundations of Language* **6.2**, 220–240.

Katz, Jerrold (1972) *Semantic Theory*, Harper and Row, New York.

Katz, Jerrold and Paul Postal (1964) *An Integrated Theory of Linguistic Descriptions*, MIT Press, Cambridge, MA.

Keenan, Edward (1972) 'On Semantically Based Grammar', *Linguistic Inquiry* **3.4**, 413–462.

Keenan, Edward, and Bernard Comrie (1977) 'Noun Phrase Accessibility and Universal Grammar', *Linguistic Inquiry* **8.1**, 63–98.

Kempson, Ruth M. (1977) *Semantic Theory* (*Cambridge Textbooks in Linguistics*), Cambridge University Press, Cambridge.

Kenny, Anthony (1963) *Actions, Emotion, and Will*, Humanities Press.

Kim, Jaegwon (1973) 'Comments on Lewis' "Counterfactual Analysis of Causation",' *Journal of Philosophy* **70**, 570–572.

Kintsch, W. (1974) *The Representation of Meaning in Memory*, John Wiley and Sons, New York.

Kirsner, Robert W. (1977) 'On the Passive of Sensory Verb Complement Sentences', *Linguistic Inquiry* **8.1**, 173–179.

Klein, Ewan (ms) 'VP and Sentence Pro-forms in Montague Grammar'.

Kripke, Saul A. (1972) 'Naming and Necessity', in Donald Davidson and Gilbert Harman (eds.), *Semantics of Natural Language*, Reidel, Dordrecht, 253–355.

Ladusaw, William (1977) 'Some Problems with Tense in PTQ', *Texas Linguistic Forum* **6**, 89–102.

Lakoff, George (1965) *On the Nature of Syntactic Irregularity*, Doctoral dissertation, Indiana University. (Published by Holt, Rinhard & Winston as *Irregularity in Syntax* (1970).)

Lakoff, George (1968) 'Instrumental Adverbs and the Concept of Deep Structure', *Foundations of Language* **4**, 4–29.

Lakoff, George (1970) 'Repartee', *Foundations of Language* **6.3**, 389–422.

Lakoff, George (1970a) 'A Note on Vagueness and Ambiguity', *Linguistic Inquiry* **1.3**, 357–359.

Lakoff, George (1971) 'On Generative Semantics', in Leon A. Jakobovitz and Danny D. Steinberg (eds.), *Semantics: An Interdisciplinary Reader in Philosophy, Linguistics, and Psychology*, Cambridge, 232–296.

Lakoff, George (1972) 'Linguistics and Natural Logic', in Donald Davidson and Gilbert Harman (eds.), *Semantics of Natural Language*, Reidel, Dordrecht, pp. 545–665.

Lakoff, George, and Stanley Peters (1969) 'Phrasal Conjunction and Symmetric Predicates', in D. A. Reibel and S. A. Schane (eds.), *Modern Studies in English*, Prentice-Hall, Englewood Cliffs, NJ, 113–142.

Lee, Gregory (1971) 'Subjects and Agents II'. *Working Papers in Linguistics #7*, Department of Linguistics, the Ohio State University, Columbus.

Leech, G. (1971) *Meaning and the English Verb*, Longman, London.

Lees, Robert B. (1960) *The Grammar of English Nominalization*, Mouton, The Hague.

Lees, Robert B. (1970) 'Problems in the Grammatical Analysis of English Nominal Compounds', in Manfred Bierwisch and Karl E. Heidolph (eds.), *Progress in Linguistics*, Mouton, The Hague, pp. 174–86.

Lehiste, Ilse (1973) 'Phonetic Disambiguation of Syntactic Ambiguity', *Glossa* **7.2**, 107–122.

Levi, Judith N. (1975) *The Syntax and Semantics of Non-predicating Adjectives in English*, University of Chicago dissertation.

Lewis, David (1969) *Convention. A Philosophical Study*, Harvard University Press, Cambridge, MA.

Lewis, David (1970) 'General Semantics', in *Synthese* **22**, (1970), 18–67. (Reprinted in Davidson and Harman (eds.), 1972.)

Lewis, David (1973) *Counterfactuals*, Harvard University Press, Cambridge, MA.

Lewis, David (1973a) 'Causation', *The Journal of Philosophy* **70**, 556–567.

Loeb, Lewis E. (1974) 'Causal Theories and Causal Overdeterminization', *The Journal of Philosophy* **71.15**, 525–544.

Lyon, Ardon (1967) 'Causality', *British Journal for the Philosophy of Science* **18**, 1–20.

Lyons, John (1963) *Structural Semantics*, The Philological Society, Oxford.

Lyons, John (1968) *Introduction to Theoretical Linguistics*, Cambridge University Press, Cambridge.

Lyons, John (1977) *Semantics*, Cambridge University Press, Cambridge.

Marchand, Hans (1960) *The Categories and Types of Present-Day English Word-Formation*, Second Edition, C. H. Beck'sche Verlagsbuchhandlung, München.

Marchand, Hans (1972) 'Reversative, Ablative, and Privative Verbs in English, French, and German', in Braj Kachru, Robert Lees, Yakov Malkiel, Angelina Pietrangeli, and Sol Sapota (eds.), *Issues in Linguistics: Papers in Honor of Henry and Renee Kahane*, pp. 636–643.

McCawley, James D. (1968a) 'Lexical Insertion in a Transformational Grammar without Deep Structure', *CLS* **4**, 71–80.

McCawley, James D. (1968b) 'The Role of Semantics in a Grammar', in E. Bach and Robert Harms (eds.), *Universals in Linguistic Theory*, Holt, Rinehart, & Winston, New York, pp. 124–169.

McCawley, James D. (1970) 'English as a VSO Language', *Language* **46**, 286–99.

McCawley, James D. (1970a) 'Where Do Noun Phrases Come From?' in R. A. Jacobs, and Peter Rosenbaum (eds.), *Readings in English Transformational Grammar*, Ginn & Co., Waltham, MA, pp. 166–183.

McCawley, James D. (1971) 'Pre-Lexical Syntax', in O'Brien (ed.), *Report of the 22nd Roundtable Meeting on Linguistics and Language Studies*, Georgetown University Press.

McCawley, James D. (1971a) 'Tense and Time Reference in English', in Fillmore and Langendoen (eds.), *Studies in Linguistic Semantics*, Holt, Rinehart & Winston, New York, pp. 97–114.

McCawley, James D. (1973) 'Syntactic and Logical Arguments for Semantic Structures', in Osamu Farjimura (ed.), *Three Dimensions in Linguistic Theory*, TEC Corp., Tokyo, pp. 259–376.

McCawley, James D. (1974) 'On Identifying the Remains of Deceased Clauses', distributed by the Indiana University Linguistics Club.

McCawley, James D. (1976) 'Remarks on What Can Cause What', in M. Shibatani (ed.), *Syntax and Semantics VI: The Grammar of Causative Constructions*, Academic Press, New York, pp. 117–130.

McCawley, James D. (1978) 'Conversational Implicature and the Lexicon', in Peter Cole (ed.), *Syntax and Semantics: Pragmatics*, Vol. 9, pp. 245–259.

McCoard, Robert W. (1978) *The English Perfect: Tense-Choice and Pragmatic Inferences* (*North-Holland Linguistic Series* 38), North-Holland Publishing Company, Amsterdam.

Miller, G. A. and P. N. Johnson-Laird (1976) *Language and Perception*, Harvard University Press, Cambridge, MA.

Mittwoch, A. (1971) 'Idioms and Unspecified Object Deletion', *Linguistic Inquiry* **2.2**, 255–259.

Montague, Richard (1968) 'Pragmatics', in R. Kiblansky (ed.), *Contemporary Philosophy: A Survey*, Florence, pp. 102–122. (Reprinted in Montague, 1974.)

Montague, Richard (1969) 'On the Nature of Certain Philosophical Entities', *The Monist* **53**, 159–194. (Reprinted in Montague 1974.)

Montague, Richard (1970) 'Pragmatics and Intensional Logic', *Synthese* **22**, 68–94. (Reprinted in Montague, 1974.)

Montague, Richard (1970a) 'English as a Formal Language', in B. Visentini, *et al.* (eds.), *Linguaggi nella Societa a nella Tecnica*, Milan. (Reprinted in Montague, 1974.)

Montague, Richard (1970b) 'Universal Grammar', *Theoria* **36**, 373–398. (Reprinted in Montague, 1974.)

Montague, Richard (1973) 'The Proper Treatment of Quantification in Ordinary English', in J. Hintikka, J. Moravcsik, and P. Suppes (eds.), *Approaches to Natural Language*, Reidel, Dordrecht. (Reprinted in Montague, 1974.)

Montague, Richard (1974) *Formal Philosophy: Selected Papers of Richard Montague*, ed. by Richmond Thomason, Yale University Press, New Haven.

Morgan, Jerry (1969) 'On Arguing About Semantics', *Papers in Linguistics* **1**, 49–70.

Newmeyer, F. J. (1974) 'The Regularity of Idiom Behavior', *Lingua* **34**, 327–342.

Newmeyer, Frederick (1976) 'The Precyclic Nature of Predicate Raising', in Masayoshi Shibatani (ed.), *Syntax and Semantics: The Grammar of Causative Constructions*, Vol. 6, pp. 131–164.

Partee, Barbara (1973) 'Some Structural Analogies between Tenses and Pronouns in English', *Journal of Philosophy* **70**, 601–609.

Partee, Barbara (1974) 'Opacity and Scope', in M. Munitz and P. Unger (eds.), *Semantics and Philosophy*, New York University Press, New York, pp. 81–101.

Partee, Barbara (1975) 'Montague Grammar and Transformational Grammar', *Linguistic Inquiry* **6.2**, 203–300.

Partee, Barbara (1977) 'John is Easy to Please', in A. Zampolli (ed.), *Linguistic Structures Processing*, North-Holland, Amsterdam, 281–312.

Partee, Barbara (to appear a) 'Montague Grammar and the Well-Formedness Constraint', in F. Henry and H. Schnelle (eds.), *Syntax and Semantics* 10, Academic Press, New York. (Paper originally given at the Third Groningen Round Table.)

Partee, Barbara (to appear b) 'Montague Grammar, Mental Representation and Reality', in Ohman and Kanger (eds.), *Proceedings from the Symposium on Philosophy and Grammar, June 1977.*

Perlmutter, David (1971) *Deep and Surface Structure Constraints in Syntax*, Holt, Rinehart & Winston, New York.

Perlmutter, David, and Paul Postal (to appear) *Relational Grammar.*

Postal, Paul M. (1969) 'Anaphoric Islands', *CLS* **5**, 205–239.

Postal, Paul M. (1970) 'On Coreferential Complement Subject Deletion', *Linguistic Inquiry* **1.4**, 439–500.

Prince, Ellen (1973) 'Futurate *Be-ing* or Why *Yesterday Morning, I was leaving on the Midnight Special* is OK', unpublished paper, read at the 1973 Summer Meeting of the Linguistic Society of America.

Prior, A. N. (1967) *Past, Present, and Future*, Oxford University Press, Oxford.

Putnam, Hilary (1975) 'The Meaning of "Meaning",' in Keith Gunderson (ed.), *Language, Mind and Knowledge*, (*Minnesota Studies in the Philosophy of Science*, Vol. 7), University of Minnesota Press, Minneapolis, pp. 131–193.

Putnam, Hiliary (1978) *Meaning and the Moral Sciences*, Routledge and Kegan Paul, London.

Quang Phuc Dong (1970) 'A Note on Conjoined Noun Phrases', *Journal of Philosophical Linguistics* **1.2**, 31–40.

Quine, W. V. O. (1960) *Word and Object*, The MIT Press, Cambridge, MA.

Reichenbach, H. (1947) *Elements of Symbolic Logic*, University of California Press,

Berkeley.
Rescher, Nicholas and Alisdair Urquhart (1971) *Temporal Logic*, Springer Verlag, New York.
Rodman, Robert (1976) 'Scope Phenomena, "Movement Transformations", and Relative Clauses', in Barbara H. Partee (ed.), *Montague Grammar*, Academic Press, New York, pp. 165–176.
Rogers, Andy (1971) 'Three Kinds of Physical Perception Verbs', *CLS* **7**, 206–222.
Rogers, Andy (1972) 'Another Look at Flip-Perception Verbs', *CLS* **8**, 303–315.
Rose, James H. (1973) 'Principled Limitations on Productivity in Denominal Verbs', *Foundations of Language* **10**, 509–526.
Ross, J. R. (1967) *Constraints on Variables in Syntax*, Doctoral dissertation, MIT, Cambridge, MA. (Distributed by the Indiana University Linguistics Club.)
Ross, J. R. (1969) 'Auxiliaries as Main Verbs', *Journal of Philosophical Linguistics* **1**, 77–102.
Ross, J. R. (1970) 'On Declarative Sentences', in R. A. Jacobs and Peter Rosenbaum (eds.), *Readings in English Transformational Grammar*, Ginn & Co., Waltham, MA, pp. 222–272.
Ross, J. R. (1972) 'Act', in Donald Davidson and Gilbert Harman (eds.), *Semantics of Natural Language*, Reidel, Dordrecht, pp. 70–126.
Ross, J. R. (1972b) 'Doubl-ing', *Linguistic Inquiry* **3.1**, 61–86.
Ruttenberg, John (1976) 'Some Difficulties with Cresswell's Semantics and the Method of Shallow Structure', *University of Massachusetts Occasional Papers in Linguistics* **2**, 58–69.
Ryle, Gilbert (1949) *The Concept of Mind*, Barnes and Noble, London.
Saarinen, Esa (1978) 'Backwards-Looking Operators in Tense and Logic and in Natural Language', in J. Hintikka, I. Niiniluoto and E. Saarinen (eds.), *Essays in Mathematical and Philosophical Logic*, D. Reidel Publishing Co., Dordrecht.
Sadock, Jerrold (1974) *Toward a Linguistic Theory of Speech Acts*, Academic Press, New York.
Sadock, Jerrold (ms) 'Almost'.
Sapir, Edward (1949) *Selected Writings in Language, Culture, and Personality* (ed. by D. Mandelbaum), University of California Press.
Saussure, Ferdinand de (1915) *Cours de Linguistique Générale* (translated as *Course in General Linguistics*, McGraw-Hill, New York, 1959).
Scheffer, Johannes (1975) *The Progressive in English* (*North-Holland Linguistic Series*, Vol. 15) North-Holland Publishing Co., Amsterdam.
Schmerling, Susan F. (1975) 'Asymmetric Conjunction and Rules of Conversation', in P. Cole and J. Morgan (eds.), *Syntax and Semantics 3: Speech Acts*, Academic Press, New York, 211–230.
Scott, Dana (1970) 'Advice on Modal Logic', Karl Lambert (ed.), *Philosophical Problems in Logic*, Reidel, Dordrecht, pp. 143–174.
Shibatani, Masayoshi (1976) 'The Grammar of Causative Constructions: A Conspectus', in M. Shibatani (ed.), *Syntax and Semantics VI: The Grammar of Causative Constructions*, Academic Press, New York, pp. 1–42.
Siegel, Muffy (1976a) 'Capturing the Russian Adjective', in Barbara Partee (ed.), *Montague Grammar*, Academic Press, New York, 293–309.
Siegel, Muffy (1976b) *Capturing the Adjective*, University of Massachusetts dissertation.

Smith, Carlota S. (1978a) 'The Syntax and Interpretation of Temporal Expressions in English', *Linguistics and Philosophy* **2.1**, 43–100.

Smith, Carlota S. (1978b) 'Constraints on Temporal Anaphora', *Texas Linguistic Forum* **10**, 76–94.

Stalnaker, Robert (1968) 'A Theory of Conditionals', in N. Rescher (ed.), *Studies in Logical Theory* (*American Philosophical Quarterly* Supplementary Monograph Series).

Stalnaker, Robert, and Richmond Thomason (1970) 'A Semantic Analysis of Conditional Logic', *Theoria* **34**, 23–42.

Stalnaker, Robert, and Richmond Thomason (1973) 'A Semantic Theory of Adverbs', *Linguistic Inquiry* **4.2**, 195–220.

Talmy, Leonard (1976) 'Semantic Causative Types', in M. Shibatani (ed.), *Syntax and Semantics VI: The Grammar of Causative Constructions*, Academic Press, New York, pp. 43–116.

Taylor, Barry (1977) 'Tense and Continuity', *Linguistics and Philosophy* **1.2**, 199–220.

Tedeschi, Philip J. (1973) 'Some Suggestions for a Semantic Analysis of Progressives', *University of Michigan Papers in Linguistics* **1.2**, 157–168.

Thomason, Richmond (1970) 'Indeterministic Time and Truth Value Gaps', *Theoria* **18.3**, 264–281.

Thomason, Richmond (1974a) 'Deontic Logic as Founded on Tense Logic', Unpublished paper presented at the Temple University Conference on Deviant Semantics, December 1970.

Thomason, Richmond (1974b) 'Home Is Where the Heart Is', Unpublished paper, University of Pittsburgh.

Thomason, Richmond (1976) 'Some Extensions of Montague Grammar', in B. Partee (ed.), *Montague Grammar*, Academic Press, New York, 77–118.

Thomson, Judith Jarvis (1971) 'The Time of Killing', *The Journal of Philosophy* **68.5**, 115–132.

Tyler, S. A. (1969) *Cognitive Anthropology*, Holt, Rinehart, & Winston, New York.

Van Fraassen, Bas (1969) 'Presuppositions, Supervaluations and Free Logic', in K. Lambert (ed.), *The Logical Way of Doing Things*, Yale University Press, New Haven, CT.

Vendler, Zeno (1967) *Linguistics in Philosophy*, Cornell University Press, Ithaca, New York.

Verkuyl, H. J. (1972) *On the Compositional Nature of the Aspects* (*Foundations of Language, Supplementary Series, Vol. 15*), D. Reidel Publishing Co., Dordrecht, Holland.

Vermasen, B. (1967) Review of Katz and Postal (1964) and Katz (1966), *Synthese* **17**, 350–365.

Vetter, D. C. (1973) 'Someone Solves this Problem Tomorrow', *Linguistic Inquiry* **4.1**, 104–108.

Waldo, James H. (to appear) 'A PTQ Grammar for Sortal Incorrectness', in M. Mithun and S. Davis (eds.), *Proceedings from the Albany Conference on Montague Grammar, Philosophy and Linguistics*, University of Texas Press, Austin.

Wall, Robert (1972) *Introduction to Mathematical Linguistics*, Prentice-Hall, Englewood Cliffs, NJ.

Wall, Robert, Stanley Peters and David Dowty (to appear) *Introduction to Montague Grammar*.

Wekker, H. Charles (1976) *The Expression of Future Time in Contemporary British English* (*North-Holland Linguistic Series 28*), North-Holland Publishing Co., Amsterdam.

Winograd, T. (1972) *Understanding Natural Language*, Academic Press, New York.

Wittgenstein, Ludwig (1958) *Philosophical Investigations*, The Macmillan Company, New York.

Wojcik, Richard H. (1973) *The Expression of Causation in English Clauses*, Doctoral dissertation, Ohio State University.

Wojcik, Richard H. (1976) 'Where do Instrumental NP's Come From?' in M. Shibatani (ed.), *Syntax and Semantics VI: The Grammar of Causative Constructions*, Academic Press, New York, pp. 165–180.

Woods, W. A. (1970) 'Transition Network Grammars for Natural Language Analysis', *Communications of the AMC* **13.10**, 591–608.

Wright, Georg H. von (1963) *Norm and Action*, Humanities Press.

Wright, Georg H. von (1968) *An Essay in Deontic Logic and the General Theory of Action* (*Acta Philosophica Fennica*).

Zimmer, Karl (1964) 'Affixal Negation in English and Other Languages: An Investigation of Restricted Productivity', Supplement to *Word* **20.2**, Monograph 5.

Zimmer, Karl (1971) 'Some General Observations about Nominal Compounds', *Working Papers on Language Universals*, Stanford University 5, C1–21.

Zimmer, Karl (1972) 'Appropriateness Conditions for Nominal Compounds', *Working Papers on Language Universals*, Stanford University, 8, 3–20.

Zimmer, Karl (1976) 'Some Constraints on Turkish Causativization', in M. Shibatani (ed.), *Syntax and Semantics VI: The Grammar of Causative Constructions*, pp. 399–412.

Zwicky, Arnold (1972) 'Remarks on Directionality', *Journal of Linguistics* **8**, 103–109.

Zwicky, Arnold (1978) 'Arguing for Constituents', *CLS* **14**, pp. 503–512.

Zwicky, Arnold, and Jerrold Sadock (1975) 'Ambiguity Tests and How to Fail Them', in John P. Kimball (ed.), *Syntax and Semantics, Vol. 4*, 1–36.

INDEX

Note that words with meanings analyzed in this book are listed in the *Lexicon* of the English Fragment on pp. 364-368, along with their translations and page references to their discussions earlier in the text. Likewise, the *Syntactic Rules* of the Fragment are listed on pp. 356-360 with page references to earlier discussions, as are the *Lexical Rules* on pp. 360-361.

Studies in Linguistics and Philosophy

1. *H. Hiż (ed.): Questions.* 1978 ISBN Hb: 90-277-0813-4; Pb: 90-277-1035-X
2. W. S. Cooper: *Foundations of Logico-Linguistics.* A Unified Theory of Information, Language, and Logic. 1978 ISBN Hb: 90-277-0864-9; Pb: 90-277-0876-2
3. A. Margalit (ed.): *Meaning and Use.* 1979 ISBN 90-277-0888-6
4. F. Guenthner and S.J. Schmidt (eds.): *Formal Semantics and Pragmatics for Natural Languages.* 1979 ISBN Hb: 90-277-0778-2; Pb: 90-277-0930-0
5. E. Saarinen (ed.): *Game-Theoretical Semantics.* Essays on Semantics by Hintikka, Carlson, Peacocke, Rantala, and Saarinen. 1979 ISBN 90-277-0918-1
6. F.J. Pelletier (ed.): *Mass Terms: Some Philosophical Problems.* 1979 ISBN 90-277-0931-9
7. D. R. Dowty: *Word Meaning and Montague Grammar.* The Semantics of Verbs and Times in Generative Semantics and in Montague's PTQ. 1979 ISBN Hb: 90-277-1008-2; Pb: 90-277-1009-0
8. A. F. Freed: *The Semantics of English Aspectual Complementation.* 1979 ISBN Hb: 90-277-1010-4; Pb: 90-277-1011-2
9. J. McCloskey: *Transformational Syntax and Model Theoretic Semantics.* A Case Study in Modern Irish. 1979 ISBN Hb: 90-277-1025-2; Pb: 90-277-1026-0
10. J. R. Searle, F. Kiefer and M. Bierwisch (eds.): *Speech Act Theory and Pragmatics.* 1980 ISBN Hb: 90-277-1043-0; Pb: 90-277-1045-7
11. D. R. Dowty, R. E. Wall and S. Peters: *Introduction to Montague Semantics.* 1981; 5th printing 1987 ISBN Hb: 90-277-1141-0; Pb: 90-277-1142-9
12. F. Heny (ed.): *Ambiguities in Intensional Contexts.* 1981 ISBN Hb: 90-277-1167-4; Pb: 90-277-1168-2
13. W. Klein and W. Levelt (eds.): *Crossing the Boundaries in Linguistics.* Studies Presented to Manfred Bierwisch. 1981 ISBN 90-277-1259-X
14. Z. S. Harris: *Papers on Syntax.* Edited by H. Hiż. 1981 ISBN Hb: 90-277-1266-0; Pb: 90-277-1267-0
15. P. Jacobson and G. K. Pullum (eds.): *The Nature of Syntactic Representation.* 1982 ISBN Hb: 90-277-1289-1; Pb: 90-277-1290-5
16. S. Peters and E. Saarinen (eds.): *Processes, Beliefs, and Questions.* Essays on Formal Semantics of Natural Language and Natural Language Processing. 1982 ISBN 90-277-1314-6
17. L. Carlson: *Dialogue Games.* An Approach to Discourse Analysis. 1983; 2nd printing 1985 ISBN Hb: 90-277-1455-X; Pb: 90-277-1951-9
18. L. Vaina and J. Hintikka (eds.): *Cognitive Constraints on Communication.* Representation and Processes. 1984; 2nd printing 1985 ISBN Hb: 90-277-1456-8; Pb: 90-277-1949-7
19. F. Heny and B. Richards (eds.): *Linguistic Categories: Auxiliaries and Related Puzzles.* Volume I: Categories. 1983 ISBN 90-277-1478-9
20. F. Heny and B. Richards (eds.): *Linguistic Categories: Auxiliaries and Related Puzzles.* Volume II: The Scope, Order, and Distribution of English Auxiliary Verbs. 1983 ISBN 90-277-1479-7
21. R. Cooper: *Quantification and Syntactic Theory.* 1983 ISBN 90-277-1484-3

Volumes 1–26 formerly published under the Series Title: Synthese Language Library.

Studies in Linguistics and Philosophy

22. J. Hintikka (in collaboration with J. Kulas): *The Game of Language*. Studies in Game-Theoretical Semantics and Its Applications. 1983; 2nd printing 1985
ISBN Hb: 90-277-1687-0; Pb: 90-277-1950-0
23. E. L. Keenan and L. M. Faltz: *Boolean Semantics for Natural Language*. 1985
ISBN Hb: 90-277-1768-0; Pb: 90-277-1842-3
24. V. Raskin: *Semantic Mechanisms of Humor*. 1985
ISBN Hb: 90-277-1821-0; Pb: 90-277-1891-1
25. G. T. Stump: *The Semantic Variability of Absolute Constructions*. 1985
ISBN Hb: 90-277-1895-4; Pb: 90-277-1896-2
26. J. Hintikka and J. Kulas: *Anaphora and Definite Descriptions*. Two Applications of Game-Theoretical Semantics. 1985 ISBN Hb: 90-277-2055-X; Pb: 90-277-2056-8
27. E. Engdahl: *Constituent Questions*. The Syntax and Semantics of Questions with Special Reference to Swedish. 1986 ISBN Hb: 90-277-1954-3; Pb: 90-277-1955-1
28. M. J. Cresswell: *Adverbial Modification*. Interval Semantics and Its Rivals. 1985
ISBN Hb: 90-277-2059-2; Pb: 90-277-2060-6
29. J. van Benthem: *Essays in Logical Semantics* 1986
ISBN Hb: 90-277-2091-6; Pb: 90-277-2092-4
30. B. H. Partee, A. ter Meulen and R. E. Wall: *Mathematical Methods in Linguistics*. 1990
ISBN Hb: 90-277-2244-7; Pb: 90-277-2245-5
31. P. Gärdenfors (ed.): *Generalized Quantifiers*. Linguistic and Logical Approaches. 1987
ISBN 1-55608-017-4
32. R. T. Oehrle, E. Bach and D. Wheeler (eds.): *Categorial Grammars and Natural Language Structures*. 1988 ISBN Hb: 1-55608-030-1; Pb: 1-55608-031-X
33. W. J. Savitch, E. Bach, W. Marsh and G. Safran-Naveh (eds.): *The Formal Complexity of Natural Language*. 1987 ISBN Hb: 1-55608-046-8; Pb: 1-55608-047-6
34. J. E. Fenstad, P.-K. Halvorsen, T. Langholm and J. van Benthem: *Situations, Language and Logic*. 1987 ISBN Hb: 1-55608-048-4; Pb: 1-55608-049-2
35. U. Reyle and C. Rohrer (eds.): *Natural Language Parsing and Linguistic Theories*. 1988 ISBN Hb: 1-55608-055-7; Pb: 1-55608-056-5
36. M. J. Cresswell: *Semantical Essays*. Possible Worlds and Their Rivals. 1988
ISBN 1-55608-061-1
37. T. Nishigauchi: *Quantification in the Theory of Grammar*. 1990
ISBN Hb: 0-7923-0643-0; Pb: 0-7923-0644-9
38. G. Chierchia, B.H. Partee and R. Turner (eds.): *Properties, Types and Meaning*. Volume I: Foundational Issues. 1989 ISBN Hb: 1-55608-067-0; Pb: 1-55608-068-9
39. G. Chierchia, B.H. Partee and R. Turner (eds.): *Properties, Types and Meaning*. Volume II: Semantic Issues. 1989 ISBN Hb: 1-55608-069-7; Pb: 1-55608-070-0
Set ISBN (Vol. I + II) 1-55608-088-3; Pb: 1-55608-089-1
40. C.T.J. Huang and R. May (eds.): *Logical Structure and Linguistic Structure*. Cross-Linguistic Perspectives. 1990 ISBN 0-7923-0914-6
41. M.J. Cresswell: *Entities and Indices*. 1990
ISBN Hb: 0-7923-0966-9; Pb: 0-7923-0967-7
42. H. Kamp and U. Reyle: *From Discourse to Logic*. Introduction to Modeltheoretic Semantics of Natural Language, Formal Logic and Discourse Representation Theory. 1991 ISBN Hb: 0-7923-1027-6; Pb: 0-7923-1028-4
43. C. S. Smith: The Parameter of Aspects. 1991 ISBN 0-7923-1136-1

Studies in Linguistics and Philosophy

44. R. C. Berwick (ed.): *Principle-Based Parsing:* Computation and Psycholinguistics. 1991 ISBN 0-7923-1173-6
45. F. Landman: *Structures for Semantics*. 1991 ISBN Hb: 0-7923-1239-2; Pb: 0-7923-1240-6
46. M. Siderits: *Indian Philosophy of Language*. 1991 ISBN 0-7923-1262-7

Further information about our publications on *Linguistics* are available on request.
Kluwer Academic Publishers – Dordrecht / Boston / London

Printed in the United Kingdom
by Lightning Source UK Ltd.
111583UKS00001B/163-165

9 789027 710093